'A GENERAL PLAGUE OF MADNESS'

THE CIVIL WARS IN LANCASHIRE, 1640–1660

'A General Plague of Madness'

The civil wars in Lancashire, 1640–1660

STEPHEN BULL

CARNEGIE

'A General Plague of Madness': The civil wars in Lancashire, 1640–1660

Copyright © Stephen Bull, 2009

First edition

Published by Carnegie Publishing Ltd
Carnegie House
Chatsworth Road, Lancaster LA1 4SL
tel: 01524 840111
www.carnegiepublishing.com

ISBN 978-1-85936-105-4 *limited edition hardback*
ISBN 978-1-85936-191-7 *softback*

British Library Cataloguing-in-Publication data
A catalogue record for this book is available from the British Library

Designed and typeset by Carnegie Book Production, Lancaster
Printed and bound in the UK by Jellyfish Solutions Ltd

Contents

Acknowledgements

M ANY PEOPLE AND INSTITUTIONS have helped make this book possible. Although the Lancashire Record Office, the Local Studies Library, and the Harris Library in Preston have taken the brunt of many requests for obscure texts, at least a dozen other libraries and archives, mainly in the North West and London, have made valuable contributions. These include particularly the Manchester City Archives, the Derby family archive at Knowsley, courtesy of the current Lord Derby, and the Chetham Library; a fuller list is included as part of the bibliography at the end of this work. Museums, galleries and stately homes have also provided valuable assistance – notably my own colleagues at Lancashire County Museums and Gawthorpe Hall, but also Warrington Museum, the Harris Museum in Preston and York Castle Museum.

Individuals who have assisted in a wide variety of different ways – and over a very long period of time – include Professor Michael Mullet and Dr Jean Turnbull at Lancaster University; Professor Charles Esdaile at Liverpool; Dr Alex Craven at Manchester; Lord Shuttleworth; former County Archaeologists Gill Chitty and Ben Edwards, and current incumbent Peter Iles; Peter McCrone (DEFRA); Susan Bourne at Towneley Hall; John Barratt; Alistair Hodge; Mike Seed; Emma Tate; David Ryan; the late Professor Austin Woolrych; John Tincey; Stuart Reid; Keith Matthews and John Convey.

This work has been many years in gestation, having its first roots in 1991–92 and a Lancashire County Museums 350th anniversary exhibition on the wars. This was shown in Preston and Bolton, and accompanied by a brief booklet *The Civil War in Lancashire*. Seven years later *Bloody Preston: The Battle of Preston, 1648*, the first full-length study of one of Cromwell's greatest victories, finally appeared. A further decade has been required to finish the hopefully not over-ambitious project of a complete history of the wars in the county. Staging posts along this home straight have included two Lancaster University Civil War study days, in 1999 and 2005. Reflecting the key importance of religion in the history of this period, the last of these took as its title *God's War*.

Stephen Bull, Fulwood, 2009

Measurements and spellings

I N mid-seventeenth-century England many forms of measurement were gloriously inexact: miles, for example, were standardised across the country only after this period. Distances as given in quotations are repeated here, but where possible modern figures, taken from recent maps, have also been given. Time also tended to function on a very 'local' basis, and was only completely uniform and exact after the coming of the railways. Times given in contemporary sources have therefore been treated with some scepticism, and effort has been concentrated upon achieving the correct chronological order – and on determining whether events happened before or after dark.

During this period (and until 1752) the Julian calendar was still in use in Britain. As if determinedly to confuse later scholars, the new year in this calendar began not on 1 January but on the 25 March following, Lady Day (the Annunciation, exactly a full pregnancy term before the birth of Christ). Thus contemporary documents refer to the execution of Charles I as taking place on 30 January 1648, whereas our present, Gregorian calendar presents this date as 30 January 1649. (As a Protestant country, England had simply ignored the papal reform of the calendars which had been set out as early as 1582.) For simplicity, in this book all dates between 1 January and 25 March have been modernised to the Gregorian calendar; thus, within these pages Charles met his fate on 30 January 1649, and Lancaster was burned by the royalists in March 1643.

Happily the seventeenth-century Englishman, and especially the seventeenth-century Lancastrian, regarded orthography as completely unimportant. This has the interesting effect of men writing precisely as they spoke – spelling was phonetic and often varied not only from region to region but person to person. This was not regarded as 'incorrect'. Accents and dialects therefore sometimes show through, often giving the seventeenth-century manuscript or printed book a more truly authentic 'voice' than anything produced since. Where possible original spellings have therefore been retained. Dictionaries actually appeared in the first decades of the seventeenth century, but few people possessed them, and in any case their initial purpose was definition rather than pedantic spelling. It is likely that the obsession with the standardisation of spelling began only after the introduction of the dictionary, and since pronunciation still varied, may indeed originally have been intended by lexicographers essentially as an aid to getting their words in the right order.

In the case of people or places mentioned outside direct quotations these have been given consistency in the interests of intelligibility. So it is that the various Asshetons, and other spellings, have been rendered as plain 'Ashton' while 'Seaton' is preferred to 'Seton'. Likewise places such as 'West-Chester', 'Leverpoole', and 'Armeschurch' have taken their modern forms of 'Chester', Liverpool, and 'Ormskirk' outside direct quotations.

Younger readers will have no direct experience themselves of using pre-decimal Sterling currency. Before the early 1970s the pound sterling (£, L, from Latin *librae*) was divided into twenty shillings (*s.*, from Latin *solidi*, not actually an abbreviation for shilling), which in turn were divided into twelve pennies (*d.*, from the Latin *denarii*). From the thirteenth century until 1960 pennies could be quartered into farthings (from the Anglo Saxon *feorthing*, a fourth part). In the seventeenth century a frequently used monetary unit was the mark. There was never a coin of this value, but it was often used in accountancy and law. In this period it equalled 160 pennies, or two thirds of a pound, i.e. 13*s.* 4*d.* One half or one quarter of a mark (6*s.* 8*d.* or 3*s.* 4*d.*) are common sums in seventeenth-century documents, often as court fines. The guinea, which older readers will remember as a common term before decimalisation, was actually a coin first minted just after our period, in 1663.

Introduction

L ORD DERBY, Lancashire's highest-ranked nobleman and its principal royalist, once offered the opinion that the English civil wars had been 'a general plague of madness'. Complex and bedevilling, the earl defied anyone to tell the complete story of 'so foolish, so wicked, so lasting a war'. Yet attempting to chronicle and to explain the events is fascinating and hugely important. Both nationally and at the county level, the impact and significance of the wars can hardly be over-stated: the conflict involved our ancestors fighting one another, on and off, for a period of nine years; almost every part of Lancashire witnessed warfare of some kind at one time or another, and several towns in particular saw bloody sieges as well as at least one episode characterised as a massacre; nationally the wars resulted in the execution of the king; in Bolton in 1651 the seventh Earl of Derby himself was executed for high treason. In the early months of the civil wars many could barely distinguish what it was that divided people in 'this war without an enemy', as the parliamentarian Sir William Waller famously wrote; yet by the end of it parliament had abolished monarchy itself and entered upon what turned out to be a relatively short-lived experiment in republicanism. Over the ensuing centuries this period has been described variously as a rebellion, as a series of civil wars, even as a revolution.

Lancashire's role in these momentous events was quite distinctive, and relative to the size of its population particularly crucial. Some of this was because of geography: the proximity to Ireland was critical, while the position in respect to Wales and Scotland was not without importance. Significant, too, were the presence of a mainly royalist Yorkshire across the Pennines and the role of Cheshire so close across the Mersey. Lancashire was thus at the centre of the wars, even if it was located several days' journey from London: it lay in the middle of the 'British archipelago'. Equally significant was the social composition of the county: the long-established position of the Derby

1

The seventh Earl of Derby, prominent royalist nobleman in the Lancashire civil wars.

family, and the growing but essentially localised impact of textile production and organised commerce in the south-east of the county. Lancashire also has a serious claim to be considered as the place where the real war – the shooting war, rather than the war of words – actually began: the first attested death due to military action took place on the streets of Manchester.

Yet what was even more singular was the role of religion. God bulked large and terrible in the seventeenth-century mind. God spoke personally to the Puritan, and in different ways was equally dominant in the lives of Catholics. Apart from the foreboding walls of Lancaster castle, churches were often the most significant buildings a Lancastrian ever saw, and it was denomination which marked a man as 'one of us', or 'one of them'. In Lancashire this division was starker than in any other place in England. The established church held a statistical majority, but there was a higher proportion of Catholics here than in any county, and a smaller, but vigorous, low church faction. We now refer to these reformers as Puritans, and tend to have a somewhat simplistic view of what might be regarded as their fundamentalist belief: but usually they saw themselves simply as more 'exact' Christians, who listened more closely to the biblical word than most. Some were indeed the fanatical killjoys of popular belief, or eccentrics; some did regard themselves as specifically 'chosen' by God; but many others were cultured and surprisingly ordinary men. Most regarded the reformation of the church as incomplete, and took issue with the Arminian innovations in the Church of England, which in the 1630s were being championed by Archbishop Laud.

Estate – or class to use a modern but not interchangeable term – was important, but in Lancashire, as virtually everywhere, the war was not a simple case of gentleman against commoner. Establishment figures were to be found on both sides. In no way was this war for democracy – the term would have meant nothing to most Lancastrians of the time. Parliament represented specific interests as much, or even more, than the king's supporters. It was, however, often portrayed as a war fought to uphold ancient liberties, or against 'oppression' by the royal party. Both sides strove to represent themselves as the party of continuity, of public safety, peace, and not least importantly, as the upholders of true religion. The nobility may have been natural royalists, but the remainder split for many other reasons, not least significant of which was their God. That 'fundamental' opinions helped to whip up hatred of an enemy should come as no surprise, although as the great historian Conrad Russell put it, 'to say that the parties were divided by religion is not the same thing as to say that religion caused the Civil War'.

At first, most Lancastrians were reticent about the notion of fighting one another. In the minds of Lancastrians it appears that the war was 'caused' somewhere else – London, Rome or Ireland – depending on point of view. Arguments can be made, moreover, that key characters, such as Lord Derby, or Richard Holland, did not really want to go to war at all. Some of the parliamentarian leaders were good friends of future royalists before war came, and the majority of Lancashire leaders, on both sides, were pillars of their communities in the years leading up to war.

Yet it would be a serious mistake to assume that what held true in the summer and early autumn of 1642 was still taken for granted just six months later. The depth of division and the sheer destructiveness of the war are difficult to exaggerate. By 1644 the war was all-encompassing. Campaigning was no longer seasonal, and local government, in so far as it existed, was now designed essentially to provide troops and pay. As the war progressed moderates became less moderate, and with the passage of years radicals, and radical solutions, came to the fore. Many unusual concepts, inconceivable in 1642, were embraced more or less willingly in 1649.

In this sense at least 'neutralism', though it existed in a form, died an early death. Men may have joined the fight reluctantly, given up their goods, money and horses grudgingly, but once battle was joined all were consumed to a greater or lesser extent in its fire. And, with anything up to 10,000 Lancastrians under arms at any given moment, and with a demographic structure biased towards the young, it can rightly be claimed that the proportion of adult male combatants to the population as a whole rivalled that of either of the world wars of the twentieth century. Conscription in a form we might recognise was acknowledged in 1643. There were specialists, professionals, arguably some 'mercenaries' – but most of the soldiers in the ranks were 'ordinary' men. Many were 'civilians in uniform': others were merely civilians, armed with clubs – 'clubmen' – or with hunting weapons, pikes and bills.

To a very small population, many of whom used little cash at all, the cost of the war would be almost incomprehensible. The parliamentarians kept better records than their opponents, and we know that the parliamentarian county committee alone would swallow up to £3,000 in cash every month: what the royalists used, and how much was plundered, requisitioned, or destroyed – and how much lost, because men fought rather than farmed – can only be guessed at. Money eventually gave out, sometimes food was exhausted, and promissory notes, particularly those given out by the losers, proved to be worthless. Some fortunes were made through the purchase of enemy estates

The gatehouse of Lancaster Castle. Lancaster Castle sits on top of a prominent hill overlooking the city and the river Lune. It is by far the most imposing fortified building still surviving in Lancashire.

PHOTOGRAPH: CARNEGIE, 2009

at knock-down prices, but those who actually gained from the war financially were very few and far between.

A good case can be made for stating that the English civil wars were the most destructive, and most costly, conflict in terms of both lives and goods, that Lancashire has ever experienced. On the other hand, the determination of the contestants, and the fury of the battle, sieges, fires, plagues and famines does not appear to have been matched by a concomitant level of atrocities and lasting bitterness. Sixty years after the civil wars 'papist' was still an insult, but 'cavalier' and 'roundhead' were acquiring more comfortable historical resonances.

The only serious history of the civil wars in Lancashire was that of Ernest Broxap, published nearly a hundred years ago, in 1910. It was a good history, and remains a useful book despite the passage of time. Certain aspects of the local war have since been illuminated in some detail, as for example the role of the gentry, the Commonwealth administration, the Derby family, and the transactions of the Lancashire Committee with Cheshire. Nor is it just that a great deal of new scholarship has now to be taken into account. Generally speaking county record offices did not exist in 1910, and Lancashire's was not established in anything like its present form until 1940. This has brought much that is new to light, including quarter sessions papers and church registers. Perhaps even more significantly many documents have been transcribed and reprinted – as for example by the Chetham Society and the Record Society.

A county study is still relevant today, for the history of England lies in its shires. The military organised at county level, as did the law, and taxation was largely assessed and collected at county level. Emissaries from central government, from king or parliament, went out to the counties. Lords lieutenant of the counties raised the only armies that had existed in the years leading up to 1642. Parliament's war effort would eventually encompass 'associations' of several counties, and a form of 'national' army controlled from the centre in the shape of the New Model, but this was not how it started out. Parliament's first ability to fight was based on respected members of the local community calling out the militia, or raising other troops, at county level. Other contributions to the cause, like the London Trained Bands, or the navy, were the exceptions to this basic rule. The 'county committee' was the visible manifestation of parliament in the country, and its main forum in the localities. 'The county' therefore had its own distinctive life and history within the story of the wars. Lancashire's story was exceptional, and twice – in 1644 and especially in 1648 – the course of the war within the county was of crucial importance to the course of the national conflict. In the very wet August of 1648, indeed, the entire outcome of the Second Civil War, the life of the king, and the institution of a Britain's only period of republican government, depended entirely upon the outcome of a single battle that took place in Lancashire.

For many years some have regarded military history as somehow separate from the mainstream, somehow unworthy of serious analysis and consideration. The war in Lancashire demonstrates the fallacy of this argument. The war finally began over who had the right to direct the military, and its opening moves were almost entirely concerned with control of recruiting and physical resources such as munitions. The way the war was fought, its costs, and the capture of territory influenced not just the outcome, but the objectives of those doing the fighting. There was, in fact, a symbiotic relationship between the nature of the war and the development of the political history.

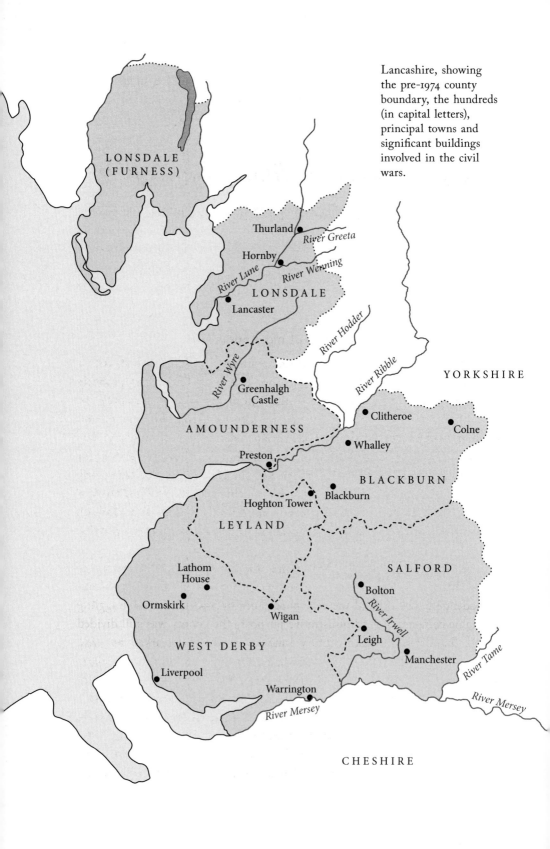

Lancashire, showing
the pre-1974 county
boundary, the hundreds
(in capital letters),
principal towns and
significant buildings
involved in the civil
wars.

LONSDALE
(FURNESS)

Thurland
River Greeta
Hornby
River Lune
River Wenning
LONSDALE
Lancaster

River Hodder

River Wyre
Greenhalgh
Castle

River Ribble

YORKSHIRE

AMOUNDERNESS

Clitheroe
Colne
Whalley

Preston

BLACKBURN

Hoghton Tower
Blackburn

LEYLAND

SALFORD

Lathom
House
Bolton
River Irwell
Ormskirk
Wigan
Leigh
Manchester
River Tame

WEST DERBY

Liverpool
Warrington
River Mersey
River Mersey

CHESHIRE

CHAPTER ONE

People, county, military: Lancashire in the seventeenth century

The hundreds of old Lancashire

On the eve of the English Civil War Lancashire was primarily rural, with a population of not more than about 150,000. It was physically, and probably intellectually, closer to the medieval world than to our own. Perhaps only one in ten Lancastrians lived in a town.[1] It was also geographically remote, and parochial, in the sense that when Lancastrians referred to their 'country' they were just as likely to mean Lancashire as England. As recently as 1610 in his book *Britannia* William Camden had viewed the bleaker parts of the county with 'a kind of dread'. Holderness, in his much more recent *Pre-Industrial England*, would place sixteenth-century Lancashire, together with Durham and the West Riding of Yorkshire, as 'among the poorest and least peopled counties'.

There was more than one Lancashire, for Lancashire was a county of considerable contrasts, with differing lifestyles, religions and regions, and both the moderately well off and the very poor cheek by jowl within its straggling geographic compass. For administrative purposes the county was still divided into six 'hundreds', a tenth-century innovation which demarked an area, assessed at one hundred 'hides', which had its own court and meeting place. Though the idea of 'hides' was now quite archaic, the hundred was still relevant in terms of local government, and the recruiting and organising of militia.

The English hundreds were by no means of a standard area, and Lancashire exemplified this diversity in both scale and character. Leyland hundred, for example, could be traversed easily, on foot, in a day: Lonsdale hundred, was a vast tract of mountain and moor with pockets of agricultural activity and

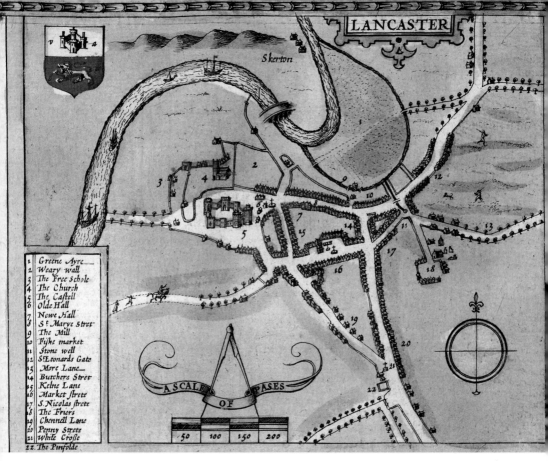

Speed's 1610 plan of Lancaster, which originally appeared as a detail in his county map of Lancashire. The whole built-up area is less than five hundred yards across, and is dominated by the Norman castle on its prominent hill above the river Lune. The town had changed relatively little by the time of the civil war.

medieval fortifications. 'North of the sands', in the northern part of Lonsdale, were the beginnings of small-scale industry, including charcoal burning, mining and iron works; these were juxtaposed with sheep, often grazing areas that had been monastic lands until a century before the civil wars. Despite the presence of metal-working there was little or nothing urban about Furness, for even its most major settlements would qualify as no more than villages by modern standards. Separated by the treacherous sands and water of Morecambe Bay the southern part of Lonsdale was less rugged, but dominated by the river Lune, which gave its name to the hundred as a whole. Much of the land was pastoral, although arable land predominated on the eastern flank of the river. The scenery of south Lonsdale was commanded by significant, if outdated, medieval castles: Thurland and Hornby were noteworthy, but they were minor compared to the mighty Norman keep at Lancaster. Though no longer much of a defence against modern artillery, Lancaster Castle was no antiquarian symbol, for it still housed a court and jail – and from here more serious criminals, condemned at the assizes, would be led out to their deaths at the gallows. Lancaster with its castle, small port, and royal dynasty was also the historic county town. Important though Lancaster still undoubtedly was, its significance was more administrative and ceremonial than economic, its population probably little more than 1,000 souls.

About half of Amounderness hundred comprised the familiar low-lying Fylde: but Blackpool and Fleetwood did not yet exist, and the coast here was a mainly desolate stretch where the last serious population upheaval had been settlement by the Vikings more than half a millennium before. Kirkham and the surrounding agricultural land might have had modest importance for the Fylde, but maps also show substantial tracts of undrained land, with Marton Moss to the west, and Pilling Moss a significant feature north of the river Wyre. Low and boggy western Amounderness contrasted with the eastern part of the hundred, where the land rose up into the rough Pennine landscape of the Yorkshire border, the Forest of Bowland and its environs, where the most productive land was devoted to cattle and sheep.

The medieval 'forests' did not necessarily denote trees or woodland. They were areas set aside for hunting, primarily for the king, as Manwood's *Laws of Forest* put it in 1598,

a forest is a certain territory of woody grounds and fruitful pastures privileged for wild beasts of the forest, chase, and warren, to rest and abide in, in the safe protection of the king, for his princely delight and pleasure. Which territory of ground so privileged is mered and bounded with unremovable marks and meres ...

Though woodland remained widespread, the general picture of the sixteenth and seventeenth centuries was one of retreat. From the 1550s commissioners began to parcel out common land on a substantial scale, while the crown often prospered from fines levied on those who had transgressed against its real or imagined royal forest rights, rather than attempt to maintain all of the historic forest assets. Moryson in his *Itinerary* of 1617 also remarked how gentlemen of this 'prodigal age' preferred rather to improve their revenues by 'disparking' the land and keeping cattle.[2]

Easily the most significant town in Amounderness was Preston, which owed its importance to its market and its geographic position as a major

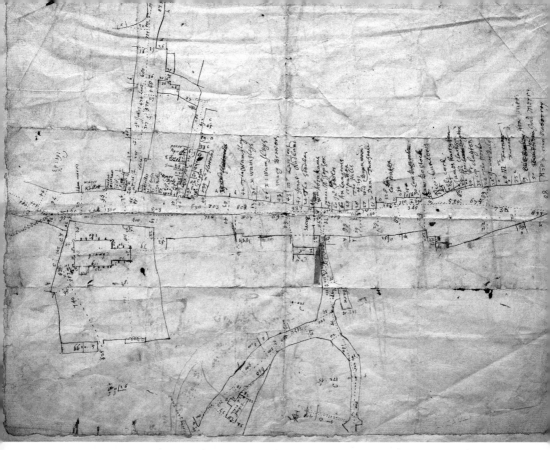

This is a detail from one of a remarkable series of late seventeenth-century survey maps which survive for both Preston and Lancaster and attributed to Richard Kuerden. This detail shows Preston parish church (*left*), with Church Street (or Churchgate) extending eastwards. The names of some of the occupiers are given and the Church Street town bars can be seen around the centre of this detail.

crossing point of the Ribble. 'Proud Preston' was both a conduit for agricultural produce, and a site of potential strategic significance, although the old wooden Norman castle at Penwortham across the river was long since ruined, leaving a desolate mound. Famously Preston's internal trade was regulated by its Guild, a medieval institution of surprising resilience and longevity.

In 1630–31 plague had struck Preston, killing a large if unquantified percentage of the population. As Alexander Rigby reported to his brother George in July 1631, the pestilence was not merely confined to Preston itself, but spread across surrounding towns and villages, 'The sickness in these parts increaseth much, and disperseth. It is now in Fulwood, Cadeley, and in Kirkham; so that the inhabitants and bordering neighbours leave their howses and seeke and resort to forrin places.' In Penwortham, where the number of burials had been just 34 in 1630, at least 132 were buried the following year. Eventually the epidemic would reach far to the north and west. The 'fearfull infection' spread into the 'pore Fylde', causing 'miserable distresse'; and local folklore has it that the disease reached Dalton in Furness carried 'in a parcel of ribbons', and ultimately killing 360 people, which, if correct, was much of the population. Rigby himself considered sending his children to Cheshire where they might be safer. Another letter, sent to George Kenyon a few weeks later, attempted to put his mind at rest by assuring the recipient that its bearer lived at Ellel, just south of Lancaster, an uninfected area. To be doubly sure that he had not caught anything the messenger had refrained from drinking on the way. Another precaution put in place by justice of the peace Roger Kenyon was to cease having books delivered in case they, or their porter, was a plague carrier, 'till God make it less dangerous'. At the other end of the social scale the unfortunate vagrant Henry Towneley of Bolton was suspected, together with his wife and family, of having been begging within infected areas. They now 'laid in the highways about Bolton', and were construed as a serious threat to public health. The constables of Bolton therefore obtained a writ from the Bishop of Chester, allowing them forcibly to deport the family to Huncoat, high on the moors near Burnley, thus preventing the 'affrighting of the country'.

Most people avoided infected areas altogether if they could, and indeed by mid-August 1631 orders arrived from London for the 'restrayning of travellers' and 'ordering the people at home for the better prevention of the infection'. Law officers in the Fylde actually appealed to Lancaster to excuse either them, or felons, from having to travel up to the county town for their cases to be heard. The authorities in Blackburn, mindful of 'God's mercifull deliverance' of their town hitherto, were not minded to tempt providence any further, and therefore asked permission to bar all persons not known to abide in plague-free areas. This ban would extend to 'all or moste of the common people'. Darwen did not escape infection, and was 'restrained from church and market' as a precaution against the spread of disease: as a result it was unable assist other blighted areas.

It was therefore understandable that when the epidemic was at its height in Preston fuel ran out, and nobody could be persuaded to bring it in. The judges of the assize at Lancaster therefore suggested that 'some convenient place' near Preston should be earmarked, and both food and fuel dumped there so that the purchasers could emerge to collect them later while the vendors avoided contagion. Nevertheless things got so bad that a collection of 'three score pounds' per week was ordered from the rest of the county for the relief of the town until 'the ceasing of the said sickness'. Roger Kenyon later determined that £856 5s. 5d. had been disbursed, the maximum number of persons receiving the benefit being 1,390. This was probably a majority of the inhabitants, since other accounts show that three quarters or more of the total population received assistance at this time. Interestingly individuals received varying amounts being anything from 8d. to 12d. each at different times.[3]

According to figures put together by Sir Gilbert Hoghton and other justices meeting at Hoghton Tower the population of Preston dipped as low as 887 in late August 1631, although this figure certainly excluded refugees who managed to flee and return at a later date. It might also have omitted babes in arms. Estimates of the number of inhabitants in Preston at the time of the civil war have been put as low as 1,000, and for many years afterwards there would be no more than 2,000 Prestonians.

Just to the south of the Ribble was Leyland, Lancashire's smallest hundred. Blessed with fertile arable farmland, it was a little wealthier than the northern parts of the county. Certainly the area had at least its share of country seats and gentlefolk, with Park Hall at Charnock Richard, Bank Hall Bretherton, Mawdsley and Euxton halls, Astley Hall at Chorley and

Astley Hall, Chorley, home of the royalist Charnock family. Originally built in the sixteenth century, the house retains many seventeenth-century features.
PHOTOGRAPH: AUTHOR

other houses prominent in the landscape. It was at Carr House, Much Hoole, that the celebrated young curate and astronomer Jeremiah Horrocks first observed the transit of Venus, in 1639. The settlements of Chorley and Leyland themselves feature on contemporary maps, although neither had a large population. Leyland appeared in the Domesday Book, and boasted a church with a twelfth-century foundation: nevertheless it was commonly referred to as a 'village'.

Except perhaps for widespread Catholicism, Leyland hundred can be seen as rather more like the rest of England than many parts of the shire. Leyland hundred was very much 'central Lancashire', and as such it would soon be at a crossroads of military strategy and supply. Of particular potential strategic importance was Hoghton Tower, ancient seat of the Hoghtons, just five miles from Preston at what might be considered the gateway to Blackburn.

Bordering Leyland and inland from Amounderness was Blackburn hundred, a rather larger space which encompassed both a part of the eastern Pennines, and part of the fertile Ribble Valley. The hundred owed its name to the parish and town of Blackburn, a settlement whose Christian heritage stretched back to at least the Dark Ages. The area was one of particular contradictions. In some respects it was one of the most advanced parts of the county, for the manufacture of fustians was already well established here – and this was one of the few indicators of Lancashire's future industrial pre-eminence. Coal was also being mined near Burnley. Yet if part of Blackburn hundred looked to the future, a substantial part looked to the past. For the Forest of Pendle was wild, bleak and backward. The most important recent event here had been the notorious Lancashire witch case of 1612, an episode that would be taken as a legal model for other counties. Though the 'Pendle Witches' were undoubtedly the most notorious of their age, belief in magic and the supernatural was widespread and enduring. Documents for a number of Lancashire cases of 'enchantment' survive, and although the subject was by no means as sensational in the 1630s as it had been in the reign of James I, the matter was still brought, from time to time, to the attention of the courts. In 1638, for example, Peter Winn brought forward the case of Anne Spencer of Lathom, 'a knowen wich', who was accused of having 'greiviously tormented' Sara Cross by witchcraft until she died.[4]

In Blackburn hundred there was also at least one pocket of endeavour that we might fairly characterise as cutting edge 'science'. The Towneleys of Towneley Hall were recognised as particularly interested in natural phenomena, and Christopher Towneley collected the papers of northern astronomers including not only Horrocks, but William Crabtree and William

Gascoigne. As Sir Edward Sherburne would later observe, Christopher Towneley, 'stuck not for any cost or labour to promote' both astronomical and mathematical studies. Richard Towneley conducted experiments that involved taking thermometers and barometers up hills and down mines. Amazingly Robert Boyle generously referred to his own work on the relationship of pressure and volume in gas – which finally culminated in 'Boyle's law' – as 'Mr Towneley's hypothesis'. Gascoigne's micrometer, arguably a crucial idea for the industrial revolution of the eighteenth century, would be improved and brought to the attention of the Royal Society, by Richard Towneley, in 1666.[5]

Blackburn hundred was also surprisingly 'gentrified', having as many families of quality and title as either Amounderness or Leyland. The hamlet of Walton-le-Dale alone boasted a baronet, an esquire, and two 'gentlemen'. Yet what constituted the gentry class was always difficult to define precisely, and a title, or pretensions, were not always backed by hard cash. Many

Towneley Hall, home to the Towneley family for five centuries until the male line died out in the 1870s.

Gawthorpe Hall, Padiham, near Burnley, Lancashire. Largely reconstructed in the early seventeenth century, Gawthorpe was home to the Shuttleworth family, and for much of the war effectively the key parliamentarian headquarters in East Lancashire.
PHOTOGRAPH: CARNEGIE, 2009

Lancashire gentlemen had incomes of less than £100 a year – and plentiful burdens in terms of expenses and taxes. Very few Lancastrians were truly rich. Yet some of the gentry families of Blackburn hundred would be key players in the civil war, the Shuttleworths of Gawthorpe Hall being perhaps the most significant.

An example of the other extreme of Blackburn hundred's social scale was the case of Thomas Sagar, a married man from Ribchester. Having become seriously mentally ill, his family were forced to restrain him, and he became a 'chained lunatic'. Whether his deranged condition had anything to do with the war is unknown, but in early 1643 his wife was forced to apply to the magistrates for financial relief. As an illustration of the total lack of public health provision, and the precariousness of life in seventeenth-century Lancashire, there can be few better examples. Education does not appear to

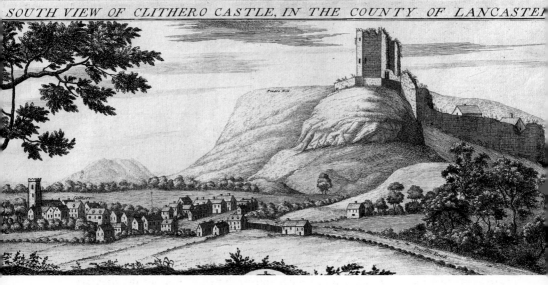

SOUTH VIEW OF CLITHERO CASTLE, IN THE COUNTY OF LANCASTER

A detail of Bucks' view of Clitheroe town and castle, 1727. The perspectives are awry, but the basic disposition of castle keep upon its rock above the town is accurate enough.

have been a strength of Blackburn hundred either. Schools were few, and that at Clitheroe came in for particular criticism. About 1630 Sir Raphe Ashton was of the opinion that the governors of the school were incompetent, and the schoolmaster himself was 'fitter to keepe hogges than bring up youth'. Blackburn's own grammar school had been founded as early as 1509, but lacked its own premises, lessons being held within the parish church.[6]

The entire south-west corner of Lancashire was occupied by sprawling West Derby hundred. Low-lying but of relatively poor soil, the area was dominated by the holdings of the Earl of Derby. The main Derby residence at this period was Lathom House, not far from Ormskirk. Clever marriages, and accident of inheritance, had brought the Lathom estate into the Stanley family patrimony in 1390. The original Lathom House was undoubtedly grand, regarded as a 'Northern Court', a haven of wealth and political influence in an otherwise backward area. Given how little visible survives today – even the precise location of the house is a matter of debate – it is surprising that this substantial defended residence was ever there. The author of the *Discourse of the Warr* in Lancashire was able to state that the Earls of Derby were 'esteemed by most about them with little lesse respect than kings'. William Stanley, the sixth Earl of Derby, had been born in 1561 and was thus an octogenarian by the time civil war was looming. From middle age he had progressively handed over much of his responsibilities to his son James, who retained the title Lord Strange until the death of the father in 1642. James, then aged 35, duly became the seventh Earl.

Despite the Derbys' pre-eminence it would be a mistake to regard the Stanley family position as in any way omnipotent. The vicissitudes of the Wars of the Roses had found them on the winning side in 1485, and this had helped to make their fortune. Yet royal favour could be fickle, and failure to produce an heir had caused both dynastic and financial crisis for the family in the 1590s. As relatives of the Stuart royal family the earls were natural allies of the crown, but equally, under the wrong circumstances, they could be regarded as competitors or substitutes in any battle for the throne. While the monarch might view the Earl of Derby as a convenient mechanism for keeping one of the wilder corners of the realm in some sort of order, the task on the ground would be politically complex. The demands of the centre were not necessarily in accordance with family interest, nor would they be accepted in full as a matter of course by those who owed allegiance to the Earl. Religion was perhaps the most obvious case in point, since many Lancastrians were Catholic, and the state was Protestant. As one recent commentator has

A large number of vessels are depicted in the Mersey in this painting of *c*.1680 by an unknown artist. Liverpool was a major North West port, whose strategic importance in relation to Ireland was to play a part during the conflict. The castle can be seen to the right in this view, with the Tower on the river front in the centre. In the background may be seen Everton hill, where Prince Rupert was to set up his headquarters in 1644.
LIVERPOOL RECORD OFFICE

observed circumstances constrained the Earls of Derby 'to seem to be all things to all men'.[7]

Liverpool, despite its medieval castle, harbour, and access to the Mersey – allowing the import and export of coal and textiles and significant trading contact with Ireland and the Stanleys' holdings in the Isle of Man – was as yet relatively insignificant, with a population of under 2,000. The town had been affected by plague in 1609, and in the 1620s there were dozens, rather than hundreds, of christenings annually. Even at the end of the century, and after much new building, Celia Fiennes would describe a settlement of 24 streets with only one parish church and a chapel. Liverpool was thus smaller than Wigan. Even so, compared to the relatively empty countryside around it, Liverpool was a place of note, and, because of its maritime location, of significant strategic importance. During the war one parliamentarian report would describe it as 'a market towne and of great resort, a garrison towne and the cheeffe port of theise parts'. Its access to Catholic Ireland could be seen as potential, or threat, depending on one's political sympathies.

Wigan was a town of more than 2,000 before the civil war, proportionately more significant than it is today. Its produce included copper, pewter and brass, and it already benefited from local coal mining. The Wigan coalfield, which lay close about the town, had been recognised as early as the fifteenth century, and its exploitation had started in earnest in the sixteenth. By the 1630s extraction was of some thousands of tons per year, with this area almost certainly the most significant coal producer in the county. Potential for further development was apparent, but doubtless held back by the difficulty of transporting large volumes of coal any great distance in a time of poor roads, pack animals and relatively small carts. Nevertheless, the Wigan area was also important for its corn and cattle. The latter were the famous black Lancashire longhorns, some of which may have been driven as far as London to find their market.[8]

Salford hundred occupied a substantial, south-east corner of Lancashire, and as such shared long boundaries with both Yorkshire and Cheshire. In many ways it was both more outward- and more forward-looking than other parts of the county. The contrast between the towns to be found here and some of the rural backwaters of north Lancashire could be considerable. The early growth of industry in south-east Lancashire took place outside the old 'corporate' towns: in Manchester, Rochdale and Bolton trades grew up and expanded beyond the reach of old restrictive practices, and regulations that had been formed for a different age.

Manchester was pre-eminent, different. So much was clearly apparent to contemporaries, even to those from other parts of the country. As Arthur

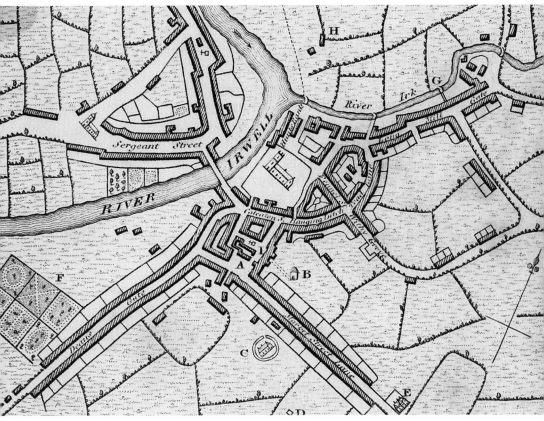

Manchester in 1650. This version of a now-lost mid-seventeenth-century map of the town is from Baines' map of Manchester dating from 1824. The rivers Irwell and Irk bound Manchester to the north and west, with Salford opposite. This is not an easily defensible place, but Manchester did witness the first named fatality of the wars.

Trevor put it in 1642, Manchester is 'the very London of those parts'. Local pretensions were underlined by a petition to the new parliament in March 1641 which urged the foundation of a university in the town, a proposal with considerable local support which might have come to fruition were it not for growing unrest over the following year. Manchester was certainly the largest and most cosmopolitan town in Lancashire, with an estimated population of about 4,000 in 1642. Mancunians were already acknowledged locally as the 'most industrious' people of the North. Visitors were interested to note that even many of 'the very children' were maintaining themselves by their labour. The town's relative prosperity owed much to its growing cloth trade, weaving linen yarn for Ireland and other markets, and working imported 'cotton wool', as it was then called, into fustians and other textiles adding value and a profit to the finished wares. The Irish trade was well enough established that a spot near Smithy Door became customary for the merchants to meet, and fittingly enough to be known as the 'Patrick Stone'.

Manchester products also found their way to London. According to Lewis Robert's *Treasure of Traffike* some of the Manchester merchants purchased their 'cotton wool' from the Mediterranean and Turkey in London. This was then transported north and worked in Manchester. Such was the profitability of the trade that it was possible to return it to London for sale, some even getting back to 'foreign parts'. Despite this success the textile trades of the south-east Lancashire towns were still essentially small scale. Spinning and weaving were jobs for families or individuals, performed mainly within the home or small outbuildings. Nor was the manufacture of yarn or cloth necessarily an exclusive employment: family incomes were frequently supplemented with small-scale agriculture, husbandry, service, trade and barter.

Manchester goods for the capital included not just cotton, but linen commonly called 'Stockport cloth', rugs, yarn, and baize. Smaller scale enterprises were carried on by 'chapmen' who rode to the metropolis to sell their little goods and trinkets at the London fairs. As there were bridges across the Mersey at Warrington, Stretford and Stockport, communication with Cheshire was probably easier than that across the Pennines. Chester, still the most important town in the North West, was within relatively easy reach and formed a gateway to both Ireland and the Midlands. Although it had no town wall, Manchester was not entirely defenceless. The river Irwell was a substantial obstacle on the west, with a lesser boundary marked by the Irk to the north. As it turned out some of the buildings provided substantial enclosures from which a determined force might make resistance.

Yet Manchester's relative modernity and commercial bustle was at best comparative, and, set against London, Bristol or Norwich, Manchester was but a pinprick on the map. As yet trade with the Americas, or any overseas territories, was infrequent and most Mancunians – and Liverpudlians – looked little further than the rest of the British Isles for their windows on the world.

The court leet records of the mid-seventeenth century present a colourful – near medieval – view of a town still far from its future Victorian splendour. In 1640 Edward Richardson; Margery Bowringe; widow Francis Hallie; Richard Whitworth senior and William Hardman all found themselves referred to the court for 'layinge dunghills in severall places in the high ways within the town of Manchester'. Others were singled out for 'emptyinge of stinkinge water and other excrements' into the gutters, and the theme of foul ditches and clogged drainage continued through the century. As in many other Lancashire towns plague was still an occasional visitor, a particularly serious outbreak having occurred in 1605. Fresh visitations were considered likely enough for a six-acre field near to the town to be designated as a potential isolation area shortly afterwards. Here the townspeople would have liberty to build huts in which the sick could be placed, and bury them if they fell victim. Justice in seventeenth-century Manchester could often appear strange through modern eyes. In April 1648, for example, the town authorities would order the erection of a 'cuck stool' or ducking stool for the punishment of offenders, but not long afterwards the constables were themselves criticised for their failure to put one up: as a result Mary Kempe, a convicted 'common scold', went without her dunking.[9]

By the early seventeenth century Manchester had its own beadle to look at the problem of vagrancy on a stipend of 1s. per week. Additionally he was allowed 4d. for every vagabond that he whipped – thought by some to be the origin of the term 'a fourpenny one'. More enlightened was the attitude of those who set up charities upon their deaths. The Virginia Company contributed £30 to a fund by means of which yarn was purchased for the poor to work on. In due course the finished product would be sold, the proceeds supporting the workers and going toward more materials.[10]

Lancashire was a poor county in relative terms, yet not all Lancastrians were poor. A sprinkling of gentry families lived quite well. Lancashire manor houses of the period could be quite ambitious in terms of plan and internal arrangements, and a significant number exceeded twenty bedchambers: there were 28 at Lytham Hall in 1634, and 24 at Rufford in 1620. Beds and bedding were particularly expensive items, with probate inventories suggesting that about half of the cost of the total furnishing of the Lancashire gentleman's house went upon the family sleeping arrangements. In 1618, for example, Richard Ashton of Middleton was found to have £312 worth of furnishings in his house, a full £150 of which was invested in beds and bedding.

Dining rooms, parlours, and studies all featured in Lancashire's halls, and though books were a relatively expensive commodity, libraries were also found in the best homes. Robert Hesketh is likely to have been one of the most avid readers, with a collection of books valued at £50 in 1620. Lord Derby's library was the most splendid, as might be expected, with 265 books – 54 of them having gilded bindings. Butteries, cellars and brew-houses were often connected to the main dwelling and around the model Lancashire hall were found numerous outbuildings and related properties containing farms, stables

Contemporary woodcut showing drinkers at an alehouse. The 'pot boy' on the left might indeed be very young – pubs were the subject of local legislation, but age was not taken into consideration until much later. Note the tobacco pipes, a common accompaniment to drink at this time. Pipes were often purchased pre-filled, the tobacco being more expensive than the clay pipe itself, which was regarded as semi-disposable.

and sometimes mills. The better off frequently had what has been described as 'a self contained community with its own staff living on the spot and providing to a very considerable extent for its own needs' – Rufford had at least 20 servants, Dunkenhalgh more than 30.[11]

Though land and agriculture were still regarded as the bedrock of wealth and status in Lancashire, fortunes were already being made from trade and industry. One good example was the happy prosperity of Salford's leading citizen, Henry Wrigley. This man's substance came essentially from his business as a linen draper and money lender. His status as a merchant was further enhanced by his London warehouse, although his attempts to establish a monopoly over West Indian cotton were overtaken by the war. There were also quite a few small tradesmen, who were, though by no means rich, perfectly comfortable by the standards of the day. John Breres, a tanner of Chorley who died in 1614, left behind him goods, chattels, and a list of bills to clients that showed him to be worth almost £300. His prize possessions included not just cattle, and stocks of yarn, wheat, malt, barley and flax, but small luxuries such as pewter and brassware, cushions, and some silver spoons that were valued at 30s. Lawrence Breres of Whittle-le-Woods, a kinsman who died just after the Restoration, boasted an inventory of goods valued at £186, despite being described, modestly, as a 'yeoman'. His property included seven cushions; four beds; at least two chairs and five stools; various other pieces of furniture including a desk; some pewter – plus the usual stock and equipment for farming and husbandry. His clothes alone were assessed at £4.

Religion and society

Lancashire had about 60 parishes during the civil war period, with some 63 parish churches and 118 chapels recorded in a survey of 1650. This suggests that there was at least one officially established Anglican place of worship for every thousand head of the population. This, however, was but part of the story. At 1650 it was noted that 38 of the churches and chapels were without a minister, usually for want of 'maintenance'. In a poor county the church was also relatively poor: the incumbents of 17 of Lancashire's parishes had incomes of £40 *per annum* or less. Curates were far worse off, with 51 of them bringing in less than £15 each year. The worst paid clergy were thus earning little more than might be expected by a common soldier. Moreover the parishes were far from even in size, and the distance to a church could be considerable. Church attendance was not therefore as high as it might otherwise have been.[12]

One of the most God-forsaken places was the land around Admarsh chapel in Bleasdale, which had 'neither minister nor maintenance'. The local population were said to be 'careless people, knowing nothing of the worship of God, but live in ignorance and superstition, and six miles from any Church or Chapel'. The Yorkshire divine John Shaw regarded north Lancashire generally as a desert in terms of religious instruction. At Cartmel he claimed to have found a man who had only once heard of Christ, and then had no real comprehension of who he was. Most Lancastrians were devout, at least nominally, but cynicism was not unheard of. Though most atheists and non-believers kept quiet, at Pendle in 1626 a man was brought to court for uttering the blasphemy that 'God when he did one good turn did two bad, and that if God were there he would cut off his head'.[13]

On the face of it all was conformity and uniformity – a national Christianity with the king as head of the Church, and the localities in agreement. A strict hierarchy led from the congregation of the faithful through their local curate and vicar, up to the bishops. Landowners and nobility had a significant role in the appointment of junior clergy. Senior churchmen sat in parliament by right, but owed their ultimate allegiance to the monarch. The monarch was responsible to God. The Church was not merely seen as an outward expression of spiritual belief, but as the very cement of society. In a non-technological age with limited horizons for the majority, it could realistically be claimed that, for some at least, the Church was their lives. For the many it was intrinsic and integral. With other national institutions comparatively weak, the structure and influence of the Church were, perforce, of prime importance.

Yet in Lancashire all was not harmony. The Reformation had failed to reach – or else failed to convince – a substantial minority of Lancastrians. Catholicism survived, particularly outside the major towns, and with great depth and strength in the west of the county. A majority of the convictions for recusancy reported nationally in 1641–42 were in Lancashire. For the establishment this was an ongoing threat, associated in suspicious government minds with rebellion, subversion, and to loyalties to parties outside the kingdom. Most suspect were those Jesuits and others who had actually gone abroad, to train at Douai and other continental seminaries, and then come back to import the poison. As the Privy Council had observed to the then earl of Derby in 1574, Lancashire was 'the very sink of popery'. Nevertheless, not all habits were conscious, or necessarily subversive. At the beginning of the reign of James I in 1603 both Catholic and non-Catholic Lancastrians were noted as making the 'sign of the cross', or crossing themselves with more than usual frequency. The peasantry in general did not shed old beliefs easily; nor did they as a matter of course embrace new ideas, and in some instances did not understand them.[14]

If Lancashire had more than its share of religious reactionaries, and ancient conservatism which stretched back to, and beyond, the reign of King Henry, it also had a strong strain of innovation in the contrary direction. On the other wing of Christianity were the radicals of the 'low' Church, 'fundamentalists' in the broader sense of the term, who saw God in his word, not in any outward forms. Again, the inspirations came from outside the county: but usually either from London, the universities, or from parts of northern Europe where Protestantism was especially vibrant and vocal. It is convenient to regard those of Low Church persuasion as 'Puritan' – a handy and descriptive portmanteau – but in reality many were far more inclined to Presbyterian ideas, faithful to the word and distrusting of innovations not mentioned in the scriptures. Some relative few were more 'independent' of any obvious category, and the term itself would later gain currency, and a specific political meaning.

Unlike Catholics, who were ultimately followers of Christ through the see of St Peter and his holiness at Rome, or the devotees of the established church with their conforming trust in God and King, Puritans had far more risky

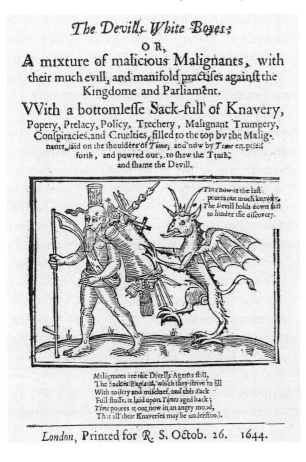

The Devills White Boyes:

OR,

A mixture of malicious Malignants, with their much evill, and manifold practises against the Kingdome and Parliament.

With a bottomlesse Sack-full of Knavery, Popery, Prelacy, Policy, Trechery, Malignant Trumpery, Conspiracies, and Cruelties, filled to the top by the Malignants, laid on the shoulders of *Time*; and now by *Time* emptied forth, and powred out, to shew the Truth, and shame the Devill.

Time now at the last pours out much knavery. The Devill holds down fast to hinder the discovery.

Malignants are the Divells Agents still,
The Sack is England, which they strive to fill
With misery and mischief, and this Sack
Full stuff, is laid upon *Times* aged back;
Time poures it out now in an angry mood,
That all their Knaveries may be understood.

London, Printed for R. S. Octob. 26. 1644.

How 'malignancy', 'Popery', and 'knavery' were all linked in the popular parliamentarian press with the work of the Devil. From a pamphlet printed in London, October 1644.

personal horizons of religious authority. At the extreme Puritan thinkers also had more urgent and unstable concerns, for a literal belief in the bible as the word of God perforce accepted Revelations, as well as Exodus and Genesis. To suggest that further reform was required along fundamentalist lines opened the door to not just to reorganisation of the church, but potentially to millenarianism, and other things likely to 'turn the world upside down'.

Many Protestant nonconformists, either secretly or openly, would accept little or no religious hierarchy. For the more moderate this stopped at a suspicion of bishops, and a reluctance to accept any innovation from the centre that looked like 'popery'. For the most extreme nothing – no minister, no King, no authority – could come between them and their maker. Personal conscience was all. At the very least this prevented 'Puritans' from becoming a monolithic, organised body. In its fullest manifestation the result was many sects, which would actually multiply as the shackles of central authority were weakened by war. In Lancashire during the civil war period nonconformists were never in a majority anywhere: indeed in sheer numbers they were generally far inferior to the Catholics. Even so, there was a significant concentration in the south-east of the county, and the incidence of Puritanism has also been associated more generally with market towns – where trade and the new religion appear to have fed one upon the other.[15]

Serious Catholic–Protestant violence appears to have been fairly rare in the twenty years leading up to the civil war. Nevertheless there were instances, one of the best illustrations of which is undoubtedly the Ashton *versus* Blundell case which rumbled on for a decade from the early 1620s to the early 1630s. It began, unremarkably, with an accusation of recusancy against Edward Rice, a yeoman of Little Crosby. Rice was bound over against a sum of £20 to appear at Lancaster assizes in August 1622. His non appearance eventually led to the issue of a writ for the seizure of goods and chattels, and accordingly Sir Ralph Ashton, sheriff of Lancaster, dispatched bailiffs to recover items of the appropriate value in 1624. However, as soon as the bailiffs had secured two oxen and a 'nagge' they were set upon by an angry 'troupe of people', numbering about fifty, armed with 'pykeforks, longstaves and muckroukes, one speare or pyke for warre and other weapons'. This gang of 'Popish recusants' rapidly snatched back what had been taken, and one of the bailiffs, William Cowper, was knocked to the ground and wounded.

It was now suggested that not only had there been a dangerous Catholic-inspired riot but that others were complicit in helping Rice to hide his goods, and that William Blundell, the local Catholic gentleman, was actively encouraging his tenants and friends in physical resistance to legal authority. By September 1624 the law was after the 'obstinate recusant' William Blundell himself. Again the bailiffs returned, and again they were violently resisted. Blundell's cattle were driven away into a fenced enclosure to the side of his hall, and a new fracas ensued, allegedly watched by Blundell. Emilia Blundell, his wife, was observed by one of the bailiffs standing on a wall laughing as her servants laid into the men who had been sent to take their property. Bailiff Richard Hardman was seriously hurt, by his own account being in pain and 'in danger of deathe' for a period of seven weeks. His son ran for medical help but was chased from Little Crosby by what he later claimed were 16 armed persons, who shouted that they were going to kill him so that he would 'tell no tales'. A surgeon later attested that Richard Hardman had sustained a two and a half-inch deep, 'verie dangerous' chest wound.

Complaints were now made by Ashton to the Court of Star Chamber. At the examination of these events, held in Wigan in 1625, the Blundells denied all the charges put to them, and instead blamed Rice and his brother for the violence. When confronted with evidence of a recusant graveyard at Harkirk, where the bodies of Catholics were being interred at his behest, Blundell protested that in fact this was being used merely because the rector of the Established Church was refusing burial. His little cemetery was not therefore a recusant plot, but a mercy provided to those 'refused at the Church'.

One would have thought that the involvement of Star Chamber and the calling of Blundell before the authorities might have quietened the situation. However, in August 1626, new attempts were made to confiscate goods from William Blundell and others in lieu of unpaid fines for recusancy. Now Robert Mawdsley the Deputy Sheriff and Edward Moore JP organised posse of 20. Predictably the result was another riot, with at least 14 'yong rash fellowes' from Little Crosby entering the fray, but according to Blundell's account it was the authorities who were the heavy-handed aggressors. Among other things it was said that an old woman was beaten, and called 'Demme Dyke', being 'the name of a famous witche'. Obviously this time the posse achieved its aim for they took away with them cattle, swine, and other items to a value of well over £100. Another enquiry under the direct auspices of the court of Star Chamber ensued, and Blundell was ordered to pay heavy fines and dispossessed of Crosby Hall. Only in 1631 did a personal letter from the King to the Lord Treasurer pardon Blundell, and reduce his fines to a manageable level. Little wonder then that we should find Blundells and Ashtons on opposite sides of future conflict, and Blundells loyal to the King.[16]

If religion was a highly contentious area, then by modern standards local administration and law and order were extremely patchy – again a point well illustrated by the Blundell case. Justices of the peace were important arbiters, but are likely to have been limited and inefficient in their impact. Though there may have been more justices in the sixteenth century, by 1640 there were only 39 for the entire county: and this equated to about one per 4,000 of the population. Part of the problem went back to the religious issue again, since Catholics could not hold office, and many of the gentry in the remoter parts of the county were Catholic. Justices usually had other interests, and it is obvious that in most of Lancashire's scattered communities at any given time no JP was readily to hand. Comparative calculations also suggest that Lancashire JPs actually dealt with proportionately fewer cases than their colleagues in more prosperous counties: yet there is no suggestion that Lancashire was any more law abiding, and possibly it was less.

When cases did reach the courts there was a quantum leap between the petty and the serious. Minor cases before the magistrate or the quarter sessions

might lead to a fine which might, or might not, be paid. Serious criminal cases
went to the assizes at Lancaster where the death penalty was available for a
range of crimes. The idea of any significant term of imprisonment was unusual,
if not completely impractical, given the lack of facilities for incarceration in
most areas. Holding poor people was fairly pointless in any case since they
were in little position to finance their captivity. Corporal punishment and
shaming therefore filled more important roles than we might expect. Moral
stigma could also be a significant if cruel enforcer of conformity. In cases
of bastardy for example the mothers of illegitimate children who could not
find support from the father, or their family, were likely to get short shrift
where maintenance from an already poor community might be concerned.
This disapproval could be forcefully backed up with an officially sanctioned
whipping. Nevertheless Lancashire had relatively high rates of illegitimacy,
and Sefton, where a full ten per cent of children were born out of wedlock
in the 1630s, must have been close to being the bastardy capital of England.

    Clearly such daily regulation as there was in the localities usually devolved
to part-time local officials, some of whom were unpaid. High constables served
for the hundreds of the county, but at the really local level petty constables and
churchwardens were probably the two most important figures. In townships
petty constables were clearly vital, although their quality and competence
varied tremendously. Given the difficulties of maintaining harmony in isolated
villages, the lack of any real method for examining petty or moral crime, and
the often thankless nature of the task, being constable was rarely popular. In
many of Lancashire's villages the office was therefore a duty which was carried
out in rotation – with office-holding passing from one head of household
to another by 'hedge-row' or 'house-row'. In some townships the office was
shared out between just a handful of families, and the duty came round to
each more frequently than was welcomed. Most minor crimes and disputes
were probably settled locally long before they ever reached a justice of the
peace, let alone a formal court. The constable was therefore as much a local
mediator, and voice of consensus, as an officer of the law. Perforce there was
very little to distinguish him from his neighbour, who might well be the
constable the following year.[17]

    There is some evidence, however, to suggest that petty constables of the
rural hamlets and those of significant towns were rather different in kind
and in station. At the upper end of the local stratum Manchester's constables
of the period 1632 to 1648 included a number of persons styled 'gentleman',
and apothecaries, clothiers and chapmen. On the other hand quite few of
the rural constables were illiterates who signed papers with a cross – their

'mark'. Though considered for such a position, George Page of Clitheroe was specifically excused duty as constable on the grounds of poverty.

The churchwarden was far more important in seventeenth-century Lancashire than in the modern era. His job encompassed not only maintenance of the church, but keeping accounts, and disbursements to the poor, and sometimes during the civil war period payments to maimed soldiers. As dictated by the 1601 Act the churchwarden was, together with the overseers of the poor, part of the official machinery of the Poor Law. In small rural communities both the churchwardens and constable were likely to be significant figures – particularly if the clergyman was an absentee and there was no JP in the vicinity. However, depending on the size of the village or town, there were likely to be other people with official tasks, such as clerks to administer markets; ale-tasters and 'streetlookers' who dealt with obstructions in the streets or encroachments upon the highways. Moderate-size towns might well have a score of such appointees: Manchester could number over a hundred.

Liverpool's structure of local administration and regulation was particularly well documented in the Liverpool Town Books. As might be expected the senior local figure was the mayor, with John Walker in post from 1641, and James Williamson installed in 1643. The mayor's oath dictated that he swear allegiance to the crown, obey His Majesty's laws, and uphold the liberties and franchises of the town. A requirement introduced in December 1641 was, that 'for the tyme being and soe evey Maior shall on his owne costes fynd the two preachers that preach every exercise day togeither with the preacher belonging to this Towne'. Though modest, these measures were a doubtless indication of a growing puritan sympathy amongst certain classes in the town. Traditionally the church-going of the mayor was attended by the sergeant and bailiffs, whose ceremonial presence was enhanced, like that of the Lord Mayor of London, by the carrying of arms. New halberds were purchased for this honour guard in 1648.

Nor was the symbolism purely decorative: the mayor of Liverpool retained local legal status, presiding over the portmoot court. Here minor cases including assaults, what we might now term health and safety violations, morality issues, and the like were tried. The town book records many instances of bastardy, blasphemy, and scuffles, as well as of dumping manure and refuse. Pretending to be a free man was also punished. Defamation of the legitimate officials of the town and mayor were severely frowned upon. In 1643, for example, Liverpudlian Henry Haskaine was called to account for abusing bailiff Massam, 'calleing him a hollwharted knave, a base knave and a Cheating knave and for offering to lay violent hands upon him'.

The two bailiffs were second in place only to the mayor, and their work combined that of local tax collector with senior court official. Though they were invariably men of prominent local families their work inevitably brought them into conflict with ne'er-do-wells, and those genuinely aggrieved at the legal system. After the outbreak of hostilities in 1642 their stance appears to have been essentially parliamentarian, and this may have led to a general tendency to assume that Liverpool was actually more against the king than was the case. Mayor John Walker certainly appears to have had royalist sympathies – being threatened with both imprisonment and transportation under parliament.

Other significant Liverpool officials included the recorder and town clerk – the former quite literally recording legal and official proceedings in writing, the latter dealing with many administrative matters including the issue of warrants. The 'Stewards of the Hall' were the most junior legal officials of Liverpool, and one of their main duties was to furnish the hall, the upper floor of which was the court. Being Liverpool town sergeant was quite lucrative before the civil war, for the position had brought with it a fee of 4d. for 'everie Tickett or warrant' that he issued. A curious arrangement introduced in 1630 also provided that everyone arrested by the sergeant should pay him 2s. 6d. If the accused could not be proved guilty, the plaintiff then had to pay the sergeant instead. For a while the sergeant thus had a pecuniary interest in arresting anyone and everyone, but it was not to last. Fees became such an 'inconvenience and preiudice to everie freeman' that in 1642 it was decided that the sergeant's perquisites should be scrapped. Instead there was reversion to the ancient system where his wages were collected 'everie Christmas' from the burgesses.

Lower down the social and administrative tree were other officers with more specialised remit. These included 'registers of tanned leather', who enforced regulations concerning leather; 'levelookers' who were supposed to check the quality of food in the markets and 'alefounders' whose task was to certify that ale and bread were wholesome and reasonably priced. 'Booth setters', 'board setters' and 'scavengers' also had their roles to play in commerce, and the smooth operation of the town, ensuring that stalls were set up properly and rubbish cleaned away. Around the outskirts of the town were others whose official job was of an essentially agricultural nature. These included a 'hayward' who looked after the crops on the town field, 'moss reeves' and 'burleymen' helped ensure rights of way and prevented encroachments on common land.

The 'free burgesses' were the leading citizens of seventeenth-century Liverpool, the numbers of whom appear to have grown substantially in the decades leading up to the civil war. By 1629 there were no fewer than 337. They included the local nobility, gentlemen, esquires, and some of the officials who held other posts within the town hierarchy. At the height of the war, in 1644, there were no fewer than 454 burgesses, including 46 military officers. Whilst many of the burgesses were clearly wealthy men, or had status in other walks of life, not all would have been rich – and some were quite modest tradesmen. Among the less exalted were to be found a couple of 'husbandmen'; a blacksmith; a cooper; a yeoman and a brewer. Given the number of burgesses, and the relatively small population, a sizeable percentage of adult males residing in Liverpool must have had free burgess status. Importantly this bestowed upon them exemption from the town's customs, and from some tolls. Existing 'free' men could bring their offspring into the ranks of the free burgesses for a payment of 3s. 4d., but freemen could also be elected from outside the town through family or other connections, usually being admitted upon a charge of anything ranging from £1 to £7. Probably the cheapest free burgess was Thomas Darbisheire who was admitted for nothing in 1647 on the basis that he kept the town clock in good order.

Interestingly the civic oath sworn by the free burgess placed upon him responsibilities as well as rights. He was, in effect, swearing to be a good citizen and a religious conformist, agreeing that if he should,

> heare of any unlawfull Congregacions, conventickles, Ryottes, Routes or unlawfull assemblies or other disordered tumults to be had or made, or lyke to be procured had or made by day or night within this town … yow shall give warninge and notice thereof to the maior or his deputie or bayliffes with all speed. And all and every other thinge or thinges which shall either touch or concerne the advancement or prefermentes of the common welth and state of this towne … you shall for your part doe accomplish, fulfil, performe and observe to the best of your abilitie, power, knowledge and witt.

All this was to be performed with the help of God. Such sworn sentiment was the cement of local society.[18]

The county as 'Armye'

Perhaps surprisingly the military was also an essentially local matter. There was as yet no 'standing' army, and the early Stuarts had very few men under arms. During peacetime the only men the monarch was likely to have available were a few bodyguards, such as the yeomen of the guard, and a few gunners, retained as a nucleus for the royal navy and to garrison key fortifications, mainly in the south and east of England. When an army was required, this would have to be recruited specifically for the purpose in hand, and the mechanisms used were based on the counties and the hundreds, having their roots in medieval systems, better suited for a feudal than an early modern society. The key figures were the king's lord lieutenant of the county and his deputies, who would put in train the directions received from the monarch and his advisors. Parliament had as yet no role in recruiting or the command of military forces, although by now its approval for raising the extraordinary sums needed to pay and equip armed forces through taxation was likely to be necessary. Nevertheless for short periods small forces could be maintained on purely local resources.[19]

What did already exist in the counties was the old 'militia' system. Under precedent which went back beyond medieval feudal obligations to Anglo-Saxon England, the monarch had the right to call out all men aged between 16 and 60 for military service on his behalf – and on occasion this is exactly what was done. As might be imagined, however, youths of 16 without training, and men of 60, possibly with some experience but well past their physical best, did not make for an efficient military force. Moreover, this mass levy could be of only fleeting utility, since without the majority of the male population the local economy would quickly break down. Harvest time in particular would be likely to call a halt to hostilities. Besides, men called out under such a method were probably liable only to serve for a certain number of days, and it was not likely that an enemy would deign to fight according to such a timetable.

The solution to finding soldiers suitable for modern war was the so-called 'trained band'. By the sixteenth century it had become customary not to use everyone liable to call out in a disorganised throng, but to list those eligible for service as 'able men' and then to select from the many a relatively small number to be trained and armed to a better standard. Leaving the bulk of the population to go about their normal business was a more sustainable proposition: but those left behind still had responsibilities, most importantly to provide arms, horses and pay according to their wealth and status. By 1621, for example, anyone worth £10 a year per annum in returns from land was likely to be required to provide a set of armour, plus half the cost of paying a soldier. Exact burdens varied not only with time but also from county to county, with total numbers for each area set by central government. The fact that Lancashire was less well off than many counties is apparent in that

Detail of the famous window in St Chad's church Farndon, Cheshire, depicting a
fifer and drummer. Though based on continental illustrations, the figures are likely to
approximate to the appearance of Lancashire soldiers of the period. Cheshire troops
were involved in a number of the actions in Lancashire, including the defence of
Manchester, the fighting around Warrington, and the siege of Lathom.

PHOTOGRAPH: CARNEGIE, 2009

relatively few expensive cavalry were demanded, and that up to eight persons
were banded together to pay for one horse.

Musters of the part-time soldiery were held, though not very often, and
according to the most authoritative estimate were called as infrequently as once
every three years in quiet times. Nevertheless, training had become an integral
part of the muster by the 1570s, and professional 'muster masters' were often
employed for their specific expertise. Grumbling about waste of time and the
curtailment of liberty were now assuaged at least in part by the introduction of
pay, the troops mustered being entitled to a sum which equalled or exceeded
that earned by the ordinary working man. Commissioners for the enforcement
of rules on the keeping and breeding of horses with a view to having a ready

supply in war were appointed in 1580. As might be expected, the increased threat from Spain increased interest in the militia, and by the time of the Armada in 1588 several days' training each year was an official requirement. In Lancashire there was certainly an awareness of the danger of having Catholics, declared or otherwise, in positions of military authority. An undated document of the reign of Elizabeth, for example, speaks of 'instructions, given at the Queen's Command' that 'none suspected in religion have the charge of any number of soldiers'.

As yet there were no barracks or arsenals anywhere save in the relatively few fortresses, which marked parts of the Scottish border and south coast. The custom therefore was to keep the militia 'embodied' as briefly as possible, sending the men home as soon as might be after training, or marching them out of the county under direction of an appointed 'conductor'. A fragmentary paper of 1602 records that in that year the county supplied 100 men to the service of the state. These were drawn out of the hundreds, 24 from West Derby, 19 from Amounderness, 18 from Blackburn, 16 from Lonsdale, 14 from Salford and just 9 from Leyland hundred. 'Coat and conduct money' was intended to cover the costs. The men were to receive 8d. each per day, while the conductor in charge would be given 16s. The cost of coats, and presumably any other materials required, was set at 4s. – a figure which would not have provided very much even in late Elizabethan England.

The only real alternative to disbanding or marching the troops out of the county was the politically contentious idea of billeting troops on the populace. At best, this led to financial loss and inconvenience: at worst it could turn into riot and wholesale destruction. In some parts 'billeting' was therefore regarded as a form of punishment, or as a measure to subdue the population of an area. Not surprisingly billeting was avoided, and notes made by one Lancashire member of parliament about 1630 suggest that in some circles the issue was viewed essentially as one of the perhaps necessary evils of the king's prerogative. It was something that might however be traded, perhaps against agreement for more rigorous treatment of Catholics.[20]

In the absence of storehouses the custom was for arms and armour to be kept at home, and a gentleman might well have one or more armours and weapons hung on the walls of his hall. The only real alternative was the church, with the church tower doubling as armoury; and late sixteenth-century Lancashire documents do indeed refer to the dispersal of armour to parish churches. In 1595, however, a specific recommendation had been put forward by the Lancashire justices of the peace. Under this scheme dedicated stores were to be set up at Lancaster, Preston, Chorley, Ormskirk, Whalley and

Manchester – one for each hundred of the county. An order was made to this effect, and though not everything may have been achieved immediately militia armouries in the Lancashire hundreds were the order of the day prior to the civil wars. This arrangement would have far-reaching consequences.

With peace in the early part of the reign of James I the militia appears to have relaxed back into its pre-war condition. On at least one occasion both Lancashire and Cheshire failed to submit a certificate of the musters they were supposed to have held, and there was a revival of the corrupt practice of 'borrowing' equipment. The mutual advantage of this trading of munitions between adjoining areas was that only one set of arms and armour had to be bought and maintained – and considerable savings could thus be made. Even when there were enough firearms to go round there were problems because they were of different bores, a problem specifically complained about in Lancashire.

At the accession of Charles I in 1625 the militia was suddenly shaken out of its torpor. With foreign war on the agenda again, there were demands for an 'exact' and well-disciplined militia, and requirements that the latest drill, as laid down in the 1623 manual, should be practised. A surviving document in a deputy lieutenancy letterbook suggests that this drive in no way bypassed Lancashire, a formal 'view and muster' of the trained bands being required that year, along with a check on armour and horses and repair of the warning beacons. In 1626 sergeants who had previously been employed in the Low Countries were brought over to England to drill the home troops. The plan initially was that they would remain for only three months, but in the event many stayed much longer. The sergeants were instructed to meet with the local trained band officers first, then train with one company at a time using

Charles I silver crown, showing an equestrian portrait of the king, against the backdrop of his war-time capital at Oxford, engraved by Thomas Rawlins.

the local corporals to pass on knowledge to the ordinary soldier. Having attained a basic level of proficiency, the companies from the locality could then be brought together for larger scale practice. A least a fragment of the West Derby muster paper for 1626 survives in the British Library collections.[21]

In Lancashire the loyal men of the militia took oaths both of allegiance and supremacy as part of their induction, so that no Catholics, other than those of the closet variety, can have borne arms in this pre-civil war period. The deputy lieutenants of Lancashire returned encouraging reports on proceedings. According to these, 1626 saw intensive training, with many men receiving almost weekly individual coaching; progressively larger groups were mustered, with full companies meeting twice a fortnight. Three of the four Lancashire sergeants certified their bands fit for immediate service. In view of the 'great pains and charges in attending musters, training, exercising, and disciplining', the deputy lieutenants ordered that all trained soldiers were to be excused duty as constables, churchwardens or similar. Two years later particular attention was applied to the cavalry, and a muster of well-equipped horse was reported,

A musketeer, from the drill book by Jacob de Gheyn. The musket was the key infantry weapon of the civil wars. It was not remarkably accurate, nor swift to load, but was devastating when used by formed bodies of troops at close ranges.

though apparently the efficiency of the foot had slipped back somewhat in the meantime. In 1629 the muster masters were put on a more professional basis with the payment of set fees, Lancashire's £50 cost for this purpose being levied from the county. So it was, as Gervase Markham remarked, that the state made 'every severall Countie' an 'Armye'.[22]

The basic building block of the county militias was the infantry company, and the smallest unit was the individual musketeer. Markham provides us with an ideal description of his arms and equipment, which the muster master was to examine, being a

Comb-cap [ridged helmet?], sword and belt, Bandeleires [bandoliers] with Bullet – bagg, wherein is Mould, worme, screwe, scourer, Bullets, [ammunition and tools for cleaning the gun and making shot] a sufficient rest, with a string, and the rest so small that it maye goe, into the Barrell of the Musquet. He shall see that the Musquett be of true Lengthe, and Bore; and to that end he shall have a gage, made according to the kings true

Pikeman with 'charged' or levelled pike. The pike was the anti-cavalry weapon par excellence, although infantry could also be engaged at 'push of pike'. Infantry armour was seen less and less as the wars progressed. This illustration is drawn from Jacob de Gheyn's drill book *Wapenhandelinge* which first appeared in 1607.

height and Standard, and that with that gage he shall trye every Musquett Downe to the Bottom; he shall see that the Stocke be of sound wood, and true proportion, the nether end shodd with Iron; the Locke, Tricker, and pan, serviceable, and the scouring sticke, strong, and sufficient.

The muster system appears to have been run much better in the 1630s than previously, but we should be cautious lest we overstate this new warlike efficiency. Though small-scale training was much more frequent, the assembly of large bodies of men was only possible occasionally, Markham suggesting that a general muster once a year was thought 'excellent'. Ammunition expenditure was also limited, suggesting that the amount of musket practice that took place was not great. A 'General View' of the Lancashire militia taken in 1635 shows the county forces organised by hundreds, with just under 2,000 sets of equipment available for front line duty. These were divided into 31 'harnesses' for 'demi-lances', or heavy cavalry; 133 for horse; 1,123 muskets, and 481 corselets for pikemen. The best provisioned area was West Derby hundred, where 346 muskets; 133 corselets; 42 horse and eight demi-lances were on hand. Lonsdale had the weakest stockpile of munitions, with equipment for just over 200 soldiers.

The 'Certificate of the Musters' which survives for 1639 gives us much greater detail. Here we see that each hundred drew forth a select 'trained band' out of its militia for more complete training. Every area provided an identical

Two panes of the Farndon stained glass windows, showing a drum, pikes, halberds and swords.

PHOTOGRAPH: CARNEGIE, 2009

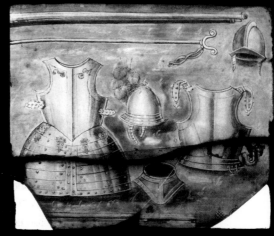

Two panes from the Farndon stained-glass windows, showing a musket, a bandolier, armour and various other accoutrements of war.

PHOTOGRAPH: CARNEGIE, 2009

infantry complement of 100 men – comprising 70 musketeers and 30 pikes – but the weaker cavalry component varied from hundred to hundred, from 2 to 7 lances, and from 7 to 24 horse. There were also three 'petronels', but quite why a few of these antiquated weapons were included with the 'trained men' is unknown. The infantry companies from five of the hundreds were led by a captain: Robert Charnock for Leyland hundred; Henry Byrom for Salford; Roger Nowell for Blackburn; William Farington for Amounderness and George Dodding for Lonsdale. No captain is listed for West Derby, but this may be because the Earl of Derby or his nominee was expected to lead this in person. Three other officers are also named, Richard Shuttleworth as captain for the 25 lances; John Atherton as captain of the 77 horse, and Henry Dattine, provost marshal. The trained bands together could thus be expected to field what was effectively one well-prepared infantry regiment of 600 men, and two troops of horse, one weak and one strong.

Interestingly the 1639 'Certificate' provides a separate table for the much stronger 'untrained' complement, which totalled 7,400. Though untutored, this massive body of men did have quite a few weapons, with 346 muskets in West Derby alone out of more than 1,000 guns held in reserve. Match, powder and ball were stored in the steeple of St Nicholas' chapel in Liverpool. Men who had neither musket, nor horse, nor bill, nor pikeman's equipment, were listed as 'pioneers' – and presumably would have been expected either to labour on fortifications, trenches or roads, or to appear in the field with whatever club or implement came to hand. As with the trained troops the untrained were organised by their local hundred, under a colonel or captain. Several of these 'reserve' officers would play important parts in the civil wars, notably Sir William Gerrard; Edward Rawstorne; William Farington and Sir Gilbert Houghton for the royalists, and Alexander Rigby and John Starkey for parliament. The total militia strength for Lancashire was thus between 8,000 and 8,500 troops of all categories, and this gives us some idea of what the county would be able to achieve in war.[23]

A particularly detailed and instructive example of what may well have been a typical rural unit of the militia at the outbreak of the civil war is provided by Captain Parker's Bowland company. In 1642 this recruitment area around Browsholme was technically just inside West Yorkshire, though virtually surrounded by adjoining Lancashire. Parker had 93 men, whose names were recorded on a company muster list under the area from which they hailed. Each settlement, including the villages of Waddington, Newton in Bowland and Slaidburn, provided from about nine to a dozen men. Next to the name the company clerk inscribed either an 'M' or 'C' depending on whether that individual was armed with a musket, or equipped with a 'corslet' or thigh-

left Pikeman's 'pot' helmet, from the York Castle Museum collection.

right Pikeman's armour or 'corslet' from the York Castle Museum collection. At least in theory the London armourers had a monopoly on armour production. Relatively small quantities of armour were kept in the counties in the militia stores and churches for the use of local forces.

length pikeman's armour. From this it can be deduced that Parker's company comprised 67 musketeers and 24 pikemen.[24]

The musket was the more modern weapon, deadly at close ranges, though slow to load by modern standards. The pike, typically 16 or more feet in length and tipped with a metal point, was the weapon of choice for dealing with cavalry. This worked particularly effectively if the pikemen stood shoulder to shoulder and several ranks deep and presented a forest of spikes which sensible horses would avoid at all costs. Pikemen could also be useful against other infantry, closing with their pikes levelled against the enemy at 'push of pike'. They might similarly be deployed in situations such as the storming of towns, where their armour would be at a premium, though here full-length pikes might be discarded in favour of swords or shorter pole arms.

How the armour and weapons were provided for Parker's Bowland company is demonstrated by another document, which makes clear that some pieces, or at least the cost of them, was levied from individuals, while others came from 'the common charge'. Thus it is that 'John Parker gentleman' provided a pikeman's armour, while Oliver Marton, Thomas Kinge and other named individuals provided muskets. Although some may have carried the weapons that they themselves gave, it is clear that those 'fit to beare this charge', and those actually equipped with the arms, were not synonymous.

A hierarchy of status in who is called upon to provide what is also apparent. Gentlemen were deemed fit to provide armour, which other sources suggest could cost about £3 a set, while others found muskets which were

Diagram showing the 'ancient' way to draw up an infantry regiment – the 'p' stands for a pikeman, the 's' for a musketeer, or 'shot'. From Gervase Markham's *Souldiers Exercise*, 1639.

cheaper. The 'common charge' doubtless included smaller contributions from the less wealthy. That something similar operated a few miles away on the Lancashire side of the old county boundary is suggested by papers for Dutton and Ribchester. Eight leading citizens from Dutton were to provide a like number of muskets, while seven persons from Ribchester were charged with finding nine muskets.[25]

At the time the pike was regarded a more ancient and honourable weapon than the musket, despite the fact that it was proving less deadly than firearms, which could send 'messengers of death' over a distance. The tradition that in 1642 pikeman's armour was provided by gentlemen, whereas firearms were commonly purchased by lower strata of society, may have reinforced this old-fashioned perception. Parker's company ratio of almost three muskets to each pike is especially interesting, as is the fact that the lists for Dutton and Ribchester mention no pikes or corslets. Theorists of the early seventeenth century had suggested that armies should carry equal numbers of pikes and muskets, with a figure of two muskets to one pike becoming more normal towards the time of the civil war. By the end of the period muskets would feature even larger in the inventories. A high number of muskets was thus following the most up-to-date thinking, though equally this could have provided for an easy expansion of the company by the addition of pike or bill men, without armour, in time of emergency. Interestingly evidence from other parts of the country in the decades prior to the civil wars suggests that militia recruits were often graded according to stature, previous training, and age, and thus matched to the most suitable weapons or duties. Tall, active young men were thus most likely to end up trailing a pike, while the small and unfit with no previous experience were probably material for the pioneers, lucky to get the use of a spade.

Whether the Lancashire militia wore 'uniform' at the outbreak of the civil war must remain an open question. We certainly have references to officially purchased 'coats' about this time, and we do have sources for specific costumes in the late sixteenth century. One document, talking of men being equipped at Ormskirk in 1577, speaks of a 'white doublet' over which was worn 'a coat of watchet' in the 'fashione gascoine'. Remarkably this was decorated with a double red and yellow stripe 'two fingers broad', which ran down the hose, as well down the coat. What may be a later paper mentions that the pikeman's coat was of 'broad blew', the cost of the cloth for which was '8s. the yard', each garment containing a yard and a quarter of the material. It is therefore perfectly possible that the Lancashire trained bands wore blue coats in 1642: but the fully trained element of the militia was merely a part, and even if these had uniforms it is unlikely that the large numbers raised after the outbreak of war can all have received clothing immediately. Moreover, there were men from the old militia on both sides.

That not everything was obtained all at once, or without difficulty, for the county militias of 1642 is attested by a further, undated, note to be found among Captain Parker's papers. This bemoans the lack of a pike for 'Master White's man', and a musket for 'Mr Standish's man'. The cost of his brother's coat was also yet to be paid for. To make up shortfalls the constable of Newton was to collect £3 11s. 8d. 'for the common men'.

In total Lancashire in known to have paid some £7,200 for arms and ammunition in the period from 1638 to 1640. With a pair of pistols costing about 18s. and infantry firearms costing less than £1, this would probably have been adequate to arm at least 2,000 troops. It was principally with this weaponry that the opening campaigns of the civil war in the county would be fought.[26] This model of local support for the military did not die with the coming of civil war, nor even would it be entirely extinguished with the advent of the New Model army late in 1644. Similar methods for putting county, or 'militia', forces into the field continued throughout the period. From 1648, for example, we have the example of Captain William Rawlinson's troop of Furness horse – whose establishment, curiously enough, was set at 73½ horse. Of these the town of Ulverston would provide support for 15; smaller settlements paid in proportion, giving maintenance to anything between two and nine cavalry according to their means.[27]

It may fairly be claimed that it was the question over the ultimate control of the militia which in the end turned verbal conflict in London into a national conflict. By the autumn of 1641 there was argument about who had the right, first to appoint personal guards for the king and the parliament house, and then about the control of the militia. The need to raise men to deal with rebellion in Ireland, or the possibility of an Irish, Catholic threat to England, made it necessary to transfer this quarrel from the debating chambers to the shires. At this point each locality had to make up its mind what to do. More debate was had, and more ink used upon the question of the militia than any subject, with the possible exception of religion, during the first year of war. How Lancastrians responded to the fast developing national situation is of great interest and consequence well beyond its borders.[28]

CHAPTER TWO

'The fittest subject for a King's quarrel': the causes of civil war

THE STORY of the English civil wars is an extraordinary one, and this
was realised even by contemporaries who had little of the perspective of
history upon which to base their judgements. The Lancashire author of the
Discourse of the Warr in Lancashire was not alone in marvelling at how much
evil could be unleashed when 'corrupt and unmortified lust', boiling in the
hearts of men, was freed by the breaking of the reins of 'civill government'.
It was by no means clear how people could be turned so completely against
their 'dear neighbours' – who so quickly became 'deadly enemies'. How was
it that civil war broke out in Lancashire, as elsewhere? The national causes
of the civil wars are arguably the best researched aspect of the conflict.
Nevertheless, there are still arguments, even about basic definitions. For some
the war remains 'the great civil war', or wars; for others it was a 'rebellion'
against the king and authority more generally; for others again, a 'revolution',
or, even *the* English revolution. To some commentators the whole idea of an
'English' civil war is a misnomer since the fighting in England was just part

left Equestrian statue of Charles I, Charing Cross, London. In 1678 to honour the
memory of his 'martyred' father Charles II had this statue, by the French sculptor
Hubert Le Sueur, re-erected on top of a plinth designed by Christopher Wren. The
statue had actually been commissioned during the Personal Rule by Charles I's Lord
Treasurer Weston, and had been duly erected at Weston's Roehampton home. In 1647
Puritans in Parliament had voted to pull down the Eleanor Cross that had stood on
this site at Charing Cross, and Charles II took advantage of the now empty site. Thus,
rather ironically, for the last 360 years Charles I has found himself looking rather
mournfully straight down Whitehall, past the place of his own execution outside the
Banqueting House, to Parliament, where the statue of Oliver Cromwell still stands
right outside Westminster Hall, where Charles had been tried for treason.

PHOTOGRAPH: CARNEGIE, 2009

of wider wars which engulfed much of Britain from 1638 to 1651. For them there was actually a war of 'three kingdoms' – though arguably Ireland was not really a 'kingdom' at all. There have also been widely differing points of view over whether the civil wars were caused by long-term factors, building over decades, or, as is now more commonly accepted, the reasons for the conflict should be sought principally in the period of two or three years leading up to the outbreak of war. At one extreme some have pointed to 'origins' and 'causes' which stretch back as far as the early sixteenth century, at the other there are those who see the essential crisis as being that of late 1641 and the early months of 1642.[1]

Though there have been significant variations in emphasis over the intervening centuries, the three inescapable national factors that can be listed as 'fundamental causes', appear to have been religion, power and money. It could be argued, too, that this was the correct order of importance, for in the paradigm of the period God was by far the most important factor. Legitimate power flowed from God, and love of money ran an extremely dubious third. John Rushworth recalled that the precise reasons parliament gave for taking up arms were 'the defence and maintenance of the religion, the King's person, honour and estate, the power and privilege of Parliament and the just rights and liberties of the subjects'. Even so, the power struggle was more complex than 'king or parliament', because the conflict was set in train by war over Scotland and Ireland – and questions of how far the king's writ ran in his other realms. Neither was the power battle simply a matter of who could make law – the king, his advisors, or parliament – as conflict was ultimately sparked by one major dispute. This would be over who had the power to call out an army: it was what Charles I himself would call 'the fittest subject for a King's quarrel'. Control of the military was also arguably the most immediately offensive claim of the unpalatable 'Nineteen Propositions' put forward by parliament in June 1642, for, without the power to enforce anything, a king might be no king.

Religion was certainly an important aspect, if not the key factor: but again it was not a simple doctrinal battle of Catholic against Protestant. The royalists saw Protestant nonconformists as overturning the natural order, and the king's rights as head of the established church. Parliamentarians would usually portray Catholics as the enemy within, and Archbishop Laud and his compatriots as dangerous innovators.

Money, despite its theological position of theoretical unimportance, was a perennial and stubborn headache. The debate over what might be a legitimate tax, the use of monopolies, fees, and fines, and parliament's real or pretended right to regulate the king's purported financial abuses stretched back many years before 1642. It has also been claimed that the whole episode was just part of a 'general crisis' of seventeenth-century Europe, in which the cost of war outran the monarch's ability to raise funds. In this view one war – which could not be afforded – occasioned a spiral of violence, with more fighting being triggered by unpaid armies and campaigns of loot and sequestration designed to meet the costs of pay and supplies. Such a picture comes close to Conrad Russell's final point of view that parliament in particular may have blundered into the war through ignorance, or meanness. Low taxation could not be squared with increased public spending on war; England, Scotland and Ireland could not be reconciled with a dual monarchy, or the idea of 'Britain'; and there was a fundamental inability to accept religious pluralism.[2]

Both sides would claim that they were defending the established order against innovation and subversion. To the royalists it was the parliamentarians who were rebels against the lawful king and established church: to the parliamentarians it was the royalists who were malignants, misdirecting his majesty, usurping the time-honoured rights of free-born Englishmen, and who would betray the country to foreign papists. Many parliamentarians, particularly early in the war, would have it that they fought for 'king and parliament' – the old order – rather than as rebels against a lawful king. The 'rights' for which they stood were the traditional rights of law and of Magna Carta, ideas older than the Stuart monarchy. As Richard Hubberthorne, Lancashire Quaker, would later put it, the struggle with the king was mounted

> in a Defensive way, for our Rights and Liberties ... Upon which account and for which causes we freely brought in our Moneys, Plate, Horses, Arms and other Habilliments of warre, and many choice spirited men freely adventured their lives, with all that was outwardly near and dear to them, Liberty of conscience so called, and Religion, seeming therein included.

Many of the general factors thus had a resonance in remote Lancashire, but without the national context it is extremely doubtful whether any significant conflict could have broken out spontaneously in the north of England. As Russell put it, 'the English Civil War was not the result of an outburst of anger in the localities, but a failure of the political process at the centre'. Such was certainly the case in Lancashire. Nevertheless, the gentry and, to an even greater extent, the lower orders focused on the local arena – and specifically the county – for the most important aspects of their lives. One's landlord, family, and most personal economic activity was likely to be within the county. Unless one was a nobleman with lands in other areas and a place at court, or a merchant with wider interests, most social, economic, cultural and emotional ties were firmly local. Manchester and, to a lesser extent, Liverpool did have significant trading connections with far-flung places, but most Lancastrians' attention was focused on the parochial, the familiar and the nearby. Deference was to head of family, social betters, and clergy – all of whom were part of the local scene. The local court of quarter sessions was more than a legal arbiter, and might include administrative disputes, poor relief, road repairs and other matters within its ambit. Kevin Sharpe has even argued that the House of Commons was really a 'seminar of the English localities'. In the Lancashire case there are indeed clear indications that the local emphasis was different, unique even, within England.

When it came to finding Lancashire members for the London parliament, the local process was often one of 'selection', determining consensus and natural place, rather than adversarial politics. The franchise was limited, without a voice for the lower orders or women, and often there was no voting at all, with 'natural' leaders going to parliament uncontested. It would, however, be wrong to say that 'ordinary' people had no political importance at all. Literacy was limited, and evidence is admittedly slender, but husbandmen and yeomen did become churchwardens, even constables. In armies they might sometimes advance further beyond their natural station – a circumstance which would become quite widespread later in the wars. In the corporate towns artificers and cloth workers could sit on juries and fill other minor positions. Moreover, even in this very hierarchical society, there was an element of governance by consent, the higher orders depending at least in part upon maintaining the deference and economic usefulness of the remainder. In the Lancashire instance we can see how this chain of dependence reached even to Lord Derby, and how desperate many people would be to avoid shattering their local community.

Though different arguments can be made for the significance of long- and short-term causes of the war, it does seem reasonable to suggest that Charles's reign without a parliament, the eleven year 'personal rule', delayed or sidestepped many political conflicts. It probably also made them much worse: when parliament eventually was summoned to answer the needs of financial crisis precipitated by war with Scotland, it was in a comparatively strong position. Parliament appeared to hold critical purse strings. As Sir Ralph Hopton put it during the Short Parliament of 1640, 'The Revenues

Colonel Richard Shuttleworth of Gawthorpe (1587–1669). Shuttleworth was very
unwilling to declare his hand too obviously early in the war, but eventually his family
contributed more to the Lancashire parliamentarian war effort than virtually any other.
A key member of the Lancashire Committee, his sons also led troops in the cause.
Remarkably Richard was a staunch Presbyterian who managed accommodation with
the New Model, and later survived the Restoration.

of the Subject is the myne of the kingdom'.[3] Nationally final division into royalist and parliamentarian camps did not occur until 1641–42, with many of the gentry not apparently choosing one side or the other until they received the commission of the king or parliament. This picture is largely confirmed within Lancashire, where many decisions were left unmade even in the early summer of 1642. There were some waverers who had not decided where their allegiance lay even at the time of Edgehill.

'Ship money', the levy first imposed by the king in the mid-1630s and ostensibly intended to pay for ships for the navy, is an interesting case in point. Undoubtedly it was a real and mounting grievance, and has popularly been linked with the parliamentarian cause, but there was little or no specific connection with the way Lancashire divided in 1642. The initial assessment for the county was a modest £475, with an additional £15 and £8 from the ports of Liverpool and Lancaster respectively. Liverpool grumbled, but the full sum was collected within a couple of months. In August 1635 a further call required a total of £3,500, including £160 from the corporations of the towns of Preston, Wigan, Lancaster, Liverpool, Clitheroe and Newton. The towns paid up, but there were complaints, particularly from the clergy of the rural areas, and the 'poorer sort', that the assessments were inequitable. Nevertheless Sheriff Humphrey Chetham was successful in his task, managing to collect from all but the 'verie poor' and a 'few refractorie persons'.

In 1636 the assessment of what was fast becoming a regular and ever increasing tax, was fixed at £4,000. Even so, Sheriff Richard Shuttleworth of Gawthorpe managed to find almost exactly 99 per cent of the total. Some objections were forthcoming, and as a result Wigan, which pleaded poverty, had its contribution reduced from £50 to £20. In 1637 the new sheriff, Roger Kirkby, had rather less success, and was held personally responsible for a shortfall of £120, although he never appears to have paid it.

Only in 1640 did opposition finally reach levels where the collection became unworkable. Constables failed to make assessments, and some even refused to attend meetings. Robert Holt, the exasperated sheriff of that year, was forced to report the 'backwardness of the people' and the 'great trouble' experienced in collecting money. As he put it, the 'county in general bends themselves against the tax'. Three hundreds finally contributed £1,300, but nothing was to be had from Amounderness and Lonsdale. In the event both these areas were basically royalist in 1642 – and as a local 'cause' ship money appears, at worst, to have been part of a background of discontent. It does not seem to have been a factor which decided Lancastrians one way or another.[4]

The forest clearances and enclosures of land, which have been cited as one of the lesser causes leading up to the 'Great Rebellion', certainly had an important impact on Lancashire in the decades before the war. Parts of Amounderness and Blackburn are known to have been particularly affected. Some of the royal lands in West Derby were sold off by the crown in 1628, and acquired by Lord Derby in 1639. Around Clitheroe those who occupied what had once been crown lands had a rude awakening following a judicial investigation and a significant price hike. Establishing definitive links between these events and the war is difficult, however, especially since many of the places involved remained more or less well disposed to the king in 1642. It also has to be admitted that this is an area as yet inadequately researched.

It has, however, been possible to make a direct connection between at least one the local enclosure episodes and the later parliamentarian cause. The disputes over Fulwood and Broughton had festered from as early as the fifteenth century, right through to the civil war. The crux of the issue was whether the historic rights of the crown, and the traditional rights of local 'commoners' to use the land, were superseded by those of squatters and local landowners who cut down trees, enclosed the area, and claimed it for their own. Later the problem was exacerbated by royal attempts to use the matter for fund-raising, making retrospective prosecutions and charges for these encroachments. One small parcel of land over which there was a particular wrangle was the Boys Lane area on the boundaries of Fulwood and Cadley. Originally the property of a religious foundation, various petitioners disputed whether it had ever been part of the old 'Fulwood Forest', or indeed part of the Duchy of Lancaster. The land had therefore been leased to William Boys about the turn of the century. James I had entered the fray in 1623, leasing all the wastes of Fulwood and Cadley to Henry Percy. This gentleman now found himself opposed by the Corporation of Preston, which pointed to an earlier Duchy Court decision in its favour. It looked as though the dispute might reach an accommodation when Percy accepted £150 from the corporation to buy him out. The corporation offered the use of the lands to tenants, old and new, in return for rent, but the result was a riot. Long-term users of the land, who had paid 10s. a year for the privilege, felt they had been dispossessed and cheated. Many of the hedges and enclosures were torn down. The problem rumbled on, with a further attempt at a court settlement in 1627.

In 1639 there was another outburst of vandalism when local people objected violently to the king's agents who were undertaking further fencing and digging out dykes in Fulwood and Cadley. Edmund Hatch and Thomas Browninge, employees of John Gregory, apprehended John Gregson late at night, near a newly demolished fence, and accused him of its destruction. Busybody Margaret Tasker gave the workmen a good piece of her mind, telling them that they need not bother digging since their dykes would be pulled down soon enough. One of the crew, Ralph Turner of Ingol, desired her to 'hold her peace' – but she rebuked him threatening that like as not he would wind up dead. A few days later John Gregory and his men found cattle wandering loose amongst their works, and took them into Preston. Gregory and his assistants were then apprehended by ten or a dozen people including Richard Walmesley, Richard Singleton, William Singleton, Thomas Harrison, Katherine Bonney and others who demanded their animals back and overthrew Gregory and his men in a 'tumult'.[5]

The lawyer who represented the accused citizens against the crown was Alexander Rigby of Goosnargh, future parliamentarian leader. The court's decision was no whitewash for the king, but decided upon 'a commission' to examine witnesses and establish the facts of the matter. Though it seemed likely that the enclosure was legal, and the violence punishable, the court also took a dim view of the kidnapping and possible ransoming of the local people's cattle. Interesting as this ongoing squabble was in social-historical and economic terms, it is stretching credibility to see such a specific issue as a major cause of the war which broke out three years later. Nevertheless, such episodes were matters affecting people's livelihoods. They also smacked enough of repression to be recalled when many from east Lancashire joined the struggle during the first year of the war. As the author of *A true and full relation of the troubles in Lancashire* would put it in December 1642,

> For now the men of Blackburn, Padiham, Burneley, Clithero, and Colne, with those sturdy churles in the two forests of Pendle and Rossendale have raised their spirits, and have resolved to fight it out rather than their Beefe and fatt Bacon shall be taken from them.[6]

There were also parallels in other areas, with evidence of anti-enclosure rioting with similar disturbance identified in no fewer than 26 counties just before and during the war.

Cases of local links between disputes over rent and dues and the political allegiances of 1642 have also been identified. One instance that has been studied in some detail is that of Sir George Middleton of Leighton Hall and his estates at Yealand in South Lonsdale. On the death of Sir George's father in 1640 his tenants refused to pay the entry fines that he levied upon them, and accused the family of being exploitative landlords. Sir George riposted that costs had risen and rents fallen, and so he was acting within his rights to recoup his position. The case was further complicated by the fact that the Middletons were Catholic, and indeed had more outgoings than most similar families. Part of the money raised was thus extracted to pay unavoidable costs, levied, at least indirectly, by the crown.

When war came the tenants sided with parliament, some of them becoming soldiers, as Sir George complained, merely 'to oppose him and his family under pretence of serving Parliament'. In the middle of the war Leighton Hall was seized, a group of the occupiers not only plundering its goods but destroying deeds and other documents. Sir George saw this as a deliberate plot, a 'confederacy' led by Richard Robinson, to destroy evidence of the Middleton family's rights and possessions. However, we should be wary of thinking of the events at Leighton Hall as some sort of 'peasants' revolt', as Robinson was a former bailiff on the estate and some of the others were yeomen who had also held positions of responsibility. It would appear that although local issues had not caused the war, in the Yealand area they were a crucial factor in choice of allegiance and gave opportunity for the settling of old scores.

Another case in which matters of property became conflated with those of religion was that of the Walmesleys. When Thomas Walmesley died in March 1642 his south Lancashire estates were inherited by his son Richard, who was still a minor. His tenants accused the family as 'papists', and in 1643 mother and son were driven from the county. The tenants now refused to pay rents and took back their tithes, even though it appears that the properties were never officially sequestered by parliament.[7] Personal interests probably became reasons for 'acts of war' more often than we realise. One Lancashire royalist prisoner named Moreton insisted that he had been held 'by some trowpers of Manchester' not because he was an enemy combatant, but 'upon a pryvatt quarrell for taking of powder & other goods belonginge to one of Manchester'.

God's war?: Catholic and Protestant

Religious disagreement is one consistent thread running through the years leading up to 1642. 'Settlement' of religion was seen as the key, but illusive, goal after which so many strove throughout much of the period. Put simply Charles' enemies saw him as a crypto-Catholic, determined to lead the English church back to Rome. For those of a low church persuasion the evidence was clear. Queen Henrietta Maria was a French Catholic whose faith was indulged at court, and the king's religious reforms, as expressed through Archbishop Laud, smacked of popery and superstition. Ultimately it seemed probable that England would be betrayed to foreign powers. That there had been Catholic plots to overthrow the monarch in the reigns of Elizabeth and James lent dreadful credence to this point of view. On the other side of the coin the king's supporters were inclined to view their religious opponents as dogmatic and intolerant crackpots, sectarians whose opposition to bishops and established religion was bound to lead to anarchy and strife. According to one's point of view, either high or low church could be portrayed as subversive: ritual led to Rome; lack of ritual led to diversity, independent thought and social chaos.

On the national level there were many who viewed religion as a principal cause of the war. As the royalist Earl of Clarendon put it,

> I must not forget – though it cannot be remembered without much horror – that this strange wildfire among the people was not so much and so furiously kindled by the breath of Parliament as of the clergy. These men, having crept into, and at last driven all learned and orthodox men from, the pulpits, had from the beginning of this Parliament, under notion of reformation and extirpation of popery, infused seditious inclinations into the hearts of men against the present government of the church, with many libellous invectives against the state too. But since the raising of an army and rejecting of the king's last overture of a treaty, they contained themselves within no bounds, and as freely and without control inveighed against the person of the king ...

Lord Derby said that his Puritan opponents 'mocked God' by their stance against established authority.[8]

The fact that Lancashire was the most Catholic county in England, with the 'old religion' surviving over much of its northern and western parts, would be highly significant. Many of the county gentry were Catholic, although the relative numbers have sometimes been overstated. Research suggests that the most important concentration of Catholic gentry was in West Derby hundred, where there were some 73 families, comprising rather more than one-third of the leading households of the area. Nevertheless, the proportion in Amounderness was actually higher, where the 51 Catholic families made up almost half of the total. Generally speaking Catholics were more frequently to be found in the countryside than in the towns. The unevenness in the total distribution of Catholics can make Lancashire look like two different countries, even before the outbreak of war. In Amounderness more than one person in nine was a declared Catholic, and many more were doubtless practising the faith in secret, with some others uncommitted or apathetic. In the deanery of Manchester Catholics were outnumbered by hundreds to one. Nevertheless, on paper at least, the Anglicans were in at least a small majority pretty well everywhere.

Catholics were discriminated against in law – and 'recusants' had to pay fines for not attending the established church. This very fact makes an assessment of exactly how many Catholics there were in the county extremely difficult. In many instances the head of a so-called 'church papist' family would attend the established church the minimum number of times required to escape financial penalty, yet continue to attend mass covertly at other times. Some attended the state-sponsored church regularly, but went to mass on occasion. Determining the status of such individuals, and distinguishing them from an ordinary lax, or inattentive, churchgoer is often impossible. In 1638 one preacher at Denton reported that not only did people fall asleep in his church, but that there appeared to be some who came to church explicitly to do so.

By the seventeenth century, the penalties for Catholics were usually no more than financial, although the disbarment from official office could also be a stiff punishment. In a few instances Catholic priests did still pay with their lives. Lancashire did have its own martyrs, such as Father Edmund Arrowsmith, who was put to death at Lancaster in 1629. It is not enough, however, to see Lancashire Catholics simply as a minority faced with state-sponsored oppression. Tolerance and intolerance ebbed and flowed with the attitude of the monarch and the changing of the international scene. The number of declared Catholics actually increased tenfold in Lancashire during the latter part of the reign of Elizabeth and the early part of the reign of James I. By 1604 there were 3,516 known recusants in the county, plus a further 521 persons who refused communion. The numbers multiplied under Charles I, whose laxity on the subject was widely noted. Interestingly the period 1641 to 1646 would see something of a purge of Catholic priests; nevertheless the total number put to death during this entire period, over the whole country, was only 21.[9]

It has reasonably been suggested that this official picture of burgeoning Catholicism was produced less by the actual increase than by the willingness of Catholics to declare themselves in what had become a more lenient climate. Except in the period immediately after the famous Gunpowder Plot of 1605 general recusancy laws were often neither rigorously nor universally enforced, and prosecutions were aimed first and foremost at disloyal subversives, or at priests who had trained abroad. In 1640 new proclamations were issued preventing papists from coming within ten miles of a royal court, and keeping them within five miles of their homes. This may have appeared a prudent and stringent measure, but how this was to be properly enforced was unclear – and with the queen a Catholic any practical application of this measure was clearly going to be awkward.[10]

The fact that Catholics were coming more out of the shadows gave some credence to the accusation that they were multiplying rapidly, and probably helped to encourage a reaction from the opposite side of the religious spectrum. Public 'popery' challenged the status quo in a particularly dangerous way. As one of Richard Heyrick's finest rabble-rousing efforts put it in 1641,

> Popery has multiplied abundantly. In Lancashire it has superabounded above a hyperbole; the mass has outfaced our Christian meetings, Jesuits have jeered our ministers, confronted and abused authority.

At the same time Alexander Rigby would report that there had been 15,000 indictments for recusancy at the last sessions of the Amounderness hundred. If true, this suggested not that a tenth of the population were Catholics, but that anything up to 40 per cent of households in this area were Catholic. To many, and particularly to observers from outside the county, this was a shocking revelation. There were only two reasonable conclusions: either Catholics were indeed multiplying like wildfire; or there had long been a huge and secret body of the foreign faith lurking unseen beneath a devious veneer of conformity. Remember, too, that Catholicism was inextricably linked in English minds with the threat of foreign invasion, and an atmosphere of heightened suspicion and fear was hardly surprising.

It has been suggested that this was the nub of the difference between the war in Lancashire and the war in other counties. A strong Catholic presence prompted a strong reaction – and the two fed off each other. Comparative study would tend to reinforce this conclusion. Religion appears indeed to have been less significant as a motivation in areas where there were very few Catholics. In Cheshire, where there were quite a number of Catholics, but far fewer than in Lancashire, the puritan response was less rabid. Nevertheless religion is still cited as a significant factor in Cheshire. As Anthony Fletcher has remarked, it is Lancashire which provides much of the outstanding evidence of 'anti-Catholic hysteria' and 'nowhere else in England was Catholicism so deeply rooted as the hundreds of Amounderness, Leyland and West Derby' and nowhere else was the ideological conflict 'felt so keenly'.

It is certainly apparent that though the Lancashire puritan clergy had diverse attitudes on many issues, they were united in their staunch opposition to Catholicism. Not all assumed that the pope and the antichrist were synonymous: but their objections to the very idea of a pope were many and deep-rooted. For Christopher Hudson of Preston a key issue was that popery actively encouraged sin and immorality through the sale of indulgences, so that,

> by the Popes disposition a man may be a sodomite, may marry his owne sister, may sinne against the law of god and the law of nature, and yet escape unpunished.

Moreover, in so doing the pope appeared to claim, through his ability to grant absolution 'from sinne and all other things', that he can 'do whatsoever God himselfe can'. In the eyes of Hudson and others this was surely the greatest blasphemy.[11]

The Lancashire petition of 1640 was essentially a religious affair, roused ostensibly by fear of Catholicism as well as suspicion of 'innovation'. Local men, albeit of a specific viewpoint, spoke up against the 'intollerable burdens laide upon our painful and Godly ministers'. Merging of good English reformed practice with Popish superstitions could only lead to trouble.

Catholics had been viewed as a potential military threat since before the Spanish Armada. That Catholics should be disarmed had been a continual and recurring theme for decades. In the 1580s it was decided that recusants should no longer hold arms suitable for the militia musters, but could be allowed such edged weapons that were deemed necessary for the defence of their homes and families. Muskets and the like had to be disposed of, but could be sold on to approved buyers. Orders imposed in 1585 were repeated in 1596 and 1599; disarming reached the statute book in 1606 in the wake of Gunpowder Plot. A proclamation was made to the same effect in 1611. Under Charles I recusant disarming was revived in 1625: but how completely it was in fact achieved is questionable, for not only was it often unclear who was a Catholic, whether all their arms had been rendered was impossible to judge. In the late 1620s certain leading Catholics on the national stage were specifically excluded from the disarming provisions.

In Lancashire some local officials were themselves closet Catholics, or in other instances were reluctant to cause confrontations with influential neighbours who preferred a live and let live policy. Nevertheless the proportion of total disarmings which were carried out in Lancashire in the wake of

1625 was extraordinary. Over the whole country we know with certainty of the confiscation of weapons from 253 individuals: no fewer than 97 of these were Lancastrians. This was almost double the number recorded in Northumberland, the next most significant county in the list, where 58 persons were disarmed. Rather more than a third of the definite cases of Catholics being disarmed in the whole country therefore came from Lancashire. It is noteworthy that there were complaints that many stashes of arms had been missed, and that the weapons recovered were old, and probably not the entirety of those held by the Catholics. There have also been suspicions raised that one of the disarmers, Sir Richard Hoghton, was a Catholic himself in all but name, and that Thomas Covell, the county gaoler to whom some of the weapons were entrusted, was a Catholic sympathiser. Whether disarming was genuine, or comfortable rhetoric, prior to 1641, is thus unclear.[12]

That the parliament in London linked, very closely indeed, Lancashire and possibility of a Catholic uprising is confirmed by an order issued in August 1641 that 'Commissioners, or Committees, may be forthwith sent into the Countries of most danger'. The purpose of these visits was to ensure that Catholics, being an 'extraordinary cause of danger', be disarmed, according to the law. Parliament's judgement was that the top six potential hot-spots were Yorkshire, Lancashire, Cheshire, Staffordshire, Hampshire and Sussex. Lincolnshire and Nottinghamshire were added to this worrying list shortly afterwards. The obvious danger seemed to be confirmed just three months later when London tailor Thomas Beale reported overhearing two men in Moorfields discussing a heinous plan. Instigated by Catholic priests, this plot would see a mass assassination of puritan MPs and peers, and rioting in the city. There would also be papist risings in six counties, among which Lancashire was prominent. 'Beale's Plot' may have been wildly exaggerated or complete nonsense – but it was believable enough to command attention, and the Lancashire connection added verisimilitude.[13]

In February 1642 another horrifying tale would emerge following the examination of a 'poor', but apparently credible, gentleman by Lancashire justices of the peace. Richard Lathame was first fingered to the authorities by 'friends' who had grown suspicious following utterances he had made 'in some passion'. The frightening information was then drawn out of him with 'no little difficulty'. Lathame's statement, probably obtained under duress, was that when Mr Barlowe the Catholic priest had been arrested in a coal shed at 'Moreless House', the law officers had failed to discover there 'nine or ten' barrels of gunpowder and a firearm. This was just part of a plot involving Edward Reeding 'a Romish secular Priest' who travelled between recusants' houses saying mass. Reeding had drawn Lathame himself into the design, swearing him to secrecy by placing his hand on a crucifix and making him swear by 'Almighty God', Christ, the Virgin, the Saints and various holy objects to keep the plot secret.

Reeding had then taught Lathame how to make 'balls of wildfire' using frogs' grease, brimstone, and other ingredients, and gave him two shillings for his expenses. When Lathame had enquired the purpose of producing these incendiaries the priest had told him that he was just one of many ready to advance the Catholic cause, as several of his neighbours, including Richard Sale and Richard Shuttleworth were already stockpiling arms and explosives. It was, so Reeding had said,

> generally resolved amongst Catholics, that when the Irish Designs were a little over, a respectable part of the said Irish should be landed in Lancashire, and the Recusants of that County would be ready to rise in Arms, and join with them ... they would have their agents, at one Instant of Time, to fire all the principal Towns in the Country.

Lathame had protested, so he said, that it would be difficult for him to resign himself to kill his neighbours or to commit arson. In response the priest had told him to steel himself to the task, for 'it was no sin, nor any way the breach of Religion or good Conscience, by any means to destroy Heretics'. Lathame was still uneasy, for though he had been bred 'a Romish Catholic', he was horrified by the prospect of such 'bloody designs', and so he had not only failed to make any fireballs, but wrestled with his conscience until deciding to reveal all. The Lancashire justices had of course instituted a search, but had found no gunpowder. This did not reassure, however, since many of the Catholics' houses 'made anciently of the Purpose for private Conveyances' might still conceal munitions. Holes and corners that could conceal priests might equally contain powder or muskets. All of this troubling intelligence was conveyed to London and read out in parliament. The perception that Catholics were everywhere, and had malign intent, was widespread. Moreover, the threat appeared to be growing, and becoming more specific in nature. As John Osborne told Henry Oxinden on 27 July 1642, 'The papists are upon Lancashire and threaten some heavy doom to befall the Protestants in those parts'.[14]

It is often less well appreciated that, like Catholicism, extreme, or merely nonconformist, types of Protestantism also met with official disapproval. In Dugdale's account Lord Derby specifically claimed that the war itself was caused by the unfairness of the execution of Strafford, and by his enemies' false claims to act in the name 'of God'. The word 'puritan' does not properly define all the shades of low church Protestant belief, but does serve as a convenient way to describe those who regarded the reform of the church under Elizabeth I as having been in some way incomplete, or not having gone far enough. At the time the name 'puritan' was regarded by many as a term of abuse. At least one contemporary regarded the name as 'ambiguous' and therefore essentially useless. Another wit had it that a puritan was 'one that loved God with all his soul, but hates his neighbour with all his heart'. Nevertheless, puritans were not a separate religion, as few extremists had broken completely with the established church prior to 1642 – rather 'Puritans' and 'Anglicans' represented two polarities within a broad national church which had taken shape under Elizabeth, and were still developing.

By any measure puritan gentry families were a relatively small minority within the county. Arguably the most Protestant town was Manchester, which had absorbed many of the continental reformers' ideas. For minister Richard Heyrick, Manchester was the most godly town of the county, 'a Goshen, a place of light'. Yet it was run at least a close second by Bolton, 'the Geneva of Lancashire'. Salford hundred as a whole had at least 47 gentry families which have been defined as 'puritan', and while a large majority of townsmen actually conformed to the established church, Catholics were a very small minority in Salford hundred, and zeal for the word of God was widespread. The similarity in geographic distribution of early industry, urban centres and puritanism has long been remarked. As one commentator has put it 'the saints were thick on the ground wherever cloth was manufactured'.

Lancashire Protestants had clashed with authority as early as the Hampton Court conference of 1604. Here Lawrence Chaderton of Oldham, the master of Emmanuel College, Cambridge, had pleaded the right of Lancashire ministers not to wear the surplice or to make the sign of the cross at baptism. He met with no success, and though government policy was not strictly enforced at this time the bishop of Chester was forced to remove several non-conforming ministers. In the 1630s, after Laud became Archbishop, more Protestant ministers were removed. These included William Bourne, a fellow of Manchester College and Richard Mather, chaplain of Toxteth. Some of the ejected divines continued to minister to congregations outside the established church. In hindsight this appears to have done little to silence low church opposition to the establishment, and perversely may even have stirred up further trouble.[15]

In 1641 Lancashire was one of the first counties to call for the abolition of government of the church by bishops, and the most northerly so to do. In the famous 'Root and Branch' petitions Lancastrians were disproportionately well represented, with approximately 4,500 signatures. This was slightly more than the relatively well-populated Suffolk, and more than double that achieved in Norfolk. This is all the more surprising when we consider the reforming reputation of East Anglia, and the almost complete support of that area for parliament during the war. It may have been that Lancashire's high turnout of anti-episcopalians was more a reflection of organisation than sheer numbers, but nevertheless the figures are startling. There was certainly a strong correlation between those places which had at least a vocal minority campaigning for an end to bishops, and those that either sided with parliament, or would soon fall to parliament. As early as 14 July 1642 Lancashire MPs agreed a composition for a new commission for the ordination of ministers, so religious reform and military preparation advanced together – though the former may have led the latter, at least by a week or two, chronologically speaking.

In pockets alternative Protestant religion was clearly well rooted. In any case Laudian innovations were but patchily received, as one alarmed visitor to the county commented in 1637,

> all the orders of the church go down the wind, for they call surplices the rags of Rome; they do it at Preston and Manchester, and will suffer no organs, nor sign no children with the sign of the cross when they are christened and the altars are pulled down.

The lack of a surplice was commonly taken as a sure sign of a non-conforming low church minister, and one which the authorities started to look out for in order to correct deviation from the established course. In just one example in 1637 John Broxopp, vicar of Ormskirk, was brought before the consistory court for his failure to dress appropriately. He offered the somewhat lame excuse that his surplice was in the wash.

Very quickly puritan ministers became identified as keen sermonisers, and there were instances where prescribed services were changed to insert longer sermons. Doubtless many puritans were more enthusiastic about their faith than some of those in the mainstream, and were committed to expounding upon it as frequently, and for as long, as possible. For the authorities, however, the sermon was often identified as the vehicle of deviation from the established line, as preachers might follow the set forms and texts for much of the service and then insert the ideas of reformers, or their own eccentric interpretation in the sermon. Some ministers went as far as to hold religious gatherings outside the church, in other buildings, their homes, or even in the open air. Such 'conventicles', or clandestine meetings, were forbidden, but there was a fine line between innocent gathering and alternative service. In at least one Lancashire instance people caught out visiting the minister's house in suspiciously large numbers protested that they were merely there to hear the major points of the church sermon again, and to help those who had not understood. This was not intended to produce 'any faction', but to reinforce the accepted teachings.

Another mark of nonconformity was the manner, and for that matter the place, in which baptism was performed. Puritan ministers often took to using a dish or bowl, and avoided the pomp of utilising the medieval stone fonts which were such a common feature in parish churches. Seen from the minister's own point of view this was not so much an act of subversion, as a homely convenience and a symbolic break with the more ritualistic tradition of the Catholic past.

Sunday observance was a particularly important issue in the county. Low church ministers frequently complained that the lord's day was not being marked with due reverence, and attempted to force the populace to abandon any frivolous activity on a Sunday. Some of the more fun-loving Lancastrians petitioned James I on this point when he visited Hoghton Tower. As a result James rebuked 'the puritanes and precise people' for punishing peasants who followed lawful recreation and 'honest exercises upon Sundaies and other holidaies' after the services and sermons. As might be expected, every advantage was taken of this licence, and James was later forced to rule on what was legal. As published for the whole country in 1618, this would become the 'Book of Sports', which legitimised 'Maygames, Whitsun Ales, Morris dances, the setting up of Maypoles and other sports'.[16]

We should not, however, fall into the trap of regarding all of the Lancashire puritan ministers as killjoys who would rather be Protestant martyrs than use ceremony of any description. Some could not even be clearly defined as puritans in a strict doctrinal sense, being merely less ceremonious, or more literal, or even more lackadaisical, versions of their more orthodox brethren. Doubtless there were some who genuinely had not bothered to learn the latest form, or who could not afford the right garments. There were also others who were genuinely open-minded, and more flexible in their ministrations. One Lancashire preacher was quoted as regarding 'ceremonies as things indifferent', in the sense that he worried not whether they were performed or omitted. There was also a concept, albeit not very widespread, of 'Christian liberty', in which an element of choice came into the matter, usually on the part of a patron or vicar, in allowing the use of some ceremony and the dropping or abbreviating of others. Doubtless such pragmatism could be helpful where there was strong Catholic competition, apathy on the part of the people, or practical obstacles to holding a service at all.

Neither was being 'puritan' a certain badge of moral probity. In 1636 Sir Ralph Ashton of Whalley, a relative and comrade of his more famous parliamentarian civil war cousins at Middleton, was found guilty of 'incest and adultery' with Alice Kenyon, Jane Whittakers, Elizabeth Holmes *and* others. These several liaisons resulted in a number of children, whom Ashton did actually support (providing, incidentally, his prosecutors with just the evidence they were looking for). His fine was £300.[17]

Religion was undoubtedly one of the major local factors in the war. This was not, however, just a matter of Catholic against Protestant, but a more encompassing schism, for in the seventeenth century religion governed far more of everyday life than it does in the modern Christian world. Without a permanent police force, and no compulsory schooling, religion was also a mainspring of social control. With 'livings' commonly in the gift of magnates, the nobility and the church were often opposite sides of the same coin. The church and the alehouse were the centres of news and discussion, the places where people were likely to form a view of the wider world, and unless one lived in a significant town, virtually every important event would take place in one or the other. Perhaps the two benefited from antithesis: rousing godly sermons being balanced by the more bawdy gossip and ballads of the tap room. Alehouses were also famously regarded as 'the nursery of naughtiness': brawls and immorality were both thought to be readily found – or available – there. Alcohol consumption *per capita* is high in modern North West England, and so it was, doubtless enough, at the time of the civil war. Clitheroe may lay some claim to the most spectacular over-provision of drink, having one alehouse per 15 inhabitants in 1645, when a much more normal ratio would have been one drinking place per seventy or eighty of the population.

That puritan ministers tended to have the most violent reaction against drink was no accident. In the most extreme examples alcohol was seen as a direct competitor for the soul of the drinker, even a work of the devil. Christopher Hudson, lecturer at Preston in 1631, railed against

the multitude of alehouses, which are the nests of Satan where the owls of impiety lurk and where all evil is hatched and the bellows of intemperance and incontinence blown up to the provocation of God's wrath in the subversion of the kingdom.

The promotion of puritan JPs in Lancashire has been linked directly with an increased rate of closure of unlicensed alehouses, the enforcement of Sabbath observance, and other 'measures of social control'. In 1647 a memorial against alehouses obtained the signatures of over 800 ministers and 'godly' laymen.[18]

However, we should not be too sweeping in our generalisations about the opposition of religion and drink, since in 1626 two ministers of the county were themselves discovered to be keepers of unlicensed alehouses. Individuals also fell prey to the temptations of strong drink. Soon after the civil war Mr Gilbody, the minister of Holcombe, was suspended for a number of misdemeanours including tippling in an alehouse where fiddles were playing. Henry Newcombe enjoyed a good game of billiards, and this was only one of several games and pastimes usually found in public houses.[19]

Whether one attended a church, as most people did, and which one, was critical. The mass, held more or less in secret, was the mark of a community as well as of specific belief. Congregations may have been more isolated in Lancashire, and there were also sparsely populated swathes with little religious provision, but this did not mean that religion was not an extremely important force for forming opinion. Religious concerns were strongly reflected in the petition to the Commons of 12 March 1642 in which many future parliamentarian supporters put forward their aspirations for a 'National Synode of able Divines'. This meeting would not only settle differences of doctrine, but put an end to the 'Civil Warre of the Church' which in their opinion was already raging. The disarming of recusants was seen as necessary to security.

In the important case of parliamentarian Colonel Ralph Ashton of Middleton religion appeared to play a direct role in choice of allegiance. Ashton was a convinced puritan, who followed his conscience with his wealth by sponsoring the Reverend Thomas Pyke. His parliamentarian conviction was no doubt further reinforced by his educational background as he had attended Sidney Sussex College and Cambridge – the same *alma mater* as Oliver Cromwell. Alexander Rigby of Goosnargh was just one of several other parliamentarians who actively advanced the religious cause through the sponsorship of ministers, in his instance in the particularly inhospitable environment of the countryside around Preston. Gratton has suggested that eventually as many as two-thirds of all Lancashire parliamentarian officers could be described as 'puritan' – though the inability to define such a term accurately must make this a somewhat vague statistic.

When the county divided in allegiance, it was certainly on what Anthony Fletcher has called 'starkly religious lines', with the 'puritan' stronghold of Manchester balanced by royalist garrisons such as those at Eccleston, Ormskirk, Prescot, Warrington and Wigan.[20] In Lancashire the majority of the established church, and almost all Catholics, were, in spirit at least, on the side of the king. A minority of the established church, and almost all of the Protestant nonconformists, were with parliament. This degree of polarisation was probably unique to Lancashire. At its most extreme the Puritan–Catholic enmity could be viewed as a struggle of annihilation. As Richard Heyrick put it in a sermon of 1639, long before open war,

> The quarrel betwixt Rome and us is not like Ceasar and Pompey, which should be chief, but like that betwixt Rome and Carthage, which should not be. If Rome prevail we shall not stand; and if we prevail they should not stay long.

The fact that ordinary Catholics had kept themselves isolated, and usually as quiet as possible, and were not by law allowed to bear arms, would prove significant disadvantages to the king's cause in Lancashire. For encouraging them to take up arms and fight on his behalf would give a huge propaganda coup to his enemies. In the beginning Lord Derby dared make no overt use at all of what was potentially a considerable source of manpower. Indeed, early on he instructed that previously confiscated 'recusants armes' that were now in store in Chorley should be delivered over to Captains Charnock and Standish; these were to be used in the king's cause, certainly, but they should only be issued to 'confirmable protestants', and freeholders at that. In the early stages of war, there were clearly scruples both about religion and about property qualification. Poor people and Catholics were just too big a gamble to be given arms: or, from another viewpoint, being seen to enlist such soldiers was too much of a political risk.

There were many incidents during the conflict that attested to the depth of religious feeling, with Catholics and nonconformists particularly singled out for vilification by the opposition. One of the earliest was an episode when Wigan cavaliers, having seized the puritan chapel at Hindley, stole its Bible. Tearing it to pieces, they stuck leaves of it onto stakes around Wigan – deriding it as the 'Roundheads' Bible'. On the other side of the coin the religious agenda of many of the Manchester parliamentarians is even more obvious. As early as May 1642 a gathering of Catholics near Lancaster was presented to the public as a threat to the established order, and a rallying point for those who were worried that existing provisions were soft on Catholics and potential traitors, which indeed were virtually synonymous.

The *Discourse of the Warr* relates that it was those with 'best affection to Religion' (i.e. puritans) who were the first to take up arms, and it was God that 'pointed them out'. One of their prime objectives was to complete what the Reformation had failed to do, and pull down way side crosses 'erected through superstition as alsoe some in Market Townes – witness Preston and others – taking out of churches the Booke of Common Praier, Surplisses, Fonts and breaking downe of Organs wher they found any'. In some places mockery and satire were deployed: having 'disarmed' Bury, parliamentarian troops entered the church and 'took away the Surplysse and put it on the back of a Souldier and caused him to rid in the Cart of Armes ... to be matter of sport and laughter to the Behoulders'.

'A horid, cursed, and barbarous Rebellion': the Irish question

Arguably it was the Irish rebellion, which broke out in late 1641, that made civil war in England all but inevitable. The crisis in Ireland made a new army necessary: an army needed money; and the raising of money through taxation would require the co-operation of parliament. For parliamentarians such as Pym and his party this was a fresh opportunity further to circumscribe the king's influence. In the early hours of 23 November, by a narrow majority, parliament passed its 'Grand Remonstrance', a general indictment of the king's policies at home and abroad. The message was clear: the king stood accused of being incompetent in choosing his advisors, and in directing the forces.

Geographic proximity made Ireland a more serious issue for Lancastrians than for many other Englishmen, for given a favourable wind Dublin was within easier reach than was London (in September 1639 the Earl of Strafford had made the crossing from Dublin to Chester in just thirteen hours when the normal journey time from Manchester to London was measured in days). Victims of, and witnesses to, the atrocities perpetrated on Protestants in Ireland would not take much longer to reach the mainland. It was what the *Discourse of the Warr in Lancashire* would call a 'Horid, cursed, and barbarous Rebellion of the Irish Papists' – a clear and present danger to the people of Lancashire.

The effect of the Irish troubles on Lancashire is graphically illustrated by the account books kept by the Manchester constables. Odd refugees and a few sick soldiers from across the Irish Sea had been arriving in the town for years. In 1641, however, the trickle swelled from an occasional curiosity to a problem that consumed a significant proportion of the constable's budget. A handful of cases now rose to over a hundred individuals, and many of the unfortunates

An Exact and true Relation

of the late Plots which were con-
trived and hatched in Ireland.

1. A Coppy of a Letter sent from the Lord chiefe Iustices and Privy Councell in Ireland, to our parliament here in England.
2. Their last Proclamation which they published concerning those Traytors.
3. The whole Discourse of the Plot revealed by Owen Ockanellee who is now in England.
4. The dangerous and extraordinary deliverance of the party who narrowly escaped with his life.
5. The reward the Parliament hath confirmed upon him.
6. The true Relation of the whole Treason related by the Lord Keeper, to the Honourable House of Commons the first of November. 1641.

London Printed for Francis Coules, 1641.

Title page to *An Exact and True Relation of the Late Plots Which were Contrived and Hatched in Ireland*, November 1641. Very real fear of the revolt in Ireland was both a cause of great anxiety in England, and something to be manipulated for propaganda purposes and political gain. Lancashire's geographic position at the heart of the British archipelago put it in close proximity to the seat of the troubles.

were women and children. Notable among these were Elizabeth and Mary Hubbarde, two Irish women with eight children between them who arrived in Manchester that September. These had to make do with a grant of 18*d*. In January 1643 an Irish woman with ten children appeared at the constable's door seeking support. We may only speculate how many people arrived from Ireland and survived without assistance, went to other Lancashire towns, or indeed reached the Manchester authorities only to be turned away.[21]

Putting an army into the field in Ireland to suppress rebellion was a double-edged sword. Parliament had reluctantly authorised the raising of a

Irish atrocities, seventeenth-century style. Rebellion in Ireland in 1641 fuelled genuine
fears that conflict would cross the Irish Sea to Lancashire, where there were many
Catholics. Refugees from the conflict sought aid in Manchester adding first-hand
evidence to the panic.

force of 6,000 foot and 2,000 horse in England, to be commanded by James
Butler, Earl of Ormonde. Additional numbers were committed by 1642, and
these were raised both in England and Ireland. There could be no guarantees,
however, that the king might not decide to use his 'Irish' army elsewhere:
or indeed that troops raised in England, ostensibly for Ireland, would cross
St George's Channel at all. Parliament's nervousness on this point was well
illustrated when in April 1642 they sent down a letter to the local officials of
Lancashire and Cheshire, via the hand of John Moore, demanding to know
why 'horse troops' there 'so long' had not moved on, and by whose neglect
this had occurred.[22]

   Once the rebellion in Ireland was under way, parliament was quick to
discern what it portrayed as the true cause and culprits. As evidence presented
to the Lords on 7 March 1642 put it, 'that the Rebellion in Ireland was
framed and contrived here in England, and that English Papists should have
risen about the same time, we have severall Testimonies and Adverts from
Ireland'. This was confirmed both by 'suspicious meetings and consultations'
and by what was apprehended as be the 'seditious carriage' of Catholics in
England. The objectives of the rebels were thought to be the maintenance of

bishops, recovering of the royal prerogative, and ultimately 'the queen's pious intention' of restoring the Catholic faith in England. This last was confirmed by 'original letters' directed to the Pope's nuncio, Count Rosetti, by 'a Priest in Lancashire'.[23]

Some of the accounts of what happened in the rebellion across the water may have been exaggerated, but fear of Irish invasion was clearly a very strong local reason for conflict – and it is mentioned time and again in contemporary documents. This was made particularly obvious in the petition of 12 March 1642, when parliament was lobbied by its potential supporters in Lancashire for the appointment of Lord Wharton as lord lieutenant. The petitioners were keen that the Crown should be established 'upon the old and sure foundation of impartiall justice, nationall lawes and the subject's love', and that 'innovations' should be expunged from the Church, while the laws against Catholics should be enforced. The immediate threat, however, came from across the Irish Sea. Moreover, Lancashire Catholics were seen as a fifth column,

in regard the course of these great affaires, so highly concerning the safetie, plentie, and quiet of the Kingdome hath been much interrupted by some whose sinister ends or corrupted understandings (capable of no amendment) hath made them active for the introduction of publike calamities. And your petitioners being seated in the mouthe of danger, and having fresh and daily spectacles of the Irish cruelties presented to their eyes, cannot but chuse but apprehend feare from the noveltie of so great barbarism, and lest the kingdom (for want of timely ayds) being lost, the war (or rather the massacre) should be transported hither from the opposite shore, where the number of Popish Recusants, and the opportunity of landing, may invite an invasion …

In the eyes of the petitioners the only recourse was to put the militia in 'a posture of defence', secure the ports, and disarm all recusants.

The Lancashire petition directed to the king that May was animated by similar sentiments. His majesty had abandoned London for York early in 1642, and the 'Knights, Esquires, Ministers, Gentlemen and Freeholders' of the county were anxious that he should return to his 'great Councell'. His absence from the heart of the administration not only encouraged 'Popish malignants' but exposed his Lancashire petitioners to the possible 'Fury of a Forraigne Foe'. The longer the king was away the greater the damage to the affairs of the kingdom, and the longer it would take to subdue 'the Rebels in

Ireland'. As late as June 1642 there were still many in Lancashire who hoped that conflict could be avoided. Given that even the parliamentary committee had serious doubts about fighting at this time it is reasonable to suggest that a many Lancastrians, at this eleventh hour, were either undecided or seekers after peace.[24]

Fortuitously the Irish threat – perceived or real – was actually slow to have a material impact upon the war in England. The main reason for this would not be lack of will on King Charles's part, but the almost insurmountable complexity of the Irish problem. For in 1642 there were not one or two factions in Ireland, but at least four.

First there was the main body of what London saw as 'rebels', the Catholic Confederacy, or the 'Confederation of Kilkenny', which came to dominate the largest land mass, though not the richest areas. The most articulate of the confederates sought complete tolerance for Catholicism as well as political and economic concessions – despite the fact that they continued to claim that they were loyal to the Crown. Willing to enter into a truce with the king, and prepared to put resources at his disposal, they nonetheless continued to be a problem. Entering into any sort of pact with those who had slain his subjects, and particularly former rebels who were Catholics, might further inflame public sentiment against him and was bound to remain extremely difficult.

Second, the royalist party in Ireland retained its grip on Dublin, the traditional seat of power within the 'pale', that part of Ireland regarded as wholly within the administrative control of the central government. Beyond this significant enclave the king's loyal subjects were in dire straights, little more than pockets of resistance in the south and west, with their backs to the ocean. Short of supplies and with little immediate prospect that king or parliament would come to their rescue, they were as yet in no position to offer any military help to anyone but themselves.

Third, parliament was a considerably smaller minority force in Ireland at this early stage: small groups of parliamentarians might however complicate matters, acting as a spoiling device making it more difficult for others to achieve their aims. Fourth, and rather more significant, were the Ulster Scots, intent on the preservation of their lands in the north, much of which had been granted to them by the late King James. A sort of peace existed between king and Confederates, and between parliament and Scots, but this was not the same as ready-made alliances with agreed goals. It would be late in 1643 by the time matters were sufficiently resolved to allow any significant numbers of troops to be released to fight for the king in England.

As G.R. Elton has observed, none of the things that have been traditionally argued as long-term causes of the war actually dictated when or how conflict might be ignited – indeed it is arguable that there was no 'high road' to civil war – in Lancashire, as anywhere else. Moreover Charles was essentially the head of three kingdoms or dominions, and England was in fact the last to rebel against him. In this context the English civil war can be seen as just a part of the 'War of the Three Kingdoms' – or a 'British Problem'. War with the Scots was certainly an important short-term cause of the crisis in England. The need for ready money abruptly ended Charles's eleven-year personal rule with the recall of parliament. The Scottish problem aggravated religious and financial grievances in England, and may well have acted to embolden Charles's English critics. Scotland was also linked to Ireland, through settlers, religion, and other factors, and turbulence there was at least in part a backlash against the success of Scottish reformers against the king.[25]

In attempting to mediate between the parties the Duke of Hamilton was one who gained the thanks of neither. Yet he was unusually perceptive when he pointed out that, on the one hand, the king risked provoking rebellion in England if he tried to suppress the Scots by force, and on the other the rebels threatened sparking off a war with no foreseeable end. In Lancashire, as in many other parts of the country, there was antagonism to the enforcement of the king's military programme to fight the Scots, and it has been suggested that Ralph Ashton and Roger Kirkby were elected as MPs on their reputation as men committed to reform.

The Long Parliament had made great inroads into what they saw as their natural grievances, and in doing so it is reckoned that they had deprived Charles of over half his normal revenues. Charles's cause was weak: the hated Earl of Strafford, the king's lord deputy in Ireland, had gone to the scaffold that May, and Archbishop Laud languished in the Tower. Belated, and arguably misguided, attempts at conciliation helped ensure that the king no longer had a significant powerbase in parliament with which to continue a political struggle. Eventually it appeared that the king had only one significant power left: power itself, military force. This then was the final straw: who would answer the call to arms of king or parliament?[26]

Gentlemen and townsmen

The English civil war has sometimes been portrayed as a 'class' war, or a war of the town against the country. Although the term 'class' itself is certainly anachronistic if applied to the seventeenth century, it is fair to question whether factors such as wealth, social station or place of residence were important determinants of allegiance during the war. We see echoes of these ideas in the Lancashire case, but at best they are over-simplifications. In places such models seem to apply very well – we, see for example, a majority of townsmen in south-east Lancashire siding with parliament – but in general the formulae are apt to break down as soon as the detail is examined. The three peers of Lancashire, Lords Derby, Molyneux, and Morley and Mounteagle all sided with the king, but the picture concerning the lesser gentry was far less clear-cut. Indeed of the almost 800 gentry families who have been identified, the allegiances of almost two-thirds are unknown or unclear. Many were militarily inactive at the outset. Of those allegiances we do know, a majority were for the king, with a little under 150 opting for the armies of his majesty and not quite 100 fighting with the parliament. Yet these bald statistics by no means tell the whole story. There is some evidence that the parliamentarian families were more active in their cause than their opposite numbers, and at the same time the most active of the royalists were more likely to fight outside the county – with the king's forces on the national stage.[27]

However, the influence of the local magnate does often seem to have been a more significant factor in choice of sides than political idealism. As Blackwood has pointed out, it is likely that the personal influence of the earl of Derby was at least a partial explanation of the prevalence of royalist gentry in West Derby hundred. Half of the extensive Derby estates were in West Derby, and the value of his patronage was not inconsiderable. As a contemporary account put it, his 'great hospitalitie' brought 'much love and applause'. Moreover the Molyneux family of Sefton were also influential royalists in this area. In south Lonsdale a similar, but smaller, grouping of royalist gentry lived around the cavalier nobleman Lord Morley and Mounteagle. In one instance it appears that it was personal antipathy to the leading members of the Derby family which was the deciding factor. Thus it was that Sir Thomas Stanley of Bickerstaffe, who had previously been locked in a property dispute with his more famous kinsmen, threw in his lot with parliament.

Though James Lord Strange (who became seventh Earl of Derby upon the death of his father William, the sixth earl, in September 1642) has been described as a 'fanatical royalist', his aims and actions were not dictated by a simple, blind obedience to the king. The Derby influence had been built up over centuries, and the standing of the family depended not only on royal beneficence, but on the respect of, and the material contributions made by, his tenants, allies and retainers of the north west of England. In short it would profit Lord Derby very little if he retained the confidence of Charles

I while his estates were overrun and his people turned against him. Lord Derby's motives in the period 1638 to the early part of 1642 were therefore subtle, if not ambiguous. If never openly disloyal to the crown, his role in the House of Lords was not that of unquestioning lackey. He did not oppose the Triennial Act, which required a summoning of parliament every three years, nor the abolition of Star Chamber; nor did he attempt to prevent the outlawing of Ship Money.

On the other side of the coin Derby upheld the king's right to choose his own ministers, and deplored the impeachment of the Earl of Strafford. In war with Scotland he was a faithful servant of the crown. His essentially pragmatic approach to religion was to ignore both Puritans and Catholics who enjoyed their devotions unobtrusively without making problems for him. At the same time he confided to his journals that his best servants were neither 'puritan nor Jesuit'. Derby succeeded in remaining a genuinely popular character with much of his natural constituency until 1642. Personal charm and civility went a long way. As he later advised his son, a smile and a flourish of the cap cost nothing, and might, under the right circumstances, serve to reap considerable dividends.[28]

As lord lieutenant of both Lancashire and Cheshire the earl had been obliged to raise forces in the county for the king's unpopular Scottish wars. The result was a good deal of criticism. In 1641 he had a genuine sympathy for those who now feared that Lancashire could be the next target for the Irish rebels, and the victim of internal strife. Thus it was that he wrote to colleagues in the House of Lords explaining what was fast becoming a panic, because 'wee that live soe neere to Ireland have a bad advantage of knowing ill tidings there sooner then you doe'. On 16 November 1641 Lord Wharton read out a letter to lords which he had received from Lord Strange, expressing extreme disquiet about the state of the county. Strange was now, so he said, on his guard against 'some in that county that were stronger than he', and that furthermore 'if ever Need was to look to Lancashire in our Time, it is now'.[29]

Viewed from court Lord Strange's warnings looked uncomfortably close to the position taken by the king's opponents. Indeed the opposition would remain hopeful for many months that the Derby family would eventually come down on their side, and might even make useful local figureheads around whom resources might be gathered. Under such circumstances it would be much of Lancashire, rather than just the Manchester area which might be counted parliamentarian. At the same time local complaint finally gave way to a pamphlet of February 1642 in which Peter Haywood accused the noble lord of gerrymandering, acting arbitrarily in raising troops for Scotland, and illegally advancing the position of recusants. Lord Strange defended himself in the Lords, but it was all too obvious a sign that local consensus and traditional deference were well on the way to breakdown.

From this time on it was also the case that Strange's 'middle way' stance gained him no love, and a lot of backbiting, in court circles. Neither was he helped by the fact that the religious policies of the crown were often at variance with local sentiment. His position was thus sufficiently far from that of the core members of the court, and apparently detached and open-minded, that despite difficulty with his previous conduct the opposition in Lancashire still regarded him as a potential leader in early 1642. Naturally he refused to have anything to do with such a suggestion, the results of which would have been even more inimical to Derby family interests than either the status quo, or a premature declaration of unquestioning support for a hard line royalist position. Yet his defence of personal and local interest left question marks which were slow to go away.

Charles may never have been as distrustful of Lord Strange (soon to be the new Lord Derby) as some commentators would have us believe, but on the other hand these things would not naturally recommend him to any position of leadership. Moreover when it came to war he was not an experienced soldier – there was no reason to pick him as a senior officer for the main army in the field. Nevertheless, he was clearly the key figure in the North West, and not to accept him as such was to risk alienating a significant part of the kingdom, and lose a handy pool of potential recruits. Even so, there was much to be gained from the local perspective from avoiding war on Derby lands. Thus, although Strange was theoretically the king's foremost soldier in the region, he was, at the outset at least, something of a reluctant warrior. As one commentator has put it, he was no fanatic, but 'a cautious man whose life after 1640 was dominated by an overriding ambition to maintain and then restore his family's predominant local position'.[30]

To those royalist leaders who were influential Lancashire noblemen before the war we should add at least one who was ennobled during the conflict. Charles Gerard, son of Sir Charles Gerard of Halsall, was also related to the royalist Fittons of Gawsworth. Described as gallant and honest, Gerard soon showed an aptitude for war. Other family members were also committed fighting royalists, one brother, Edward, being promoted to Colonel, another a cavalry commander. Two of his uncles fought, one being mortally wounded at Ludlow in 1645. The same year Charles Gerard's own efforts were marked by advancement to the peerage as Lord Gerard of Brandon.

Though the effect of any one individual was less pronounced than that of Lord Derby the parliamentarian grandees also exerted personal influence in their own localities. The Hollands and Ashtons, for example, were well respected in Denton and Middleton. Indeed, the parliamentarian county committee of Lancashire was not at odds with 'the continued retention of control by the traditional county elites' and relatively few of the leading parliamentarians were 'new men'. Nevertheless only some of the existing elite were represented in the parliamentarian ranks, and the fact that Lord Derby remained loyal to the king would be of critical importance in retaining a majority of the landed classes on the side of the crown. As might be expected, justices and the legal profession were well represented in the Lancashire parliamentarian leadership, and in this Alexander Rigby and his family were prime examples. In some instances Rigbys were able to share out local legal offices between them.[31]

Yet nothing appears to have been predestined, and there are many whose allegiance would have been difficult to predict merely from their circumstance. As Ann Hughes has put it,

In Lancashire ... most of the gentry were royalists but any differences between royalists and parliamentarians were subtle. Rising gentry and declining gentry were in a minority on both sides which were thus largely composed of families of stable fortunes. There were prospering families on Parliament's side, while the king's followers included the more spectacular failures, and the most indebted. The Lancashire royalists included reactionary, paternalistic and progressive landlords, coal speculators and 'commercial tycoons'; it is hard, therefore, to characterise them as defenders of a feudal social order. Furthermore, Lancashire royalists, like royalists in Suffolk or royalist members of the Long Parliament, were younger than their parliamentarian counterparts; a finding which those who associate youth with radicalism have used to support the argument that it was monarchy which represented the avant-garde.[32]

It took a brave, or foolish, man to opt openly for the opposition where one side or the other had the support of the key nobleman in an area. Nevertheless it did happen, and the middling and lower orders of society could be surprisingly radical. In 1642 many Lancashire yeomen and husbandmen did sign the protestation to 'maintain the religion established against Popish innovations and to protect the freedom of Parliament', though by doing so they may have genuinely believed that they were upholding the established order rather than defying the king. It was also observed that yeomen's sons sometimes fled their home locality, avoiding the king's recruiting parties, and made their way to towns, where, intentionally or accidentally, they might land up fighting for parliament. Whether such incidents were a deliberate political choice, a vote for adventure, or mere generational rebellion against parents can only be judged on individual cases.

As far as the towns were concerned it is certainly true that the comparatively modern town of Manchester, with its growing trade and industry, was a parliamentarian stronghold. As Lord Clarendon would observe, it had been so 'from the beginning', being proud of its wealth, and implacably opposed to the king. Rochdale was similarly for parliament, as was Low Church Bolton, famously the 'Geneva of the north'. Nevertheless not all towns were for parliament, and many, including Manchester, harboured a minority opposition. Salford had royalist sympathies, but was not big enough seriously to challenge its larger neighbour across the Irwell. Liverpool, Lancaster and Bury were all mixed to some degree, with Liverpool and Lancaster both adapting readily enough to changes of regime with the swinging fortunes of war. In Liverpool a parliamentarian political majority appears to have been temporarily achieved as a form of protest vote against the nearby Molyneux family of Sefton who were for the king. Even so at the outset the mayor and part of the council were royalist. Preston and Warrington were for the king but nothing like as vociferous as the town of Wigan, once described as the 'most maliganant in all the county'. So it was that though there was some correlation between towns and the parliamentarian cause, the issue was by no means clear cut.

The willing and the unwilling

Although most Lancastrians had some sort of opinion, it was not easy to translate nascent sympathy for king or parliament into hard cash or soldiers. There was also a strong body of neutral sentiment: or to be more accurate, a large body of moderates, many of whom would actually join the war later, who saw peace as serving the best interests of all concerned. Indeed it would take most of 1642 to mobilise the resources of the county, and it may be argued convincingly that at the outset Lord Derby himself would rather have maintained a nominal loyalty to the king while keeping the peace within Lancashire. There were many who were aware that war would be expensive, interfere with trade and agriculture, and might be injurious to dynastic interests. William Farington, later identified as staunch and committed to the cause as any Lancashire royalist, was almost apologetic about raising the Wigan militia for the king. On the outbreak of hostilities he wrote to parliamentarian gentlemen of his acquaintance explaining that this was 'only for the preserving of peace and quietnes of the county', definitely not for any purpose of aggression.[33]

The royalist regiments raised in Lancashire eventually proved to be as good as any in the king's armies, but it would be an exaggeration to suggest that they were a crack body of volunteers. On occasion Lord Derby was happy to take whomever he could get. Adam Martindale reported that his brother Henry was no willing soldier, knowing not

> where to hide his head for my Lord of Derby's officers had taken up a custom of summoning such as he and many other persons, upon paine of death, to appear at generall musters and thence to force them away with such weapons as they had, if they were but pitchforks, to Bolton; the reare being brought up with troopers that had commission to shoot such as lagged behind.

Others went to war relatively happily. Adam Hodson of Aspull was induced to join the king's forces by a bounty of 20 shilings, a red coat, musket and knapsack, all of which were provided by his sponsor, the comfortably-off yeoman farmer, Ralph Wood. Disillusionment set in later: Hodson served six months, but for about half this time received no pay at all.[34]

Perhaps surprisingly many Catholics stood aside, particularly during the early stages. Some lacked motivation; others may have been genuine neutrals; but it is also probable that there was awareness that by taking up arms they would have been in breach of the laws of the land, and likely to bring discredit to the cause. A clear route out of this dilemma was found only in September 1642 when Sir William Gerard (in income terms the county's wealthiest royalist), Sir Cecil Trafford, Thomas Clifton, Charles Towneley, and other leading recusants of Lancashire, petitioned the king to have their arms 'redelivered' for the defence of his majesty and 'our own families'. As hostilities had now commenced, and was rebellion under way, the king had adequate grounds to allow Catholics to take up arms 'against unlawfull violence and force'. Naturally the fact that Catholics were now openly in arms on the royalist side was a propaganda gift to the opposition: the parliamentarian *Discourse* gloats that having 'thrust themselves into the Warr without any calling', Catholics then 'brought upon them a greater burden of evill than they needed'. The parliament contended that papists were now effectively 'licensed to rise'. On 22 November 1642 the *House of Commons Journal* pointed out that

Lancashire specifically needed supplies of finance for the war because it was faced with a 'general Rising of the Papists there'.[35]

Not all Catholics availed themselves of the opportunity of rallying to the royalist colours, and some would remain aloof, or lukewarm, throughout the war. Eventually, when the conflict was won, the Committee for Compounding would identify just 151 'papist delinquents' and 760 recusants worthy of legal sanction and fines – although records spoilt by damp and other causes might account for perhaps a further 90 more. Of just under 600 key royalists who took up arms in the county we have documentary proof that a little more than a quarter were Catholic.

Taken at face value this would seem to suggest that the Catholic contribution to the royalist war effort in Lancashire was modest, but this fails to take account of several factors. Most importantly the Committee for Compounding was primarily interested in money, and there was no point in bringing poor people in front of it. Secondly there were certainly royalist Catholics who slipped through the net: death and fleeing abroad being only the most obvious causes. By one attempt at statistical computation it has been estimated that a total of 42 Lancashire royalist gentlemen lost their lives in the civil wars, and of these a full 30 were Catholics. Even allowing that this total may be an underestimate it suggests that a majority, rather than a minority, of the county royalist leadership were of the 'old faith'. Moreover the proportionate importance of Catholics in key military roles in Lancashire cannot be denied.

According to statistics compiled by Peter Newman 13 of 21 royalist colonels identified as coming from Lancashire were Catholic. This compared to 15 of 52 for Yorkshire, one in three for Westmorland, and 3 of 15 in Cumberland. Over forty per cent of all the Catholic colonels in the country came from the six northern counties. All in all Newman suggested that about a third of all the royalist northern armies were Catholics, and nothing has yet emerged to seriously challenge this statement. Indeed most recently Gratton has tended to revise the estimate for Lancashire up rather than down.[36]

There are also good reasons to suppose that the count of royalist Catholics in certain parts of Lancashire was an underestimate. Catholics who lived in predominantly parliamentarian areas were well advised to keep a low profile, managing to escape notice, or more likely be identified as Catholics but not as active supporters of the king. One of the most interesting cases of a Catholic gentleman caught between a rock and a hard place was that of Sir John Talbot, who lived perilously close to Blackburn. He was noted as a 'great papist, but one that hath ... stood as neuter betwixt King and Parliament'. In what appears to have been an attempt to ingratiate himself with the Manchester garrison he invited leading parliamentarians to his house, 'promising them very kind usage and some further courtesies by way of complyance with them'. Sir Thomas Fleetwood may have been a Catholic royalist, but kept all bases covered by supplying a horse to the opposition when it looked as though he was on the losing side.[37]

On the parliamentarian side there were also examples of initial reluctance among the troops – or rather, among the occasional soldier-civilians whom the local authorities wished to turn into full-time fighting men. In October 1642 John Braddyl reported to Richard Shuttleworth at Gawthorpe that he had conferred with Mr Halstead of Rowley regarding the muster of the Burnley 'Parish men'. Yet Halstead had shirked his duty, explaining that he needed 'help for disciplining of the people'. Braddyl therefore suggested that in a few days' time a meeting should call the men of the parish together, so that both Halstead and Braddyl could address them. Nevertheless, Braddyl himself was reluctant to take even this modest step without Shuttleworth's explicit approval, preferably by return, using the bearer of this plaintive missive for the reply.

A meeting of parliamentarian sympathisers was certainly convened at Padiham in October 1642, but again the response was not overwhelming, as a letter in the Shuttleworth correspondence relates,

> a good parte of the Hundred did in some seasonable manner make their appearance, but not soe fully as we expected, which was excused through the occasion of housing their corne.

On the practical side match and powder do not seem to have reached Richard Shuttleworth until 6 November, and even then it seems unlikely that the parliamentarians of the Burnley area were ready to march immediately. Despite this tardy start, the *Discourse* was of the opinion that the companies raised in Blackburn hundred eventually 'proved stout men and were of good repute for hardness and manhood'.[38]

At the same time the parliamentarian leadership of Blackburn hundred was extremely reluctant to come out in open opposition. Richard Shuttleworth actually received a summons to the royalist muster at Warrington. As late as 20 October he was writing back to Lord Derby in semi-apologetic tones,

> I humbly begg pardon if I do not; according to your letter requiring, waite upon your Lordship tomorrowe at Warrington. It is noe personall

opposition against you that detaynes mee, for I thinke you have understoode my love.

The parliament men were in arms, so he said, only 'for our owne safety' against the 'popish party'.

Some men stayed at home, hoping perhaps that their absence would go unnoticed for the time being, or might be construed as loyalty by both sides. As John Barratt has put it, 'the inhabitants of many outlying areas of the kingdom clung to the hope that the war would pass them by'. And in 1642 this aspiration was not as unlikely as might now appear. England had been at peace for many decades, and even in the sixteenth century Spanish and French incursions had been essentially limited to the south coast and Ireland. Earlier still the Wars of the Roses – a major and protracted conflict – had had periods of peace, and regions which saw relatively little impact from the fighting. To many people, therefore, it did not seem unreasonable to hope that, given good relations with one's neighbours, lip-service to crown and parliament, and some luck, that God might let the scourge of war visit elsewhere. Sadly this only delayed the cataclysm, and might actually have made it all the more protracted.

CHAPTER THREE

'Up in arms':
the siege of Manchester, 1642

T HE DATE when the English civil war began – being a protracted flurry of flag raisings, speeches, riots, musters and the sending of commissions – is difficult to pin down precisely. In this respect Lancashire was no exception, and as in many parts of the country the opening moves were attempts to influence local leaders and to secure magazines. Frustrated in its attempts to pass a bill under which it would effectively gain control of the militia against the Irish threat, parliament eventually decided to take unilateral action. Thus the 'Militia Bill' became the 'Militia Ordnance'. Now, however, it began to seem more and more likely that parliament's forces would be needed in England. With the active support of Alexander Rigby Lord Wharton was appointed lord lieutenant for Lancashire by parliament on 5 March 1642 – a position that he did not actually accept until about three weeks later. An uneasy period ensued in which the county now had two lord lieutenants: Lord Derby for the king, Wharton for parliament.

Perhaps what might be considered the first overtly military action of the English civil war took place in neighbouring Yorkshire. Here the king attempted to take Hull at the end of April, although the refusal of that town to admit Charles and the somewhat half-hearted blockade which followed were long on posturing, and short on actual violence. On 27 May parliament declared that the king, influenced by his evil counsellors, had started war. In the absence of any other legitimate authority, it argued, responsibility for governing the country devolved upon parliament; parliament therefore stated that orders coming from any other source but itself were invalid. Now the most important thing was that the king's design of raising an army should be frustrated. Interestingly the entry in the *House of Commons Journal* for 28 May 1642 shows that it was Lancashire that was uppermost in the members' minds when the practical business of preventing the assembly of forces by the king was being considered. The orders to the county sheriffs were directed, not equally to the country as a whole, but to 'the Sheriff of the County of Lancashire, and all other Sheriffs of the Kingdom of England, and Dominion of Wales'. Instructions to the lord lieutenants were framed similarly, with Lancashire the first county to be mentioned. A few days later parliament put forward its 'Nineteen Propositions' in which it claimed the right to appoint civil and military officers, control fortresses, and regulate reform of the Church and laws on Catholics.[1]

Militias and magazines

The royalist 'commissions of array' were generally issued early in June, although the Lancashire document may have been received a day or two earlier. The commission of array was an impressive looking Latin document, actually a revival of an old device commanding the raising of troops in each county for the king. The London parliament had this development under discussion within days – noting that the king's summons applied to the north, and specifically Lancashire, Cumberland, Westmorland and Yorkshire. From Lancashire Sir Thomas Stanley reported that Lord Derby had departed for York, whilst 'Mr Gerrard' had arrived to recruit a troop of horse 'out of Lancashire and Cheshire' which was also destined for York. Lancashire gentlemen George Middleton of Yealand and John Girlington apparently also attended upon the king; Girlington was knighted, and Middleton was created a baronet. His majesty's favour was not misplaced, for in the ensuing months both men would become prominent in the royalist cause. By 13 June parliament had decided to send down to Lancashire four of the county's members of the Commons: Ashton, Shuttleworth, Rigby and Moore. These would form the nucleus of a committee for the 'preservation of peace of that county', and frustrate the plan of the king's 'wicked' councillors to start war. Despite this apparently pacifist mission their first duty would be to put the Militia Ordnance into action in coordination with the deputy lieutenants, calling out the 'trained bands, and other forces' to suppress the royalist attempts at raising troops. They were also to make sure that mail from parliament was not 'intercepted or stayed', and to ensure that no 'recusant arms, or other ammunition' left the county. Catholics were to be confined 'to their dwellings'. Within a few days a parliamentarian committee was indeed assembled in Lancashire.[2]

Battle lines were drawn, but as yet very few were either prepared, or willing, to fight. Despite the arrival of the MPs with clear instructions, many

The key royalist garrisons in the winter of 1642 following the failure of the siege of Manchester.

LONSDALE

Lindale

Dalton

Thurland Castle

River Lune

Hornby Castle

LONSDALE
Lancaster

River Hodder

River Ribble

YORKSHIRE

Key:

1. Warrington: 300 men including two 'Welsh companies.

2. Wigan: 300 men.

3. Preston: 200 men.

4. Leigh: outpost of 20 men.

5. Brindle: one company, 50–100 under Captain Somner.

Rossall Hall

River Wyre

Greenhalgh Castle

St Michaels on Wyre

Myerscough Lodge

Poulton

AMOUNDERNESS

Lytham Hall

Kirkham

3. Preston

5.

Clitheroe

Colne

Padiham

BLACKBURN

Blackburn

Chorley

LEYLAND

SALFORD

Rochdale

Bolton

Bury

Lathom House

Ormskirk

2. Wigan

4.

River Irwell

Middleton

WEST DERBY

Salford

Manchester

River Tame

Liverpool

Prescot

Newton

River Mersey

River Mersey

1. Warrington

Hale

Stockport

CHESHIRE

in Lancashire were still debating whether or not they would actually take up arms. Sir William Brereton, the Cheshire parliamentarian, attended one of the vital meetings of the Lancashire committee, and attempted to persuade his colleagues to proceed with resolution in executing the Militia Ordinance, there being no other means by which they could counteract the threat of 'being plundered by Papists, or other malignant spirits'. Nevertheless, as he reported back to John Hampden in London on 18 June, there were still plenty who would not take the final irrevocable step without clear assistance from outside the county,

> these gentlemen, who were of a contrary opinion, and seemed not to apprehend so much danger (perhaps knowing something of their own knowledge which might incline them thereunto), and did out vote the rest, declared that they conceived, that, if they should enter upon the Ordinance for the militia, they were not able to prosecute and go through with the execution thereof, and therefore thought fit to suspend the same; which I fear may much disadvantage and prejudice the cause, unless Lord Wharton come down in person, or some assistance be speedily sent from the Parliament.

It might have been expected that Lord Wharton, as parliament's lord lieutenant for Lancashire, would have made his own active intervention at this juncture, but it was not to be. Wharton had been appointed lord lieutenant for Buckinghamshire as well as Lancashire, and had also accepted a commission to lead a force in Ireland. At best he was a figurehead, and a name to conjure with: at this stage everything depended upon the men on the ground – their fears, aspirations and resources. Only Manchester and its surrounding area was actually 'up in arms', the town being 'forward and well affected' to make good its defence.

By now Lord Strange had attended the king's court at York, and, having been set to his task of raising support for the royalist cause, arranged a public meeting at Preston on 20 June to read out the royal declarations. Both supporters of the king and adherents of parliament hurried to the moor outside the town, but there appears to have been a preponderance of royalist glitterati present, including Lord Molineux, Sir Thomas Tyldesley, Sir George Middleton and Sir Edward Fitton.[3] In time the throng numbered more than a thousand. Various accounts survive of the undignified shouting match which ensued upon Preston Moor. According to the parliamentarian pamphlet *Lamentable and Sad Newes from the North* it was the opposition which had the loudest voice: the pamphlet claimed that the Lancashire committee members who were present, including Alexander Rigby, prevented the reading of the king's letters. Lord Strange,

> in contempt of their order from the Parliament departed with some of his friends and cryed out, all that are for the king go with us, 'crying for the king, for the king', and so about 400 persons, whereof the most part were popish Recusants went with him and ridde up and downe the moore and cryed, 'for the king, for the king', but far more in number stayed with the Committee and prayed for the uniting of king and Parliament with a generall acclamation.

In Alexander Rigby's own version of events the undersheriff, Thomas Danson, and others did succeed in reading out the king's documents, including the commission of array, complete with its great seal of England. The parliament men now countered with a reading of their instructions which 'were applicable to the present passages and the Militia of the County'.[4]

Despite the brave gloss put upon these events by the parliamentarians, it looks as though for practical purposes they had lost the argument. Lord Strange now began to enlist troops, and one parliamentarian correspondent doubtless expressed the thoughts of many others, when, feeling 'beset by papists' he decided he could no longer show his face upon the moor. Acting upon the instructions of the royalist leaders William Sumpter, a servant to William Farington, began to empty the town magazine, and take away the barrels of powder. Rigby's remonstration with the sheriff that this was contrary to the 'Order of the Lords and Commons' went unheeded. Violence could have resulted, but Rigby was surely right to exercise discretion in a town where his friends were sorely outnumbered. After the event he rationalised that it would have been more trouble than it was worth to come to blows over a relatively small stock of ammunition. Parliament's supporters promptly withdrew, and Richard Shuttleworth was among the first to make off. On 24 June Rigby remarked somewhat archly that Shuttleworth had been suddenly 'called away from Preston to Manchester', but for some unaccountable reason he had still not appeared in the town.

The parliamentarian stand at Manchester

About the same time, but with much less public upset, the magazine at Liverpool also fell into royalist hands. Large parts of the county, and most of its munitions, were drifting, bloodlessly, into the king's control. Almost by default the parliament men were forced back on Salford hundred and Manchester. If Manchester could not hold on to its supplies there would be no parliamentarian power base of any note within the county – and arguably no war on Lancashire soil. The men of the parliamentarian committee therefore took pre-emptive action, and Ralph Ashton, acting on Rigby's warning, raided the college where the powder and match had been stored on Lord Strange's orders. When the royalist commissioners of array arrived to demand them back, they met with outright refusal. Lord Strange now rode towards Manchester, his arrival at Bury with armed men causing 'a great terrour and amazement' among parliament's supporters.

How critical these local supplies of arms and ammunition actually were was underlined by the fact that the king, having given up London, had insufficient weapons for his field army. In certain counties Charles therefore ordered the militia to give up their arms for the benefit of the national struggle. In response some of the Lancashire hundreds made the decision not to appear in arms should the king visit the county in person. This logic does not seem to have been strictly limited to one side, since not only would the king's supporters have thereby have been more likely to be able to keep their arms for local defence, but parliamentarians, real or potential, would have avoided a clash which would have ruined the fiction that they were for 'king and parliament'. As a neutral stance, avoiding turning up with a gun also had much to recommend it.

Rumour ran riot, the Lancashire committee warning London that not only was the king himself expected to march on Manchester, but that all manner of nefarious designs were afoot, including 'great Insurrections' of Papists, malignants and their supporters.[5] In a show of strength the shops of Manchester were shut and the militia was called out to drill. They were paraded 'well furnished with musketts and pikes, and completely trained by the Captains that were there, and there was a greate shoute for halfe an houre "for the king and Parliament, for the king and Parliament". It was all, as one commentator put it, an 'ill omen to the peace of England'. For if this 'be the beginning of civill war, God knows … when the ending will be'. As the puritan author of *Lancashire's Valley of Achor* reasoned, if the royalists had failed in its attempt to cheat Manchester of its magazine, now they were likely to try to 'despoil' the place by force.

In the meantime Alexander Rigby continued a shuttle diplomacy, relaying demands from parliament in London that the opposition should desist in their warlike preparations and return the various magazines to their rightful places.

During this process one of parliament's missives was detained by a sentry set by Sir Gilbert Hoghton near Walton-le-Dale. Sir Gilbert called Rigby before him, and in a display of remarkable chivalry gave him his letter unopened and invited him to dinner. Amazingly Sir Gilbert's other guests were Sir Thomas Tyldesley and Mr Dawton, a recusant: they ate together in civility, Rigby remarking to two of the king's key supporters in Lancashire that, 'he could like them well, if they were not so familiar with Papists'. Yet not all were as gentlemanly, and another man guiding parliament's messengers was dealt with rather less politely: Roger Haddock of Chorley was set upon by a gang of cavalier ruffians, being beaten with 'very sore stokes' which 'broke his head to the very scull'.

Despite this martial flag-waving, minor brawls, and goading from both king and parliament, in Lancashire both sides remained unwilling to strike the first serious blow. An account of a military clash just outside Manchester, which supposedly occurred on 4 July 1642, was published in London, although it seems that this was much exaggerated if not entirely fictional. As with so much else coming from Yorkshire or the capital, the intention appears to have been to whip up support for one or other of the factions. In fact the Mancunians and Lord Strange appear to have negotiated a very curious compromise, or a tacit understanding, designed to leave neither with serious loss of face. Lord Strange would be allowed to enter Manchester with his immediate entourage, be invited to a dinner, and to hold further discussions. He would be allowed to remain until the following Monday morning, and an attempt would be made to decide some formula upon which the future of the Manchester magazine might be settled.

What exactly went wrong when Lord Strange came to town for his banquet on 15 July is very difficult to determine. It may be that showing the royalist noblemen just how strong and determined the Manchester militia might be was part of a plan to overawe the opposition. Perhaps another fist fight developed which simply got out of hand. Possibly one of the royalist party made an ill advised attempt to read the commission of array – as is suggested in *Lancashire's Valley of Achor*. In any event it seemed that things were under control until,

Captain Holcroft, Sir Thomas Stanley and ... Birch who were appointed Commissioners for the Militia, began to strike up their drum to put the Militia in execution, in another part of town; which when my Lord Strange and my Lord Mollineux heard, they came and met them and some blows passed on both sides, but two men of ... Birch his company are shot, one of which dyed this morning ... Birch was shot at twice, yet escaped with some few blows, by means of a coach that stood in the street.

Another account more sympathetic to the royalists has it that it was the sheriff who first confronted Holcroft's militia, demanding in his majesty's name that they 'lay down their armes, keepe the peace and cease the tumult'. Lord Strange 'missing his owne horse' had to make his undignified exit on foot, only narrowly missing assassination when his irate kinsman Sir Thomas Stanley, and another man, fired two pistols at him from a window. After finding a mount, Lord Strange had to fight his way through the throng. As he and his companions forged a passage, they were struck at from the rear by men with swords and one of these assailants was pistoled. Captain Birch may or may not have ordered the militia to fire, but the weather was inclement and the powder in the soldiers' muskets was damp – or they lacked resolution to fire a volley into men who were running away – and no more killing occurred.[6]

At least one of the descriptions speaks of a number of men 'wounded mortally', but we know of only one definite fatality: Richard Parcival of Kirkmanshulme, a 'linen webster'. He was buried in the collegiate church on 18 July 1642. Traditionally Parcival is stated to be the first fatality of the English civil wars, although on the face of it this seems unlikely given the blockade of Hull and the various minor altercations which preceded the Manchester skirmish. Nevertheless, Richard Parcival is the first attested casualty whose name we know, and it is partly upon this fact that the contention rests that the civil war started here, in earnest, in Lancashire.[7]

Not everyone in Manchester saw the intervention of the militia and the eviction of Lord Derby as a good thing. On 29 July a body calling themselves the 'better sort of townsmen' – either neutrals or royalist sympathisers – published a description of the action in which they blamed Sir Thomas Stanley, and Captains Birch and Holcroft for the violence. According to this version it was these extremists who were the 'disturbers' of the peace, their actions amounting to 'treachery'. With good will, it was thought that his lordship and Manchester could still be 'on very fair terms'. If these sentiments can be entertained it suggests that Broxap's explanation of the incident in which he says that there were in fact two major parties in Manchester at this time can be given some credence. In such a scenario it is plausible that some of the townsmen – neutral, or moderate parliamentarians in sympathy – offered a genuine reconciliation with Lord Derby, which was promptly wrecked by the militia call to arms. Although Lord Strange continued to raise troops, for the time being he backed away from further confrontation with Manchester, and he concentrated his immediate efforts upon supporting the king's cause on the national stage. Arguably this was a course of action he would live to regret.

In a significant show of solidarity with the crown Strange now suggested that the royal standard should be raised, and the army gathered, at Warrington. This idea was probably rejected as impractical and geographically inconvenient, given Lancashire's relative isolation and distance from the seat of the main action; instead, the king raised his flag at Nottingham, on 22 August 1642. Nevertheless the fact that Charles had not chosen Warrington was interpreted as a snub by critics of Lord Strange. There are also said to have been mutterings about his ancestors who had deserted Richard III at the vital moment at Bosworth with such dire consequences. Undeterred, his lordship raised about 2,000 Lancashire men, and a similar number from Cheshire, and during August led them off to join the main royalist army at Shrewsbury. Dugdale's account states specifically that the units raised for the king's field army were 'three regiments of foot and three troops of horse' – a little under 4,000 men at full strength: Derby himself would later claim the contingent to have been 3,000 'good men'. It has been suggested that two of the regiments raised at this time were commanded by members of the Gerard family of Halsall: Charles Gerard, who had previously fought in Scotland and the Netherlands, and his uncle Sir Gilbert. Four other Gerards featured among the senior officers of these units. Certainly, more than one Gerard would fight at Edgehill, along with many other Lancashire royalist soldiers.

It probably appeared that the best had been made of a bad job. Lord Strange had done his duty to the crown, and given the cause strong material backing: at the same time sending troops out of the county suggested that the ensuing mess of battle and destruction would befall people far away from Lancashire. Actually this act of duty, and pious hope of local peace, sowed the seeds of disaster, massively weakening the potential Lancashire royalist forces just at the time when an extra couple of thousand troops could have made a vital difference in the local arena. It also seems that, despite the intention of keeping Lancashire arms in the county for its own defence, the royalist troops took their militia equipment with them. One account of a few weeks later speaks explicitly of the arrival in Chester of 260 horse loads of arms, which had been gathered 'out of the north'.

That all was not well in the North West was apparent to King Charles almost immediately, as was related by the Earl of Clarendon in his *History of the Great Rebellion*,

As soon as the king came to Shrewsbury he had despatched his letters and agents into Wales, Cheshire and Lancashire, to quicken the levies of men which were making there, finding that the Parliament had been very solicitous and active in those counties of Cheshire and Lancashire, and that many of the gentry ... were deeply engaged in their service, and the loyal party much depressed. His majesty himself, leaving his household and army at Shrewsbury, went in person (with his troop of guards only) to Chester, presuming that his presence would have the same influence there it had had in all other places, to compose the fears and apprehensions of all honest men, and drive away the rest. This fell out accordingly; for being entertained with all demonstrations of duty by the city of Chester, those who had been most notably instrumental to the Parliament withdrew themselves, and the nobility and gentry – and indeed the common people – flocked to him ... Yet in Nantwich in Cheshire, and Manchester in Lancashire, there was some show – by fortifying and seditious discourses – of resistance and disaffection. For Manchester the Lord Strange undertook, without troubling his majesty further northward, in a very short time to reduce that place ...

Seacome later put these events in an even less positive light, suggesting that in fact Lord Strange had wanted to command the Lancashire troops as a brigade of regiments in the king's army. Charles had other ideas, and gave command of Derby's regiments to others, ordering him to return to Lancashire to check the progress of the rebels there, which, so far, he had so obviously failed to do. Not surprisingly, Lord Strange responded in high dudgeon, and only with difficulty did the king placate him, saying that with the enemy on the march this was no time 'to quarrel amongst ourselves'.

Lacking the strength to take immediate military action, the next act of the Lancashire parliamentarians was symbolic. In mid-September Lord Strange was impeached in parliament, and lawyer Alexander Rigby was one of the members given the task of drawing up the indictment. Naturally this parliamentarian document portrayed his lordship as a 'malicious' traitor who had raised a force to levy war – and the death of Parcival was specifically described as 'murder'. Interestingly it was not parliament that was seen as rebelling against the king, but Lord Strange and his cronies who were viewed as 'in open and actuall Rebellion against the king, Parliament, and Kingdome'. Both sides claimed that it was they who upheld the established order, and that it was the other who had committed the heinous crime of attempting to overthrow the state.[8]

The siege of Manchester, September 1642

Meanwhile, the Mancunians took advantage of Lord Strange's absence to begin preparing the town for a more organised resistance. Having the advantage of few experienced military leaders they engaged the services of a German professional soldier, John Rosworme, who, according to his own account, had recently fled to Manchester from Ireland. For a retainer of £30 every sixth months they would have the benefit of his 'advice and skill' – principally in fortifications, but also in the other military arts. Fortunately for future historians, Rosworme went unpaid for part of the time, and this led him to compose a whining, lengthy and detailed appeal to parliament, which included an important description of the events in Manchester that autumn.

My first aime was to set up good posts and chains to keep out the enemies horse; which by contrivance of a false alarum, and by the help of the Country's coming in, upon the ringing of the bels backwards, devised

German professional soldier John Rosworme, hired by the parliamentarian faction to defend Manchester in 1642.

purposely for this end, I safely performed, though many tongues had doomed me to death, if ever I attempted it. This was done upon Wednesday 22 of September 1642.

Having by this devise drawn some armed men into the town I earnestly pressed, that they might be carefully provided for, heartened and encouraged; for I was confident that in lesse than a week, that the enemy would make a reall approach, and then these men would stead us ...

In that small time of preparation which I had, I fortified and barricadoed up every streets end, with the addition of mud wals, which were unfinished when the Earl came upon us. I advised how our men should be assigned through each part about the town; but Salford bridge, the onely place of manifest danger, greatest action, and least defence, upon others refusall, I undertook myself: though by my engagements I was not bound to fight at all, but to advise and direct only'.[9]

Although Rosworme's account makes it appear that he was the mainstay of Manchester's defence, many parliamentarian supporters from Salford hundred and beyond had in fact repaired to the town – probably over a period of about two weeks leading up to the siege. One contemporary account dates Rosworme's works mainly to the period after 13 September – attempts to start before this date being met with local opposition, and threats to interfere physically with the erection of barricades. After this time royalist movements did much to persuade those who doubted the point of such preparations. Some of the defenders of the town came from far beyond the sound of Manchester's bells. Key figures who marched into town included Colonel Richard Holland, the town's parliamentarian governor, who hailed from Denton, as did Robert Hyde. Captain Robert Bradshaw arrived at the head of 150 of the Ashton tenants of Middleton, and Captain Edward Hyde and his company came in from Cheshire. Pro-parliamentarian accounts state that at least in part this migration into Manchester was stimulated by the behaviour of Sir Edward Fitton and other royalist leaders, who even yet were plundering the countryside and disarming any they suspected of disloyalty to the king. Others no doubt were alerted by the 'posts immediately sent into the country to give them notice', mentioned in the *True and Faithfull Relation*.[10]

Moreover the Manchester militia was itself gaining strength and experience, having been 'encouraged first by some Justices of the Peace, afterwards by the Ordinance for the Militia ... whereby sundry of them became skillfull musquetiers and active pikemen'. Richard Radcliffe, the captain of the Manchester militia, responded to the hour with resolution 'cheerfully and couragiously' and upon the beating of the drum, gave a rousing speech promising to 'maintaine the libertie of their persons, and the propriety of their goods, with the utmost hazard of their lives'. A contemporary parliamentarian account numbers the defenders at 1,000, and this would appear to be a safe, conservative minimum. Despite the preservation of the magazine in the town, ammunition was not yet in plentiful supply, so the casting of shot was hastily commenced. The *Discourse* speaks of gunpowder being manufactured at the college, and near disaster when a candle caused a minor explosion that blew some of the slates from the roof, 'and terrified the workmen'. A

A true and faithfull Relation of the
befieging of the Towne of

MANCHESTER

in Lancafhire upon Saturday the 24.
of September.

Together with the manner of the feverall Skirmifhes and
Paffages betwixt the Earle of *Derby* the befieger with
his 4500.men, and the Souldiers in the Town
being only 1000.or thereabout.

Alfo a Declaration of the Lords and Commons in Parliament to the Inhabitants of the faid Towne.

And laftly, the manner of the raifing of the faid Siege, having continued untill Saturday the 1. of October, as it was
credibly reprefented unto the Houfe of Commons
from a godly Minifter in the faid Towne,
and appointed to be printed
and publifhed.

He Towne of *Manchefter* having fome Malignants
in it, and multitudes of Papifts neere unto it, and
being reputed a Religious and rich towne, hath
been much envied and often threatned by the po-
pifh and Malignant partie, and therefore the
Townef-men being incouraged firft by fome Ju-
ftices of the peace, afterwards by the Ordinance
for the *Militia* did in a peaceable manner exercife and traine up their
A   youth

Title page to *A true
and faithfull Relation
of the besieging of the
Towne of Manchester
in Lancashire upon
Saturday the 24 of
September*, 1642.

Continuation of Certaine Remarkable Passages has it that the townsmen even took to recasting the bells of the church into cannon: but if this was so it must have been after the siege had started, as the bells also served the town's early warning system.

On Saturday 24 September the bells rang backwards again and the alert was sounded in earnest. Any defenders still outside made their way into Manchester, armed 'abundantly' with 'Muskets, Pikes, Halberts, Staves, and such like'. Even so, the royalists did not appear on the scene immediately, due, it was said, to the breaking of a wheel on one of the gun carriages which slowed their march considerably. About nine on the Sunday morning the royalist colours came into view. The command had been split, so that part surrounded Manchester from the south, and part confronted the inhabitants across the Irwell. Lord Strange set up a command post at Alport Lodge, about half a mile from the town. Deliberately, the king's supporters presented an imposing sight, numbering 2,000 at the least, and in some accounts double this figure. It is likely that about half a dozen small guns accompanied the troops, estimates on either side ranging up to as many as eight or nine. In

Cannon fire, *c.*1640, from an illustration which has popularly been associated with the siege of Manchester, but whose original provenance is unclear.

the ranks were not only Lancastrians but men from Cheshire and north Wales. With Lord Strange was most of the local royalist hierarchy including Lord Molyneux, Sir Thomas Tyldesley, Sir Gilbert Hoghton, Sir Alexander Radcliffe and Sir John Girlington.

Two gentlemen were sent out to enquire what Lord Strange should require of the town: one was promptly taken captive, and the message was sent that Manchester was to yield immediately. The town resolved to keep him out. Lord Strange did not attack straight away, but sent a further message on the Monday morning. This demanded the surrender of all the arms in Manchester, and promised to 'use the Towne kindly', but with the veiled threat that otherwise 'fearfull ruines' would ensue. This demand was likewise refused. Obviously the royalists had not entirely wasted their time since their arrival the previous day, for by now the artillery was in position, and fire commenced.

The fight was first begun by the Lord Strange his forces, which were in and about an house of Sir Edward Mosleys called the Lodge, where they planted some of their ordnance; and at the same time was seconded by an assault they made upon Salford Bridge, they having possessed themselves of the town of Salford, which adjoyneth to Manchester, save only the water betwixt, but did not joyne with them in common defence. But God so ordered the matter, that the cannons played in vain, and therefore they assaid to enter the town, and to beat our men from their works, which not being able to doe, they sent some of their souldiers to fire two barnes and eight or ten dwelling houses about twelve roods from our works, which being effected, the enemies with great shouting ('the towne is our owne, the towne is our owne') renued their assault, but by the valour and courage of Captain Bradshaw and his souldiers were beaten back, and many of them slaine. The wind at first blew the flame and smoke in the faces of our souldiers, to their great annoyance and the endangering of the town. But God that rides on the wings of the wind did very seasonably turn the wind till the rage of the fire was abated.

The royalist assault on Salford bridge had been something of an act of bravado – pouring men through a confined space which was commanded from the higher ground of the churchyard. Smoke and flame from the attempt to burn the town hindered both sides. Casualties were high. Nevertheless, the attackers had obtained a lodgement in a house at the foot of the bridge, and intermittent fire continued from here long after the assault had foundered. Rosworme, defending Salford bridge itself with some thirty musketeers, had given the royalists 'hot entertainment', and also claimed some of Bradshaw's glory, having sent him additional reinforcement at the vital moment of the action.

Sometime on this momentous day Colonel Holland also found time to write to Richard Shuttleworth at Gawthorpe asking him not only for reinforcements in his defence of Manchester, but specifically for matchcord for his muskets. Clearly copious shooting was having an impact on supplies, and if the siege turned out to be protracted there was a danger of his muskets falling silent. For the time being, however, nothing would be forthcoming from Blackburn hundred. Holland was clearly frustrated with the attitude of the Blackburn men, appealing to them to honour 'the realitie' of the 'association which both our hundreds have entered into'. What the enemy were now doing should surely bring them to their senses and realise that their public duty should take precedence over the 'private concerns' of either the harvest or the courts. What was holding the Shuttleworth clan back from declaring their hand at this early stage was not merely logistics, but political prudence. As was explained in later correspondence, the family had interests in other parts of the county which would be vulnerable to seizure as soon as they declared openly for parliament. Moreover, there was a danger of being seen as aggressors if they were to send out troops from their own locality before 'actuall violence had broke out there'.[11]

The next day, Tuesday 27 September, the attackers surrounding Manchester attempted to catch the parliamentarians off guard, beginning with a concentrated bombardment of Rosworme's position. This obviously had shock value; as Rosworme himself recorded, it was

> a strange noise and terror to my raw men, sixteen of them took to their heels; the rest, some for feare of my drawne sword, others out of gallantry, resolving to dye, than to forsake me, and the safety of their town. I was now few in number, but found some pitie from other gallant hearts, who voluntarily came in to my assistance, making up my number [to] 28.

Despite this drama, the royalists had in fact switched the main focus of the action to the Market Stead Lane area, where Captain Radcliffe and his men were waiting. An infantry attack here quickly faltered, allowing the victorious parliamentarians to sally out and take several prisoners. Others were killed and royalist stragglers in the vicinity were put to flight. With battle petering out during the afternoon, Strange again appealed for surrender, and a truce was agreed until the following morning.

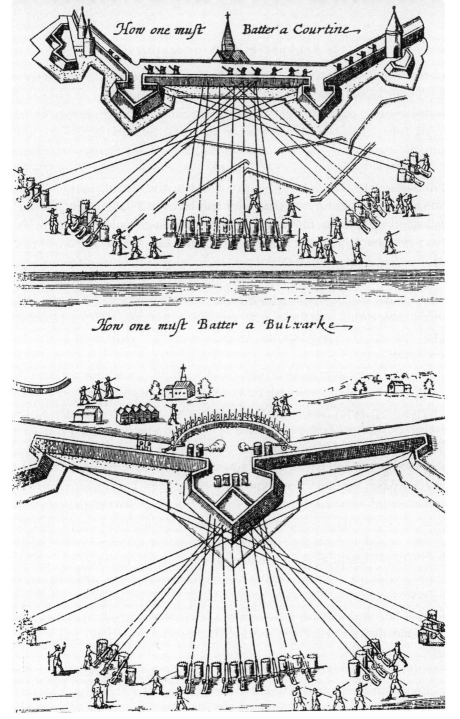

Contemporary textbook illustration showing how to batter curtain walls and bulwarks with cannon. Rarely did it prove possible to gather effective battering siege trains of artillery during the Lancashire campaigns. When Rupert achieved this at Liverpool in 1644 the town fell fairly quickly. When this was not done, as at Manchester and Lathom, for example, either failure or very protracted siege was the result.

On Wednesday morning negotiation continued: and even at this stage it was by no means clear that all Lancastrian supporters of king or parliament had a burning desire to fight one another. Some of the gentlemen of the town, were, as one eye witness put it 'inclinable to condescend'. At about this dramatic time – or very soon afterwards – Lord Strange must have received the news of the death of his father, the elderly Lord Derby. From henceforth James Lord Strange would be the seventh Earl of Derby. Whether this traumatic development had a significant bearing on what followed is impossible to determine, but it is difficult to believe that it did not have some impact on the operation of the royalist command in the final days of September. Lord Derby now sent, what was on the face of it, a very conciliatory message to the town, the import of which was that if the Mancunians would surrender to him 100 muskets he would withdraw and march away – thus could honour be satisfied on both sides. Colonel Richard Holland, the governor, was apt to seize upon this chance of a peaceful resolution.

Colonel Rosworme the professional soldier and Master Bourne the preacher interpreted this as defeatism, and gave rousing speeches to the soldiers – thus propping 'up their hearts against any dangers'. On being consulted, the parliamentarian soldiers are supposed to have said that they would now fight 'to the last drop of bloud'. Bradshaw's men swore in a 'general shout' that they would only part with 'their armes and their lives together'. Holland was mortified, but the die was cast. A reply to Lord Derby's summons was prepared and sent out. According to the *True and Faithfull Relation*, this pointed out that the defenders of Manchester could in no way believe that his majesty would wish his loyal subjects to give up their arms – lawfully borne for their own defence 'against malignant enemies and multitudes of bloudy Papists'. Moreover, the men of Manchester had no desire to suffer the same outrage as had their brethren in Ireland. Derby's men appeared to operate by the same 'hellish principles' as the Irish Catholic rebels, and there was no reason that they should trust him. In short they would not give him so much as a 'rusty dagger'.

Unsurprisingly this uncompromising – not to say insulting – message led to an immediate resumption of hostilities, and a fresh volley of cannon balls. One of these scudding shot is said to have killed a bystander who 'stood gazing on top of a stile'. By Thursday 29 September it was clear that the initiative had passed decisively to the defenders. That morning about 200 parliamentarians sallied out from Deansgate intent on recapturing a house which had been occupied by the royalists; a fierce skirmish ensued, to which the royalists committed about 100 foot soldiers and a troop of horse. After some time the king's men were driven off, some of them into the river, where an officer and two men were drowned. The body of Captain Snell was later found with two rings 'worth £20' on his fingers. There were a further dozen casualties on either side. The same day, the 29th, a sniper positioned in 'Manchester Steeple' got in a lucky shot which killed Captain Standish of Duxbury who was on the Salford side of the water marshalling his troops. According to parliamentarian sources, this was a particularly demoralising blow, many of his men deserting soon afterwards.

On Friday Lord Derby's men continued to make a show playing,

upon the town with the Ordnance and musket shot from Salford and the Lodge, and cast up a trench before the end of Deanes gate, as if he had intended to make a long siege. The Ordnance did make holes in divers houses, and battered down a piece of a chimney but did little harme. This night his Cannons were removed. On Saturday he sent that prisoners might be exchanged for prisoners, and that plundering should cease on both sides. It was answered that our side had not plundered any house, but that his Lordships forces had plundered so many that ten thousand pounds would not make a recompense. Prisoners were exchanged according to his Lordships motion. Aboute noone on Saturday his forces removed away from the town.

So the royalist army packed up and marched away. Parliamentarian propaganda claimed that some of Lord Derby's soldiers 'wept', while others protested that they had 'great unwillingness to fight against Manchester'. Behind them they left over a hundred dead, many of them killed in the attempted storm of Salford bridge. The graves of some of the fatalities were later found in the fields about the town, five 'in the sands of the river'. A few more had been carted away as far as Didsbury for interment. By comparison parliamentarian casualties had been light, the number of their dead perhaps not more than ten. Some in the victorious party put their success down to two factors: the hand of God, and the miserable Manchester weather which had dampened the attackers, their powder and the fires which had been lit in the attempt to burn the parliamentarians out. *Lancashire's Valley of Achor* claimed that the reasons for the repulse of the Lord Derby were clear – the profane willingness of the royalists to fight on the Sabbath, and the 'Armies of Prayers' and 'Legions of Angels' which had supported the 'godly' side from all over the kingdom.[12]

Sir Thomas Tyldesley of Myerscough near Garstang, Lancashire royalist (1592–1651). The Catholic Tyldesley was no youngster when war broke out in 1642, but he was arguably the king's most active supporter in the county. He also fought with the main royalist field armies at Edgehill and Marston Moor. He was killed at Wigan Lane.

Prayer was in fact all the Lancashire parliamentarians could have hoped for. Only when the siege was over, and the dead buried, did parliament give serious consideration to how 'speedy relief' might be sent into Lancashire. On the afternoon of 5 October it was proposed by the Committee for the Safety of the Kingdom that troops from Norfolk and Suffolk might be sent northward 'if they can be spared from the Lord General's army'. Characteristically the crisis also resulted in the formation of another committee, initially to be known as the Committee for the Raising of the Thousand Dragoons – later rechristened the Committee for Lancashire Dragoons. This finally reported to the lower house in late November, and there was certainly an attempt to recruit dragoons, who were to report to two London public houses for enlistment. Yet by then events had long since overtaken talking, and it appears that no 'Lancashire dragoons', or indeed dragoons for Lancashire, materialised at this time. Stephen Bowtell, writing in *England's Memorable Accidents*, did claim that the required dragoons had been found among 'men came out of Holland in the ship that was forced by a leake to put into Yarmouth'. No evidence has yet been found that these troops, if they existed, did get to Lancashire.

There is reason to believe that eventually some of the money designated for the Lancashire dragoons found its way into the coffers of the army of the Earl of Essex. *Mercurius Aulicus* likewise had it that the men intended for Manchester went to fill up the ranks of parliament's main field army in the south. All in all parliament's ham-fisted and belated, small-scale attempts to help Manchester that autumn could only reinforce the opinion that London's ability to intervene was as yet very limited. Neither had very much, if any, assistance yet materialised from elsewhere in Lancashire beyond Salford hundred. As a despairing Edward Johnson of Manchester wrote to friends on 12 October, 'for ayde from the parlement forces or any other wayes we have noe hope of any'. Parliamentarian correspondent Thomas Jesland of Atherton was still bemoaning the absence of reinforcements in early December. Had a useful force come to Lancashire's assistance promptly he believed that there would by now be no 'masse-monger' or 'malignant of note' left at liberty'.[13]

A bigger and more important idea which did begin to grow, albeit slowly, was the concept of a 'Northern Association' of parliament's forces. For mutual support the 'well affected' of the 'Counties of York, Lincoln, Nottingham, Derby, Stafford, Chester, Lancaster, Northumberland, Cumberland, Westmorland, County Palatine of Durham, and Town and County of Newcastle' were called upon to work together. The plan was that they would 'associate themselves, and mutually aid, succour and assist one another, by raising Forces of Horse and Foot, and leading them into places which shall be most convenient and necessary … suppress and subdue the Popish and Malignant party'. Lord Fairfax would have the commission to lead such combined 'forces out of their own Counties' – a novel idea when most militias expected to work only within their own areas. The suggestion had much to recommend it, and indeed much of parliament's war effort would later be expressed through such associations. For the time being, however, this concept of 'big battalions' and strategic mobility was far beyond the reality of what could be achieved in the beleaguered, royalist-dominated north the early months of hostilities.

Only much later would parliament's Northern Association have a serious impact on the war in Lancashire: even then the Northern Association forces were mainly drawn from the north-eastern counties, with the emphasis on Yorkshire. Lancashire's contribution to the association never appears to have been great, and was always secondary to operations undertaken at the behest of its own committee.

More systematic supplies of money for Lancashire also received somewhat belated parliamentary consideration in the face of what the members now portrayed as a general 'Catholic' revolt in the county. Funds were not, however, voted directly, but facilitated by means of loans for which 'Mr Thomas Case' and others might pledge money or plate. In return the investors would have the 'public faith' that they would be repaid, plus 8 per cent interest. Clearly the reinforcing of the local war chest by any means was welcome, but such a roundabout route of supply cannot have been effective immediately – nor is it yet clear how much was raised by means of such loans.[14]

On 6 October parliament gave a formal declaration of thanks to the 'well affected gentlemen' and others of the county of Lancashire who had resisted Lord Derby.[15] The royalist army fell back on Warrington, and while they were stationed there a summons was received directing them to reinforce the king's main army. Again Derby divided his force: while he remained in Lancashire, some of his best troops, including those of Sir Thomas Tyldesley, set off for the south. Not all of these went willingly. In the days before the existence of a standing or national army, Englishmen called out to fight often regarded their responsibility as beginning and ending with their county. Nevertheless, any dissent on such account was dealt with in a day or two, and about 10 October the king's Lancashire reinforcements were on the road. Tyldesley took many of his Amounderness men with him, 'not suffering' it was said, 'any of them to returne home but compelled and forced them to march with him after the king'.[16]

For the royalists nationally as well as regionally the failure to take Manchester was a serious setback. For this the Earl of Derby would reap much criticism, a good deal of it from his own side. Clarendon had it that the job had not been 'fortunately performed' because it had not been 'resolutely pursued'. There was some truth in this accusation, but there were also obvious military ineptitudes. Before attempting to secure Manchester, Derby had already divided his strength and taken many of his best men to the king at Shrewsbury: had he attempted to reduce the town first, he would most likely have been able to bring overwhelming strength to bear. As it was he had given the opposition just enough time to organise themselves and to draw in support from the surrounding area. Derby also appears to have been deficient in artillery, the few small guns being inadequate to the task. The royalist tactics were also suspect: they had neither attempted to storm the town immediately, nor set about a systematic siege. Instead, they had waited for some time before resorting to brief cannonades, followed by rushes which apparently lacked coordination. Very probably Lord Derby had hoped to avoid serious action on what he regarded his own turf, and believed that once the king was in the area Manchester would either capitulate, or, under pressure, come to some sort of terms. At best this was a miscalculation.

Interestingly, and despite the bloodshed at Manchester, Colonel Holland had not given up all chance of a negotiated peace, at least in the local area. Acting in concert with Richard Shuttleworth at Gawthorpe, Peter Egerton, John Bradshaw and others, there were attempts to fix a meeting with royalist gentlemen at Blackburn on 13 October. On the royalist side Roger Nowell of Read, a relative of Shuttleworth, acted as middleman. Perhaps there was a feeling that Blackburn was not safe enough territory for the parliamentarians, and the time and place was renegotiated to Bolton on the 18th. In the meantime Holland received direct instructions from London not to attend. So it was that a frustrated Holland was forced to write to Shuttleworth and John Starkey, explaining parliament's opposition 'to any treaty' and giving his apologies – though he, more than any other, desired the preservation of peace. The meeting never happened. Sadly John Rosworme's opinion of Richard Holland as a coward seems to have wide acceptance, while the equally probable explanation that he was a moderate, a seeker after peace, seems to have been largely ignored.

Another overture to peace which came to nothing was reported in the *Perfect Diurnall* of 7 November. This story had it that Lord Kilmorey, in consultation with Brereton, had put forward a proposal that Manchester should cease fortifying activities, and its arms be laid down. In return the royalists would withdraw their forces from the Manchester area, and no attempt would be made on the town. Effectively Manchester would become part of a neutral zone which would also be extended over Lancashire and Cheshire. The 'gentry and freeholders' of Manchester replied that they had done nothing in the first place to generate Lord Derby's wrath. Since he had come against them 'God, Nature, Law and Conscience' bound them to defend the town. Not long afterwards parliament set its face against all such local peace proposals.

These episodes were doubly sad, since there is some evidence that Lord Derby would have acquiesced in an accommodation. As Holland was portrayed on the parliamentarian side, so was Lord Derby on the royalist, whose enemies insinuated that he might be disloyal to the crown. To clear himself Derby wrote personally to Charles offering to 'pick the calumny off the lips' of his detractors 'with the point of the sword'. Even so he did admit that it was no sin to search for peace, provided that 'such a peace contains not a conspiracy against the king and the true religion'.[17]

Had the king's main army that gathered at Shrewsbury met with overwhelming success in the autumn of 1642, the royalist debacle at Manchester would have become a relatively unimportant footnote of history. As it was, the main royalist field army confronted the Earl of Essex at Edgehill in Warwickshire on 23 October. Among the Lancastrians present on the field were Thomas Fanshawe, MP for Lancaster, Lord Molyneux and his regiment of foot, and Sir Thomas Tyldesley. Though bloody and protracted, Edgehill was not the decisive engagement that both sides were seeking. The royalists claimed a technical victory, for they struck a heavy blow against the Earl of Essex, who withdrew, thus opening the way to London. Yet the royalists were unwilling, or unable, to grasp the nettle which might have led to an early end to the war. Both sides had been stunned by this clash of 30,000 men, and both had taken losses. The king's army crawled on to Oxford, and calls for negotiation proved inconclusive. Only in mid-November did the royalists reach Turnham Green in their attempt to capture the capital, and by then it was too late to seize the city, which the enemy had already reached and reinforced.

CHAPTER FOUR

'All barbarous crueltie': the struggle for Lancashire, 1642–43

FOLLOWING ROYALIST FAILURE at the gates of Manchester rumour circulated that the king intended to install the Earl of Newcastle as his 'Lord general of Cheshire and Lancashire', recalling Lord Derby to attend his royal person at Oxford. In fact, the turn of events was rather more than a personal humiliation for Lord Derby, since Manchester and its immediate environs had been the one significant obstacle to a county broadly united behind the king. Had Lancashire been pacified in 1642, it would no longer have needed much by way of garrison, and could have offered more coherent support to royalist comrades in neighbouring counties. It could also have made more regiments available to the king's field army in the south. At the same time it has been reasonably argued, by Broxap and others, that it was the very attempt to support the king's ventures on the national stage which fatally weakened royalist efforts in Lancashire. Some of this was apparent at the time, for as Clarendon observed, the royalist 'fair expectation of Cheshire was clouded by the storms that arose in Lancashire'. That the Lancashire royalists, and Derby in particular, had sought to push the war away from the county, and to fight it on the territory of others, was certainly apparent to well-informed commentators at the time. Within eighteen months royalist William Legge was offering the opinion that he despaired of 'any good of Lancashire, who, to divert the war from themselves have exposed their own quarter to be lost'.[1]

The outcome at Manchester may not ultimately have been a deciding factor in the national war, but failure to secure this key town left a running sore, on which local parliamentarians could capitalise and cause mischief within a north-west region otherwise sympathetic to the royalist cause. Not dealing with the problem decisively during the early months of the following year would have serious long-term ramifications. While royalist fortunes reached their zenith nationally in the summer of 1643, Lancashire remained mired in a local struggle in which, little by little, the parliamentarians would gain the upper hand. Fresh supplies of powder finally reached the Manchester garrison on 22 October, but for the time being it was the royalists who retained the initiative, and at least nominal command of most of the county. This control looked most questionable in east Lancashire, where currents of support were already running for the parliament. For this reason, it was here that Lord Derby's supporters would strike next.

Campaigns in east Lancashire, October 1642

During the early months, the war had passed central and east Lancashire by. Sir Gilbert Hoghton was for the king, and Hoghton Tower on the Leyland and Blackburn hundreds border was a royalist stronghold: conversely, the Shuttleworth family, and much of the Burnley area, was for parliament. Even so no serious action had so far taken place. Perhaps rightly the Manchester parliamentarians regarded many of those in Blackburn hundred as fence-sitters who were waiting to see which side was likely to win before entering the fray. Nevertheless this uneasy peace would soon be shattered.

Perhaps unfairly some later historians would also see self-interest and avarice as the key personality traits of the cautious 55-year-old Richard Shuttleworth and his brood. It is therefore fitting that the very name of his seat at Gawthope Hall, Padiham, has been interpreted as derived from the Old Norse for 'farmstead of the cuckoo'. As the Reverend Whitaker would fume two centuries after the events of the civil wars, Shuttleworth senior was,

> A wary, fawning man, who knew how to serve the time, in the worst sense of the words and fattened along with his brother sequestrators upon the spoils of better houses than his own. In the dialect of the neighbourhood he is yet remembered by the name of *Old Smoot*, a term which conveys no bad idea of the demure and plausible hypocrite of those times.

Of his eleven children no fewer than eight were sons, five of whom would take up arms for parliament: Richard the younger, Nicholas and Ughtred all eventually reached the rank of colonel, commanding regiments; Barton served as a major; and William was a captain at the time of his untimely death.

Through royalist eyes Richard Shuttleworth was a cynical opportunist. Yet he also appears to have been a genuine and careful presbyterian – to whom reckless risk-taking would have been not only an anathema, but an affront to God. The Shuttleworths had been at Gawthorpe since at least as early as 1388, and much of the recent family fortune had been accrued during the Elizabethan era through profits from the legal profession. Parts of the proceeds had been spent on the extensive remodelling of Gawthorpe Hall during the period 1600 to 1605 under the supervision of the Reverend Lawrence Shuttleworth. *Old Smoot* had inherited the estate in 1608, after Lawrence had died childless. Yet while Lawrence has been described as 'puritanical', Richard actually acquired a reputation as something as a patron of the arts, hosting companies of players and musicians at the hall. In 1618 and 1638 he was high sheriff of Lancashire. Clearly there was too much at stake to throw away on some uncertain adventure.[2]

Practical matters aside, Richard Shuttleworth also had to look deep into his conscience. If he had done so while sitting in front of his own fire, he would not have been able to avoid the words which the Reverend Lawrence had caused to be inscribed upon the mantle: 'Feare God, Honor the kinge, Eschewe Evil, Doe Good, Seek Peace and Ensue it'. What was moral, what would accord with religious conviction, and what was politic could be very different things. There would be no precipitous action – though Richard himself had been one of the MPs sent back to the county some months earlier with a brief for immediate mobilisation. Cavalry had not ridden over the hills to the rescue of Manchester in September 1642. Nor would they ride at all, until the threat was too great, or the time was right and he could be certain of local support. This was undeniably slow in coming.

The Shuttleworths certainly proved subtle in their policy in the early months of the war. For while they were attempting to cajole the militia into arms for parliament, one of their main activities in the autumn of 1642 was the establishment of a spy network focused on royalist areas. As a letter written by Richard Shuttleworth explained, it was

needfulle we should have information of some other parts of this county, what they did and what business there was on foote at tymes as they might fall out, as namely at Wigan, Ormischurche or Warrington.

To these ends it was necessary to recruit 'faithfull honest and knowing gentlemen' whose efforts should be concentrated on military intelligence, 'tending to armes or force or what designes & how and where intended'. His correspondent, George Rigby, offered a number of potential informants including Joseph Rigby of Aspull, Alexander Thompson of Wigan and

Henry Ashurst of Ormskirk. Infiltrating Warrington was clearly a tricky problem, but for this task two further names were put forward, John Dunbabin and a 'Mr Gerard' who were respectively in the wool and clothing trades. Their work may perhaps have influenced them to take sides with Mancunian business contacts, rather than with their nearer neighbours who were predominantly royalist.

This spy ring quickly bore fruit; before long information was being fed to Colonels Ashton and Rigby regarding companies raised by 'papists' at Wigan, Lathom and Ormskirk. There was even some counter-espionage effort. The unfortunate Henry Haddock was arrested as a royalist spy and brought before Colonel Starkie. As he had a personal reference and a business cover story provided by a lady of quality it appeared that he might be released promptly. However on being searched it transpired that he was carrying upon him a suspicious 'note or wryteinge', and so he was detained.

Perhaps the most important outcome of Richard Shuttleworth's espionage was what appears to have been a surprisingly accurate picture of the overall strength and dispositions of the enemy. At the end of October an estimate was made that the royalists had about 1,400 men. Of these between 300 and 400 were thought to be in Warrington, with 300 each in billets at Preston and Ormskirk. Wigan was thought to have 200 enemy soldiers. Smaller detachments of 100 each were at Eccleston and 'Pressberye', possibly Prescot. As far as we are able to determine the parliamentarian spies had done their job very well, and in all probability had got the enemy strength correct to within about 100 men. The locations of at least three of the four the main bodies were also correct.[3]

Clearly there were many opportunities for parliament: nevertheless the populace of Blackburn hundred was decidedly mixed in its allegiance. Prominent royalists gentry families included the Towneleys of Towneley Hall, near Burnley; the Nowells of Read; the Bannisters of Altham, and the Sherburns of Little Mitton and Stonyhurst. Many were Catholic. Thomas Birtwistle of Huncoat Hall, a declared recusant, had priests in his family and was one of several in Blackburn hundred reputed to hide them from the authorities about his home. Perhaps surprisingly recent research suggests that the royalists may even have enjoyed a numerical majority in the hundred in 1642. Gratton identifies 58 officers who fought in the civil wars domiciled in Blackburn hundred, and of these no fewer than 37 fought for the king. A surviving set of documents drawn up by the constables as late as 1655 lists a couple of hundred persons who were still regarded as 'delinquents' – or of royalist persuasion – several years after the wars had ended. Those who were suspected to have carried arms against parliament over the period of conflict were a varied bunch, including Catholics, and some were listed as 'under age' at the time of their offence. Probably the least dangerous of these people was John Barker, 'taken away by his father at 10 years old' and returned home 13 weeks later, binding himself to a local tradesman for a seven-year apprenticeship.

In the autumn of 1642 the power which might be drawn from the Blackburn locality was latent rather than actual. Activists had to be careful, as it was by no means clear which party might gain the upper hand. Opportunities would arise gradually with circumstance, and perhaps as staunch royalists were drawn away to other theatres of war. For the time being however a false move at the wrong moment could easily have led to dispossession, or the need to flee. As it was, and had lives not been at stake, the opening moves in east Lancashire would have appeared more comic than serious.[4]

Belatedly both sides had realised that the arms kept for the militia of Blackburn hundred were as yet insecure, and that neither side had yet successfully claimed all the resources of the area. If the war was to drag on, then money, materials, and men would all be needed, and it was only by physical domination of the countryside that there could be proper exploitation of resources and taxation. So it was that in October Sir Gilbert Hoghton returned to the Preston area after the abortive siege of Manchester, lit his beacon at Hoghton Tower, and began recruiting afresh in order to launch a campaign to secure east Lancashire. The 52-year-old Sir Gilbert had previously served in parliament, but he was one of the king's staunchest supporters, and now appeared to be his moment to shine in the cause. Drawing troops principally from the Fylde and from Leyland, he gathered a little force, thought to number perhaps 300 men, in Preston some time in mid-October. News of this development quickly reached Clitheroe, from whence the bailiff wrote to Richard Shuttleworth at Gawthorpe, apologising that it was 'these distractive times' that forced him to trouble him, but that he ought to warn him of Sir Gilbert's movements. The fear was that the royalists were intending to march up the Ribble valley, and seize Clitheroe and its castle. Clitheroe was in a panic unnecessarily, however, since Hoghton had his eyes on somewhat easier pickings. The royalists marched via Hoghton and struck out for Whalley. Here they appear to have met with little or no resistance, and by 17 October they had carted the militia arms stored here back to Blackburn.

It was only with this provocation on their very doorstep that the parliamentarians were finally stirred to action, that same day oulde Colonel Shuttleworth (having recieved inteligence of his Designe) had a Randavous of the Clubmen of Blackburne Hundred upon Houley Moore where they had a consultation what course to take about those Armes the general vote being not to let them goe out of their Hundred but either to Reskowe them or adventure themselves to the Hazard. Soe that night hearing that Sir Gilbert with his companie and the Armes had taken up their quarters at Blackburne they silently fell down upon Blackburne beating up their quarters, tooke many of Sir Gilbert's souldiers prisoners, seazed upon the Armes.

According to one version, the attack had been cunning, with two groups, one coming from the Darwen Street side, the other from the bottom of Church Street. Too late royalist guards posted on the parish church had opened fire, then the enemy were upon them. The whole action had taken no more than a couple of hours. Though there was doubtless some stout work with clubs and swords in the streets of Blackburn, and there is reference to fighting on 'Hinfield Moor' (Whinney Hill), it seems unlikely that there were high casualties on either side. Trapped, Sir Gilbert escaped by jumping from his horse into a field, and disappearing into the darkness in the direction of Preston.

As yet there appears to have been no particular animosity on either side. The royalist prisoners, including Sergeant Roger Haddock, were brought before Colonel Shuttleworth, who gave them a thorough wigging, exhorting them to be 'honest men' in future, and to stay at home. He then let them go. One wonders whether Sergeant Roger, and Henry the spy were related. Another remarkable feature was the apparent democracy of the parliamentarian posse, whose 'club men' appear to have fought as much to protect their locality as for any particular political ideal.[5]

In some counties 'club men' eventually gained the status of what was effectively a 'third force' – fighting to keep both armies out of their locality. Such appears to have been the case in Worcestershire, Dorset and Wiltshire, particularly late in the conflict, where there was war-weariness and popular resistance to the war in general. There is little or no evidence that this was the case in Lancashire. Almost always where 'club men' are mentioned in the Lancashire context they were poorly armed levies, or local volunteers, fighting for one side or the other. Reticence, peace-mongering, and indifference were all encountered – within the armies, as in the civil population – but the concept of taking up arms to stop war does not accord with the local evidence. There would never be any 'third force' in Lancashire.[6]

Though the parliament men had successfully defended east Lancashire in these October skirmishes, they were under no illusion about the permanency of the situation. Indeed, there would be one or more false alarms concerning further royalist forays from Preston during the next few weeks. The parliamentarians of Blackburn hundred were particularly worried that the enemy now appeared to be raising cavalry, while they themselves not only had 'no horse at all', and were short of arms and ammunition.

On 6 November Adam Bolton wrote from Manchester to Richard Shuttleworth at Gawthorpe, by 'speciall messenger with all speed', warning that there was intelligence that Sir Gilbert was about to march with 'renewed forces'. The Manchester parliamentarians wanted to know if the threat was serious, and whether immediate reinforcement should be sent. The very same day Thomas Birch set out from Manchester carrying with him not only another letter assuring the Blackburn men of the Mancunians' support, but even more vitally 223 lb of match cord, and 170 lb of gunpowder. Just two days later John Nowell and Richard Lister of Clitheroe wrote to Gawthorpe with information that Lord Derby and Sir Gilbert were 'makinge great preparations' against Shuttleworth and his adherents. They reported that they were experiencing difficulties with some recalcitrants who owned arms, but they also protested that they had yet to receive any summons to serve parliament. Nevertheless Nowell and Lister promised their 'best assistance' to the cause. For the time being, however, these alarms came to nought.[7]

Chowbent, November 1642

Another hot spot that November and December of 1642 would be the disputed boundary area between parliamentarian Manchester and royalist Wigan, where both sides were now putting out patrols to stake their claims to the resources of the locality. Parliamentarian sources claim that it was Lord Derby's men who were making a 'great spoyle' of the country – and doubtless the royalists held much the same opinion of the opposition. Parliamentarian sympathisers pleaded for, and were granted, support from the Manchester garrison to protect their livelihoods. Matters came to a dramatic head on Sunday 27 November at Chowbent. Now subsumed into Atherton, Chowbent lay a couple of miles north-east of Leigh. As the parliamentarian correspondent Thomas Jesland related in *A True and Full Relation of the Troubles in Lancashire*,

> ... as wee were going towards the church, a post [messenger] rode through the countrey, informing us that the Earle's troopes were coming towards

Chowbent: whereupon the countrey presently rose, and before one of the clocke on that day we were gathered together about 3000 horse and foot, encountring them at Chowbent ... and beate them back to Leigh, killing some and wounding many. Where you might wonder to have seen the forwardnesse of the young youths, farmers' sons, who indeed were too forward, having had little experience of the like times before this. And so we over-rode our foote being carried with a fervent desire to overtake them, and do some notable service upon them, so we drove them to Loaton common, where they, knowing our foote to be far behind, turned their faces about, and began to make head against us. Whereupon a sharpe although a short Incounter, but when they perceived our full and settled resolution, they made away as fast as their Horses could carry them.[8]

The parliamentarians claimed to have killed, wounded or taken prisoner as many as 200 of the enemy. In view of the fact that their own losses were stated as just three, all wounded, this seems an improbably high number. Nevertheless, the parliamentarians of south-east Lancashire were beginning to show that they had offensive spirit as well as the ability to defend their own district. Many of the other particulars of the fight ring true, for it may easily be imagined that the parliamentarian horse, much of it seeing action for the first time, was quickly out of control. Riding impetuously ahead of, and through, its own infantry, excitement seems to have got the better of them. It was fortunate that the enemy were themselves not better prepared.

It was probably only a few days later that a reconnaissance in strength by the infantry companies of captains Bradshaw and Venables probed westwards. According to *Lancashire's Valley of Achor* their purpose was to 'plunder a papist's house near Wigan', but meeting with superior forces they were forced to abandon the enterprise. On 15 December, at Westhoughton, Bradshaw and Venables tried their luck again. This time, however, the royalists of Wigan had organised better, and managed to outflank the parliamentarian raiding force with superior numbers. A sharp skirmish began, during which the parliamentarian captains attempted to extricate themselves from the trap which was closing round them. *Lancashire's Valley of Achor* claims that the parliamentarians' ammunition supply caught fire, cutting short their ability and will to resist. God, this deeply puritan account reasoned, had allowed this 'foul blow' to humble them, and serve to warn them of the danger of complacency.

The parliamentarian captains now called a parley, and, realising the hopelessness of their situation, laid down their arms and surrendered to the enemy. 'Eight score' soldiers were marched off into royalist captivity. Captain

Venables, a Cheshire man, later destined to lead the parliamentarian forces in Ulster, was held in captivity at Lathom for some time. Bradshaw, 'a very moderate man and of good parts' was actually released very quickly, but was probably already sick or wounded, for he died not long afterwards. While this disaster 'was a great greef and discouragdgment to the Parliament party all the county over', it was in fact a relatively minor setback in the broader scheme of things, and it is likely that other than the prisoners and Captain Bradshaw, relatively few on either side were lost at Westhoughton.[9]

Revenge was now becoming a motive in this tit-for-tat local battle. On Christmas Eve it was the royalists who were caught at a disadvantage while they were foraging in the vicinity of Leigh. The Manchester garrison were swiftly appraised of the situation and marched out rapidly to confront them. Rosworme states that on this occasion the enemy were 'shattered' at Chowbent, and although many of the parliamentarian counter-attack force must have spent a cold Christmas Day on the march they were back home again within three days of leaving. A number of the king's men were taken prisoner in their turn. While the *Discourse* celebrates this success, it makes it clear that already parts of Lancashire were paying a high price for the war. Theft, plunder, looting and requisition were all much the same thing in the short term, whomsoever had made off with the goods: 'Thus the County was divided and at Defyance one neighbour with another and many pore men were forced to leave their dwellinges and seek Refuge where they could find it, in Yorkshire or elsewhere.'[10]

Sir Gilbert Hoghton and Blackburn

It was also on Christmas Eve 1642 that the war finally returned to Blackburn, albeit in a desultory and rather amateur fashion. Following the autumn skirmishes the parliamentarians had 'caused some fortifications' to be made about the town. It has been reasonably speculated that these were earthworks at the main entry points to the town: at the top of Northgate on the Ribchester road; by the bridge at Whalley Banks on the Preston road; near the Darwen Street bridge; and somewhere on the Burnley side. On 24 December Sir Gilbert Hoghton again tested the resolve of the defenders, approaching the town by means of the lane from Mellor and Samlesbury, and then 'set down' his forces as if to begin a siege. *Lancashire's Valley of Achor* claims that the royalists had vast strength, with three guns, one of which was, 'their god (the greatest field piece)', but given the available resources it does not seem credible that the king's men can have numbered more than 1,000.

A detail of a mid-eighteenth-century manuscript map of Blackburn preserved in
Lambeth Palace Library. The parish church can be seen prominently just below the
centre of this detail.

BY COURTESY OF LAMBETH PALACE LIBRARY

The *Discourse*, perhaps more reliably, refers to a single small piece of artillery. This was positioned, under cover of darkness, by the house of a 'husbandman', whose real name is frustratingly absent from the reproduced document, but who went by the nickname of 'Duke of the Bank'. This location has since been identified as Bank House at Higher Bank. From here the gunners fired off a number of rounds, but with little effect. The *Discourse* stated that their best shot was the one which 'entered into a house upon the south side of the churchyard and burst out the bottom of a fryen pan'. The defenders returned fire with muskets, and even sallied out, but with even less impact, no casualties being identified. No attackers appear to have come within a quarter mile of the town itself. Though this little action has been glorified with the title of siege, it seems more accurate to describe it as a raid, or perhaps a reconnaissance in strength. In any event Sir Gilbert and his men stole away 'upon Christmas day night', his soldiers and clubmen being 'glad of it that they might eate their Christmas pyes at home'. The only person to have a really unhappy festive season was poor 'Duke', whose barn the royalists ignited before retreating, having already robbed him of his 'provision of Meale and Beefe and the like'.[11]

At the end of 1642 the focus of action shifted naturally to Preston. In the absence of success in the Manchester area, Lord Derby doubtless reasoned that his best chance to reorganise and dominate the county was from its geographical centre. Parliamentarian sources state that the meeting held there between Lord Derby, Sir John Girlington the high sheriff, and 'many more great Papists' on 10 December 1642, was specifically to levy an assessment of £7,800 on the county with which to prosecute the war effectively. As outlined in the pamphlet *Orders Concluded By the Lord Strange and his Adherents*, the money was to be used for the upkeep of 2,000 infantry and 400 cavalry, and the 'provision of a magazine and ammunition'. Just how expensive the war might ultimately prove was demonstrated by the pay lists published for the royalist troops, in which a captain of horse was to receive as much as 15*s*. a day, with 9*d*. going to each 'common' foot soldier at the other end of the scale. With a single officer swallowing £274 a year, even several thousand pounds would not go far.

Recent research suggests that raising money for the king's cause in Lancashire was no easy task. While attempts were made to exploit existing structures and systems within the royalist areas in 1642, use was also made of the resources of the nobility and gentry, with Lords Derby and Molyneux making significant personal contributions. Collection of the new royalist assessment in early 1643 was by no means a foregone conclusion. On 25

February one collector of funds was moved to remark that 'most of the hundredths have failed to contribute and bring in their money'.[12]

On the other side parliament in London realised that the burden of resisting Lord Derby and his 'divers Murthers and Robberies' was too great for Manchester alone to bear: all those who reaped the 'benefit' of resistance should therefore expect to pay for the privilege. On 26 January 1643 it therefore granted the Lancashire committee specific powers to force any who were 'of ability', and had not yet contributed, to pay 'such sums' as they deemed 'fit and reasonable' to the war chest. Any who resisted could be compelled to cooperate, or, if needs be, imprisoned. Some reorganisation, and a fresh endorsement of the committee was also made in February, essentially as a preamble to tightening the financial screws yet further. With both sides demanding contributions, a long war would either ruin the county, or men would go unpaid. The *Discourse* suggests that the earl's expensive designs would have brought the county 'to beggery', but for the resistance of the two parliamentarian hundreds. It can be argued, however, that eventually the county was effectively bankrupted by the predations of both king and parliament, and even then many troops went unpaid at least some of the time.[13]

Such evidence as there is suggests that after the departure of the royalist regiments to join the king's field army, and the east Lancashire debacle, Lord Derby's forces within the county were dangerously depleted. According to one document, prepared on the order of the earl on 30 December 1642, the main garrisons loyal to the king at that date were Warrington, Wigan and Preston, with smaller outposts at Leigh and Brindle. These were to be organised as follows,

Leigh to be kepte with 20 men and 2 horses. There is already in Leigh 20 men Armed; victualls for viii daies, £12 in money; vizt. Xs [10s.] a peece to the 20 men and xls [40s.] for the Lieftennante: and 2 dragooners appointed to go thither this day. At Warrington 300 men, whereof the 2 welch Companies to be parte ... At Wigan alsoe 300 men, vizt. The Companys of Captaine Chernoke of Captaine Chisnall & of Captaine Barrow; if these make not 300 men, they must be made up upon further consideracion alsoe 100 dragooners & a troope of horse. At Preston 200 men under under the Command of Captaine Houghton and Captaine Farrington to be supplyed with Armes where defect may be found. At Brindle, or in the most conveniente place thereabouts by the advise of Sir Gilbert Houghton the Company of Captaine Somner ...

Though there were additional officers mentioned, and doubtless 'club men' could be called upon to volunteer, or be pressed, the picture is of little more than 1,000 royalist troops, about three-quarters of them infantry, in the central and southern parts of the county at the end of 1642. Indeed, the document also mentions at least one other unit that was to be 'paid and disbanded' over the winter. There is also an implication that not all the formations were either fully armed or up to strength. This picture of the royalist fortunes so early in the war is far grimmer than many accounts would hitherto have us believe, and certainly gives credence to the point of view that the policy of fighting the war for the king outside the county had catastrophically weakened Lord Derby's defence of the royalist position in Lancashire.

Ironically sending men out of the county could prove doubly expensive; because not only were troops sent south or east lost to the local struggle – it could cost to deliver them. It is recorded of John Woodworth of Eccles, for example, that though his normal pay was 1s., a further 6d. was given for the fact that his service was out of the 'county'. Troops, particularly those of the trained bands, who served in or near their own home town or village could often be expected to find their own accommodation. This was not the case when men were far from home for long periods, which entailed either more money or looting and billeting on civilian households.[14]

To recruit more men and to galvanise them to fight a protracted war would take a concerted effort, and in Lancashire this was arguably a more difficult task for the royalists than for parliament. For those who fought for parliament the 'defensive' argument had proved particularly apt: the king had raised an army at York, and Lord Derby had attempted to seize Manchester. Parliament's supporters had little choice – they had to resist or to acquiesce in the king's domination of the county. Parliament fought against popery, the threat from Ireland, innovation in the Church, and the chicanery of those who would exploit them financially or otherwise. They supported traditional liberties – whatever these were – and the system of 'king and parliament'. What the royalists were fighting for was less clear – certainly they did not want to be seen as fighting for Catholicism, or as in favour of any sort of repression. Many indeed were royalists by default – because they did not want to fight against the king, or did not want to be perceived as 'in rebellion', something which was viewed with horror and a sin against God and order. The natural state of the Lancastrian was therefore that of the moderate royalist, but turning this apathetic equilibrium into fighting spirit – and physical support for a definite 'cause' – was not easy.

Some statement of the justice and 'traditional' fairness of the royalist case was therefore required. As in so much else it was Lord Derby who was expected to take the lead. How widely it was applied is unclear, but there is a manuscript source which speaks of 'an oath imposed by Lord Derby upon Lancashire'. Those taking the oath were expected to swear that they would,

> to the uttermost of my power and with hasard of my life maintain and defend the true Protestant religion established in the Church of England, His Majesty's sacred person, his heirs and lawful successors, His Majesty's just powers and prerogatives and the just powers and prerogatives of parliament against the forces now under the Earl of Essex and all other forces whatsoever.

Rather like the enemy claim to fight for 'king and parliament', this was an oath which virtually anyone, with the possible exception of an active and public Catholic, could have taken. It was a claim to the political middle ground – as well as to the moral and religious high ground. As might be expected, parliamentarian sources rubbished Derby's oath. Nevertheless it was taken seriously, the pro-parliamentarian *Lancashire's Valley of Achor* speaking of how friendly forces intervened just in time to prevent the enemy imposing the oath upon the populace of Preston in February 1643.[15]

Following the raising of the king's standard, Lord Derby had also issued his own manifesto, or 'protestation'. As quoted in the *Discourse* this read as an appeal for help against rebellion, and a call to duty in favour of not only the king but established religion and the status quo. Yet it was also a generalised plea for peace,

> Whereas our Sovereign Lord King Charles hath set up his Standard Royall and hath required the Aid and Assistance of his Subjects for the Suppression of such Armies and Forces as are raised without his Majesties consent. And whereas by our Duty and Aleadgeance all Subjects are bound to assist the king against all force and might raised within the kingdome against him or his commands. In manifestation therefore of the sinceritie of our hearts and loyalty to our Sovereign and our duty to our Country to avoid all misinterpretations of our Actions wee whose names are hereunder written doe hereby declare before God and the World that wee will maintayn and defend the trew Protestant Religion the person honour Just and known Prerogatives of King Charles our only supreme Governour and the Just and known Privileges of Parliament and the Liberties of the Subjects of this Kingdome. And we do lykewise declare that wee will assist

the king for the Defence of his person and for suppressing of all forces and armies under what pretence soever Raised without his Majesties consent. And whensoever these forces ... shall be quietly laid downe or otherwise suppressed and dispersed We will quietly and peaceably lay downe all Armes and doe our utmost endeavour that all other Inhabiting within this County shall doe likewise ...[16]

War in the balance, spring 1643

The significance of events in the Manchester area had not been lost upon parliament in London. Though reinforcements earmarked for Lancashire during 1642 may never have arrived, a large consignment of powder was received in October, and Scottish professional soldier Sir John Seaton was dispatched to co-ordinate parliament's forces. He appears to have assumed his command in January 1643. Though he proved competent enough for immediate purposes, Seaton was an outsider of overbearing character. As the parliamentarian minister John Tilsley put it to a friend in February 1643,

> Truly, Sir, we owe (subordinate to God) a great deal to Sir John Seaton: things are artificially and methodically done, past what they were before, he is a man of wonderfull care and unwearied industry, onely rather too harsh for our northern notty rigged dispositions; had he the meek spirit and smooth tongue of S.M. [Sergeant Major] Sparrow, he were peerlesse, and without parallel doubtlesse.[17]

Whatever personal doubts the Lancashire parliamentarians may have harboured about their new leader, he was initially blessed with either organisational skill, or extreme luck, managing to co-ordinate a swift winter campaign which would begin to undermine royalist control. The opportunity to strike was first perceived through intelligence from Blackburn. Colonels Shuttleworth and Starkie had news that royalist Preston was but poorly prepared and with only a slender garrison. All being well the enemy would not be expecting that the parliamentarian forces, few in number and so recently on the defensive, would have the temerity to take the initiative.

Preston falls to parliament, February 1643

On Monday 6 February Sir John marched out of Manchester accompanied by the doubty Sergeant Major Sparrow, Colonel Holland and other officers

Major campaign movements of 1643. The royalists make progress in most regions except in Lancashire: the Earl of Newcastle advances to York while Rupert and Hopton succeed in the West Country.

NORTH SEA

SCOTLAND

Inverness

Dundee

Firth of Forth

Edinburgh

IRELAND

Londonderry

Belfast

Dundalk

Galway

Dublin

Wexford

Cork

Isle of Man

IRISH SEA

Cardigan Bay

Bristol Channel

Plymouth

Solway Firth

Carlisle

NEWCASTLE

Durham

Lancaster

Preston

Halifax

Manchester

Warrington

Chester

Natwhich

BRERETON

Wem

Shrewsbury

Stafford

York

Adwalton Moor

Hull

Lincoln

Newark

Nottingham

The Wash

Norwi

Coventry

Leicester

QUEEN

Northampton

Gloucester

Oxford

London

Bristol

Roundway Down

HOPTON

Southampton

Isle of Wight

at the head of three Manchester foot companies. A similar number of troops joined the army from Bolton, and by the Tuesday night the little army had reached Blackburn. Here the force was brought up to strength by four or five more companies from Blackburn hundred led by Captain Nowell and others. According to Tilsley's account the parliamentarians now numbered a little over 1,500, being 'about 900 or 1,000 firemen, horse and foot, and about 600 Bill men, Halberdiers and Club men'. There may even have been more, since another account claims the presence of 2,000 'club men' in addition to the properly armed troops.

Though rain threatened, the night of Wednesday 8 February proved to be fine, and the parliamentarians made good progress. According to the *Discourse* Seaton's men found the Ribble bridge passable, and formed up in a close among the fields north of the river. From here locals sympathetic to the parliamentarian cause led some of the troops around the town towards the House of Correction, so as to make an entry via 'Fryars Gate Barrs' – presumably the modern Friargate. Meanwhile the main body prepared to attack from the east and north. To manoeuvre so close during the hours of darkness without coming to grief was a considerable achievement.

The next day before dawn the attackers 'fell on with notable resolution' the main assault being made from the east. Though Preston had no town walls to compare with York or Chester, brick walls surrounding individual plots proved to be a significant obstacle. *Lancashire's Valley of Achor* has it that some of the royalist defenders had loopholed the walls and poked their muskets through to fire on the attackers. The parliamentarian troops ran stealthily forward and grabbed hold of the muzzles, directing them harmlessly away. In another place the attackers found their way blocked by an earth rampart defended by pikemen; this they circumvented by means of a small party of twenty men who broke in through the front of a house, and then came out at the back taking the defence in the rear.

Cheshire parliamentarian Sir John Booth and Colonel Holland are said to have disputed whose troops should have the honour of entering Preston first, but in the end it was Booth who encouraged his men to scramble over or between the walls to get to grips with the enemy, 'behaving himselfe most bravely' in the vanguard. Seaton took a more direct approach, attacking the strongpoint of the church head on,

The Major General behaved himself gallantly at the end of Church Street where the entry was made; our musquiets beat them from their centeryes and from the steeple. There dyed of the Popish party, the Major of the

Town (Master Adam Morte) who killed one of the Collonells men with push of his pike, but afterwards lost his own life for it, together with his son, and also M. Radcliff Hoghton, captain of the horse, (and brother to Sir Gilbert Hoghton) Sergeant Major Purvey, (lately come out of Ireland) and the Popish Doctor, Dr. Westby, with two or three Lieutenants and others more of quality, are likewise slain, and divers others which I saw were mortally wounded, and to some procured Surgeons ... My Lady Hoghton, my Lady Girlington, and Mrs Townly, were also taken as prize. We tooke three pieces of ordnance, a murdering piece, a great number of musquiets, and many horses, with two or three colours, and divers were pillaged to a purpose. Few friends have suffered to any value; there were but two barrells of powder found in the town. We had only three or four common souldiers, not an officer slain on our side; we gave the enemy no leisure to annoy us with their guns, our entry was so quick, and the execution done was most with the sword.

Perhaps 200 royalist soldiers and gentlemen fled from Preston, and Sir Gilbert Hoghton was said to have departed so quickly that he left his hat behind. The fight was over in little more than an hour. With the royalists taken by surprise, and as we now realise vastly outnumbered, active resistance was probably shorter still. However, the parliamentarian troops were keyed up with such 'fear and fury' that they rampaged through the streets breaking the windows with staves, 'which was to no purpose and pittifull to behould'.[18]

Despite the vandalism and excitement, the seizure of Preston had been relatively bloodless, and it is unlikely that the total casualties were more than a few dozen. Nevertheless the taking of the town was of both practical and symbolic importance. It lay roughly at the centre of the county, astride the main north–south route, and holding Preston was well calculated to interfere with enemy communications. At the same time it allowed easy access to those nascent parliament men in the Fylde, who were otherwise powerless to assist the cause. The capture of Preston was similarly a boost to morale, and would bring more of the surrounding area under the control of the parliamentarians. As the *Discourse* observed, the taking of Preston could also be seen as a blow against Catholicism, for it had been there that many 'Papists of eminency' had taken refuge in the winter of 1642. John Rosworme who had been with the attackers was afterwards ordered to refortify the town: but as subsequent events will demonstrate, little more of consequence was done than under the royalists. The one new work described by the *Discourse* as having been erected at this time was, 'a strong sconce upon the marsh to command the fords over

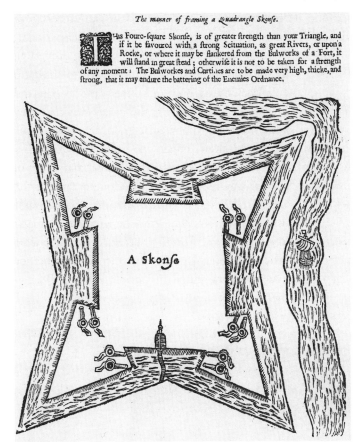

The manner of framing a Quadrangle Skonse.

This Foure-fquare Skonfe, is of greater ftrength than your Triangle, and if it be favoured with a ftrong Scituation, as great Rivers, or upon a Rocke, or where it may be flankered from the Bulworks of a Fort, it will ftand in great ftead; otherwife it is not to be taken for a ftrength of any moment: The Bulworkes and Curtines are to be made very high, thicke, and ftrong, that it may endure the battering of the Enemies Ordnance.

A skonfe

A 'sconce' or fortlet, as depicted in Robert Ward's *Animadversions of Warre*, 1639. Similar small earthworks were used on a number of occasions during the conflict in Lancashire, notably as part of the otherwise slender defences of Blackburn and Preston.

the Ribble both ways'. No modern evidence of this fort has been found, but it appears probable that since the main ford joined Preston to Penwortham it would have stood somewhere in the vicinity of the current Broadgate or above Strand Road, where the river ran at this time.

Tragedy at Hoghton Tower

With Preston in the hands of parliament, the way was now open to deal decisively with Hoghton Tower, which had already proved itself to be a royalist headquarters of some significance and of great nuisance value. Accordingly a small expedition of about 300 men, consisting of three companies of mainly Blackburn troops, was put together to march on Sir Gilbert's fortified house. According to reports Hoghton Tower was equipped with 'three pieces of great ordnance', but the garrison was estimated to be as few as 30 to 40 musketeers, so again numbers would be on the side of parliament. The parliamentarian pamphlet, the *Punctuall Relation* of 14 February 1643, takes up the story,

> Our men approaching near the said tower first shot against it to summon it, whereupon they in the Tower desired half an houres time to consider what they should doe ... after which the result of the parley was that they would deliver up the Tower to our men upon quarter, which was by our men granted unto them as they desired. Whereupon our men (thinking all had beene as was pretended to them) entered the Tower; and Captain Starkey of Blackeborne, a worthy gentleman, and his Company, were the first that entered into the said Tower, and in the same found good store of armes and powder strewed upon the stairs; wherefore he with his company going into the upper rooms of the said Tower to search for more, were most treacherously and perfidiously blown up by two of them whom they had before given quarter, who had a traine of powder laid, and when Captain Starkey and his men, to the number of above one hundred, were

Hoghton Tower as it appears today, much rebuilt after the catastrophic explosion during the first Civil War.

above in the House, gave fire to the said traine, and blew both him and his men, with the top of the house up, threescore whereof were afterwards found, some without armes and some without legges, and others fearefull spectacles to looke upon.

According to the author there was now 'no treaty or cessation' given by the enemy that could be relied upon. Only the 'Pope and the Devill' would be likely to pardon such an act of treachery.

Intriguingly not all parliamentarian sources agreed that it was the royalists who were to blame for the explosion at Hoghton Tower. *Lancashire's Valley of Achor* said that it was the largely the soldiery's own sin and laxity which caused the misfortune that befell them. Entering the tower burdened with 'the weight of their swearing, drunkennesse, plundering and wilfull waste at Preston', they had carelessly set light to the powder with their own muskets' match cords. The only other possibility was that their pipes, filled with 'that great Souldiers' Idoll, Tobacco', had caused the accident: so it was, the puritan account went, that parliament's men had been taught a salutary moral lesson about profanity and drink. The *Discourse* also refers to what it called a 'fearfull accident' through 'want of heedfullnesse'. Either way, royalist subterfuge, or careless accident, the Hoghton Tower explosion had been an unwelcome postscript to the success of Preston.[19]

A 'verrey hot skirmish' as Bolton holds out

Just a few days after the taking of the tower the royalist force from Wigan chanced its hand against Bolton. Whether this timing was based on intelligence that many of the enemy were occupied at Preston and Hoghton Tower, or whether it was happy accident that they chose a moment when the enemy were relatively weak and off guard is not clear. That this foray was extremely dangerous was acknowledged by the parliamentarian press. However it is questionable quite how much of a superiority in numbers the royalists had managed to obtain. The *Punctuall Relation* records the garrison of Bolton in mid-February 1643 at about 500, being five companies under Colonel Ashton and Captains Buckley, Schofield, Holt and Ashust. The royalists by contrast are noted as marching under 'eleven colours' with 'two companies of dragooners', and 'some troops of horse' as well as cannon. Since it was usual to have a 'colour' flying over every company of foot the suggestion is that the royalists numbered about 1,500. Whether there really can have been so many, just six weeks after Lord Derby listed his total strength throughout the county at little more 1,000, must be dubious. Among the royalist commanders were thought to be Sir Gilbert Gerard and Charles Anderton of Lostock.

Whatever the exact strength of the attacking force, its initial tactics were good. On Thursday 16 February they succeeded in marching virtually the whole way from Wigan to Bolton undetected, moving with the guidance of 'malignant' country folk. They got to within a mile of the town 'marching furiously' before the parliamentarians had 'any certaine intelligence' of what was happening, and by then the royalists had moved to surround their target. The dilemma then was the same as had faced Lord Derby at Manchester the previous autumn: to surround and besiege, or to rush the enemy immediately. This time the royalists dispensed with the preliminaries and went for the more dramatic option, as the *Punctuall Relation* tells,

> The enemy gave the first assault at Bradshaw gate end of the Towne, where the Town had three sconces, but the enemy set upon our men that were in them so resolutely, that they beat them from their workes, and forced them to retreat and leave them, and to runne with much difficultie and hazard towards a mudde wall and chaine which they had a little nearer the towne to save themselves.

Among the last to save themselves from the royalist onslaught was Captain John Ashurst, with 24 of his men, who were cut off and embroiled in hand-to-hand fighting.

> There was sixty enemies got between him and home; and yet after sharpe bickering and the losse of a man or two, hee got safe to the chaine, having slaine one man with his owne hands, and his souldiers two or three more with their but ends of their muskets. When the enemy had gained these out-workes, they came furiously upon the mudde wall and chaine, and had thought to have broke through all, but there was such a sharp service for a great while together as I think had seldome beene heard of. They played sore upon our workes with their ordnance, and shot quite through our mudde walls which were two yards thicke, and one of their bullets, after it had runne through, hit a man on the leg and broke it. They shot iron bullets of five and six pound weight: they also came up to the breast of our workes, even upon the mouthes of our muskets.

'Mud walls', more properly earthen ramparts, were one of the few things which could hope to resist the power of artillery. Quite how much earth was required to resist an iron round shot is often not appreciated. As can be seen from this passage six feet was hardly sufficient to stop a ball from a field gun. According to Eldred's *Gunner's Glasse* an amazing 23 feet of earth was needed to stop the shot from a full sized siege or 'whole' cannon, preferably banked to a height of eleven or more feet. Just a 20-foot section of such a defence would need something of the order of 5,000 cubic feet of earth. As can be imagined to build such hills of soil, and to revet them with wood or turf was a prodigious effort. To hire engineers and labour and to pay for very many artillery proof defences stretched even the king's purse in peacetime. In war local people could be pressed for the work, or given promises of payment later, but diverting the efforts of men, women and even children into such gargantuan enterprises could not but help having an adverse impact upon the local economy. Little wonder then that the defences of Bolton were not of the best in the early months of 1643.[20]

Despite the inadequacy of their works, the parliamentarian foot finally succeeded in making a stand, and receiving the enemy 'valiantly', then 'played on them so fast that they could not enter there'. The troops it was said, 'fought like lyons', and at one point Colonel Ashton himself was forced to join in the fire fight, firing 'as fast as he was able'. Some of the royalist attackers therefore deviated to the left,

and entered five houses at the end of the Towne, the first being a Malignants, into which they were freely suffered to come into, and so out of those houses they played onto the reere of our men that kept the Fort, and the rest played as fast on the front of them, insomuch that our men were forced for a while to give ground from their works. Whilst they thus shot out of the houses, they slew two of Captain Bucklies men, and killed Sergeant Major Leighs horse under him; as he was getting on the back of another, he was shot through the arme, yet hee and his men stood to it very courageously, and he called forth a squadron to goe against the houses the enemy had taken. And one Scoles, his man, the first shot he made kild two of the men that had shot Sergeant Major Leigh in the arme, then two of our men entered one of the houses with the great end of their muskets, and cleared that house, and entered the next, where there was such a threshing as was never heard of before, for besides the hand blowes that past, the enemy was so desperate that three times they came to the end of their muskets, and catcht hold of them as they went off.

Captain Ashurst and 16 of his men then succeeded in breaking into the back of another house behind the enemy who came at them 'very furiously'. Ashurst kept his cool and ordered his men to fire a volley, which 'beate them away'. According to *Lancashire's Valley of Achor* one or more of the royalists involved in these vicious house-to-house struggles had armed themselves, 'in their wittie malice', with spiked maces mounted on six foot staffs with which they could thrust or smash alternately. The pamphlet *Speciall Passages* tells us that 'stormes of bullets' actually 'powdered' the flimsy wood, daub and wattle houses with their impact.

Following this crescendo the attack ebbed, though the royalists started a fire which consumed three houses. This the defenders only escaped by hastily pulling down another house to create a firebreak between the conflagration and the rest of the town. By now the fight was all but over, and, screened by the fires, the royalists withdrew back towards Wigan. Not long afterwards parliamentarian reinforcements began to arrive in Bolton, club men from Middleton, Oldham and Rochdale, and the redoubtable Captain Radcliffe at the head of 'two hundred fresh souldiers from Manchester'. Further skirmishings and plundering also occurred at Little Lever, even before the fight at Bolton had drawn to a conclusion. The parliamentarians now had at least as many, and possibly more men than the enemy. Any chance the royalists had had in securing Bolton was now gone. It had been the sharpest 'bout' fought so far.

The parish clerk of Bolton recorded that this 'verrey hot skirmish' had lasted about four hours. The *Punctuall Relation* tells us that the enemy departed with 'two or three cartloads of dead bodies', besides a dozen dead and others mortally wounded that they were forced to leave behind. Though the royalists probably departed with a larger number of their casualties, just 15 people were buried in Bolton churchyard after the fight: five parliamentarian soldiers, six royalists and four civilians. Among the latter was Alice Rothwell, a daughter of Nathan Rothwell. Since other parliamentarian sources admit to eight or ten fatalities on their own side, and the wounded usually considerably outnumber the dead, it seems reasonable to suggest that the total casualties were upwards of 50, a majority of them royalists. As usual many more were claimed.[21]

Lancaster and the Fylde

Just a few days after the struggle at Bolton, the parliamentarians settled upon a rather more ambitious design. With Preston, Hoghton Tower and much of east Lancashire secured, as well as the Manchester region, the county and the royalists had effectively been split. There now appeared to be two major areas of enemy resistance offering serious obstacles: the south-western part of the county, and the straggling, sparsely populated north. Of these south-west Lancashire, encompassing Wigan, Warrington, Lathom and Ormskirk, looked the most problematic. For not only were these the places likely to hold the strongest royalist garrisons, this was the traditional heartland of the Derbys. It was also the very seat of Catholicism, home to many Catholic gentry familes – the Blundells, Fazakerleys, Gerards, Mainwarings and the Billinges to name but a few. Here a parliamentarian force would very likely be behind enemy lines – with many problems, and few friends of note. Even some of the few parliamentarian families in that area were divided in their loyalties.

North Lancashire, and Lonsdale hundred in particular, were less-known quantities. Lancaster may have been nominally for the king, but how strong the town was as a military garrison was unknown. Recent researchers have suggested that in fact the place was covertly for the parliament, or perhaps divided. In early 1643 Sir John Cansfield's attempts to recruit for the queen's horse in Lonsdale had met with mixed results – and one account even spoke of 'revolt' among the draftees. There were certainly pockets of sympathy for the cause of parliament 'north of the sands', but many relatively isolated settlements had not yet been called upon to make serious commitments, or to fight in their own locality. While West Derby in the south-west was known to be a hornets' nest, Lonsdale might just rally to parliament given the right pressures and incentives.

For these reasons a cautious approach to north Lancashire was adopted, and a reconnaissance in force would determine the strength of the opposition. The result was better than many parliamentarians would have expected,

> From Preston there was sent Sergeant Major Birch to Lancaster, to view whether the Townes were fortified strongly against him or no, who finding no great opposition, with his owne company entered the Towne, and after the Towne joined with him, and they went against the Castle, wherein was Master Kirby, one of the Knights of the Shire, and Sir John Girlington with some other forces, who perceiving they were not able to resist, stole away out of the Castle, and so Captaine Birch took possession of it.

The *Discourse* contends that the royalists had neglected Lancaster, thinking it safe while Lonsdale was still in their hands. Now the enemy had the castle, and released the felons and debtors they found there.

The *Santa Anna*

So it was that parliament's grip on Lancashire gradually expanded, and by March 1643 half the county was under its control.[22] Like the royalists before them, however, the parliamentarians who now held Lancaster found that it was ill-prepared for war. Most importantly it was dangerously short of modern artillery, for without its own guns there was little prospect of the town making any serious defence against recapture. It was therefore widely thought that the sudden, unexpected appearance of a possible source of cannon, at the very moment they were most needed, was nothing short of divine intervention: a shipwreck at the mouth of the river Wyre was, as Nehemiah Barnet, puritan minister at Lancaster would put it, '*God's Lift Up Hand For Lancashire*'. The news that Birch and his men heard was that contrary winds had driven the *Santa Anna*, 'a Dunkirke ship, a man of war, that came from Spaine, furnished with one and twenty peeces of Brasse and Iron Ordnance' onto the coast not far south-west of Lancaster. Here she was stranded, her cannon waiting to be requisitioned. The *Discourse* claims that the Spanish vessel was not initially grounded, but that having been buffeted by storms, the ship's crew, and the raw recruits for the Spanish army in the Low Countries that she was carrying, had grown 'feeble and weak'. The ship had then drifted 'into the ebe seas upon the back of Rossall' and now the disorientated mariners had become hopelessly lost. The bleak coast offered little clue as to where they were, and so the crew had fired the ship's guns in the hope of attracting attention. A pilot boat duly appeared, and the ship had been landed 'upon Rossall side'. The few country people who put in an appearance were overawed with this 'wonder', being as great a ship as had landed in Wyre water in living memory.[23]

In the event it was not Birch's men from Lancaster, but four companies from Preston under Sergeant Major Sparrow which actually set out for Rossall to lay claim to the *Santa Anna* for parliament. Yet they were not the only ones. Similar tidings had reached the Earl of Derby at Lathom, and the easy pickings promised by the ordnance from the *Santa Anna* was just as great a temptation to the royalists. Stanley set out at the head of a troop of horse, and crossed the ford across the muddy Ribble downstream from Preston, heading north, on 4 March. That night he halted at Lytham Hall, enjoying the hospitality of the royalist, Catholic Clifton family.

Had the timing been different, Derby's horse and Sparrow's foot might have come together in battle in the Fylde. As it was Sergeant Major Sparrow was near Poulton when he received intelligence that the Earl was in the vicinity. Usually of course the presence of the Earl of Derby betokened a significant royalist force: moreover Spaniards were Catholics, and there was no guarantee that if it came to a fight they would not side with the king's men against him. An international incident would have been the likely result. One source also suggests that Derby had a few foot with him as well. So Sparrow gathered his men together, and sent out scouts to discover the enemy's position. By the time that reports came back that the royalists were riding through Layton Common, 'swords drawne', it was too late. Lord Derby had slipped past on the way to his prize, and Sparrow's men, being dismounted, would have been at a disadvantage in any race. Sparrow had also to take extreme care that his infantry, though more numerous than the royalists, were not caught unaware by the cavalry.

So it was that the parliamentarians took the apparently strange decision to double back across the Wyre near Mains Hall, and carry on towards the coast along the eastern bank of the river. Sparrow has been criticised for this manoeuvre ever since, but there was certainly some logic to what he did. He kept his force between the enemy and Preston and Lancaster, thereby preventing the royalists from surprising these towns. Moreover, the river would have stopped Derby's horsemen from making a sudden attack upon his foot soldiers, who could have had plenty of time to retire or form up for action. It has also been suggested that part of the booty had already been taken off, and now lay on this shore. Had Sparrow been lucky the ship might even have been accessible from the eastern bank – but he was not.

Lord Derby, more single-minded in his venture, reached the *Santa Anna* in short order, and in so doing overtook and captured Colonel Dodding and Mr Townson of Lancaster. This pair were watching the ship and had been expecting that their friends would turn up at any moment. 'Drunk with joy' at the prospect of the captured guns, they were easily surprised and overcome. Yet Derby did not have everything his own way, since he was now in possession of the vessel but had too few men and no suitable wagons to shift the guns. Neither could he afford to wait until the enemy had gathered in overwhelming force and trapped him against the Irish Sea coast, defeating his little band and probably capturing the king's chief representative in the North West. The royalists therefore gathered some weapons from nearby Rossall Hall, and secured the 'chiefest persons', male and female, who had been aboard the *Santa Anna*. The ship was set on fire, and Derby's troop mounted up for a brisk ride back to Lathom. The sight of the burning vessel was impressive,

The Ship being on fyre, alwaies as the fyer burned it down to the ordenance they discharged till it was burned down to the watter, the Ordenance falling some into the bottom of the Shipe and some into the watter.[24]

Although Sparrow was chided for thinking only of his 'whole hyde', parliament was now free to begin the salvage of the wreck. Boats were sent down from Lancaster, and the guns were successfully raised from the river bed and floated back up the coast to the castle. At Lancaster castle they were not immediately put into use, presumably because the gun carriages and other equipment would have been consumed or damaged when the *Santa Anna* went up in flames. Despite the salvage effort, it is also unlikely that ammunition still aboard would have survived the conflagration. Whatever powder could not have been carried off by the royalists would have exploded, or been soaked, and gathering all the individual roundshot from the water would probably have been impossible.

Some commentators suggest that at least part of the ammunition was carried off and piled on the shore before the fire, and a good case has been made for associating three large shot found locally over the intervening years with the wreck of the *Santa Anna*. These were exhibited at the old Dock Street library, Fleetwood in the 1970s. Weighing from 30 to 45 lbs, these would have fitted substantial 'demi-cannon' or similar large-calibre guns. Interestingly Sir John Seaton's account speaks specifically of the recovery of 22 guns, 'whereof 8 were brass, 2 demi-cannons, one minion, five sacres whereof 3 were broke and made useless'. The ordinary crewmen and the soldiers aboard the *Santa Anna* received less attention. The *Discourse* relates that those who were not sufficiently interesting to be carried away with Lord Derby were simply left behind, starving and impoverished. Some 'died in the Country of extreme povertie of bodye' – while 'the rest ... went southward and were never heard more of'.[25]

Lord Derby appeared to have lost out during this manoeuvring in the Fylde and Lonsdale, but this was only the first round of a longer fight. Much of the Fylde remained for the king; in addition to the Cliftons Lord Derby could count on the support of a number of Catholic gentry in the area. Among these were the Butlers of Out Rawcliffe, the Westby family of Mowbreck, and the Bradleys of Brining. Scottish parliamentarian commander Sir John Seaton took the somewhat exaggerated view that all in the 'Fyld Countrey' were papists. According to the *Discourse* Fylde royalist Captains Singleton and Bamber had ridden through the Fylde area a few weeks earlier, and although the local response had been less than overwhelming, there had been no actual opposition. Parliamentarian sympathisers at Bispham and Warbreck had simply taken to their homes until the 'Popish Captains' passed on their way. Given that Derby had no reason to suppose that Lancaster was now impregnable, and with some support for the king in the Fylde, continuing the campaign in the west of the county was probably a far more inviting prospect than attempting to tackle the nest of rebellious vipers that was Manchester. Royalists resources were still slender, and only by keeping their grip on north and west Lancashire could they hope to keep up the flow of recruits and resources so necessary to the cause.

Having used the intervening week to gather greater strength from West Derby and Leyland hundreds, Lord Derby marched from Wigan on 13 March 1643 at the head of about 1,000 men. The *Discourse* makes this advance sound like a colourful procession, including not only a 'little piece of Ordnance', but 'vagabond women' – or camp followers – to attend to the needs of the soldiers. Despite such encumbrances, the royalist troops made good time, for within forty-eight hours his lordship was back at Lytham Hall, and his men were resting in quarters around Kirkham, while a general summons was issued to the Fylde to rise for King Charles. It is difficult to tell with how much enthusiasm this was greeted. On the one hand the royalist *Mercurius Aulicus* speaks of the 'great cheerfulnesse' of the country people in coming forward to contend with the wearying 'insolence and tyrannie of the Rebels'; on the other hand the pro-parliament *Discourse* claims that the unwilling conscripts virtually had to be hauled from their homes at gun point,

> The Earle by his officers that night issued out Warrants all the Fylde Country over commanding all above 16 years old and under 60 upon payne of death to be and appeare before his Honor at Kirkham the next morning by 8 of the clock in their best weapons to attend the king's service, which was obeyed of all the Country. And having taken a view of them being come from Lytham Hall to Kirkham, great words and threats were used by his officers against any that showed unwillingness to obey their commands. And he, with his officers being ready every man was commanded upon pain of death to march. Over the club men thus sodenlie raised there were Captaines appointed. John Hoole of Singleton was maid a Captaine and one John Ambrose of Plumpton Parish an other.

Whatever the quality of this levee, it certainly had numbers on its side, with *Mercurius Aulicus* claiming that 3,000 answered the summons. On the parliamentarian side Seaton's account refers to an 'infinite' number of bill men – suggesting that many peasants had armed themselves with agricultural bills in just the way that their ancestors might have done during the wars of the middle ages. A body of regular troops under Sir John Girlington and Sir Thomas Tyldesley joined the throng soon afterwards. Royalist sources claim that these units numbered about 600 soldiers, of whom half were musketeers. Most likely this body was a mixture of veterans of Tyldesley's own regiment, reinforced by Yorkshiremen.

Adding the various contingents together gives a total of well over 4,000 men for Lord Derby's royalist army in the Fylde at this point. This is probably an overstatement, but there were certainly many under arms and the pressure on resources was considerable. As might be expected, the parliamentarian account stresses the amount of plundering in which the royalist force now indulged. Naturally, too, they singled out the 'dwellings of the Roundheads', from whom they stole horses, pewter, brass, and bedding, 'and what els they could carry' up to the value of £20 a time. Most outrageous, however, was the theft of 'Mr William Swarbreck's Books' – put simply 'whoever had the tytle of Roundhead in their way, from them they took what they lyked'. Such a mighty and unruly force with little visible means of support could not be kept in being for very long, and so Lord Derby determined to advance immediately in the direction of Lancaster.[26]

The burning and capture of Lancaster, March 1643

On the morning of 18 March a surprised parliamentarian garrison found the host at their very gates, issuing them with a summons to surrender. The parliamentarians did not yield, but manned their battle stations as Derby's hordes swept towards them. One parliamentarian account has it that the defenders put up a significant resistance, volleys of shot causing 'two or three of their colours to fall at once, and bodyes lye on heaps'. At this the attack faltered, some of the royalists taking cover 'amongst the hedges, and at the back of the houses'. Some now managed to creep closer and set light to some of the properties. Dugdale's picturesque account is that it was Lord Derby himself who revitalised the stalled attack, 'leading on his men himself, with a half pike in his hand ... to the second assault, which did the business'. The royalist sources suggest that Sergeant Major Sparrow may have had as many as 600 defenders, but there is no reason to think that he had many more than his original four companies. In any event there did not seem sufficient to hold both town and castle under this pressure, and when the enemy burst into Lancaster 'severall waies', the garrison conducted a fighting retreat towards

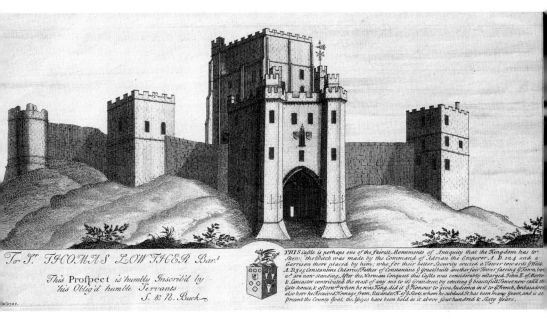

To Sʳ THOMAS LOWTHER Barᵗ

This Prospect is humbly Inscrib'd by
his Oblig'd humble Servants
S. & N. Buck.

THIS Castle is perhaps one of the fairest Monuments of Antiquity that the Kingdom has to Shew; the Ditch was made by the Command of Adrian the Emperor A.D. 124 and a Garrison there placed by him; who for their better Security erected a Tower towards ye West. A.D 305 Constantine Chlorus, Father of Constantine ye great, built another fair Tower facing ye Town, both wᶜʰ are now standing. After the Norman Conquest this Castle was considerably enlarged, John E. of Morton & Lancaster contributed the most of any one to its Grandeur; by erecting ye beautifull Tower new call'd the Gate-house, & afterwᵈˢ when he was King, did it ye Honour to give Audience in it to ye French Ambassadors also here he Received Homage from Alexander K. of ye Scots, whom he subdued. It has been many Years, and is at present the County Goal; the Assizes have been held in it above four hundred & sixty Years.

Lancaster Castle in the early eighteenth century, before the extensive alterations of that period: an engraving by S. and N. Buck.

the safety of the castle. One who did not make it inside was Captain William Shuttleworth, who fell right at the castle gate.

Having been stoutly resisted, and taken casualties, the royalist reaction was predictable, and for the time, legal. Looting and killing immediately broke out, as the lurid *Lancaster's Massacre* reported,

> the enemie entered the town, and killed man, woman, and children, with all barbarous crueltie, dragging poore people from their houses and cutting their throats with butchers knives.

There appears to have been no direct assault upon the castle itself, from which the parliamentarian troops could do little but watch the town burn. Despite some killings, it seems unlikely that the massacre became general, and that the troops were brought under control fairly quickly, as it was reported that the mayor, and some of the 'most seditious' townsmen were taken alive.

Royalist sources claim that the retribution was selective, but they did concede that arson had taken place. It was said to have been done purposefully, so that Lancaster could not become 'a receptacle to beaten Rebells'. The Earl of

Derby reported that since his summons had been rejected, he had 'made bold to burn the greatest part of the town'. It is thought that about 180 buildings were destroyed: in some properties the cattle burned in their byres. Human deaths are more difficult to assess, but given that most of Sparrow's troops escaped to the safety of the castle, and that there are direct reports of just one high profile fatality, they are more likely to have been measured in dozens than in hundreds. Lord Derby would later deny that there was any wanton slaughter, or that he bore any personal responsibility, but the explanation he gave to Prince Rupert has something of an ambiguous tone,

> There were no women or children suffered, or any but those that did bear arms, for so I gave directions to my soldiers, except some three or four, that I think as likely to be killed by them.[27]

Taken at face value the sack of Lancaster looked like a royalist victory. On closer inspection the result was a blunder – or at the very least a waste of Lord Derby's precious resources. Failure to take the castle had effectively left the field in the hands of the enemy. Worse, the destruction in the town had not only damaged the opposition. As the *Discourse* pointed out, the king actually had few real enemies in Lancaster town, and the blow had therefore fallen upon friends and neutrals as well as upon supporters of parliament. The enemy were therefore free to depict the royalist campaign as one of robbery and terror, a *chivachie*, or raid through the county. Like Prince Rupert, Lord Derby was well on his way to gaining a reputation as a ruthless plunderer. The word 'cavalier' had originally meant any gentleman on horseback, or cavalry soldier. Now the parliamentarians would apply the term as an insult, to their unprincipled and intractable enemies, high-handed and vainglorious criminals who cared nothing for anyone or their property. Whatever the objective facts, parliament, by contrast, would eventually be able to capitalise on its claim to be the party of law and order.

Preston and Lancaster change hands

The sense that the fiery raid on Lancaster had actually achieved little was heightened by the news that a parliamentarian relief force under Major General Seaton and Colonel Ashton had set out from Preston. The royalists therefore withdrew from Lancaster, and Sparrow's little garrison emerged cautiously from the castle to repossess the devastated town. It had been a narrow call: the castle had been poorly provisioned, and it would have been dubious whether the defenders could have withstood any sort of siege. According to Seaton's own account, however, the parliamentarian relief force was in no way a mortal threat to Derby's army. Lack of coordination between himself and Ashton, and mutiny in Preston itself over the insensitive way Seaton managed the army, had threatened the whole venture from the beginning.

The unrest started over an apparently trivial incident. One of the parliamentarian troops discharged his musket in Preston one evening, after the watch had been set. Seaton, incensed by this dangerous indiscipline, gave the unfortunate man what he called 'a knok or two'. At this his colleagues also boiled over into violence, and 'about 100 mad men with polaxes' rampaged after their Scottish commander. The bold Seaton, in fear of his life, ran away and hid – at one point actually leaving the town for a while. At some juncture during this undignified galloping to and fro Seaton suffered a bad fall from his long-suffering horse and took to his bed. The historian Broxap felt that the ugly mood of the rank and file was already exacerbated by want of funds and supplies; given parallel events in other counties, this is quite plausible.

Against this background Colonel Ashton appears to have made a false start, making it as far as Garstang before Derby burned Lancaster. There was now an exchange of messages. Seaton claims that he ordered Ashton, who 'had no courage to go on' to remain at Garstang, between Preston and the enemy. However, Ashton held a council of war with his officers who urged him to return to Preston, which he duly did. We lack Ashton's side of the story, and it is equally possible that it was Seaton whose morale had crumbled and Ashton wanted to return precisely because of the risk of a potentially disastrous mutiny in his rear. Colonel Shuttleworth with his Blackburn troops now also appeared on the scene in Preston, and began using all his persuasion to 'appease' the unruly troops. It is very possible, being outnumbered by veteran parliamentarians from Manchester, Bolton and Blackburn, that the Preston men, newly converted to the cause, were now cowed into conformity.

Whatever the precise detail, order was somehow restored enough for the parliamentarian expedition to set forth afresh from Preston. Yet the misfortunes of the ill-fated relief had only just started. Derby's army advanced south to Ellel, while the parliamentarians marched north to Cockerham. The accepted story, as published in London and reinterpreted by later historians, is that Lord Derby, having the better intelligence, and lacking the strength or resolution to fight, now craftily avoided his enemy and slipped past them on the road to Preston. While it is probably true that many of the country people of south Lonsdale had a residual affection for the king, and would have been likely to give Lord Derby's commanders accurate information there is probably more to the story than this. The apparently maladroit manoeuvrings of 19 and 20 March 1643 therefore require a more detailed consideration.

When Major General Seaton's little army of eleven companies of foot and 'some few ill mounted horse who durst not looke the enemie in the face' approached Ellel it was dubious whether he had much more than 1,000 men under arms. Moreover, Seaton states that he had no artillery. Given his particular lack of horse and guns, he therefore marched 'in a closse way'. By this he may have meant that his units marched bunched up for mutual strength, or more likely, that his march was directed to take best advantage of features such as enclosed fields, hedgerows, sunken lanes and other topography. In so doing he would have exposed his force to as little danger as possible in the face of an enemy whom he believed had guns and plenty of horses – these arms being better suited to more open terrain. Such a stratagem was no recent fad, but deeply ingrained in military literature and theory. As Vegetius had explained as early as the Roman period,

> a large part of a victory depends on the actual place in which a battle is fought ... if we are strong in cavalry, we should opt for plains; if it is in infantry, we should choose confined places, obstructed by ditches, marshes or trees.

Little wonder then that the parliamentarian army, which appears to have been weak in virtually everything, but particularly cavalry, chose to march 'in a closse way'.

Also implicit in Seaton's narrative is caution, and this was understandable for several reasons. As we have seen, Lord Derby's army was strong: but even if he had as few as 2,000 or 3,000 men he would have outnumbered the parliamentarians by about two to one. It would have taken a very brave, very skilled, or very foolish commander to attack Lord Derby's victorious army head-on at such odds. Seaton, by turns lucky and bumbling, and poor man-manager that he was, did at least have experience. Such experience would have told him that an attack in open country would have been unlikely to succeed. Caution was also valid because battle was not the key objective. His main purpose was the relief of Lancaster, and he would have been correct in his appreciation if he had thought that the castle itself was still in a position to be relieved. Seaton's final motive for avoiding battle, or at least not seeking it out too aggressively, was that his command, or at least his control of it, was already shaky. He had left behind him in Preston four companies of foot,

500 club men, and a troop of horse under Captain Duckenfield. The senior officer present there was Colonel Holland. Between a third and a half of the parliamentarian strength was therefore nowhere near Cockerham, and there must have been good reason for such a serious fragmentation of the command in the face of the enemy. Two obvious suggestions are that Preston was still restless, and fundamentally still royalist, and required a strong garrison: or, equally worryingly, part of the parliamentarian army in Lancashire already regarded Seaton's claim to leadership to be illegitimate.[28]

On the other side of the coin, it would seem that Lord Derby was not anxious for battle either. He may have felt weak, or exposed, as the parliamentarian accounts claim. Equally, much of the campaigning to date had centred on the seizing or storming of towns, and in the eyes of the royalist leaders Preston was probably a greater prize than a potentially bloody and inconclusive fight with a portion of the parliamentarian army. The town was one of the few genuinely strategic targets in central Lancashire, and its 'liberation' from the enemy was a worthy objective. It was also the case that with a large force, many of whom were a poorly armed levy, loitering around the countryside for any length of time was not really a viable option. The royalist supply chain was weak, or non-existent, and Derby was already isolated from his south-west Lancashire power base. Remaining in sparsely populated north Lancashire, even among friends, would have entailed living off the country in such a way as to ensure its alienation. Conversely lack of food and plunder would have been likely to lead to further indiscipline in the ranks.

So it was that Seaton and Derby passed, probably within two miles of each other, and not a shot was fired, although the royalist scouts had certainly located the enemy. As the *Discourse* relates, the Earl lingered just long enough to avoid Ashton's men

on purpose to avoid the meeting of the Colonell having received Intelligence of his coming. And when he had ceratin knowledge that the Colonell was marching one way to Lancaster he came the other way to avoid him and being quit of him he then marched spedily towards Preston, his design being to surprize Preston that night. Yet he made a stay in the lower side of Fulwood More taking especiall care to stop all Intelligence from Preston of his coming soe that there was no word of him so near till very late that night that the Scoutes sent out of Preston discovered him who brought a fearfull allarum into the towne. And then preparation was made for resistance. The Fryars Gate Barrs was strongly guarded with men, but the nearer the Earle approached the Towne the lesse and weaker it waxed for the Townes men were generally disaffected to the Parliament.

The night of 20 March can easily be imagined. There were perhaps 400 loyal parliamentarian troops beginning to gather to make a stand in the gloom, but they were probably outnumbered by local club men, many of whom had been active supporters of the king only weeks before. Other townspeople would have had little desire to be 'defended' – a staunch stand against Lord Derby could only mean plunder and possibly death. Any Catholics in town that evening, and likely there were many lying low in the face of what they might perceive as occupation, would having been praying that Lord Derby's arrival would be swift and preferably bloodless. 'Foreigners' from other parts of the county whose sympathies lay with parliament now glanced about them in paranoia.

> Strangers of the Parliament part that were accidentally within ... their care was more how they might provide for their safetie, leave it, and escap ... which many did. Ould Colonell Shutleworth of the first got his horse and [headed] homeward. Many strangers were cruelly betrayed by base and false Hostlers who had boulted the Stable doors uppon their horses and avoided out of the way the keyes thereof soe that they could not have them but were taken loosing their Horses and some having their horses were glad they escaped ... Then the Earles forces coming up to the Fryars Gate Barres discharged that little peece of Ordenance they caried with them divers times into the towne the Clubmen shouting vehemently. At last without any resistance they entered and their Horse coursed about the Towne to the East end and to the Ribble Bridge, which they guarded that none could fly that way. Thus was the Earle possessed of the Towne againe for the king. Many Prisoners were taken.[29]

So it was that the parliamentarian garrison of Preston melted away and gave up the town in the face of a few roundshot. *Mercurius Aulicus* claims that there was something of a fight, but even in this account there were very few 'ten or a dozen' killed. Most made good their escape. Those that were left either changed sides or were captured. As usual there was plunder to be had – focused this time on the goods of those collaborators who 'had showed themselves favourers of the Parliament partie when they had the towne'. Key properties robbed were Edmund Wearden's house, and the shop of Henry Tailor. The *Discourse* has it that the royalist club men were now discharged, making their way home with their plunder. This must have reduced the earl's numbers considerably, but there was good reason for their dismissal since to maintain such a force in being for a protracted length of time would have been very difficult.

Oddly the royalist and parliamentarian positions in north Lancashire were now effectively reversed, with the king's men back in charge in Preston, and the parliamentarians in Lancaster. Of the two parties it was the latter who were faced with the greater dilemma, since they were now virtually a force trapped behind enemy lines. This mounting crisis appears to have been the final straw concerning the local committeemen's attitude to Major General Seaton, who demanded the apparently impossible; with part of the army to march again on Preston, and part to stay as a garrison in Lancaster castle.

> I wes to march from Lancaster with the troupes about 2 of the clok again but no sogior would stir in regard they were weried, having marched 20 myls. The next morneng being reddie to march, none wold stay in Lancaster. Coll Stanlies 3 Companies who were into it caused beat there drums in spyt of my teeth, & when I caused schut the gates, they swore they wold fyre the Canons & the castle & be gone, so that I was faine to cause set open the gates, none of Coll Schutleworth regement wold stay, so that I was in a greater perplexitie than ever. At least two of Coll Hollands regement sayd, Sir we will stay if yow stay, but not els …

Seaton therefore acquiesced, determining to stay at Lancaster while others marched south, but 'about midway' the party that had set off for Preston were greeted with the news that it had fallen. Seaton was appraised of the position by letter – and as he himself related – those about him more, and then less, diplomatically told him to mount his horse and depart. It was on Sergeant Major Sparrow's advice, so he said, that he set off for Clitheroe, by night, to save himself.

By 25 March the disgruntled Scottish general was back in Manchester penning the letter describing his misfortunes. Had he been with the vanguard marching on Preston, he claimed that he would have attacked the town again, 'or died in the place'. As it was, his troops had retired on Chipping and Ribchester, whilst Seaton – more unpopular than ever – was afraid to go out of his lodgings for fear of being killed. Having agreed to remain in Lancashire for only three months, he thought it best to leave, 'if I can get away with my lyfe'. Pleading impoverishment and other woes, the erstwhile parliamentarian commander of Lancashire disappears from the narrative at the end of March. A unified command under a parliament nominee had much to recommend it, but in practice the experiment had been fraught, for reasons of local suspicion, practicality, and not least Seaton's own deeply flawed and abrasive character. How little impact he had is illustrated by the *Discourse*, which barely acknowledges his existence.[30]

Momentarily at least parliament's forces in the county were off balance, 'much dejected by these disasters', as the *Discourse* put it. About this time Colonel Holland wrote to a friend that he was under orders to march for the relief of Wem in Shropshire, but that 'sicknesse, diseases, and other disasters of warre' had taken their toll. The two regiments in question amounting to no more than 600 men, and these 'so discouraged and mutinous through want of pay and clothing that it is feared that they will refuse to march'. It seems very possible that Lord Derby would now have liked to have attempted to take Manchester. Yet despite his successes during March 1643, his overall strength was no greater than it had been the previous autumn. Capitalising on local advantage would prove extremely difficult.

A second royalist attack on Bolton, March 1643

On 28 March 1643 the royalists attempted to bluff Bolton into surrender, followed by a surprise night attack. Evidence as to the exact course of events is scanty, the only substantial account appearing in *Lancashire's Valley of Achor*. This contends that Lord Derby, 'encouraged by so manifold successe', was in hopes of 'gaining all'. He therefore advanced on the town on the day following the 'National Fast',

> The Enemie made no neare approach till three of the clock; so soone as they began to draw into a Body upon the Moore, our Cannoneer drew his Cannon into a Croft on the backside of the Towne, and at the second shot killed two horses neare a mile off. Then a Messenger came to summon the Towne into submission, but they resolved not to change the tenure.

The parliamentarian troops were thus alerted, but as nothing happened many were stood down again after sunset to take part in prayers with the local minister and townsmen. At the end of prayers, the royalists delivered what was described as a 'furious assault'.

> The enemy came on desperately, even to hand blowes, and some of them leaped upon the works, where they found Club-law. The enemy retreated,

and left ten men dead. After this they made no assault till Bury forces
were come into the Town … They then made an assault upon the South
end of the towne; by the advantage of the darknesse they came close to
the Mud-wall. Here they hoped to prosper by fire, as at Lancaster, but the
light discovering their nearnesse to danger, they fled for safetie. After this
they marched towards the West, but finding it a busie and warm corner,
they hasted off, and came on no more.[31]

Lancashire's Valley of Achor is a highly coloured and not incontrovertible
source, yet there is supporting evidence for a sharp, if limited, action at Bolton
on 28 March. Parish records relate the burial of '23 of the Earle of Darbeyes
men all in one cave' on 29 March, and the interment of 'two soldiers sleyne' on
4 April. Roger Dixon, 'a soldier' was buried a week later. It is likely that 'one
cave' indicates a single cavity, or mass grave, while there is every possibility
that the other three soldiers were men who died of wounds. This tallies fairly
closely with the *Valley of Achor*, which refers to 23 men 'left upon the ground'
by the enemy, and one youth on Bolton's side, 'shot through the arme'.

Brought to a reverse against Bolton, albeit a relatively minor one, Derby's
most successful offensive to date finally ground to a halt. At first glance this
looks like an anti-climax due to lack of will, but the royalist efforts over the
last few weeks had been concentrated and prodigious, and their troops can
have been scarcely less exhausted than those of the enemy. In less than a month
the earl and his immediate entourage had ridden the better part of 200 miles.
In the course of this campaign Lancaster had been burned, Preston seized,
and Bolton unsuccessfully attacked. Large numbers of troops had been raised,
and some disbanded. There had been night marches, forced marches, scouting
operations, plundering, requisitioning, and a dozen logistical problems. All
this had taken place with fewer troops, within the confines of one county, but
in terms of distances travelled and actions fought, it was still a performance
to rival that boasted by parliament's New Model Army later in the war.

In view of what has been claimed for what has, rather inaccurately, been
called 'Cromwell's Army', this begs many interesting questions. Certainly a
significant difference between these local royalist efforts in 1643, and those
national efforts of the parliament two years later, was in the matter of
sustainability. When Lord Derby's resources ran short, there was no central
well upon which he could draw, and what he gained in the facility to take
swift local decisions he lost in his inability to keep paying and feeding for
protracted lengths of time. There is little evidence of any assistance from
royalist headquarters in Oxford, nor indeed from royalists in other parts of

England. Though there was some mention of Welsh troops, contribution from either Ireland or Wales had been slender. In early 1643 the royalist war effort in Lancashire had been largely isolated from what happened elsewhere, and the net flow of men and resources was still outward. Only in 1644 would this position be reversed, and even then local requirements would be subsumed within the national. For the time being it looked as though the Lancashire royalists were beginning to run out of steam.[32]

Parliamentarians attack Wigan, March 1643

As if to confirm that parliament's forces were regaining their equilibrium, the Manchester forces marched on royalist Wigan at the end of March 1643. Colonel Holland was in command of the expedition, with Colonel Ashton and a mistrustful John Rosworme among his key officers. According to Rosworme's account, the parliamentarians mustered over 2,200 men, as there were '2,000 foot, most part good Muskettiers, the rest Club and Bill men, and to my best remembrance about 200 or 300 horse, besides eight Peece of Ordnance, and no want of ammunition or provisions'. The blow fell upon the hapless Wigan on April Fool's Day: in the vanguard of the attack was Colonel Ashton. *Lancashire's Valley of Achor* has it that the defenders managed to bring their assailants under artillery fire killing two men during the approach march, but so 'venterous and daring' were the parliamentarians that they carried on, realising that to halt under fire would be suicide.

In less than an hour Ashton's troops – by now seasoned veterans – had overcome the initial resistance and forced their way into the town. Quite a few of the enemy were captured immediately. The fight was not however over,

> Whilest the Towne was taken, the Enemy having for a refuge observed and fitted the Church and steeple adjoyning for their advantage, fled thither as many as could, and killed from thence, I dare say, more men, after the taking of the Town, than we had lost in the whole assault besides.

So it was that confused fighting continued for some time, with perhaps a hundred royalists ensconced in the church and steeple, shooting out into the crowded streets. In Rosworme's version there was now a sudden 'alarum' when a reserve of enemy cavalry appeared on the scene. The parliamentarian horse accordingly squared up to this new threat, and the royalists held off. News reports that the Earl of Derby's main force was about to descend upon them proved to be premature.[33]

Nevertheless Holland was now in a serious dilemma – Rosworme depicts him 'shaking in an agony of fear'. Some estimates put the royalist forces in the area as strong as 1,400, and 500 of Ashton's musketeers were already sent off to reinforce Bolton. Rosworme says that there was now a heated argument between himself and Holland, with Colonel Holland directing a strategic withdrawal, while Rosworme, in a paroxysm of frustration, demanded the right to attempt a close assault upon the church. Ironically the defenders of the church surrendered just as the parliamentarian main body was pulling out – a total of 86 men being taken.

Whether Wigan ever was the prime target, and whether Holland had intended to hold it in the long term remains a moot point. The town, as *Lancashire's Valley of Achor* put it, was 'not so gloriously achieved as obscurely left'. One possibility was that the Lancashire parliamentarians had learned from their recent experiences at Lancaster and Preston, and saw that attempting to hold a royalist town with a weak garrison was, at best, a waste of time. That Rosworme might have exaggerated the situation is suggested by the *Discourse*, which barely mentions this hit-and-run attack on Wigan, making it appear merely as a prelude to an attack on Warrington. The parliamentarian pamphlet *Manchester's Joy* puts a far more positive spin on the whole episode, stressing that not only was this a victory 'obtained without any considerable prejudice to the Manchestrians', but that Wigan had been sacked of valuable loot. The town was the major 'place of receipt for papists goods and treasure', and not only munitions but papists' 'goods to the vallue of twenty thousand pounds' had been seized. Many of the enemy had been killed and copious prisoners were claimed. As Derby had treated Lancaster, similar measure had been handed down to Wigan by the Manchester men.

Warrington and the battle of Stockton Heath, April 1643

Whatever the real objective at Wigan the 'big picture' was the taking of Warrington. The plan was that both the Cheshire and Lancashire parliamentarians would descend on Warrington town simultaneously, thereby surrounding the opposition and cutting off all hope of relief. Concentrating the resources of the two adjoining counties would also mean that the royalists would be substantially outnumbered. Doubtless, the hatching of this strategem was aided by the fact that during March Sir William Brereton, the prominent Cheshire parliamentarian, had been elevated to chief all of parliament's forces in that county, so unifying the local command. Moreover, Brereton was well connected in Lancashire, having been appointed a deputy lieutenant for

Lancashire before the war, and was related to both Colonels Richard Holland and Ralph Ashton. The Warrington plan was excellent in theory, but in practice it proved difficult to marshal the disparate parliamentarian forces. The royalists were also present in strength, being commanded by Lord Derby himself. As the *Discourse* observed, 'Warrington the Earle did Garrison for the king, strongly fortifying it with Gates, Mounts and an engine devised and placed upon the Bridge to stop the passage over it'.[34]

The first parliamentarians on the scene were the Cheshire companies of Captain Ardern, who approached the town from the south on 3 April. However, Lord Derby had either much improved his tactical skills, or was well advised that day. Taking advantage of the fact that the enemy were as yet in small numbers he sallied out of Warrington. Derby caught the enemy ill-prepared, and brought them to battle on Stockton Heath, where he 'slewe some of them'. Sir William Brereton, arriving soon afterwards with more Cheshire troops was likewise brought to an abrupt halt.[35]

The pamphlet *Mercurius Aulicus* was cock-a-hoop with this performance, giving a typically pro-royalist view of the proceedings which it reported on Saturday 8 April

> The first news of this day was a double defeat given by the Earle of Derby to Sir William Brereton, at Warrington in Lancashire, a towne very neare the borders of Cheshire. Brereton coming thither upon an hope of hindering the Earl's proceedings, who was going with part of his forces towards Manchester. But Brereton being well beaten at the first onset, with the losse of many of his men and some of his colours, and had no minde to go away till he had perfected the Earles victorie and his own overthrow, and therefore drew into the field againe with the accession of some new forces from Manchester, to play double or quits. Which being perceived by the Earle of Derbie, hee purposely held off from accepting the battaile till the duske of the evening, and then sent some of his owne men under Brereton's colours to make towards them; who being taken and indeed mistaken for theire own party, were suffered to joyne with them or come very neare them upon the one side: and then the Earle charging very hotly upon the other, they made a great impression on both sides, and having caught them in a trapp, defeated them with great slaughter and little labour.

How many were actually killed at Stockton Heath and other skirmishes around Warrington in early April is unclear. Very probably the total losses to both sides were no more than a few dozen. It does appear that Brereton did manage to place a battery on Moot Hill, and got as far as occupying Sankey, within a mile of the town, but that the co-ordination and strength required to take Warrington were lacking. Parliamentarian propaganda claimed that the failure to take Warrington was due to humanitarian motives rather than defeat, as Derby's men had set fire to part of the town, and were likely to reduce the rest to 'utter desolation' had the attack been continued.[36]

Nevertheless the royalist account of the use of darkness and captured colours is interesting for it suggests that, as in other parts of the country, there was little at this stage to distinguish the combatants friend from foe, other than the flags that they carried. Armies certainly had no homogenous costume, though individual colonels often attempted to give their own regiments uniform-coloured coats. So it was that battles could occur in which a rainbow of different uniform appeared for either side, with both the royalists and the parliamentarians having men arrayed in blue and red for example. Early in the war in particular it is likely that quite a few units had no uniform at all, going into action in civilian costume, with perhaps the addition of bandoliers for their ammunition, and 'snapsacks' for the carrying of food. Some impromptu fighters such as 'club men' probably even lacked these basic pieces of equipment, fighting quite literally with clubs, staves, daggers and agricultural bills. Old stocks of bows even survived in certain parts of the country and saw limited use, though documentary evidence of archery during the wars is lacking in Lancashire.

In set-piece actions where commanders had time to deliberate, 'field signs' could be adopted, with all of the men perhaps wearing a piece of white cloth or paper in their hats, or maybe a sprig of foliage. Alternatively, a conscious decision could be taken not to have a sign – trusting that the enemy would be obvious by the fact that they had selected one. Even so, there were instances when both sides opted not to have a sign, or even selected the same one. A substitute, which might *in extremis* prevent a soldier from being run through by his comrades, was a battlecry or password, although the difficulty of getting entire armies to remember these, or to distinguish them in the hubbub of action, can be imagined.[37]

Despite a good deal of bloodshed, and many miles of weary marching, the Lancashire winter and spring campaigns of 1642/43 had proved largely inconclusive. Neither side had yet succeeded in gaining the upper hand. While one or other of the protagonists gathered strength in one area to push forward – here to Lancaster, there to Preston, here again to Wigan – it weakened itself in another. The enemy had then been able to capitalise on the weakness to

Troops drawn up for battle, from a detail in a scene depicting an action in the Thirty Years War, with cavalry foreground, and pikes flanked by musketeers in the distance.

make a gain of its own. Meanwhile, holding on to towns sympathetic to the enemy had proved no easy task under pressure, and the opposition had often succeeded in fleeing or blending back into the civil population. The core forces of both sides were small: getting larger armies depended upon impressment or mass call-outs. In the face of inadequate funds, and lack of supplies, holding larger forces together for long enough for them to make a lasting impact was proving extremely problematic.

Neither side was winning clearly by mid-April 1643. Arguably, perhaps, Lord Derby was losing ground by missing another opportunity to put an early end to the war. Whilst royalism was beginning to go forward in other areas, the Manchester parliamentarians had made a surprisingly good effort from an unpromising start. They may not as yet have had very much to show for their efforts, but remaining in the game at all against what appeared to be poor odds was remarkable. It is sometimes said that wars are won not by the best generals, but by the side which makes the fewest mistakes. In Lancashire the combatants had shown plenty of spirit, and often remarkable stamina – but no really inspirational leader had appeared to sweep all before him. Now one side was about to make a mistake that almost proved fatal.

CHAPTER FIVE

'Brave and victorious': the war turns for parliament

T HROUGHOUT the first six months of the wars in Lancashire most of the military action had taken the form of sieges, storms, small skirmishes and more or less deadly street fighting. Neither side had shown much inclination to seek out the enemy in the open field – and on at least one occasion this had been deliberately avoided. The battle of Read Bridge, also known as the battle of Whalley, was therefore something of a new departure as it was fought mainly in the open countryside, between Padiham and Whalley, with further fighting in and around Whalley itself. Nevertheless Read Bridge was an encounter battle, not the result of a planned strategy designed to bring the enemy to a single decisive action.

The battle of Read Bridge, Whalley, April 1643

In mid-April 1643 the Earl of Derby had called a general muster of his Lancashire forces at Preston, with the idea of renewing his offensive. This would be an attacking campaign to the east to clear Blackburn hundred, the main parliamentarian power base outside Manchester. The result of his muster was an army of perhaps 3,000 – one contemporary estimate specifying 2,000, another a maximum of 5,000 men. Although we do not know the precise figure, a high number is credible, because Derby had recalled his levee *en masse* back to the colours, what the *Discourse* refers to as his 'Club [men] of the Field'. Apart from Derby himself, the key contingents were led by Lord Molyneux, Sir Gilbert Hoghton and Colonel Tyldesley. According to the parliamentarian account, *A True Relation of a Great and Wonderfull Victory*, the royalist force numbered eleven troops of horse, 700 foot 'and infinite club men'. The *Discourse* also refers to a single artillery piece. This body of troops was one of the largest so far gathered in the county, although it was neither the best armed, nor the best trained or disciplined.[1]

Leaving Preston, Derby's army marched east, keeping to the north bank of the Ribble until they reached the little town of Ribchester about noon on 19 April. They then crossed the river and marched on towards Salesbury. Then they turned left, to Whalley, the 'clubmen according to their practice plundering in most of the townes they passed by or thorrow'. The people of Whalley could do nothing about it. As one eighteenth-century account put it, the inhabitants 'thereof not expecting such as visitant were very much surprised and not being properly provided for defending themselves against so potent an enemy, they calmly submitted'. The first parliamentarian force to raise the alarm was two troops of cavalry at Dunkenhalgh Hall, a body of horse unlikely to have been more than 100 strong. Given the impossibility of confronting a royalist army by themselves, they sent word back to Colonel Shuttleworth at Gawthorpe to 'raise the Country', and fell back on Padiham. The messengers found the parliamentarian main body ill-prepared: Shuttleworth's companies had been dispersed or stood down, and in any case were 'also wanting ammunition and Pouder'.

Had the royalists now attacked with all speed it seems probable that the unprepared enemy would have been swept before them, leaving north-east Lancashire open to the royalists. As it was Derby was cautious, or his force too unwieldy and difficult to control. Shuttleworth and his comrades therefore had a few hours' grace, and, given the situation, reacted remarkably smartly. The alarm was raised on the 19th, the day the earl's force had crossed the Ribble, and by the following morning 'all the firemen' – or musketeers – had been mustered. This was all the more remarkable as according to one account they had had no pay in the last five weeks. They were joined by a few club men and cavalry. The initial strength of the parliamentarians may have been as few as 500 men, but most authorities assume that there were somewhat more than 500, plus the cavalry, and contemporary reference to reinforcement during the day of the battle makes it likely that eventually they had 1,000 troops in the field. In any event they were still outnumbered by the royalists by about two to one.

As the last of the parliamentarian outriders scampered away from Whalley they took with them a couple of horses, and a no doubt protesting 'Mr Lathams' whom they accused of being a 'great Papist'. With the powerful royalist force now in occupation of Whalley, and Lord Derby himself enjoying the reluctant hospitality of Captain Ashton's home at Whalley Abbey[2] the most obvious course open to the parliamentarians was to retire again. Indeed, the author of the *Discourse* states that the leadership had indeed decided that a strategic retreat was sensible. However, the rank and file demanded to stand and fight – shaming their captains into a more confrontational frame of mind.

How they then managed to spring such an effective ambush at Read Bridge is therefore open to some speculation. One account describes how it was one of the commanders of the parliamentarian cavalry who first saw that he could lure the enemy advanced guard within range of the parliamentarian foot hiding behind a wall. The *Discourse* states that either the parliamentarians had 'intelligence from others that the enemie would [pass] that way', or that they correctly guessed the royalist line of advance. Another convincing idea is that the men of east Lancashire were now well aware of the plunder and disorder that the royalist army brought in their wake. Their apparent resolution was perhaps less because of a desire to win a battle for the ideals of parliament than to protect their homes and livelihoods from the Preston rabble surrounding the more seasoned regiments now set to descend upon them. In any case topography, and lack of defined objective on the part of the royalist army, played significant parts in the debacle which followed.

The exit to the narrow defile or 'hollow dingle' at Read Bridge. Here the royalist cavalry were ambushed by the parliamentarian foot as they made their way up from Sabden Brook. The large body of mounted troops was constricted by the terrain and routed back down the slope. This sudden upset led ultimately to total defeat.

PHOTOGRAPH: AUTHOR

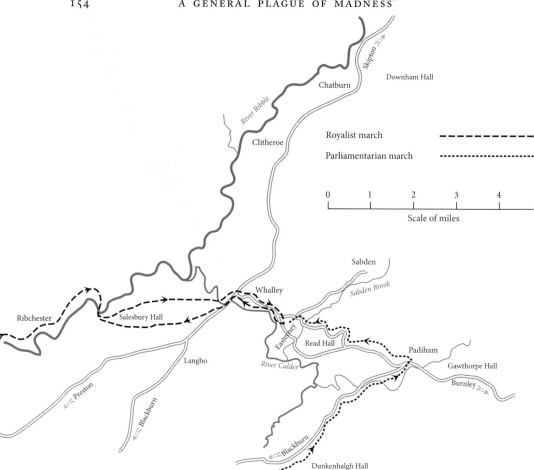

The area of Read Bridge and Whalley in April 1643. The running battle which marked Lord Derby's somewhat ignominious failure against the rather smaller forces of the East Lancashire parliamentarians, is known as both the battle of Read bridge, and the battle of Whalley. Casualties were relatively light, but the action marked a significant turning point in the war in Lancashire.

Near Read Bridge the Sabden Brook is not very deep, but occupies a small, steep-sided valley. On the Read side the track way bends off to one side. Any unit of troops crossing the river in a hurry, without first scouting the opposite bank, thus runs the risk of being taken by surprise as it rises out of the depression. Whether lured by an easy victory over the retreating parliamentarians, or merely impetuous, this was exactly what happened to the royalist cavalry. Tyldesley's regiment of horse was in the van as the king's men approached Parkhead, and one account has it that Sir Thomas paused to speak to a local woman to check his location and seek intelligence of the enemy. On receiving no useful information save that he was now near the house of Roger Nowell of Read, he continued with his troopers on up the road. As they mounted out of the 'hollow dingle' they were tempted forward by the first sight of a smaller body of the enemy. Very probably there was an exchange of fire, as numbers of pistol and carbine shot have been found within a hundred yards or so of the current river crossing: but the parliamentarian troopers were not staying to be overwhelmed by greater numbers. They turned about and made off, pursued by Tyldesley's men. Little did the royalists know, however, that they were riding straight into the trap. The parliamentarian infantry had 'planted themselves in the fields' on either side of the highway on the far side of the water, 'with their muskets readie charged'.[3]

E.F., an officer with the parliamentarian horse, describes how about 150 of the royalist horse followed his men to a point where the parliamentarian militiamen were concealed behind a wall. Then,

> I made as though I fled, they pursued me, when I knew they were in the command [within effective range] of our men, I advanced again and shot off my pistoll (being a sign for our foot); whereupon our men discharged with a great showt; the enemies horse fled in great disorder, we wounded many, took forty prisoners, some horse and 60 musquets ...[4]

It is likely that this crashing surprise volley was delivered fewer than a hundred of the parliamentarian foot. Yet, being fired from close range, by men covered from the enemy by a solid wall, into cavalry – probably in a narrow formation – on the defile of the track way, the result was devastating. Nonetheless, with Lord Derby having numerous reinforcements in the vicinity, this comparatively small setback should certainly not have proved catastrophic.

The shock and the sudden casualties proved too much, however, and Tydesley's cavalry routed. They fled back down the hill, and the parliamentarians, elated by their easy victory, rushed after them. *Lancashire's Valley of Achor* claimed that the resolution of the righteous parliamentarians was fired up by God, their elan against superior numbers being 'against all sense and reason'. Sir Thomas himself took the wrong track attempting to rejoin his command, landing up on the way to Easterley farm, and only extracting himself from the confusion with difficulty. The remaining royalist resistance crumbled quickly as the melee was pushed inexorably back a mile and more towards Whalley. The parliamentarian troops 'pursued them hotly', capturing some of the enemy club men on the way.

At Whalley Lord Derby managed to regain a semblance of order, rallying his command on the abbey, where E.F. reports that the royalist cannon was brought into action. This does not appear to have caused serious loss to the victorious parliamentarians, but it did buy some time to give the royalist foot a chance to reform near the river. Some of Derby's men took cover in the church and tower, and it seemed that all might not be lost. The check, however, was momentary. One of the royalist captains fell mortally wounded, shot through the eye, and the royalist levies were 'amazed' by the hullabaloo raised by the enemy charging down upon them. Moreover, despite the support from the abbey, many of the royalist foot were in a poor position with their backs to the river Calder, and now they panicked:

> The Earles Clubb men being in the Reare of his Army hearing the great noyse of shoutting, apprehending it fearfully fled through the river in much haste, he being most happie that could get through it with most speed and run the fastest away. Noe Command of the officers nor force of the horsemen could make them turne again or staye, but gone they would be; which wrought soe upon the rest of the Armie that they lykewise turned their backs and fledd soe disorderly and confusedly that (as relation was) the Earle himselfe had much adoe to cause them to take their Ordenance with them.[5]

Sir Thomas Tyldesley and others who had been pushed back in the first clash attempted to rejoin the fight, but no intervention was of any use. Captain James Collier of Tyldesley's regiment was one of those who fell into captivity.

Parliamentarian officers were now struggling, not to push their soldiers forward, but to hold their men back to keep the pursuit from going completely out of hand. The parliament foot ran through, and under, the hedgerows and

> played upon them with our muskets, and routed their foot, which fled over the water, their horse still facing us, our men still pursued them to Lango-green, where Captain Ashton and myselfe with much ado caused our first men to stay still till more came up, then our men shot; their horse fled; then all our horse came up and pursued them through Salisbury Park, and to Ribchester.

The parliamentarian foot giving chase were exhausted and wet, some of them having waded through water 'to the chin', in order to get at the opposition. Having driven the royalists 'out of the Hundred', their charge was truly blown, and the east Lancashire men now considered that their job for the day was complete. The parliamentarian force thus rallied back on Padiham.

The battle of Read Bridge had been untidy and unplanned, but in fighting on home turf and retaining the initiative throughout the action a significant victory had been won. Some accounts refer to up to 300 royalist dead, although this is probably a significant overestimate. Parliamentarian casualties were certainly extremely light, and Blackburn hundred was now secured. This success might not have been the result of great generalship by Colonel Shuttleworth, but it was not a fight that could easily have been afforded to be lost. If luck had smiled upon the parliamentarians in east Lancashire the abortive local campaign of April 1643 still had important repercussions for the king's supporters. If not suspect already, Lord Derby's qualities as a general were now exposed as relatively slender, and with the waxing of parliament's fortunes in the county he would begin to slip ever more into the background.

South Lancashire and the Fylde, April–May 1643

Read Bridge had been no battle of annihilation, nor was it, even by civil war standards, a particularly large or lengthy engagement. Nevertheless, its impact was considerable, and, it may be argued, a psychological blow to Lancashire royalism out of proportion to its material importance. The *Discourse* paints a picture of the Earl of Derby at Mr Fleetwood's house at Penwortham after the battle, 'dismayed and disconsolat'. If not betrayed, he certainly had reason to feel let down. His force easily had the strength to confront the east Lancashire parliamentarians, but it had run away in short order. Derby, was, so it was said, in a 'very sad pensive condition by reason of the dastardlines which appeared in his Army'.

If Derby was in a trough, Colonel Ashton was determined to make capital in the wake of Read Bridge. Parliamentarian designs on Wigan and Warrington had been frustrated too long, and now appeared to be the time to strike a decisive blow. So it was that on 22 April 1643, just two days after the battle of Read Bridge, he set out for Wigan again. The parliamentarian journal *Certain Speciall Passages* takes up the narrative,

The noble and renowned Manchesterians under the command of Collonel Ashton, with about 22 hundred horse and foot, and marched towards

Cavalry drill illustrations from John Cruso's *Militarie Instructions for the Cavallrie*, Cambridge, 1632. The 'three quarter' armour shown here was becoming increasingly rare at the time of the civil war, but still used by heavy cuirassiers, and by some officers.

Wiggon, where Collonel Tilsley commanded for the Earl of Derbie with 9 troops of horse and 700 foot. But when brave and victorious Collonel Ashton appeared before the town, the enemies were immediately smitten with astonishment of heart, durst not stand to it, but fled away from thence to Latham, leaving Wiggon to their possession: whereupon the noble Collonel demolisht all the outworks and fortifications, burnt the new gates and posts that had been set up, took an oath of the townsmen never to bear arms against the king and Parliament, and then this brave Collonel pursued the enemie in their flight to Latham, whereupon the Earl of Derbie and his companie fled thence to a town called Prescot, thinking there to have drawn the countery to him, but the brave Manchesterians pursued them close, thither also and the enemie was forced to flie back to Latham.[6]

The *Discourse* states that Wigan was actually bombarded for a while before the parliamentarian troops entered. Whether or not this was so, Wigan was now being despoiled for the second time in the space of three weeks. Captain Chisnall was taken prisoner, and the parliamentarian soldiery looted whatever they could. Behind them they left not only a sorry, but a bizarre spectacle, 'Great heapes of Woollen Cloth of the Drapers being laid in the streets'. Neither Sir Thomas Tyldesley nor Lord Molyneux were apt to tarry in south Lancashire, and retired first to Ormskirk before turning north to the Ribble, which they forded below Preston. Having rested their tired regiments in quarters around Clifton and Kirkham, a fresh alert that the enemy were advancing upon them sent them scurrying further northward. Not long afterwards they were to be found north of Lancaster on their way out of the county. At Broughton-in-Furness Tyldesley was finally among friends; here he was partially re-equipped, and made the decision to make for Yorkshire, though according to the *Discourse* Molyneux's men returned into Lancashire.

Apart from natural depression and exhaustion, and the desertion of many of his troops following the reverse at Read Bridge, other explanations have also been advanced for Derby's somewhat supine reaction to the Manchester men's advance into his natural heartland. Most important of these is the idea that he had been positively ordered not to engage again, nor to risk such of his force that was still available to him. This is probably putting it too strongly, but there is certainly sufficient evidence to suggest that Lord Derby now had some hope of receiving help from outside the county. His best course would therefore be to hold off until he could unite the Lancashire royalist forces with those coming to his rescue. By doing so he might hope to catch the enemy off guard and outnumbered.

Queen Henrietta Maria had returned from the continent, landing at Bridlington on the east coast in late February 1643. With her she had brought 2,000 cases of pistols, £80,000 in cash, and 'over a thousand old, experienced soldiers'. It was said that this year-long expedition had involved not only pawning her own jewellery, but some of the crown jewels and even the king's pearl buttons to obtain funds. This windfall had been a valuable fillip to northern royalist morale, and there was even speculation that she might remain in the north as 'she-generalissima'. Now everyone wanted a share of these new resources. Lady Derby wrote a direct and personal appeal for her help from Lathom. Apparently this was 'a doleful letter' begging 'speedy aid', for unless 'she did not send some aid, at least 3,000 horse and foot' disaster beckoned. With the rapid deterioration of the situation in Lancashire it appears that the queen did intend to intervene directly. Just the day after the fall of Wigan she was writing to the king of her intentions, which with hindsight appear ridiculously over optimistic,

... my proposition is this – to detach from the body of the army 2000 footmen and 1000 horsemen, 200 dragoons and some cannon and send them at once into Lancashire to join with the Earl of Derby and to clear out that county, which I hope can be done in ten or twelve days.

Unsurprisingly there was no ten-day lightning campaign to 'clear' away the parliamentarian forces which had just spent six months painstakingly and expensively establishing their dominance in the county.

A few weeks later the master plan had changed out of all recognition. Now the queen intended to march upon Halifax via Leeds and Bradford. This having been achieved, Manchester could be taken and Lord Derby restored to his rightful position in the county. This was another pipe dream, and probably Derby recognised it as such. If so, he was very quickly proved correct, as few of the ambitious designs for Yorkshire would be fulfilled in the short term. Moreover at Wakefield in May 1643 the renowned parliamentarian commander Sir Thomas Fairfax achieved what must have been regarded as a surprise victory over the superior numbers of royalist George Goring. This was a 'hott incounter' – during which the parliamentarians had stormed the barricades with 'unspeakable courage'. In this 'Miraculous Victory' 27 enemy colours were seized; Goring himself was taken prisoner. There would be no miracle relief force from Yorkshire, which had plenty of problems of its own. As so often was the case, stories of big new forces coming in from outside the county to aid one side or the other would be proved false.[7]

Derby himself ventured to York in an attempt to encourage the queen to strike westward with all haste, but the appeals now fell on deaf ears. The national requirements were imperative – together with the Earl of Newcastle and his troops the queen's march would be to the south. Thomas Tyldesley's experienced Lancashire soldiers would remain on what Derby doubtless saw as the wrong side of the Pennines. Tyldesley would march via Newark with the army to Burton on Trent, where his courageous part in the storming of the town would be marked with a knighthood. Though Cavendish returned to York, Tyldesley and many of the Lancashire troops would become part of the king's main army in the south fighting at Bristol, Gloucester and Newbury.

Royalist retreat and Warrington attacked, May 1643

In the meantime royalist fortunes in Lancashire were going steadily from bad to worse. When it was realised that Warrington might be the next target governor Colonel Edward Norris made a general call-out of the militia of the surrounding area on behalf of the king. His summons used the broadest imaginable definition of the term, the document of 14 May demanding 'all able men ... within the age of 60 yeares and above the age of 16 yeares' to come to the defence of Warrington with 'best armes' and provisions for 'four days'. In the event supplies would prove grossly inadequate. It may also be speculated that in the absence of the troops of what now approximated to Lancashire's regular royalist army, the 'best armes' of any levy were likely to be less than ideal. The Manchester troops sallied forth on 20 May, to meet up with their old allies, the Cheshire forces of Sir William Brereton, outside Warrington. Taking advantage of a windy night, which helped cover the noise of their activity, the parliamentarian advanced guard crept within 'half musket shot' of the town.

By the morning of 22 May the besiegers' cannon were wheeled into place, letting rip with salvoes of ball. According to Vicar's *Parliamentary Chronicle* one of the main points of aim was the church. Though there was no 'storm' of the town, there were certainly casualties on both sides. Warrington parish records note the burial of at least seven soldiers between April and June 1643, being men from the contingents of 'Captain Ashton' and 'Captain Barrow'. Six fatalities are recorded in contemporary journals. By 27 May the Warrington royalists had lost stomach for the fight. With 'bread and other necessaries being scarce', Norris was forced to the negotiating table. As a result of his prompt surrender relatively good terms were obtained and further bloodshed averted. His officers were allowed to depart with 'horse and pistols', while his men were to leave unarmed. Sir George Booth entered the town in triumph. The parliamentarian *Perfect Diurnall* crowed that the 'considerable worth' of Warrington was now at the disposal of the victors, virtually the whole county being purged of 'papists' and 'evill members'. To the *Kingdom's Weekly Intelligencer* the religious implications were crystal clear: whereas Lancashire and Yorkshire had more 'Papists than in all England besides', nevertheless 'God had shewed his power more in a handfull of men against these numerous and potent enemies of the Gospel' and the enemy had been routed.[8]

The royalist command had little compassion for losers. Things had taken so poor a turn in Lancashire that many senior royalists were now counselling the removal of Lord Derby. Clarendon considered that Charles only retained him only for fear that if he imposed another over his head, Derby might be tempted to sabotage the war effort in the region out of spite. Although his skill and courage could be questioned, to date his 'fidelity, without doubt, was blameless'. Frustrated by what must have seemed a bewilderingly swift and catastrophic turn of events, Lord Derby reluctantly accepted the orders he was given to make good the Isle of Man against the parliamentarian navy and rebellion. His journey thence was via Lathom. He later stated that he made what provision he could to put his house in a state of defence, specifically laying in money and ammunition against the evil day when the 'insolence and affronts of the enemy' might be visited upon his home. Interestingly while official correspondence upholds the idea that the king was grateful for Lord Derby's efforts, and that the threat of revolt in the Isle of Man was genuine and serious, there are also suggestions of dramatic rifts in the royalist camp in certain sources. How accurate Seacome's narrative on this point is may be open to question, but here it is stated that Derby saw the Isle of Man as a form of 'banishment'. His view of Lord Molyneux as given in this account is also revealing – Derby having apparently stated in private that his lordship, in the end, gave him 'as much trouble as the enemy'.[9]

On the parliamentarian side sudden success and virtual freedom of much of the county was a heady cocktail after months of gruelling and uncertain campaigning. Having chased most of the remaining royalists northwards, Ashton's troops fell upon the Fylde, marching via Garstang and St Michael's. An orgy of plunder followed, in some instances stealing from their own supporters, though the *Discourse* excuses Colonel Ashton himself as being absent at the time.

> From Mr Parker of Bradkirk they took a great many Cattel and out of his house all they found worth Cariage, leaving his house in a very sorry condition. In Kirkham they plundered from them that were soldiers in their own army and had been in that expedition with them so disrespectless were they and greedie. And all the way they passed to Clifton and from it they drove a great store of Cattell. Att Preston falling at discord among themselves about dividing of them and about the Ordenances they caried which was a matter of sadness to their friends and wil be an infamie to their Reputation in future generations when pretending conscience and good will of the Cause to be the motives of their taking up of armes did bring odium upon themselves by their base covetousness, violence and oppressions.[10]

The battle of Adwalton Moor, June 1643

Parliamentarian success in Lancashire in the early summer of 1643 might have been further reaching still were it not for events in adjoining West Yorkshire. With the Fairfax family involved in an increasingly desperate struggle against the Earl of Newcastle, the Yorkshire parliamentarians were keen to draw support from Lancashire: and for once the Lancastrian parliamentarians were in a position to respond. As a result a number of companies from the Manchester area were marched east across the county border in support of

Sir Thomas Fairfax. The precise number of Lancashire parliamentarians who fought in Yorkshire in June 1643 is unclear; estimates of up to 12 companies numbering from 700 to 1,000 men in total being given in various places. In either instance the number was significant, given the relative smallness of Fairfax's army at this time.

Despite this useful support a very difficult strategic position had developed by the end of June. Lord Fairfax, holding Bradford with perhaps 4,000 men and few provisions, was apprised of the approach of Newcastle's much larger army. Given the apparent hopelessness of the situation bold measures were called for, as was later reported by his son Sir Thomas Fairfax,

> The Earl of Newcastle marched with an army of 10 to 12,000 men to besiege us, and resolved to sit down before Bradford, which was a very untenable place. My father drew all the forces he could spare out of the garrisons hither. But seeing it not possible to defend the town, but by strength of men, and not having above ten or twelve days provision for so many as were necessary to keep it; we resolved, the next morning very early with a party of 3,000 men, to attempt his whole army as they laid in quarters, three miles off.

Fortune on this occasion did not favour the brave. For when the parliamentarians came up to the enemy at Adwalton (or Adderton) Moor on 30 June they found them, not helpless and unprepared in their billets, but 'in Battalia', or drawn up ready to fight. If Sir Henry Slingsby's account is to be believed the royalists were not only ready but marching towards their enemies, and Newcastle's advanced 'forlorn hope' struck 'unexpectedly' with the parliamentarians. Sir Thomas Fairfax suspected treachery – but the vigilance of Newcastle's piquets and scouts may have been good. Perhaps both sides really were surprised, making this a genuine 'encounter battle'.

The parliamentarians were now forced into a very unequal stand-up fight, in which the Lancashire men formed part of Sir Thomas's 'main battle', along with 500 men from Halifax and surrounding garrisons. One source claims that the Lancashire troops were in fact in the rear of this body. In any case the parliamentarians at first gained ground, forcing their way over Whiskett Hill, but then, not far from the villages of Drighlington and Adwalton they were confronted by superior numbers. The cavalry charged and counter-charged, the parliamentarians giving their adversaries 'sharp entertainment' before the foot of both sides came on, fighting from hedge to hedge. The issue appeared to hang in the balance until Colonel Kirton's pikes joined the fray, and the royalist artillery found its mark among Fairfax's cavalry. The parliamentarian command fragmented, Lord Ferdinando and Sir Thomas losing contact in the struggle. Both were forced to withdraw independently, and in disarray. Bradford was taken for the king on 1 July.

Though perhaps half of the parliamentarian troops would make good their escape, the Yorkshire flank would, for the foreseeable future, remain a threat to the parliamentarian cause in Lancashire. The Earl of Newcastle was pleased enough with himself to summons Manchester to surrender on 5 July – carefully pointing out his Protestant credentials and his horror that his men had been slandered as an army of 'Papists'. This was probably only grandstanding, and the Manchester men, who had seen much worse over the previous twelve months, would answer in similar vein a few days later. They were not the aggressors, and since God was their protector they had nothing to fear. All being well the almighty would now direct them to return the violence of the papists, and other malignants, upon themselves.[11]

Hornby, Thurland and the battle of Lindale Close

Within the county of Lancashire there was for a little while little active resistance to parliament. With Preston secure, Colonel Alexander Rigby was able to return to the area, armed with a commission to raise fresh troops for parliament, putting the 'Hundreds of Laylond and Amounderness into a posture of warre which he was diligent to doe within a little time'. Given that Preston in particular had hitherto proved itself for the king, and difficult to manage at the best of times, Rigby's new units also drew on officers from outside Leyland and Amounderness. One of these was Major Downes, a Derbyshire gentleman, and another the young captain of horse, Edward Robinson. This Robinson had previously raised a troop of horse which served under the command of 'ould Colonell Shutleworth'. He may well have been the author of the *Discourse* itself. Fresh supplies of ammunition also appear to have been obtained about this time: on 3 June parliament ordered 50 barrels of powder, with match and bullets, to Lancashire via Hull.[12]

Parliament had unquestionably gained the upper hand, but there were still pockets of royalists under arms. Lathom, doubtless acknowledged as a hard nut to crack, could be left for the time being. As so often, however, Lonsdale was going its own way and required more immediate attention. Thurland and Hornby castles were now garrisoned for the king, and, as the pamphlet *Certaine Informations* remarked, also gave refuge to many 'disaffected ladies and gentlewomen' who had fled there from elsewhere. Also the royalist

THE EAST VIEW OF HORNBY CASTLE, NEAR LANCASTER.

THIS Castle is beautifully situated on a Hill, round the foot of which runs the river Wenning. It was founded by Nicholas de Mont-on and after belonged to the Noble Families of the Harringtons & Stanleys Barons de Mont Aquila or Monteagle, descended from mas Stanley Earl of Derby: William Stanley the third & last Baron of Monteagle of that Name, left only a Daughter named abeth, who married Edn.d Parker Lord Morley, and had a Son William, who was restored by K James 1.st to the Barony of Monteagle.

N.B. delin S. B. Sculp. 1727

Hornby Castle. Parts of the surviving fabric dates from the medieval castle, but most of what we see here is sixteenth-century in date, and not built primarily for defensive purposes, although the site above the river Wenning is a good one.

forces of Westmorland had taken advantage of the struggle focused on south Lancashire to intervene. Having marched across the county boundary, they had now sat down before Lancaster, bringing war and siege back to the town for the third time in four months. To make matters worse, Sir John Girlington's men who held Hornby were now foraging round about, bringing what parliamentarian Colonel Alexander Rigby called 'robbery and murder' to this part of the county.

In the event Lancaster would be easily relieved by Colonel Ashton. On hearing of his advance the Westmorland troops promptly decamped, having 'begirt' the castle for twenty days without bringing about its capitulation. From Lancaster Ashton marched three companies on in the direction of Hornby castle, which stands on a hill overlooking the crossing of the river Wenning about nine miles north-east of Lancaster. The great central tower, its main feature, had been mainly erected in the sixteenth century, but on an earlier base. This edifice was certainly impressive, but not of the latest design. According to parliamentarian sources the enemy, apprised of their coming, attempted a close range 'ambuscado' or ambush from outside the castle grounds. Despite a volley from a range of 'half musket shot', Ashton's troops were not to be discouraged and it is claimed that his scouts managed to secure a prisoner 'that had escaped out of the castle, who gave us true information of the state of things'.

To all intents and purposes Hornby appeared secure on its mound, apparently impregnable from all directions except via the main gate, and it was here that the garrison had focused their main defensive efforts. Taking into account their intelligence windfall, Ashton's 'venturous' troops now hatched an imaginative plan to take the castle. While a diversion was made at the main entrance, the real attempt to enter would be made on the other side, scaling a wall and coming in through the large and relatively vulnerable glass windows. The troops would be guided by the man that had previously escaped from the castle. As *Lancashire's Valley of Achor* explained,

> The Companies drawn out for this Designe, accommodated with scaling ladders, great Hammers, Ropes, Mattocks, and some combustible matter for the Gates, were appointed to play upon that side towards the Gates, to draw them to that side, where the rest were to force their entrance. The fore Forces played upon the Castle and Church not without great danger of Iron and Stones, till they put fire to the Gates which smoaked them further off: The back forces were as busie at the Window, scaling and hammering; Which undaunted resolution to enter by the Gates and Window, speeded the cry of the Enemy for Quarter, which was speedily granted, the Gates opened and the Castle entered. In this assault, for two hours space, we lost but two Common soldiers, a third dangerously wounded, some other hurt with stones but not mortally.

The author of the *Discourse* confirmed much of this detail, remarking that he himself later examined the windows through which Ashton's men had climbed, marvelling that 'it was a great adventure the windows being very high from the ground'. On 6 July 1643 parliament issued an order that Hornby was to be demolished. To what extent this was carried out is unclear, but from what now remains it appears that the tower survived, with much rebuilding of other parts in the intervening centuries.[13]

Given the fate of Hornby castle, the garrison of Thurland, less than five miles away, seem to have promised to render or demilitarise their little fourteenth-century fortress at some date in the near future. This undertaking was apparently given the very day after Hornby fell, but the soldiers holding

Thurland, being what one puritan commentator called 'heretics' – actually Catholics – were not to be trusted. Thurland had been in the Girlington family since 1605, and Sir John was not going to give up his seat without a struggle. Within a few weeks it must have been clear that Thurland – far from being given up or disarmed – remained a defiant stronghold. As the *Discourse* put it, 'Sir John, his wife and many disperat cavaliers' had 'strongly fortified it' with 'provision out of the country as alsoe ammunition'.[14]

By the beginning of August Alexander Rigby had gathered the strength with which to force Thurland, and he was on the march to what he called this 'out angle of our county'. Though the sources are slender, there is sufficient evidence to suggest that this new parliamentarian expedition was stronger than the three companies brought by Colonel Ashton to Hornby a month earlier. The *Discourse* mentions 'forces' from Salford and Blackburn hundreds, and 'companies newly raised from Preston', which is suggestive of at least four companies, and probably many more. They also had more than 200 cavalry. More important perhaps were 'some pieces of ordnance' also mentioned, as these would have had the potential to create a breech in medieval stonework.

Rigby's method may not have been the swiftest, but it was textbook and methodical, beginning by surrounding the site with his infantry at a distance from the castle. Rigby himself took up residence in Hornby castle, while Captain Edward Robinson, and presumably others, found a billet at Tunstall just a few hundred yards to the north-west of Thurland. The parliamentarian army now appear to have dug one or more redoubts, and positioned their battery so as to begin the pounding,

> The maine bodie of his foote or his mayne guard was at the house of Mr Cansfield about half a mile from the Castle. It was moited [moated or entrenched] about so that it could not be come to. He planted his Ordnance on the East side of the Castle in a very fair plot betwixt Cansfield and it. They plaied oft against it with little execution. It was stronge.

Moreover the garrison showed spirit and no sign of surrender, shooting back desperately whenever they 'spyed occation', causing many casualties. One fatality was Captain Edward Breres of the 'volunteers of Preston', shot dead when he came too close to the walls. Worry was also created by the fact that the parliamentarians were under observation by royalist forces from Westmorland, the border with which was only about four miles off to the north. It was dubious whether Rigby was going to be left to his own devices, and indeed whether Thurland could be reduced under these circumstances.

Not long afterwards the besiegers received the disquieting news that a relief force was on its way, marching out of Cumberland under the command of royalist Colonel Huddleston of Millom. He was reported to be accompanied by all the 'malignant gentry' of Westmorland and Cumberland, plus two Lancashire gentlemen, Roger Kirkby, and Colonel Rigby's namesake, Alexander Rigby 'of Burghe'. Rather than be caught from behind while attention was riveted on the castle, Rigby gave orders for the majority of his men to abandon the leaguer, leaving just a skeleton force sufficient to prevent those in the castle from coming out to create mischief. His main body now formed up for the march into Furness, the plan being to intercept Huddleston on his way – perhaps taking him by surprise. In the event the two forces made contact at Lindale, about three miles from Cartmel, on Sunday, 1 October 1643.

Colonel Rigby's letter to parliament takes up the story:

> ... to this end they drew together part of Cumberland forces into Fournes [Furness], and with them the strength of that place, to the number of about 1600, intending the next day to March into Cartmell towards us, and then to add to their forces, and in their way they tooke and imprisoned divers of the best affected, and caused the rest of them to fly out of the Country, who posting to us, I forthwith took 500 foot, 2 Drakes, and 3 small Troopes of Horse, parcel [part] of my forces at Thurland, and with them in one day I marched almost 30 miles, over mountains, and thro Sea sands and waters, within two miles of the Enemy, and the next morning, being the Lords day, we found the enemy in the Field, standing with a body of Horse and another of foot in a posture to receive us, upon ground chosen for their own advantage: and when we were within a half mile of them, we committed ourselves to Gods protection, and began our worke with publike prayers for his blessing upon us: and those done, we speeded up to the Enemy with such Resolution and Courage in all the Captaines and Common Souldiers, as by their deportment I might have rather deemed that they had made hast to have saluted their friends than to have encountered their enemies.

So the parliamentarians charged – their identifying cry of the day being, fittingly enough, 'God with us', that of the royalists, 'In with Queen Mary'.[15]

Rigby claims that even before his men clashed with the royalists, the enemy's hearts were so struck 'with terrour' their horse shied back. Then 'our foot gave a shout, our Horse pursued, theirs fled; their foot dispersed and fled; they all trusted more to their feet then their hands'. The rout was unstoppable, and within quarter of an hour the parliamentarian horse were riding down the fugitives, some of whom were killed, others driven into the waters of Morecambe Bay. The list of prisoners was impressive, including not only Colonel Huddleston but two captains, an ensign, and about 400 soldiers. Also taken were six foot colours and one horse colour, plus the royalist magazine wagons drawn by eight oxen, some horses and a large store of arms. The *Discourse* is rather less triumphalist in its description, but does make explicit mention of the capture of 'four or five Ensignes or cullers of brave silk'. So ended the 'battle' now commonly known as Lindale Close.

Broxap has suggested that Lindale Close proves that Colonel Rigby was a man of 'considerable military skill'. Yet his prowess cannot be judged objectively merely on the strength of Rigby's own letter. There is another description, less flattering to Rigby, and probably unseen by Broxap. Its almost comic opera content contains the strong suggestion that, although the royalist force at Lindale was reasonably numerous, precious few were trained soldiers or properly armed. This account, by one Thomas Park, is worth quoting at length because it adds further detail, as well as serving to balance Rigby's own opinion of himself:

Colonel Rigby, continuing his siege of Thurland Castle ... was let know, that Mr Kirkby, Mr Rigby, and Colonel Huddleston, were in commotion in Furness, and that they had gotton together 1500 horse and foot many of them out of Cumberland, young Mr Pennington being there with a company, and the rest of Furness; they were about 200 fire men, and the rest club men and they kept their rendezvous at Dalton. Whereupon Colonel Rigby, at the earnest desire of divers of Furness who fled thither, marched with seven or eight companies of foot, and three troops of horse, all firemen, except about 20, who had pikes: they were all complete and stout fellows. I being a prisoner at Hornby Castle at that time, and three weeks before, was appointed to go with the Colonel: and the last of September they came to Ulverston, and rested that first night; and early the 1st of October, 1643, being Sunday they set forward and had prayers on Swartmoor; which being ended, they marched forward till they came in Lyndal; and there the foot halted; but the horse went on to Lyndal cotte, and drew up in a valley facing, and shouting at Huddleston's horse, who were drawn up on the top of Lyndal close, who did shout also in return; which lasted about an hour, while the foot were receiving powder and shot, and match; which being ended, the foot marched up to the horse: when the king's horse fled; whereupon they raised a great shout, and did pursue them very hotly.

Park claims that the royalist fatalities were a mere handful: their enemies none at all. The rout was followed by the jubilant parliamentarian 'common soldiers' plundering Dalton. At Cartmel one of the portals of the priory is still traditionally known as 'Cromwell's door'. The old wooden door may indeed have been shot at by parliamentarian troops, but as is so often the case with Civil War folklore there is no evidence whatever that Oliver Cromwell was actually ever present in person.[16]

Whether or not Lindale was a victory of any importance, the *Discourse* confirms Rigby's return to Preston 'in triumph'. Most of the parliamentarian troops were ordered back to Thurland, the defenders of which now realised that their chances of relief had shrunk to near zero. Two days later Sir Philip Musgrave, the royalist commander in Westmorland and Cumberland, negotiated the surrender of the castle. Sir John Girlington and his lady were lucky to be allowed to depart for Yorkshire. Within the next few weeks Rigby had Thurland 'demolished'. Whether parts of it were burned as well is unclear: Rigby certainly had problems with his 'common soldiers', who wanted to set light to the remaining 'combustible materials'. Huddleston was sent down to parliament in London in the charge of Robert Fogg, for disposal at their pleasure.

The *House of Commons Journal* makes it clear that Huddleston was in London in the keeping of parliament a few months later. Having considered the matter they ordered that since he had been taken in 'actual arms against the Parliament' he be 'kept in strict custody' in the Tower, 'till this house give further order'. The destruction of Thurland castle was approved retrospectively, and Rigby was thanked for his actions. The 'diligent' Mr Fogg was given £100, plus expenses, or rather, was entitled to take such a sum out of the 'rents and profits' of Huddleston's estates. As was so often the case parliament's rewards, if they came at all, they came at someone else's expense.[17]

Autumn and winter 1643:
parliamentarian adventures outside the county

With victory in north Lancashire Colonel Rigby was in a position to consolidate his hold on Leyland and Amounderness hundreds. The *Discourse* suggests that a restructuring of the forces drawn from these areas now allowed him to put such captains in place as 'he did especiallye confide in'. Doubtless it also gave opportunity to screen out any local men from the ranks whose natural sympathies had lain with the king. What he managed to achieve is an interesting reflection on local allegiances, as well as perhaps population and willingness to fight.

The majority of the parliamentarian forces of Amounderness were infantry. For the Preston area a 'Mr Clayton', an 'Antient Gentleman dwelling about Fulwood More' was made captain, with the 'freeholders of the hundred under his conduction'. Kirkham was split into two companies for recruiting, with Captain Richard Wilding of Kirkham taking one half and Captain William Pateson of Ribby the other. Poulton and Bispham were to furnish a total of four companies, the captains being Robert Jollie of Warbreck, William Hull of Bispham, Richard Davis of Newton and Rowland Amon of Thornton. Captain Bare took an area north of the river Wyre. Stalmine, Hambleton and the 'townes ajacent' managed a further two companies under Richard Smith and George Carter of Hambleton. Garstang likewise was to have two companies, led by Captains Fyfe and White, and a further Woodplumpton company was under Captain Duddell. The St Michaels' company was to be led by William Swarbrick. Colonel Rigby's own company was raised in Goosnargh, his son filling the position of lieutenant colonel. In Lytham parish the recruiting effort was poor, for though George Sharples was appointed captain only a few would 'raise with or follow him'. A few months later a troop of horse was raised under Captain Thomas Whittingham of Whittingham, and there is reason to suppose that some others also received horses in the winter of 1643.

What is fascinating about this apparently bland list is that had Amounderness managed to recruit to its full strength in the autumn of 1643 this former royalist area would have expected to support the better part of 2,000 men under arms – a sizeable percentage of the adult male population. As it was, reluctance to join the colours and perhaps failure to persuade men to change sides, left significant holes in the plan. Lytham was obviously obstructive, but it is noticeable that Preston, easily the largest town in the area, appears only to have been called upon to produce a single company. The central and northern part of the Fylde, by contrast, seems to have been able to raise at least several hundred men, with Kirkham, Poulton, Bispham and Garstang being surprisingly significant contributors. The picture given of Leyland hundred by the *Discourse* is far less complete, but mention is made of two further companies under Captains Henley and Walton. Money for arms, drums and colours came from the sequestered estates of local Catholics.

Lancashire recruiting efforts also received a welcome fillip in the shape of a new ordinance passed by the London parliament on 27 October. This allowed the county deputy lieutenants, or the committee, 'to raise, levy or imprest' such 'soldiers, chirurgeons, and gunners' as they needed to make up the numbers required by parliament. In short, formally sanctioned conscription had arrived in the county. The force now established was 'three thousand soldiers', with as many gunners, surgeons and trumpeters as the committee thought fit. Together with this requirement came the power 'to do everything, for the providing of monies, and all manner of necessaries, for the accommodation and support of the forces raised, or to be raised, within the said County'.

Most of the newly raised troops were 'called to Preston and there a whole week together exercised and trained having provision out of the towns where they were raised, saving beeffe, and to furnish them there with, the Commissaries brought of the sequestered Cattell of Papists who were there killed and dressed for them.' Many of the men from Amounderness and Leyland would find themselves on the Yorkshire border that winter, providing a guard lest the Yorkshire royalists should take it into their heads to invade the county from the east. As the *Discourse* explained,

> There was a strong Guard kepte by the Lancashire forces at a paseage into both Counties at a place called Blakston Edge, for that Winter the Cavaliers possest much of this side of Yorkshire, as Leeds, Halifax, Wakefield, Bradford and other places all up to York.

Certaine Informations states that some 1,200 men were garrisoned in Rochdale, and a further 800 at Blackstone even before the summer was out. Just before Christmas another body, including Captain Pateson and 'some of his souldiers', marched down to Liverpool via Wigan and Prescott, where it was feared that royalist ships sailing around the coast had designs on the town. In the event this proved a false alarm since only one vessel actually entered the harbour, and this for the purpose of rendering itself to parliament.[18]

Late in 1643 parliament had such a hold on Liverpool, a town of decidedly mixed sympathies, that the bailiffs were able to tour the streets in the company of the sergeant rounding up supposed enemies. As an order of 21 December in the Town Book explained,

> Wheras it apeares That divers Papists and other ill affected persons or Malignants and such as have borne Armes against the Parliament or theire wives and Children are as yet inhabittinge and remain within this

Town of Liverpoole, who are suspected to give Intelligence, and doe other ill offices there it is ordered … That all such Papistes and Malignantes, except such as are Prysoners as also theire wives Children and families, shall within fourteen days after notice hereof depart and remove out of the said Towne, upon payne to be plundered and deprived off all their goods and personall Estate whatsoever.

The fortunes of the Lancashire parliamentarians had so generally improved by October 1643 that, in addition to defending the frontiers, forces could now be sent beyond the county boundary in support of the cause in adjoining areas. This was very fortunate for the parliamentarian cause. It was extremely bad luck, or at least bad timing, from the royalist perspective, for at long last the Marquis of Ormonde, commander in chief of the king's forces in Ireland had agreed a ceasefire or 'cessation' with the rebels, and the king had high hopes for the intervention of Irish troops in England. With Lancashire virtually secure, and following Sir Thomas Fairfax's victory at Selby in Yorkshire, parliament would have the resources at hand with which to parry this new threat. Interestingly, the Earl of Clarendon considered that the principal purpose of the import of troops from Ireland was not to regain the north, but to go to Oxford in the spring of 1644 where they would become a key part of the king's main field army. Nevertheless, the king gave Lord Byron 'leave to employ them upon landing'.

So it was that about 4,000 'Irish' troops were shipped across to Flintshire. The parliamentarian garrison at Hawarden surrendered not long afterwards, and Sir William Brereton, the parliamentarian leader in Cheshire, had little option but to fall back. With Lord Byron (a Nottinghamshire royalist magnate of Lancashire descent) appearing from the south with 1,000 cavalry from Oxford, and Ashton's Lancashire militia on the march to Brereton's aid, the scene was set for a significant confrontation. Perhaps surprisingly, at least a proportion of the royalist troops here were also Lancastrians, being, according to one authority at least, parcelled out to bolster the Anglo-Irish foot regiments of Major General Ernle, and Colonels Gibson, Robert Byron, Warren and Hunckes.[19]

In late December 1643 Brereton and his Lancashire allies attempted to relieve Nantwich from the north, but on Christmas Day the royalists managed to concentrate perhaps as many as 4,000 troops against Brereton. The result was a fierce Boxing Day action in and around Middlewich. Here the parliamentarian forces are thought to have lost about 500 men, and became so scattered that they had to desist from their relief attempt. As the

Perfect Diurnall reported, the royalists had responded to good intelligence, and managed to surprise the parliamentarian troops, putting them to rout. Lord Byron, the 'bloody Braggadocio', was now determined to seize Nantwich before the enemy could intervene again, and duly attempted to storm the town at dawn on 18 January 1644. The royalist infantry used scaling ladders and hurled themselves against the sconces at the ends of the streets, eventually gaining a foothold in the town. Yet the defenders of Nantwich were made of stern stuff, and managed a counter-attack which ejected Byron's tired men. Many royalists were killed, some hundreds of their bodies decorating the works at Wall Lane, Welsh Row, Beam Street, Hospital and Pillory Streets.

On 21 January a new parliamentarian force left Manchester under Sir Thomas Fairfax, strong in cavalry, and partly composed of troops that he had brought with him from the Lincolnshire area. By 24 January this fresh relief effort had reached Delamere where they swept aside the relatively few royalist troops there to oppose them. The next day they were near Nantwich. Here they found Byron ill prepared. He had been reluctant to abandon his siege, and now bad weather had swollen the river Weaver and damaged the wooden bridge at Beambridge, which facilitated communications between the various parts of his army. Fairfax now moved rapidly on towards Nantwich in the hope of joining forces with the garrison before the enemy could react, but Byron launched a spirited attack, catching the parliamentarians in the flank and rear to the north-west of the town.

The Lancashire regiments of John Booth and Colonel Richard Holland turned to face the enemy, and were hotly engaged by Robert Byron's regiment. The result of the battle appeared uncertain until John Lambert's cavalry waded in and the defenders of Nantwich, alerted by the sound of gunfire, sallied out to join the fray. Whereas the parliamentarians had been in danger of being enveloped an hour earlier, now the royalists found they were being assailed in the flanks and rear. Following a sharp fight Byron's men attempted to break off the action, some of them fighting their way back to Acton church. The dead of the battle have been reckoned as being as few as 300; but 1,500 royalists including many senior officers had been captured. Among those taken were also some of the Irish auxiliaries and '120 women, many of whom had long knives'. Doubtless the riposte issued to the Irish was of particular satisfaction to the Lancashire parliamentarians. In any case the victory was decisive, and, like Lancashire, Cheshire was now fundamentally a county under the control of parliament. The Earl of Newcastle reluctantly concluded that the king would have to allow both counties to 'lye fallow for a while', while royalist efforts were concentrated on the North East.[20]

It has been suggested elsewhere that parliament's failure to deal with Lathom in late 1643, and the first weeks of 1644, was effectively a 'local demilitarisation pact'. However, as we have seen, the Lancashire parliamentarians actually had far more important things to do during this period; and Lathom was surprisingly secure within its fortifications. The Lancashire royalists lacked the strength to be any more than a local nuisance. With the New Year the situation would change, and for the royalists things looked increasingly bleak.[21]

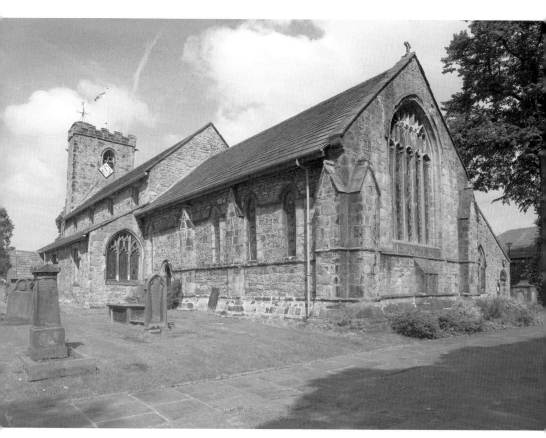

St Mary and All Saints parish church, Whalley. Lord Derby's troops occupied both Whalley Abbey and the church on their retreat from Read Bridge, but in spite of further fighting failed to stem the enemy advance. Read Bridge was the most important engagement in Lancashire's own civil war.

PHOTOGRAPH: CARNEGIE, 2009

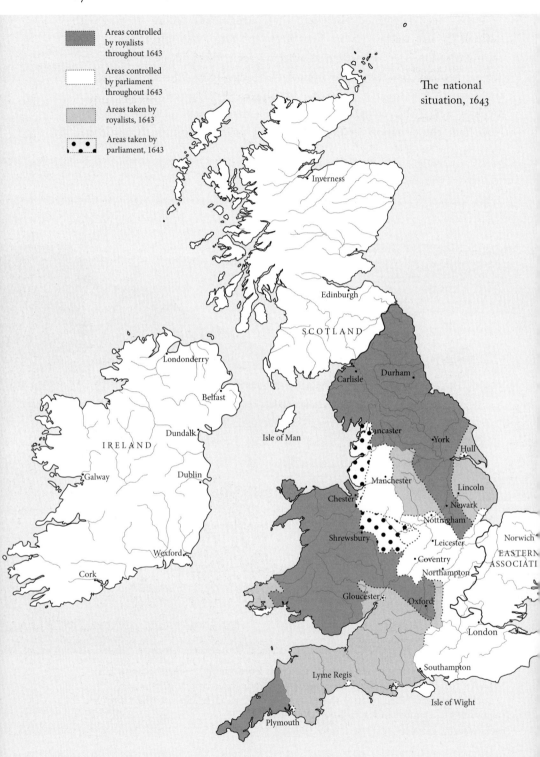

Areas controlled
by royalists
throughout 1643

Areas controlled
by parliament
throughout 1643

Areas taken by
royalists, 1643

Areas taken by
parliament, 1643

The national
situation, 1643

Inverness

Edinburgh

SCOTLAND

Londonderry

Belfast

Dundalk

Isle of Man

Carlisle   Durham

Lancaster   York
                              Hull

IRELAND   Manchester   Lincoln

Galway   Chester   Newark

Dublin   Nottingham

Shrewsbury   Leicester   Norwich
                                            EASTERN
                    Coventry   ASSOCIATI

Wexford   Northampton

Cork   Gloucester   Oxford

                                        London

                              Southampton

                    Lyme Regis

                              Isle of Wight

        Plymouth

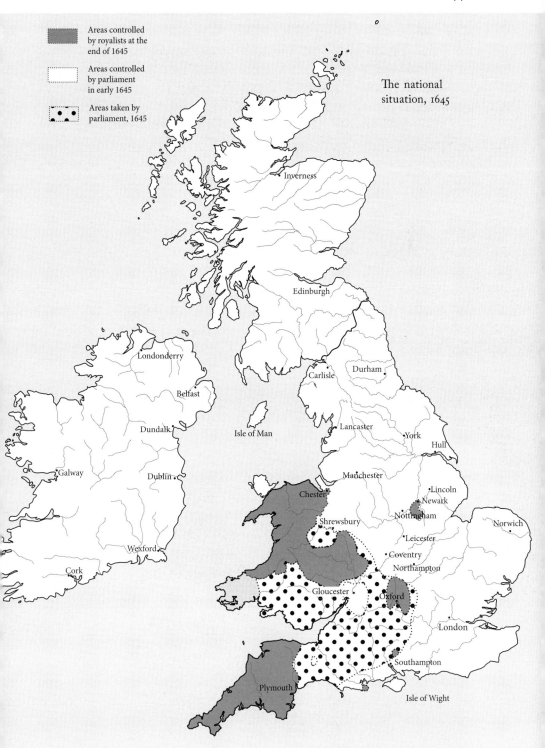

Areas controlled
by royalists at the
end of 1645

Areas controlled
by parliament
in early 1645

Areas taken by
parliament, 1645

The national
situation, 1645

Inverness

Edinburgh

Londonderry

Belfast

Dundalk

Galway

Dublin

Wexford

Cork

Carlisle

Durham

Isle of Man

Lancaster

York

Hull

Manchester

Chester

Lincoln

Newark

Shrewsbury

Nottingham

Norwich

Leicester

Coventry

Northampton

Gloucester

Oxford

London

Southampton

Plymouth

Isle of Wight

Charlo
de la T
de Tho
James
Strang
7th Earl
-ted fo
Lathor
to surr
B. 15

CHAPTER SIX

'Stealing the earl's breeches': the first siege of Lathom House, 1644

B Y EARLY 1644 it must have appeared that the war in Lancashire was all but won for parliament. Nationally there were also signs that the war might be turning decisively: on 19 January, for example, the first of the Scottish regiments, joined with the king's enemies under the Solemn League and Covenant, crossed the river Tweed and marched into England. As we have seen, a significant threat was lifted, just a week later, when the first of the king's Irish contingents came to grief at Nantwich. In February parliament showed its increasing determination by replacing its unwieldy Committee of Safety by bringing together twenty-one Englishmen and four Scots in a new Committee of Both Kingdoms, designed to direct the war in a much more nimble manner. This move attracted jibes that power had now moved conclusively from the legislature to the executive, and that all that was now lacking was 'a dictator'.

Locally Lancashire royalist resistance was reduced to pockets, and of these only two, Lathom House and Greenhalgh castle near Garstang appeared to offer substantial problems. Around Lathom there were still intermittent incidents, as the royalist defenders came out to forage, or parliamentarian patrols attempted to contain them. One such, reported in early February, saw the garrison skirmish with Captain Hindley's troop of parliamentarian horse. The royalists claimed the capture of a number of the enemy, including the

left   Charlotte de la Tremouille, Countess of Derby (1599–1664). The French-born wife of the seventh earl is probably the best-remembered character of the civil wars in Lancashire. Her fame rests primarily upon her sterling defence of her family home during the first siege of Lathom.

NATIONAL PORTRAIT GALLERY

wounded Lieutenant Dandy. Specific individuals suffered particularly badly from the royalist depredations. As parliamentarian sympathisers the houses and herds of Richard Smithson and Henry Simkin were natural targets. Edward Rigby of Orrell appears to have been one of the biggest losers, with £200 worth of goods spirited away: among his losses were cattle and horses, brassware, and bedding.

On Saturday 24 February 1644 the committee at Manchester finally decided to grasp the nettle and deal with this annoying threat to Lancashire's future peace. Colonels Ashton, Rigby, and Moore would advance on this 'nest of brigands' forthwith. In overall command would be Sir Thomas Fairfax, victor of Nantwich, and rising star of parliament's forces in the national arena. According to the *Briefe Journall of the Siege*, the main surviving account, Lady Derby received 'some broken intelligence' of this resolution as early as the following morning.[1] This came from a 'secret friend' who was familiar with the enemy intentions, and advanced warning proved invaluable, giving her a few days to use 'all diligence and care to furnish her house with provision and men'. One lurid account adds the dramatic detail of a woman who crept repeatedly through the enemy lines with reports, but who was finally caught and tortured for her pains. These were perhaps the first signs that, in Lady Derby, the parliamentarians faced a thoughtful and determined opponent.

Charlotte de la Tremoille, now Countess of Derby, was born at the Château of Thouars, in the department of Deux Sevres, France, in 1599. Her pedigree was considerable, her father being Claude de Tremoille, Duc de Thouars, and her mother Lady Charlotte Brabantine, a daughter of William the Silent. As her biographer observed, she was not a fit child, as 'her mind was stronger than her body'. It was in 1626 that she married James Stanley, Lord Strange, thus creating a highly suitable dynastic match with a family similar in social standing to her own. She was five years older than her husband, and no great beauty, and it would have been reasonable to question whether this was simply a marriage of convenience, were it not for the evidence of her letters. These speak of the 'utmost affection' of James, and the 'happiness and peace of mind' enjoyed by the couple from the outset. She 'thanked God' that her mother had taken such care for having married her 'so happily'. Charlotte was also well received by the elderly Lord Derby, who addressed her in French calling her 'lady and mistress of the house, a position that he said he wished no other woman to hold'.

Charlotte will for ever be associated with events at Lathom, but it was not her only home, and periods were spent at Knowsley, on the Isle of Man and in London. For a time after the marriage, for example, she had appeared at court as lady of honour to the queen. She had nine children, of which two, her daughters Mary and Catherine, were present during the siege. Her eldest son, Charles, was named after the king; another of her daughters was named Henrietta Maria, after the queen. Any difficulties in the relationship with her husband came down to money, and to Lady Derby's background. A substantial marriage settlement, and continued support, were expected from the family in France, but whether this was ever paid in full is unclear. Certainly payments were late, and a cause of some anxiety. During 1627, for example, she received only £1,200 from France – a handsome sum to most at that time, but grossly inadequate as a contribution to the leading noble family of Lancashire. At least some of the money that did come was reinvested in land and local assets, as for example the rectory of Ormskirk. In return Charlotte received an income of her own from lands in Lancashire, Yorkshire and Cheshire.[2]

As to Lady Derby's background, her correspondence makes clear that there were quite a few Lancastrians who did 'not love foreigners', a negative feeling which was doubtless enhanced by war with France soon after her marriage. Nevertheless, this antipathy could have been far worse, for at least Charlotte was a Protestant. In her early forties at the time of the siege, she was described as 'a well built, almost fleshy woman, having large eyes, heavy eyebrows and a prominent nose ... at once haughty and humble. She was pious, and would, out of pride, stubbornly hold to a cause she regarded as her duty ... and would look with contempt upon anyone who offended her code.'[3]

Lady Derby's defence of her home came in part also from the quality of those who shared the task with her. Not all were from the immediate locality, although it would appear that the majority were Lancashire men. William Farington of Worden Hall, usually described as Lady Derby's 'chief advisor', was a notable county royalist who had served as sheriff and commissioner of the array. Over the last two years he had campaigned extensively for the king in the area, including the siege of Manchester and the storming of Preston. The chaplain was the Reverend Samuel Rutter, later Bishop Rutter, originally of Burscough. The Stanley family had sponsored him to Westminster School and Oxford, and now he repaid the debt by standing by Lady Derby in her hour of need. The 'Major of the House' and effective military commander under Lady Derby's titular direction, was Captain William Farmer, a 'faithfull and gallant souldier', a seasoned Scottish professional who had fought in the Thirty Years War in Europe.

The other captains present were Henry Ogle of Whiston; Edward Chisnall of Chorley; Edward Rawstorne of New Hall, Preston; Molyneux-Ratcliffe of Ordsall; Richard Foxe of Prestwich, and Captain Charnock of Charnock.

Though Captain Charnock appears in Seacome's narrative of the siege, and not the *Briefe Journall*, he is memorialised in a contemporary painting, which still hangs in the family home at Astley Hall, Chorley. This unflattering image, with balding hair and damaged eye, gives rise to his popular local nickname 'one eyed Charnock'. Traditionally the injured eye is attributed to a wound in the civil war. Despite having Astley Hall, the Charnocks were by no means wealthy gentry, having sold much of their other property, and being in considerable debt by 1642.

Half a dozen lieutenants completed the list of royalist officers at Lathom House. Three of these, Worral, Heape and Kay were from the Bury area. Lieutenant Penketh came from Penketh near Warrington; Lieutenant Walton from Wigan, and Lieutenant Brethergh from Childwall near Liverpool. The young Edward Halsall was also present, though it is not clear whether he held any particular military rank. As Lady Charlotte's steward Mr Broome supervised the domestic staff, who also provided a useful pool of labour during the siege. The ordinary soldiers numbered about 300, and there is mention of

Lieutenant, later Captain, Kay, one of the royalist defenders of Lathom under the Countess of Derby.

Nothing above ground survives of the civil war Lathom House. This photograph, in May 2009, shows the shows the refurbished west wing of the eighteenth-century house.
PHOTOGRAPH: CARNEGIE, 2009

a dozen cavalry. Particularly valuable were some 'selected marksmen' who took turns to keep watch from the towers and battlements: as we shall see at least some of these were armed with rifles. Rifles were rare at this period; they were expensive and slow to load, but the ideal weapon for a sniper defending from the cover of solid masonry. With rifles the marksmen had the advantages of both range and accuracy over any attackers, and height made it possible to overlook enemy works. Having fired a shot the sniper would be able to duck down under the battlements to reload at leisure.

For a fairly small garrison there was a good supply of artillery. According to the *Briefe Journall* there were six 'sakers', two 'sling pieces', plus one or two 'murderers' in each tower of the house. The 'saker' was a field gun firing a ball of about five pounds in weight, with a range of about 400 yards even without elevating the barrel of the piece; 'slings' were much smaller. 'Murderers' were short-barrelled, rather old-fashioned pieces, but well designed to fire multiple shot at point-blank range. They were thus ideal to sweep confined spaces such as courtyards, or to clear the ditches around towers and other defences. It is therefore likely that the house had over twenty pieces of artillery in total, of

Artist's impression of Lathom House in an engraving from Draper's *House of Stanley*, 1864. No contemporary image of this substantial fortified house appears to survive, so much of what we now know is based upon written and archaeological sources.

which six were capable of causing serious damage to the enemy at a considerable distance from the walls. Powder supplies were apparently adequate for the task in hand – but finite, and had to be used sparingly, the author of the *Briefe Journall* stating that want of powder was 'our greatest fear'.[4]

Early in the siege, before the attackers had dug and manned their full encirclement, it even proved possible to bring some communications in form the outside. Lord Derby himself related, how,

> When Latham was besieged in the year 1644, my wife, some children, and good friends in it, I did write letters to them in ciphers as much in as little compass as I could. I rolled the same in lead, sometimes in wax, hardly as big as a musket bullet, that if the bearer suspected danger of discovery he might swallow it, and physic would soon find it again. I have writ in fine linen, with a small pen, which hath been sewed to the bearer's clothes, as part of the linings. I have put a letter in a green wound, in a stick, pen, &c.

The location and layout of Lathom House

No standing vestige survives today of the civil war Lathom House. The layout and even the precise location of the house have, in fact, long been subjects of debate and controversy, and there is relatively little by way of contemporary description. The house is thought to have been built, or substantially enlarged, around 1496. At its heart was the Eagle Tower, and its other towers and outer walls were arranged around at least two courtyards. Weber's poem *Flodden Field*, written in the mid-sixteenth century, contains the following lines spoken through the character of the second earl,

> Farewell, Lathom, that bright bower,
> Nine towers thou bearest on high,
> And other nine thou bearest in the utter walls,
> Within thee may be lodged kings three.

The picture is therefore of a substantial building, fit for a king, or kings, which had nine major towers, and surrounding walls in which were a further nine turrets.[5]

Brief as this is, there is some agreement with a much fuller description provided in Seacome's *House of Stanley*, which apparently draws upon the manuscript by Bishop Rutter. Assuming that the bishop's words have been transcribed correctly this should be a reliable account, as Rutter himself was an eyewitness. As the most substantial picture this is worth quoting at length,

> Lathom House stands upon a flat, upon a moorish, springy, and spumous ground and was encompassed with a strong wall of two yards thick; upon the walls were nine towers, flanking each other, and in every tower there were six pieces of ordnance, that played three one way, and three the other: without the wall was a moat eight yards wide, and two yards deep; upon the back of the moat between the wall and the graff, was a strong row of pallisades around. Besides all these, there was a high strong tower, called the Eagle Tower, in the midst of the house, surmounting all the rest; and the gate house had also two high and strong buildings, with a strong tower on each side of it; and in the entrance to the first court, upon the top of these towers, were placed the best and choicest marksmen, who usually attended the earl in his hunting and other sports, as huntsmen, keepers, fowlers, and the like; who constantly kept watch, with screwed guns and long fowling pieces, upon those towers to the great annoyance and loss

In Manchester Cathedral are several sixteenth-century wood carvings which relate to the Derby family, including an end panel of a choir stall which represents the Eagle and Child story. This is one of two miserichords which are thought to show Lathom House, with a central polygonal tower, a curtain wall with towers and a pedimented gatehouse.

of the enemy, especially of their commanders, who were frequently killed in their trenches, or as they came or went from them. Besides all that has hitherto been said of the walls, towers, moat, &c., there is something so particular and romantic in the general situation of this house, as if nature herself had formed it for a strong hold, or place of security; for before the house, to the south and south west is a rising ground so near it, as to overlook the top of it, from which it falls so quick, that nothing planted against it on those sides can touch it further than the front wall; and on the north and east sides, there is another rising ground, even to the edge of the moat, and then falls away so quick, that you can scarce, at the distance of a carbine shot, see the house over that height; so that all batteries placed there, are so far below it, as to be little service against it: and, let us observe, by the way that the uncommon situation of it may be compared to the palm of a man's hand, flat in the middle, and covered with a rising round about it, and so near to it that the enemy, during the siege, were never able to raise a battery against it, so as to make a breach in the wall practicable to enter the house by way of storm.[6]

This description has been the cause of much argument over the years, and has been frequently cited as evidence to support the theory that the 'old' fortified Lathom House of the Stanleys, and the 'new' eighteenth-century Lathom house, a mansion designed by Giacomo Leoni, were actually on different sites. Within the last decade, however, modern archaeology and topographic observation have dispelled this misapprehension. Numerous investigations and excavations now firmly support the conclusion that the old and new buildings were on the same site. Perhaps most critically a dig conducted by Mark Fletcher made,

> ... the discovery of the massive rock cut ditch (and presumably moat) apparently backfilled prior to, or during the construction of the eighteenth-century great house [that] strongly suggests that the site of the medieval house is beneath, or immediately to the east of, the site of the later building.

Further work indicated that the original sectional dimensions of this ditch were 13 metres wide by over 2.5 metres deep, substantial in any terms, and fitting for a very strong defence. Its size was thus somewhat greater than the figures mentioned in the Seacome account. The course of this chasm was suggestive of an enclosure about 300 metres east to west, and somewhat less north to south, around much of the current site. Part of the enclosure's course agreed with the eighteenth-century garden ha-ha, a sensible and cost-effective reuse of the existing defensive landscape. Taking the original length, depth, and width of the ditch into account makes it obvious that there must once have been many thousands of cubic metres of spoil. Such a volume of material could well have been used to form substantial earthen banks.[7]

In addition to the West Yorkshire, Matrix, and Lancaster University Archaeology Unit digs, evidence has also been gathered by the Lathom Archaeological Society. Examination of the rubble from building works

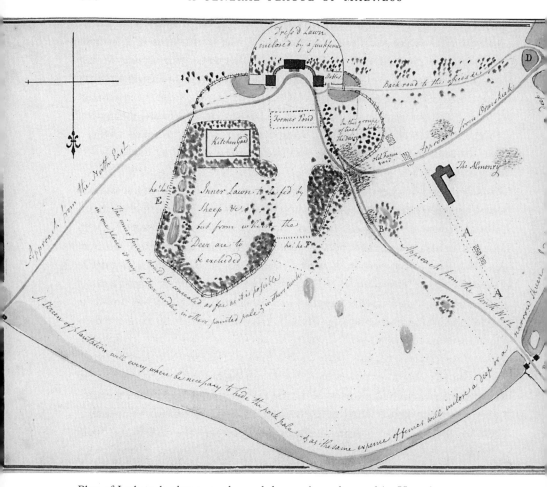

Plan of Lathom landscape garden and deer park, as designed by Humphrey
Repton *c.*1792. Recent archaeological work suggests that at least part of the massive
seventeenth-century defensive ditch followed the line of the later garden ha-ha feature.
The main body of the old Lathom house, besieged in 1644 and 1645, is believed to have
lain between the north-eastern corner of the eighteenth-century house and the kitchen
garden.

FROM REPTON'S 'RED BOOK' OF LATHOM, LANCASHIRE RECORD OFFICE

carried out from 1996 to 2004, has tended to confirm the observations made
by the Reverend Buxton as early as 1889. Much of the material used in the
construction of the later Leoni house was indeed recycled from the old seat
of the Stanleys, and included not only wooden beams but pieces of stone,
window tracery, and dressed blocks from one or more earlier structures.
Dendrochronology tests on wood samples made by the Ancient Monuments

Laboratory showed that a significant number of the timbers used in the construction of the Leoni house were felled in the fifteenth century. Moreover, having been cut after 1475, and forming a distinctive grouping chronologically, it is almost certain that they date to the work done on the medieval Lathom House by Sir Thomas Stanley about 1490. Crop-mark evidence seen in many aerial photographs from 1941 onwards may be less conclusive, but has suggested several sites for what might well be civil war besieging earthworks.

In the nineteenth century Buxton also noted the discovery of musket balls, stones inscribed with the Derby crest, and the reuse of at least one 'ancient' rubble wall within the later structure. Since then Lathom Archaeological Society members have discovered over 1,000 small shot scattered over the entire site, in every possible state of preservation; from the near perfect and unfired, to those which have been massively distorted by having been shot into hard surfaces from close range. Given all these factors, it may now reasonably be concluded that the old and new Lathom Houses occupied virtually the same site, and that the eighteenth-century builders, very sensibly, had shown little desire to move many tons of existing building materials any great distance.

The accumulation of modern archaeological evidence thus accords reasonably closely with the observation made by Sir Thomas Tennant about 1780, that, 'the ancient Lathom, the celebrated seat of nobility and hospitality, stood between the north-east offices of the present house and the kitchen garden'. It also agrees with the late nineteenth-century statement of George Lea that the new Lathom was built 'upon the site of the old'. Obviously the main structure lay within a substantial outer enclosure. However it is certainly the case that the entire area has since been extensively landscaped; interesting watercolours pertaining to proposed work on the eighteenth-century gardens having resurfaced very recently.[8]

The main problem which presents itself is how to reconcile what Rutter saw in 1644, with the evidence on, and under, the ground today. In 1910 Broxap was not convinced that this could be done at all. By 2005 the only building extant was the 'west wing' of the new house, essentially a stables and coach house. As late as the 1990s this was semi-derelict, with parts of the grounds occupied by a scrapyard. Plans to convert the remaining structure into a hostel came to nothing, and finally conversion to luxury apartments was approved, with contributions towards conservation made by English Heritage. Much of the remainder of the old footprint of the site is now covered with gardens and trees. A few hundred yards to the north-west, down across the pasture, lies the early sixteenth-century Lathom 'Chapel of St John'. In its neat grounds near to the road is the old 'Cromwell's Stone', moved here from Damsteads

The 'Cromwell stone' in the grounds of Lathom Park chapel.
PHOTOGRAPH: CARNEGIE, 2009

in 1978. Two deep hollows in its surface were traditionally said to have been used by the besiegers for casting shot – something that appears unlikely if not absolutely impossible. At first glance, and particularly close up, there is little relationship between Rutter's Lathom and what we have left in the landscape.[9]

Nevertheless, when we bear in mind that the purpose of Rutter's description was essentially a military topography and explanation of the defence, the relationship between old and the contemporary is suddenly much clearer. For example his statement 'upon a flat, upon a moorish, springy, and spumous ground' does not mean that the whole site was flat and boggy, but that the 'flat', or plateau of the house, was itself within, or upon, a larger waterlogged, or moorish, area. The surrounding land has had much drainage work done in the intervening centuries, and examination of the west wing of the new house, when in ruined state, also revealed at least one relieving arch within the masonry. Such arches were incorporated over hidden watercourses to support a building. This also agrees with a statement in the *Briefe Journall* regarding springs rising to the south-east. The Golforden, a brook mentioned in Leland, still exists despite being hidden from view for part of its course, and has been identified with the Spa Brook. In living memory parts of the nearby Plough Lane have also been flooded in bad weather. The drastic changes to the drainage patterns around the area of the former house were explained at least in part by Derbyshire Caving Club in 1998, when the investigation of a large lined culvert showed where considerable volumes of water could have been redirected.

Likewise when Rutter states that Lathom lay as if within the palm of a hand, he is being very literal – and referring to the immediate environs only. A palm is higher on one side than the other, and so it is that the site nestles behind the rise of what is now the Pilkington glass site. The old Lathom was clearly not on the crest of the hill, a point which is confirmed by the *Briefe Journall* which refers to 'higher ground' south-east of the house from which water could flow. As we see from Ordnance Survey maps, the land rises gently to the south, and the 50-metre contour skirts around what was once the approximate perimeter of the old house, with the land dropping away gradually in other directions. This can be practically demonstrated by walking along Hall Lane and along the road to Westhead village, as, from vantage points, the site appears, and then disappears according to the undulation of the land.

Around the perimeter of the house were not only the outer walls, but, as described in the *Briefe Journall*, 'a deep ditch, fenced on each bank with strong pallisades' and within the walls a lining of 'earth and sods, two yards thick, by the industry of the soldiers'. There can be little doubt but that the 'deep ditch' is that recently rediscovered by the archaeologists. Such banks and ditches would indeed have prevented observers from seeing much of the house from ground level, and made it very difficult for the besiegers' guns to have been aimed at the base of the inner walls where they could have done most damage. When it was surrounded by banked earth, with rising ground to one side, the simile of Lathom being as within the palm of a hand, appears eminently reasonable.

Desultory siege and negotiations, spring 1644

The approach of the parliamentarian besieging force in February 1644 was leisurely, even casual, suggesting the actions of an army which believed itself to be in a position of overwhelming strength. On the face of it this was so,

His Excellencie Sᵣ Thomas Fairfax Kᵗ Generall of the forces raised br the Parliament.

Printed for John Partridg. Edua Bower Pinxit   W. Marshall sculpsit

Sir Thomas Fairfax (1612–1671). Born in Yorkshire, 'Black Tom' Fairfax had gained considerable military experience even before the civil wars. Soon after the outbreak of hostilities he was appointed second-in-command to the Northern Association army under his father, Ferdinando, Lord Fairfax. He campaigned extensively in Yorkshire, Cheshire, Lincolnshire, and Lancashire, before being promoted to command parliament's New Model Army in early 1645. In 1649 he distanced himself from the execution of the king, and resigned his commission in 1650.

since between them the Lancashire colonels had succeeded in gathering over 2,000 men – a superiority of about seven or eight to one over a garrison which could have no immediate prospect of relief. Fairfax may therefore have regarded the reduction of Lathom as essentially a formality, if not a local matter, which would have had no great strategic bearing on the war. So it was that when the army arrived on 27 February they took quarters a mile or more from the house, and on the following morning Fairfax deputed a Captain Markland to go to the house with a letter offering her ladyship surrender upon honourable terms. He was given a cunningly evasive response. Lady Derby expressed surprise that, given she had personally offered parliament no offence, she should be asked to give up her home. Moreover, this was such an important decision, touching both her 'religion and life', and her loyalties to king, husband, and family, that she needed a week to consult, and then to frame her reply.

Fairfax realised immediately that these 'demures and protractions' were a play for time, and denied the countess her delay, asking instead that she should meet him at New Park, a short distance from Lathom, and here they would discuss the matter face to face. In her turn Lady Derby turned down this new suggestion, saying it would be more 'knightly' if Fairfax should wait upon her, rather than she upon him. This was agreed in general terms, but a further exchange of letters was required to work out which of the parliamentarian officers should enter the house and upon what conditions.

Finally, on 2 March, Colonels Ashton and Rigby entered Lathom to put forward a new set of terms. Whether Fairfax accompanied them, as had originally been proposed, is doubtful: although Seacome's account says that he was there, it is confirmed by no other source. Seacome also has it that the visitors were greeted with a display of military pageantry and strength, Captain Farmer seeking to make clear that taking the house by force would be an extremely expensive option. The conditions now presented were that all arms would be surrendered, but that Lady Derby and all in the house would be allowed to depart. If she so wished she could go to Knowsley or the Isle of Man, and maintain twenty musketeers for her personal protection. Fairfax would recommend to parliament that she continue to receive the revenues of her husband's estates within West Derby hundred. This compromise was rejected, mainly on the grounds that until parliament had agreed that she could keep the revenue it could be no treaty at all. The colonels departed empty handed, and, observing the Sabbath, took no further action on Sunday 3 March.

On the Monday Colonel Ashton returned to Lathom to hear a set of counter proposals offered as an alternative way out of the impasse. What the

Captain Robert Charnock (1604–53), of Astley Hall, Chorley. Charnock fought on the royalist side and was present at a number of actions including the siege of Manchester. Sometimes described as 'one eyed Charnock', he is believed to have lost his eye in the defence of Lathom.

defenders asked for was never a realistic proposition, but just about served as a basis for continued negotiation: Lady Derby should have a month during which she would prepare to leave; she would then take with her everyone from the house, its artillery, and all the small arms and go to the Isle of Man; her weapons would no longer be used against parliament, but on the other hand the enemy would quarter no soldiers at either Lathom or Knowsley; no one on her estates, her neighbours or friends were to suffer financially or otherwise. Not surprisingly Lady Derby's terms were given short shrift, but Fairfax did offer that if the garrison was stood down the next morning, and 40 parliamentarian soldiers were allowed inside, he would give her the month she needed to put her affairs in order. She could then go to the Isle of Man with everything except the artillery, which would remain behind. Lady Derby refused these terms, and negotiations were concluded. As the *Briefe Journall* put it, 'her Ladyshipp could scrue them to noe more delayes', but she was now prepared to hazard their 'utmost violence trusting in God both for protection and deliverance'.

By the next morning it was apparent that the parliamentarians had begun their siege works, digging by night to avoid observation. These works

were begun about musquett-shott from the house, in a stoopeing declining ground, that their pioneers by nature of the place might be secured from our ordnances on the towers, and soe in an orbe or ringe-worke cast up much earthe everye day by the multitude of the countrey people forced to the service.

It has reasonably been suggested that these first works were begun from a base somewhere in the Tawd valley, and that one of the main entrenchments was a significant fortification at Spa Roughs. This fits the picture on several grounds, not least its accordance with Draper's account in the *House of Stanley*. It is also in agreement with the folk traditions surrounding Cromwell's Stone when in its original location. Perhaps most importantly it makes topographical sense given lines of sight from what we now know to be the location of the house, and the likely range of the weapons involved. When in the dip of the Tawd valley the workers would have been out of sight and at a distance of almost half a mile from the defensive perimeter. They were therefore all but immune to royalist observation or fire. As their trenches crept closer greater security was required, but Spa Roughs, at a distance of several hundred yards, can still be regarded as a forward base or jumping-off point, rather than a final position.

It has been argued by some that Spa Roughs is just too far from the site of the original house to have been the location of a parliamentarian work. Nevertheless it does have much to recommend it as a base for lines of circumvallation. Such lines, made around a besieged place, and the besieging army, would have served to protect the camps of the parliamentarians against an attack from an enemy without. Given how active the defenders proved to be, and how the siege would eventually be raised by an army approaching from outside, protection from the rear was extremely necessary. There is no reason therefore that all of the parliamentarian works should be within range of the garrison, nor indeed that they should all face inward towards Lathom House.

The industrious digging went on for several days, but about 10 March six local gentlemen were allowed into the house to make a direct appeal to Lady Derby. This petition pointed out that not only did the siege put her own life at risk, but it also impoverished the whole country round about. The royalists portrayed this as a ploy by the enemy to undermine their morale – but equally some or all of the petitioners may well have been genuine. The peasantry were being forced to dig siege works and neglect their normal duties, while the well off were doubtless helping, willingly or unwillingly, with contributions of finance or provender. If this persisted for very long, poverty and hunger were the likely result. The countess heard them out with 'all curtesy' and explained what had transpired so far, but would not be swayed from her resistance. She recommended that they petition the besiegers instead, to which they had little to say but, 'God bless the king and the Earle of Derby', before making their departure.

The next day Captain Ashurst came in from the siege lines with a final offer. Lady Derby was free to leave now with anything she pleased and the entire garrison, yielding up the house. She could leave up to one hundred people behind to complete the arrangements, but these would also have to go within ten days. Any weapons taken from the house could no longer be used against parliament. Though Ashurst was 'even and civil' in his deportment, Lady Derby accounted this move a sign of weakness, and, with a speech of defiance, vowed not to buy 'peace with slavery'.

On 12 March, in the first serious act of violence, the defenders seized the initiative, an action described in detail by the *Briefe Journall*:

… the nexte day, beinge Tuesday, a hundred foote, commanded by Captain Farmor, a Scotchman, a faithfull and gallant souldier, with Lieutenant Brethergh ready to second him in any service, and some 12 horse, our whole cavalerie, com'anded by Lieutenant Key, sallied out upon the enemy: and because the sequel of every busines dependeth upon the beginning, the Captayne determined to do something that might remember the enemy that there were souldiers within. He marcht up to their workes without a shoote, and then firing on them in their trenches, they quickly left their holes, when Lieutenant Key, having wheel'd about with his horse from another gate, fell upon them in their flighte with much execuc'on; they slewe about 30 men, took 40 armes, one drum and six prisoners. The main retreate was that day made good by Captain Ogle, a gentleman industrious to returne the curtesie w'ch some of theire party shewed to him when he was taken prisoner in the battell at Edgehill.

Allowing for the fact that this is an unashamedly royalist account, and that some of the casualties were likely to have been conscripted labourers, Farmer's lightning sally using horse and foot must still have come as a considerable shock. Its main impact was to keep the enemy permanently on edge, but it was also said that the prisoners revealed that the parliamentarian plan was one of long-term starvation of the garrison, rather than of all-out assault.[10]

Little happened for the next few days, although from time to time the garrison gave their besiegers 'night alarums' to keep them on their toes. The sources are not explicit as to what form these harassments took, but given the spirit of the garrison, and the means to hand, odd sniping at any figures seen in the works by moonlight, and small patrols on darker nights are possibilities. The sudden beating of drums or the sounding of trumpets would also have served to make the besieging troops rush to arms, anxious to prevent a repeat of the previous bloody nose. On the other side of the coin the *Discourse* speaks of the parliamentarian's seizure of the windmill, and a work in the park, early in the proceedings which had previously been thorns in the besiegers' side.

With outlying pickets cleared, the parliamentarian engineer Mr Browne was now able to plan siege lines which could be 'drawne by degrees' ever closer. By completing the encirclement communication with the outside world was made ever more difficult, and the options of sally parties reduced. Trenches and works also enabled the attackers to move around the house in greater security. At first the pioneers and their civilian auxiliaries dug forward using 'Basketts and hurdles' to cover them as they worked. Later they had a more elaborate system, being 'a kind of testudo, a wooden engine running on wheeles, rooft towards the house, with thick plancks', under the protection of which the men toiled with spades and shovels. Water courses added complexity to the engineering, and the royalists believed that one of the enemy miners' objectives was to cut off the water supply to the house, though given its deep well this would have been unlikely to succeed. It was probably also intended that a deep tunnel would eventually undermine the walls: to achieve this, and to allow the troops to reach the walls, a plan was conceived to drain off the moat. This was never achieved, although the *Discourse* states that a good deal of work went into this design. Again archaeology has tended to confirm the

Firing a mortar, from Malthus' text book *Pratique de la Guerre*. This siege engineer is lighting the fuse of the bomb with one hand. Next the match cord held in the other hand would be applied to the breech to launch the missile. Mortars were the only weapon capable of lobbing large quantities of explosives over walls into fortifications.

written record, with what has been described as 'a water management cut' related to the moat, of possible civil war date, being discovered in 1997.

On 17 March 1644 the defenders attempted a more serious night raid on the enemy's new trenches which were now creeping their way around the back of the house. The soldiers of the garrison drew lots again to see whom luck would choose to participate, and then,

at 3 o'clock in the morning, Captain Chisnall, a man of knowne courage and resoluc'on, Lieutenant Brethergh, and Lieutenant Heape, with some 30 musketeers, issued out of the backe gate to surprize the enemy in their new trenches; but they discovering some of the light matches ran faster than the Captayne or his souldiers could pursue, secureing their flight in a wood close by, where, not willing to engage his souldiers in unnecessary dangers, hee left'em, onely killing 2 or 3, and chasing the rest in flight.

What had happened to alert the parliamentarians may require some explanation. Most muskets of the period were matchlocks – in which the main charge in the musket was ignited by means of a 'match', a length of smouldering cord set in the lock mechanism. Evidently, as the sally party crept forward, the enemy had caught sight of the glowing red tips of the cords in the darkness and made off. Although the defenders' spirited actions had caused relatively small loss, they had interfered with the progress of the works, for as yet there was not 'one mount for ordnance' – and without artillery in a position to batter the gates or walls, there was no chance of making a breach, and little hope either of forcing a surrender.

Finally, two nights later, the besiegers did succeed in dragging up a cannon. On the Wednesday morning the gun commenced a desultory fire, discharing just three 24-pound shot. The first of these made little impression on the wall, so the barrel was elevated against the higher 'pinacles and turrets' which were more vulnerable to artillery. Having made this display of strength, Fairfax attempted to reopen negotiation, his main excuse for doing so being a letter that Lord Derby had sent him, requesting that his wife and children be allowed safe passage from the house. The messenger was Reverend Jackson, a chaplain to Alexander Rigby, whom her ladyship found 'sawcy and zealous'. Lady Derby afforded Fairfax due credit for his courtesy, but firmly refused any such offer. By this time Fairfax himself was summoned away to more pressing duty. For one of parliament's most distinguished commanders he had achieved remarkably little during his time in front of Lathom House.

For the better part of a week no significant progress was made by either side, until on 25 March the demi-cannon and culverin which the parliamentarian gunners had brought to bear fired seven rounds. A lucky shot, ricocheting off the ground, penetrated the great gates and the defenders were forced to stop up the entrance using 'beds, and such like implements'. The painfully slow bombardment continued for the remainder of the month, with relatively little effect except on the 29 March when

one of our men, vainely provokeing danger with his body above a tower, was shott to a present death. In the afternoone, they played 4 cannons, one

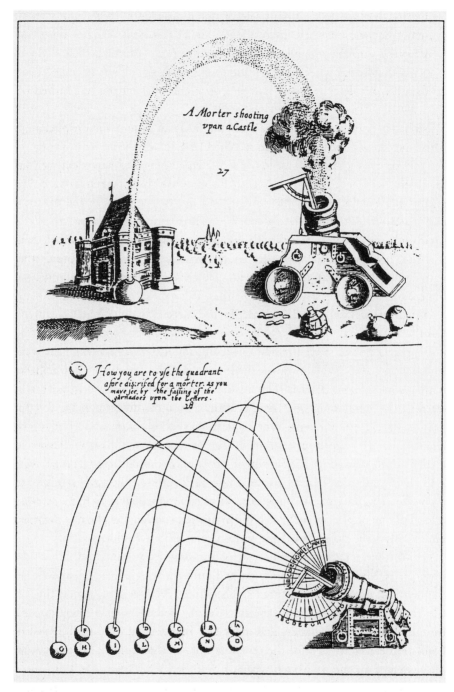

Textbook illustration showing how to shoot a mortar against a castle. High angle fire was the key characteristic of the mortar, but mortars and their shells were expensive and technical pieces of equipment.

wherof, levelled to dismount one of our ordinance upon the great gates, strucke the battlements upon one of our markes-men ready to discharge att the cannonneere, and crusht him to deathe.

On 1 April, by way of variety, the parliamentarian artillerymen fired off six rounds of chain shot and 'barres of iron'. These would have been well calculated to damage wooden buildings, and kill anyone unfortunate enough to get in the way, but were of no use against fortifications.

Two days later there was a much more frightening and potentially serious development. The parliamentarians had emplaced their mortar well within range, and now they fired three times,

loaden with stones, 13 inches in diameter, 80 lb in weight. It was planted about halfe a musket shott southwest from the house, on a riseing earthe, convenyently giveing the engineere a full p'spect of the whole buildinge. Theire worke to secure it was orbicular, in forme of a full moone, 2 yards and a half of rampier above the ditch.

The weapon was thus securely covered in its own earthwork, in a position eight or nine feet higher than the ditch surrounding the house, very probably within what is now the footprint of the Pilkington laboratory. In an era of warfare dominated by sieges, the mortar was the terror weapon of the day, for unlike ordinary guns which fired at low trajectories, mortars were designed to lob their projectiles high into the air – over any intervening rampart or earthworks. To make them doubly effective they were usually used with 'granadoes', grenades or shells, which exploded on arrival destroying whatever lay within the target area. The psychological impact of sudden death from above was considerable, as the *Briefe Journall* put it, even 'the stoutest souldiers had no hearts for granadoes'.

Problems facing the besiegers

The threat posed by the mortar was clearly significant, and it is no surprise that it helped to galvanise Farmer and his compatriots into renewed, even desperate action. In retrospect, the apparently mighty parliamentarian investment force was facing significant problems which were to prove more and more crucial as time progressed. The first and most obvious was the lack of clarity in command. Sir Thomas Fairfax was initially the senior figure, but the majority of the troops on the ground were not hitherto part of his army.

In this instance his approach was not particularly 'hands on', nor can we be sure for how long he was actually present at Lathom. He does not appear to have regarded Lord Derby's house as a high priority assignment; nor does he seem to have wished to deal unduly severely with Lady Derby. Fairfax's own memoirs dismiss his participation in the siege of Lathom in a few curt lines, which appear to absolve him of any interest, let alone responsibility,

> ... we took in several garrisons in Cheshire: Lathom only in Lancashire held out; which was besieged by the forces of that Country, but afterwards raised by Prince Rupert.[11]

With Fairfax's departure, almost with a sigh of relief, the burden devolved upon the Lancashire committee men. The unease between Rigby and Holland on the one hand, and Ashton on the other has been widely remarked. Whether Rigby was as blinded by malice as his detractors would have us believe is uncertain, but his control of events was certainly insecure. Both the *Discourse* and the *Briefe Journall* speak of Rigby as having responsibility, but Lathom lay within West Derby hundred, so Peter Egerton, parliament's colonel for the hundred, would also have had a legitimate claim. One source states indeed that Egerton was the commander for a period after Fairfax, with Major Morgan as his principal engineer. Colonels Ashton and Moore are stated to have been at Ormskirk early in April. Ashton had clearly fallen out with Rigby very seriously, for in a letter of the following year he vowed never to serve with him again.

The second problem faced by the besiegers was the perennial problem of finance. The trouble was not merely that the funds for the siege were inadequate, but that the way money was obtained and distributed was proving inefficient. Captain Birch was said to have objected to the siege in general on the grounds of its disproportionate cost, and the way that the money was raised. In his opinion sequestration of enemy property was proving inefficient and possibly corrupt. Straightforward plunder was unlawful, although the laws of war made many types of property seizure legal under certain circumstances, for example when sequestration orders were in place, after the storming of a town, or on the specific order of parliament. Confusingly parliament could both give permission to take property, or retrospectively endorse such confiscations made in its name. The giving of promissory notes was also acceptable, though whether anything was ever paid against them would depend on both luck and who happened to be winning when the time came for repayment. Any taking of goods and funds by the enemy was naturally portrayed as robbery.

A rather fanciful nineteenth-century impression of the capture of the parliamentarian mortar at Lathom House. Despite this slightly comic image Lathom would turn into a bitter siege where the taking of prisoners was eventually regarded as a luxury and starvation was the final weapon.

The parliamentary financial system, in which the local committees collected their own local taxation, had not been fully implemented until well into 1643. Even then there were many instances of inequality or lack of clarity. Humphrey Chetham, one of Lancashire's key parliamentarian money men, was instrumental in fixing the 'rates' against which actual sums might be gathered. Basic to the process was the pre-war county 'rate book' – new versions being produced eventually in 1645 and 1648. However even if the pre-war book had been perfect there was no way it could take account of the ebb and flow of war over the countryside, which had been repeatedly milked, more or less violently, by either side. Parliament's imposition of the 'excise' tax on alcohol, tobacco, cloth, leather and certain other goods did not come in until July 1643, and does not seem to have been collected with any great efficiency in Lancashire until later. To call it unpopular would be a gross understatement. Another problem, assuming that funds could be more or less legally collected, was who was entitled to draw them, and how they should be accounted for. The detail of this was still unresolved as late as the first siege of Lathom.

An attempt to sort out the Lancashire committee's finances was clearly made at this time, but parliament's ruling on this matter was not made until 20 May 1644. Parliament's decision was that for Cheshire Sir William Brereton's signature would be sufficient for the release of funds. The formula for Lancashire was illustrative of the fact that parliament had no single commander with supreme authority within the county. Here parliament required that two of the deputy lieutenants, who were also members of parliament, should put their hands to receipts in order to obtain payment. Any Lancashire colonel who was not an MP was thus at a serious disadvantage when it came to obtaining resources; moreover, the new system required two acting in concert – perhaps against the objections of others. Even then the decision was really too late to have to have any practical impact on the conduct of the siege at Lord Derby's house. Money would be short at Lathom – and one of the key incentives keeping troops in the field there remained the prospect of plunder from the house. However, if the house did not fall soon, there would be no plunder.[12]

The third factor hampering the parliamentarians at Lathom was the rotation of the troops employed in the siege. As the *Discourse* tells us, 'the companies that weare to keepe the siege came out of their severall Hundreds by turns'.

When the League[r] had been about one fortnight, companies out of the Fyld country were called up, Captaine William Pateson with his companie being the first. He with his companie were seaven weekes compleat. All the companies had their provisions brought them by those severall townes or places where they were raised as also their paye and were ordered to such and such as might receive them, some nearer the League[r] and some further off. They weare upon duty every third day and night. It was a very costly siege to the county. There was needlessly spent against it in shot and powder an infinite quantity. Some was alwaies shooting at nothing they could see but the walls.

The administrative nightmare is easy to imagine, with troops marching many miles to get to Lathom, attempting to bring all their provisions with them, and then spending one day in three actually in the lines. Had fresh men been encamped locally, this might have helped. As it was, no one can have arrived on the scene ready and rested, and the problems of feeding green troops into trenches they did not know, under sniper fire, can easily be imagined. Moreover the suggestion is that no more than a small percentage of the parliamentarian army can have been in the siege lines at any given moment; indeed a figure of about 700 is mentioned in the *Briefe Journall*. It was therefore perfectly possible that, despite being constantly under pressure, the royalists' sally parties could achieve decisive local superiority wherever they chose. Farmer therefore had only to make sure that his tactics were hit and run, never tarrying long enough to allow Rigby and Egerton to get their men to the vital spot.

In view of what has been written about the mortar and bombardment the final, and perhaps conclusive, parliamentarian weakness is a considerable surprise. The hitherto undisclosed Achilles heel of the Lancashire parliamentarians before Lathom was that their artillery and logistics were totally inadequate, if not a sham. Things were so bad, indeed, one is almost inclined to wonder whether the first attempt on the house was actually a gigantic bluff. There is mention of only two siege guns, and one mortar: three sakers completed the artillery. For all the posturing and bravado, the defenders actually outgunned the attackers, a situation which made achieving a break-in all but impossible. The heavy guns had to be brought close, so as to concentrate their fire on a short section of the defences: but as soon as they were close enough, counter bombardment and sniping would intervene. The mortar itself was also something of a hollow threat. The tragic truth is that it had a maximum of about six granadoes to fire – and so much of the time was limited to shooting stones, or nothing. The weapon itself had been begged from Sir William Brereton's Cheshire forces – when it arrived Rigby was shocked to discover it had little or no ammunition. While the engineers cast about for suitable rocks, Rigby wrote pleading to Sir William,

We have already presumed upon the confidence we have of our interest in you and your affections to the public, and now having your mortar, it cannot be so useful to us as you desire, unless you please to furnish us with half a dozen or more shells for granadoes for the mortar piece, which I earnestly entreat from you to be delivered to this bearer for the more expedition in the work which now detains us from other services, and what satisfaction you shall desire for them you shall receive, if not from the rest of the Deputy Lieutenants then from me. If any shells shall be left at the end of the work they shall be returned with the mortar by me.[13]

The majority of the parliamentarian rank and file marching back and forth to Kirkham and other distant parts were doubtless unaware of the true facts: from the above it appears that Ashton did know – and may well have encouraged Rigby to desist in his folly. Two who certainly must have known the truth were the senior parliamentarian engineers, Browne and Morgan. Their thoughts on facing a major nest of well-armed 'malignants' with inadequate artillery, and little more than stones for their key weapon are not recorded. The first of the precious granadoes was fired on 4 April: chosen men of the garrison however were already alert, being ready with 'greene and wett hides' to extinguish any conflagration that it might cause. In the event they were not needed, with the missile sailing right over the house.

Lady Derby takes the initiative

Four days later the defenders launched yet another of their spoiling raids. This time almost half the garrison participated, and the action degenerated into fierce hand-to-hand fighting over the enemy earthworks,

> About 11 o'clock, Captain Farmer and Captain Mullineux Rattcliffe, Lieutenant Penckett, Lieutenant Woorrale, with 140 souldiers, sallyed out at a postern gate, beate the enemy from all theire worke and batteries, which were cast up round the house, nail'd all theire canon, killed about 50 men, took 60 armes, one collours, and 3 drumes; in which acc'on Captain Rattcliffe deserves this remembrance, that with 3 souldiers, the rest of his squadron being scattered with execu'on of the enemy, he cleared two sconces, and slew 7 men with his owne hand. Lieutenant Woorral, ingageing himselfe in another worke among 50 of the enemy, bare the fury of all, till Captain Farmer relieved him, who, to the wonder of us all came off without any serious wound. The sally port was this day warded by Captain Chisnall, who with fresh men stood ready.[14]

The signal to attack and to retire was given by Captain Fox who raised flags accordingly upon the Eagle Tower. The royalists claimed to have suffered only one fatality in the melees. Chillingly the *Briefe Journall* also states that they took only one prisoner. According to the royalist version of events Rigby had previously agreed to exchange prisoners, only to renege on the deal. The result was that the garrison, being in no condition to keep captives, no longer took them. This of course resulted in a 'greater slaughter than either her Ladyship or the Captaynes desired'. Whatever the explanation, it was now clear that men trying to surrender were being killed on the spot. Unsurprisingly the remainder of this blood-drenched night was 'one continued allarum', with 'nothing but shoutes and cryes' among the enemy, as if the 'cavaleers had still been upon them'. Bitterness was not the sole prerogative of Colonel Rigby.

Royalist accounts similarly stress the growing dastardliness and desperation of the enemy leaders. A piece in *Mercurius Aulicus*, for example, suggests that Colonel Moore would happily have killed Lady Derby with a shot from a cannon during one of the several parlays. Only the fact that the cannoneer was more gallant than his officer was said to have saved the life of the Countess. The legend of the 'Lady of Lathom' was already growing by the day, and it is not too fanciful to suggest, that in royalist circles at least, it was actively encouraged.

On 12 April the bombardment resumed with two shots from the mortar, and some shooting from the parliamentarian sakers, one ball from which whizzed through the 'claye walls' and entered the window of Lady Derby's chamber. Continued slow battering over the next few days demonstrated that though the great raid had been a success, efforts to disable the parliamentarian guns had been at best only partially effective. Unless there was time to smash a piece with hammers or drag it away, 'nailing' a gun was the usual method. Banging a nail into the touch hole could put a piece out of action quite effectively and quickly, but was usually only temporary, as with the right tools nails could be removed. On 16 April the mortar finally demonstrated its potential,

> ... about 11 o'clock they played their mortar piece with stone, and p[er]ceaving it struck within the body of the house, they cast a granadoe att the same levell, which fell into an old court, strikeing about half a yard into the earth, yet rose again with such vyolence in the bursteing, that though its strength was much lessened, and deaded with earth, it shooke down the glasse, clay and weaker buildings neere it leaving only the carcase of the walls standing about it, yet without hurt of any person, saveing that 2 woemen in a neere chamber had theire hands scorcht, to putt them in mind hereafter that they were in the siedge at Lathom. The morter peece was now more terrible than formerly, insomuch that the captaynes, to prevent the souldiers feares, lodged in the upproomes within clay walles, as not esteeming the force of the granadoe: and one thing more now happily lent more courage to our men, that one of their engineers, mounting the rampier to see the fall of the granadoe, was happily slaine by a marksman from one of our towers'.[15]

Another account has it that one of the mortar shells, possibly this one, 'shivered all the room', where the ladies were present, but actually hurt no one.

On Saturday 20 April, following another lull in the action, the parliamentarian gunners finally managed to bring their pieces to bear on what they thought might be a key target. They fired thirty shot from their demi-cannon and culverin against a postern tower, part of which was vulnerable as it stood outside the 'mote and pallizadoes', causing some damage. Still the lie of the land caused problems, with the result that only a yard of the wall could be hit squarely. Again the royalist marksmen came into play, and one of them, firing through a 'porthole' in the tower, killed one of the gunners. That night the defenders made good the damage, while the enemy brought the mortar back into action, a precious granadoe falling short of the target. After a brief respite on Easter Sunday there was further shooting on the Monday, and after dark two or three men from the garrison crept out. Again the parliamentarians spotted the glowing match cords moving in the dark, and this time opened fire with everything that came to hand.

On 23 April the parliamentarian gunners gave up on the outer wall, directing their fury against the Eagle Tower instead. A large breach appeared in a staircase, and two shot scudded through Lady Derby's own chamber, forcing her to move her bedroom elsewhere. Impressive as this was, a breach in an internal tower advanced the attackers very little, as the opening was not accessible to troops beyond the outer wall. That night the defenders employed a new variation on an old ruse, by embedding glowing match cords in balls of clay, which they threw out of the house into the siege lines. The parliamentarians responded as predicted, shooting at non-existent targets. Shortly afterwards a further appeal for surrender was correctly interpreted as a sign of weakness. Lady Derby tore up the insolent communication with well-calculated theatricality. The unfortunate parliamentarian drummer who had delivered it was threatened with death, but then allowed to return to his own lines, dismissed as the 'foolish instrument of traytors pride'.

Though the besiegers' mortar was now silent for lack of bombs, the defenders were probably in ignorance of its impotence, and still regarded it as the key threat. So it was that a plan was hatched for an even more ambitious night sally, with the mortar itself as the main target. Captains Chisnall and Foxe, seconded by four lieutenants, were to lead the assault, while Captains Rawstorne and Rattcliffe were to secure the retreat and man the walls with other troops. Farmer held a small final reserve, ready to assist wherever danger required. About four in the morning of 26 April,

Captain Chisnall and 2 Lieutenents issues out of the easterne gate, and before hee was discovered, gott under theire canon, marching straight upon the scouts where they had planted their great gun. It cost him a light skirmish to gayne the fort: at last hee entered: many slayne, some prisoners, and some escaping. Now by com'and of that battery the retreate being assured, Captain Foxe seconds him with much bravery, beating upon their trenches from the easterne to the south west point, till hee came to the work which secured the mortar peece, which being guarded with 50 men, he found sharp service, forceing his way through muskett and canon, and beateing the enemy out of the sconce with stones, his muskett, by reason of the high worke, being unserviceable.

Within a quarter of an hour the shooting and stone throwing had secured the enemy trenches in this sector, and the royalists, in possession of one of the sconces, were able to line it with musketeers. Mr Broome and Lady Derby's other servants now levelled a way across the works, and,

with ropes lifting the morter-peece to a low dragge, by the strength of men drew it into the house, Captain Ogle defending the passage against another companye of the enemye which played upon their retreate. The like endeavour was used to gayne their great gunnes; but lying beyond the ditch, and being of such bulke and weight, all our strength could not bringe them off before the whole army had fallen upon us.

Two royalist soldiers fell mortally wounded during the retreat back to the house, but the diarist has it that even prostrate they continued to shoot, thus aiding the escape of their comrades. How many parliamentarians were killed was not clear, but arms, three drums, and five prisoners were taken, Captain Chisenall showing 'mercy as well as valour'. One of those captured was Browne the engineer. The mortar now lay in the grounds of Lathom, like 'a dead lyon', the royalist soldiers taking it in turns to pose with a foot on the beast, and joke with their friends. Rigby had suffered a 'shamefull defeate'.[16]

Parliamentarian troops kept positions around Lathom for another month, and issued at least one more summons to surrender, but siege had degenerated into a half-hearted investment on the off-chance that the defenders' provisions would become exhausted. The ever upbeat royalist *Mercurius Aulicus* reported an incident in May in which some of the enemy troops, believing that the siege was at last over, attempted a rush on the house, only to be driven back by cannon fire. This may or may not have happened, but given the failing spirits of the besiegers the story was all too believable.

Outside the walls Rigby wrote to the committee in Manchester of his 'anxiety and fatigue'. Money began to run out, and soldiers were going unpaid. Rigby protested that he had spent a good deal of his own resources on the enterprise, but as the *Briefe Journall* put it this was 'cheape talke' – the men needed cash or loot, and the once plausible prospect of plunder from Lord Derby's property was now becoming increasingly unlikely. Rigby's reputation had now sunk to its lowest ebb: as the melodramatic Victorian account penned by Guizot de Witt would later portray him, the former lawyer turned soldier was now exposed as 'a bad man, a robber and a hypocrite'.

Heavy rain gradually filled the trenches and the mine, leaving those already 'wearied with extraordinary duty' soaked and dispirited. Some soldiers melted away; another simply ran out of the works in broad daylight and surrendered. On 26 May the defenders perceived a slackening of the encirclement, fewer men than usual arriving to relieve those in the trenches. However there was also intelligence received that Prince Rupert was on the march with an army to rescue Lathom. Between midnight and one that night the parliamentarian army 'stole away'.

With the enemy gone and help on its way, the garrison had time to take stock. The *Briefe Journall* claimed that only six royalists had died in the defence, while the enemy had about '500' dead. This was probably a gross exaggeration – Colonel Moore's correspondence refers to far fewer being killed in the sallies of early April – but it was certainly true that the parliamentarian losses were many times those suffered by Lady Derby's men. Believably, the royalist propaganda paper *Mercurius Aulicus* reported dead bodies around the house, causing a 'loathsome' sight and stench. The *Discourse*, well disposed to the parliamentarian cause, admits that Lathom's snipers were 'very good marks men' who killed many. Their most deadly technique was in watching the besiegers' loop holes, firing as soon as the view through was obscured, thereby killing enemy observers. Moreover the siege lines were brought so close to the house that 'it was the death of many pore honest men'.

Months of work, and the construction of no fewer than eight small sconces or forts, had resulted in nothing 'but the loss of men's lives and the spending of much treasure and victuals'. Had the mortar been applied to its best advantage, the writer of the *Discourse* was of the opinion that the house would have been yielded in a short while. As it was the wonder weapon had fired only four granadoes and a few dozen stones. New research makes us aware that the parliamentarians were in fact far less strong, and the royalists less weak than we might have suspected. Some of the killing was also far from gallant and honourable. Nevertheless the legend of this romantic episode is unlikely to be dimmed – most especially the reputation of Lady Charlotte, who, as the *Scottish Dove* would put it soon after the event, had stolen the earl's breeches in his absence, to 'play the man'.[17]

Prince Rupert.

CHAPTER SEVEN

'Prince Robber' in Lancashire, 1644

T HE INTERVENTION of Prince Rupert in Lancashire in May 1644 was
one of the most crucial turning points of the war in the county. Almost
overnight hard-won parliamentarian superiority would be overthrown, and
a dramatic revival of royalist fortunes saw besiegers become the besieged.
Rupert's 'thunderbolt' also had a much wider significance, as for the first
time the national conflict and the war in the county became virtually
synonymous.

Prince Rupert's objectives in coming to the north of England were strategic
and national, largely a response to pleas for assistance in Yorkshire. The outline
of the king's strategy was laid in April at a conference at Abingdon. While
the Oxford army defended what was effectively the royalist capital, Prince
Maurice would take Lyme. Prince Rupert, his brother, would go north to
join the Earl of Newcastle, stopping the Scots in their tracks, and freeing the
north. Given a successful outcome Rupert and Maurice could then rejoin the
king to complete the victory in the south of England. From a more specifically
Lancashire perspective Lord Derby now appealed both to the prince's sense of
honour in seeking his assistance for his wife at Lathom, and also held out a
more tempting prospect. With the enemy committed to the siege of Lathom in
large numbers, the garrisons of towns such as Liverpool and Warrington were
weak. They might therefore be picked off with comparative ease. Clarendon

left Prince Rupert, Count Palatine of the Rhine and Duke of Bavaria (1619–82).
Prince Rupert, a nephew of Charles I, gained early military experience on the
Continent in the Thirty Years War. Arriving in England in 1642 he was soon one of
the king's most senior commanders, campaigning extensively throughout the country.
His 1644 intervention in Lancashire briefly and dramatically revived royalist fortunes in
the county. Portrait *c.*1642 attributed to Gerrit van Honthorst.

NATIONAL PORTRAIT GALLERY

even suggests that Lord Derby promised Rupert at least 2,000 men on the successful relief of Lathom, and 'a considerable sum of money'.[1]

Still aged only 24 in 1644, Prince Rupert of the Rhine was a son of the king's sister Elizabeth and her German husband, Frederick the Elector Palatine. From his early years, and with service under the Prince of Orange in the Thirty Years War, Rupert had been trained in military affairs. Portraits by William Dobson show a handsome, soulful, emotionally intense youth. Despite appearances or rumours to the contrary, Rupert was religiously sound by English standards of the day; indeed his father had lost his lands for his Protestant faith. The Prince had come to England to fight for his uncle in 1642, winning an early reputation as a general of horse with the victory at Powick Bridge. For those who fought with him he was a dashing and courageous, if sometimes hot-headed, commander who 'put that spirit into the king's army that all men seemed resolved'. Lord Derby said that his mere presence was worth more than all the reinforcements 'newly landed hear from Irelande', his appearance being calculated to strike 'a terror' to the 'wicked partie' of the enemy and give new life to those weary royalists who had for so long been banished from their own counties by the war. His key qualities as a general were a complete willingness to throw all into the action when he believed that this would win the day, and an awareness of the latest continental ways of waging war, specifically those introduced by Gustavus Adolphus and the Swedes.

For those who fought against him there was another view. Prince Rupert was seen as Prince Robber, an arrogant and ruthless aristocratic bandit, a mercenary opportunist. This was the 'bloody Prince' who had sacked Birmingham in April 1643, burning as he went. In Sir John Meldrum's famous epithet, he was a 'fierce thunderbolt that strikes terror amongst the ignorant'. Upon hearing that Rupert was marching north the first reaction of the wry correspondents in the parliamentarian *Perfect Diurnall* was to suggest that he was more likely to plunder York than to relieve it. Rupert also gave rise to some of the more bizarre stories and legends of the war. In Lancashire a rumour circulated concerning one of the Reverend Herle's parishioners at Winwick. Herle said the man was able to 'plainly discern in Prince Rupert's dog' the features of a female spy and camp follower. This was interpreted as 'enchantment' – being obviously some form of witchcraft or devilment on the part of the royalists.[2]

Rupert left Oxford at the head of some cavalry on 5 May 1644. At Shrewsbury he was joined by about 8,000 horse and foot, including an Irish contingent under Henry Tillier. On 16 May the royalist army advanced northwards, making first for Whitchurch, as one parliamentarian account noted, 'plundering most fearfully all along, and especially taking men and horses'. Some Cheshire men who gave up their goods and animals to Rupert were doubly cursed, being royalist supporters already forced to hand over much of their property to parliament. William Davenport of Bramhall, was a particularly good example of this double jeopardy. Part of Sir William Brereton's cavalry had visited him in early 1643, taking away not only eight muskets, eight sets of pikeman's armour but other equipment to the value of £40, plus £7 in cash. Thereafter he had had to make regular payments to help support the Nantwich garrison and various 'loans'. On New Years Day 1644 Captain Francis Duckenfield and other parliament men had returned to clear out most of his horses, and various other things including a drum. Then, five months later, Rupert's army came as something of a final insult,

> by whom I lost better than a hundred pounds in linens and other goods at Milesend, besides the rifling and pulling in pieces of my house. By them and my Lord Goring's army I lost eight horses, and besides victuals and other provision they ate me three score bushels of oats. No sooner was the Prince gone but Stanley's cornet, one Lely, and twenty of his troop hastened their return to plunder me of my horses which the Prince had left me.

Parliamentary sequestrators would come again just a couple of months later.

Through Stockport and into Lancashire

Whether new recruits were willing or pressed, Rupert's forces were swollen to almost 10,000 as they crossed Cheshire. Progress of Rupert's increasingly impressive army was somewhat slow, according to the author of the Carte manuscript, 'by reason of the roughness of the wayes, and weather'. Nevertheless, avoiding direct confrontation with the garrison of Nantwich, Rupert's force reached Knutsford on 24 May. The last serious obstacle between the royalist army and Lancashire was the Mersey, and it was at Stockport that the local parliamentarians belatedly resolved to intercept the Prince on what they hoped to be favourable ground.

Here the regiments of Henry Mainwaring, Robert Duckenfield, and local militiamen, totalling perhaps as many as 3,000 troops, took up a position to block the prince's advance. First on the scene were some of Rupert's horse, a reconnaissance in force which the parliamentarians were able to repel,

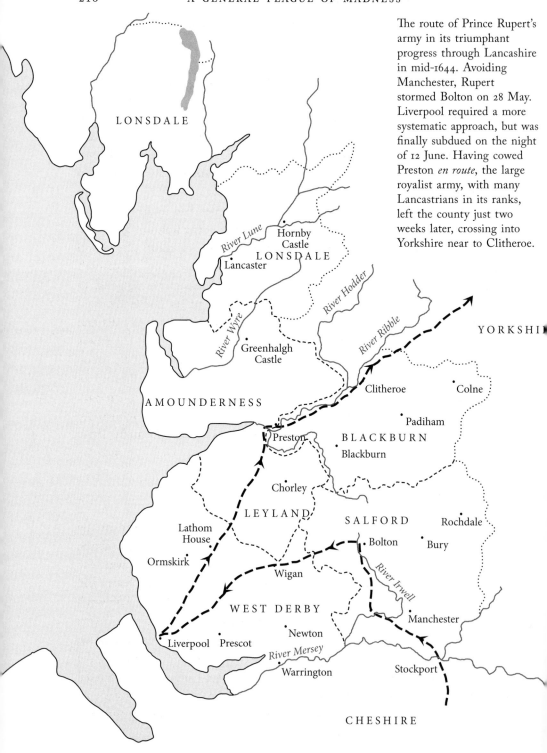

The route of Prince Rupert's
army in its triumphant
progress through Lancashire
in mid-1644. Avoiding
Manchester, Rupert
stormed Bolton on 28 May.
Liverpool required a more
systematic approach, but was
finally subdued on the night
of 12 June. Having cowed
Preston *en route*, the large
royalist army, with many
Lancastrians in its ranks,
left the county just two
weeks later, crossing into
Yorkshire near to Clitheroe.

LONSDALE

River Lune

Hornby
Castle

LONSDALE

Lancaster

River Hodder

River Wyre

River Ribble

YORKSHI

Greenhalgh
Castle

AMOUNDERNESS

Clitheroe   Colne

Padiham

Preston   BLACKBURN

Blackburn

Chorley

LEYLAND   SALFORD   Rochdale

Lathom
House   Bolton   Bury

Ormskirk

River Irwell

Wigan

WEST DERBY   Manchester

Newton

Liverpool Prescot

River Mersey

Warrington   Stockport

CHESHIRE

apparently without serious loss to either side. Then, at about six in the evening, the royalist foot began to arrive in numbers; then,

> the cunning Rebells withdrew themselves, and lined hedges through which he [Rupert] was to passe with their Musketeers. Which being perceived by the Prince, he commanded Colonell Washington with some Dragooners to scour those hedges; he performed the service with such speed and courage, that the Rebels in great affright fled towards the Towne; whom the Prince followed so close upon the heeles, that he entered pel mel with them, and so tooke the Towne, together with all their cannon.

So it was that the prince's army 'beat their way over the passe' of Stockport and into Lancashire. Thomas Malbon's account claims that Duckenfield and many of the enemy actually fled across the county border into Lancashire. Lord Denbigh, whom the Committee of Both Kingdoms had expected to intercept the royalist force, proved quite powerless to intervene. When quizzed later about his impotence to prevent the ensuing tragedy he was quite definite at whose door the blame should be laid. The forces of Cheshire and others had been quite willing to follow his orders, but those of Lancashire,

> which should have made up the greatest Body of Foot, found excuses, and would not appear at the rendezvous I had appointed, though several Orders were sent ... But I will not insist longer upon this Particular those worthy Gentlemen of Lancashire having suffered so much for such an Omission, which might have proved fatal to these Kingdoms, if God by his Goodness had not prevented it.[3]

The effect of Prince Rupert's entry into the county at the head of the largest army in the region was immediate and electric. The siege of Lathom, which had already slackened considerably, was now abruptly abandoned. The investing force would indeed have been trapped between a hostile house and a relieving force in their rear triple their own number had they not desisted. Rigby's army was gathered together and marched to Eccleston Green. Rigby has been accused of indecision in the extrication of his men after the failed siege, but given how quickly Rupert was able to cross the Mersey, and the limited time available, this is probably not a fair charge. He may have intended to have made for the relative safety of Manchester, but the chance of an encounter battle was just too great. So it was that the dispirited parliamentarians made instead for Bolton.

The sack and 'massacre' of Bolton, May 1644

The sack of Bolton by Prince Rupert's army on 28 May 1644 is generally regarded as the most infamous incident of the civil wars in Lancashire. Some commentators have even argued that it was the worst atrocity of the entire war in England. There have even been comparisons with the awful sack of Magdeburg during the Thirty Years War in 1631.

While this may be an exaggeration, it is clear that the Bolton 'massacre' was in a different league to much of the skirmishing which up to that point had characterised the war in the region. Hitherto even the bloodier storms had stopped short of the killing of women. The fury of the sack of Bolton was exacerbated by a number of factors, not least of which was that the defenders put up determined resistance, leading to heavy casualties among the attackers. At the time there was a general assumption that an immediate and bloodless surrender would lead to the mildest of terms, but defenders waiting for the enemy to bring up its cannon would suffer stricter sanctions. If those holding the garrison contested a storm, and fought hand-to-hand in the streets, there was no guarantee that any would be granted quarter.

Another aspect which pointed towards a bloody resolution was the sheer number of troops packed into a small area. Under normal circumstances it would have been surprising if the town could have put as many as 500 militiamen to its defence, but on 27 May Alexander Rigby's army of about 2,000 men had arrived at Bolton, having fled out of Rupert's path from the abandoned siege at Lathom. Other ill-armed 'club men' also joined the ranks at this hour of need, so that over 2,500 now stood in defence of the town. The physical defences were minimal, but there are references to a 'mud wall' around at least part of the perimeter. This would have been a useful barrier to bombardment, but would not form an insurmountable obstacle to determined infantry. Though the parliamentarians had little time to put the place into order, there were now as many fighting men within the confines of Bolton as there were non-combatants.

To make matters worse the seizure of Bolton was seen as a settling of old scores, even, by some, as a sectarian grudge match. Bolton was regarded as one of the most strongly Protestant towns in england, the 'Geneva of the North' no less. Two previous attacks on Bolton had been driven off, and at least in roundhead propaganda there was an assumption that 'godly' preachers and their flocks were now being singled out for special treatment. The royalist army included many Irishmen, according to recent research perhaps as many as 4,000, and from the defenders' perspective it seemed as if their worst

Colonel Alexander Rigby (d. 1650). Rigby had almost the archetypal profile for a parliamentarian leader, being a Member of Parliament and Puritan lawyer. He was an original actor in the Lancashire County Committee and an active go between for parliament and the county. He was not however particularly successful as a military commander, the nadir of his fortunes being arguably Lathom and the catastrophe of Bolton in 1644.

nightmare was about to come true. A force of barbarous Irish Catholics was to be unleashed upon them in exactly the way they had feared ever since the Irish rebellion of 1641. Moreover, Lord Derby was now back from the Isle of Man, ready to right the humiliations of Read Bridge and Manchester, as well as the affront more recently offered to his wife at Lathom. It might not be too much to suggest that, by showing his zeal in the royalist cause now, before Prince Rupert, Lord Derby was seeking his own rehabilitation as much as the downfall of his enemies.

And so the stage was set. At about two in the afternoon of 28 May the royalist army was detected on the moor about a mile to the south-west of Bolton. The bulk of Prince Rupert's field army was now swollen by the forces of Lord Derby and his Lancashire contingent. The royalists were a leviathan on the landscape, appearing like 'a wood or cloud'. The royalist army may have numbered as many as 12,000 in total, though Sir John Meldrum's intelligence report of a few days later put the figures at 4,000 horse with 7,000 foot, supported by 14 field guns. This mass was split into 'severall bodies', from which issued scouts approaching to discover the most advantageous line of

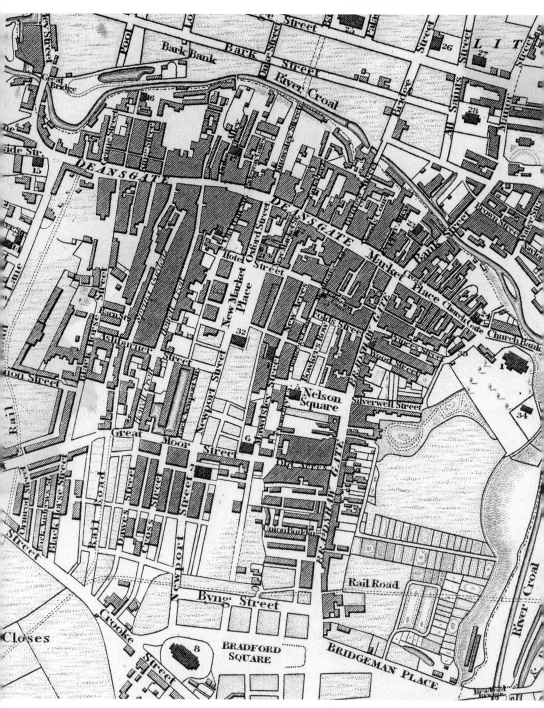

Central Bolton in the early nineteenth century, from Baines' map, 1824.

advance. With Bolton having but little in the way of fixed defences, and the royalists wishing to resume their field campaign without protracted delay, no trenches were dug, and no siege was undertaken. Instead, Bolton was to be attacked head-on, marched over, and pushed to one side.

In the front rank of the royalist army four regiments of foot, Rupert's own, Colonel Tyldesley's, Colonel Ellis' Welshmen, and an Irish regiment, prepared themselves for action. By now it was raining, but with a brisk assault settled upon in the style we have learned to associate with the prince, his men 'fell on'. Yet they were matched with equal determination, if the main parliamentarian account is to be believed,

> Our Commanders were very couragious, and our soldiers very hardy, and both resolved to stand to it, and in the first encounter gave them about halfe an houres sharpe entertainment, were close in discharge, as the enemies confessed after, and repulsed them to enemies great losse and discouragement, and in their retreat cut them down before them in great abundance, and they fell like leaves from the tree in a winter morning.

The Welsh and Tyldesley's put up the hardest fight, apparently getting right over the earthen rampart before being overcome, and forcibly ejected from the town. Seacome's account adds the gory embellishment of some of the attackers, left behind by their comrades, 'murdered in cold bold'. Rupert, unsurprisingly, was 'irritated and ruffled'.[4]

In the brief pause before the next onslaught it is said that Lord Derby appealed to the prince to have the honour of leading the attack in person. Rupert acquiesced, and the earl took up his station at the front of two companies of Tyldesley's foot. Though Tyldesley's may have formed the spearhead, the second attack was upon a wide front, from any direction that it was 'possible to make any approaches', and backed by horse as well as foot. The fact that the cavalry were deployed in the attack rather confirms the absence of a continuous physical obstruction, and was also unusual in that horses were generally seen as a liability in street fighting, where there was a poor field of view and little opportunity to charge. It was also a particularly lethal decision: for horses running out of control in confined spaces, under fire, were almost bound to lead to mayhem.[5]

The royalists now charged again, this time 'drunk with blood' as one parliamentarian eyewitness would later describe it. One account states that some of the royalist cavalry did indeed come to grief, trapped in the narrow space by enemy infantry. Nevertheless the overwhelming assault from all directions worked its fury in a few minutes. The account of the carnage still has the power to shock three and a half centuries after the events:

> At their entrance, before, behinde, to the right, and left, nothing heard but kill dead, kill dead was the word in the town, killing all before them without any respect, without the town, by their horsemen pursuing the poore amazed people, killing, stripping, and spoiling all they could meet with, nothing regarding the doleful cries of women and children, but some they slashed as they were calling for quarter, others when they had given quarter, many hailed out of their houses to have their brains dasht out in the streets, those that were not dead in the streets already pistoled, slashed, brained or trodden under their horses' feet with many insolent blasphemous oathes, curses, and challenges to heaven itselfe, ... But I forbeare many sad things that might be inserted, the usage of children crying for their fathers, of women crying for their husbands, some of them brought on purpose to be slaine before theire wives faces; the rending, tearing, and turning of the people naked, the robbing and spoiling of all the people of all things that they could carry.[6]

As Rushworth's account described everyone in the town now 'endeavoured to shift for himself': soldiers, civilians and horses were now running in all directions to escape the carnage.

The orgy of violence and plunder which followed the storming of Bolton has been the subject of more than one lurid description. Captain Horrocks fell, and Sergeant James Siddall was reported to have been finished off with a pistol as he lay helpless on the ground. Septuagenarian Katherine Seddon was run through with a sword, while preacher's widow Alice Gregg was stripped of her fine clothes and left cowering in her under-smock. One of the most controversial fatalities was Captain Bootle. According to some witnesses he was dispatched personally by Lord Derby himself, after he had been granted his life, but the facts of the case were disputed.

The prime target of the wrath of the victorious cavaliers was undoubtedly Rigby's little army, which broke and fled in the direction of Bury, hacked at and ridden down as they ran. So it was that the victory was pursued not only in the town but 'some miles around, in out houses, fields, highways and woods', with the 'killing, destroying and spoiling' of many.

Appalling as it undoubtedly was, the degree to which this slaughter contravened contemporary rules of war is open to debate. To those failing to withstand a storm there was no guarantee of 'quarter' – and money and goods were generally recognised as the right of any soldier who had taken the extreme risk of walking into the cannon's mouth to take a town. As one royalist account explicitly stated, the town was rightfully the 'souldiers rewarde'. From what we know of the casualties themselves it also appears that the military dead far outnumbered the civilian. Nevertheless the 'woefull work of plunder' was widespread, Adam Martindale being just one who recorded people who now had little or nothing upon which to subsist. Even the rich, it was said, were 'asking bread'. On 30 May Sir John Meldrum summed up the situation by describing the enemy as 'potent and vigilant', now 'in the bowels of its wasting and spoiling, and flushed by the taking of Stockport and Bolton'.

How many actually died when Bolton fell is a matter of controversy. The highest number of fatalities mentioned in any source appears to be an incredible 1,800, the lowest as few as 200 or 300. The true death toll lies somewhere between these figures. The parish register records 78 'slayne on the 28 of May', of whom two were women. This is but part of the picture, since it is likely that these are merely the townspeople who were known, and could be identified, on the spot. To these should be added Rigby's men who were killed nearby, or in the rout from the town. Parliamentarian sources admitted that these amounted to the better part of 200, and the actual number may have been rather higher. The *Discourse* names Captain Faith of Waddicar, Captain Duddell of Wood Plumpton, and Captain Richard Davie of Poulton among the fatalities, together with 'most of their companies'. Both Captain William Dandy, and his son, a lieutenant, are also listed as dead. Equally the royalists did not enter the town at the first charge. At least one account suggests that Rupert's army suffered 200 losses while forcing their way into the town.

Other references to fatalities have been found elsewhere. In 1648 a Mrs Fiffe of Garstang Mills gave an official deposition that she had lost two sons, and a son-in-law, in the service of parliament at Bolton. Another woman widowed by the action at Bolton was identified in similar documentation a few years later. At Bury the burial of seven 'strange soldiers' was reported on 30 May – and there is a very good chance that these were fugitives from the storm who expired after the event. This register also notes the burial of 'a strange souldier, a cavallier' on 10 June. Some of the royalist dead were described as being 'buried in the chancell of the Church' at Bolton, but others were laid in 'obscure places' – as one might have expected, given that common soldiers, particularly those from other parts of the country, were unlikely to have been given expensive funerals. Some of the injured of 28 May will have recovered; others died, weeks or months later. On the other hand, some of those reported dead were later discovered to be safe, like the 'four worthy devines' whose demise was reported in the *Perfect Diurnall* of 10 June. Some defenders who took refuge in the church do appear to have been spared. Though Alexander Rigby and many of his men did in fact escape, the damage to his army was described by the Earl of Manchester as a 'sore blow'. Rigby himself had been lucky indeed, mingling undiscovered among the royalist troops before fleeing all the way to Bradford. For the time being what was left of his force was not sufficiently strong to form any type of independent command. Effectively a decisive battle had taken place within, and around, a town. These points together make it seem reasonable to suppose that the total dead at Bolton, on both sides, were the better part of 700 to 800, of whom only a minority were civilians. This agrees reasonably with the account in the Carte manuscript, which speaks of 1,000 men fallen in the 'streets and fields', though this royalist document assumes that the dead were essentially those of the enemy.[7]

The effects of the storm of Bolton also went well beyond the tragic and the local. The author of the Carte manuscript claims that, in addition to the casualties inflicted on the enemy, the royalists took 600 prisoners, 50 officers, more than 20 colours and 20 barrels of powder in addition to 'match and armes in great quantity'. The colours were given as trophies to Lady Derby, and the earl presented the prince with a £20 ring by way of gratitude for his timely intervention. The prisoners, bound in pairs, were sent south for distribution over Cheshire and Shropshire. In Manchester a sense of doom and isolation was felt as the enemy marched with impunity within a few miles of the town, plundering and 'heathenishly' ravishing. Heyrick's letter *Prince Roberts bloudie carriage at Bolton*, explained how in Manchester, a town already 'over-burthened' with the billeting of troops, there was every danger of the rich becoming the poor, and the poor beggars. Salford raised a special collection for the relief of Bolton's distress, while the parliament in London belatedly voted extra funds for the maintenance of its army in the county.[8]

Just a few days after the fall of Bolton the generals of the parliamentarian forces besieging York were reviewing their options with increasing gloom.

> ... we all conceive Lancashire is in great hazard for the present to be brought under the enemy's power, the town of Manchester excepted, which is well fortified and has Sir John Meldrum to command, and at least 5,000 well armed men and sufficient store of ammunition, but no means are left to us to prevent the spoil of Lancashire without apparent hazard of the loss of this country [Yorkshire], for by this accession of

forces Prince Rupert's army is so increased as we think it not safe to divide our men, and send a part to encounter him in Lancashire. If we should raise our siege before York and march with all our forces against him, it is his discretion to avoid us, and either pass by another way than that we take, and so come into Yorkshire, or else retire into Cheshire, whither if we should pursue him, it would be in the Marquis of Newcastle's power in our absence to recover all Yorkshire again and increase his army to as great strength as ever it was.

Only if Rupert came into Yorkshire, and parliament's combined forces could meet him in the field could the position be reversed.[9]

The storming of Liverpool, June 1644

Within a few days Rupert's army was replenished and reordered, and though it might have been better for the royalist cause had he made directly to raise the 'great and close' siege of York, he was 'prevailed upon' for further help in Lancashire. An additional motive for doubling back to Liverpool was to open up the port to aid communication with Ireland. In addition to the Lancashire royalists, an important voice in favour of the taking of Liverpool was Rupert's second in command, Lord John Byron. He argued that not only would possession of the port secure 'intercourse betwixt these parts and Ireland', but that it would be strategically important in helping to keep any Scottish threat at bay. It was also true that there were quite a number of closet royalists in the Liverpool area, hitherto cowed by parliament's upper hand in the county, who would now come forward to join the colours. As Sir John Meldrum put it, those in 'the country thereabout who formerly lurked as neuters do now show themselves in arms for the Earl of Derby'. Whether these factors were worth a delay, which might have led to the fall of York in the meanwhile, must remain an open question.[10]

The defences of Liverpool were incomplete in 1644, but they were certainly much stronger than those of Bolton, earthworks having been commenced as early as 1642. In December 1643 parliament had also ordered that 'five iron pieces' be taken out of the stores and conveyed north by ship 'for the better defence of Liverpoole'. The town's location also had some natural strength in that the wide sweep of the Mersey, the pool itself, and marshland, covered substantial parts of the town's circumference. Moreover, the garrison appears to have been warned of the prince's coming. Later in the year Meldrum would think the defences of Liverpool little inferior to those found around many

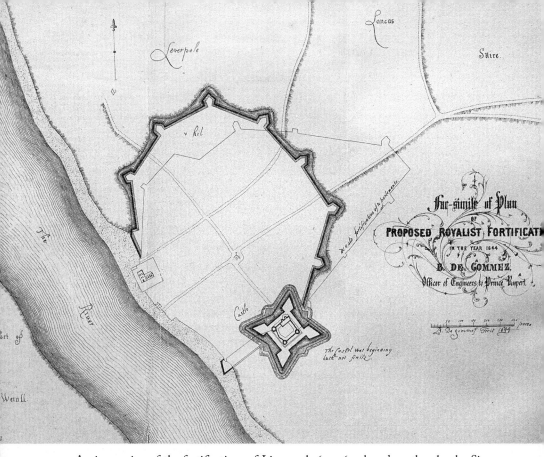

Within the image (map labels): Leverpole · Lancas · Shire · v hil · The ... · River · Castle · The castel was beginning buth not finle. · ould fortification of the parlements · Werall · ort of

fac-simile of Plan
of
PROPOSED ROYALIST FORTIFICATI
IN THE YEAR 1644
B. DE GOMMEZ.
Officer of Engineers to Prince Rupert.

An impression of the fortifications of Liverpool 1643–1644 based on the plan by Sir Bernard de Gomme. The works seen in faint outline and denoted by the legend 'the ould fortification of the perlements', were certainly completed in reality. How much of the more substantial intended royalist works were dug prior to the fall of the town is open to question. De Gomme was an expert in Prince Rupert's entourage who had previously acted for Henry Prince of Orange on the Continent as early as 1637. He was knighted in 1645, and worked in England again after the Restoration. This version of the plan was produced by Royal Engineer W.G. Ross in the nineteenth century, working from British Library, Additional Manuscript 5027, a.3.69.

towns on the continent, requiring a garrison of 'at least three hundred men'. Seacome gives us a detailed description of Liverpool's defences:

> Upon the Princes arrival near Liverpool, he was inform'd that it was well fortified with a strong and high mud wall, and a ditch of twelve yards wide, and near three yards deep, inclosing the Town from the East end of the street called Dale, street, and so Northward to the River, and from Dale Street end East, and South East, being a low marshy ground, was covered with water from the River, and Batteries erected within to cover

and guard against all Passage over or thro' that water. All the street ends
to the River were shut up, and those to the Land inclosed with strong
Gates, defended by Cannon; all useless Women and Children were sent to
their friends in the Country on both sides of the River. There was also a
strong castle to the South, surrounded with a Ditch of twelve yards wide
and ten yards deep, from which to the River was a cover'd Way, thro'
which the Ditch was filled with water, and by which when the tide was
out, they brought in Men, Provisions, and stores of War ... In and upon
this Castle were planted many Cannon, as well to annoy the Besiegers at a

A later copy (now in the Athenaeum at Liverpool) of an original map supposedly held
among the Leland papers shows civil war deployments at Liverpool. The seven streets
of the town are protected by a mud wall fort and several gun emplacements as well as
the castle.

BY COURTESY OF THE ATHENAEUM, LIVERPOOL

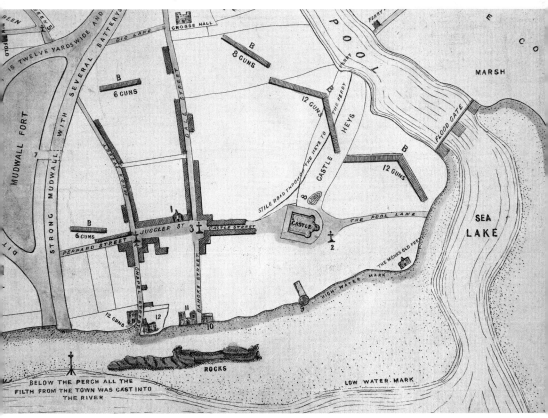

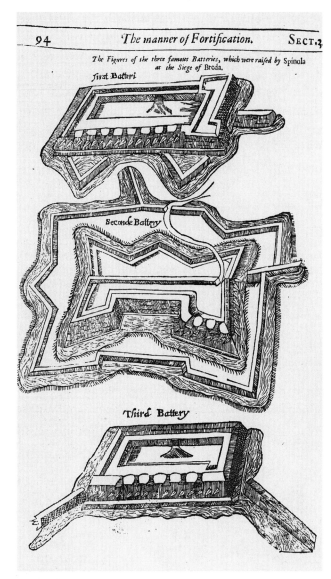

GENERAL PLAGUE OF MADNESS'

94   *The manner of Fortification.*   SECT.3

The Figures of the three famous Batteries, which were raised by Spinola
at the Siege of Breda.

First Batteri

Seconde Battery

Third Battery

Types of gun battery
used during the wars
in the Netherlands,
from Robert Ward's
*Animadversions of
Warre.* Earthwork
gun batteries saw
at least limited use
in Lancashire, as at
Liverpool for example,
where Prince Rupert
deployed a significant
train of artillery in
1644.

Distance, as to cover Ships in the Harbour ... and at the Entrance whereof
was a Fort of eight Guns to guard that, and to prevent all Passages by the
River side at low water'.

The castle was technically long out of date, having been built in the
thirteenth century, and not in the best state of repair, but the massive gatehouse
and substantial round towers are apparent on contemporary illustrations. It

occupied an area of about fifty yards square. In addition to solid defences the defenders also piled up sacks of wool so as to protect themselves from observation and small arms fire. 'Outhouses' which would have given enemy troops cover in their advance on the town were pulled down, thus improving fields of fire. In May 1644 parliament supplied the defenders with an additional 100 muskets, rests and bandoleers, for the 'defence and saftie' of the town. On 1 June some 44 barrels of powder were ordered by Committee of Safety to be taken from the navy store to Lancashire, together with an unspecified quantity of artillery. However, it is highly unlikely that this last would have got as far as Liverpool before its investment. The order may indeed have been a somewhat belated reaction to the earlier news that Rupert was marching on the county.[11]

If Liverpool had weaknesses these were that parts of it were low-lying and could be overlooked from the hills to the east, and that its people were by no means uniformly parliamentarian in allegiance or sympathy. In December 1643 it had proved necessary to warn any inhabitants disloyal to parliament that they might be 'expulsed and removed forth of the towne'. More seriously it was suspected that malignants were passing intelligence to the enemy. The Irish threat was also ever-present: in February 1644 Sir Thomas Fairfax wrote to governor Moore warning him that 'a very vigilant eye' was needed for the guarding of the sea, and to prevent the 'landinge of the Irish which are nowe daily expected'. Parliament had also found that there were limits to Liverpudlians' willingness to play the soldier. As recently as March 1644 there had been difficulties with mounting a reliable round-the-clock guard as,

> Divers of the inhabitants of this towne have refused and contemptiously neglected contrarie to divers orders to appear with their best armes at the beating of the drumme.

Defaulters were warned to expect a fine of 12*d*. or even a spell in prison.[12]

The first of Rupert's scouts reached Everton heights, above Liverpool to the east, on 6 June, and were soon able to make some assessment of the town. At first sight the outlook was not particularly promising: there were moderately good defences, and starving out the garrison was probably impossible given that it could always be restocked by sea. Rupert put a brave face on the enterprise, saying that a 'parcel of boys' could take the town. Nevertheless an attempt to rush Liverpool in the same manner as Bolton would have been extremely costly to the attackers, with no guarantees of success. At Bristol the previous year, under not dissimilar circumstances, Rupert's army had suffered heavily, losing many of its senior officers. There were occasions when common sense reined back the prince's legendary dash, and this was one of them.

The royalists deployed so as to cut off Liverpool from the landward side. As trenches and approaches were prepared, Rupert set up his headquarters at the Beacon, a mile or more from the town. Tradition has it that his forward billet was in a cottage in the village of Everton, a nearby road later being named Rupert Lane in his memory. James Stonehouse's version of this story, penned in the Victorian era, has it that Rupert's abode still stood 'on the site of Eastbourne Street' until its demolition in 1845. It was

> a long low one-storeyed building which was known as 'Prince Rupert's Cottage'. In it – so it is said – the Prince took up his quarters during the siege of Liverpool in 1644. This cottage was constructed of wood, mud, and stone and was thatched with straw. It contained four rooms, and the kitchen had a tiled floor … When the building was demolished an armoire or wardrobe was removed from it to the Collegiate Institution, which was said to have been in use at the time of Prince Rupert's sojourn. Behind the cottage was a raised mound, which at one time was used as a bowling green. The mound has been dignified by the learned as having been constructed by the Prince for the reception of a battery.

Away from the front line, the prince also made use of what had been John Moore's house at Bank Hall.

Before long Rupert's artillery was in position and bombardment commenced. While holding part of his force in reserve a rota system was used so that the royalist troops manning the frontline trenches were relieved twice a day. For a week the besiegers concentrated their artillery upon locations where it might later be possible to effect a breach, and sappers dug painstakingly forward to prepare jumping-off points for the attackers. The prince now had perhaps 16 guns at his disposal, some of them heavy culverins, and he was determined to use them to maximum effect. It was said that 100 barrels of powder were used as the artillery battered monotonously against the northern end of the town. Some of the guns were set up in batteries near to London Road, a spot where bodies dating from the time of the siege are also said to have been discovered in the nineteenth century. The area around St George's Hall has also been suggested as a possible battery site, based on the evidence of its location and distance from the defences.

Parliamentarian accounts in *Mercurius Britannicus* speak of two early attempts on the rampart which failed with heavy casualties on the royalist side. These are largely confirmed by the evidence of the Carte papers which note that,

> The matter was disputed very hotly until the tenth day of June with muskett and great shott without measure out of the towne and from shipps, upon which day our line approached within a coites cast of the gate where our great shott had almost filled the ditch with the ruines of the sod wall, and about noone a furious assaulte was made by our menn where a terrible fight was on both sides above the space of an houre uppon the workes, the Enemy resolute, ours not seconded retreated with some losse.

The defenders of Liverpool did receive reinforcement of the town by water, but by 12 June the writing was on the wall. The vastly superior royalist army was now right up against the defences, and the garrison was withdrawn from the area under greatest threat. Under cover of darkness royalist troops crept forward before unleashing their final attack: by three in the morning it was all over.

Though we lack the detailed and blood-curdling accounts which accompanied the 'massacre' at Bolton, it was clear that the attackers were out of control for some time here too, exercising what they regarded as their legitimate right of plunder. Some of the defenders at least received no mercy. One of the royalist officers, Caryll, brother to Lord Molyneux, a 'blud-thersty Papest', was later specifically accused of killing several 'with his owne hands'. A letter written by Lord Byron suggests that resistance was weak, and that, of the 400 defenders, some were killed and others 'had quarter'. Among the defenders, Adam Martindale reported that despite talk of quarter,

> Rupert's men, upon their first entrance, did ... slay almost all they met with, to the number of three hundred and sixty and, among other, divers of their own friends, and some artificers that never bore arms in their lives, yea, one poor blind man: yet the first that I met with offered me quarter before I asked.

Tradition places the worst of the mayhem in the vicinity of Old Hall Street where the Old Hall of the Moore family was ransacked and various out buildings burned. The majority of the buildings on Lord Street are also reported to have been destroyed. Assessors would later tot up the damage and destruction of bombardment and storm at about £900.[13]

Several factors, however, made Liverpool's taking less bloody than the sack of Bolton. It is possible that the attackers would have been greeted as liberators by at least some of the Liverpudlians. Moreover, the fact that the seizure was carefully planned, and advanced by stages, gave the defenders time to prepare their actions. The majority appear to have withdrawn in good order to the vicinity of the castle, and from here offered the surrender of the medieval fortress in exchange for their lives. The governor Colonel Moore – 'a worthy member of that Rebellious Junto who sat in Westminster' – went a stage further, and, having prepared before-hand, slipped out of Liverpool by ship with some of the key parliamentarian players. The enemy, and some of his supposed friends, would portray this as cowardice, but the absence of their main adversary may have helped stay the hand of at least some of the victorious royalists at this heady moment. Moreover, it may be contended that once Rupert's army and its cannon were at the gates the fall of the town could only have been a matter of time.

On 13 June parliament gathered in London still unaware of the night's dramatic events. Following prayers it ordered that the Committee of Both Kingdoms should meet, 'presently, and receive information of the state of Lancashire, and take into their special care to order relief for that county'. In a fine-sounding declaration the Commons further ordered that any 'publick monies', including customs and excise, raised in Liverpool could be employed 'for the safety and defence of the town'. Had the royalist soldiers now in possession of Liverpool been able to hear this pious proclamation, it would probably have enhanced their enjoyment of their plunder still further.[14]

Whatever the real facts, the stormings of Bolton and Liverpool were soon portrayed as acts of savagery, new depths in an increasingly depressing conflict. Bolton in particular came to be compared with some of the worst outrages of the Thirty Years War in Europe. The contemporary Cheshire observer Thomas Malbon, wrote of the events at Bolton and Liverpool as having, 'more creweltie than there was in any place since the begynngne of the warres'.[15]

The triumphant royalist army had the sense to avoid attacking Manchester. Though it was arguably quite powerful enough now do to so, in either late May or June, this would have taken time. It would also have needed men to be left behind to form a garrison – very probably Rupert had decided that the effort required would have been disproportionate, and of only limited usefulness in terms of his overall strategy. Nevertheless John Rosworme claimed that the enemy did attempt subtle means against the town. Specifically he suggests that about this time a concerted effort was made to bribe him, with 'a very great sum of money' to deliver Manchester to the prince, whereafter Rupert would give him 'great preferments' in his service. Rosworme reports that he listened very carefully to the treacherous proposition – not because he was a potential traitor, but to 'fish out' the enemy stratagems. Even so he must have been tempted, given that he regarded the townsmen's underpayment of him as 'injurious and most unthankfull unworthiness'.

How serious a proposition this betrayal might have been is difficult to judge. Rosworme's inflated opinion of himself was that he could have sold Manchester to the enemy 'man, woman and childe' very easily. There is independent confirmation of some sort of conspiracy, resulting in Peter Heywood fleeing the town in May. On the other hand, given the Mancunians' spirited resistance to date, it is difficult to believe that things could have been quite so simple. Other accounts note that Sir John Meldrum and a Scottish regiment arrived in Manchester about this time to reinforce the local troops. Documents from Furness show that all, or part, of Dodding's cavalry regiment also repaired to the town in late May 1644, on the approach of the royalist army. If Rupert had ever intended to chance his luck these reinforcements would have been more of a factor in his decisions than the subversion of a handful of individuals.[16]

Lancashire had experienced a royalist whirlwind. Rupert's army had taken Stockport, Bolton and Liverpool in less than three weeks, and most of Lancashire now lay at his feet. In the relatively brief time available he now did what he could to reorganise royalist administration of the county. Probably the most important matter was the establishment of a committee of local gentry in Liverpool, whose main task was to supervise the collection of money. The governorship of the town was given to Sir Robert Byron, brother of Lord Byron. Certain other fortresses were also entrusted to men from outside the county. In these particulars Rupert treated Lancashire much the same as he had his other territories, and by the standards of the time these measures had a certain logic. It has been suggested, with some truth, that Rupert was intent on integrating Lancashire within what he might have seen as a national royalist system.

The most important omission from these arrangements, however, was Lord Derby. He does not appear to have played a significant part in the new committee, nor was he given a command in Rupert's field army. The Court, and Prince Rupert himself, may by now have viewed Derby as insufficiently dynamic, parochial in outlook, even vacillating: but leaving him out of the new organisation was potentially an error. By replacing Derby's patronage with his own Rupert doubtless made his own position more important, but with many looking directly to the prince, Rupert's personal presence became much more of a necessity if the cause was to thrive in Lancashire. Moreover, and despite his later reputation, Derby was no extremist, and had done much to defend the fabric of local society. Lancastrians were not yet used to looking for leadership from outside, and much of their natural adherence to the crown had come from the traditional relationship between themselves and their local landowners. Without a local and obvious head to the hierarchy, there was a potential danger that Lancashire royalism would fragment. Previously unswerving royalists might even begin to ask political questions, rather than simply accepting that their interests lay with those who appeared to control their daily livelihood.

Rupert aims to relieve the siege of York, June 1644

Yet Lancashire had never been the principal focus of Prince Rupert's northern adventure. The great city of York was still being besieged by a sizeable parliamentarian force. And if York were lost Charles' crown might also be lost; and if York could be relieved by the royalists, the 'rebel armies of both kingdoms' might be beaten, and Rupert could then return south to help the king regain London and overall political control. With these larger concerns in mind, Charles wrote to Rupert on 14 June 1644, both to congratulate him on his personal success, and to urge haste for a decision at York. Five days later, on the 19th, Rupert set off from Liverpool at the head of 13,000 men, leaving Sir Robert Byron as Liverpool's governor, and the town garrisoned by the regiment of Colonel Cuthbert Clifton. At Lathom he broke his march. Here he promoted Captain Rawstorne to the rank of colonel, and made him governor of Lathom in the absence of the Countess, who had already departed for the Isle of Man. Rupert also directed some improvement to the physical defences. Yet his impact on Lathom's strength was almost certainly in the negative, for he also promoted Captain Chisenhall to colonel and took both Chisnall and his newly raised Lancashire regiment with him when he left.[17]

The majestic royalist army, swollen further by cavalry reinforcements, headed on towards Preston. Here the mayor William Cottam attempted to ingratiate himself by inviting Rupert to dinner; the prince responded by having this politically suspect individual and his bailiffs, Captains Benson and Patten, arrested. Now turning east, Rupert brushed aside some harassment from Colonel Shuttleworth's remaining parliamentarian forces in east Lancashire before leaving the county near Clitheroe about 24 June. Preston's mayor was deposed in Skipton Castle for safe keeping two days later, and languished here for about three months. While ridding himself of Cottam and his companions, Rupert also picked out a new horse, a beast called 'Shottenherringe'. The fact

Dauentny

Brimidgham

Rupert – as 'Prince Robber' – in action, as depicted in parliamentarian propaganda.
The prince's reputation as dashing general or terrible plunderer went before him. The
dog at his horses feet is based on fact, because a poodle called 'Boye' accompanied him
on campaign.

that his new mount was actually the property of the Earl of Cork was dealt
with by a short note promising his lordship 'satisfaction' later.[18]

Rupert would relieve York, but in little more than a week his proud, and
hitherto all conquering, army would be shattered on the field of Marston Moor.
Though Rupert's army may eventually have grown to over 15,000 men on its
final approach to York, it was still somewhat outnumbered by the combined
forces of the Scots, Lord Fairfax and the Earl of Manchester's armies, which

were besieging the city with over 25,000 troops. Nevertheless, intelligence of the imminence of his arrival was enough to make them desist in their efforts and begin to shake themselves into posture for battle on the Knaresborough road, not far from Long Marston. Rupert, however, had already out-thought his enemies, and advancing from the north, via Boroughbridge, successfully relieved York on 1 July 1644. Many of the delighted defenders immediately emerged to seek supplies and to plunder the dumps of ammunition and boots which the allied forces had left behind. Another 3,000 men were now available to increase the royalist ranks.

Had this been the end of the affair Prince Rupert's northern campaign might have been accounted a success, but the enemy still had massive armies near at hand, and Rupert's interpretation of relieving York was to make sure that it was not besieged again as soon as he had left. Moreover the allied commanders were not simply going to allow Rupert's army to march away. So it was that when the royalists emerged from York the next morning the Scots and parliamentarians scrambled to block their path by occupying the low ridge of cornfields and scrub overlooking Marston Moor. For much of 2 July it appeared that an impasse had been reached. Rupert was blocked, and now waited some time for the Marquis of Newcastle's men to join him from York. The allies, meanwhile, were not yet ready to attack, nor immediately willing to sacrifice a position of advantage.

Only in the afternoon did the artillery begin to fire, and as late as early evening Rupert was still under the impression that the main action might be postponed until the following day. Now, and probably unintended by the commanders of either side, a skirmish commenced over guns which had found their mark on the royalist horse of Molyneux and Byron. The young prince was used to seizing the initiative, but this time it was Lieutenant General Cromwell, at the head of the left wing of the parliamentarian cavalry, who charged first. What had first appeared to be something of a non-event escalated rapidly into the largest battle of the civil wars. With the allies pushing forward on their left, the royalist cavalry now attacked successfully on the other wing until much of the horse was spent. Next the bulk of the allied infantry advanced, grinding its way painfully over the royalist foot. For some hours the result was unclear – and indeed several of the commanders fled or were wounded – but in the end Rupert's army, the king's great hope in the north, was decisively crushed.

Since it has been reckoned that eleven regiments that were present on that Yorkshire battlefield were wholly, or partly, raised in Lancashire, it is probable that several thousand Lancastrians fought on the royalist side. A good number will have died on 2 July 1644. In beating Rupert and the Marquis of Newcastle, the allied army of Generals Fairfax and Manchester, and the Scots, also struck a body blow to the royalist cause in Lancashire, and it was arguably one from which the king's cause would never fully recover. Marston Moor took away the powerful threat of Rupert's national field army, and with it many local royalist troops who could ill be spared.[19]

William Cavendish, Earl of Newcastle, Yorkshire royalist (1593–1676). Although he did not fight in Lancashire, the Earl of Newcastle's performance east of the Pennines had a considerable influence on what happened to the west. In the event Lord Derby and Cavendish were rarely able to coordinate their actions to any worthwhile effect, with Derby beaten in 1643, and Cavendish ruined by the defeat at Marston Moor.

OLIVER
CROMWELL

1599
1658

CHAPTER EIGHT

'A fatal blow':
the aftermath of Marston Moor

PRINCE RUPERT'S campaign in the north had raised royalist hopes high. The *Discourse* did not exaggerate when it suggested that in late June 1644 'halfe of the county' of Lancashire was back in royalist hands. Yet the fruits of Rupert's intervention in the north would evaporate almost as swiftly as they had come. On the other side of the Pennines the royalist Marquis of Newcastle, who still had troops under arms, and could have struggled on longer in Northumberland and Durham under more propitious circumstances, fled the country. It was said that one of his parting remarks was that he would 'not endure the laughter of the court' by going to Oxford. The Duchess of Newcastle excused her husband's swift departure for Hamburg on the grounds that his exit was honourable since his treasure and ammunition were exhausted. King Charles, for his part, viewed his resolution as 'discontent'.

It has been said, with only modest exaggeration, that Marston Moor was not a battle for York, nor a battle for Yorkshire, but for 'the north'. Sir Thomas Fairfax would claim that the royalist enemy had 4,000 dead at Marston Moor. This is undoubtedly slightly too high a figure, but modern research still suggests that the cost to one of the biggest royalist armies ever assembled was about a quarter of its number killed, wounded or captured. Foot soldiers

left Sir Hamo Thornycroft's (1850–1925) statue of Oliver Cromwell takes centre stage at Westminster, right outside Westminster Hall where the treason trial of Charles I took place in January 1649. Mindful of Cromwell's terrible historical legacy in Ireland, the Irish Nationalist Party objected furiously to public money being used for the statue, and so, in 1899, Thornycroft's Cromwell took his place here thanks to the generosity of the wealthy Liberal peer Archibald, fifth Earl of Rosebery.

PHOTOGRAPH: CARNEGIE, 2009

were certainly injured aplenty. Just one ordinary Lancashire man to return wounded was George Richmond of Chipping. Under the Commonwealth he would claim that he had been 'taken by force' to fight in Captain Robert Swinglehurst's royalist company, where he was 'maymed'. Though the infantry had suffered the biggest blow, men of quality were killed in numbers. As Captain Clarke would put it 'the battaile fell heavy upon Prince Rupert's old souldiers and the gentrey'.

One of the fallen officers who hailed from Lancashire was the old Catholic campaigner Colonel Charles Towneley, of Towneley near Burnley. Tradition has it that his wife Mary was in Knaresborough at the time of the fight, and went to the battlefield to seek out his body. Here she wandered the bloody field disconsolate and without success, until she met with a parliamentarian officer. This gentleman told her that it was better that she leave the scene of slaughter, which would only distress her further, and in any case he would not risk that she be molested. One of his troopers then lifted her up behind him on his horse. As she was carried away she enquired the name of the officer: the trooper told her that it was one Oliver Cromwell. The story was apparently related by the lady herself, many years after the event.[1]

Towneley was in no way unique, a significant minority of the royalists at Marston Moor being Catholics. Like him, some were Lancashire Catholics. Even more alarming to the allied forces representing the parliament, half a dozen regiments were 'Irish' – or at least crown forces that had been based for a long time in Ireland. These were still not necessarily liked, even by those who fought shoulder to shoulder with them in the royalist ranks. West-country royalist Lord Hopton, who used two such regiments in the south, described them as,

> bold, hardy men, and excellently well officered, but the common men were verie mutinous and shrewdly infected with the rebellious humour of Englend, being brought over merely by the virtue, and loyalty of theire officers, and large promises, which there then was but small meanes to performe.

At Nantwich both Lord Byron and his brother had commented on the unreliability of the troops from Ireland, a few of whom deserted to the enemy during the battle, with more changing sides afterwards. So it was that despite the propaganda regarding the fearfulness and cruel treachery of soldiers from Ireland, the initial approach of some parliamentarian commanders to these troops was pragmatic. For the most part they were seasoned professional soldiers, and their political views, if they had any, could be ambivalent.

Parliament's increasingly dim view of 'Irish' forces was expressed less than a month after Marston Moor, though the timing may have been purely fortuitous. In their opinion any 'well grounded peace' could not include the Catholics, nor the Irish, certainly not those who had had the temerity to fight or lend support to the enemy. As the proposition to the Commons put it,

> ... all Papists and Popish Recusants who have been, now are, or shall be, actually in Arms, or voluntarily assisting against the Parliament, shall expect no Pardon ... all Persons who have had any Hand in the Plotting, Designing and Assisting the Rebellion of Ireland, shall expect no Pardon ... all Irish Rebels, whether Papists or others, who have, or shall come from Ireland, and have assisted, or shall assist, in this War against both Houses, shall expect no Pardon.[2]

After the battle of Marston Moor the parliamentarians resumed their siege of York; but though they immediately summoned Sir Thomas Glemham the royalist governor to surrender, he gamely sent them back 'defyance', insisting that he would keep the city for the king as long as he could. Words and spirit would not be enough. Over the next few days siege guns were dragged into position, and preparations were made to storm the town. Glemham could see no way in which the coming struggle could end other than in defeat, ruin of the town, and possibly even slaughter. Accordingly, after a further day's negotiation, York was surrendered to the parliamentarian forces on 15 July. Glemham and his men were allowed to depart, colours flying and drums beating, along with their personal weapons; the artillery and other 'furniture of Warre' had to remain.[3]

A couple of days after the great battle near York Rupert himself had retreated on Richmond. Following brief discussions with the Earl of Montrose he then fell back via Wensleydale into Lancashire, arriving at Hornby about 8 July. In his wake would later follow Lord George Goring and many of the redoubtable 'Northern Horse', cavalry which had formerly been part of Newcastle's command, and much of which survived the debacle at Marston Moor. Still about 2,000 strong, the Northern Horse made its way via Westmorland and Cumberland, attempting to rejoin the prince or other friendly forces. With a total of perhaps 6,000 loyal troops still under his orders in the area, Rupert might yet have consolidated his hold on Lancashire.

Some of his orders of this time appear to confirm that this was indeed his intention. Sir John Mayne (or 'Mayney') was dispatched to secure Furness and raise more men for the king; the garrison of Skipton castle was increased, and there was talk of acting in concert with Montrose on the borders. Rupert's activity in the Kirkby Lonsdale area has been interpreted as preparation for fresh action, which terminated abruptly when news of the surrender of York filtered through. In the event Sir John Mayne's mission can hardly be described as an overwhelming success. Henry Slingsby speaks of Mayne's 'broken shattered regiments' even before he reached the area, where he was forced to engage in skirmishing with local parliamentarians outside Dalton. Threats from the south and from the Scots made him desist prematurely from his endeavours.[4]

In truth Prince Rupert appears to have been undecided as to what to do next, or was uncharacteristically overwhelmed by the show of concerted and unprecedented enemy strength he had met at Marston Moor. The shock of so serious a loss must have been considerable, even to a seasoned commander. The parliamentarian *Perfect Diurnall* optimistically refers to Rupert's army of about this time as 'broken forces'. Whatever Rupert's state of mind after the battle, it took a few days for him to make up his mind. So it was that he lingered in the county, or perhaps more accurately busied himself, for nearly two weeks, much of this time being spent around Preston and Garstang, where it is likely that he would have viewed the little garrison at Greenhalgh castle. He also visited Lathom again briefly on 21 July, reaching Liverpool a day or two later. Manchester, an enduring island for parliament in this turbulent sea of royalist change, he left unmolested. By the 24th Rupert was out of the county going south, enjoying the hospitality of royalist Chester on his way. Goring, a son of the Earl of Norwich with strong interests elsewhere in the country also went, leaving the brave but often unruly Northern Horse in Cumberland in the capable hands of Sir Marmaduke Langdale.[5]

Sir Marmaduke, a character destined to become important in Lancashire's civil war history, was a dour Yorkshireman, now in his mid-forties. One commentator described him as 'a very lean and much mortified man', almost a 'ghost' who haunted the enemy. Nevertheless this disturbing demeanour was balanced with devotion to the king's cause, and a considerable gravitas in his counsel and presentation which was widely respected in the royalist camp. Langdale had experience in wars on the continent from as long before as the 1620s, and had served as high sheriff of Yorkshire from 1639. Not unlike many future royalists, he had initially opposed certain aspects of the personal rule of Charles I in the 1630s, but had rapidly rallied to the king upon the outbreak of hostilities. He campaigned extensively from 1642, and was one of two

Sir Marmaduke Langdale, later Baron Langdale of Holme, Yorkshire royalist (1598–1661). Langdale was a seasoned campaigner, who raised a troop of horse for Charles I early in the war. Later he commanded the Northern Horse, fighting at Marston Moor and campaigning in Lancashire. In 1648 he led the entire northern royalist army.

brigade commanders of the Northern Horse at Marston Moor. His brigade, of about 800, consisted largely of troops drawn from Yorkshire, Lancashire and Derbyshire, while that of his opposite number, Sir William Blakiston, was drawn from Northumberland, Durham, Cumberland and Westmorland.

Sir Marmaduke's spartan image scarcely made him popular. Sir Henry Slingsby compared him to Caesar, being 'severe and precise in exacting discipline', leading his men to endure hardship by personal example. There was, however, cold method in his personal eccentricity. Apart from his copious experience, another reason for Langdale's rise to prominence at this juncture may have been his personal relationship with both Rupert, and his mother the Queen of Bohemia with whom he had corresponded in the 1630s.[6] Langdale proved to be a useful commander, in many ways the ideal figure to retain order in the Northern Horse.

With hindsight a number of Rupert's strategic decisions at this time were highly questionable. The Earl of Clarendon certainly had reservations about

Rupert's conduct after Marston Moor, his criticism in his *History of the Great Rebellion* being about as unguarded as it was reasonable to expect regarding close a relative of the king. Clarendon believed that

> ... if Prince Rupert had stayed with the army he marched away with, at any reasonable distance, it would have been long before the jealousies and breaches which were between the English and Scotch armies would have been enough composed to have agreed upon renewing the siege – the Scots talking of nothing but returning into their own country, where the Marquis of Montrose had kindled already a fire which the Parliament of Edinburgh could not quench. But the certain intelligence that the prince was marched away without thought of returning ... reconciled them.[7]

The royalists in Lancashire, summer 1644

If Rupert's grand strategy was flawed, his more limited tactical decisions had dreadful repercussions for Lancashire. Having gone west after Marston Moor, and having already assumed effective control of the county, many of the king's active supporters gravitated to the North West, rallying to his aid. Despite losses, there still remained a substantial force of cavalry and a reservoir, albeit a depleted one, of public support. Given these circumstances it would seem that two courses of action were conceivable. The first would have been to capitalise on the situation in Lancashire, bringing his troops together to face any threat, and meeting it on the ground of his own choosing. Victory here would have allowed Lancashire to remain royalist even though Yorkshire had been lost. A mere show of strength might have been enough temporarily to dissuade the enemy from launching an attack. In the event of failure in such a venture Rupert himself would still have been likely to make an escape to the south. The second possible course of action would have been to take as many men with him to Chester as possible straight away. The royalist forces would then be at their maximum possible strength further south. Rupert did neither of these things very successfully, and the county would be lost again. He was, it has been noted, very concerned about the situation on the Welsh border. Nevertheless, when he left Lancashire at the end of July 1644 the royalist forces there were not in the best of order, and, worse, Rupert seems to have departed without leaving a clear chain of command. Lord Derby may not have been the best of leaders in the past, but he was a leader, and one who commanded a significant measure of deference within the county. Lord

Byron was now the senior royalist in Lancashire, and his defence rested on the reliably friendly West Derby hundred, and the town of Liverpool with its access to Ireland, but quite what else was expected of him was unclear. If Rupert had a master plan for what Lancashire should do after he had gone, we are no longer acquainted with it.

Despite industry in strengthening certain Lancashire royalist garrisons, some simply melted away after the departure of Rupert and the main royalist force. At Clitheroe, for example, Captain Cuthbert Bradkirk of Wray, an officer of Tyldesley's regiment, had gone to some trouble to secure the old Norman keep for the king. He repaired the gatehouse, and laid in great store of provisions, including 'meall, mault, beef, bacon, butter, cheese and such like'. After Marston Moor some of his ill-gotten plunder was simply tipped down the castle well, and he and his company fled 'without taking any leave'.

While royalist control wavered, particularly in former parliamentarian areas, there were still enough men loyal to the king roving Lancashire to make a serious fight of it. By mid-August 1644 there were three main royalist units in the county. The most potent of these was the Northern Horse, now under Sir Marmaduke Langdale. This body spent some time in the Carlisle area, but with the growing threat from the Scots, and the increasing possibility that a strong body of parliamentarian troops would manage to interpose themselves between Carlisle and friendly forces in the south, Langdale had decided upon a march into Lancashire. His intention appears to have been to join with other royalist forces in the Lathom area and then to make for Chester. Another body, again essentially of cavalry, was commanded by Lord Molyneux. Numbering a few hundred these were similarly mainly survivors of the Marston Moor campaign, where, during the battle, they had formed a reserve in Lord Byron's second line together with other Lancashire horse and Prince Rupert's own cavalry regiment. Now Molyneux's men were back on their old south-west Lancashire stamping ground, handy for the defence of Liverpool, and to provide patrols against enemy incursion.

Tyldesley's battered regiments of infantry and cavalry were also back in Lancashire. Since May they had marched from Cheshire, fought they way through and around Lancashire, then marched across to York and back. Now they were billeted in the Fylde. Thus they had covered about 350 miles – the infantry entirely on foot. At Marston Moor both horse and foot had fought, the foot being in the front line. All had been heavily engaged, the infantry so much so that they had run out of ammunition. Quite a few were killed or wounded, including, presumably among many others, Captain Edward

Bradley, and soldiers John Swinglehurst and John Butler. In later years a common soldier, John Hilton of Wheelton, claimed that day to have received no fewer than 18 wounds. Lieutenant Edward Cripling had remained behind in York.[8]

Lord Derby, effectively sidelined, had no control of these elements: nor would he take a leading role in the fresh round of fighting about to break out in south Lancashire. Some authorities place him back in the Isle of Man as early as the end of July, but there is contemporary evidence to suggest that Derby remained at Lathom until some time in August. Thereafter he may have spent a little time in Cheshire, recruiting to support the defence of Liverpool. Parliamentarian sources on the earl's whereabouts at this time are confusing: one document, published on 10 September, is probably in error when it claims that he was at still at Lathom at that time; the *Perfect Diurnall*, meanwhile, has him skirmishing against Sir William Brereton. Either way he was certainly back in the Isle of Man by early autumn, his influence at an all-time low. Derby later said that his enemies used this episode to portray him as a 'neuter' to the cause.[9]

The battle for control of Lancashire, late summer 1644

By 8 August 1644 it appears that parliament had decided that royalist forces should finally be expunged from Lancashire. As we have seen Sir John Meldrum was now the senior parliamentarian officer in the Manchester area, and had reinforced the town as early as the beginning of June with a Scottish regiment and another of 'Lancashire men', previously under the command of Lord Fairfax. The scene was set for yet another campaign on Lancashire soil.

A Scottish professional soldier of lengthy experience, Meldrum appeared a very suitable candidate for the task in hand. Now aged about 60, he had been an officer for more than 30 years. As early as 1611 he was ranked as a captain, and had been awarded his knighthood in 1620 for service in the Low Countries. Though the ill-fated expedition to La Rochelle was arguably a low point in his career, he had also served successfully under the great Swedish king and military innovator Gustavus Adolphus. The civil wars were a natural arena for his talents, and together with Sir William Waller he had taken part in the reduction of Portsmouth in 1642, and had fought at Reading and Hull over the following year. He had then taken charge of part of the Earl of Manchester's Eastern Association, capturing Gainsborough from the enemy in late 1643.

His record had been marred by one serious setback, for at the end of February 1644 Meldrum had laid siege to the royalist stronghold of Newark. Despite forces under his command numbering over 7,000, drawn widely from the north and east Midlands, he was faced with strong earthwork defences and a determined resistance. The royalists held out until mid-March when Prince Rupert appeared with an army of similar strength, undertook a daring night march, and trounced Meldrum in battle. Newark was relieved, and much of Meldrum's military hardware fell into the hands of the enemy. Parliament did not lose confidence in him, however, and a victory over the prince's acolytes in the royalist heartland of west Lancashire would have appeared the ideal thing to remove any blot from his military record.[10]

Happily for Meldrum the tools for the job were to hand, and he appears to have raised a combined force of about 1,500 horse, 3,000 foot and five guns from both Lancashire parliamentarian resources and the reinforcements which he had brought into the county. The *Discourse* suggests that Meldrum's army at this date was composed specifically of the 'forces of Salford and Blackburn Hundreds with the remainders of Amonderness and a Regiment of the Yorkshire Horse'. His expedition set out from Manchester about 10 August 1644, probing westwards and attempting to locate the main body of the enemy which he believed to be in West Derby hundred. The royalists were not about to oblige him with a set-piece battle, and while some avoided the parliamentarians by heading towards Liverpool, the majority, including Molyneux, Langdale's Northern Horse, and Tyldesley's men retired into the Fylde.

In the event not all of the royalist detachments got away cleanly, and a few hundred horse were detected by men of Colonel George Dodding's regiment heading south-west from the Preston area in the direction of Ormskirk. In all probability these were intending to reach the safe haven of Lathom, where they would be beyond parliamentarian reach. The *Perfect Diurnall* takes up the story,

> Lord Ogleby and Col. Hudleston marching towards Latham House in Lancashire, encountered with Colonell Doddington not far from Preston, and at first the dispute was very difficult, but Colonell Shuttleworth received an alarm upon this engagement (his quarters being neere), delayed not any time to rescue the first undertakers; upon whose approach Colonell Doddington's men were put in great courage, and these two valiant Colonells, being joined together, charged the enemy with such brave resolution, that they were put into disorder, and many of them slaine

in the place. The enemies party, consisting of about 400 Horse, of which number was taken about 50 or 40 prisoners; the rest being totally routed, thought to have secured themselves in flying to Latham house, but finding the siege there well maintained, were most of them taken in the action; the men of note which were taken prisoners, were Lord Ogleby himselfe, Lieut. Col. Hudleston, Mr Maxfield, and Cornet Grimes.[11]

This account appears to be the best that we have of the skirmish, but it is one which leaves a number of questions, not least of which is where this action actually occurred. 'Not far from Preston' is unhelpful, and we should be aware that the *Perfect Diurnall* was a London publication whose editors were unlikely to have been particularly familiar with Lancashire geography. Other accounts speak of skirmishing all the way to the outskirts of Liverpool, and of another minor action in the vicinity of Wigan about this time. Broxap mentions 'near Walton' as the main site of this running fight. This does not seem totally satisfactory either, and there may have been some confusion between Walton, near Liverpool, and a different action at Walton-le-Dale, near Preston, the next day.

Significantly the *Discourse* contradicts the *Diurnall*, stating clearly that it was Colonel Nicholas Shuttleworth who took Lord Ogilvy and Colonel Huddleston, almost by accident. Shuttleworth and part of his troop of horse had been 'desirous to go to Preston if possible (it being the fair there)', but they were uncertain whether their appearance would be contested so they rode up cautiously. On the 'Coppe at Walton [le-Dale]' they met with 'some of the king's part, skirmished with them and put them to the flight'. Pursuing the enemy they managed to apprehend the officers, whom they then took prisoner. A few more royalists were encountered on the hill leading to the Ribble Bridge, and one cavalier, 'a brave portly man', put up a stout fight of it at the bridge end before they managed to kill him. They then made off back to Blackburn with the captives with 'great difficulty', though managing to preserve 'honour and safetie': sadly they were unable to determine the name of the opponent for whom they had such respect.

Perhaps the most likely explanation of the events of 11 to 15 August is that Meldrum sent a number of cavalry patrols of varying strength out across south Lancashire in an effort to find, and preferably pin, his illusive enemy. More than one of these made contact with enemy detachments, some of which fought, while others scurried back on either Lathom or Liverpool as opportunity allowed. Not all escaped. Colonel Dodding with a strong patrol of his regiment certainly defeated a royalist patrol, although it remains unclear exactly where this took place. By accident or design one or more parliamentarian scouting groups also investigated Preston, where it was discovered that the enemy grip on the town was slender, and the guard on the bridge virtually non-existent. It is known for sure that the 'Lord Ogleby' was James Ogilvy, Earl of Airlie, who was reported as being captured in Lancashire carrying despatches to the king from the Earl of Montrose. He may have joined a larger royalist patrol deliberately, or perhaps his armed escort was caught up in the fighting purely by chance. Ogilvy was one of the luckiest men in the entire civil war period: he would ultimately be captured no fewer than three times, and though excluded from pardon and condemned to death at least once, was still alive half a century after the wars had ended.[12]

The most important thing to emerge from these tip and run skirmishes was the intelligence gathered that there was no concentrated body of royalist forces between Liverpool and Preston, and that the chief quarry was thus likely to be found either around Preston or in the Fylde. Accordingly Meldrum turned north with a view to retaking Preston. His army reached the town late in the evening and brushed aside the few remaining enemy. By the end of 16 August he was in occupation of Preston.

It was now known, however, that the royalists were not far away. They were in the Fylde, they were hungry, and predictably enough the plunder and looting of that benighted area had begun all over again. Moreover this pestilential enemy was increasing in strength. As the *Discourse* related,

To that Armie in the Fylde that fled thither out of Darbie Hundred to avoid Sir John Meldrum ... came Colonell Goring's force [the Northern Horse] from northward into the Fyld Country, also being strong in number, for (as report was of such that saw them) before the last Companies were marched over that Bridge at St Michael's Church, the first Companie was judged to be at Kirkham. They filled the parishes of Kirkham, Poulton and Lythome, that night quartering at some House 20, some 40, some 50, and at some 60 men, most of them Horsemen. Sunday following they ranged, some of them three or four myles from their quarters, to pilfer and plunder without any respect to any persons, as well from their friends as Enimies, yea some in the Country when they came in said they were their frend, that when they went out cursed them ... For they took away all they could, leaving not any Horses they could meet withal. Besides, they forced the Country to thrash and winnow their corn, it being Sunday, for their horses, yea Winnowing in the open fields or lanes, without any Clothes, so disrepective were they ... And wherever they saw any fatt Cattell in any man's Closes or Sheepe, they fetched them to their quarters and killed them. They left not many pullen [poultry] in any place where they saw them, as also young geese. Thus they spoyled the Country that night and day, and had harmed it much more, if they had staid one other night.[13]

Equally offensive to the good citizens of Kirkham and surrounding areas were the sexual habits of the licentious cavaliers, for the royalist cavalry 'caried along with them many Strumpets', whom they termed 'Leaguer Ladies'. These 'they made use of in places where they lay, in a very uncivill and unbecoming way, who outwardly appeared otherwaies disposed'. Luckily for the few remaining chickens, and the morally outraged farmers of the Fylde, these goings-on were cut short by the alarming news that Meldrum and the parliamentarian army was less than a day's march away.

The royalist and parliamentarian armies appear to have reacted to each other's presence roughly simultaneously. The king's men cast aside their whoring, saddled up, and made for their appointed rendezvous at Freckleton on 18 August, carrying along with them not only their women, but 'drink in barrels, bread, flesh, roasted and cold, or what other provisions they had'. Langdale, who would have liked to cross the Ribble the same day, was disappointed to discover that the tide was high and the river unfordable anywhere in the immediate area. They were therefore forced to camp upon the marsh, or in Freckleton itself. The outlook was made all the more miserable by rain as it was 'sore wet' that August day, and this made it still less likely they would be able to cross anywhere west of Preston.

Meldrum, who appreciated that it was likely that the enemy would attempt to head south, had decided to put the river between himself and the royalists. This would have had the useful benefit of placing a significant barrier in their way, and a tactical advantage would accrue to the parliamentarians if the enemy attempted a disputed crossing. His horse headed off first, soon reaching their objective of a moor near Penwortham, on the other side of the Ribble from Preston. The *Discourse* states that the infantry and baggage were just packing up ready to follow them when there was a sudden change of plan. The new command was 'Toward the Fyld Country: to the enemy'.

This change of orders has yet to be explained satisfactorily, but there are a number of possible reasons why Meldrum suddenly decided to head straight for the enemy, even though much of his cavalry was at that moment on the wrong side of the Ribble. The first of these is that the Penwortham plan may have been merely a ruse all along. By sending his cavalry across the river he could have been hoping to mislead the royalists into thinking that no action was imminent. By not telling his own troops in advance, and possibly not even informing his own officers, this stratagem would have been kept secret, even in the event of prisoners being taken or attempted betrayal. Another possibility relates to the reinforcements that Meldrum's army received during the night. According to the *Discourse* a regiment of infantry carrying 'Black Cullers' reached him from Cheshire. This was Booth's regiment, a very useful addition to his infantry strength. Additionally Colonel Dodding's hard-working Furness cavalry now appeared on the scene. Though now tired, the *Discourse* relates that they had recently been recruited up to strength in Blackburn hundred, and would have made a splendid sight with their newly issued guidons. Taken together, these extra troops might have given Meldrum the confidence that he now decisively outnumbered his enemy, and should attack while the odds were on his side. Lastly, there is the somewhat prosaic explanation that Meldrum simply changed his mind: perhaps as the result of a new scouting report, or a council of war.[14]

So it was that Meldrum's infantry and artillery set out along the north bank of the Ribble, but burdened with guns, carriages and baggage on ground 'soft with quickmires' they made slow progress. Some of the larger equipment appears to have difficulty even clearing the fortifications of Preston. Sir John, doubtless frustrated, gathered to himself 'some that could direct him the way', and rode to the head of the army where his exhortations would do most good. Eventually they made Lea Hall, where, doubtless with some incredulity, it was discovered that the enemy had plunged deep into the Ribble and was already crossing. Realising that there was now every chance that the royalists would escape, Meldrum gave orders that as many infantry as possible should mount up behind the cavalry troopers and ride, two to a horse and as fast as possible, and attempt to intercept the enemy. Some few of the royalists were actually caught at Proud Bridge, Freckleton, and shots were exchanged. One or two were killed, but most of this group of stragglers made off. As the *Discourse* explained, 'it being marsh ground and many pooles and holes nor very passable for strangers'.

Almost all of the royalist army therefore made it across the Ribble, and also managed to avoid some of Ashton's Lancashire parliamentarian troops who were currently billeted about Hesketh Bank. The very wet royalist horsemen then marched on to Meols. Local tradition has it that they replenished their ammunition by stripping the lead from the roof of Halsall church, turning it into musket and pistol balls. Meldrum, meanwhile, had little choice but to turn round and march back to Preston. It was said that had he been just an hour quicker his army would have caught the enemy part in the water and part preparing to cross. The result of catching the royalists at their most vulnerable would doubtless have been a stunning victory. As it was, Meldrum was not about to give up, and though he now directed Dodding's men to reinforce the effort at Greenhalgh castle the pursuit would be renewed the following morning. He would find his enemy, unprepared, near Ormskirk. The people of the Fylde gave thanks both for Meldrum's arrival, and for his departure, since they were acutely aware that had he decided to stop with them his men would have continued the feast of their produce where Byron and Langdale had left off.

The battle of Ormskirk, August 1644

The battle of Ormskirk, fought on the evening of 20 August 1644, was one of the more important civil war engagements in Lancashire. It could indeed have been as significant in its own way as the fateful battle of Read Bridge a year earlier. A sizeable force of royalists, strong in cavalry, drawn not only from the county but many other places, faced a determined parliamentarian effort to clear Lancashire for a second time in eighteen months. A good deal was at stake, but the result has gone down as one of the damp squibs of history. This is perhaps partly due to the poor performance of the royalist army and their apparent willingness to give up more easily than we might expect. By all accounts the battle was over remarkably quickly. It is also true, however, that the surviving sources of information for Ormskirk fight are both more confusing, and less copious, than they are for many other actions. We might therefore argue that the significance of the battle has been relatively understated.[15]

As was so often the case with sudden routs a major cause of the royalist downfall was poor intelligence. Lord Byron's own account is particularly telling,

> I thought of nothing less than fighting that day, as having no intelligence of the enemyes being so neere, and came onely from Leverpoole upon a pacing nagge to advice with Sir Marmaduke what was fitt to be done.

So it was that a little before dusk the royalist commanders were about to open their conference somewhere on the fields just to the south of Ormskirk. Nearby were about 2,700 royalist troops, the majority of them cavalry, a few

Ormskirk parish church, with its peculiar combination of spire and tower. The Derby chapel here is the last resting place of thirteen Earls of Derby and 33 members of the family.

PHOTOGRAPH: CARNEGIE, 2009

of them infantry of Sir Thomas Tyldesley's regiment. Some of the horse were still mounted, but it would seem likely that many of the men would by now have either been preparing food or readying themselves for the night.

Suddenly this tranquil scene was interrupted, as Byron put it, by an 'alarm'. Enemy cavalry were already in the town of Ormskirk, and threatening the unprepared royalists with a sudden overthrow. Byron's first instinct was to get out of the way of danger as quickly as possible. As many troops as were available drew up 'in battalia' and faced in the direction of the town. While this rear guard, comprising Lord Molyneux's brigade 'and some dragoons', numbering perhaps 1,400 men, made good the retreat, the remainder of the command rallied back towards Aughton Moss. Very probably many of the royalists retired along what is now the route of the A59 in the general direction of Aughton, struggling to reform their units as they did so. Nevertheless Meldrum's men were not about to let their disarrayed enemy slip away quite so easily and 'came fast on', the parliamentarian cavalry being quickly seconded by their infantry.

The first of the parliamentarian foot into action were men of Booth's regiment, and it may not be coincidence that one of the lanes to the north of the main road to Liverpool, a little more than a mile from Ormskirk, still bears the name 'Booth's Lane'. The *Perfect Occurrences* of 28 August states that Booth's men succeeded in catching up with a body of the enemy, and now fired into them, vastly increasing their confusion in the gathering gloom. Now the parliamentarian horse followed up bravely and 'totally routed them'. At least one commentator has suggested that it was Tyldesley's careworn and under-strength foot which bore the brunt, and that their sudden recoil was due more than anything to their lack of ammunition with which to reply. They may indeed have had new musket balls, cast from church lead, but without powder, or with powder damp from the Ribble, their weapons would have been useless. Whoever flinched first would succumb to panic; royalist regiments first bunched together, then fell over one another in their haste to quit the field.[16]

Byron stated that the Northern Horse were first away under Langdale's orders, while the retreat was being covered by Molyneux, but that the volley 'of muskett shots' fell so 'foule' upon Byron's own troops that they were 'utterly routed'. Thereafter

> ... the enemye's horse, taking advantage of the disorder, charged into the lane (through which we were to passe) tooke and killed some, and strooke such a terror into the rest that they would not be stopped until they came to Liverpool.

Byron claimed that he attempted to rally some of the royalist horse in the lane and was lucky to escape capture. Sir Marmaduke Langdale's version was that Byron's actions were foolhardy, attempting to take command of Molyneux's troops and engaging himself when there was no need, thereby suffering a 'repulse' which had been avoidable. The very brief account contained in the *Discourse* agrees that the royalists were taken by surprise, with the parliamentarians falling upon them so 'fearsly that they fled in a most confused manner towards Liverpoole and Hailles Ford ... Many were slayne in the Rhublshawe many taken prisoners and many leaft their horses and fled into the feildes thereabouts to hide themselves, and night coming on they escaped'. *Perfect Occurrences* goes as far as to suggest that Byron and Molyneux were themselves among these fugitives, abandoning their mounts and hiding in a 'Corn Field'.[17]

This embellishment may be parliamentarian propaganda, but precise details of the brief fight, and much longer rout, must have been difficult to ascertain, even at the time. Given the limited amount of information that we do have, and the areas of agreement between the various sources, it would appear that much of the action occurred around the vicinity of Moss Delph Lane and Gaw Hill Lane, roughly mid-way between Aughton and Ormskirk. With the better part of 5,000 troops involved, the entire area between the railway line now to the east, and Clieves Hills in the west, might reasonably be thought of as part of the battlefield.

Following the battle the defeated royalists retreated in the direction of Liverpool, and were perhaps fortunate that nightfall coincided with their peremptory departure, for otherwise their destruction might have been total. As it was their routed troops eventually regained some order, and the survivors succeeded in rallying once they had put some miles between themselves and the parliamentarians. Not long after the cavaliers retired across the Mersey and into Cheshire.

Whether the Northern Horse had performed particularly badly must remain open to question. Defeated commanders often claim that their disappearance from the field is a strategic withdrawal, or an 'advance to the rear', but it is difficult to judge if this is the case with Langdale's command at Ormskirk. The Northern Horse had performed remarkably well at Marston Moor and would in the future achieve further considerable feats of arms. Both Byron and Langdale, or Langdale alone, might have been motivated by the desire to keep this important unit in being, and felt that to commit it upon such unfavourable terms was rash. Perhaps there was a belated realisation that saving as many men as possible, and taking them south as soon as possible, was the best outcome that could be hoped for.

On the other hand, large bodies of cavalry insufficiently supported by infantry could prove extremely skittish under fire. Moreover, the Northern Horse was an unusual, and somewhat disparate, formation whose name belied the fact that it was an amalgamation of many small regiments which had mainly been raised in the first eighteen months of the war, drawn from seven counties. Their local attachment to Lancashire, and to the Ormskirk area in particular, was thus less strong than in the ranks of Molyneux's troops. The somewhat rough and ready approach of the Northern Horse to war was certainly reinforced by the fact that their supply train was inadequate: even before Marston Moor one account speaks of the 'great drove' of looted cattle that marched with them, providing meat, quite literally, on the hoof. Nor were their weapons, or horses, considered to be of the best type. Wading across the Ribble, so soon before the Ormskirk fiasco, is likely to have compounded problems, and may have led to the jettisoning of carriages, or other heavy equipment, while Meldrum took the less direct but more certain course of avoiding the water.[18]

As might be expected the parliamentarian press claimed a resounding victory. Bullish reports incorrectly stated that Sir Thomas Tyldesley was either dead or captured, perhaps even that his corpse had been 'stript' and lay unidentified among the fallen. Another account noted that '1,000 horse' had been taken in the pursuit. This is a high and suspiciously round number, but there can be little doubt that the royalists had lost well into three figures, counting dead, wounded and captured. The *Perfect Diurnall* may well have made a close estimation of the truth with its claim of 300 prisoners taken. Certainly the 28 August edition of *Perfect Occurrences* listed 33 'chief prisoners', including Colonel Sir Thomas Prestwich of Hulme, Lieutenant Colonel Cottington, six captains, six lieutenants, four cornets and an assortment of 'gentlemen', clerks and quartermasters. It is perfectly credible that each of these persons of 'quality' could have been outnumbered by a factor of eight or nine 'common' soldiers, bringing the total count of prisoners to around 300. At least three of the officers taken, Captains Anderton (of Burnley), Brooks and Butler, came from Tyldesley's foot, which tends to suggest that the unit was indeed hard hit, and that part of it at least had been overwhelmed.

The names of a few of the royalist dead are also recorded: Colonel John Haggerston, Captain Thomas Anderton, Captain Richard Walmsley and Edward Preston, gentleman volunteer. Applying the same multiplier to this short list suggests that the royalist fatalities numbered perhaps a few dozen; doubtless there would have been a greater number of wounded. Little information survives concerning parliament's dead, but we can be reasonably sure that since the king's forces bolted quickly these were few. One parliamentarian casualty we do know was John Morrison, for whom £4 in expenses was later paid out, 'beinge rune through the bellie at Ormskirke'.[19]

The real significance of the battle of Ormskirk, however, was neither material nor numerical. It was Lancashire's final battle after Marston Moor, the last chance of local royalists to hang on to a significant portion of the county in the face of parliamentarian resurgence. Poor intelligence, low morale and confusion of command threw that chance, slender as it might have been, firmly away. The *Discourse* suggests that within 14 days of the fight at Ormskirk many cavaliers from the neighbouring counties of Westmorland and Cumberland who had fought in Lancashire now decided that no further purpose would be served by remaining. Rather, they decided to 'put themselves upon the mercy of their own country, and steale back again in smale and great companies'. So it 'pleased God of his goodness to give freedom to the County of all Forces of the king's part save that within the garrison of Liverpoole, Lathom and Greenall [Greenhalgh] Castle'. As Byron himself summed it up, Lancashire was now 'destitute of all forces' save those that were penned up in these few garrisons.[20]

Marmaduke Langdale was equally disposed to write off Lancashire at this stage, writing to Prince Rupert that, '... we resolved there was noe hope to continue in Lancashire, and in Westmorland would be as ill, and Cheshire in the same condition'. Unless the king was prepared to relieve 'these northern counties' again, he could see little to encourage him. The best remedy of all would have been the 'speedy returne' of the prince himself, but Langdale cannot really have expected a quick return to the heady days of May when the king's forces had held a decisive military superiority and initiative. The Earl of Clarendon was unequivocal in laying the blame for the loss of the north as a whole at the feet of Prince Rupert and the Marquis of Newcastle. Neither would ever offer the king what Clarendon would deem to call a fit 'excuse' or 'vindication' of their actions, nor could they reasonably be called to do so thereafter, since the 'times grew so bad' and 'the king's affairs succeeded so ill', that there was no opportunity. In Clarendon's view Marston Moor, and the month that followed, were indeed 'a fatal blow'.[21]

CHAPTER NINE

The end of the first civil war,
1645–46

W**ITH THE DEFEAT** at Ormskirk the surviving Lancashire royalist garrisons were effectively isolated, with no mobile royalist forces left within the county, nor indeed anywhere near enough to come to their aid. During 1644 the North had featured significantly in national events. Prince Rupert had sought to swing the war with a decisive thrust through the region. Briefly he prevailed for the royalists in Lancashire, but in attempting then to raise the siege of York had suffered a major reverse at Marston Moor. Decisively, then, by the end of August the king's faction in Lancashire was both militarily defeated, and – with the departure of Prince Rupert, Lord Byron, Langdale, and the Earl of Derby – leaderless.[1]

Liverpool falls to parliament

Into this vacuum, the parliamentarians stepped with quiet efficiency. Sir John Meldrum was quick to contain Liverpool. As the *London Post* of 10 September explained, he soon dug approaches, thus bringing 'the siege very neer unto their works and to their walls'. John Rosworme, the defender of Manchester, was instrumental in this activity, as master of the ordnance, giving directions 'for divers works'. By ship Colonel Moore cut off hope of relief from the seaward side. According to the *Discourse* Meldrum also had opportunity to demonstrate his humane side:

showing himselfe very charitable and bountiful to such pore men of the

left The rather forlorn remains of Greenhalgh Castle, near Garstang.
PHOTOGRAPH: CARNEGIE 2008

Parliament's part as were prisoners within it [Liverpool] by exchanging some and buying others out with money.

Parliamentarian hopes of a swift resolution to the siege of Liverpool were high; the morale of the defenders was depicted as very low indeed, and the inhabitants as 'deeply distressed'. Meldrum's opinion was that there was a good possibility of reducing the defenders 'by famine', and that the chance of a royalist revival within Lancashire any time in the near future was extremely unlikely. So rather than tackle the remaining enemy garrisons head on, by attempting to storm them, he deputed others to hold these points in check while cooperating with other parliamentarian forces to neutralise external threats. So it was that when Sir William Brereton sought out his help he departed for the Welsh border with as many of the Lancashire troops as could be spared. The result was a battle under the walls of Montgomery castle on 18 September 1644, which resulted in another defeat for Lord Byron and his Welsh and Irish allies.[2]

Sir John later reported to the parliamentarian Committee of Safety:

I was, by the earnest invitations of Sir William Brereton and Sir Thomas Middleton, easily persuaded to concur with them for the Relief of Montgomery Castle, besieged by the king's forces. I resolved to contribute my best Endeavours in that Expedition, as well in regard of the importance of the service, as that Leverpoole was not to be attempted suddenly by such forces as I had … whereupon I went along with the Yorkshire, Lancashire, Cheshire and Staffordshire Forces (which amounted to Three Thousand Horse and Foot), and marched to Montgomery Castle in Wales, which was by a great deal of Industry and Resolution taken in by Sir Thomas Middleton, together with a great deal of Powder, Match and Brimstone, which (coming from Bristoll) was prepared for the relief of Shrewsbury, Chester and Leverpoole.

As Meldrum approached the castle the enemy withdrew, but the next day, 'being the 18th of September', the royalists took

advantage of the Weakness of our Quarters, the Third Part of our Horse being employed abroad for victuals and Forage. Their Horse and Foot came on with great courage, resolving to break through our Forces and to make themselves Masters of a Bridge we had gained the Night before, which would have cut off the passage of our Retreat. It pleased God to dispose so of the Issue of the Business (by the Resolution of the Officers and Soldiers of Horse and Foot) the Enemy did lose the Advantage they had in the beginning and were shamefully routed by the Pursuit of the Victory which continued for the space of three miles.[3]

Among those captured at Montgomery was leading Lancashire royalist Sir Thomas Tyldesley, recently promoted brigade commander in Byron's army. Tyldesley was a significant prize in his own right, and Sir John planned to make maximum capital on this good fortune. Colonel James Wemyss, Meldrum's countryman and parliamentarian master of the ordnance, had been captured in June 1644, and the Earl of Essex, parliamentarian Lord General, was desperate to have him back lest he be tempted over to royalist service. Meldrum therefore suggested an exchange of prisoners.

The Lancashire parliamentarian colonels were, however, horrified by this proposal, and Meldrum was forced to refer the matter back to parliament's Committee of Both Kingdoms in a letter to London:

Upon an imagination I had that both Houses of Parliament would have been glad to have exchanged any of the like quality with Col. Weem [Wemyss] Master of the Ordnance to Sir William Waller, who is now a prisoner at Ludlow [having been taken prisoner at Cropredy Bridge], I proposed to Major-General to Sir Thos. Tillisley, who has been Major-General and Colonel of foot, that if he would procure Col. Wemes his liberty, I would use my best endeavours to set him [Sir Thomas] free, but upon discourse with the Lancashire Colonels I find [Sir Thos. Tyldesley] has been a great enemy to the country, and was the first man who drew blood in Lancashire in that cause, upon which account I have stayed the exchange until your pleasure be known therein.

Sir William Brereton's understanding of the Tyldesley case was that it was Colonel Shuttleworth who was instrumental in making sure that Sir Thomas stayed in captivity, his 'enlargement' at the present being viewed as extremely 'prejudicial' to the conduct of operations. In the event Meldrum's exchange plan remained unfulfilled, and Tyldesley was imprisoned in Eccleshall castle. Despite negotiations initiated by the royalists the following year, he remained in prison. Eventually transferred to Stafford, he managed to escape to continue the struggle for the king's cause in the Midlands.[4]

The fresh disaster visited upon the royalists at Montgomery both allowed Brereton to turn his attention to Chester, and gave Meldrum even greater freedom of action in Lancashire, whence he had returned by the end of September 1644. Back in front of Liverpool, he was quick to issue Sir Robert Byron a summons to surrender. The royalists were offered a stark choice: to render up Liverpool along with its arms and ammunition and the officers in the town could expect good conditions, with the soldiers 'of what nation soever' having 'free passage to their Country or dwelling houses without molestation, or to march to any part of the kingdome in safety (Cheshire excepted)'. If the royalists failed to deliver the town, the consequences would be harsh:

> you may expect noe other quarter but such as the subjects of this Kingdome (being sensible of the butcherly cruelties as have been practised in Ireland, and here in Lankashire and highly exasperated against such natives as have brought in strangers to ripp up the Bowells of their owne native country by invading England) will give.[5]

Given recent history at Bolton, Liverpool and elsewhere, this dreadful threat, aimed essentially at the troops from Ireland and those who had brought them to Lancashire, had considerable force. Yet it was also posturing in part, and may have contained an element of bluff since it appears that there was still little chance of a successful storm of the town. Meldrum had even met something akin to passive resistance when it came to renewing a vigorous prosecution of the siege of Liverpool. It was, he reported, difficult

> to bring back the Lancashire foot to their quarters before Liverpool, in regard of their want of obedience even to their own officers, the unseasonableness of the weather, and the time of harvest. They have had no pay for 18 weeks, and have been much pinched for want of victuals ever since they have been under my charge, the country being so wasted and spoiled by Prince Rupert's two journey's ... During my being abroad the enemy has taken divers of our men while sleeping upon their guard.

Nevertheless the hardships of the penniless besiegers that dreary October were mirrored, and exceeded, by those of the starving defenders of Liverpool. By 7 October Lord Byron was reporting to Prince Rupert his opinion that his brother in Liverpool would be unlikely to hold out more than another fortnight, unless resupplied, and this was now 'almost impossible' due to the fact that the 'Rebells' had gained possession of the Wirral as well as investing the town on the Lancashire side. Lord Byron was convinced of the loyalty of the royalist officers, but the soldiers, like their parliamentarian opposite numbers outside the walls, were growing 'extreame mutinous for want of pay'. Some had already slipped out of the town and run away.

Many who remained within Liverpool were war weary, but the prospect of actual surrender left them in a quandary. Following the terms of the September summons Irish troops, and others that the king had imported from across the Irish Sea, were understood to be barred from the mercy of parliament: Meldrum might well now have felt that he had *carte blanche* to dispose of them as he wished, and this could have included slaughter. A further exchange of letters in mid-October tended to reinforce this dire outlook, with Byron refusing another offer of relatively lenient terms, dismissing it as 'insolent', and Meldrum reminding him that those who brought 'strangers' to invade England were not in any position to be so dismissive. Sir William Brereton, who had become more intimately involved in the fate of Liverpool through his intervention on the Wirral, predicted that the 'obstinacy' of the 'grand Papists and Irish rebels' in the town would lead to their 'absolute distruction'. God's purpose, he thought, was to reckon with them for their past deeds, most notably the blood shed at Bolton.

The national picture tended to confirm the gloomy outlook for any Irish now falling into the hands of parliament. As Clarendon would later report,

> There had been lately in some service at land some prisoners taken of the king's troops, and, upon pretence that they were Irishmen, as many as they thought to be of that nation were all hanged, to the number of ten or a dozen. Thereupon Prince Rupert, having about that time when he heard of that barbarity taken an equal number of Parliament soldiers, had caused them likewise to be hanged upon the next tree. This the Parliament declared to be an act of great injustice and cruelty, and appointed the Earl of Essex to expostulate with Prince Rupert, in the letter they caused to be very rudely penned for him, and to send a copy of their ordinance enclosed in the said letter, with expressions of reproach for the prince's presumption in making an ordinance of theirs the argument to justify an action of some much inhumanity. Prince Rupert returned such an answer as was reasonable, and with sharpness equal to the provocation, and sent it to the Earl of Essex.

The impasse at Liverpool was broken only by mutiny and defection within the town on, as related in the *Perfect Diurnall*:

PSAL. 20.7.
Some trust in Chariots, and some in Horses, but we will remember the name of the Lord our God.

PRO. 21.31.
The horse is prepared against the day of battail, but safety is of the Lord.

London, Printed by *Andrew Coe*, 1644.

'Some Trust in Chariots and Some in Horses, but we will remember the name of the Lord our God'. Frontispiece from John Vernon's *Young Horseman*, 1644.

About fiftie of the English souldiers two or three days before made escape out of the Garrison, and drove away most of the cattle about the town, and came to Sir John Meldrum, which the English-Irish within the Garison perceiving, and that they were now in a desperate condition, for that quarter was before refused them, consulted together, and seized upon all their commanders or otherwise secured them, and thereby delivered up the town to Sir John Meldrum, laying down their lives at his feete, who no doubt will recompense this exploit by showing them more mercy than otherways they could have expected.[6]

Despite earlier bloodcurdling statements, Meldrum did indeed show compassion, and allowed those Irish who gave themselves up to depart on oath that they would not take up arms against England again. English troops from the Liverpool garrison were permitted to return home, although a few of the key commanders were kept captive. Strictly speaking Meldrum had disregarded parliament's directions in so doing, but he was successful in protesting that he was unaware of the 'Ordinance of Parliament against the Irish' at the time the terms of surrender were fixed. His leniency was retrospectively sanctioned by parliament on 9 November.

The *Discourse* confirms this version of events, remarking on the royalist soldiers' 'distaste at their Officers' who were delivered prisoner to the enemy. There were to be no mass executions, and Meldrum appears to have been as good as his word, but the officer prisoners were carried off to Manchester where both Colonel Cuthbert Clifton and Captain Richard Butler died during their incarceration. Robert Byron survived in captivity. Some of the troops who had come from Ireland were promptly shipped back to Dublin, but the royalist command were now desperate to have every man available on the English mainland. Many were therefore swiftly turned round, and at least 160 of them found themselves in Chester again, where, on Lord Byron's orders, several were punished for mutiny before the remainder joined this new beleaguered garrison. As the chronicler Randle Holme reported, on the morning of Saturday 9 November the gibbet was mounted by the 'Cornmarket House' in Chester, and here, 'Four souldiers with papers on their brests were hanged, whereupon was written in text letters, "Theis men dye for trechery in betrainge of Liverpoole"'.[7]

On the other side the final fall of Liverpool was greeted with joy, and most likely not a little relief. The *Discourse* reports the 'Roundheads' celebrating with 'bonfyres' and singing 'praises to God'. On 4 November 1644 parliament itself declared a public thanksgiving. Quite what to do with Liverpool now was another matter, as it was clear that the town would never be a model of loyalty to parliament. Some counselled that it would be as well to destroy the fortifications; others that, given its strategic importance, the proximity to Ireland and its innate vulnerability, a substantial garrison was required. In the event a garrison of 300 foot and a troop of horse was decided upon, but again it was a vexed question as to who should be in command. The Lancashire colonels disagreed about this, leaving Meldrum to report to parliament that 'the partialities and divisions of the gentlemen here are so great that I cannot but leave Liverpool in the hands of Colonel Moore'.

Even then things were slow to settle down, local rivalries having been further embittered by the death and destruction visited upon the town in both sieges. The new regime was outraged at the 'great company of our inhabitants' that had been 'murthered and slaine by Prince Rupert's forces', but it proved difficult to identify specific culprits, perhaps because the sympathies of potential witnesses still lay with the king. One highly unpleasant – and perhaps malodorous – reminder of the fighting was provided by the inadequacy of the shallow graves in which the victims had been buried. As a result the town council decided to give the bailiffs powers to send out anybody they picked 'with a spade or wiskett for the better covering of them.'

Part of the problem in Liverpool appears to have been continuing local dissatisfaction with Governor Moore, ex-royalists thinking of him as the enemy, and local parliamentarians regarding him as a coward who had abandoned them in time of need at the climax the first Liverpool siege. On the parliamentarian side there were calls for an enquiry into how the town had been lost to the royalists, so that 'whose neglect or default' had caused the spilling of 'innocent blood' could be discovered. By mid-1645 Moore was out of office and the town was under the governorship of Major John Ashurst.[8]

Interestingly it appears that at the time of the fall of Liverpool Meldrum would have liked to have come to a settlement with Lord Derby, now on the Isle of Man, for peace in the Lancashire area. Effectively this would be a royalist capitulation to be sure, under the terms of which both Lathom and Greenhalgh would be abandoned or destroyed, but it could also be one which allowed the Earl to retain his title and a portion of his lands. Such an arrangement had much to recommend it from a local perspective: Derby would be freed from his now self-imposed exile; Lancashire's torment of destruction would draw to a close; and Meldrum would be able to claim victory, enabling some his forces at least to be deployed against royalism elsewhere. A less obvious effect would have been a reconfirmation of Lord Derby's stance as the leading royalist to be dealt with regarding Lancashire, rather than Lord Byron or Prince Rupert.

Letters were sent, and meetings involving proxies arranged. Meldrum's agent in these proceedings was Major Ashurst: for Lord Derby William Farington and John Greenhalgh were granted safe passage into Lancashire. Discussions apparently reached quite an advanced stage, as was reported by Ashurst on 21 November,

> I find the Earl inclinable to give satisfaction to both Houses of Parliament, if he may have the least testimony under the hands of the Earls of Pembroke and Salisbury that upon the demolishing of the fortifications

and garrisons of Lathom House and Greenhalgh Castle, he may expect to have fair and noble dealings.

Later it was even suggested that Derby might be willing to come to London.

These intriguing possibilities came to nothing. Parliament excluded Lord Derby from any possible pardon under the terms of the 'Propositions of Uxbridge', presented on 24 November, which were expected to form the basis of national negotiations with the king. Parliament thereby accorded Derby the status of the third most dangerous royalist after Prince Rupert and Maurice, his brother. Under this threat Derby was extremely unlikely to come to any form of accommodation. Moreover, when Charles I finally got to see the Uxbridge proposals between late November 1644 and January 1645, his reaction was predictable: 'There are three things I will not part with – the Church, my crown and my friends; and you will have much ado to get them from me'. So it was that attempts at finding a way to peace went nowhere, and at least in the Lancashire instance, appear to have made the prospect less likely.[9]

Greenhalgh Castle

While the sorry events of Liverpool's capitulation were being played out, Greenhalgh Castle in north Lancashire was supposed to be contained by the combined efforts of Colonel Dodding, his Furness cavalry, and Major Joseph Rigby, the younger brother of Colonel Alexander. Proceeding here in August 1644, they made their headquarters, or 'maine guard', in the little market town of Garstang, less than a mile from the castle walls. That they were not entirely successful is suggested by the fact that the garrison, commanded by Captain Nicholas Anderton of Lostock, a gentleman who had previously trained as a Catholic priest in a continental seminary, was able to sally out. He ultimately maintained the castle, a strongly built but old-fashioned edifice, for many months.

From the account given in the *Discourse*, Anderton's success, his religion, and the sympathies of the local people, were no coincidence, 'manie desparat Papists' having filled the garrison. Garstang was itself essentially a Catholic town. Nor did Dodding's men endear themselves to the population, the 'northern men' living off local produce 'without pity', and putting the countryside to 'extraordinary charges'. From the limited amount of information we have, it also appears that the besiegers, at least initially, had no artillery. So it was that Anderton's garrison vexed the country thereabouts extreamly, fetching in, in the night time many honest men from their houses, making a commoditie of it, They sallied out often upon the Leaguiers and killed some. They stood it out stoutly all that winter.

At one point the besiegers attempted to undermine the castle, with the objective of filling the cavity with gunpowder and blowing a breach in the walls. They failed because of the sandy soil, which would not admit of a mine gallery.

At last this Anderton died and then those within being discoradged they were glad to come to a composition to deliver it up upon conditions – which were that they might go to their own houses and be safe. It was ordered that the Castle should be demolished and made untenable and all the timber taken out and sold, which was done. And so it lyes ruinated, It belonged to the Earl of Darby. It was very strong builded so that it was thought impregnable with any ordnance whatsoever, having but one dore into it and the walls of an exceeding thickness and very well secured together. Thus was Amunderness freed of visible enemies.

So was the siege Greenhalgh concluded in early June 1645. Now the only other garrison left in Lancashire was Lathom.[10]

The end at Lathom; Lancashire troops at Chester

The second siege of Lathom apparently began before the end of August 1644, but at first the very few parliamentarian troops available had little more than a watching brief. In the absence of either Lord Derby or his wife the house was under the charge of Colonel Edward Rawstorne, and for several months he took every opportunity of the laxity of the enemy to forage far and wide. The *Discourse* suggests that indeed for much of the period from the late summer of 1644 until early 1645 there was no investment worthy of the name:

Lathom House Intertained many disperat Caviliers into it, fetching in provision out of the Country of every side especially from Roundheads for there being no Guard upon them for all that Winter 1644 they ranged abroad into the Country in the night time taking many men prisoners and keeping them in durance till they would buy themselves forth with much money. For which purpose they kept a party of Horse within Lathom

House and did oft ryd ten or twelve myles in the night tyme and come again ere it were day. It was a great terror to many people of that sid of Ribble Watter ...[11]

Occasionally royalists even ventured beyond the Ribble, crossing the river covertly at night, and ranging as far as Westby Hall – on missions which the parliament men might well have characterised as looting and kidnap. On one occasion a small party raided the stables of Major Robinson's horse, but were prevented by the bravery of a few men of Kirkham, 'with some women who had their Aparons full of stones', who foiled their designs 'in the nicke of tyme'. The parliamentarian John Wood waded into the enemy first, kicking aside a trooper who attempted to pistol him, before slashing about him with his sword. The royalists made off, one of them bleeding from Wood's sword cut, later escaping via Woodplumpton and Penwortham. Their only prize on this occasion was the unfortunate James Clitherall of Eccleston who was carried away for ransom.

After the fall of Liverpool in November 1644 things might have been expected to improve: in fact the situation deteriorated, since some of those allowed to leave the town at its capitulation made their way to Lathom. As a result the compass of Rawstorne's garrison of early 1645 may have been larger than that successfully defended by Lady Derby the previous spring. In addition to the main house, there were also troops in 'the Lodge', later known as New Park House, and another house nearby which contemporary chroniclers identify only as 'a gentleman's house'. According the parliamentarian newspaper *Perfect Occurrences* it was the Lodge which was garrisoned by the 'Irish rebels'. The royalist defenders were now organised under their officers into troops and companies so that Major Munday and Captain Kay commanded the cavalry, with the infantry led by Captains Charnock, Farington, Molyneux-Ratcliffe, Nowell and Worrall, many of whom had held similar positions during the first siege. Colonel Rawstorne remained in overall charge. The Reverend Rutter continued to serve as chaplain, although we know that a second clergyman, Peter Travers, former rector of the parish church of Bury, was also present with the garrison. When parliament discovered this fact they sequestered the rectory, and handed its profits over to 'orthodox divines' sympathetic to the parliament.[12]

Reporting to the Committee of Both Kingdoms, Meldrum insisted that the parliamentarian forces on the ground for the job of reducing Lathom were inadequate, and other resources well-nigh non-existent. Stomach for a formal protracted close siege, involving trench warfare in wintry weather, was totally lacking. Indeed the Lancashire colonels under his command had told him plainly, 'that if I should press the soldiers on an approach which would require them to lie in trenches without shelter, where there was neither money nor victuals, they would all be gone do what we could to prevent it.'

After this time we hear little more regarding Meldrum's involvement with Lancashire. This was probably a setback for the parliamentarian cause, since his energetic hand had been instrumental in far greater results than his countryman, and predecessor parliamentary nominee, Sir John Seaton. By the summer of 1645 we find Meldrum engaged in the siege of Scarborough castle. Here he was mortally wounded and died on 21 July; the castle surrendered the very next day.

Whether it was Meldrum's goadings and complaints, or whether Lancastrians eventually became exasperated with the arrogance of royalist raids, before the end of 1644 there were signs of a new seriousness of purpose in the parliamentarian camp. There was now a will to rid themselves of the 'outraigious dealings' of the cavaliers of Lathom, once and for all. The parliamentarians were, however, disinclined to hurry their activity: for even if the house did not fall immediately, a tight investment would at least 'stay their Robbing'. In January 1645 a fresh magazine of munitions was carted down from Manchester to Ormskirk, at the not unreasonable cost of 10s. About the same time Colonel Egerton was appointed commander of the investing troops. His progress would be systematic rather than dramatic, as was described in the *Discourse*,

> Colonell Egerton was the man agreed upon to be Governour of it. He was to have forces for it out of all the County. The siege was not laid so close to the House as at the first, nor did the Leaguer lie in trenches: But a great ditch was draune round the House a good distance from it which was much Troublesome to pass over and the Leaguer lay a good distance from it, as convenient as possible and the whole County bore their charge.

There was one bout of skirmishing around 'Gilliburne's house' about this time, and pro-royalist accounts give Rawstorne at least one victory over Egerton. During a spirited night sally it is described how the royalists managed to capture a good deal of enemy powder, and the Roundhead commander was forced to 'fly away in his shirt and slippers'. Be this as it may, at last the royalists were successfully contained. In late February an interesting exchange of prisoners from Lathom received the formal sanction of parliament: it was approved that the royalist Colonel Uriah Leigh, and his servant 'prisoners to the Parliament', should be traded for Lieutenant Colonel Rigby (son of Colonel Alexander Rigby MP), and his servant, 'now prisoners at Lathom'. To make sure the young Rigby was released Leigh would give Colonel Alexander £1,000 as surety.[13]

To prosecute the siege more effectively was obviously proving difficult in view of the range of tasks the parliamentarian Lancashire committee still had to undertake. How surprisingly stretched resources were at this late date was illustrated by a letter sent from Manchester by Colonel Ashton on 22 March to Sir William Brereton in response to his request for further assistance in Cheshire,

> As for the forces which are desired out of Lancashire in regard our soldiers which are in common pay are all abroad in public employment – in Cheshire and in blocking up Lathom and besieging Greenhaugh Castle and guarding the frontiers of the County against Skipton – we know not how to perform what is expected of us. But we are sending to the captains of the new raised companies here about which consist of husbandmen and such like ... The prisoners you sent here are very troublesome to this town and the charge of them ... occasions a stronger guard than otherwise would be needful.

Just three days later Colonel Egerton wrote to Speaker Lenthall in London in similar vein, outlining the specific problems he faced before Lathom. He still had no more than a few hundred troops, most of whom had been got together only by his own efforts, and due to both enemy activity and indiscipline among his own men he had been forced to pull well back from the walls. It would take several more months to improve on this situation, but with the coming of better weather there was also a new threat to contend with. During the winter months the Lancashire committee had been complacent in the knowledge that there was no royalist field force near enough to come to the aid of Lathom. In April 1645 this pleasant conceit was abruptly punctured. Intelligence was gained that the king's main field army was about to march north to join forces with 'those of the two princes in Hereford and Worcester shires'. In fact enemy ambitions were greater still, according to one royalist account:

> For although the whole Design of the Winter past was to march Northward for the relief of those parts, and particularly Pomfret [Pontefract] Castle;

yet this march was more hastened under the Pretence of relieving Chester, then besieged, and in danger to be lost; though the true cause was, the earnest Desire of Prince Rupert to be revenged of the Scots for the defeat he had received the year before.

How close the Lancashire parliamentarians were to the Presbyterian Scots was well illustrated by a visit the Scottish commanders to Manchester at this very time. Here they appear to have been well received as allies: or at the very least plied heavily with drink. The constables' accounts show that the provisions laid in for the occasion included at least 29 gallons of beer, a 'pint of sacke' and some lemons, the purpose of which was not immediately apparent. Tobacco worth a total of 16s. was provided explicitly for the entertainment of the Scots' commanders.[14]

The prospect of another major campaign in the north was now very real, and doubtless made all the more vivid by the presence of Sir Marmaduke Langdale and a revived Northern Horse in the royalist ranks. Indeed that February 37 of the officers of the unit had actually signed a 'Northern Horse Petition to goe Northward'. Their explicit intention was to succour and encourage those 'valuable and considerable' parts of the north loyal to the king 'enthralled under the pressures and insolencies' of parliament, and to relieve the garrisons currently under threat. In Cheshire Sir William Brereton believed that the main royalist field army would indeed come to the aid of Chester, and then 'strengthen themselves in Lancashire' before a general attempt on 'the north'.

By 12 May Charles himself was at Droitwich. Leicester was stormed at the end of the month, the 'cruel massacre' being described by Major Leonard Watson as 'not much unlike the sack at Magdeburg'. Brereton, who had hoped to gather both Scottish and Sir Thomas Fairfax's 'New Modelled' army forces to his aid, but had failed in his design, took the prospect of the intervention seriously enough that when the king's forces arrived at Market Drayton he immediately desisted in his investment of Chester. He then retreated into Lancashire, where he would be likely to receive more local support. At a muster on 'Barlow Moor' Brereton's troops were supposed to join forces with the Lancashire regiments of Colonels Holland and Ashton, but the Cheshire leader was disappointed with the result, 'very few of them came up', Colonel Holland's being 'in a very great mutiny' and refusing to march. One of the chief reasons for this lacklustre response was doubtless the annoyance of Lathom, which as Brereton put it, continued to 'very much puzzle this county'. Another was an outbreak of plague which had struck in Manchester.

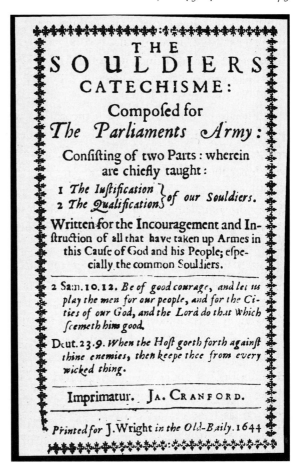

THE
SOULDIERS
CATECHISME:
Compofed for
The Parliaments Army:
Confifting of two Parts: wherein
are chiefly taught:

1 *The Iuftification* }
2 *The Qualification* } *of our Souldiers.*

Written for the Incouragement and In-
ftruction of all that have taken up Armes in
this Caufe of God and his People; efpe-
cially the common Souldiers.

2 Sam. 10. 12. *Be of good courage, and let us
play the men for our people, and for the Cities of our God, and the Lord do that which
feemeth him good.*

Deut. 23. 9. *When the Hoft goeth forth againft
thine enemies, then keepe thee from every
wicked thing.*

Imprimatur. JA. CRANFORD.

Printed for J. Wright *in the Old-Baily.* 1644

Title page of the
parliamentarian *The
Souldiers Catechisme*, 1644,
a pamphlet intended for
the 'encouragement and
instruction' of 'all that have
taken up arms in this cause
of God and his people'.

As it transpired, the king's army was defeated decisively by the New Model
Army at the battle of Naseby on 14 June 1645. This was not immediately the
end of the matter. Charles himself retired on Bewdley in Worcestershire with a
force of 4,000 cavalry, but renewed his calls to the Marquis of Ormonde, Lord
Lieutenant of Ireland, for 'Irish assistance'. Then, having followed a tortuous
path through Wales, he reappeared at Raglan, where he spent much of July
raising Welsh forces. Charles now realised that there was a high chance the
war would end in his 'ruin', but expressed his determination to Prince Rupert
that he would 'neither abandon God's cause, injure my successors, nor forsake
my friends'. The king hoped, very soon, to be at the 'head of the greatest
army' that he had possessed all year. Doubtless this was over-optimistic, but
the possibility of another royalist cavalry chevauchée through the North West,
or attempts at the relief of Lathom or Chester, must have helped to galvanise

the minds of the Lancashire committee men. Doubtless there were many who believed his target to have been Chester, York or Liverpool. In fact his meanderings took him by a convoluted route to Doncaster, before he retired once more to the relative security of Oxford.

By the first week of July 1645 – technically almost eleven months into the second siege of Lathom House – the parliamentarians were finally present in some strength, with 4,000 men in position according to one account. The besiegers had mounted their artillery so as to cover the Lodge. As *Perfect Occurrences* reported

> Our forces having blocked up those rebels in this garrison, sent them a summons to deliver up the said garrison to Parliament, but they refused, saying that they would keep it good for their King by whose authority they were put in there. Whereupon our forces placed their batteries, and plaid upon the House [i.e. the Lodge], and having made some breaches in it, marched up close to the enemy and stormed them; and it was a very hot fight of both sides for the time it lasted, and we had divers hurt and some slaine, as in so hot a storme as that was could not be avoided: but our brave men followed on so gallantly, that notwithstanding the violent opposition of the rebels, yet our men brake in upon them, killed and tooke them alle.

The parliamentarian troops claimed that they had killed 40 of the enemy, with several wounded and 60 captured, plus 12 officers variously put out of action, and 'a supposed' Catholic priest also taken. Along with 100 weapons and various baggage and powder barrels, the victorious soldiers captured 'Popish books, beades and crucifixes'. The Irish portion of the garrison quartered in the lodge was effectively liquidated.[15]

How close the siege now became, and how difficult it now was for the defenders to communicate with the outside world, is illustrated by stories repeated in a Victorian description of the second siege. According to the first of these, the Reverend Rutter actually conspired to keep contact with friends of the Derbys outside the walls by means of a female go-between. She was captured and tortured, having her fingers burned off in an attempt to extract information. The members of the garrison now resorted to the services of a trained dog which carried despatches written in cipher hidden in his collar; he had completed several missions until shot by a soldier just after he had crossed the moat. The inhabitants of Lathom were now so tightly constrained that there was nothing to buy or sell and money appears to have become meaningless: the bored and hungry royalist soldiery pooled the coins from their purses and pockets and used them as stakes and tokens in games of 'span-counter', the pastime that we now call shove-halfpenny.[16]

Though the Lodge had succumbed to cannon and storm, earlier experience had taught the parliamentarians to treat Lathom House itself with greater respect. No efforts were spared to prevent supplies entering the house, but this time the approach was far more circumspect. In August two of Lord Derby's officials, Mr John Sharples and Mr Paul, were captured by parliamentarian troops: the story they told was that they were on a mission on behalf of the earl to instruct the garrison of Lathom to treat with the enemy in an attempt to gain the best terms possible. Given that Derby had entered into at least indirect discussions with Meldrum a few months earlier this seemed plausible. The gentlemen were therefore brought to Lathom, and were allowed to cross the siege lines in order to deliver another demand for surrender. This was sharply rejected, and the emissaries reappeared from the house. As civilians who had presumably acted in good faith, they were allowed to return to the Isle of Man.

The continued resistance of Lathom after August 1645 has been portrayed as either glorious, or pointlessly obstinate, depending on point of view. Hope remained that relief might yet be forthcoming from outside. Following his first venture to the north and subsequent retreat Charles I had once more found his way to Wales, and to his familiar stamping ground of Raglan. By 18 September he was again on the march, headed across the Welsh mountains for Chester, his aspiration being of going through Lancashire to join up eventually with his Scottish supporter Montrose. In a letter to Major Ashurst Brereton stated the opinion that it was Charles' specific intention to relieve Skipton and Lathom, 'and then to recruit his foot in Lancashire, where Manchester will almost as easily be entered as attempted', unless there was an army at hand to stop him.

On arriving at Chirk the king sent an appeal for the garrison of Chester to hold on just one day longer, as relief was at hand. Not much later he was indeed riding across the Dee bridge into the city, accompanied by his Life Guard and the horse of Lord Gerard. If any messages at all were finding their way into Lathom by this time, it must have appeared that a raising of the siege could perhaps be tantalisingly close. On 24 September, however, the king's army found itself trapped between the former besiegers of Chester and the troops of Sydenham Poyntz's Northern Association army. Battle was joined at Rowton Heath. As at Ormskirk, Booth's regiment was prominent in the action, as was Langdale's Northern Horse, and again as at Ormskirk the royalists were soundly defeated, with 1,000 men killed, wounded or captured.

After Rowton Heath it seems that the defenders quickly agreed terms for the submission of the house The Lancashire committee were heartily sick of the trouble and expense of the second investment, now well into its second year. It was agreed that Lady Derby could return to Knowsley; Lathom was to be being disarmed, but could remain occupied by the earl's retainers. This relatively easy end to the siege was probably vetoed from one, or both, sides. In one version of events the royalists, seeing that they had a negotiating advantage, pressed their luck too far and also demanded to keep their artillery: in another an outraged member of the Committee of Both Kingdoms in London could not stomach such leniency and demanded more from the surrender. Either way there was no capitulation at the end of September, and the siege dragged on. It may well have been the relatively supine attitude of the Lancashire men to their royalist cousins inside the house which was one of the factors that influenced parliament to make sure that fresher troops from outside the county became involved.[17]

It was also the case that the Lancashire parliamentarian forces were at risk of being dangerously over-stretched. On 26 October the committee wrote to their opposite numbers in Cheshire explaining, in reply to the latter's urgent calls for help that,

> We have also at the same time received an alarm from the north by the retreat of the forces which escaped at Sherburn [in Elmet] and fled into Scotland. For the repelling of which we sent towards them above 200 horse and all the forces from Lonsdale Hundred. We are endeavouring to our utmost power to strengthen our frontiers against Skipton, by whom we are much infested, and to draw with all speed unto the parts towards Chester all the rest of the forces of the county not employed at the Leaguer at Lathom. We have given out orders (and hope they will be obeyed) for the speedy marching of seven troops of horse into your county for your assistance …

For several more weeks the defenders of Lathom clung on in hopeless deprivation. Finally, 'towards Christmas', they were driven back to the negotiating table, as Thomas Malbon put it, by 'famyne, wante of victuals and other necessaryes'. As was recorded in the *Discourse*,

> … their provision waxing low and scant and how to come by more was

not so easy to them as formerly, therefore was their couradg somewhat abaited and qualified as to admit of a parley with the Colonells. A place was appointed where they met yet could they not agree. They bore it out with much seeming Audacitie – that they would stand it out even to Death unless they might have such Conditions as they proposed. Thus the parley broke off and they returned into the House againe. When they were gone Colonell Alexander Rigbie said to the rest of the Colonells and Commanders then present that he was persuaded that notwithstanding their seeming stoutness and highnes of stomacke they could not hold out long and the smell and taste of their garments bewraied it.[18]

Rigby's prophecy was soon proved correct. Terms were set forth on 2 December, and the next day the garrison marched out. Some debate remains concerning the precise form of the surrender, as there is some doubt whether the surviving texts of terms were actually applied. However, it does appear that, other than their lives and liberty, the brave defenders were ultimately able to salvage very little. Rawstorne himself was able to maintain some dignity, riding out with his personal arms and £10 in money. Everyone else was stripped of their weapons and cash before being turned loose. All other things were the spoil of the victors, namely 12 cannon, other weapons and ammunition, and a 'greate store of rich prize and pillage'.

Final royalist defeat in Lancashire, December 1645

With the end at Lathom, the end also came for royalism in Lancashire. As the *Perfect Diurnall* put it, by this means 'the whole County of Lancashire is absolutely freed and reduced under the obedience of the Parliament the enemy having not any one garrison in that County'.[19]

Interestingly neither Rigby nor Egerton negotiated the final capitulation which was between the Cheshire parliamentarian officer Colonel John Booth, one-time governor of Warrington and son of Sir George Booth, on the one part, and Colonels Roger Nowell and Edward Vere, clerk Peter Travers, and Andrew Broome 'gentleman' servant to Lord Derby, on the other, all of whom acted on behalf of the governor Rawstorne. As a result it appears that a good deal of the plunder went to Cheshire troops who had been called in over the last few weeks to relieve some of the long-suffering Lancashire men. As might be expected, this whisking away of the prize, after such a long period of toil and hardship, incensed the Lancashire parliamentarian soldiers.

Ironically many of the Lancashire soldiers were now serving in Cheshire, or on their way there, whence they had been sent to assist in the siege of Chester: but when the news of the fall of Lathom reached them the reaction was electric. As Colonel George Booth observed on 20 December, Ashton's regiment,

> are broken out into such a mutiny that they are tumultuously run towards Lathom, vowing to cut the throats of those in the house. Yet their officers are gone after them and, if they can prevail, intend to bring them over to Runcorn.

This was not so easily achieved however, for two days later a shame-faced Ralph Ashton (the younger, now commanding his father's former regiment), was forced to admit that his unit was 'dispersed', with many 'gone to their own homes, some to Lathom House and, I am afraid, to the Committee in a contemptuous manner to require their arrears'.

The reaction of senior Lancashire parliamentarian officers to the crisis of Christmas 1645 was more measured than that of their men. Nevertheless they were assiduous in attempting to make sure that, having put so much effort into the taking of Lathom, their forces should not be denied a major share in the spoils. The committee therefore engaged in an exchange of letters with both the Cheshire committee and with Sir William Brereton, commander of the besieging force at Chester, demanding that their men should be paid there. The Cheshire committee replied that the Lancashire men had already been paid by them as much as they were able, and indeed that they had received more to date than soldiers from Staffordshire, Shropshire, Wales and indeed Cheshire. Moreover, the Cheshire committee was anxious to point out that it was the lack of payout from Lathom which had caused the mutiny. The Cheshire committee had received no funds from this source, so in its turn it pleaded with the Lancashire committee 'to give satisfaction to your soldiers'.

This was not what Lancashire had wanted to hear. Their own officers and men had told them a different story: £10,000 had been sent for the paying of the parliamentarian troops at 'the leaguer' of Chester – and the Lancashire men had not had their share. With regard to prize money from Lathom the Lancashire committee 'had not yet anywise disposed of the same'. This unedifying wrangle went on for some time, with promised additional Lancashire forces for Brereton at Chester not arriving. In answer to his repeated calls for help the Lancashire committee penned him the somewhat plaintive response from Preston, that,

Although it hath pleased almighty God to deliver that strong hold of Lathom up into our hands, yet by reason of the long siege there our treasury is so much exhausted that we are not able to give the soldiers that reasonable satisfaction which their pains and endeavours to deserve ... we have so long fed our men with our promises and small performances by reason of our wants that ... we hear they absolutely protest that without a fortnights pay they will not march, neither foot nor horse.[20]

They might well have added that though the intervention of the Scots had helped to bring victory a step closer it was also costing the English counties dear. In February 1645 the committee had been saddled with a further assessment of £730 to pay for this military assistance, and it looked as though this additional cost would continue to accrue for some time. Sequestration of royalists' property had helped the committee's financial plight to some extent, but many of these estates were worth a good deal less now than they had been in peacetime. As Colonel Egerton would remind parliament, 'the whole county is extremely exhausted, and they have been plundered of horse and cattle by both sides; and land is so cheap by the great quantity of sequestered land untilled and unstocked that the well affected from whom we receive our greatest relief can make very little of their estates'. Rather than demanding yet more of a county that had done so much for the cause, the committee warned the Speaker that further demands could cause Lancashire's unpaid forces to implode. London should be sending Lancashire money, not the other way about.

It was lucky indeed that no new royalist army lurked in the wings to come to the aid of Chester, for had such an army existed it must be suspected that the unpaid parliamentarians might indeed, even at this eleventh hour, have cracked like a brittle twig. As it was there were few royalist troops left, and Sir William Vaughan in Wales was too weak to make any serious attempt at relief. So the besiegers' festive gifts to Chester were cannon shot, stones, and flaming 'granadoes' to batter the town into submission, and a significant part of the Lancashire forces assisting in the siege regained their composure. A parliamentarian council of war held on Christmas Day at the Red Lion in Whitchurch, for example, records the presence of a detachment of the Lancashire troops, horse under Major Jackson, and foot under Major Peter Brooke and Captain Aspinwall. Similar numbers continued to man the trenches around Chester.

Shuttleworth's horse were deployed to the south-west of Chester to prevent supplies reaching the town from the Welsh side, but clearly these men were feeling considerable hardship, and it was their Cheshire hosts who had to provide them with 'horsemeat' or fodder for their mounts. On 29 December, however, a body of enemy cavalry crept past them while they were at Dodleston, about four miles south-west of Chester, and brought fresh supplies into the city. Brereton and his colonels were angry that Shuttleworth's men paid so little heed,

> If your horse will not obey order and do duty as they are commanded, they will be rather a burden than a help unto us. Then they had better return to Lancashire than continue here so unwillingly and unserviceably. For so many of them to go, to the Northgate is both senseless and unnecessary.

Ashton's foot regiment was still effectively absent without leave, despite the 'great pains' taken to bring them back into line. Brereton remarked darkly that there were 'evil spirits abroad' conspiring against his efforts. If the parliamentarian troops were in an under-fed, impecunious and uneasy alliance, things were far worse for the royalist defenders within Chester. As at Lathom, it was hunger and deprivation which took the greatest toll, Lord Byron reporting that the citizens and soldiers alike were becoming 'very impatient and mutinous'. On 30 January 1646 commissioners representing the two sides met to discuss terms. After protracted discussions eighteen articles were finally agreed, although some of the royalists failed to ratify the terms. On 3 February the royalists marched out, and Chester was surrendered.

If Lancashire was financially exhausted by the campaigns and pillage of 1642–44, the final straw came with the fifteen months spent investing Lathom for the second time. Interestingly the crisis point came not simply as the result of a cumulative lack of pay, but as an issue of fairness, with the long-fought-for reward being snatched away, it seemed, by others. The first, and better documented of the sieges had been bad enough, but the Lancashire committee seems to have come perilously close to disaster as a result of the eventual victory over Lord Derby's home. Taking the fight deep into Cheshire also placed considerable strain on the patience of those who had now spent more than three long years at war. Reluctance to serve in other counties was no mere xenophobia, or local prejudice; it was extremely difficult, in practical terms, in winter when supplies and pay were deficient. Towards the end, the war in Lancashire and Cheshire alike had become a war of attrition, and parliament prevailed at last by a margin considerably narrower than many now imagine.

Reform of the Lancashire committee

Though parliament was clearly in the ascendancy in Lancashire during 1645 and 1646, the situation was far from resolved and settled. Belatedly London had realised that it had continuing leadership issues in the county, as well as dire problems of finance. This begs the question as to how the committee had operated prior to August 1645, and why indeed reform was attempted at this juncture. The primary purpose of the county committee had been military, but its historical importance was arguably much greater, since, other than parish and manorial courts and the quarter sessions, in most parts of the kingdom it was the first real example of local government covering a wide range of issues at the county level.[21] Certainly the uses to which it was finally put, and the interests which it represented, were much wider than that of the Duchy, whose functions were curtailed and then temporarily ended by the war.

Our knowledge of the operation of the Lancashire committee early in the war is frustratingly scant. Odd fragments tell us that the committee was not specifically elected, while on important questions its procedure was not unlike a miniature version of the London parliament itself, with votes following debate. Once action was joined, formal meetings can only have been irregular, or poorly attended, since many of the key players would also be military commanders who were campaigning in the field with their regiments. Of the county's five MPs, Ralph Ashton, John Moore and Richard Shuttleworth appear to have spent the majority of their time in the county. William Ashurst and Alexander Rigby spent more of their time in London, being perhaps best regarded as the chief spokesmen for Lancashire at Westminster, although Rigby in particular also campaigned extensively during the first civil war.

Recent analysis of surviving papers suggests that 12 individuals played pivotal roles in the parliamentarian committee from its inception until its reorganisation in 1645: and that perhaps a total of 20 individuals were regular attendees. The names of Peter Egerton, Thomas Birch, Richard Holland, Alexander Rigby, John Moore, John Booth, Sir Thomas Stanley and Ralph Ashton are readily familiar to us as leading fighters in the field. John Bradshaw, lieutenant colonel in Ashton's regiment, was also a particularly diligent member of the committee. Sir Richard Houghton and Richard Howarth appear to have come to prominence only during 1645. Some have suggested that the committee was divided in some way into 'peace' and 'war' parties, and that its internal politics were played out along these lines. While some members were obviously more bellicose than others, this is undoubtedly too simplistic, since as matters progressed the tenor of changing times and the geography of conflict appear inexorably to have swung the whole committee towards war.

There is a clear impression that during the earliest period, following the first declarations in the summer of 1642, the moves of the committee were essentially defensive, reactive even, to royalist initiative. As Manchester and the surrounding areas of Salford hundred were the only ones on which parliament could rely, it is tempting to assume the Mancunians were in a *de facto* position of leadership. Most members of the committee were established pillars of society. If parallels with other counties hold good, it may well be that the committee initially regarded themselves less as a parliamentarian county committee, and more as traditional deputy lieutenants – who happened, it was true, to have been confirmed in their appointments by parliament. They were thus foremost an established body of military organisation and supply, and one which represented the existing order of society. Their role was in no way 'revolutionary', at least in these early days.

As time progressed, however, the remit of the committee and its various sub-committees appears to have expanded; a total of nine separate bodies are mentioned in contemporary papers. For example, a special committee was established in May 1643 for the 'punishment of scandalous clergy'. Some scholars have regarded the additional committees formed during the course of the war as entirely separate; others have asserted that, essentially at least, the main Lancashire county committee and its offshoots were one and the same thing. Either way, many of the personnel were the same, and the meetings appear to have taken place at the same, or similar, venues. The relationship between the main committee and the others was thus very close, and may have been different only in that the persons present changed their title, or the subject of discussion, or reduced or increased in number accordingly. This was certainly the case in Suffolk, Staffordshire, Westmorland and Cumberland. Cheshire's arrangement, with a main body meeting at Nantwich, was certainly similar to this model of 'one body, several functions', but does not seem to have been formally graced with the title of county committee.

As an MP who drew much of his strength from south-east Lancashire, and had quickly declared his hand, Ralph Ashton was a natural committee leader, balanced perhaps by the more cautious and conservative Colonel Holland, governor of Manchester. Nevertheless, declared decisions seem almost always to have assumed a collective character. This may be interpreted as simple fact, a desire to show unanimity, a willingness to subsume authority under the parliamentarian banner, or even calculated scheming to avoid sole responsibility in the event of failure. Though his regiment continued to take the field, Ralph Ashton senior ceased to have a military command early in 1645, because as an MP he was subject to the Self Denying Ordinance, designed to separate the political leadership of the country from a more professional army.

With the slow emergence of the Shuttleworths as key military figures in east Lancashire, and with Read Bridge and the victories of the spring of 1643, the power picture altered subtly. The fall of Preston, and later other areas of north Lancashire, doubtless also helped transform Alexander Rigby from a theoretical and political player to a practical military leader. Colonel Egerton, who actually hailed from Salford hundred, emerged as commander of the West Derby forces raised by parliament. Despite this fragmented picture, with committee members often doubling as field commanders, and the practical difficulties of formal meetings, there were some remarkable examples of practical cooperation with one or other of the Lancashire colonels marching to each other's aid or cooperating in joint expeditions.

Ironically it appears to have been just when parliament was beginning to win that the divisions in the leadership became most apparent, with damaging differences in opinion emerging, for example over the conduct of the second siege of Lathom. In some counties, sooner or later, such situations led parliament to nominate a sole supremo, as was the case with Cheshire. Interestingly Sir William Brereton, the Cheshire parliamentarian leader, was related to both Colonel Richard Holland and Ralph Ashton, as his mother was a Holland of Denton.[22]

For Lancashire London's response was less clear-cut. The attempt to impose Sir John Seaton as military commander from outside at the beginning of 1643 was a messy failure, and it may reasonably be argued that ultimately parliament's continued success in the county was in spite of, rather than because of him. Lancashire was technically a part of the Northern Association, and briefly at least in early 1644 its commander, Sir Thomas Fairfax, was accepted as parliament's leader in Lancashire, though not as Lancashire's parliamentarian leader. Happily for Fairfax he had other matters to concern him, and his time in Lancashire did not hold him back from the ultimate prize of lord generalship of parliament's New Model Army, which was voted through the Commons on 21 January 1645. Sir John Meldrum's position in late 1644 may theoretically have been analogous to that of Seaton, but happily for both Meldrum and parliament he was as successful as Seaton had been a failure. He was also lucky in that in the wake of Marston Moor the tide of war was flowing with parliament. This is not to say that his time as commander was without controversy; and his historical record might also have been helped by the fact that he moved on – and died gloriously – when he did.

A number of factors exacerbated what was potentially a quarrelsome power vacuum in the now essentially parliamentarian Lancashire of mid-1645. Apart from the departure and subsequent death of Meldrum, the shortage of resources of all kinds, including money, and the need for Lancashire soldiers to serve elsewhere played their parts. In financial terms it would appear undeniable that the Lancashire parliamentarian war effort achieved greater success than the royalist, but this success was at best comparative. The appeals for voluntary loans made in 1642, on promise of an 8 per cent return, achieved nothing spectacular, while the costs rose inexorably. Compulsory loans, introduced in 1643, were an inefficient form of raising funds, and the committee became dependent on weekly assessments levied at parish level.

The excise was even more unpopular, and more than one 'tumult' was associated with its collection in the county. Nevertheless the Lancashire committee does seem to have benefited to some extent from the excise, for example when at the end of August 1645 an order was made for £2,000 to be paid out from London. Yet even with what would appear to be a simple disbursement of tax revenue there were complexities. The money was to be paid out to James Wainwright 'whose Receipt shall be a sufficient Discharge unto the said Commissioners of Excise', but equally if there was prior call on the funds already collected anyone else who was able to provide the money could do so and be reimbursed their capital, plus 8 per cent at a later date. It was probably also the case that since this payment coincided with the reform of the committee, parliament saw financial relief and administrative reform as linked.

For the first eighteen months of war the Lancashire parliamentarians' special relationship with London appears to have produced scant financial advantage. Such figures as we have suggest no significant net inflow of 'London Monies', and, as today, a significant proportion of the revenues of the London parliament were themselves garnered in the provinces. Though contributions from the centre do appear to have picked up somewhat later, the traffic was in fact in both directions, with Lancashire making specific contributions to the Scottish Covenanter army, forces in Ireland, and, from 1648, the New Model Army itself. Something which may have made a positive contribution to the Lancashire parliamentarians' cashflows was the role of individual businessmen and merchants. Such men not only carried weight in the City of London, but, if sufficiently wealthy, could act as private conduits of funds – being in London, and paying out sums on behalf of the committee locally. Lancashire parliamentarian business financiers included men such as Thomas Markland, Thomas Stones, a London haberdasher originating from Hoole near Preston, and the Rodes family of cloth merchants from Rochdale. Evidence is lacking, however, as to how much these contacts helped, or indeed, to what extent these men benefited personally from official transactions intended to finance the military.[23]

In terms of material resources parliament does seem to have helped Lancashire from time to time; support of this kind was not forthcoming from the king to his supporters in the county. Most importantly parliament had access to gunpowder stores and to ships. We thus see evidence of powder being delivered out of the navy or other stores for the use of the county; it was often too late to aid the specific cause for which it was sent, and it was sometimes intercepted *en route*, but it was hugely useful nonetheless. Likewise the intervention of parliamentarian warships on the Lancashire coast both mitigated the threat of royalist intervention from Ireland, and made it more difficult for the enemy to retain Liverpool and other points which might have been saved had the king managed to gain control of the seas. The Liverpool situation was thus an inversion of what sometimes happened in the south of England where, for example, Lyme Regis was able to hold out for parliament against apparently overwhelming force due to support from the sea.

Depending on one's point of view, sequestration – a regulated version of the 'spoils of war' introduced in 1643 – was a godsend or a pernicious evil. Much of what was raised by this means went directly to fund the war effort. Surviving evidence is far from comprehensive, but statistical work done on sequestered estates in West Derby hundred suggests that about 40 per cent of the proceeds was devoted to soldiers' pay, and a similar sum was spent on garrisons and supplies. A smaller portion was expended on the expenses incurred in what could be quite a complicated and protracted series of financial arrangements which often took into account the interests of the family members of the royalist gentleman under sequestration. Sequestration appears to have been particularly significant from late 1644, when parliamentarian forces, drawn mainly from Salford hundred and central Lancashire, formed what was effectively an army of occupation in the west of the county. At least once London suggested that the committee would be able to continue to finance its activities by further 'discovery' of hitherto untapped royalist estates.

The activity of the Lancashire committee may appear inefficient and at times dilatory, but we need to remember that for much of the time it acted largely independently. It is also the case that compared to some of the committees in the North West it was quick to form, ultimately successful in the conduct of its campaigns, and tolerably representative of the county elites. This certainly could not be claimed of every county committee: the Westmorland committee encompassed only one gentry family of note, plus what one commentator has called 'insubstantial gentlemen and other minor persons'; its impact on the local war, let alone the national, was limited, and even its continued survival in the face of royalist domination appeared questionable; it was ultimately topped up with previously neutral figures and moderate former royalists. Meanwhile, the smaller Cumberland committee boasted a single knight, and had some military success, but again its impact was far inferior to that of the Lancashire body.[24]

It was certainly the case that with parliament's 'new modelling' of their main field army at the beginning of 1645 there was a renewed call to reform the arrangements which had grown up during the war on a more established, regulated basis. As Oliver Cromwell so eloquently put it to the House of Commons, 'if the army be not put into another method, and the war more vigorously prosecuted, the people can bear the war no longer, and will enforce you to a dishonourable peace'. So it was that MPs who were also army officers had to lay aside their military commissions as a result of the Self Denying Ordinance.

Interestingly it has also been suggested that the reconstitution of 1645 was intended to make the committee less purely military, and in so doing to pave the way for peacetime conditions. It could also be argued that local separation of military command and political power was seen from the centre as a good way of preventing Lancashire's MP commanders from becoming too demanding or rebellious. Nevertheless what amounted to a local 'remodelling' of parliamentarian resources would have some unforeseen effects.[25]

Discussions during August 1645 led to the publication of new orders published in the *Lords Journal* of 29 August: these were intended to address simultaneously the issues of raising money and the composition of the Lancashire committee. The result was entitled an '*Ordinance to raise money in Lancashire; and to appoint a Committee there, for Regimenting the Forces of the County, and appointing the Officers, &c.*' Interestingly, rather than appoint a new single commander, the existing committee was vastly expanded and formalised, and little was said about matters of practical command. Under the ordinance no fewer than 28 persons were appointed to the committee. Many of these were familiar names such as Ralph Ashton, Richard Shuttleworth, Alexander Rigby, Thomas Birch, Peter Egerton and George Dodding; but there were also relative unknowns, as for example Robert Cunliffe of Sparth in Blackburn hundred, and William Knipe 'gentleman'. The wealthy gentleman and political moderate Sir Robert Binlosse (or Bindloss) of Borwick was included, presumably because of his financial interest (and in the event appears to have profited from his engagement through the purchase of former royalist estates). From these 28 members a smaller standing committee, of seven or more, was to be selected, composed of at least one member from each of Lancashire's hundreds for the transaction of routine business.[26]

The committee was intended to meet at Preston 'once in every month at the least', although in case this could not be done safely they could nominate another 'fit and indifferent' location within Lancashire. The standing committee was to 'sit constantly', also at Preston. The choice of Preston is interesting, and not immediately obvious given the town's generally pro-royalist stance. It can be explained on geographical grounds, as being near to the centre of the county – or perhaps there was a definite will to avoid Manchester, and spread political influence further abroad. Preston may also be regarded as the 'compromise' candidate in that it was neither Manchester, nor Liverpool, not as inaccessible as Lancaster, nor as close to potentially vulnerable borders as Warrington or Lancaster.

The powers of the committee were essentially financial, 'to assess and tax all such Sums of Money upon the said County as the major Part of them shall think fit, by the accustomed rule for the assessing of the said County, commonly called the "Soldier's Lay"'. The total raised each month was not to exceed £3,000, and this to include contributions to the Northern Association. 'Assessors' would make reports to the standing committee, and likewise provide copies to the actual collectors of money. Any persons aggrieved that they were 'over rated' were to 'complain' to the standing committee within six days. Alexander Norris of Bolton was appointed treasurer to the Lancashire committee, being empowered to make payments against the signature of three or more of the standing committee. The main purpose of the fund was to cover arms, ammunition, 'cloaths' and pay. Remarkably the ordinance also ordered a sweeping reorganisation of the Lancashire regiments, which were now to be,

> reduced into Two Regiments of Foot, and One Regiment of Horse, neither of which Regiments of Foot shall have in them above Ten Companies, nor the Regiment of Horse above six Troops, at the most; and that all common Soldiers now in Pay within the said County be taken into the said Three Regiments; and that the Commanders and Officers of the said Regiments shall be appointed, placed and displaced, by the Consent and Agreement of the said Committee.

Pay scales were to be set by the committee, so as not to exceed the pay of that in the New Model Army. Deputy lieutenants of the county who held estates within Lancashire were barred from commanding regiments, and officers above the rank of lieutenant were to receive no more than a quarter pay if residing in their own county and not on active service. No officers or men were to 'meddle in anything', such as requisitioning horses, money or goods in Lancashire, without committee approval. Whether this deliberately left open the possibility of requisitioning goods elsewhere was left unspoken. Officers' claims for arrears of pay were to be submitted by 31 December 1645, with deductions for free quarter and any other money obtained, as for example through profits gained as a result of sequestrations. Money obtained from the enemy in a fight or 'storm' was an acknowledged perquisite of the job, and excluded from the back pay calculation. Presumably these accounts also covered the pay of the commander's companies, for otherwise no mechanism for the paying of arrears to the other ranks was specified.

Muster rolls were to be prepared for each unit, and musters held by a 'commissary of the musters'. Payment to units was on a per capita or 'poll' basis, numbers being determined according to the commissary and signed by him. Pay was to be equally distributed between the units, not unfairly allotted. 'Keepers of magazines' were also to be appointed, who would issue arms on the instruction of the committee. As in the militia system of old, the able-bodied men of the county would also be listed, in addition to those actually serving in the three regiments, but those thought 'not fit to be trusted', on the say so of seven or more of the committee, would be excluded. Town dwellers were allowed either to put themselves down as potential recruits, or to 'find a man' to bear arms in their stead.

It is difficult to know precisely how far, or how quickly, the provisions of the ordinance of August 1645 were carried into effect. References to the various Lancashire parliamentarian regiments for the period from September 1645 to early 1646 are confusing, but clearly the forces were kept well over the notional establishment strength throughout this period. Mention is made of nine troops of Lancashire horse at Whitchurch, this being half as many again as the ordinance's total establishment. Despite the non-appearance of Ashton's regiment, 400 Lancashire infantry are recorded as being present at Chester in December, while a further 500 foot had been recorded as 'sent to Skipton' and Liverpool's garrison was numbered at 300. At the end of October 1645 there was also a reference to 'some volunteer companies' being maintained for the defence of the southern part of the county.[27]

On the face of it the back-pay provision of the ordinance seems unlikely to have been carried out very quickly, or satisfactorily, since if money had appeared promptly one of the major reasons for the mutiny would have disappeared. We do know, however, that Sir Ralph Ashton, William Ashurst, and the MPs who had formerly served as Lancashire colonels now spent much of their time in Westminster, though they returned to the county from time to time. The names of the other members appear with greater or lesser frequency on surviving committee correspondence. The clauses regarding the membership of the committee were therefore probably adopted fairly quickly, and in full.

CHAPTER TEN

War without conclusion
and the 'Province' of Lancashire

A CCORDING to the *Discourse* Lancashire was in 'a reasonable quiet posture' after the final reduction of Lathom, and fortunately the harvest of 1646 appears to have been fair. So it was that corn and other necessaries were reasonably plentiful 'and cheap' after a period of dearth. Many counties would be less lucky.[1] King Charles surrendered himself to the Scots army at Newark in May. The royalist capital of Oxford surrendered in June. One of the few Lancastrians to go on fighting after the king himself had capitulated was Sir Thomas Tyldesley, who had by now become commander of the royalist horse in Staffordshire. Following defeat at Cannock Chase, and near capture, Tyldesley had made for Lichfield. Besieged and bombarded, the garrison had finally found themselves confined to the cathedral close. After twenty weeks Tyldesley surrendered on the orders of the king, on 10 July 1646.[2]

The end of the first civil war in Lancashire, coinciding with an increasing availability of bread, came as a blessed relief. Some soldiers, probably a minority, simply turned in their muskets and – paid or unpaid – went home. Garrisons, however, continued to be manned, and many units remained embodied: as standing armies were virtually unheard of in England prior to 1642, their continued presence remained a resented drain upon society. For the *Discourse* it was the foreign influence of a 'rude company of Yorkshire Troopers', ordered to guard Lancaster Castle, that was the most insupportable burden. The Yorkshiremen were apparently,

> the cruellest persons that ever this County was pestered with. They were an unmeasurable torment to the Hundreds of Lansdaile and Amonderness – men that could not be pleased with any quarters either for themselves

of their horses and for their own advantage would quarter themselves (as farr from the Castle) at the bottom of the Fylde country.

This nuisance was only terminated when part of the castle was demolished, and the horse guard posted without the castle was dispensed with. Warrington apparently also retained its garrison for some time, but parliament ordered its disbandment in March 1647.[3]

Liverpool's attitude to its continuing military role was ambivalent. It actually raised a petition that it should be allowed, 'being a garrison town', to keep its 'mud walls' which it did not want altered. Some may have wished to retain this protection, but it is also possible that it was feared that the earth embankments would be replaced with masonry – which would have been expensive, and could have demanded the demolition of buildings to accommodate them. When it came to troops, the governor asked that the townsmen themselves should be enlisted, but the populace refused, sending him the message that they would come to his aid 'in case of danger, not otherwise'. They did at least maintain an armed 'night watch' throughout 1646, but in a spirit of egalitarianism the council allowed able-bodied men selected for the task to be enrolled 'under what captain they please' for this tedious duty.[4]

What was particularly tragic about the end of the war in 1646 was that really it solved very little. The king's armies had been defeated and his garrisons reduced, and many were thankful for this. Yet in terms of politics and religion this put the country not much further forward. Charles still believed in his God-given right to rule, and in his peculiar privileges as head of church and state. Parliament was still opposed to what they saw as tyrannical innovations. Neither had members of parliament grown to love Catholics or bishops, and military victory had, if anything, emboldened their opinions – 'puffed them up' as Clarendon put it. At the same time winning the war undermined the pragmatic unity which had sustained them so long. What had held together moderates, the army, Presbyterians, the Scots, Independents and fellow travellers had not been so much any ideological common purpose as opposition to 'malignants'. Now that the enemy was militarily powerless, the old cause was liable to fragment.[5]

Serious stresses had indeed begun to emerge within the coalition as early as mid-1644. Despite the success of Marston Moor in the north, the royalist victory at the battle of Lostwithiel in Cornwall had clawed back some of the lost ground. The Earls of Manchester and Essex appeared to have lost stomach for the fight, and quite how such a locally based rag-bag of different forces that existed at that time could have brought the war to an early conclusion was difficult to imagine. As one contemporary put it, God seemed 'not to favour the great officers'. General Sir William Waller, writing to the Committee of Both Kingdoms, put it more bluntly, 'an army compounded of these men will never go through with your service, and till you have an army of your own, that you may command, it is in a manner impossible to do anything of importance'. The upshot had been the creation of the New Model Army, which first took to the field in April 1645. This new force brought together seasoned soldiers from Manchester's Eastern Association army, and the armies of the Earl of Essex and Waller. Three significant consequences resulted from this amalgamation. The first was a purging of unsatisfactory generals, who were to be dismissed by means of the Self Denying Ordinance which prevented members of either house exercising military command. Bulstrode Whitlocke went so far as surmise – probably correctly – that the primary objective of the ordinance was 'the outing of the Lord General', Essex. That the original ordinance did not get by the House of Lords ultimately mattered little, since by a process of 'naming of the officers' much the same result was achieved, and a revised version of the Self Denying Ordinance was passed later. The new force would thus be led from the outset by men who were soldiers first and foremost, committed to driving the war to a successful conclusion. Sir Thomas Fairfax, whom we last met, fleetingly, at the siege of Lathom, became Lord General of the New Model. As neither a radical, nor a member of parliament, Fairfax was arguably one of the few real stabilising influences on the situation. Contrary to popular myth, Cromwell was not, at this stage, an army commander but still an MP and a lieutenant general of horse under Fairfax. His survival as both MP and military leader was frowned upon by moderates, who took exception to the fact that he had not been removed under the precepts of the Self Denying Ordinance; uniquely, indeed, renewal of his military commission had to be approved by parliament specifically.

The second major consequence of the formation of the new army was that, being an amalgamation from several areas, supplied from the centre, principally the capital, the New Model was very much a 'go anywhere' force. Unlike most of the county forces, its umbilical was long and elastic. This relatively good supply system, standardisation of weaponry, uniform, command and procedure, were keys to the New Model's success, but led inexorably to the third significant consequence. This was that the New Model, owing little to any one county, and much to parliament, looked to parliament for a resolution of its problems and the granting of its aspirations. A pay dispute in the Lancashire militia impacted hard on one county, but men's homes and communities were never far away. Pay came ultimately from one's peers, neighbours, village, kith and kin. Communities fought together, paid together, died together, and, certainly in the instance of Lancashire, sometimes starved together. Even if one county among parliament's forces should be temporarily paralysed this would not be a total disaster in the great scheme of things, since there were many others, in other counties and associations of counties, fighting under the same banner. Conversely the New Model would take its grievances direct to parliament, in the way that parliament in 1640 had taken its grievances directly to the king. Happily for parliament arrears of pay, and the awakening of the realisation of its own great potential political power, did not reach any final crisis point before the royalists were effectively extinguished in 1646. When the war was over, however, there were idle hands and many unresolved issues for those whom God had so clearly favoured in battle. Going without pay to their widely scattered homes – or worse to Ireland – would not be options for the soldiers of the New Model.

It is arguable that it was the exertions of the New Model which were the main instrument in bringing the first civil war as a whole to a successful conclusion. However, the direct impact of the New Model on the north during this period was limited. The force was paid for mainly by a monthly assessment of £45,000 laid on the seventeen counties of East Anglia, the Midlands and the south east. Its officer corps was drawn primarily from these areas, plus London. Its campaigns, extensive as they were, had been limited essentially to the midlands and south – indeed, according to Sprigge's narrative, the New Model did not advance further north than Leicestershire at any time before the king's surrender. Moreover, though the New Model superseded certain forces, it did not replace either the county militias or the Northern Association army which had taken an important role in the fight.[6]

Clearly many parliamentarians had not actually considered what to do in the event of victory. The king was in no way inclined to be quietly compliant, and even the manner of his surrender appears to have been designed to sow dissension amongst the allies who had defeated him. As Clarendon described it,

It was very early in the morning when the king went to the Scot's Generals lodging at Newark, and discovered himself to him. The General either was, or seemed to be, exceedingly surprised and confounded at his majesty's presence, and knew not what to say; but presently gave notice of it to the [Parliament] committee, who were no less perplexed. An express was presently sent to the Parliament at Westminster, to inform them of the unexpected news, as a thing they had not the least imagination of. The Parliament was so disordered with the intelligence, that at first they resolved to command their General to raise the siege of Oxford, and to march with all expedition to Newark; but the Scots commissioners diverted them from that ...

Many Englishmen had fought the king as a last resort, in a 'defensive war': such parliamentarian moderates felt they were acting to restore their ancient rights against innovation by 'malignants' – foreigners and Catholics who misled Charles Stuart – and attempted to pervert legitimate royal authority as expressed in the ancient yet unwritten English constitution. With fighting over and 'his Majesties person' delivered from this evil thrall, there appeared no reason why a peace settlement with the king – under which his power would be limited but still significant and balanced by the people's will as expressed in parliament – should not be negotiated. Yet the world, and the realities of power, had changed. Not only was the king a prisoner but the House of Lords had dwindled in numbers and influence. The Commons were certainly a major force to be reckoned with: but within the Commons real power over policy came from the Committee of Both Kingdoms. It would be difficult to replicate the old order, even had there been sufficient demand so to do.

Less easy to satisfy than the moderates would be those who had thrown themselves into a far less limited sort of war, and specifically the soldiers who had actually borne the brunt of the fighting. Having fought, taken casualties, and put up with many a hardship, few fighting men are willing to believe that they have ventured their lives for nothing, or for trivial alterations to their condition. In the months following the cessation of hostilities in 1646 this was particularly truly felt: many soldiers were unpaid, or underpaid, and were bent on a significant financial or political price. Among the most dissatisfied, and becoming more radicalised as time progressed, were the men of the New Model Army. The army would become even more politicised after June 1647, when Cornet Joyce seized the king from his existing place of captivity at Holmby House.[7]

As had so often been the case during the war constitutional and political issues were alternately muddied and sharpened by their religious dimension. High churchmen and Catholic sympathisers were now effectively silenced. Altar rails, superstitious images, pictures and organs were already officially suppressed. As early as 1642 the Commons had put the question of the abolition of episcopacy to a committee of the whole house. Now, after the slow-moving cogitations of the Westminster Assembly, the Church of England

Charles I (1600–49) after the First Civil War, from a contemporary woodcut. In his hand he holds the Newcastle 'Propositions', one of many attempts at a negotiated settlement after the end of fighting in 1646.

would be a reformed body, without bishops, but with significant powers in the hands of the clergy. While the detail remained debatable, the idea of some form of presbyterian settlement does seem to have enjoyed significant support. On the other hand there was a large body of Independent opinion, which viewed any form of theocracy with alarm, sought to allow a much freer association between ministers and their flocks, and even a general rejection of state-regulated worship. Broadly speaking presbyterians were associated with those content to make a negotiated settlement with the king. Independency was increasingly connected not only with sects which were genuinely independent of the established church, but with the leaders of the New Model Army and those who had vigorously prosecuted the war to final conclusion. Indeed the New Model Army had been referred to in pamphlets as the 'Independent' army as early as 1645. Given these mixed and sometimes contradictory standpoints it is no wonder that a lasting settlement proved impossible to obtain between 1646 and 1648. As Gerald Aylmer has suggested, perhaps the real surprise was that the 'hopelessly divided' grouping which backed parliament had actually managed to forget its differences long enough to win the 'Great' Civil War in the first place.[8]

The Scots were a third factor. They had the king, but their detailed objectives were different to either of those of the main parties now emerging in England. Ideally they would seek not only presbyterianism in both kingdoms, but a settlement which improved their position relative to England, and provided financial compensation for their outlay on the war. Also desirable was an arrangement which gave them influence over the man, who, after all, was king of Scotland as well as England. Opposition to bishops and overweening royal power had been a glue holding the alliance together: now these essentially negative goals were all but achieved the Scottish–parliamentarian united front would drift apart. Just to complicate matters further, not all Scots were of one opinion: some remained loyal to the Stuarts of old, others, including the Kirk, would remain opposed to any 'engagement' with the king against their allies in the English parliament.

The counterpoint to parliamentarian and Scottish divisions was Charles' own intransigence. The first attempt to reach an accommodation with the king came as early as the end of July 1646 when parliamentary commissioners, led by the Earl of Pembroke, reached him at Newcastle. The terms they laid before Charles were predictable, even surprisingly lenient under the circumstances. The key points demanded were a presbyterian church for England, and the exclusion of ex-royalists from public life. In fact royalists were more or less already excluded, and some form of presbyterianism was now seen as all but inevitable. Though urged by the Earl of Loudoun to accept these Newcastle Propositions, Charles rejected them. With nothing decided, parliament managed to secure the £400,000 required to pay off the Scots, and by early 1647 the Scottish army had departed from England, leaving Charles behind.

Where Lancashire's parliamentarian leaders stood against this background of shifting political negotiation would soon become obvious. The majority of those who mattered were either in sympathy with a presbyterian course, or at least sufficiently content to go along with it. On 25 August 1646 the county presented a petition to parliament, supposedly signed by 12,578 people, 'well affected gentlemen ministers, freeholders and others of the County of Lancaster' in favour of presbyterianism, and against 'sectaries, heretics and schismatics'. Not surprisingly, perhaps, about half of the signatures were collected from Salford and Blackburn hundreds, the traditional heartland of parliamentarian support in the county. Outright royalists were excluded from this settlement. Nevertheless, the petitioners contended that they were no extremists, but were moderates in their opinion, what they were wont to call of 'a golden mediocrity'. This essentially religious document also included an explicit plea for 'a safe and well grounded peace in the three kingdoms'.

Presbyterianism in Lancashire

On 5 September the Lords and Commons formally abolished the titles of the bishops and archbishops. Just a week later parliament was considering a proposal that Lancashire would be divided into nine classical presbyteries, a move that would finally be sanctioned in December 1646. Thus was the most Catholic county in England reformed along presbyterian lines, an arrangement which would hold for more than a decade. Broxap was accurate in his claim that it was Lancashire which furnished the example of the 'most completely organised system of Presbyterian government in the whole country'. How much this was a popular solution, or an unpopular measure imposed by the victors of war, or indeed was seen as a way of circumventing future interference from the centre, can only be speculated. As the petitioners themselves pointed out, it might have been viewed literally as the only practical way to avoid schisms and further confusion. Nevertheless the *volte face* was total, and represented a significant triumph for the county's low church minority.[9]

The new presbyterian 'province' of Lancashire was organised in nine 'classes' or areas. Within each area every parish was represented by a minister and lay elders, initially two per parish nominated by parliament, but later six or more were elected. This local presbytery directed the individual parish in all matters relating to church membership, sacraments and morals. Each classis held its meetings at a central town, for example Manchester or Bolton, and each classis in its turn sent representatives up to a provincial synod. This synod met mainly at Preston, but later also at Wigan or Bolton. As might be expected, the 'first' classis was Manchester, its surrounding area including Oldham, Flixton, Eccles, and Ashton-under-Lyne – and the representative ministers here would be the old Puritan campaigner Richard Heyrick and Richard Hollingworth. The second classis was Bolton and district, encompassing Bury, Middleton, Rochdale, Deane and Radcliffe. Manchester and Bolton, with their lengthy Puritan pedigrees, had a particular axe to grind when it came to the setting up of the new system. Adam Martindale commented that Hollingworth, along with John Tilsley of Deane, and John Harrison of Ashton-Under-Lyne, were, very zealous [usually called Rigid] Presbyterians that were for setting of the governance of the Church of Scotland amongst us ... and the utter extirpation of Independencie root and branch as schismaticall and inconsistent with the Covenant.

The third classis coincided roughly with Blackburn hundred, covering Whalley, Chipping and Ribchester. The fourth covered a large area of south Lancashire around Warrington and Wigan, including Prescot, Holland and Leigh. The church of St Nicholas at Liverpool was still a chapel of ease to Walton parish, and so Liverpool itself was not explicitly named as a classis, but was encompassed by the fifth which included Walton, Huyton, Sefton, Ormskirk and Aughton. The sixth classis was essentially the area of Leyland hundred, including Croston, Leyland, Standish, Penwortham, Hoole and Brindle. Preston and the Fylde comprised the seventh classis; Lancaster and south Lonsdale formed the eighth, and Furness including Ulverston, Dalton, Cartmel and Kirkby the ninth.[10]

What really stands out in the composition of the classes however is the names of the nominated lay elders, which included Ralph Ashton, Richard Shuttleworth, John Moore, William Ashurst, Alexander Rigby and George Dodding. Essentially therefore the key members of the presbyterian church were the members of the parliamentarian Lancashire committee. The fact that the synod and the committee both met in Preston can only have facilitated and underlined this unity of political and religious influence. Preston parish church and the town hall were only yards apart, and the image of the powerful trooping across the road in solemn procession to their devotions is vivid. The remembrance that Preston was still one of the most, if not the most, Catholic town in the kingdom makes this impression all the stronger. There were some indicators of broader membership, however, and, in at least one instance, army participation. This is the case of Zachary Taylor, a former army chaplain who became a member of the Bolton classis, representing Bury. By 1654 he would also be the headmaster of Rochdale grammar school.

What some local Puritans may well have welcomed as God's new reign on earth began at Preston on 16 February 1647, with the first meeting of the provincial synod. The 'Church of Christ', so it was said, was now 'restored' to the hands of those whom God himself had chosen. The first meeting of the Lancashire provincial synod predated that in London by about three months. The first 'resolution' of the Lancashire synod was a statement of purpose, for having removed both the bishops, and 'the Book of Common

Prayer with all its burdensome and unnecessary ceremonies', it intended that it should embark on a different path. Yet its members saw themselves as no extremists – they were indeed intending to adopt a middle route, the golden mean, 'betwixt prelatical tyranny and popular anarchy'. This new version of the Church of England, essentially answerable to itself, would encompass the 'old godly nonconformists' and 'moderate conscionable conformists'. In practice it would have little to do with the king, but quite a lot to do with parliament, particularly as in Lancashire MPs, committee and synod membership was interwoven, and sometimes synonymous. Indeed, at the very first meeting the elders declared themselves 'bound to yield in all due subjection to the civill powers'.[11]

Holding the Church together was undoubtedly a key objective. In a thunderous 'Solemn Exhortation' of about the same date, the synod railed against the

> miserable disorders, errors and offences which like a flood have broken out, continued and risen to so great a height amongst us to the high dishonour of the name of God, the great hindrance and shame of the gospel, and the trampling of holy the things and precious pearls thereof under the feet of dogs and swine.

Their job would be to frustrate the 'advancement of Satan's seat amongst us'. They would 'stand fast' to 'the Solemn League and Covenant and all branches of it'. Obviously the synod thought that it was of moderate intention: but in no way was it lax in the deliverance of its own opinion.

How encompassing the presbyterian church of Lancashire would actually be was questioned by the Bury delegation at the third meeting of the provincial synod on 25 March 1647. It was then asked whether 'malignants' could in conscience be admitted to communion 'without admission of their faults', given that they had 'their hands in blood'. Whether this was a rhetorical point or whether a serious answer was expected we shall probably never know, as the records are fragmentary. Nevertheless the idea that the synod could exercise, in effect, a form of excommunication was a strong one which does seem to have appealed to the members. In July the synod stated its own power to summon persons before it, and to define who was 'approved' as a communicant, as well as endorsing the role of patrons. A little later the synod spoke up in favour of the 'ancient reputed bounds' of the individual parishes, and inveighed against parishioners 'promiscuously' receiving the 'Lord's Supper' at different parishes without the consent of their own parish. Baptism was not to be allowed in private houses, and ministers who had originally been ordained by bishops were to have their status confirmed by the synod.

How far the presbyterian poachers had become gamekeepers would be illustrated after the Second Civil War, when the Bolton classis, doubtless more active than most, introduced a ticket system to admit the faithful to communion. Anyone deemed to be unsuitable could be denied entrance: Richard Haywood was suppressed, and effectively barred from the church. The provincial synod ruled that this had taken things too far, and overturned the suppression. The Bolton elders appear to have shown their displeasure by not attending the next meeting of the synod, and were duly censured for this also. None of the incumbents of Bradshaw chapel met with much approval from the classis, three unsuitable ministers being put aside between 1649 and 1653. Thomas Blackburn of Rivington lost his post for a minor litany of crimes including baptising the children of Catholics, and of kneeling on his first approach to the desk or pulpit of his chapel, a dangerously superstitious, or even popish practice. A few years later John Isherwood met censure for a clandestine marriage.[12]

Yet another who attracted the ire of the Bolton classis was Michael Briscoe, minister of Walmsley chapel. Briscoe was identified as 'ill affected to the government' and called upon to answer to the elders. The upshot was that he went to Scotland to serve as an army chaplain – a solution which would doubtless have appealed to his Independent leanings. Nevertheless the problem did not end there, since when he returned to Walmsley some years later he found the doors of his former chapel locked against him. His chequered career then took him back and forth to his native Ireland – and led to direct appeals to Cromwell before his final ejection from his post after the Restoration in 1662.

One of the most endearingly barmy characters to cross the path of the strictly minded Boltonians was Ellis Bradshaw of Tonge, a man with a fascination for astronomical and meteorological phenomena, to which he ascribed his own very peculiar brand of explanation. As early as June 1648 he was accused of neglecting his duties and 'hazarding the peace and quiet of the congregation', as well as, and perhaps most importantly, slandering the elders. Undaunted, Bradshaw produced a pamphlet the following year entitled *A New and Cleer Discovery*, in which he described how he had determined, with the aid of 'scripture and reason', that the moon had nothing to do with tides. In early 1650 he followed up with the sensational scoop *A True Relation of Strange Apparitions seen in the Air, on Monday 25 February, in and about the Town of Bolton in the Moors*. This exciting interpretation of sun haloes did nothing to calm his neighbours, and it seems likely that he soon fled to London where his racy tracts continued to appear for a long time afterwards.

All in all, the shifting political scene after 1648, non-attendance, the attendance of the unsuitable, and probably a lack of widespread popular support, seemed to suggest that presbyterianism in Lancashire was an experiment with a limited future. Certainly after the Second Civil War the presbyterians were weakened, and the Lancashire province met with no lasting success. The 1650 survey of church livings confirmed that financial issues and practical problems accompanied theological difficulties. In Manchester it was complained that 'thyths and rents' were not flowing as they should to Richard Heyrick, the warden, or the minister, and in any case the titles of dean, sub-dean, and chapter which had accompanied the status of a collegiate church had recently been scrapped by parliament. 'Some inhabitants' were holding out on their contributions, but whether this was as a result of financial hardship due to the wars, religious scruple, or just taking advantage of opportunity is unclear. Asset-stripping of church land had in any case received formal sanction by 1649, when parliament had decreed that assets other than cathedrals, churches and burial grounds were to be sold off to assist the army getting to Ireland.[13]

The Lancashire presbyterians also had a point when they suggested that they were beset with 'fanatics': and as Independents gained ground in parliament after Pride's Purge things would get worse. As one London MP would observe from the orthodox perspective, 'those that came out of the North are the greatest pests of the nation'. Gerrard Winstanley, leading theorist of the Digger sect, was born in Wigan; Lawrence Clarkson, the Ranter, came from Preston; and James Webster, the Grindletonian, was actually schoolmaster at Clitheroe in the 1650s; the Seekers would also attract several Lancashire congregations. But arguably it was George Fox and the Quakers who would have most lasting impact in the county. Fox experienced his famous vision of a 'great multitude waiting to be gathered' on Pendle Hill in 1652, and several of the other important landmarks of his religious career also took place within the county. His wife, the wealthy widow Anne Fell, was domiciled at Swarthmoor Hall in Furness, and it was at nearby Ulverston parish church that he received a celebrated beating. From the Quaker perspective this would become one of the most famous examples of vicious religious persecution and bigotry: from the point of the parishioners, no doubt, it was simply the noisy eviction of a somewhat crazed itinerant who had disturbed the service.[14]

CHAPTER ELEVEN

'Routed and defeated': the Second Civil War, 1648

T HE YEAR 1648 would see Lancashire back at the epicentre of war. As in the early summer of 1644 national and the local conflicts would become closely intertwined. This time, however, the warring parties would not simply besiege, storm, and manoeuvre their way to a battlefield beyond the county, but would fight the climactic action within its confines. The battle of Preston, fought that August, was not only one of the biggest and bloodiest of the entire nine-year drama. Arguably it was also the most important battle, politically and militarily, of the civil wars. The stakes were enormous, and upon its outcome the entire political direction of the three kingdoms hung. It was a turning point, and for the king was to prove fatal. It would propel Oliver Cromwell to the forefront of the national stage, proving him to be one of, if not the, leading general of his times. Arguably this was the real starting point of Cromwell's ascent to power. It was certainly a major factor in Charles Stuart's journey to execution. The outbreak of the Second Civil War was provoked by several factors, but much of the fuel was provided by the fact that the end of military action in 1646 had not solved the major constitutional issues. The king was beaten on the battlefield, but his will was unbroken. On the other side it would be difficult for the victors, hitherto united by their desire to beat the royalist forces, to come to a clear-cut opinion of what it was that they wanted from the peace.

Oliver Cromwell (1599–1658). Huntingdonshire gentleman Oliver Cromwell rose to become the towering figure of mid-seventeenth-century England, eventually being created Lord Protector in 1653. His direct role within Lancashire was limited to the vitally important Preston campaign of 1648.

NATIONAL PORTRAIT GALLERY

303

Though arguably more rapid, the slide into the second conflict was even more messy and less clear-cut than it had been into the first. Six months before its outbreak it would have been extremely difficult to predict which parties and causes might be aligned on the opposing sides. The former allied ranks opened ever wider with agitation by Leveller activists within the New Model in the summer and autumn of 1647, increasing suspicion of the army in parliament, and the Scots drifting further away from their former friends. Lord General Fairfax protested that although he might cut the head off the 'Hydra' of army insurrection, there were always plenty more to take up the cudgels of those that had been dealt with, however sternly. There were also petitions raised against the county committees. England came perilously close to anarchy. Though the Lancashire soldiery does not appear to have been motivated in the same political manner as the New Model, lack of pay was still an ongoing issue. In August 1647 the Lancashire committee was moved to plead the case to London. The Speaker was then informed that the huge sum of £20,000 was required, 'otherwise we are afraid we cannot possibly keepe them in a peaceable Condicion ourselves'. It was not a good time to ask for a large sum of money. Complaints were also raised about the behaviour of soldiers *en route* for Ireland.[1]

The cost and arrogance of the New Model were significant causes of an increasing rift between the Westminster members and the army, and the tax burden of supporting forces was an important national issue. For the journal *Mercurius Rusticus* the excise tax, free quarter and the monthly assessment were all matters of concern, but it was the assessment which was especially invidious. In November 1647 its opinion was that this monstrous tax of £60,000 a month would 'swallow up all the money, & consume the trade of the kingdom' just to keep soldiers 'in their idleness, mutinies and rebellion against the Parliament'. For presbyterian parliamentarian Denzil Holles the former burdens of supporting the king's administration now looked like 'flea bites' compared to what was now being visited upon the country. Lilburne's regiment marched to Corkbush field near Ware, carrying papers in their hats with the slogan 'England's Freedom: Soldiers' Rights'.

While Leveller mutiny was effectively quelled, and the 'Putney debates' of October and November 1647 went some way to reunifying the rank and file with the grandees of the New Model, it is also arguable that these events crystallised the military as a political force. The genuinely new *Agreement of the People*, with its implications of much expanded, if not universal, suffrage, was extremely worrying to those with a major stake in the traditional arrangements of power and society; it was duly repudiated. Getting men out of the army and back to peacetime occupations was extremely desirable, both because it could be hoped that this would reduce financial burdens, and that it might take the military out of politics. Yet disbandment without pay was itself a serious grievance, and soldiers not paid by one faction might be pushed into the camp of another. During the early months of 1648 parliamentarian forces were reduced to what, with hindsight, appears a parlous state. Nationally about 20,000 men were disbanded – with the bulk of these reductions falling upon the provincial forces. The Northern Association in particular was left with only five regiments. In retrospect this diminution appears foolhardy, but at the time it was a practical demonstration that parliament was committed to reducing the crushing financial burdens on a country already impoverished by war.[2]

An 'engagement' between king and Scottish royalists

The king could see only what he had predicted: jealous rebels falling out one with another over their ill-gotten gains. Escaping from Hampton Court in November 1647, he made his way via Farnham to the south coast, Lymington, and eventually across the Solent to the Isle of Wight. Colonel Hammond of Carisbrooke was naturally astounded, 'surprised', and 'very much discomposed', to find Charles Stuart, almost literally, in his back yard. He was torn between 'Duty to his Majesty, and my gratitude for this fresh obligation of confidence, and my observing my trust to the Army'. There was never any real prospect of Hammond turning royalist, however, and parliament was soon informed of the development. If anything Charles had weakened his position by flight, and any trust that had been established was now being eroded. Parliament did present 'Four Bills' to the king at Christmas 1647 – but these were rejected, and for the time being negotiations were broken off. Behind the scenes new talks were already well under way: between royalists and Scots, for a new 'engagement', under the terms of which Charles might be restored as king in fact as well as in name.

The key figure military figure among the engagers was James Duke of Hamilton, a noble courtier to the house of Stuart of many years' standing. Actually Hamilton had a stake in political affairs on both sides of the border. Born in 1606, the young James attended Oxford, and inherited his titles in 1625. At court he served as both a gentleman of the bedchamber, and as a privy councillor, and his attentiveness was rewarded with various monopolies and perquisites. He raised an expedition to aid Gustavus Adolphus in Germany during the Thirty Years War, but it was no spectacular success, ultimately

James 1st Duke of Hamilton (1606–49). Born in Lanarkshire, Hamilton was an active courtier to the house of Stuart who had landed interests on both sides of the border, and served on the Privy Council. Leader of the Engager army in 1648, he was decisively defeated at Preston, and executed in 1649. His title passed to his brother William, who took part in the 1651 invasion of England.

providing troops for garrisons on the Oder and for the blockade of Magdeburg. During the Bishops' Wars with Scotland Hamilton had remained loyal to Charles, and was made both a royal commissioner and a general. Hamilton and his brother fled to Oxford during the first civil war, but his attempts to negotiate with the enemy had made diehard royalists suspicious of him, and he spent some time under arrest in Cornwall. Now fortunes had turned, and he appeared to be one of few realistic hopes left to the crown.

The Engagement certainly appeared to offer the king a way out, but it was also fraught with many potential difficulties, not least of which was that it was not universally popular with the Scots: the Earl of Argyll was against it, as was the Kirk, which denounced the arrangement as a betrayal of the Covenant for which many had already fought and died. As might be predicted the religious dimension was critical. To gain the support of the Engagers the king had to agree to presbyterianism in England: control of the church had been one of his major disputes with parliament, and now he was expected to give it away in exchange for a chance of military victory. Whether he would be faithful to such a deal clearly taxed the credibility of many both sides of the border. The fact that a good number of the king's supporters, particularly in the north of England, were Catholic, set up strains in the new alliance even before any troops were raised.[3]

An argument can be made for the commencement of the Second Civil War for as early as Christmas Day 1647, when serious disturbances broke out in Canterbury. The main cause of these rebels was that they objected to the banning of the festival, a stern austerity measure first ordered as early as 1644. However, it was another few weeks before armed revolt against the established power began in south Wales, in February 1648. In early April the Scots renounced their former alliance with parliament. Recruitment for the Engager army under the Duke of Hamilton began not long afterwards, with a formal levy of the Scottish shires set for 21 May. It was in early May that the seriousness of the crisis would be brought literally to parliament's doorstep, when petitioners from Surrey turned extremely nasty, burst through the guard, 'and knocked down some of the soldiers, and gave out words, that they would have a speedy and satisfactory answer; or else they will have the blood of this house'. Only with difficulty did the guard commander manage to restore order. With trouble brewing in the west, and north and on the Scottish border, as well as close to London, parliament was beset with what seemed an almost intractable strategic problem.

The Scots army alone was initially believed to number 40,000, with many thousands of royalists spread around England and Wales. Most unusually there was also royalist sentiment afoot in the navy. The establishment of the New Model under Sir Thomas Fairfax was set at 16,000 foot; 6,720 horse and 1,000 dragoons. True there were many county militiamen in the shires, and the remnants of the Northern Association still existed: but how these would react was by no means predictable. At best those defending the new regime would be badly outnumbered. It is perhaps surprising that parliament now determined to split its main army. While Fairfax and the bulk of the reliable troops of the New Model stayed to deal with Kent, his second in command, Lieutenant General Oliver Cromwell set out for south Wales. He took with him about 5,000 men, arriving at Chepstow on 11 May. The same day Kent erupted in earnest, and within two weeks there were uprisings underway from Dartford to Sittingbourne and Sandwich. Before the end of the month it was thought that there were 10,000 rebels assembled between Rochester and Maidstone, ready to march on Blackheath. Should they get there it would be only a few hours before they were at the gates of parliament itself.

Lord Byron was designated the new royalist commander for north Wales, Shropshire, Cheshire and Lancashire, and duly attempted to solicit 'eminent

persons' who had been former enemies. Though Byron's personal impact
on Lancashire appears to have been minimal, he was full of optimism for
its royalist role in the forthcoming struggle, telling Lord Lanark that with
Scottish invasion 'the greatest part of Lancashire, Cheshire and north Wales'
would declare for the king. There was some limited evidence that he might
be correct. Lancashire showed no obvious desire to take up cudgels for the
new regime, and remained mired in the question of funds to pay arrears to
its soldiers. In the former royalist stronghold of Wigan the ex-cavalier mayor
and two like-minded aldermen clung to power, and for a time at least resisted
orders for their removal. The same happened, in larger measure, in Carlisle.
Here, following an advanced foray a couple of days earlier, Sir Philip Musgrave
entered the town on 1 May 1648. Carlisle was claimed for the king, and an
attempt by the parliamentarian faction to call out the militia was nipped in
the bud.

Sir Marmaduke Langdale seized Berwick at about the same time. Here,
on 28 April, he issued his 'Declaration', effectively a manifesto of the royalist
cause in the Second Civil War, in which he explained the 'reasons and
grounds' of the gentlemen 'now in action for His Majesties Service in the
Northern parts'. Everyone, so he said, had expected that with the conclusion
of the first civil war and the dissolution of the king's armies that,

the two houses of Parliament should have proceeded according to their
many declarations towards settling religion, and a sound and well-grounded
Peace, restoring the king's Majesty to his throne, just rights, and his full
freedom, and to the glory and splendour of his royall Ancestors; that the
Queen and Prince might have been invited to return, and all Armies
disbanded, the people eased of Excise, Free quarter, and all intolerable
burthens and pressures.

Reality, in his appreciation, had been very different. A 'schismatical army'
had refused to disband; the king had been seized and 'carried up and down'
until forced to flee in fear of his life; and a new 'arbitrary power' – unlawful
as well as unjust – had been set up to 'tyranize over us'. In the face of these
new sufferings the northern royalists proposed a five-point plan to restore
order and remedy the 'great evils' of the time. These key objectives were
the restoration of the king 'to his ancient Royal rights'; a free parliament to
settle the differences in church and commonwealth; the disbanding of armies;
the reinstatement of the 'known laws of the land'; and the preservation of
union between the kingdoms of England and Scotland'. To such that might

be thinking of standing against them the royalists were prepared to offer indemnity to former enemies, to address the question of pay arrears, and then 'cordially and cheerfully embrace' those who came over to their side. Given such fighting talk, and the palpable and growing success of the royalists in Northumberland, Cumberland and Westmorland, together with the rebellion in Wales, and disturbances elsewhere, it is hardly surprising that the Engagers formed a rosy opinion of their chances of success. Intelligence filtered back to Scotland that England was in disarray and was ripe for the taking.[4]

Alarming news was now also flowing in the opposite direction. Parliamentarian supporters in Westmorland wrote to Colonel Blackmore, governor of Warrington, that the strength of the royalists in the north, 'at first despicable' was now growing daily. The enemy had either persuaded or forced the trained bands of Westmorland and Cumberland into arms, and their quarters were now at 'Kendal, Kirkby and the frontiers of Lancashire'. 'Malignant' ministers were overthrowing godly reform, ejecting their opponents from congregations, advancing the Book of Common Prayer and bringing back 'condemned ceremonies'. Lancastrians had better beware.

Despite what we see as in retrospect as obvious warning signs, according to the author of the *Discourse* Lancashire in particular had not until now been expecting expecting fresh conflict. Following 'quietness a good space', trouble arose 'unexpectedly' appearing like a 'storm'. Again the horror of war had been conjured without the county, and this time there was even less that Lancastrians could do to stop it. 'Great rumours and Newes' circulated of an 'Army out of Scotland' being led, so it was said, by Duke Hamilton, 'under pretence to set the king free from his imprisonment'. Such was the power of this story that some fled immediately, as the *Discourse* explained,

This rumour or the first Allarum of his coming by Carlisle, and so through this County was bruited in May 1648, many men flying from their houses then to avoid him who yet returned shortly again following their occations at home most of the summer.[5]

As late as May 1648 when the Lancashire forces were called back into being it was still possible to question whether the militia would fight alongside the New Model against a common enemy. As one Lancashire gentleman put it in a remarkably prophetic missive to a friend in London,

We are gathering into a body for our own defence ... Our Souldiery apprehend themselves in great straights; for if the army come down, and they joyn with them to supresse the Cavaliers, they fear and are very jealous that the army will afterwards fall upon them and suppresse them. I cannot tell, but it is conceived by many well affected to the cause we first engaged in, that if the Parliament do not new-modell the army [again], and displace such as are generally odious to the kingdom, there will scarce ever be an happy peace and settlement in the nation. For should the Presbyterian party and the sectaries joyn to suppresse the common enemy, it is (I say) very much to be feared they would afterwards clash one with another: for when those that adhere to the Covenant are put into a posture of defence, they will never (I am confident) lay down arms to become tame slaves to the Sectaries.[6]

This point of view was given considerable force by the *Declaration of the Officers and Soldiers of the County Palatine of Lancaster*, a remarkable document directed by the officers, as well as the rank and file, to both the Lancashire committee, and the deputy lieutenants of the county about 9 May 1648. Like the soldiers of the New Model, the Lancashire militia seems suddenly to have found its own political voice, but remarkably what the Lancashire men wanted, and what the New Model demanded, were very different things. Perhaps because the Lancashire men were very much rooted in a locality – and because of their natural interest in maintaining the status quo – what could have emerged as a very radical document came out as a plea for unity. It was also a restatement of the old idea, that, even as parliament men, they had fought for the 'king and parliament', not to overthrow King Charles or the monarchy. Indeed, the militia now saw themselves as trapped between the newly emerging state, and the old monarchy. They had conducted themselves as 'loyal subjects and faithfull soldiers and servants of God, King and Kingdom', but found that they were,

on the one hand aspersed as Malignants and Enemies to the state, and fit to be disarmed; and on the other as Rebels and Enemies to the Monarchy, and the kings Majestie that now is: Wee therefore thought it requisite to declare and expresse to the Deputy Lieutenants and Committee of this County, that we own the solemn League and Covenant of the three Kingdoms in every branch of it, and will not by any combination, perswasion, or terror be drawn from it. And more particularly in reference to the said aspersions, we do further expresse, that we stand for the fundamental Government of the kingdom, by King, Lords, and Commons, according to the laws of the land, and the declarations of this present Parliament, before our first engagement: that we love, desire, and should much rejoice in the regal and Regular Government of his Majestie that now is.

As might be expected the *Declaration* retained a strong religious element, not only in favour of the Solemn League and Covenant, presbyterianism, and by implication the Scottish alliance, but against Catholicism, with which they identified all the wrongs that they had combated in the first civil war.

As for Papists, Popish Persons, malignant abettors of former innovations, usurpations or oppressions, or any other disaffected persons which were or shall be in arms to disturb Religion, Righteousness and Peace, we from the bottom of our hearts do detest them, and with our lives and fortunes will endeavour to oppose them. And we in like manner do declare against Toleration of Heresie, Schism, Prophanenesse, and whatsoever is contrary to sound Doctrine and the power of Godlinesse so plainly covenanted and declared against by the Ministers of this and other Counties.

To protect this position the troops now reserved the right to decline to be commanded by any who failed to adhere to these 'honest and just principles', or favoured 'anarchy in Church or State'.

Though the Lancashire *Declaration* appeared spontaneous and from the grassroots it did have the backing of key establishment figures, notably Nicholas and Ughtred Shuttleworth, Samuel Birch and John Ashurst, and presumably much of the Lancashire committee. These four, and thirteen others, sent out copies of the document under their signatures to the Lancashire parishes, urging the ministers to publish them 'in your congregations'. By this means they sought to pre-empt those who 'pretend to religion' in their 'misunderstanding and diverse interpretations' of the Solemn League and Covenant, for their own 'private interests'. Clearly the document, and the established position of the committee, was against the Independents, or at least a renewal of the war as a battle between the victors. It is therefore difficult to characterise the Lancashire *Declaration* as in any way revolutionary, though it came from a military force, and was supported, and possibly even debated, by the troops.[7]

Sadly for those who framed the *Declaration*, events had already overtaken their stated position. With the threat of the Scots gathering to the north, and royalist forces being re-formed all around, the pious hope of keeping things as they were rapidly vanished. There was now a stark and simple choice: do nothing and have no influence upon the ravages likely to be revisited upon the county, or join forces with the New Model in a new and pragmatic parliamentarian alliance. The enemy at least was becoming clear – those 'foreign' Scottish troops who 'engaged' with the king to deliver England over to him and his innovations, old royalists, and Catholics, who as ever were depicted as the real villains of the piece. Parliament may have helped to make the decision easier: for the Commons *Journal* records that various correspondence from Lancashire was read and considered in the week leading up to 16 May, and that as a result an ordinance was drawn up for 'charging and securing' £4,000 'upon the excise, for the forces in Lancashire, now disbanded'. It therefore appeared that at least part of the old debts payable to the militia were to be settled before new action took place. In addition to imminent invasion this was a persuasive argument. On hearing that positive steps were being taken to defend the county, parliament both voted its approval and instructed that a letter of thanks be sent up, signed by the Speaker.

So it was that in the space of perhaps ten days, between the first and third weeks of May 1648, the Lancashire committee was forced to abandon its principles and take steps to mobilise in defence of the county. According to Rushworth's account, warrants were first issued at Lancaster for the embodiment of the militia, and it was here that the Lonsdale companies were gathered. Following a meeting at Preston the remainder formed up and moved north to join their comrades. The Amounderness hundred, 'both horse and foot', marched under the command of Lieutenant Colonel Rigby 'to give a stop to the enemy'.

Three weeks later the committee ordered fresh dispositions to meet the developing Scottish threat,

The Committee of Lancashire have ordered four colonels of foot and two of horse, with their regiments, now in readiness in the northern part of this county, forthwith to join with Major General Lambert's forces in Yorkshire against the enemy in Westmorland and Cumberland. Colonel Ashton is Commander in Chief, and under him Lieutenant Colonel Rigby commandeth one regiment of horse, and Colonel Nicholas Shuttleworth the other. The Colonels [of foot ?] are Colonel Dodding, Colonel Standish, who commandeth his own and Lieutenant Colonel Rigby's foot, Colonel Ashton, and Colonel Oughtred Shuttleworth.[8]

The Engager army prepares to invade, summer 1648

At the same time that Lancashire settled its determination on resisting invasion and Cromwell was wrestling with the knotty problem of south Wales, the Scots were completing their recruiting. After the Scottish army had returned to Scotland in 1647, they had been remodelled into a smaller new army of 6,000 foot and 1,200 horse. This would provide the nucleus of the Engager army of 1648. As of late May the target strength of the invasion force was set at 30,000 infantry and 6,000 cavalry. Yet given internal opposition, lack of supplies and other practical difficulties this proved to be far too ambitious a target. Previous Scottish armies of the last few years had mustered about 20,000, and aspirations were duly scaled back. Very likely the main body of Hamilton's army ultimately numbered about 15,000 men. General Lambert and Bishop Burnet gave estimates of 14,000; Cromwell reckoned their strength at 17,000.

In addition to the main Scottish army the Engagers also called upon the support of Scottish troops currently in Ireland. This so-called 'New Scots' force, under Major General George Munro, had been maintained in Ulster to uphold the 'Protestant interest' since 1642. About 2,700 New Scots were now brought across by sea to the mainland of Scotland, though they lagged well behind the main army, and Munro never really seems to have considered his force as a subordinate command, but more as an allied army. Another adjunct to the Scottish army proper was at least a few English renegades. The most significant of these was Colonel Edward Wogan, a disillusioned former troop commander with the parliamentarian dragoons. He had fled to Scotland with his men during the recent troubles in the army, expressing an 'abundance of rancour' against his former masters. Now he also contributed a few troops to the invasion force.

The somewhat disparate roots of the Scots forces was reflected in its organisation, which was very 'command heavy'. The regiments of some of the senior officers, notably the Duke of Hamilton himself, his second in Command the Earl of Callander, and others, appear to have been well up to strength. Conversely some were very small, poorly recruited, and ill-disciplined. The cavalry, often a weaker part of the Scots armies of the period, appears to have operated primarily in small troops, although when taken together they amounted to a very respectable number. The horse now operated under the overall control of John Earl of Middleton. The result was a higher proportion of commanders compared to the New Model. Some commentators have suggested that the Scots' army had no artillery at all, but since Scottish guns are certainly mentioned in contemporary accounts of the campaign it is much more likely they did have field guns but no 'train' of heavy battering pieces. Yet the general supply situation was very scant, and it appears that from the outset it was expected that the common soldiery might have to 'live off the land' for much of their needs. This would have disastrous consequences.[9]

The royalists of Northern England had got off to a quicker start in recruitment, their actions being triggered by events elsewhere in the country, and by Carlisle and Berwick, which, once taken for the king, had to be defended. Indeed the Scots complained that Sir Philip Musgrave and Sir Marmaduke Langdale were far too quick off the mark. Their appeals for immediate Scottish help were met first with prevarication, then with demands that they did not enlist Catholics. This last was almost impossible and certainly a counterproductive aspiration when so many of the northern royalists were either of the 'old religion' or sympathetic to their neighbours who were. Nevertheless Langdale succeeded in raising 1,000 men fairly quickly, and marched into Cumberland, calling men to the colours as he went. Eventually the main English royalist army in the north would number about 5,000 men.

Key figures rejoining the king's forces at this point included Sir Thomas Tyldesley, Sir Henry Bellingham, Sir Patricius Curwen, Sir Edward Musgrave, Sir William Huddleston, Sir Henry Featherston, and Colonels Carleton and Chator, all of whom contributed a regiment to the cause. Several small troops of horse were also rallied, most of them apparently being raised by the infantry colonels. The recruiting effort of the English northern royalists had been good, considering the obstacles presented by time, money, munitions and by the presence of the enemy; it was also hindered by the Allies alongside whom they would have to fight. The rapaciousness of the Scots was already legendary. As one pro-parliament pamphleteer critic would put it,

> their demeanour when they were heer last, being so full of rapine and oppression, that the weaker sort of our nation in the north ... do tremble to heare of their coming againe into this Kingdome, and the more manly and resolute party will stand on their guards, and lose their lives every man in his own defence before they will be perswaded to re-admit them. Besides they know very well that there is a party in this Kingdome, that doth so strongly hate them, that if their Covenant should hang a little lower in our Churches, their very Dogs would ... lift up their legges against it.[10]

Whether parliament truly apprehended the dire strategic position is open to some doubt, particularly when all of the varying commitments of its troops were taken into account. When parliament ordered that Fairfax provide men for an additional garrison at Bury St Edmonds in Suffolk patience was stretched to breaking point. As Fairfax's letter to the Lords of 18 May pointed out,

> I must further acquaint your Lordships, that, considering the great Occasions calling your present Forces other Ways (for the resisting of further Invasions, the subduing of those Forces and the reducing those Garrisons that already appear against you, in the North, Lancashire and South Wales, and for the suppressing of Insurrections in other parts), there is no Part of the small Force you have left for the Field can be spared to be fixed in Garrison ...

In response to the dire news from the north not very much could be done. Nevertheless Fairfax soon resolved to send Colonel Harrison's regiment of horse to Cheshire, and Twisleton's Horse 'north' ahead of Fairfax himself with two further regiments. When this deployment was complete, only five troops of the cavalry of the New Model would be left unengaged between the Trent and the Thames. Occupied in Wales, Cromwell was able to send north just 'five troops of Horse, together with some Dragoons'. As to infantry only Fairfax's own regiment was genuinely free to commence the arduous march north.[11]

Perhaps the single most important factor in parliament's success in the northern campaign of 1648 would be the quality of the scouting and intelligence work carried out by its troops. Major Sanderson of Lilburne's regiment played a key role in discovering the strength of the enemy and their intended direction of march. Accounts submitted demonstrate that in May and June 1648 he spent £4 10s. 4d. on spying and on sending messages in the service of parliament. Of this 5s. went to Thomas Gooley, 'Mr Ogle's man', for entering Berwick after its capture by the enemy, and a similar amount to an unnamed informant, sent 'to discover what Scotch troops were about Twizell'. Another man was given 12s. to 'lie at Tweedmouth' for three days to give 'timely notice of the enemy's drawing out of Berwick'. A servant of 'Mr Marshall' received 5s., specifically for intelligence of the whereabouts of Sir Marmaduke Langdale's command.[12]

English royalists were now in possession of parts of Northumberland and much of Westmorland and Cumberland, and all that faced them for parliament was General John Lambert's diminutive Northern Association, plus as many men as the Lancashire committee were now prepared to release.

Lambert was just 29 years of age in 1648, but had experience far beyond his years. He had joined the parliamentarian forces in Yorkshire at 22, and first saw action at the battle of Tadcaster in 1642. Soon promoted to the rank of colonel, he campaigned extensively, fighting at Hull, Bradford, Nantwich and Marston Moor. When Fairfax went south to command the New Model, Lambert took charge of the Northern Association but was wounded in March 1645. Thereafter he joined the New Model himself, but had been recalled to his old command at the head of the Northern Association in 1647, following a mutiny and the dismissal of Sydenham Poyntz. The popular Lambert soon restored order.

The Northern Association was essentially Yorkshire based, but when it became apparent that the main threat was in fact west of the Pennines Lambert manoeuvred his 'army', which numbered rather fewer than 2,000, on to Penrith. More than half of Lambert's men were cavalry, which improved their mobility, but his foot were limited to a single regiment: that of Yorkshire Colonel John Bright. This officer was the same age as Lambert, having raised the regiment himself when only 24. He was nevertheless described as having grown very 'valiant and prudent', and with good control of his men.

Lambert's arrival at Penrith around 16 June had a disproportionate impact on the enemy in relation to his numerical strength. Sir Marmaduke Langdale appears to have believed that the Northern Association force was rather stronger than it actually was, and to have heeded Scottish advice that he should await the arrival of the main Engager army before committing himself to all-out battle. The royalists avoided action, and Langdale wrote again to Hamilton imploring him to send 'speedy' assistance. However, the Scots were not ready to march, and would not be for almost another three weeks. By 24 June a fleeting opportunity to deal with Lambert's little army had passed, for on that day the advanced guard of the Lancashire militia trudged through appalling weather into Penrith, ready to lend their support to the cause of parliament and the defence of their homes. Harrison's regiment of horse also made a timely appearance from the south. Now Lambert had nearly 5,000 men to hand – a decent match for what Langdale's royalists could put into the field. All the Scots could yet offer was criticism that the English royalists had jumped the gun, and excuses for their own continued absence.

Despite the scale of the threat and his urgent requests for more troops of the New Model to hasten to his aid, the upbeat Lambert was now emboldened to go on the offensive. One of his first strikes was on Rose Castle, close to Carlisle, where he seized a small royalist garrison. On 1 July there was a further success in Northumberland when the royalist Colonel Tempest and 500 cavalry were worsted by Major Sanderson of Lilburne's regiment, seconded by part of the county militia. While the main body of Hamilton's army finally crossed the border into England on 8 July, elsewhere there was more positive news for parliament. As Cromwell reported back to the members, Pembroke was finally surrendered to him on 11 July. The race was now on to prevent the main Scottish–royalist army from reaching London and liberating their allies in Essex, for had they been allowed to get so far the parliamentarian regime would certainly have been at an end.[13]

The New Model clearly knew the importance of haste. In ten days Cromwell's 5,000 men marched from Pembroke to Gloucester, averaging 15 miles a day, at a time when most armies would have been happy with ten. Another week put the army at Leicester, a stiff march well out into the east Midlands which allowed them to collect recruits and supplies as well as place themselves athwart the enemy's likely route to London. How necessary this was is underlined by the fact that some of his men had now marched so hard and so long that their footwear had quite literally worn out. As one of them, corresponding with the *Moderate Intelligencer*, explained,

> Our Marches [are] long, and want of shoes and stockings gives discouragement to our soldiers, having received no pay these many months to buy them, nor can any procure unless we plunder, which was never heard of by any under the Lieutenant General's conduct nor will be, though they march barefoot, which many have done, since our advance from Wales.

Against this trenchant performance by Cromwell and his men – a 200-mile march at a blistering pace – Hamilton had little to show. During the same period the Scots army advanced barely 50 miles. On 14 July they had come up against Lambert at Penrith, and though at that juncture their army outnumbered his by almost three to one he had managed to make good his escape after a skirmish. A further fight on 17 July saw Scottish cavalry fall upon the Lancashire militia: but again the prey got away. As Captain Birch recalled,

> The Scots fell upon us before we were aware, our horse being – the greatest part – absent; drave up our horse guards within our centryes and quarters of foote, drew out parties which kept them off from us till night, and made divers works, but by day breake in the morning wee march't away, I had the rearguard of foote with major Greenlishe.

James Livingstone, 1st Earl of Callander (d. 1674), from a print published in 1647. Callander served as second-in-command to the Duke of Hamilton during the Preston campaign of 1648. Although he had continental experience and a 'reputation of great courage', it was argued that he was promoted beyond his ability – and worked poorly with the other generals.

Though there were few casualties, a lieutenant in Captain Henry Cromwell's unit was killed, and Colonel Thomas Harrison was put *hors de combat* by sword wounds sustained when he plunged over-enthusiastically into an enemy unit in an attempt to seize its colours. Lambert was very effectively wasting the enemy's time, without taking serious damage to his own forces. The Scots, as Turner recalled, were seriously hampered by 'raine and tempestuous weather'.

Parliament was certainly not insensible, nor unappreciative of, Lancashire's contribution to the fight so far, nor to its potential role in what was to come. On 20 July 1648 the Derby House committee wrote to both Ralph Ashton and the Lancashire committee as a whole thanking them for their great 'faithfulness to the service'.[14]

Even so Lambert was a realist, reluctant to take unnecessary risks given the disproportionate nature of the struggle between his 5,000 and the Scottish leviathan which had now risen to a strength of over 15,000 troops, not counting their royalist allies. Having done the job very effectively, he now fell back in the direction of Barnard Castle, keeping himself between the enemy and his own Yorkshire powerbase. The Scots took one more jab at his command where he blocked the pass at Stainmore, but again the Northern Association and Lancashire troops escaped with only trivial loss. Lambert now disappeared behind the Pennines heading south, eventually meeting Cromwell, who was marching north, on 12 August between Knaresborough and Wetherby. To have been worsted on points by a commander of Lambert's calibre was perhaps no great shame, even with the benefit of numbers. To have lost track of him entirely, and to be unaware that he had made contact with Cromwell would prove totally disastrous.

Indecision was soon added to lack of useful intelligence, for having captured Appleby castle, and seen off Lambert, as they thought, the Scottish command was still unsure of what to do next. At Kendal there was a delay as Hamilton first lingered in the hope that his reinforcements would catch up: then moved on again without them. For a long time the Scots were unsure as to which route they should take. They even remained undecided once they had got across the Lancashire border. As Sir James Turner's narrative records:

My Lord Duke marcheth on with this ill equipped and ill orderd armie of his, in which I being Colonell of a regiment, I officiated also as Adjntant Generall, or rather indeed doeing the duetie of Major Generall of the infanterie, since there was none namd for it. To relieve Langdale at Carlisle, brought us out of the roade, and trulie we never came in the right way againe; so true is the old saying, 'once wrong and ay wrong'. At Hornbie, a day's march beyond Kendall, it was advisd whether we sould march [by] Lancashire, Cheshire and the western counties, or we sould go into Yorkshire, and so put ourselves on the straight road to London, with a resolution to fight all wold oppose us. Calander was indifferent; Middletone was for Yorkshire; Baillie for Lancashire. When my opinion was asked, I was for Yorkshire, and for this reason onlie, that I understood Lancashire was a close Countrey, full of ditches and hedges, which was a great advantage the English would have over our raw and undisciplined musketeers; the Parliaments armie consisting of experienced and well traind sojors, and excellent firemen; on the other hand, Yorkshire being a more open countrey, and full of heaths, where we both might make use of our horse and come to push of pike. My Lord Duke was for Lancashire way, and it seemd he had hopes that some forces would joyne him in his march that way.[15]

Any lingering doubts the Lancashire committee might have had about siding with the New Model were soon dispelled when the Scottish army arrived on county soil. As the pamphlet *Strange and Terrible News from Colchester and the Scottish Army* reported, the Scots were evicting people, kidnapping for ransom, and stealing whatever they wanted, irrespective of whether their victims were for king or parliament. One particularly nasty trick was to ask whether civilians had taken the Covenant, 'if they answer they have, they plunder them ... as enemies to the king; if they have not ... they are plundered as Sectaries and Cavaliers'. Across in Yorkshire the arrival of the Scots was viewed with extreme alarm, as they watched their neighbours being

> invaded by a Rapatious foreign Scottish Army, joined with a Fugitive rabble of unnaturall Englishmen, endeavouring the ruine of their mother Countrey, for the satisfying of their own unbounded lusts; to which purpose they have already Marched into the Bowels of this Commonwealth, and have left some of their Forces in the next neighbouring Countrie of Lancaster.[16]

That Hamilton still had hopes of converting Lancashire to the royalist Engager cause was certainly true. Given that the king was, at least in theory, now signed up to presbyterianism, the religious card was one which could be played. Having intelligence that a number of Lancashire's preachers had taken refuge from invasion in Lancaster, where there was a strong castle, the Duke wrote thither from Hornby on 10 August in the hope of mollifying or even converting them to the Engager cause:

> Being informed that divers of the Ministry of Lancashire, upon the causeless apprehension of receiving injury from this Army, have lately forsaken their charges and benefices, and are now at Lancaster, to the inconveniences of themselves and their parishioners, for the which I am grieved; and that they should so far mistake our intentions in coming hither; it being for settled Presbyterian government according to the Covenant, liberating and re-establishing his Majesty, and for other ends conducing to the good and peace of the kingdom, according to the Declaration herewith sent, and not to harm any, (much less) the ministers of this Countrey; I therefore thought good to certifie such as have so absented themselves, may freely and without feare return to their several dwellings.

It was far too late for honeyed words to work any good. The reputation of the Scottish army had gone before it, and the preachers had fled for good reason. They duly replied, pointing out that not only did parliament itself already subscribe to the presbyterian line, but that Hamilton had in is army 'our old enemies of religion, and the kingdom's peace', the Catholics. Naturally they expressed no personal ill-will to his lordship, but they stuck to their allegiance and their 'brethren of this Province'. They would stay where they were, and hoped that Hamilton would 'act nothing prejudicially' in the meantime. Not long afterwards, however, came news from the town of Lancaster itself that the Scots were stealing the very 'crocks and pot hooks' from the population, along with 'all the beasts, sheep and horses'. Their treatment of women in particular was described as 'extreamly abominable'.[17]

Sir Marmaduke Langdale remained broadly optimistic as his force entered the county. As he explained to the royalist Sir Charles Lucas, now in arms for the king at Colchester:

In our march to Lancaster, we met with no opposition. For the town, it is rather Neutrall then cordially Loyall; howbeit, the Inhabitants pretended

Stonyhurst College, Catholic school: in 1648 the building was a relatively modest manor house, home to the Shireburn family. Cromwell stopped here the night before the battle of Preston.

The old bridge over the river Hodder, still known as 'Cromwell's Bridge' as it was here that Oliver Cromwell conferred with this officers prior to their march on Preston, and victory over the Duke of Hamilton and Marmaduke Langdale in August 1648. Built in 1562 by Sir Richard Shireburn, the bridge is also occasionally known as 'Devil's Bridge'.

PHOTOGRAPH: AUTHOR

themselves Ours: for these, much like the popular affections of most men in those parts, move and remove just as they see our Forces move.

Opponents of the king had taken themselves to the castle, but there was no hurry to capture it. Indeed, if the campaign as a whole could be resolved successfully, then the gates of all such strongholds would be opened 'cheerfully'.

'Bloody Preston', 17 August 1648

Notwithstanding the response of a group of Lancashire's senior clergy Hamilton was at last resolved to advance down the main road through the county. His left, or landward, flank would be screened by the English royalist army: but soon all was far from well. By 13 August Langdale was around Settle with about 4,000 men, when he heard the disquieting news that,

Parliament forces were gathered together, and marching towards me, I went to acquaint Duke Hamilton therewith to Horneby, where he determined for Preston, where (his army being numerous in foot) he might have the greater advantage upon his enemy in those inclosed Countries. I marched neere Clitherow towards Preston, in the march I met with the Lord Callender and divers of the Scottish Officers quartered in my way, with whom I was resolved to march to Preston, but for the present the intelligence was that the Parliaments Forces were divided, some part whereof were marched to Colne, and so to Manchester, to relieve that Towne in case we should presse upon it. This made the Officers of Horse more negligent in repayring to Preston, but Quartered wide in the Country.[18]

At some point during the night of 16–17 August any lingering complacency was shattered when Langdale received more certain intelligence that Cromwell 'with all his forces' was close at hand. Naturally anticipating action Langdale began to gather his own troops together, and sent back word, via Lord Leviston, to General Middleton of the latest developments. He then began to retire in the direction of Preston, near which he found

the Duke and Lord Callender with the most part of the Scottish foot drawne up; their resolution was to march to Wiggan, giving little credit to the intelligence that came the night before, but suffer their horse to continue in their quarters 10 and 12 miles off.

Hamilton's incredulity is perhaps understandable, but it was a crucial error. His previous definite knowledge was that Cromwell's detachment of the New Model had been fighting in Wales. It hardly seemed possible to him that in so short a time it could have marched across the country, through the Midlands, then into Yorkshire, so as to be in position to their north and east. Even less credible was that Cromwell's little army, vastly inferior in numbers to the Scots and English royalists, would now choose to go on to the offensive.[19]

This, however, was exactly what Cromwell had in mind. First he had sent scouts into the Ribble valley, then he had followed up, 'marching very sore' with his whole force, to reach Skipton on 14 August. At a council of war at the Hodder bridge two days later, he and his commanders had considered whether to go via Whalley, then south of the Ribble, and get between the enemy and their way south or to go straight ahead and attack the enemy north of the Ribble. It being decided 'that to engage the enemy to fight was our

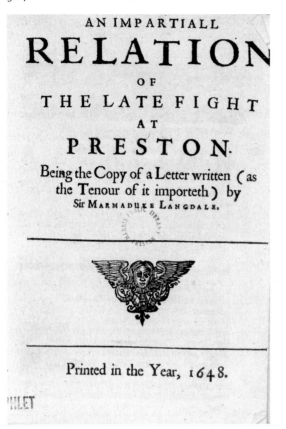

AN IMPARTIALL

RELATION

OF

THE LATE FIGHT

AT

PRESTON.

Being the Copy of a Letter written (as
the Tenour of it importeth) by
Sir MARMADUKE LANGDALE.

Printed in the Year, 1648.

Title page to *An Imartiall
Relation of the Late Fight
at Preston*, 1648, by Sir
Marmaduke Langdale.

business', the march of the New Model and its local allies continued west in
the direction of Langdale and Hamilton's unsuspecting army. After a night
at Stonyhurst, on the morning of 17 August they hurried on towards Preston.
Sir James Turner takes up the story,

> Beside Preston in Lancashire, Cromwell falls on Sir Marmadukes flanke.
> The English imagine it was one Collonell Ashton, a powerfull presbiterian,
> who had got together about 3000 men to oppose us, because we came out of
> Scotland without the Generall Assemblies permission. Marke the quarrel.
> While Sir Maramaduke disputes the matter, Baillie by the Dukes order,
> marcheth to Ribble Bridge, and passeth it with all the foot, except tuo
> brigads. This was tuo miles from Preston. By my Lord Dukes command,
> I had sent some ammunition and commanded men to Sir Mamaduks
> assistance; bot to no purpose ...[20]

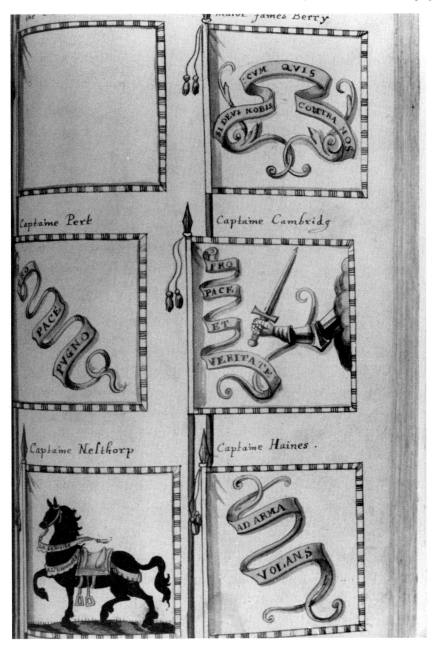

The 'cornets' or flags of Twisleton's regiment of cavalry, New Model army. The regiment was a key unit during the Preston campaign of 1648. Philip Twisleton had succeeded to what was then Rossiter's Lincolnshire regiment of horse in 1647. Captain Hezekiah Haynes was the son of John Haynes who became governor of Massachusetts and then Connecticut.

So it was that the Scots continued their ponderous movement down the Lancaster to Preston road, with their advanced parties of horse well to the fore, beyond the Ribble. First contact between the English royalists and the parliamentarians was made in the vicinity of Longridge chapel, about six miles north-east of preston. Cromwell's army was fronted by a strong screen of skirmishers drawn out from Lambert's Northern Association forces, being 500 mounted men led by Major Smithson of Lilburne's horse, and 200 foot under Major Pownall of Bright's regiment. Also available were about 200 dragoons of Okey's regiment of the New Model, a unit that had fought with distinction at Naseby, and more recently at St Fagans in south Wales. Under the circumstances, Langdale's men did the best they could. Trying to avoid having to stand on the open moor between Preston and Longridge, his men fell back by stages onto the enclosures north of Preston. A running fight now broke out, with neither side in formed bodies, as the parliamentarians pushed forward and Langdale's men gave way by stages as they retreated. As Cromwell put it, his men met with their 'scouts and outguard', and made them 'quit their ground', taking some prisoners, a 'considerable parcel of the enemy' according to Captain Hodgson. Few men had fallen as yet, but this was soon to change.[21]

It was getting towards mid-day by the time that Langdale's troops finally found a tolerably secure position behind hedges on the Preston side of Eaves Brook. Royalist skirmishers took up their posts in front of Langdale's army, lining the banks of the stream. Meanwhile the main body of the parliamentarians marched up along the road from Longridge. Langdale's army was now deployed on a frontage of about three quarters of a mile. His right flank was the firmer of the two, somewhere in the vicinity of what is now Pope Lane. Here there was little gap between the royalists and the Ribble through which any enemy could hope to penetrate. Further to the rear on this side Langdale's men were also protected by the wooded slopes which ran down to the river. The royalist left was more open, but still not an easy option for any attacker since in addition to Eaves Brook, the meanders and contours of which made for a natural defensive line, attackers would have to negotiate undulating ground to discover the termination of the royalist left from whence Scottish forces might be expected to intervene. The royalist horse appear to have been held back behind the main battle line. Langdale had found himself as good a position as any in the vicinity at which he could hope to halt his adversary: but, unless the Scots came promptly to his aid, he was still outnumbered by at least two to one. The preliminaries were over: the battle proper was about to begin.[22]

Meeting what was clearly a significant royalist position athwart the main track Cromwell decided to square up to the enemy for immediate action.

So soon as our foot and horse were come up, we resolved that night to engage them if we could; and therefore, advancing with our Forlorn, and putting the rest of our Army into as good a posture as the ground would bear (which was totally inconvenient for our horse, being all enclosure and miry ground), we pressed upon them. The regiments of foot were ordered as followeth. There being a Lane, very deep and ill, up to the Enemy's Army, and leading to the Town, we commanded two regiments of horse, the first whereof was Colonel Harrison's and next was my own, to charge up the Lane; and on either side of them advanced the Main battle, – which were Lieutenant Colonel Reade's, Colonel Dean's and Colonel Pride's on the right; Colonel Bright's and my Lord General's on the left; and Colonel Ashton with the Lancashire regiments in reserve. We ordered Colonel Thornhagh's and Colonel Twistleton's regiments of horse on the right; and one regiment in reserve for the lane; and the remaining horse on the left.

The 'remaining horse' were themselves not an inconsiderable body and are likely to have included Colonel Adrian Scroope's regiment, part of which were recorded as being at Preston. Indeed they were possibly not far short of a full regiment as at one point they were billeted at Manchester where the constables record that '400 souldiers & horse' were catered for. With them were also any Lancashire horse, including Shuttleworth's and Rigby's.[23]

The main bodies of parliamentarian troops were thus deployed out from their cramped marching columns on the lane into two major battle lines of infantry either side of the track. To the front were the foot regiments of the New Model, together with Colonel John Bright's regiment of the Northern Association. In the second rank were Ashton's men of the Lancashire militia. This much was to be expected, and a conventional approach for a set-piece action of the period. Cromwell's positioning of strong bodies of cavalry on his wings was also normal. Where his dispositions parted company with tradition was in leaving a major portion of his horse on the lane in his centre. Here they could not easily spread into line, but as Cromwell makes clear physical space for cavalry in line was limited, and weather conditions far from perfect. As early as 1610 'enclosures' with cottages and barns were recorded on the north side of Preston, on the 'waste of Preston Moor', and attempts had certainly been made to enclose parts of Fulwood by 1623. The ground was very wet and the enemy had the benefit of the hedgerows, so Cromwell was not about to contemplate a headlong cavalry assault under such disadvantageous conditions.

First to probe the royalist front line were the doughty skirmishers who had borne the brunt of the action so far. The commanders of this 'forlorn hope' were Major Pownall and Captain John Hodgson, whose account takes up the narrative,

> being drawn up by the moor side (that scattering we had been not half the number we should have been), the general comes to us, and commands to march: We not having half of our men come up desired a little patience; he gives out the word, March! and so we drew over a little common, where our horse was drawn up, and came to a ditch, and the enemy let fly at us (a company of Langdale's men that was newly raised). They shot at the

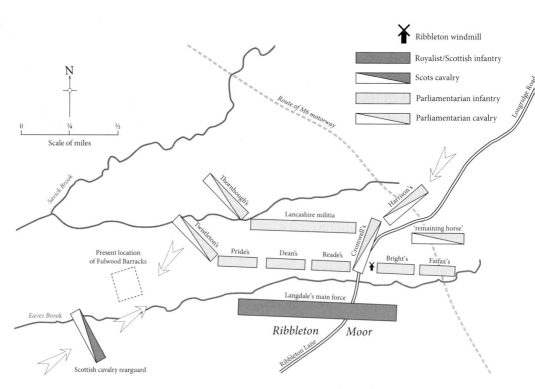

The initial deployments during the early phase of the battle of Preston at around midday, 17 August 1648. Later in the day Langdale's English royalists would be forced back on the town, where Cromwell also managed to split the larger but unprepared Scottish army in two.

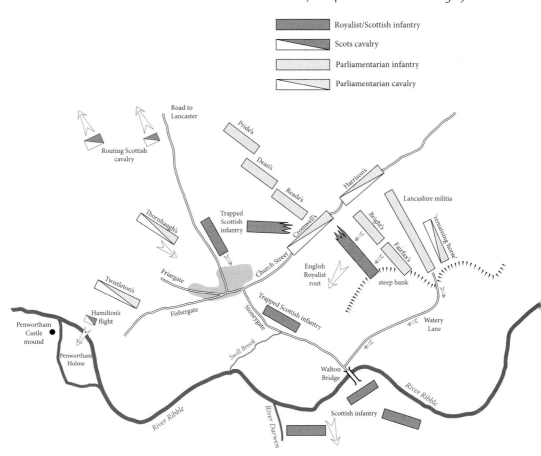

The situation at around 5 p.m. on 17 August. The parliamentarian forces had split and begun to scatter the royalists, with the Duke of Hamilton fleeing south via the ford at Penwortham Holme.

skies, which did so encourage our men, that they were willing to venture upon any attempt; and the major orders me to march to the next hedge, and I bid him order the men to follow me, and there drew out a small party; and we came up to the hedge end, and the enemy, many of them, threw down their arms, and run to their party, where was their stand of pikes, and a great body of colours.[24]

This eye-witness testimony is interesting for it suggests that initially at least some of the royalists were firing over the heads of the parliamentarian skirmishers as they pressed close to the line. This may be explained by the topography, for even today the brook nestles in a small valley, across which the parliamentarians would have had to advance. Naturally much of the royalist fire would have been directed at the formed bodies of infantry and cavalry behind the skirmish screen, who were still at the top of the slope some yards behind the 'forlorn', or advanced guard. Perhaps also this tendency to fire high was aggravated by the presence of raw troops in the royalist ranks, men who had not yet learned to aim low into the body mass of men in front of them, as Hodgson seems to suggest.

In any event Pownall and his troops were able to push through the royalist skirmishers, some of whom threw away their weapons as they ran back upon their main body, and the parliamentarian 'forlorn' was able to rush up to the hedge, from which it was now began harassing the enemy main line. From his position, virtually amongst the enemy, Hodgson could see that one party of the enemy foot lay were stationed so as to 'ambuscado' Major Smithson and his horsemen on the lane. Outflanked, however, by the swift advance of parliamentarians, these royalist infantry broke off and headed back, led by an officer who quickly got ahead of them. Hodgson did his best to capture this man, but Colonel Carleton, as it was later discovered to have been, quickly outran him. Having overcome the initial shock of contact Langdale's regiments now mounted a swift counter-attack, intended to clear away the galling marksmen who had so effectively infiltrated their position. In the face of this 'great body of colours' moving forward the parliamentarian forlorn had no option but to retire in their turn, falling back on Major Smithson's horse, but continuing to shoot at the royalists for all they were worth, 'so long as our ammunition lasted'. Both armies now, as one report put it, 'engaged couragiously', in what Cromwell called with uncharacteristic understatement, a 'hedge dispute'.[25]

It was now well into the afternoon and Langdale's fighting retreat from Longridge, followed by the hedgerow defence on Eaves Brook, must have taken up three or more hours. Clearly Langdale must have expected that the Scots would use this time productively: to come to his aid, to outflank Cromwell's right, or at least to send him intelligence of some alternative plan. In fact the warnings he had sent had gone pretty much unheeded, and the vital hours had slipped away. Despite Sir Lewis Dyves' prompting, the Scots had failed to march directly on Ribbleton, or even to get into position so to do. Baillie appears to have formed up so many of his troops as were available 'in battalia', along what is now Garstang Road in the vicinity of Moor Park. Yet they lacked clear orders, and none were forthcoming. The *Discourse* has it that the Scots were not actually very interested in helping Langdale, and that Hamilton was overheard to say that Cromwell and Langdale were best left to settle their own struggle, for after all it was only 'English dogs' that were 'killing one another'. It seems unlikely that Hamilton would actually have said any such thing, but his reaction to the crisis was at best tardy, and at worst totally incompetent. Clarendon's view was simple. The Duke was 'confounded' by the intelligence he received 'and at his wits' end knew not what to do'.

According to Bishop Burnet's account Hamilton had ridden within about a mile of what must have been an increasingly obvious battle to his left, and headed south-east in the direction of Walton-le-Dale,

passed the bridge to view the field for a convenient leaguer, and before his return Calander ordered Baylie to pass the bridge with the foot to the place the leaguer was to be. The general returning, and thinking to have found the foot still in the moor, met Baylie on the bridge, who told him that he had received orders from Calander to draw over the whole body of foot; but hearing that Langdale was hotly engaged with the enemy, he had halted there, till he saw what the event of the action might be: which the general approved, and ordered him to halt, wishing they had stayed upon the moor. Meanwhile Calander came up, and asked why they did not march: Baylie gave him the answer he had given the general, with which Calander was unsatisfied, and went away in a chafe. The general seeing him in passion studied to allay it, telling him that Baylie had stopped upon his order: Calander answered, his grace might do what he pleased, but he had given the former orders to march, which he conceived most fit to be done, pretending the necessity of having the horse and foot on one side of the river, to which the general gave way; and so Baylie marched over, and the duke and Calander returned back to the moor, where his rearguard of horse, together with two brigades of foot, stood all the while. By this time they got sure intelligence, from some prisoners whom Langdale had taken, that the enemy he engaged was Cromwell; and the general ordered Turner to send out commanded parties to Langdale's relief ...[26]

In the event Scottish aid to Langdale was too little too late. A unit of Scottish lancers did arrive at Ribbleton some time in the early afternoon, and charged Major Smithson's horse, which were forced to retreat. Burnet claims that Langdale actually succeeded in pushing his adversaries as much as 'two or three closes', back across the ground that he had just given up. John Walton, a parliamentarian commentator, states that Cromwell's left wing – Bright's and

Fairfax's regiments – was forced to concede 'a little ground'. This was but a temporary respite. In their turn the Scottish lancers were seen off by another parliamentarian cavalry formation and 'routed immediately', as witnessed by Captain Hodgson. John Walton also saw Scottish cavalry attempting to intervene, presumably on the Fulwood side of the field, where Thornhaugh's and Twistleton's regiments were now ready and waiting. The Scottish horse 'stood it for a charge or two' but, 'finding such hot service', were forced to retreat. The New Model cavalry followed them some hundreds of yards, firing into them with their pistols so much that the Scots troopers were forced to gallop off. The parliamentarian troopers were, however, sufficiently disciplined to stay their charge as soon as there was a danger that they would run into the Scottish infantry, and 'retreated in very good time to relieve our left wing'.

A detail of Bucks' early eighteenth-century engraving of the South Prospect of Preston. The steep drop to the river and the prominence of the church are both readily apparent.

A famous later representation of the fight at Walton Bridge, by Cattermole. The original bridge stood a few yards downstream of the modern bridge. On the afternoon of 17 August 1648 Scottish troops occupied the bridge, while Fairfax's and Bright's parliamentarian regiments managed to capture the high ground on the north bank of the river and fire down upon them. A rush by the Lancashire militia then forced the Scots from the bridge, initiated the royalist retreat southwards that ended in ultimate defeat.

Thereafter pressure on the English royalist front mounted steadily, as more and more of Cromwell's infantry came into action along the line. Worse, it was gradually becoming obvious that the parliamentarian forces, fully deployed, extended well beyond the royalist left. The longer the battle continued, the greater the danger that Cromwell would exploit this potentially open flank that the Scots had so signally failed to support.

Gradually Langdale's men, exhausted and outnumbered, began to give ground. As they did so they moved slowly over towards the river, shifting, deliberately, or accidentally, tighter against what was perceived as the secure flank, with the Ribble bridge to Walton-le-Dale at their rear, which might be the only good route of escape. Cromwell's report noted that the burden of the fight now fell upon the parliamentarian foot. As he told the Speaker of the House of Commons:

There came no band of your foot to fight that day but did it with incredible valour and resolution; among which Colonel Bright's, Lieutenant Colonel Reade's and Colonel Ashton's had the greatest work; they often coming to push of pike and to close firing, and always making the enemy recoil. And indeed I must needs say, God was as much seen in the valour of the officers and soldiers of these before mentioned as in any action that hath been performed; the enemy making, though he was still worsted, very stiff and sturdy resistance. Colonel Dean's and Colonel Pride's, outwinging the enemy, could not see so much share of the action; the enemy shogging down towards the bridge …

The danger to the parliamentarian left was effectively parried by Ashton's men, a couple of companies of whom plunged 'into the fire and smoke', in support of Bright's regiment.[27]

'Ribbon' hilted basket sword, found at Woodplumpton near Preston. This artefact, now in a private collection, is almost certainly a relic of the 1648 campaign.

By mid-afternoon the main royalist battle line had been pushed back from hedge to hedge, from Ribbleton into Deepdale. A near contemporary plan shows that Acregate Lane existed at this time, crossing the battlefield parallel to Cromwell's front, and it is more than possible that hedges here formed one of the main obstacles that Langdale's men now sought to defend. The report given in the parliamentarian *Moderate Intelligencer* was graphic:

> The battle on a sodain waxed very hot, and there was a furious dispute for the space of two hours or thereabouts. They had so thick lined the hedges and lanes, that they galled our horse and foot, at length our men forced them to give back, but yet the contention was very long and much ado we had to get ground upon them, till our regiments of foot came up and flank't them.

In fact it was not just one flank that royalists now had to worry about. The parliamentarians had also realised the vital tactical significance of the Ribble bridge, and fresh trouble was brewing for Langdale's beleaguered men. Ashton's militia had begun to move from their position in the second rank, marching down a narrow lane in the steep bank, out of sight, and across Fishwick Bottoms around the royalist main battle line. Now, they were beginning to emerge at the bottom of Watery Lane, by the Ribble itself, and started a fresh action against the surprised Scots who were still in the act of crossing. In the forefront of the action was the young ensign, Adam Sydall. Directed by Ashton, and his Captain Samuel Birch, Sydall advanced rapidly to the attack, as Birch's diary records, 'my ensigne, by command of General Ashton, led the pykes and colours up against the defendantes on Rible Bridge and beat them off, almost all my officers markt, none killed, divers souldiers shott and hurt, some very dangerously, most performed very well.'[28]

Belatedly the Scottish command directed 600 musketeers to the defence of the bridge position, but by now it was far too late. Claude Hamilton, the duke's brother, was felled by a musket ball through the arm. The English royalist forces, now thoroughly outflanked, with the enemy in their very rear, having fought and toiled for at least four hours, were completely undone. As Langdale himself recorded, 'The Scots continue[d] their march over the river, and did not secure a lane by the bridge, whereby the Parliament forces came upon my flankes; neither did the forces that were left for my supply, come to my relief.' As Langdale's men turned and fled, the *coup de grace* was the unleashing of Cromwell's cavalry down the lane through Deepdale. Cromwell's and Harrison's regiments, hitherto uncommitted, came splashing down the miry track, slashing about them with their swords. Any remaining resistance was soon overcome. Cromwell himself claimed that it was his troopers who were first to enter Preston, 'seconded by Colonel Harrison's regiment', charging through the enemy to clear the streets. The *Discourse* records many of the royalists killed, 'some being trodden into the dirt in the lanes with the horses' feet, the wayes were so deep. Abundance were killed in the fields on the east syd of Preston and so did drive them doune toward Ribble Bridge.'

With the English royalist army dissolving rapidly around them, the Scots were left in a dire predicament, largely of their own manufacture. Some of their cavalry had already run; two brigades of infantry were trapped north of the river and were now about to be destroyed; and the remainder of the foot were south of the bridge which was now in enemy hands. Efforts to retake the bridge were doomed to failure, with not only the Lancashire men on hand but musketeers of the Lord General's regiment and Colonel Bright's up slope of the crossing and firing down. The bulk of the Scottish cavalry was still oblivious to the unfolding disaster, strung out along the road near Wigan. Munro's troops, which would have made a useful addition at this juncture, were still a long way to the north, and would have been unlikely to arrive by evening, even had they been promptly recalled. The Scots still outnumbered Cromwell, but their dispositions were hopeless, with units strung out and scattered over a radius of at least ten miles from the main seat of the action. The New Model and its allies were acting in close cooperation at the vital point. Cromwell had the initiative, and intended to keep it.

Far from righting the situation, the Duke of Hamilton's first priority was escaping from the closing net with his life. As Sir James Turner's account explained,

> The Duke with his guard of horse, Sir Marmaduke and many officers, among others myselfe, got into Preston toune, with the intention to pass a foorde below it, thogh at that time not rideable. At the entrie of the toune, the enemie pursued us hard. The Duke facd about, and put tuo troops of them to retreate; bot so soone as we turnd from them, they turnd upon us. The Duke facing a second time, charged them, which succeeded well. Being pursued the third time, my Lord Duke cryd to charge once more for King Charles ... At that charge we put the enemie so farre behind us, that he could not overtake us so soone. Then Sir Marmaduke and I entreated the Duke to hast him to his armie; and truelie he shew here as much personall valour as any man could be capable of. We suimed the river, and so got to the place where Lieutenant Generall Baillie had

advantageouslie lodgd the foot on the top of a hill, among very fencible enclosures.[29]

Some of Hamilton's cavalry trapped north of the river never did succeed in crossing, but, having avoided the fate of many their infantry comrades, made good their escape as best they could, northwards and westwards. The tail end of Hamilton's main column, still acting under orders to head towards the bridge, were going to attempt to join him – wherever he now was, but,

> upon sight of those Horse and hearing of muskets and the defeat given to the Duke his Reare durst not come out. Great numbers of them turned not back the same way, they came but tooke other waies and fled into the Fyld Country and in great feare, as was thought, parted themselves into sundry roads or waies. For more expedition some took up a way by the Lund Chapell through Treales and up to Elswicke and so homeward. Others of them went through Kirkham and were going through it all that night and so to Thisleton whether over Wyre water or by St. Michaels is not certain. In Kirkham they were hard in their March to be very doleful and it was thought they carried some dead men with them yet, the night being dark, could not be well discerned.[30]

By late afternoon most of the surviving Scottish infantry still under command had arrived atop Walton hill, south of the river, together with the artillery, baggage, and many of the senior officers. The leading units of cavalry had finally been alerted, and were believed to be headed back to join with the main body. The remainder of the Scottish infantry north of the river was surrounded, with no escape, and no means of contact with Hamilton. As Turner observed, the enemy was between 'the bridge and us': the better part of two brigades of Scottish foot were therefore 'killd or taken'. Cromwell himself estimated that up to this point about 1,000 English royalists and Scots had been killed; about 4,000 made prisoner; and 5,000 weapons taken. Some of the parliamentarian horse were pursuing defeated fugitives of the Scottish cavalry anything up to ten miles in the direction of Lancaster. The advanced guard of the parliamentarian army had a foothold across the Ribble, and had also seized the Darwen bridge not far on, but was too exhausted, and not numerically strong enough to contemplate a frontal attack, up hill, against the Scottish infantry. A lull in the action now ensued.

Before long, however, and somewhat predictably, the Scottish commanders were again locked in dispute with each other. Hamilton had called the generals together, still mounted, for an impromptu council of war to discuss the options. According to Turner, who was present at the conference,

> We had no choice bot one of tuo, either stay and maintaine our ground till Middletone (who was sent for), came backe with his cavalrie; or els march away that night so soone as it was darke. This was seconded by all the rest, except by Lieutenant Generall Baillie and myselfe. Bot all the arguments we used, as the impossibilitie of a safe retreat from ane enemie so powerfull of horse, in so foule a weather, and extremelie deepe way, our sojors exceeding wet, wearie, and hungrie, the inevitable losse of all our amunition, could not move my Lord Duke by his authoritie to contradict the shamefull resolution taken by the major part of his officers.[31]

So it was that a plan was hatched for a covert, drumless march, away from the battlefield under cloak of darkness. To maintain secrecy the artillery and most of the stores would be left where they lay. Bishop Burnet reported that the Scots left with nothing more than their personal arms and 'their flasks full'. Just a handful of the troops were deputed to remain behind, camp fires blazing, maintaining the impression that the hilltop position was still fully occupied. After three hours the last to leave would light a train of powder, and make themselves scarce, after which all remaining munitions would detonate, so denying them to the enemy. Whether the last to leave thought better of their dangerous mission, or whether wind and rain rendered their efforts fruitless is unknown: either way they failed to destroy the Scottish ammunition dump, and before long parliamentarian scouts would be apprised of the true situation.

The Scots retreat southwards

Though the English royalist army had effectively been destroyed, and the Scots had taken a serious blow, it was by no means apparent to Cromwell quite how catastrophically the events of 17 August had struck the morale of the enemy commanders. His letter written to the Lancashire committee at Manchester that evening was extremely positive but by no means cock-a-hoop. His assumption was that the opposition had suffered a defeat, but that further exertions, supported by the Lancashire parliamentarians – and 'God's assistance' – would be required to turn this success into their 'utter ruin'. He remained concerned, moreover, that Hamilton's forces might double back across the river lower down, or alternatively head east and then make for the Whalley area, so outflanking him. The news that the Scots had stolen away into the night was therefore intriguing, and something that should be capitalised upon immediately.

Amazed parliamentarian scouts who were first on the scene on the hill above Walton-le-Dale found not just 'artillery and carriages', but 'cabins' or bivouacs that the enemy had just erected for shelter, and the enemy 'plate' or plunder in a wagon. This they attempted to move down the hill in the direction of Preston, but it overturned strewing the way with the choicest items of the Scottish baggage. In addition to the more glittering booty, the parliament men seized 20 pieces of ordnance, eight barrels of gunpowder, and four carts of other munitions. A bizarre trophy was a load of blue Scottish bonnets, items of spare uniform for troops who would no longer need them.[32]

Though Cromwell realised that Hamilton's army had a head start, his immediate order for pursuit was a bold one. It also contained inherent danger, in that he was aware that Munro's force and Tyldesley's men were somewhere in his rear in the vicinity of Lancaster. He therefore took the decision to risk splitting his force, leaving the Lancashire troops to guard the prisoners and protect his rear from any attack from the north. This would reduce the numbers that he had available for the chase to little more than 6,000 – about half the number of the Scots that were being followed. Under other circumstances this division might have been disastrous, but at this moment was an inspired choice, which did indeed lead to Hamilton's ruin. Cromwell set off south in pursuit of the enemy. Meanwhile Lancashire's forces, which had served 'so much distinction under Colonel Ashton', were encouraged to ready themselves for further efforts in the cause. By way of practical assistance £3,000 was promised, together with the observation that resistance to the Scots was undoubtedly cheaper than the alternative of giving in without a fight to those cross-border plunderers.[33]

The Scottish plan to escape and join up with General Middleton's cavalry went wrong almost immediately. Middleton's horse took the Chorley road coming north: the main Scottish force went south on the Standish road. In daylight, without the added pressure of enemy forces snapping at their heels, this mistake would have occasioned no more than a delay. In darkness, even with the Scottish horse and foot passing within two miles of each other, the upshot was a complete loss of command and the onset of confusion. One report had it that the first of Middleton's men actually reached the position on Walton hill, before the error was realised: here they found fires still burning, attended by 'some sutlers' – presumably the unfortunates who were to fail in destroying the stores, and were in imminent danger of being overwhelmed by the enemy.

Given how badly things were now going Middleton appears to have done his best to screen the retreating infantry. Near Chorley, probably a few hours later and some time after dawn, Scottish lancers blocked the path of Thornhaugh's cavalry. Colonel Thornhaugh immediately attacked at the head of his regiment, but his impetuosity was rewarded with a hero's death, Cromwell later remarking that he had been run through the 'body, thigh and head' by the enemy lances. Captain Hodgson blamed the valiant colonel's demise on the fact that he had failed to put on any of his armour. Lucy Hutchinson's near-contemporary account is probably the fullest:

> Being at the beginning of the charge on a horse as courageous as became such as master, he made such furious speed to set upon a company of Scotch lancers, that he was singly engaged and mortally wounded, before it was possible for his regiment, though as brave men as ever drew sword, and too affectionate to their colonel to be slack in following him, to come up time enough to break the fury of that body, which shamed not to unite all their force against one man: who yet fell not among them, but being faint and all covered with blood, of his enemies as well as his own, was carried off by some of his own men, while the rest, enraged for the loss of their dear colonel, fought not that day like men of human race; but deaf to the cries of every coward that asked for mercy, they killed all, and would not that a captive should live to see their colonel die; but said that the whole kingdom of Scotland was too mean a sacrifice for that brave man.

Thornhaugh died, it was said, thanking God that he had been allowed to see the overthrow of 'this perfidious enemy'.[34]

Highly coloured as this account may be, it is certainly the case that plenty of Scots fell to the swords of parliamentarian troopers on the morning of 18 August. Sir James Turner agrees that Middleton was 'hotlie pursued by Cromwell's horse, with whom he skirmished the whole way'. Bishop Burnet's opinion was that the 'wet, hungry and weary' Scottish infantry would be reduced to little more than half the number that left Scotland by the end of the day – the rest being now killed, wounded, captured or otherwise missing. That evening from Standish Moor to the outskirts of Wigan there was further skirmishing, but the Scots had little ammunition now, and neither side was in a fit state to fight a set-piece action, as Cromwell's letter recorded,

> Our horse still prosecuted the enemy; killing and taking divers all the way.

At last the enemy drew up within three miles of Wigan; and by that time our army was come up, they drew off again, and recovered Wigan before we could attempt anything upon them. We lay that night in the field close by the enemy; being very dirty and weary, and having marched twelve miles of such ground as I never rode in all my life, the day being very wet. We had some skirmishing, that night with the enemy, near the town; where we took General Van Druske and a Colonel, and killed some principal officers, and took about a hundred prisoners; where I also received a letter from Duke Hamilton, for the civil usage towards his kinsman Colonel Hamilton ... We also took Colonel Hurry and Lieutenant Colonel Innes.

Colonel Hurry [or Urry] was in fact badly wounded, shot in the head, before he fell and was captured. He was lucky to survive his injury.[35]

Cromwell's observation that the enemy successfully 'recovered Wigan' before they could be brought to battle belies the distracted, even demented, state in which the fleeing Scots now entered the town. Had the New Model men been any fresher, the campaign might indeed have ended there and then. Sir James Turner, with some of the last infantry to get away, records that one regiment of Scottish horse burst into the streets of Wigan in the darkness, apparently unsure as to which side had occupied the town. He attempted to get his men to let them pass, but the edgy pikemen mistook the order and swung their pikes towards their general, jabbing him in the thigh. The cavalry tried to screech to a halt, but in answer to Turner's cries, and the shouts from the rear ranks that the enemy was upon them, they then burst through the ranks of the foot and careered through the town disordering all they encountered. Colonel Lockheart was trampled by the stampeding horse. It was with great difficulty that any semblance of order was restored.

Few of Hamilton's army got much sleep that night – and many just kept trudging south. Turner's men beat their drums to rally as many to the colours as possible, while Sir James himself eventually fell asleep in the saddle despite the excitement and his wound.

The battle of Winwick, 19 August 1648

The next day, 19 August 1648, looked very much as though it might be a repeat of the previous day, with the battered Scots continuing their march to the south, harried by Cromwell's cavalry. Yet there was some method in Hamilton's progress, for now he was but ten miles from Warrington, and if he could put the Mersey between himself and his tormentors, survival,

St Oswald's parish church, Winwick, near Warrington. Scottish troops fled into the church after their defeat at Winwick, 1648.

even revival, might be possible. As Burnet observed, once across the river, and the bridge was blocked or destroyed, the Scots could go 'whither they pleased'. Giving the parliamentarians a bloody nose, or simply such a minor shock as might cause them to slow their pursuit, might gain enough time for the Scottish command to rally and take stock of their options. Given their tired condition and lack of powder a surprise ambush would appear to have been the only really practicable chance. Just three miles north of Warrington the topography seemed to offer the exhausted Scottish army the very opportunity they were looking for. On the road between Winwick and Newton was what was described by one commentator as 'a straight passage in that lane' that the Scots were able to make 'very stronge and forcible'. The site of this action has been identified as Red Bank, and the lane as Hermitage Green Lane. Here any troops marching along the lane would be in a defile, and at a distinct disadvantage against any musketeers who lined the surrounding hedges.

As the parliamentarian 'forlorn hope' of skirmishers entered the trap they were suddenly set upon by superior numbers. As Hodgson so evocatively described the result, the enemy 'snaffled our forlorn, and put them to retreat'.

It looked as though a decisive fight might be about to happen. Cromwell's description of the action is as detailed as any that has survived:

> We could not engage the Enemy until we came within three miles of Warrington; and there the Enemy made a stand, at a place, near Winwick. We held them in some dispute till our army came up; they maintaining the Pass with great resolution for many hours; our and theirs coming to push of pike and very close charges – which forced us to give ground; but our men, by the blessing of God, quickly recovered it, and charging very home upon them, beat them from their standing; where we killed about a thousand of them, and took, as we believe, about two thousand prisoners; and prosecuted them home to Warrington town; where they possessed the bridge, which had a strong barricade and a work upon it, formerly made very defensive.[36]

Other accounts suggest that it was Colonel Pride's regiment of the New Model which had borne the brunt of this battle, while the most stubborn resistance came from a regiment of Scottish infantry, commanded by a diminutive officer, 'a little spark in a blue bonnet', who fought gallantly until overcome by Pride's men. What finally appears to have swayed the day was local intelligence, for it was reported in the *Discourse* that local people gave Cromwell's men information on the lie of the land. So guided, many of the parliamentarian troops were able to leave the constricted lane and move into the surrounding fields, effectively outflanking the Scots. Though some horse came to the aid of the Scottish infantry, the defence now crumbled, and those that could began to fall back on Winwick church. Some threw down their arms and fled, or ran inside the old stone building for sanctuary. Many outside were caught in a 'great slaughter' as they were overrun trying to defend themselves and buy time for their comrades. However, Winwick was not won without loss. One of those who fell for parliament was Captain Cholmley of Lilburne's regiment, commander of the forlorn hope, the first to fall upon the enemy. A month later General Lambert wrote to parliament requesting that a suitable post be found for a relative as a mark of appreciation.[37]

With another substantial chunk bitten from the hard-pressed Scottish infantry, further resistance seemed questionable. Yet the rather one-sided battle of Winwick had bought a little time, as had been predicted. General Baillie managed to reach Warrington bridge with at least a portion of his troops, still formed and under orders, and now readied them for defence. Any fleeting hope that something might be salvaged from the shambles was, however, shattered by one last wrong decision by the Scottish command. For Baillie discovered that both Callender and Hamilton had disappeared. Rather than take advantage of the sacrifice the infantry had made at Winwick and rejoin them at Warrington bridge, the cavalry and senior commanders had made off, leaving Baillie and his depleted command behind to face the enemy alone.

General Turner, who was present when the messenger gave Baillie this less than cheering news, relates that the general of infantry fell into the deepest despair. He 'losed much of that patience of which naturallie he was master; and beseeched any that wold to shoot him through the head'. Turner only added insult to injury by remarking that since it was unlikely that the infantry would fight again it was pointless him staying around: so he mounted up and rode off to join Middleton. The abandoned Baillie now entered into discussions with the enemy. As Cromwell recorded in his letter to parliament of 20 August:

> As soon as we came thither, I received a message from General Baillie, desiring some capitulation. To which I yielded. Considering the strength of the pass, and that I could not go over the river Mersey within ten miles of Warrington with the army, I gave him these terms: that he should surrender himself and all his officers and soldiers prisoners of war, with all his arms and ammunition and horses to me; I giving quarter for life, and promising civil usage. Which accordingly was done: and the Commissioners deputed by me have received, and are receiving, all the arms and ammunition; which they tell me will be, as they tell me, about four thousand complete arms; and as many prisoners: and thus you have their infantry totally ruined.

A couple of hours later Baillie and his men had surrendered to Cromwell: all that remained of 20 Scottish infantry regiments now marched dejectedly into captivity; a contemporary count suggested that a total of 2,547 prisoners were taken. With them were more than 160 commissioned officers, including nine colonels and lieutenant colonels.

The long road to Uttoxeter

With the surrender of Baillie, the campaign moved off out of Lancashire to the south, but by now the important action was over. The Scots were a spent force, reduced to a fraction of their former strength. What had once been well over 20,000 men was now reduced to a mere 5,000 or so under arms and control of their officers, and even this fragment was definitively split into two. The 'New Scots' of General George Munro had contributed remarkably little to the fight, and had failed even to make it as far south as Preston. Now, hearing that Cromwell was turning north again after Warrington, they retreated in short order. Sir Thomas Tyldesley had attempted to stay them, but now Munro's men were now riding back towards Scotland from the Kirkby Lonsdale area. When they were mustered at Campsie and Monyabroch at the end of the month, a fortnight after the battle of Preston, there were just 362 cavalry and 1,099 foot remaining.

Hamilton's own command, now essentially reduced to the rump of his cavalry, may have still been about 3,000 strong, but it was a sorry and bedraggled force, lacking in supplies and any hope of support. It was in no state to fight. Hard on his heels came the zealous Lambert, at the head of about 2,000 horse and a slightly smaller number of foot. At first Hamilton seems to have thought that old loyalist Chester might have been a suitable port in this particular storm, hoping perhaps to join up thereafter with Byron in north Wales. Another possible option was to outrun his adversaries, then double back to Scotland by a circuitous route: but it was not to be. Some knew the game was up and over the next few days slipped away as unobtrusively as possible, and either surrendered or made their escape as best they could. As news trickled in from one quarter or another of yet more reverses and defections, Hamilton's options shrank: Pontefract and Herefordshire were both ruled out. Finally the last of the Scottish army meandered through Market Drayton, to Stone, and at last to Uttoxeter. Bad weather had got worse, Hamilton became ill, and on the morning of 24 August the men simply refused to move. The next day the Scots surrendered to General Lambert. The campaign was over.

The *Discourse* estimated the Scottish losses during the campaign as 3,000 dead and 9,000 prisoners. Cromwell's summary to parliament, given from Warrington even before the final denouement in Staffordshire, speaks of 'two thousand enemy slain' and 'betwixt eight and nine thousand prisoners'; besides which there were a number of Scots 'lurking in hedges and private places, which the Country daily bring in or destroy'. Langdale he could not place, but his forces were 'exceedingly shattered'. Sir Thomas Tyldesley and Sir Philip Musgrave and certain other officers later went into the bag at Appleby castle. Given that a further thousand enemy troops were taken at Appleby, and that the numbers captured at Uttoxeter were 'neer upon 3,000' common soldiers, plus officers, the vast majority of Scottish and royalist forces were accounted for. By such calculations something about 5,000 were 'missing', and it is probable that some of these made it back to Scotland in the wake of Munro's force, while at least a proportion of the English royalists were able to make off and blend back in to their own localities. A few fled abroad: to France, the Channel Islands or the Isle of Man. Others were belatedly made captive, but some doubtless were murdered and robbed, revenge for the miseries they had so recently inflicted upon Lancashire. Clarendon's summation of the battle of Preston, and the fate of Hamilton's army, remains about as accurate as any that has been written in the intervening years:

> Thus was his whole army routed and defeated; more killed out of contempt than that they deserved it by any opposition. The rest were taken prisoners, all their cannon and baggage taken, and their colours. Only some of their horse, which had been quartered most backward, made haste to carry the news to their country.

Similar tidings would be received with relief in London, whence Major Berry and Captain Sexby hurried with despatches describing the action. A few days later came Capatin Pitson of the Lord General's regiment, carrying with him a hundred captured Scottish colours, cornets and guidons, the banners of a completely defeated foe. Parliament was unstinting in its praise of Lancashire's part in this overwhelming victory. On 1 September the Derby House committee wrote the Lancashire committee a glowing accolade, couched in religious terms:

> We know you cannot but have a very thankful sense of the great mercy God has bestowed upon us in that so signal victory given to this nation against that perfidious army of the Scots, who intended the conquest of this nation and were swelled to so great numbers of their own brought hither in hope of our possessions, and would further have been increased by he confluence of malignants of our own, had not God appeared for us, we having no means ready which in a rational judgement could be thought to oppose them. In this victory, those of your county had their share in the honour of retarding their march and at last for the utter breaking of that proud and insulting enemy. What this kingdom might have expected from them, they have left testimonies of it in all the places where they came.

Like praise was offered to Cromwell by the committee.

We are informed of your great success and victory ... which God have to your forces over that great army of the Scots and their adherents who had invaded this kingdom, and how evidently God was pleased to appear for us in so great a disproportion of numbers. It is alike easy to Him to save with many or with few where He will own the cause ... we do also return you thanks for your great resolution to engage them with so small a number, and for your good conduct and effectual pursuing your first victory to the total dispersing of all their foot. And we desire you to give thanks from us to all your officers and soldiers for their great resolution and valiant carriage as in all their services so in this a very especial manner, of whom as we desire to have an esteem suitable to their great merits, so we have a very tender resentment of their wants.[38]

Preston's legacy: regicide

Undoubtedly the battle of Preston was the Second Civil War's most important engagement. With Cromwell's success, ably seconded by Lambert and the Lancashire forces, the enemy abandoned all hope of victory. News of the battle reached the beleaguered Colchester garrison on 24 August; and just three days later the royalists' most significant centre of resistance in the south capitulated. Not long afterwards Cromwell was driving into Scotland, and the Scots who had supported the intervention were beset by those factions which had opposed it. In early October he entered Edinburgh unopposed, and was well received by the Duke of Argyll. The remaining 'Engagers' were toppled.

At about the same time negotiations with the captive king were reopened at Newport: but this time prevarication was not an option. Failure to make immediate political headway was met by impatience in the army. A 'Remonstrance' was presented to the Commons on 20 November in which it was required that the king be brought to trial. Two weeks later Pride's Purge ensured that the remaining members went along with this demand. Negotiations were terminated, and the king was removed to Windsor. Charles' progress from Hurst Castle to Windsor still maintained some of the stateliness of old, but once there ceremony ceased by order of the army council. The trial commenced on 8 January and was concluded with sentence passed in less than three weeks.[39]

Inigo Jones' magnificent Banqueting House in the royal palace of Whitehall held special significance for King Charles I. His father James had ordered its construction, while Charles himself had commissioned Peter Paul Rubens to paint the ceilings with an extravagant set of eulogies on his father's reign. The main hall is on the first floor; a wooden platform was erected outside at this level, and one of the first-floor windows was removed to allow for the king's final steps onto the scaffold on 30 January 1649. His executioner and assistant were not only masked, but bizarrely disguised with hair and beards, perhaps fearing that one day there would be those who would wish to track them down. In his final speech Charles proclaimed himself innocent of the charges against him. Nevertheless he was intensely remorseful of the way that he had allowed Lord Strafford to go to the block, in a way that had undoubtedly contributed to the division, rather than the appeasement of the country. His last words, naturally, related to God and religion, and a prayer that God forgive his enemies. Then Charles put down his head onto the low block, and as soon as he gave signal that he was ready, the axe swung. The onlookers at this great historical spectacle showed no great pleasure at his demise. Indeed, one witness later stated that the severing of the king's head was greeted with a groan from the crowd. The Duke of Hamilton would follow his monarch to the block a few months later.

His most loyal supporters never did accept that the war and the king's demise had been Charles' own fault, but some at least were prepared to concede that weakness of character had made the slip into conflict more likely. As Clarendon put it:

> He was very fearless in his person, but not enterprising. He had an excellent understanding, but was not confident of it – which made him often times change his own opinion for the worse, and follow the advice of a man that did not judge so well as himself. If he had been of a rougher and more imperious nature, he would have found more respect and duty; and his not applying some severe cures to approaching evils proceeded from the lenity of his nature and the tenderness of his conscience'.

He was also, to his own prejudice, an 'immoderate lover of the Scottish nation'.[40]

CHAPTER TWELVE

The search for peace and the Third Civil War, 1649–51

T HE SECOND DEFEAT of the royalists in two years was a remarkable achievement both for Cromwell and for Lancashire's parliamentary committee. Many of those who were not traditional parliamentarian supporters also breathed a sigh of relief with the departure of the Scots. A few Lancastrians even found a silver lining to an otherwise dire situation. For one thing the plundering Scots were themselves freely relieved of their goods in defeat. The *Discourse* even describes how the Scottish army was accompanied by an 'abundance of sutty [slutty?] vacabound women', who in victory had 'vexed the pore country sore'. Now they were paid back, 'home into their Bosomes', for their immoral misdeeds. Some, presumably both soldiers and women, being 'well stored with money', hid their coins 'in the feildes about Preston', returning later, where they could, to retrieve their hoards. Rumour was that Preston and some of the neighbouring places, 'lost not, but gained much by their flight'; at least, this was the jealous talk which appears to have circulated in the Fylde. Colonel Ralph Ashton also benefited from the successful campaign, with parliament finally confirming his appointment as Major General of the Forces of Lancashire on 25 September 1648. This entitled him to a salary of 40s. a day, 'over and above his pay as Colonel of Horse, and Colonel of Foot'. At long last, and arguably much too late in the day, the Lancashire parliamentarians had a clear military commander, with both roots in the locality and a successful track record.[1]

A few may indeed have profited from the great misfortunes of August 1648, but the general picture was of a county even more miserable than before. In September Lancashire appealed to parliament to help pay its soldiers who had done so much to make victory possible. Parliament effectively put matters back in the hands of the committee by referring the question to 'the Gentlemen

349

The brass memorial image of Colonel Ralph Ashton (Assheton) at St Leonard's parish church, Middleton. The accompanying Latin inscription translates as, 'Sacred to the memory of Ralph Assheton Esq., Lord of Middleton, devoted to God, his fatherland and his kindred. Of all the forces of Lancashire (levied by the authority of the supreme Parliament) the valiant and faithful commander, who with his wife Elizabeth, daughter of John Kay, of Woodsome, in the county of York, Esq., had three sons, Richard, Ralph, and John, and the same number of daughters, Elizabeth, Mary and Anna. He fell asleep in Jesus the 17th February in the year of our Lord 1650, and the 45th of his age.'

PHOTOGRAPH: CARNEGIE, 2009

of the House, that are of the county of Lancaster'. The harvest, which had held up well at the end of the first civil war, failed miserably. The only plausible explanation was God's displeasure with Lancashire: and specifically Lancashire more than other places. As the mayor, bailiffs, and ministers of Wigan explained in another appeal to London in May 1649,

> The hand of God is evidently seen stretched out upon the county, chastening it with the three corded scourge of sword, pestilence and famine, all at once afflicting it. They have borne the heat and burden of a first and second war in an especial manner above other parts of the nation. Through them the two great bodies of the late Scottish and English armies passed, and in their very bowels was that great fighting, bloud shed, and breaking. In this county hath the plague of pestilence been raging these three years and upwards, occasioned chiefly by the wars. There is a very great scarcity and dearth of all provisions, especially of all sorts of grain, particularly that kind by which that country is most sustained, which is full six fold of the price that of late it hath been. All trade, by which they have been much supported, is utterly decayed; it would melt any good heart to see the numerous swarms of begging poore.

Wigan and Ashton were now lying, as the townsmen explained, under the 'sore stroak of God in the pesilence'. No justices of the peace were presently in post; collections in church were now 'slack and slender'; and many people, on the point of starvation, were reduced to eating whatever they could, including carrion and other 'unwholesome food'. The name of the major who put his signature to this catalogue of woe was ironic ... Ambrose Jolly.[2]

The financial problems which had caused a near fatal crisis for the Lancashire committee at the end of 1645, reappeared with a vengeance at the end of 1648. The Lancashire troops were again unpaid, and in an uncanny echo of what had transpired with the New Model a couple of years earlier they were in no mood to disband meekly. Unlike the New Model, however, the Lancashire militia sentiment was still clearly presbyterian. As Whitelock reported in his *Memorials*, there were now letters being received in London stating that there were 'four thousand' of the forces of General Ashton that refused to disband: they professed 'for the Covenant, and are encouraged by the clergy'.

Parliament was certainly aware of the problem as early as 8 November 1648, for the Commons now recognised a 'present necessity' for money to get the Lancashire soldiers to stand down. Letting the issue drag on, with the troops still embodied, would only make matters worse, since it was probable that they would continue to accrue arrears of pay, resulting in a 'very great charge'. It was therefore ordered that £3,155 be paid out of the receipts at Goldsmiths Hall to Alexander Norris of Bolton, the Lancashire committee's paymaster, 'for the use of the Lancashire forces to be disbanded'. At this delicate juncture others finally lost patience with parliament; on 6 December Colonel Pride purged the London parliament of MPs perceived as hostile to the New Model by the simple expedient of barring their entrance to the building. Whether this had any bearing on Lancashire's payment is unclear: but it did not go through, since by 16 December parliament was giving formal consideration to 'repealing the Ordinance for the Militia of the County of Lancaster'.[3]

Some further explanation of how money ordered to be paid by the Commons apparently disappeared into the ether is provided by the House of Lords. A note made by their lordships on 20 December explains, with something of the air of an exasperated elder brother, how the Commons had in fact allocated the same money to two places – making the plan for 'disbanding the Forces in Lancashire', as they put it, 'fruitless'. Much of the funds had already been made over to Lord Willoughby 'for his arrears' and to 'Mr Godfrey &c. for Monies lent to the Lord Willoughby'. The Earls of Denbigh and Mulgrave were therefore tasked with drawing up a document to point out this simple fact to the Commons, and naturally the 'Lancashier Forces' would get no satisfaction.[4]

The new ordinance could not work without money, and it appears that it took the intervention of General John Lambert to convince the recalcitrant Lancashire soldiery that it was time to return home. From the limited evidence available, it seems that the popular and diplomatic Lambert reasoned with them, and may again have recommended to parliament that it should pay them immediately. In any case on 10 February 1649 the Commons were ordering that a 'letter of thanks' be sent to Lambert regarding what he 'hath done in disbanding the Forces in the North' and 'his good service therein'. It seems clear that the Lancashire military protests had been practical and financial rather than political. Never would the Lancashire militiamen pose the same threat as the Levellers within the New Model, their position being essentially conservative and local. They wanted the money they had been promised, and the freedom to enjoy the presbyterian system which had been delivered. No hint has yet been found that they wanted any of the sort of radical societal reforms which had been debated and discussed in other parts in 1647.[5]

An accommodation with Lord Derby?

There was also hope for peace on another front. Lord Derby had now been on the Isle of Man for some time, and it was joked that he had spent much of his leisure there in polishing 'his wit'. Nevertheless, in addition to catching up on his reading and compiling notes on the history and antiquities of the island, he had taken many practical steps to secure his domain, including building, or refortifying, earthwork defences. These included a fort at the Point of Ayre, and the aptly named Fort Loyal, a large rectangular work with arrowhead bastions at its corners. In this effort the earl was ably assisted by Captain John Greenhalgh of Brandlesome Hall, Bury, who had been acting as his governor here since 1640. Clearly his lordship felt great confidence in Greenhalgh, whom he described as 'a gentleman well borne', possessing his own 'good estate', and a 'valiant' man who governed well. Derby had not simply sought to consolidate his position, however, but had also taken tentative steps to begin negotiations with his erstwhile enemies. In 1647, for example, Lady Derby had travelled to London with a letter in which he suggested that his wife might talk to the parliament regarding 'his submission'. Charlotte had hopes that her discussions might be aided by either the Dutch ambassador, Albert Joachimi, or by noblemen closer to home through Scottish channels. It certainly appears that Derby's children now made some headway with regaining the house at Knowsley through the good offices of Lord General Fairfax.

Peaceful overtures were then pre-empted by the Second Civil War, and communication appears to have ceased in mid-1648, although the earl effectively stood aloof from that conflict. So it was that following the king's execution at the end of January 1649, Derby apprehended that there was a fresh opportunity to seek rehabilitation. Indeed, shocked as the family appears to have been by the sorry end of the king, the earl may well have felt that the death of Charles finally released him from his bonds of fealty to the old royalist regime, and that this was perhaps the moment to put all his efforts into securing the future of his dynasty and fortune.

Derby wanted what remained of his property back: for its part parliament wanted the surrender of the Isle of Man, and was desperately short of money. This could have been the starting point for a settlement. For a while it looked as if an accommodation might be obtainable, with Lord Derby able to return to his mainland estates on recompense to the parliament of £15,572. This pragmatic solution of a hefty fine did not take account of Lancashire sentiment, and the outrage of many at this cynical 'money for blood' deal was soon apparent. It amazed many that Derby – who had been specifically

Charles Stanley 8th Earl of Derby (1628–1672), son of James 7th Earl. The young
Charles pleaded for his father's life in 1651 to no avail. This portrait is marked as by
Adriaen Hanneman, though this has been disputed, and the whereabouts of the picture
are currently unknown.

excluded from pardon for his misdeeds at Bolton and elsewhere – was now being offered such a deal. A petition from south-east Lancashire demanded that he should suffer just as they had. The Council of State, acting through Henry Ireton, now reframed the deal in what it saw as a more acceptable form: Derby would get half his estates, parliament would get the Isle of Man.

His lordship's reaction to this apparent breaking of an agreement so close to fruition was unrestrained, and he referred roundly to his enemy's treason and his scorn for their 'favour'. No longer would he even consider giving up his watery stronghold, 'so far from delivering up this Island to your advantage … I will keep it to the utmost of my power and your destruction'. It was also said that he told the Committee of Both Kingdoms that if they sent him any further missives he 'would burn the paper and hang the messenger'. With this, communication was at an end. Derby had now burned his boats as far as any agreement with parliament was concerned.

Derby's continued identification with the royalist cause was fully confirmed in the summer of 1649 when he received Sir Marmaduke Langdale and Sir Lewis Dives as visitors to his island. Both were recognised as hardcore 'malignants', and simply offering them shelter could be construed as treason in the eyes of parliament. More than this they now signed themselves up to Derby's manifesto of defiance, calling upon all Lancashire and Cheshire men loyal to the new king to treat the Isle of Man as 'their general rendezvous and safe harbour'. Henceforth the self-appointed mission of Derby and his confederates would be 'to unanimously employ our forces to the utter ruin of these unmatchable and rebellious regicides, and the final destruction of their interests both by land and sea'. The future Charles II further endorsed this trenchant stance a few months later, when he thanked Derby for his actions and admitted him to the Order of the Garter. Perhaps most alarming to parliament was that Lord Derby maintained communication with Ireland, and that vessels from the Isle of Man were harassing shipping in the Irish Sea. This was not only nuisance 'piracy' with its attendant 'spoils and depredations' – but raised anew the old spectre of a Catholic-inspired Irish invasion.

The Irish threat was directly addressed by Cromwell, when he sailed there with his army in August 1649. The port town of Drogheda was besieged the following month and Wexford reduced in October. In March 1650 parliamentarian naval forces probed the Isle of Man's new defences but were seen off. In a somewhat more direct, but cruder, approach to the problem of the recalcitrant Derby, Colonel Birch was ordered to take his daughters from Knowsley. These were effectively held hostage against the release of parliamentarian captives. As the *Commons Journal* explained, given that,

> divers well affected Persons to the Parliament have been and still continue, imprisoned by the Earl of Derby, in the Isle of Man, and suffered much by an hard and miserable imprisonment there ... [order was given] for the seizing of the Persons of the Children and Servants of the said Earl, residing in Lancashire, and Securing of them in the Garison of Liverpoole: Which was done accordingly: And that they had given direction; that a Dispatch should be sent to the said Earl, to take notice of the hard Usage of such as he had made Prisoners for their good Affections to the Parliament; and demand them to be set at Liberty; otherwise to let them know, That a Retaliation of like Usage should be made to those of his Family, now in safe custody in Lancashire.

On 15 August 1650 parliamentary ships again tested the mettle of the defenders of the Isle of Man. According to Lord Derby's own account, he was out in a boat as the enemy approached and almost lost his life, being in 'great danger of being killed'. A shot from Captain Barlett's ship,

> Charged with muskett bullets & pieces of iron: which killed my dear friend Rus. Weston and a man that rowed, wounded Collonel Snead in a grievous manner and I sitting in the midst of them escaped.

It now seemed that James Stanley, seventh Earl of Derby, was beyond the point of no return.[6]

Political, military and religious reform

The chance of a lasting compromise between Derby and mainstream Lancashire royalists on the one part, and moderate presbyterian parliamentarians on the other, was tragically missed in early 1649. At the same time local institutions began an uncertain lurch in the direction of the Independents, in what has been described as a 'triumph of the militants'. The impact of Pride's Purge may have been first and foremost on central government, and in the facilitating of the trial of the king, but recent research suggests that the ripples spread as far as Lancashire, and the results were not inconsiderable. Now eleven of Lancashire's 14 MPs were either excluded from parliament or otherwise ceased to sit very soon after this time. According to Underdown's research, both

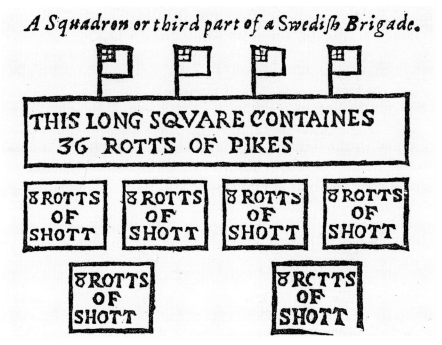

A body of infantry drawn up according to the Swedish manner to form part of a 'Swedish Brigade'. Note the pikes, muskets and colours; each infantry company had its own flag or 'colour' at this period. The Swedish methods were the most modern practice, brought over from Europe where they had been pioneered by Gustavus Adolphus, king of Sweden. From Colonel William *Barriffe's Militarie Discipline: or the Young Artilleryman*, London, 1661.

Ralph Ashtons, Sir Robert Bindloss, Peter Brooke, John Holcroft, William Langton and Sir Richard Wynn were all excluded, while William Ashurst, Thomas Fell, Sir Richard Hoghton and Richard Shuttleworth all ceased to sit for other reasons.

Some details of exactly who was excluded, and why, have been challenged in recent years, but this exodus of Lancashire MPs has been confirmed, and it had two important consequences. The first was that Lancashire, hitherto arguably over-represented in the Long Parliament, was now shunted into a position of under-representation and comparative irrelevance. Second, the messages from the centre were now pro-army – parliament now being relegated to what one royalist dismissed as 'a pretty nimble little box of instruments' to carry out the army's designs. Perhaps more accurately the 'Rump' of the parliament, of about eighty regular members, was now firmly linked to the New Model Army, and subsequent developments would contain little to suggest any sympathies with the local, more moderate, militias. In Lancashire in particular, with its presbyterian tradition strong in both church and military, this boded ill. For Humphrey Chetham in particular Pride's Purge came as shocking news, likely to impinge directly on his business interests. As his London agent put it in a letter,

> all those our Lancashire Parliament men who would have been readie to have served you therein, with many others to the number of seaventy more, were by the Armye taken prisoners and expelled the house, so that the Citty is nowe in a very sadd distraction.

Of Lancashire's MPs only two, Alexander Rigby and John Moore, appear to have remained in the Rump Parliament. How far their interests and those of the county committee were now coincident must be open to question, and the view that they themselves had become increasingly radical has much to recommend it. Rigby has been identified as a 'war party' MP supporting the foundation of the New Model, and was one of four members deputed to discuss the Leveller Agreement of the People. Both Rigby and Moore were nominated to the High Court of Justice which tried Charles I, and Moore actually signed the king's death warrant in late January 1649. Neither Rigby nor Moore would survive to receive any punishment for their part in the death of the king: Alexander Rigby became Baron of the Exchequer in late 1649, and died in the summer of 1650; Colonel Moore was with his regiment in Ireland when he died the same year. Colonel Thomas Birch's position of eminence locally in the new regime was confirmed with his election as MP for Liverpool in October 1649, following the death of Sir Richard Wynn.[7]

How far parliament became the new establishment, against which ministers of religion were now directing their ire, is well illustrated by a bill which received its first reading in the House of Commons in August 1649. This novel piece of legislation aimed to prevent ministers interfering in politics, specifically in 'declaring against the present form of civil government'. Parliament was now being criticised from the very pulpits that its puritan clergy had criticised the government of King Charles I.[8]

The ministers in the localities who criticised central government had legitimate grievances. As early as 1643 Lord Wharton had claimed that parliament was no longer limited by the provisions of the existing law, 'in these times of necessity and imminent danger'. Imprisonment without trial, billeting and new indemnities against legal action all impacted increasingly on public sympathy for parliament's cause. But it was financial burdens, far worse than those which had been imposed by the king during the personal rule in the 1630s, which most angered Lancastrians. Sequestration might have been aimed at royalists, but the monthly assessments, levied from early 1643, hit a wide spectrum of society, parliamentarians, royalists and neutrals alike. Virtually everyone was taxed by the excise of late 1643, which was applied to such staples as meat, salt and beer. A series of 'very foul riots and disturbances' over the continued imposition of the excise taxes ensued in 1650, with Manchester, Preston, Rochdale and Ormskirk all affected. Lack of either genuine representation at the centre, or obvious conduits of patronage back to the county, may well have exacerbated the situation.[9]

A fresh round of problems between local forces and the centre duly ensued early in 1650. The key issue appears to have been a restructuring of the Lancashire militia. Under the new system there would be four regiments of foot and three troops of horse. This was not necessarily much fewer men than before, but by disbanding and re-forming, a clean break would be made with the past, and it was feared that outstanding questions of arrears might be sidestepped.

Interestingly it has also been contended that the Lancashire militia reorganisation of 1650 was important for another reason, in that it marked a change from a system based on hundreds, to one in which recruitment for individual units was carried out throughout the county as a whole. New regiments for Commonwealth service outside the county do indeed seem to have been found in this way – using 'Lancashire men' rather than being bodies raised from one locality. If the 'ordinary' militia had now been reformed in this way it would indeed have been a significant departure, marking a breaking of the close paternal relationship between colonels and their troops. It could also have served to balance out dissent found in specific areas, as for example the traditionally royalist West Derby hundred. The result would probably have been a convergence between the methods and stance of the New Model and Lancashire formations.

However, the evidence does not seem to support this construction: as early as the sixteenth century armies for service outside the county had been raised from the whole county. The Commonwealth therefore followed an old pattern of recruitment which would have been perfectly familiar in the time of Henry VIII or Elizabeth. Within the locality documentation to support the idea of pan-county recruitment is lacking; moreover common sense and later practice would suggest that this was highly unlikely, if not impossible. Ideally the militia, or at least companies of it, were called together for training on a reasonably frequent basis. Had individuals had to trek from Lancaster to Manchester to join men from Liverpool and Blackburn to make up a unit which trained briefly, and then dissipated again, the result would have been at best administrative chaos. In 1643 Richard Shuttleworth had succeeded in re-forming his militia regiment in the Burnley area within 24 hours: had the suggested new county system pertained messengers would have had to ride the length and breadth of the county. Thereafter the soldiers would have had to travel anything up to a hundred miles to fall in. Delays of a week or more, and exhausted men, would have been the result. The proof of the impracticality of such an idea can be found in later periods: even in the 1860s, after the invention of the railway, for example, Rifle Volunteer companies were formed from small areas, and in some instances the majority of the men were drawn from a single parish. It is much more probable therefore that the reasons for the reorganisation of the militia in 1650 were the old and familiar ones: removal of officers seen as politically unreliable; reducing of numbers; saving of money; reforming of units to meet new 'operational requirements', or geographic and population imperatives.[10]

In the short term the changes to the local army were to be sweetened by a new instruction for money to be paid to them. So it was that on 4 March 1650 a disbursement of £1,444 was ordered out of Goldsmiths Hall. Nevertheless the changes were not achieved without mishap, and a few companies appear to have disobeyed the order to stand down, one of these being that of Captain Bamber. These troops gave out that they were intended for service in Ireland, and some heavy persuasion was required to make them stand down, but happily any serious violence was averted.

It was also during early 1650 that a new round of church reform began, driven from the centre. The aims were to some extent doctrinal, but also practical, being intended to discover the names of incumbents, the values of livings, whether 'preaching ministers' were maintained, and if churches and chapels were well placed to serve the population. Commissions were appointed to the counties, and Lancashire's held its first fact-finding 'inquisition' at Manchester on 17 June. Altogether the Lancashire commission sat 16 times, meeting at Wigan, Manchester, Lancaster, Preston and Blackburn. The findings of the commission confirm the impression of a large county with relatively few parishes. As one recent commentator has observed such gaps in the official provision could do very little to discourage the continuance of Catholicism, nor combat areas of irreligion and apathy where it was difficult in practical terms for the populace to reach either a church or minister on a regular basis.

The upshot was a series of recommendations which would see some of the larger parishes dismembered. With new churches founded, boundaries defined, good ministers installed to cover vacancies, provision would be vastly improved. It is likely that although the scale of the problems appears to have been well defined in 1650, little of the actual work to put matters right can have been achieved very quickly.

The survey is extremely interesting, however, in that it reveals how closely many of the characters who fought on both sides in the wars were intimately connected to church affairs, as patrons or lease holders, and with the collection and distribution of tithes. At Poulton le Fylde, for example, at different times both Puritan MP Alexander Rigby and leading royalist Sir Thomas Tyldesley were both involved, as well as Sir Paul Fleetwood. Rigby also had a hand in Preston's parish affairs, along with Sir Richard Hoghton and members of the Charnock family. At Middleton the parson William Ashton was probably a relative of the patron Colonel Ralph Ashton, although not all was well here, as one bold soul called to give evidence to the commission reported quite frankly:

Mr Ashton doth supply the cure at Middleton very weakely and gives not satsisfaction to his congregation, neither expounds any Chapter or Psalme, nor Catechise the youth of the said parish.

Colonel Ashton's presentation to the church at Radcliffe, Mr Thomas Pike BA, was much better received, being described to the commissioners as 'a godly preaching minister, well quallifyed in lyffe and conversacion'.

As might be expected the Derby family's role as patrons of the church was important, and though the seventh earl was in effective in exile at the time his name appears frequently in the documents of the commission. He was noted as formerly having had control of tithes, livings, or church-related properties, at Bury, Mawdesley, Bispham, Winwick, Holland and Dalton in the parish of Wigan, Childwall, Prescott, Skelmersdale, Scarisbrick, Bickerstaffe and Croston: and this list may not be exhaustive. These places were mainly, but not exclusively, within West Derby hundred, and may be taken as an additional indicator of the significance of Derby interests in the south-eastern part of the county. Lord Molyneux's church interests were more limited, but he was certainly connected to the parishes of Huyton and Altcar, again within West Derby.

Perhaps more surprisingly there are examples of royalist gentlemen, either Catholic, or later denounced as Catholics, who had significant interests in the established church. Perhaps the most glaring is Nicholas Anderton of Lostock, the die-hard defender of Greenhalgh castle. Until stripped of his powers he was patron of the church at Garstang, with the right to install the minister. Naturally he would have been unlikely to favour any reformist, and much other evidence suggests that 'papism' was rife around the parish. Sir Thomas Tyldesley's connections with the established church were not limited to Poulton, his name being connected with leases in Kirkham and Astley in the parish of Leigh.

The 1650 surveys are probably not particularly good evidence of what was achieved at the time, being essentially a listing of present and past properties and rights, together with aspirations for improvement. They are fascinating, however, in providing a map of the church-related interests of individuals, and what they reveal is a reasonably close, if approximate, correlation between religion, leaders and allegiance. They also show, in at least a number of areas, how victorious parliamentarians of a Puritan persuasion replaced existing incumbents with men more in tune with their own religious stance, and rooted out or supplanted known or suspected Catholics from the church establishment over the period between 1643 and 1650. As a picture of the continuing importance of God in the civil wars in Lancashire, they are invaluable documents.[11]

Charles Stuart and the Third Civil War

The young Charles Stuart, already acknowledged by royalists as King Charles II, took the Covenant on 27 April 1650. He also signified his intention to repudiate the Earl of Montrose. Conveniently enough this loyal Scottish nobleman was defeated at Corbisdale in Sutherland on the same day, and was soon betrayed to his enemies. Still protesting his adherence to 'fear of God and honour of the king', Montrose was hanged at Edinburgh in May. Charles opened the way to secure mainstream Scottish support, and assured himself of a positive reception in at least one of his new kingdoms. On 24 June he landed north of Aberdeen with a handful of English followers. From here he moved via the royal palace of Falkland to Dunfermline, and an uncomfortable round of discussions with the men who until so recently had been his sworn enemies. A new accommodation between Stuart king and nobles was reached not long afterwards. His Scottish coronation would finally take place six months later, on New Year's Day 1651.[12]

For a third time war was now at hand. Parliament hoped to send their New Model army north, conducted by the tried and tested team of Sir Thomas Fairfax at the helm, as Lord General, with Cromwell his able – and more politically minded – second in command. Fairfax, however, had had

King Charles II (1630–85), from a contemporary woodcut. Barely into his teens when the civil wars commenced, he was still under twenty years old when his father was executed. His adventure in Scotland led to the 1651 invasion and ultimately to the battle of Worcester, the fight at Wigan Lane, and the execution of the Earl of Derby.

scruples about the execution of the king, and had no wish to fight the Scots. Despite attempts to talk him round, Fairfax resigned his post on grounds of ill-health, and Cromwell was at last named commander of the army. About 16,000 troops were gathered for parliament at Newcastle, and they crossed the border into Scotland on 22 July 1650. Initial success in southern Scotland slowed to a snail's pace as the army came across defensive positions near Edinburgh, prepared at the behest of the able Scottish general David Leslie. Cromwell's troops reached Leith, but came perilously close to defeat before their triumph of Dunbar on 3 September 1650.

Following a serious illness in early 1651, Cromwell renewed the campaign. With fresh reinforcement, and acting in tandem with Generals Lambert and Overton, significant advances were made. Lambert finally managed to attack the Scots in the rear at Inverkeithing in July 1651, and despite a rough parity of numbers, inflicted a major defeat upon the enemy. Cromwell now advanced on Perth. The war in Scotland was now progressing well, but even with men drawn in from England and Ireland there were not enough parliamentarian troops both to conduct an active campaign of battle and siege, and to secure the border. The Scottish command was therefore still left with the problematic option of a do or die gamble: an attack into England. Though the king's generals were wary, bearing in mind the events of three years earlier, Charles II himself saw the seizure of his English kingdom as his ultimate goal. Moreover, he had been led to believe that royalism was growing in strength south of the border, and that the credit of the new regime was running low. Success in England might well bring the parliament foray into Scotland to a premature and humiliating end.

The king's mind was therefore set upon invasion, even though the result might be either 'a crown or a coffin', as he was overheard to suggest. The effective director of the invasion force under the titular command of the king himself would be Lieutenant General David Leslie: but, in an even worse surfeit of senior officers than in 1648, there would be no fewer than eight generals with the joint Scottish/English army. These included the Duke of Buckingham, Massey, and William, second Duke Hamilton, brother of the late James. Despite such an array of 'new royalist' glitterati the outlook was not brilliant. As the Duke of Hamilton remarked, going into England at a potential disadvantage appeared 'very desperate'. The Scottish army of 1651 also battled with many of the same evils which it had faced in 1648. Sir James Turner records that even before it had left Scottish soil there was 'a great deale of mischiefe'. Local people suffered 'robbing and plundering' from what were ostensibly their own troops, and disorder threatened to undermine the discipline in the army. Nevertheless, about 13,000 men were successfully mustered, and at the end of July the army left Stirling, and marched via Cumbernauld near Glasgow, reaching the border on 6 August. Near Carlisle the determination to restore order had clearly prevailed, and Charles was

> proclaimd King of England and Ireland, and with great acclamations of the armie; and severe commands made against all other robberies, plunderings and exactions; which being put in execution by hanging tuo or three, were well enough observed ...

A couple of days later the Scottish army was at Penrith, still unopposed.[13]

With the Scots slipping past into England Cromwell's strategy was briefly thrown into doubt. Voices were raised in protest and alarm. His explanation was that the method for dealing with the Scottish invasion of 1651 would be inspired by the experience of 1648. What had been managed before, with so little, could now surely be repeated under much more auspicious circumstances. As he explained to the Speaker, William Lenthall, in a letter from Leith, of 4 August:

> When England was much more unsteady than now; and when a much more considerable Army of theirs, unfoiled, invaded you; we had but a weak force to make resistance at Preston – upon deliberate advice, we chose rather to put ourselves between their Army and Scotland: and how God succeeded that, is not well forgotten! This present movement is not out of choice on our part, but by some kind of necessity; and, it is to be hoped, will have the like issue … Major General Harrison, with the horse and dragoons under him, and Colonel Rich and the rest in those parts, shall attend the motions of the enemy; and endeavour the keeping of them together, as also to impede his march. And will be ready to be in conjunction with what forces shall gather for this service – to whom orders have been speeded to that purpose … Major General Lambert, this day, marched with a very considerable body of horse, up towards the enemy's rear. With the rest of the horse, and nine regiments of foot, most of them your old foot and horse, I am hastening up; and shall, by the Lord's help, use utmost diligence. I hope I have left a commanding force under Lieutenant General Monk in Scotland.[14]

A Scottish royalist army in Lancashire again

Again Cromwell was proved broadly correct. As in 1648, smaller parliamentarian forces were able to harry and distract the invaders, while Cromwell mustered the main force as quickly as possible, ready to strike a knock-out blow. The enemy had, however, learned at least one lesson from the Second Civil War, and were nothing like as dilatory in their advance. In contrast with the month it had taken to get from the border to Lancaster in 1648, this time it would be barely a week before the king had covered the same distance. Soon afterwards the Scottish army was camping on Ellel Moor, a few miles south of Lancaster, while royalist English troops – including 'the renegade' Colonel Wogan rallied to the town.

On 12 August Charles II himself entered Lancaster. As one parliamentarian correspondent reported:

> the Scots King came thither and set all the prisoners in the Castle at liberty. Hee was proclaimed at the Crosse, and a general pardon to all persons,

except some few. That night he lodged at Aston [Ashton] Hall, some three miles from Lancaster, being Colonel Wainman's house where Hamilton lodged two days before the battail at Preston, whose fate we hope attends this young man that traces him in the steps of invasion. Upon Wednesday he lodged at Myerscough, Sir Thomas Tyldesley's house, and from thence marched through Preston. Upon Thursday, his foot having the van over Ribble Bridg, that night he lodged at Euxton-Burgh [Euxton Hall], six miles on this side of Preston, being Mr Hugh Anderton's house, who was prisoner at Lancaster, but set at liberty by the Scots. This Anderton is a bloody Papist, and one that when Prince Rupert was at Bolton boasted much of being in blood to the elbows at that cruell massacre. The last night, their king lodged at Brine [Bryn Hall], six miles from Warrington, being Sir William Gerard's house, who is a subtle jesuited Papist. This dissembling Scot trusts none so well in Lancashire for his hosts as the papists, which discovers [i.e. reveals] his gross hypocricy in taking the Covenant, and may let our English as well as Scotch Presbyters see, how they were deceived with vain conceits of this man's religion.[15]

According to the *Discourse* Charles road deliberately rode through the streets of Preston 'mounted on horse back' in order to allow his face to 'be seen of the people', thus inspiring their loyalty. He also renewed strict orders against plundering. Notwithstanding the flourish of the king's arrival in Lancashire, the response to his call was not overwhelming. The Scots had already suffered some desertions; and war-weariness, plus knowledge of how their allies could behave, seems to have limited the enthusiasm of Lancastrians for the royal cause. A good number of the inhabitants of Cumberland, Westmorland and Lancashire are said simply to have fled their homes in front of the Scottish advance. Paradoxically part of the problem appears to have been the very speed of the Scottish march. Lord Derby certainly seems to have wished to have rallied to the side of his new king, but the vagaries of the weather in the Irish Sea conspired against him, and he was unable to sail from the Isle of Man until Charles was well on his way through Lancashire. The Manx expeditionary force, only a few hundred strong, was finally able to land at Preesall Sands in the Fylde on the morning of 15 August and was by then unable to catch up with the main body. Nevertheless, the men marched straight to Weeton, where some 'Popish gentlemen of the Fylde' were given commissions in the new army.

Derby's reception might have been good among Catholics and former royalist troops, but even in his own home county it was soon very clear that he would not have everything his own way. The *Discourse* relates that after the landing at Preesall the royalist vessels which had carried him and his entourage across to the mainland were riding at anchor on the Fylde coast while their masters and sailors were in and around Preesall, 'drinking and solacing themselves'. Realising that the men whom Derby had left behind were small in number, and off their guard, some of the parliamentarian commissioners for the militia in Amounderness hundred rapidly arranged a raid. One or more vessels were seized and 'Captaine Cotherell' – a 'malignant enemie to the Parliament' was captured and dragged away. Soon he was dispatched to York 'there to be kept in durance', until trial and execution. A furious Sir Thomas Tyldesley made pursuit of the abductors, but abandoned the chase near Stonyhurst.[16]

The king and Lord Derby were not the only ones making haste. The indefatigable parliamentarian General John Lambert had been at Leith on 5 August when he heard from Cromwell that he was urgently needed far to the south. Immediately ordering General Harrison to 'march with the horse and dragoons' with 'all convenient speed', he set off at a pace even faster than that achieved by Cromwell's troops on their way to Preston three years earlier: he made it from the vicinity of Edinburgh to Lancashire in just over a week, averaging over twenty miles a day. Even though the Scots appear to have learned many lessons, Lambert again conclusively out-marched them, and now he intended to out-manoeuvre them. His intelligence was that the enemy had about 4,000 horse and dragoons and 8,000 foot, but that they were 'very sickly'.

By 13 August 1651 Harrison and Lambert were not far from Blackburn. The following day Major General Harrison wrote with an update on the movements of the armies through the county:

> Yesterday we joined on Hazel Moor [between Preston and Blackburn], and are now about 6000 Horse in the van of the enemy. The Enemy made some halt on Ellel Moor, four miles from Lancaster, but afterwards passed on thro' Preston towards Warrington Bridge, where we have 3000 foot waiting conjunction with us from Cheshire and Staffordshire. Cheshire hath been very forward in levies, most of the before mentioned foot being from thence. Six hundred of Colonel Jermie's Horse are to come to Manchester and ordered to Warrington.[17]

This accumulation of men would ultimately bring the parliamentarian army in the region near to parity with the enemy. Lambert, the senior officer

Parliamentary Major General Thomas Harrison (1606–60). The son of a Staffordshire butcher, Harrison fought at Marston Moor, and joined the New Model in 1645. His regiment fought at Preston in 1648, though he himself had been wounded earlier. Recognised by Cromwell as a zealous and God-fearing officer, he rose to the rank of major general, but was executed as a Regicide after the Restoration.

now present, was a skilful general, by no means averse to attacking superior numbers when he had a tactical advantage: but the orders were to harry and delay the Scottish royalist army, rather than to meet it in pitched battle before the main body of parliament's forces could join the fray. Moreover, his force was strong in cavalry, but still relatively weak in infantry. This might be remedied if he could join together with the Lancashire and Cheshire forces. Accordingly Lambert ordered that the parliamentarian units in the vicinity should fall back before the king, which they did, passing through the Bolton area. The next day, however, Lambert perceived that Warrington, with its constricted crossing over the Mersey, might just give him the sort of opportunity for the kind of rearguard defence in which he excelled. The bridge was barricaded as much as time would allow, and a company of foot deployed to cover the obstruction with their muskets.

A skirmish at Warrington bridge

The king's army was determined not to allow such a token effort delay them unduly. As was reported in the *Perfect Diurnall*,

A detail of a manuscript map of *c*.1580 preserved in the Lancashire Record Office showing Warrington Bridge.

On the 16 of August the enemy came down with their whole Army, and prest to passe at the bridge and Fort neer it, which we had broken down and spoyled as well as we could in so short a time. A Company of our Foot were drawn down to the Barracadoe of the Bridge, who behaved themselves gallantly, and gave the enemy opposition, till we saw cause to draw off, securing their retreat by parties of Horse, which we did because we were unwilling to engage our Army where our Horse could not doe service through the enclosures. The enemy therefore hastened over their whole army, and their King in the Van, if not forlorne, with his owne Lifeguard (as some prisoners told us since), and prest hard upon our Reare, whereof Colonel Rich had the guard, who wheeled off parties, and charged them thrice as they came on, and the Lord every time caused the enemy to flie before us.

We killed the officer that commanded one of their parties, and two or three Troopers and some Countreymen since tell us that 28 of theirs were slain in the severall skirmishes, and but foure of ours that I can heare of, there, and at the bridge. As they fell on they cried, 'Oh you rogues, we will be with you before your Cromwell comes', which made us think they would presse to engage us with all speed.

So ended the brief and inconclusive engagement at Warrington, perhaps better described as a large skirmish, or a contested crossing, rather than a battle. Royalist commentators claimed it as a victory for the new king, but strategically it had done nothing for his chances. Lambert and his compatriots were where they wanted to be, poised to harass the royalist forces and essentially undamaged by their fighting retreat from the bridge. The parliamentarian account entitled *A True and Full Relation of the Late Skirmishes at Warrington* even suggests that the guard of a single company of Cheshire troops set upon the bridge was merely to 'amuse' the enemy, not a serious defence. As one commentator has since observed the 1651 skirmish over Warrington bridge had done nothing except make Lambert retreat a little faster than he had otherwise intended. Perhaps it had also shown that the young Charles was more willing than his father had been to venture his life on the field of battle.[18]

The parliamentarians now made off south into Cheshire, from whence Lambert wrote on the morning of 17 August that ideally he would have had the bridge at Warrington broken down, so causing maximum disruption and inconvenience to the enemy, but that there had been insufficient time to complete the demolition. Accordingly he had ordered the retreat on Knutsford Heath, where there was good country for his cavalry to manoeuvre and fight, though his army's passage there had been difficult due to miles of 'close' narrow lanes full of hedges:

we having some few Pioneers, cut our waies through the Hedges, and marched our foot on the right and left, and our horse in the lanes. Our businesse at first looked very ill favouredly, the enemy having drawn up at least 2000 foot close to our rearguards before we drew off, yet through God's assistance we passed untouched for about two miles. The enemy coming on very hotly, we engaged, it not being possible to avoyd it; I commanded the rear guard, which consisted of Commissary Generals [Whalley's], Colonel Twisleton's, and mine own regiments, to charge, which accordingly they did, and routed them, and their owne men falling foule upon their other two bodies routed them also. We had the persuit of them at least a mile. We killed him who commanded the party and about eight more, and took six prisoners, besides divers wounded; this gave us time to ride two miles without any more trouble, and to draw out a new reare guard of Colonel Rich his regiment, which having done, they again engaged us, and we charged them with the same successe, killed and took the same number, and after marched quietly to Knotsford Heath, where we now are. We lost but one man in our retreat, who was taken prisoner in pursuing too far.

If this was a relatively disappointing third anniversary to the triumph of Preston Lambert did not show it, but continued with the task as resolutely as before.

Having forced their way across the Mersey as fast as was practicable it would have seemed logical for the king's army to strike out for London without delay. Yet with each passing day parliament's armies appear to have gained a better grip upon the situation, and the royalists and Scots less confidence in their enterprise. The result was a failure to grasp what in retrospect might have been the last real opportunity to end the Third Civil War quickly and decisively in the king's favour. As Sir James Turner later remembered,

> Lambert and Harriesone being beaten from Warinton bridge, and all their Cheshire foot chacd away from them, the king declind to march straight to London, from which approach it was thought that the Parliament wold have removd to Windsor; and so we went straight to Worcester, where we lay till Cromwell came and facd us; and after three or foure days respite, in which time he gatherd a great bodie of the countrey traind bands, to the number of five and tuentie thousand at least, besides his veteran armie; and then he forcd us to fight on the third day of September, with a great deale of disadvantage both for ground and numbers, bot with much greater misfortune. Here was the gros of the royall armie routed.[19]

Lord Derby campaigning again in Lancashire

Some time on 17 August 1651 it appears that Lord Derby, who had ridden out ahead of his diminutive Manx force, managed to join Charles II in Cheshire, between Northwich and Nantwich. He brought with him 'some 60 horse, most gentlemen' by way of immediate reinforcement. If he had hoped for an instant appointment as a senior commander with the field army he was to be disappointed. With his army still stubbornly stuck around the level of 12–13,000 strong Charles had more use for a loyal and able recruiting sergeant, than for yet another battlefield leader. The king appointed Derby Captain General of Lancashire, using a document already drawn up for the purpose: Captain General was a fine sounding title, with which went the instruction to return to the county forthwith and raise as many men as possible. A target suggested was 6,000 foot and 1,300 horse.

On 19 August therefore Derby regained Warrington, just inside the old county border of Lancashire. Here he met with his council of war, including many of the leading survivors of the royalist cause such as Sir Thomas Tyldesley, Lord Widderington, Sir William Throgmorton, Sir Francis Gamul and a number of former Lancashire colonels. Issuing commissions to various leaders, he then apportioned the county its recruitment targets along the long-established lines of the old hundreds. The largest were to send him 2,000 men or more. Such an ambitious call-out, encompassing most of the county, would only be feasible if a majority, including the old county leadership, had been won over to the cause. Charles' adoption of presbyterianism had been a good move to appeal to former enemies, and Derby had his royal warrant to show, but it would take much more than this if the Lancashire venture was to be the sort of success that was hoped.

In addition to raising the standard and banging the recruiting drum, Lord Derby sought out a meeting with those who had once been the enemies of the former king. On 20 August he brought together at Warrington both representatives of the existing presbyterian church and Major General Edward Massey. This officer was a shrewd and interesting choice of interlocutor, as he was both a respected former parliamentarian, and a presbyterian, as well as an experienced professional soldier who had now decided to throw in his lot with Charles II. At Gloucester in 1643 the young Massey had become something of a parliamentarian hero – holding the town against superior numbers in the face of Charles I and Prince Rupert. Now it was thought that he could win over moderate Lancastrians cast in his mould. The royalists could certainly hope that, as Lilburne would point out, presbyterians would have grown so 'bitter and envious' of the new government that they would join the king. Convincing them to act would not, however, be easy: for while many presbyterian Lancastrians had had serious doubts about the Independents and the New Model in 1648, their fear of the Scots – since amply confirmed – was probably greater. Moreover, many of the 'traditional' Lancastrian leaders of the committee were now dead, to be replaced by a new generation who had no real experience of the now distant time before the Short Parliament of 1640 when king and parliament had coexisted with some respect.

There were also other matters for the Lancashire parliament men to weigh in the balance. Perhaps the most obvious of these was that it was as yet by no means clear how Charles' overtures would go down in England as a whole. Only by waiting would they know whether they would be joining a winning popular party, or committing political, and possibly literal, suicide by attaching themselves to a lost cause at the eleventh hour. Doubtless news of parliament's debates on 12 August had reached them by this time, in which the decree of the Council of State had been reported in a pronouncement by Lord Commissioner Whitelock. The effect of this was that, 'all and every Person or Person, who shall excite, stir up, or encourage, any Person or Persons to join with the Scottish Army, or with any their party' or 'contrive or plot' should lay themselves open to a charge of high treason. Turning informer and reporting any such conspiracy back to parliament straight away might be the only way to avoid a death penalty. Perhaps not unnaturally even Lancashire moderates who might have been willing to become loyal subjects of Charles II were reluctant to declare themselves with such a threat hanging over them. Religion again came to the fore in political intransigence: Lord Derby was no presbyterian, and showed no willingness to take the Covenant: Lancastrians could therefore hesitate with some legitimacy, since Derby had not adopted the new king's position in all particulars.[20]

Amazingly Lord Derby is believed to have stayed at least one night in Warrington, at the house of John Dunbabin the draper. Assuming this to be correct Derby may have unwittingly undermined the whole campaign, for we have met the enigmatic John Dunbabin once before. In 1642 his name had appeared in Colonel Shuttleworth's papers – as that of a reliable spy for parliament. Intriguingly there is also a contrary possibility: that Derby knew full well Dunbabin's connections. If this were so, he could have been a conduit by means of which the earl sought to negotiate more effectively with his potential opposition in Lancashire, attempting to get them at least to stand aside in the current crisis. Whether Dunbabin conveyed any information to the enemy, or acted as go-between for those in Lancashire of a presbyterian leaning, is uncertain, but it was at Warrington that Derby appears to have decided upon something of a *volte face*. For hearing that Colonel Lilburne was now in the region, he rode north to Preston, and here renewed his efforts to raise troops.

Colonel Robert Lilburne, who had also been active in the Preston campaign of 1648, was a parliamentarian of long standing and impeccable Independent credentials, elder brother of the Leveller John Lilburne. Robert had joined the cause early in the first civil war, and by 1644 ranked as a captain under Edward Montague. Later, as colonel, he had headed a regiment of the Northern Association. As a regicide, his colours had been firmly and finally nailed to Cromwell's mast. Now he had received orders to remain in the North West to deal with the residue of the enemy, and prevent any additional troops reaching the main Scottish/royalist army now headed south. Thus it was that he had marched up from the direction of Stockport. He had hoped to catch Derby by surprise somewhere in the vicinity of Warrington or Wigan on 22 or 23 August, but was to be disappointed because by the time he arrived in the area the news was that the enemy had already got as far as Chorley. Having failed to intercept them, he 'marched after them towards Preston, and lay within two miles of them onely with my regiment and about 60 horse and dragoons'. That night, on hearing that Derby intended a muster in Preston the following day, Lilburne sent a patrol of 40 horse to test the enemy strength, which resulted in a small skirmish. The next afternoon his troopers were grazing their horses not far away when the enemy repaid the compliment.

The *Discourse* gives a full account of this brazen little raid executed by a band of bold young men, which it states occurred somewhere in the 'low meadows' on the Preston side of Brindle. Lilburne's soldiers,

> taking their ease being laid down by their sadles in the closes where their horses were feeding; which, as the event proved, was made known to some of the Earle's party in Preston by some secret enemy (they being all enemies thereabouts) what a prize might be had of Lilburne's soldiers horses the men being all at rest. This being sodenly apprehended by a company of yong striplings, Gentlemen's sons with other like to them, new fresh men altogether ignorant of such warlike exploits to the number of twenty two or thereabouts – these, rashlie, without order or advice, adventured upon the desperate designe in the day tyme to make a prize of the horses ... They were directed through a private way in woody, close places into the meadows.

Understandably Lilburne's officers had set their main guard in a lane on the Preston side of the spot where most of their troopers were lounging off duty, but the royalists, with their local knowledge, and diminutive raiding force, managed to creep past. So it was that the handful of youngsters leapt upon the dozing parliamentarians with a foolhardy fury. They were, however, ridiculously outnumbered and Lilburne's men were soon called from their torpor to arms, and they then

> disputed so vehementlie with the young men that they were soundly payed home for their forwardnes. None escaped but eyther slayne or taken, save one called Newsham who forsaking his horse fled into a thick Oller [hollow?] tree and there hid himselfe in the leaves thereof and at night went away.

The dead royalist hotheads included 'a lad of the north country called Knipe', a young man by the name of Butler, and the oldest son of 'Mr Hesketh of Maynes'. A serving man called Richard Wilding, who had left his employer, Mrs Stanley of Eccleston, was not killed immediately, but 'sore wounded and cut'. Carried back to Preston he had died within ten days. John Clifton of Lytham was also badly injured and taken prisoner.

Late in the evening, after nightfall on 24 August, Derby's little army packed up and left Preston. Lilburne, who was camped about three or so miles off, was soon told what was happening, but was left in something of a quandary. He was expecting reinforcement where he now stood, was weaker in number than the opposition, but thought that Derby would most likely use to the cover of darkness to move south with all the speed he could muster to catch up with Charles and the main Scottish army. Luckily three companies of Lancashire and Cheshire were now well on their way to his assistance at this vital moment. Lilburne thus decided that his best course of action would be to strike camp and advance 'hither with some confidence', harrying Derby and attempting to prevent him going to the succour of the king. Much to his surprise, it was soon determined that rather than going due south the enemy were 'bending their course towards Manchester'. It was to be surmised that Lord Derby's motive was twofold. By marching covertly on Manchester he might have hoped to catch unawares the Lord General's foot – Cromwell's own regiment – now marching to Lilburne's aid under the command of Colonel Worsley. Having done so, it might then prove possible to bring many of those who were undecided about their new monarch over to the cause. Opinion was that Derby was assured of the 'assistance of five hundred men', if only he could get to Manchester himself in strength. Lilburne now found himself in the potentially uncomfortable position of fighting in order to prevent the royalist army from stealing past him. In the event he decided that, for the time being at least, discretion was the better part of valour.

The opposing forces were now fairly evenly matched. Lilburne stated that he had with him 'my own regiment', plus three companies of foot, one from Manchester and two from Cheshire, plus an additional 'thirty horse from Liverpool' and 'fifty or sixty dragoons'. The *Discourse* broadly agrees, though it says the foot were all from Cheshire, and then contradicts itself by stating that there were two Cheshire companies, led by Captain Robert Jollie and Captain Samuel Smith, with a third 'of new raised men from Liverpool'. Very likely, therefore, the majority of Lilburne's foot came from south Lancashire and north Cheshire, with some at least from the towns of Manchester and Liverpool. This would equate to around 600 mounted men and 300 foot – a total of just under 1,000 parliamentarian troops – although at least one source suggests that he was rather stronger. Against these Lord Derby was able to pitch about 1,400 royalists, for the most part his recently raised Lancastrians, at least half of whom were infantry. Some of the other royalists were Manxmen who had come over with Derby, or men from various other parts who had previously taken refuge on the island. Though Derby had only called in his men over the last few days, it is likely that at least some were seasoned soldiers, veterans of the royalist cause during 1648 and perhaps earlier.

Lilburne's men were arguably the better organised and equipped, but had only just joined together with the local militia troops. Though the parliamentarians were still somewhat outnumbered, it seemed unlikely that it would stay that way for very long. Lilburne certainly understood that Cromwell's regiment of New Model was in the Manchester area, perhaps just a day's march away. The *Discourse* also suggests that in east Lancashire the Shuttleworth family were now readying themselves for action with their old enemy, and before long would begin to gather in the vicinity of Hoghton Tower, a few miles south-east of Preston. The problem that Derby faced was one which later military strategists might have defined as one of the 'central position'. If he could defeat one or other of his opponents – while they were alone and unsupported – he might well have sufficient strength to deal with the remainder. Lilburne's objective was to prevent this happening, and preferably rally to him sufficient forces that any pitched battle with Derby would be a foregone conclusion.

The battle of Wigan Lane, 25 August 1651

About mid-day the royalist army had made it as far as Wigan. Having marched twenty miles over the last twenty hours it was to be expected that they might now fall out and rest, taking advantage of their superior numbers of infantry to protect the buildings of the town from any incursion of the parliamentarian cavalry. Derby, however, had more aggressive thoughts in mind. As Lilburne himself reported:

> … upon the sight of our near approach, they unexpectedly put themselves in a posture of fighting with us, which then we endeavoured to decline, in regard to the very great advantage they had by their many Foote and hedges, and the danger we apprehended my Lord Generall's Regiment of Foot at Manchester to be in, we were drawing off, thinking to have marched on the left flank of them thither, to have gained a conjunction with our friends [Shuttleworth's regiment], who too, had order to march that day to me at Preston.[21]

Thus did the pursuer suddenly become the pursued, as Derby turned abruptly to confront Lilburne's little force. In doing so he effectively threw away whatever tactical advantage the town of Wigan offered, but doubtless he was aware that time was against him, and that this was likely to be one of the few opportunities that would present itself to catch Lilburne at a numerical disadvantage. According to the *Discourse* the two little armies met at the edge of town:

> The place they fought in was from Wiggon towne's end all along that broad sandie loane [lane] up to that loane end which goeth towards Mr Bradshaw's house at Hay. The Earle and his Army came from Wiggon to meet Lilburne in that loane who received them with what valour and couradge he was able. The Dispute was very hot and manly on both sides and a good space very doubtfull how it would go. The Earle's company stoutly and with much couradg beating and dryving Lilburne almost to that loane end that goes to the Hay [Haigh?]. A reserve of horse coming up to him then put the dispute out of doubt soe that the Earle having received a blow over his face turned his back and fled (some said without his hat). Captain Jollie with the other Captaines and their companies were active and serviceable in beating up the Earle's foot wherof many were slaine and the Manck [Manx] which the Earle brought with him were pore naked Snakes, those that escaped with life were scattered up and downe the Country.[22]

Lilburne's own account states that once it was clear that the royalists were emerging from Wigan, committing themselves to all out battle, he had 'resolved to trust God with the issue'. The field sign adopted by his men that day was a white band or scarf around the arm, while the royalists shouted the identifying word 'Jesu!'. The parliamentarians managed to gain an important initial advantage by lining the hedges of the lane and nearby enclosures with musketeers – and perhaps dragoons – and were thus able to fire on the royalist cavalry as they attempted to charge home on Lilburne's main body of horse. As the *Discourse* put it, 'The foot ... flanked the Earle's army bravely with much resolution upon the back of hedges'. Derby's men would never effectively overcome this initial disadvantage.

According to one version of events, Derby deployed two main attacking forces of some 300 each, commanding from the front, while Sir Thomas Tyldesley led the rearguard. Lilburne's cavalry were themselves inconvenienced by the hedges, 'our horse being not able to doe any service but in the lanes, and they overpowering us so much in foot, made the businesse very difficult'. Repeated charges shook Lilburne's cavalry considerably, and many of his horse were killed or 'spoiled' by royalist pikes. Yet the opposing combination of firepower, cover and well-trained, steady troops proved too much for the royalists. Lilburne relates that the fight lasted 'almost and hour', resulting 'in a totall rout of our enemies', who fell back through the town in complete disorder.

The battle of Wigan Lane had been relatively small, but proportionately the bloodshed was as great as virtually any battle of the period in Lancashire. As in many actions, the worst of the carnage occurred when the morale of the losers had collapsed and they had turned their backs and begun to run. Lord William Widderington was killed outright; William Throgmorton was reported dead of his wounds in the hands of his enemies; several other 'persons of quality' were also slain, along with at least 60 common soldiers. Many of the royalist colours fell to Lilburne's men, along with 400 prisoners. The parliamentarians admitted to the loss of ten dead, plus many horses, and presumably quite a few more soldiers wounded. For the Lancashire cavalier cause the most serious blow was the death of the old campaigner Sir Thomas Tyldesley, who was unhorsed and, still fighting, was among the last to fall.

On the spot where Sir Thomas Tyldesley died was later erected what is arguably Lancashire's most important surviving civil war memorial: a stone pier with a moulded cornice surmounted by a ball, standing within a triangular enclosure. It bears an inscription, declaring that it is the result of

An high act of gratitude, which convey's the memory of Sir Thomas Tyldesley to posterity. Who served King Charles the First as Lieutenant Colonel at Edgehill battle, after raising regiments of horse, foot and

The monument to Sir Thomas Tyldesley at the junction of Wigan Lane and Monument Road. Not far from this spot Sir Thomas was killed at the battle of Wigan Lane, August 1651.

PHOTOGRAPH: AUTHOR

dragoons for the desperate storming of Burton on Trent, over a bridge of 36 arches received the honour of knighthood. He afterwards served in all the wars in great command, was governor of Lichfield, and followed the fortune of the crown through the three kingdoms and never compounded with the rebels though strongly invested; and on 25th August AD 1651 was here slain, commanding as Major General under the Earl of Derby, to whom the grateful erector, Alexander Rigby, Esq. was Cornet; and when he was High Sheriff of this County (AD 1679) placed this high obligation on the whole of the family of Tyldesleys, to follow the noble example of their loyal ancestor.

The monument stood in its original position for two centuries, but was restored and moved to its present location at the junction of Wigan Lane and Monument Road in April 1886. So ended the career of Sir Thomas, once described as the 'finest knight in England'. He may never have been Lancashire's senior royalist commander during the civil wars, but he had an excellent claim to be its most persistent and active. He had always been at the seat of the action, and was present at many of the most important turning points. With his death, and that of many of his most faithful followers, the royalist cause was effectively extinguished within the county.[23]

Lord Derby did not fall at Wigan Lane, but he came perilously close, suffering one or more injuries, and having two of his horses killed as he made his escape from the field of battle. Doubtless he was much discomfited in the hand-to-hand fighting; we might doubt, however, the claim in Draper's *House of Stanley* that he received 'seven shots upon his breastplate, and thirteen sword cuts upon his beaver', as well as 'five or six severe wounds on his arms and shoulders'. According to the *Discourse*, it was not known for some time whether he was alive or dead, but pro-royalist sources state that he disappeared into a house in Wigan marketplace, leaving part of his battered armour lying in the road. Once inside, a 'good housewife' is said to have tended to him and hidden him in a 'place of privacy', where he remained concealed for some hours until the coast was clear. The hiding place has been identified as the chimney of the Old Dog Inn, from whence the earl is supposed to have fled, after dark, disguised in a trooper's coat and escorted by only three companions. Though probably romanticised, something of the sort is certainly possible since Wigan had the reputation of being one of, if not the most, royalist town in the county and was not far from Derby's ancestral seat. His chances of receiving covert assistance there were greater than almost anywhere else in the kingdom. Remaining hidden also agrees with the enemy version of events: that he was 'missing'. Lilburne's report to parliament, penned on the evening of the battle, records Derby 'sore hurt, but escaped, though narrowly'.[24]

It took Derby four days of difficult and painful travel to reach the safety of Boscobel House in Shropshire, a fairly modest timber-framed home about nine miles east of Telford. Here he was tended by sympathetic Catholic royalist William Pendrel and his wife. According to tradition it was also Pendrel who guided the earl on his way to Gatacre Park where an equally well disposed gentleman named Humphrey Elliot lent him £10 and conducted him on safely to Worcester where he met Charles Stuart and the main royalist army on 1 September. Derby appears to have been well received, soon becoming part of the royal entourage, but it is hardly likely that Charles would have been pleased with the outcome of Derby's adventures. He had expected a whole new army of about 7,000; what he got was a wounded, if loyal, nobleman. One report has it that he was so disheartened that he proposed an immediate break-out from Worcester, a desperate ride with his cavalry. However, if this ever was a serious proposition, Charles was soon dissuaded from it.

The denouement of the entire campaign came on 3 September – one year to the day after the parliamentarian victory at Dunbar – when the main Scottish royalist army met the forces of parliament at Worcester. Not to be outdone in style, nor sheer speed of marching, Cromwell and his army had stormed down the eastern counties from the Scottish border via Ripon, Doncaster, Leicester and Warwick. They progressed, so it was reported, 'in their shirts twenty miles a day', having, for ease of movement, their 'clothes and arms carried by the country'. Now, having gathered superior forces together, Cromwell was ready to crush the enemy in one climactic battle. As he himself reported,

... we built a bridge of boats over Severn, between it and Teme, about half a mile from Worcester; and another over Teme, within pistol shot of our other bridge. Lieutenant General Fleetwood and Major General Dean marched from Upton on the southwest side of Severn up to Powick, a town which was a pass the enemy kept. We, from our side of Severn, passed over some horse and foot, and were in conjunction with the Lieutenant General's forces. We beat the enemy from hedge to hedge till we beat him into Worcester. The enemy then drew all his forces on the other side of the Town, all but what he had lost; and made a very considerable fight with us, for three hours space: but in the end we beat him totally, and pursued him to his Royal Fort, which we took – and indeed have beaten his whole army. When we took his fort, we turned his own guns upon him. The enemy hath great loss ... Indeed this hath been a very glorious mercy.[25]

It is thought that 2,000 Scots and royalists were killed; 4,000 prisoners were later paraded through London. The king's army was shattered. On 5 September parliament gave formal thanks to God, for 'his great blessing'. William second Duke of Hamilton was badly wounded and died not long after the battle. General Massey, who had advanced to Upton upon Severn before the fight at Worcester, became entangled in a skirmish with the enemy at point-blank range where reportedly 'forty carbines' were shot off at him. Very badly injured, he was taken prisoner and was lucky to survive. Many of the Scottish commanders were also taken at, or after, Worcester. The Earl of Derby's faithful retainer, John Greenhalgh of Bury, governor of Man, barely survived Worcester, and it is reported that when this 'notorious malignant' realised the battle was lost he tore the royal standard from its pole and wrapped it around his body before getting away. He died of his wounds back on the Isle of Man less than a month later.

Lord Derby is reported to have fought with courage; he escaped again, and for the second time in a week became a fugitive. At least this time he knew where a sympathetic reception might be received, and after the battle it was he who conducted the defeated Charles northward. It is said that when they reached Boscobel Derby handed over his monarch to the astonished Pendrel with the words, 'This is the king. Thou must have care of him, and preserve him, as thou didst me.' Derby then took his leave.

Charles, as every schoolchild knows, tarried at Boscobel for some time, and it was here, not far from the house, that he was forced to take refuge in the foliage of the famous oak tree. The king's own account of these momentous events was later dictated to Samuel Pepys as *An Account of his Majesty's Escape from Worcester*. In this Charles states that he had at first determined to make for London – which, if true, was a mad scheme indeed. However, he found himself and his immediate companions swept along in a tide of men which would neither stand and fight, nor be got 'rid of'. Eventually he 'slipt out' of the high road 'that goes to Lancashire' taking with him about '60 that were gentlemen and officers' including not only Derby but the Duke of Buckingham, Lauderdale, Henry Wilmot (later earl of Rochester) and others. Parting company with most of them at Boscobel a day or two later, he states that he threw his fine garments 'into a privy house', further improving his disguise with a rough short haircut and rustic clothes. He talks first of hiding, hungry, in a wood near the highway close to the house, and also, of staying in a field elsewhere 'under a hedge by a great tree'. Finally he climbed up 'into a great oak that had been lop't some three or four years before' and having grown again had become 'very bushy and thick'. Here he stayed all day with bread, cheese and 'small beer' to sustain him until the coast was clear; parliamentarian soldiers actually searched the floor of the wood below. Charles would later escape to France.[26]

The Earl of Derby captured and tried for treason

Derby had already decided to make for Lancashire with all speed, perhaps with the ultimate goal of taking ship back to the Isle of Man. His immediate companions in this venture included the Scottish Earl of Lauderdale, and a small troop of horse. Just south of Nantwich Lord Derby's last disastrous and eventful last campaign came to a conclusion. At least two accounts survive recording how Lord Derby finally fell into the hands of the opposition. Captain Hodgson relates that the Scots' force as a whole was reduced to 'five or six hundred' exhausted men by the time the parliamentarian soldiers caught up with them, but it may have been fewer. Indeed, so demoralised were the royalists that,

> our musqueteers would have gone into the lane, and taken by the bridle the best like person they saw and brought him out without a single stroke, so low was the Scot brought. But the remarkable thing was, one Oliver Edge, one of our Captains, had a mind to see what was become of the forlorn, [the skirmishers] hearing a great firing; and viewing them very busy, he spies a party of horse behind him in the fields, and having no order to be there, he retreats towards the regiment, but they called upon him and asked if he was an officer; and drawing towards them about eighteen or twenty horsemen lighted, and told him they would surrender themselves prisoners; there was the Earl of Derby, the Earl of Sinclair, and a fourth. These became prisoners to one single Captain; but the soldiers fell in with him immediately.

Edge immediately granted quarter to his captives and treated them with great civility. As Derby himself would record, perhaps they were not deemed worth killing, which at least would have put him out of reach of the 'envy and malice' of his enemies. Yet Captain Edge, 'a Lancashire man', proved himself a gentleman, 'one that was so civil to me, that I and all that love me are beholden to him'. Another larger party of fugitives was overtaken further north, actually within Lancashire, an incident described in the pamphlet *Another Victory in Lancashire Obtained Against the Scots*. These, including a number of the Scottish commanders, and 600 ordinary soldiers were rounded up by General Harrison and his troopers, apparently without much of a fight. Many were then held at Middleton.[27]

Despite the promising start to his captivity, Lord Derby's fortunes would take a turn for the worst almost as soon as he was out of the hands of the front-line soldiery. He had been a thorn in the side of parliament for almost a decade, and though he had never been one of the king's most notable field commanders his royalism had proved unquenchable. As long as James Strange, seventh earl of Derby, was at liberty it seemed that there would always be a focus around which dissent in north-west England could be rallied. In parliament's eyes, as the *Discourse* put it, Derby had been 'the prime agent that sett the war afoot' in Lancashire.

Such a focus for continued royalism had to be dealt with. Yet to have accused Derby merely of having been a key royalist would hardly suffice, since probably half of England, and two-thirds of Lancashire, was for the king in 1642. What his would-be prosecutors needed was a charge that was serious and specific, and moreover, one upon which even waverers could agree. Under the recent Act of 12 August merely communicating 'with Charles Stuart or his party' had been accounted 'high treason against the Commonwealth' and therefore a capital crime. A secondary charge, but one which would no doubt have weighed more heavily within the local context, was the events at Bolton in 1644. The sack of Bolton had certainly been one of the greatest atrocities of the war, and there was definite evidence that Lord Derby had been a significant contributor. Perhaps it might even be demonstrated that he had killed a defenceless man with his own hands after he had surrendered.

So it was that Derby's captured papers were sent down to the Council of State at the end of August. Not long after, Sir Harry Vane the younger reported to parliament that their contents were sufficiently damning as to demand that his lordship be brought to trial. A vote was taken on this point on 11 September 1651, with the members agreeing to this proposal, not only for Lord Derby, but a list of other trenchant royalists and Scottish nobles. In Derby's instance, given that it was essentially war crimes which formed the nub of the case, the agency of justice would be a 'court martial, erected by the Commission of the Lord General'. This was also convenient in that military officers could be nominated to preside in the court, ultimate authority over which would be exercised by the Lord General himself, Oliver Cromwell. As one commentator observed, even before the court sat, Derby was to be 'tried at Chester and executed at Bolton'.

The trial duly opened less than three weeks later at Chester, on 29 September 1651 under the presidency of Colonel Mackworth. Others named in the court's commission included Colonels Birch, Brooke, Bradshaw, Croxton, Ireland, Carter, Twistleton and Mason. All these were important figures in the parliamentarian forces of Cheshire, Shropshire and Lancashire, although it does not appear that either of the Lancashire men, Birch nor Ireland, actually attended any of the court's sittings. Given the circumstances, Lord Derby's defence was weak, and somewhat laconic. His key points were that he had never heard of the Treason Act of 12 August 1651, and, that since he had given himself up on 'quarter', he could not now legitimately be tried for his life.

The judgement of guilty was predictable. Sentence was passed on 1 October, the court resolving that

the said James, Earl of Derby, is a Traitor to the Common Wealth of England, and an abettor, encourager, and assister of the declared traitors and enemies thereof, and shall be put to death by severing his head from his body at the market place in the town of Bolton, in Lancashire, upon Wednesday, the 15th of this instant October, about the hour of one of the clock of the same day.

In the event Derby's role at Bolton, and the death of Captain Bootle, do not appear to have formed any essential part of the judgement: nevertheless they were important in the minds of many contemporaries. Bulstrode Whitelocke, for example, immediately apprehended the significance of the choice of the place of execution, noting it as being where 'he [Derby] had killed a man in cold blood'.[28]

His Lordship really had few chances left: perhaps the best being appeal to the highest authority. It is telling that even at this stage, Derby appears to have believed that this authority was not the emaciated Rump of the parliament, but the person of the Lord General of the New Model, Oliver Cromwell. So it was that a new appeal against the sentence was prepared. In this document Derby suggested that the use of the type of court martial which he had faced was unprecedented, but basically this was a plea for mercy. No favourable response was received, nor did it appear that any such could be before the sentence was carried out.

Derby's life now hung in the balance, but one final appeal for clemency was made by Charles, his 23-year-old son, and heir to the Derby estates. An eighteenth-century account tells how

> his son the Lord Strange, having beforehand laid horses ready, rid post to London in one day and one night, got his petition read in the junto [Parliament] by Mr Lenthel, their speaker (which no man else would read or receive), but Cromwell and Bradshaw so ordered the matter that when they saw the greater part of the house inclined to allow the Earl's plea, as the speaker was putting the question eight or nine of them quitted the house, and those left being under the number of forty, no question could be put: so the Lord Strange seeing all attempts or endeavours to save his father, fruitless and of no effect, for that the grandees had resolved and determined his death: with incredible speed he returned to his father, before the hour of execution.

Given that Charles' relationship with his father had not always been harmonious, this was a magnificent effort on his behalf.

The *House of Commons Journal* for Tuesday 14 October 1651 records that the Speaker did put a question on this matter to the members, but initially only on whether Derby's plea should be read. Sir William Brereton and Mr Ellys acted as 'tellers for the yeas', while Major General Harrison and Mr Bond were those for 'the Noes'. By a vote of 22 to 16 it was decided that Derby's 'Humble Petition' should be read – which it was, but no substantive motion on it was recorded.

Justice was left to run its course. James Lord Derby now knew that he was sure to die. On seeing his son again he took his great Garter badge, denoting membership of this order of knighthood, and adorned the young man, soon to be the eighth earl, with the insignia. He is said to have asked his son, to 'Return it to my Gracious Sovereign, when you shall be so happy as to see him, and say I sent it in all humility and gratitude, as I received it, spotless and free from any stain, according to the example of my loyal ancestors'.[29]

One of the best descriptions of the execution of the Earl of Derby, though by no means an impartial one, is that given by his chaplain the Reverend Humphrey Baggerly who was with him from his time at Chester until his death. Baggerly claimed that, even before leaving Chester for Bolton, representatives of the parliament were asking him to nominate his own executioner. Derby's dry response was that, 'if those men that will have my head will not find one to cut it off, let it stand where it is'. Black humour aside, he now appears to have been resigned to his death, and prepared for it methodically. Farewell letters were written, and given to Baggerly to deliver to his family. To his servant Paul Moreau he gave money with which to go and buy rings. These were to be presented to family, friends, and trusted servants. On his way to Bolton, Lord Derby noticed the downcast countenance of his chaplain, and remarked that he could understand. Derby knew where he would rest that night, and indeed what his short future on earth would hold. Baggerly was destined to live on in an uncertain world.

According to one account the symbolism of the execution was carried so far that the scaffold built at Bolton Cross, near the Man and Scythe Inn, was actually constructed from the timbers of Derby's own house at Lathom. No risk was taken regarding any rescue, nor indeed any change of heart on the part of the people of Bolton, since there was an escort guard of sixty or more horse. On the morning of the execution Baggerly states that Lord Derby

The 'Olde Man and Scythe', Bolton, renovated in 1636. It was here that the seventh Earl of Derby spent his last night before his execution in 1651.

PHOTOGRAPH: CARNEGIE, 2009

prayed at length before mounting the scaffold, but declared himself 'content to die in this town'.

He was granted the opportunity of a last speech, which the clerk, James Roscow, diligently noted in shorthand. Though his enemies had deliberately brought him here to atone for the crimes he had committed against the town, he denied that he was a man of blood, 'as some have maliciously and falsely slandered me'. Yet if a confession was required, and royalism was a crime, he did confess that 'I love monarchy and I love my master Charles II'. At this there was some disturbance in the crowd and a trooper standing near the scaffold remarked that 'we have no king, and will have no lords'. The contemporary pamphlet *The Earle of Derby's Speech* also records a 'great tumult' in the crowd, in the 'appeasing of which there were some cut, many hurt, and one childe killed'. The earl was 'no good orator', but he continued, offering forgiveness to those that were about to take his life. Having noted that it was against all justice that soldiers should take away the life of a man who had given himself up 'on quarter', his last thoughts were for his God, his king, and an adieu to his county.

> And walking up and down on the scaffold, he said, The Lord bless you all; the Son of God bless you all of this town of Bolton, Manchester, and especially Lancashire, and God send that you may have a King again, and laws. I die like a Christian, a Souldier, and Christ's Souldier.[30]

Derby now asked to see the axe, saying to the headsman, 'come friend, give it into my hands, I'll neither hurt thee nor it; and it cannot hurt me for I am not afraid of it.' Having kissed the axe, he handed it back and gave the executioner two pieces of gold. Noticing the man wore a heavy coat he asked him to take it off, fearing that otherwise it might interfere with the swift and clean performance of his duty. Next he asked that the block be angled so that he could face the church, his Church of England, at the moment of death. There then followed a few moments of near-farce during which Derby questioned whether his neck would fit the block: his own servants were naturally reluctant to place their necks upon the wood in the midst of an already unruly execution scene, so a trumpeter of the guard duly stepped forward and demonstrated of the block's suitability for its purpose. At last Derby lay down his head and following a further short prayer he lifted up his hands, on which signal 'the executioner did his work'. At the fall of his head the crowd appeared oddly silent, 'after which there was nothing heard in the town but sighs, sobs and prayers'.[31]

CHAPTER THIRTEEN

The aftermath of war

THE BODY OF the seventh Earl of Derby was carried away from Bolton the night of the execution, to be interred later 'amongst his ancestors' in the family vault at Ormskirk parish church. According to nineteenth-century accounts, the sepulchre had a pair of wooden doors which could be opened for the edification of the curious. Inside were two coffins: one was full-size; the other one, very small, was said to contain his lordship's severed head. Such an explanation would doubtless have appealed to the ghoulish. It is more likely, however, that his undertakers had followed the practice of removing the noble entrails from the corpse during embalming, later placing them in a separate container or canopic chest. The head would most likely have been sewn back onto the body, or laid with it in the larger coffin. Such indeed is suggested by the *Discourse*, which relates how Derby's servants immediately picked up the head, and 'put it to his bodye again'. He was then placed in the coffin 'which had abundance of seeds in it to receive the blood'. An unknown hand is said to have slipped the following verse into his box: 'Wit, Bounty, Courage, all Three here in one lie dead, A Stanley's hand, Veres heart, and Cecill's head.'

Whatever the exact details, James Stanley went to his maker in at least two separate parts. It must be questionable whether, even by the standards of the time, he deserved such a fate – but his end mirrored the wretched state of much of the county of Lancashire at that time. It may not have been entirely reasonable, but there were many who blamed Derby for this destruction. What was certainly the case was that in the eyes of many Lancastrians Derby had slipped almost imperceptibly from the role of noble peacemaker, to defender of the family estates, to desperate royalist in exile, to suspected war criminal, and finally to being the treacherous lackey of foreign invaders. Derby had had his impact upon the wars; but over nine years the wars had made a greater impression upon his attitudes and reputation. The times had done him no favours. Interestingly the parliamentarian author of the *Discourse* found many good things to say about Lord Derby, and his 'honourable House of Lathom'. His family was ancient, their hospitality good, and his attitude to his tenants benign. He was personally affable and courteous, and was loyal to his sovereign. As Derby himself had advised his son, 'taking off your hat, a good word, a smile or the like will cost you nothing, but may gain you much'. The *Discourse* writer really found three faults only: he had chosen the wrong side, and, though he professed to being a Protestant, he had allowed himself to be associated with all sorts of disreputable people who were not. The third fault, crossing from the Isle of Man to the side of Charles II, had proved fatal. Had he not given his defiance to parliament in 1649, and had he stayed on his island in 1651, like as not, some life-sparing accommodation might eventually have been reached. As it was he was in league with 'God's enemies' – and God, quite rightly, had decided to 'blast all his undertakings and designs'.[1]

It has been estimated that Britain lost as many as 190,000 dead during the nine years of the civil wars, including the additional victims of disease and famine alongside battle casualties. As a percentage of the total population, deaths in the civil wars were therefore proportionately greater even than those of World War I. There were probably more than 600 battles, sieges, stormings, skirmishes and riots in which one or more people were killed. At least a quarter of the adult male population had borne arms at some point during the wars. Such measures give us an idea of the scale of the catastrophe that had befallen the kingdoms. This may not have been as bad as parts of Europe, where the Thirty Years War was raging and where Geoffrey Parker contends that in certain places enlistment and a death sentence were virtually synonymous; still, the situation in Britain was still extremely serious.

Lancashire's total population on the eve of the wars had been perhaps 150,000: of these several thousand had died of various causes. Epidemics alone had caused deaths well into the thousands, and, if the detailed research on other counties approximates to the Lancashire situation, more died from disease than in battle. The great fight at Marston Moor, the 1648 battle of Preston – 'Bloody Preston' – and the sackings of Bolton and Liverpool, had, at the most conservative estimate, led to the demise of a couple of thousand more Lancastrians. It is true that many who were killed in the county hailed from elsewhere, but, equally, many Lancastrians lost their lives campaigning in the South, in Cheshire or in Yorkshire. It is notable, for example, that the queen's own regiments under Henry Jermyn were essentially Lancashire units and included such known local recusant gentlemen as John Cansfield,

Lawrence and Gervaise Clifton and Thomas Brockholes. The regiments of the Gerard family similarly were Lancashire in origin, though topped up with Welshmen and others later on. Individually, engagements at Read Bridge and all the other minor skirmishes and stormings had not led to as many deaths. Yet when the many, and often repeated, struggles at Wigan, Manchester, Lancaster, Warrington, Bury, Blackburn, Wigan, Leigh, Hoghton, Lathom, Ormskirk, Preston and elsewhere are added together another thousand deaths would be a very modest estimate.

Taking together all war-related causes of death, a good case can be made for an approximate minimum total of 6,000 Lancastrian fatalities, or very roughly 4 per cent of the population. At the higher end of the scale of probability perhaps as many as 7,500 Lancastrians were killed or died as a result of the wars, around 5 per cent of the population. As in many wars, officers, particularly junior officers, were well represented in the death toll. On the basis of a suitably large sample Gratton claims that 4 per cent of Lancashire parliamentarian officers were killed or died of wounds and that 15 per cent of royalist leaders suffered the same fate. Proportionately Lancashire suffered a greater collective bereavement than did the country as a whole. An interesting comparison is provided by Preston in 1914–1918, when about 2,000, or less than 2 per cent of the population, were killed.[2]

At the end of the civil wars Lancashire was left in a very poor state. According to contemporaries this 'lamentable' condition was had been caused by the 'three corded scourge of sword, pestilence, and famine'. For those of pessimistic or fundamentalist religious persuasions, the wrath of God was apparent in their misery. As early as 1644 parliamentarian Colonel Peter Egerton was reporting that 'the County hath been soe extremely exhausted by continuall war that itt is not able to undergo ordinary taxacions'. The next year London was expressing similar sentiments, an official parliamentarian document referring to Lancashire as a 'miserably wasted county ...' As Lord Derby himself put it, 'No Countrie can be called Rich where war is'.

Money was voted for the relief of Manchester, although apparently nothing materialised for the next three years. Manchester was also hit by plague in 1645, and in the warmth of the summer mortality reached a frightening peak. At least 172 were buried in the town that July, 310 in August and a further 266 in September – at a time when the usual monthly toll would have been no more than 30. In this particular instance at least, disease and death appear to have approximated to the known European pattern of the Thirty Years War. A population weakened by war and shortage was hit by plague in the late summer, followed perhaps by dysentery and influenza in the autumn. Unlike today fewer succumbed during the cold of winter, once the weak had been carried away. At a minimum estimate rather more than a tenth of Manchester's population died in this epidemic. One of the few to prosper in the face of tragedy was Roger Hadocke, who received £5 1s. from the churchwardens in early 1645, for 'gathering up' money to help the 'infected poore'. People stayed away for fear of contagion, and the rich moved their families out of town. John Rosworme remained behind with a small garrison, remarking that paradoxically the miseries of the town were 'a guard to us against our Enemies', since no royalist from outside in his right mind would set foot there during the pestilence. Nevertheless, Rosworme claimed to have unmasked a conspiracy to hand Manchester over to the enemy in its hour of distress. Almost uniquely among Lancashire towns and villages, Manchester was never successfully stormed or occupied by the enemy; the town did, however, pay a heavy price both in death, and 'decay of trade'. As preacher Heyrick put it in a sermon to parliament, Manchester was 'the only town untouched by the enemy', but at that time 'the only town stricken by God'.[3]

Despite Heyrick's remarks, sooner or later many other Lancashire towns were also hit by disease. Apart from those who died violent deaths, Bolton suffered a peak of mortality in 1642, when it was struck by 'pox'. About 240 people were buried that year, an increase of perhaps 40 per cent on normal times. A majority of the victims of the epidemic were children. Further outbreaks were noted in 1647 and 1655. Though far fewer died in these later years, it has been suggested that this was because the population was markedly smaller after the sack of 1644 and other vicissitudes of war. As late as 1653 a petition was put forward to the justices of the Manchester quarter sessions regarding 'the poore widdowes, maymed souldiers and fatherless children whose husbands or parents were slayne att the surprizall of Boulton by Prince Rupert'. Claiming greater loss and hardship than the surrounding areas, the Bolton petitioners asked for speedy relief to avoid starvation. There is certainly evidence for food shortages in Bolton and nearby towns in the early 1650s, and at least anecdotal reference to a 'textile crisis', failures to pay rent, and evictions. It would also appear that bridges and other public works suffered neglect, with hard-pressed funds being used for more urgent purposes.[4]

Wigan, too, had suffered multiple blows: as a royalist town, it had been a special target for the enemy. Many of the local gentry were away, fighting or exiled, and often heavily fined. As early as 1643, when Alice Thornton passed through, she found it already 'sorely demolished, and all the windows broken'. In 1648 Wigan had been in the path of fresh devastation, topped off by the vicious famine and plague of 1649. Retreating troops had fled through Wigan during the battle of 1651. The town and its neighbouring areas were claimed between them to be home to 'full 2,000 poor'. This statement may have been an exaggeration, but we know that at least some were starving in the streets, their betters powerless to assist. Bury still presented something of a sorry picture even after the Restoration of 1660. Its population then was about 1,000, and taxation records suggest that about four in ten citizens were either permanently very poor or in a state of temporary distress. A similar number were living in one- or two-hearth cottages, working hard for a somewhat meagre living. Just one in ten could be described as 'comfortable', with only 18 souls in the entire town who were actually wealthy. Only one man then qualified for the title of gentleman.[5]

Liverpool had suffered severe if partial damage, particularly during the royalist storming of 1644. In 1645 the town was granted 500 tons of timber from royalist estates to repair the 'greate parte destroyed and burnt down by the enemie'. In March 1646 the town lobbied the Lancashire committee for relief, but with money desperately short the response was muted. The committee granted £20. This would not have gone far when it was planned to give each widow or orphan 3s. and maimed soldiers 6s. A further petition for relief was made in early 1648, in which the Liverpudlians, somewhat questionably, claimed that they had 'alwais bene well affected to the Parliament'. They went on to explain that much destruction had been caused, not just by the royalists, but by parliamentarians who had caused 'many of their howses and outhowses to be pulled downe and their gardens and orchards to be digged up' during work to strengthen the town's defences. There was some talk of a grant of £10,000, but this appears to have come to nothing. Things were still desperate in November 1648 when the mayor and aldermen passed an order that, due to the numbers of 'yong children and Beggers' on the streets, a list should be made of the vagrants and runaways. Once these had been enumerated, they would be examined to determine which belonged to the town and which did not: those who were locals were to put be into apprenticeship; those able-bodied who were not from the town could expect to be 'shipt to Barbadas' for work on the plantations. Liverpool was also visited by the plague in 1651, an outbreak which is thought to have killed 200, most of whom were buried in the aptly named 'Sickman's Lane'.[6]

At Lancaster there was also significant destruction, much of it occasioned when the town was attacked by the royalists in March 1643. As the *Discourse* had it:

Such was their cruelty that they set fyre upon the towne in several parts of it, having none to withstand them. In the hart of the Towne they burned divers of the eminent houses. That long street from the Whit croft all was burned, dwelling houses, barnes, corne, hay, cattell in their stalls. The club men plundered unmercifully carrying great packets home with them.

A good deal of the town was reported destroyed, including 90 houses, 86 agricultural buildings and a malt kiln. Some measure of the scale of the damage can be gleaned from the fact that in 1645 parliament decided that Lancaster should receive no less than £8,000 from the estates of those 'delinquents' who had been present during the action.

Warrington might have suffered less than some of its neighbours, but was still seized and fought over repeatedly. By 1647 many had been reduced to poverty, some to hunger. Town moralists shifted some of the blame from politics and war to drink, claiming it was the brewing of beer from barley that exacerbated the paucity of food in the town. Strangely recent studies of the Great Depression and other recessions suggest that alcohol consumption does indeed rise in hard times, so perhaps the anti-drink lobby was not entirely mistaken. Warrington's luckiest escape had been in 1648 when the Scots had surrendered rather than fight in its streets. Even so it was then occupied by the New Model and had to deal with large numbers of prisoners. Warrington bridge had been fought over yet again in 1651.

Ormskirk suffered an outbreak of plague – God's 'heavy judgement of the pestilence' – in 1648; a total of 33 persons were either 'confyned to their own houses' or sent out into 'cabbins' to isolate them from the rest of the community.[7] A further visitation in 1653 proved difficult to do anything about, since many of the population were already in poverty. Exactly how many of Ormskirk's population died in the wars, or of the plagues and shortages which accompanied them, will never be known. The keeping of the parish registers was abandoned between the end of 1644 and 1653 'by reason of the uncivall warres heare in England', as the vicar Will Grice recorded. Though the reasons are not usually as explicit, a number of other parish registers also ceased during the period, including those of Walton-le-Dale and Clitheroe. The registers for other places, such as Leigh, Farnworth, Radcliffe and Prescot appear very incomplete for one or more years. At Brindle the registers are patchy for the early part of the period, but in 1647 burials rise rapidly from a base line of rather fewer than 30 per annum, to more than 40 individuals. These include many children, such as 'the infants of Simsone', 'a pore child', and the 'Bastard of Georg Ryley'. In 1648 Brindle's dead numbered about 60, including several unnamed infants. There does not appear to be any mention of epidemic, though poverty, malnutrition and the Preston campaign of the Second Civil War probably played their parts.

Near Ormskirk Lathom House stood sadly dilapidated and shot about. As one witness observed, upon its ruination 'the glorie of the county was lost'. Several of its structures had either been pulled down or had fallen into the moat, and people had come from far and wide to strip lead from its roofs. Ironically some made the journey from Wigan, and are thus likely to have been former royalists. The demolition of Lathom was retrospectively approved by the House of Commons in early March 1647. According to Thomas Malbon, Cheshire chronicler, the defence of Lathom had been a general catastrophe, leading 'to the great Damage of all that countrey & in the end to the utter Ruyne of the same howse'. In 1649 the constables still protested that collecting money from local inhabitants was well-nigh impossible given the devastation and losses caused by the wars. It was not true, however, that Lathom House had disappeared entirely by the end of the civil wars. At the Restoration it was recorded that the sturdy Eagle Tower still stood, along with some parts of 'the wooden house'. A hearth tax return of 1666 records that 17 fireplaces still existed, strongly suggesting that a portion of the fortress and house had survived, or had been restored in the intervening years. It now seems likely, indeed, that some parts of the structure of the old house survived until the building of the new in the eighteenth century.[8]

Many other properties suffered in various ways, ranging from total destruction to mild inconvenience. Humphrey Chetham protested that during the ebb and flow of war his house in the medieval pele tower at Turton had been entered three times by rampaging armies. Both the property and outlying fencing had suffered, and many of the cattle had been requisitioned. Thomas Robinson of Westby, meanwhile, complained that in 1642 royalist troops had appeared at his home attempting to find him to enlist him in the king's cause. Finding him away, they thoroughly plundered his home instead, taking not only £1, which he had recently earned from the sale of corn in Preston, but his linen sheets and a flitch of bacon. At Salesbury, just north of Blackburn, the Catholic Talbot family suffered particular depredation. Sir John complained that under parliament's rule his home had been plundered 'to that extremity that the bread which my children ate was buried in the ground, thereby to preserve it for them from one meal to another'. In the end his estate was taken altogether.

Others lower down the social scale also suffered significant loss. Lawrence Breres, who spent some time with the Lathom garrison, emerged to discover that parliamentarian sequestrators had been at work on his home and goods. Among the many items seized were his cows and a 'feather bed' – probably his prize possession – his spoons, tools, and 'odd things'. The total value was £34 15s. 4d.[9]

The rectory at Winwick, formerly the home of the Reverend Charles Herle, had seen the complete kaleidoscope of war. Given Herle's parliamentarian sympathies, his abode on the outskirts of royalist Warrington had soon become uncomfortable, and he had abandoned it for London. Leaving a faithful retainer in charge, Herle had continued to get rent for a while, but soon troops were billeted there and the servant was also forced to flee. While Herle gained high-profile employment as a preacher to parliament, his parsonage was held by Sir John Fortescue until May 1643. The wheel of fortune spun again, and then the royalists left. What happened in the heady days of Prince Rupert's intervention in 1644 is unclear, but in 1648 Herle's house was at the epicentre of the Second Civil War and the important battle at Winwick. Thereafter it appears that Herle attempted to regain his Lancashire properties, with only partial success, before 1651, when the rectory is mentioned as a dressing station during the Third Civil War.

In some instances it was not the property itself that was damaged or taken, but evidence as to its ownership: over years of fighting plunder and sequestration, it could then become very difficult and expensive to prove who owned what. At Kirkham the deeds to a windmill and eight other properties went missing. 'Thornton's Tenement' resulted in a legal tussle in which the defending counsel would be Alexander Rigby.[10] In terms of general financial impact, the civil wars might well be compared with the world wars of the twentieth century, for, proportionately, the sieges, battles, fires and demolitions of the 1640s and 1650s directly affected more homes and businesses in Lancashire than did those of the early twentieth century.

On a personal scale the cost could also be vast, and financial loss did not just strike those who had been plundered or taxed. Officers and soldiers were also left badly out of pocket. For example, we have no reason to believe that Captain William Rawlinson of Graythwaite in Furness was particularly badly hit in financial terms, but his period of service under arms for parliament from October 1643 to March 1645 still cost him dear. Theoretically he should have been paid £1,633 for his pay and expenses for his 873 days of service. Part of this was paid in 'free quarter' and a little in ready money. The bulk, £1,078, was still outstanding long afterwards and was probably never paid, even in kind. Just £1 was a significant sum in 1650 when a working man might consider himself reasonably happy with 6d. a day. Colonel John Moore of Liverpool calculated that his total pay since 1642 should have amounted to £4,446 – but actually he got only half of this. He cut his losses by failing to pay at least some of his own creditors, including the London inn where he stayed on visits to parliament. The innkeeper in question was of pocket to the tune of £85, mainly through debts accrued for horses and fodder.[11]

Given even the very inadequate statistics we have, it is still apparent that Lancashire was financially ruined by the war, and that however the fighting progressed, sooner or later, one or both sides would have run out of money. In 1645 the parliamentarian committee was allowed to collect up to £3,000 in cash per month: royalist fund-raising and 'in kind' collecting would comfortably have doubled this figure. However, it cost about 5s. per week to maintain a single musketeer; a captain of foot cost £3 10s., and a troop of horse more than £50. Even allowing for the existence of just ten troops of horse and 4,000 foot, the costs would have been greater than all of the sums collected. The warring factions were thus bankrupting themselves quite quickly, before considering loss of production, destruction of property and looting, or without factoring in costs for equipment and fortifications. Thus, pay was bound to lag behind service, and this situation got progressively worse with each passing month. The population could not have stood such a situation indefinitely without starvation.

Gregory King, whose book *Natural and Political Observations and Conclusions upon the State and Condition of England* was published at Lancaster in 1696, suggests that even long after the war a quarter of the English population had a family income of less than £14 a year, and only a select few had more than £70. Lancashire was even poorer than this national average, and many were living in, or close to, poverty even before the conflict. The loss of a few pounds therefore made a catastrophic difference to the lower orders. One man who suffered in just such a way at the hands of the Scots was John Cawson of Quernmore, reduced to penury and forced to plead with the authorities for relief. He got 9d. with which to tide over himself, his wife and three children. George Halliwell of Standish had been a self-made man before the arrival of the enemy, eleven of his neighbours certifying that 'heretofore by his greate labour and industrie' he had made a 'competente livelihood'; now he, too, was forced to throw himself upon the charity of the parish. Little wonder that joining an army, anybody's army, could seem remarkably attractive, even if payment for service could be intermittent. Given such a situation, it is remarkable that the fighting could have continued as long as it did.[12]

For the Duchy of Lancaster the war also spelled at least temporary ruin. Income had been relatively healthy at almost £8,000 in the months leading up to September 1642, but thereafter revenues plunged; over the following two years just £2,391 was collected altogether. In September 1643 parliament ordered that the duchy incomes should be seized, and their own receiver general, Thomas Fauconbridge, was appointed. After March 1649 all royal claim to the estates was disbarred, and during the 1650s parts of the duchy lands were sold off.[13]

Certain episodes in the civil wars within Lancashire, such as the sack of Bolton, were undoubtedly more traumatic than what went on in other parts of the country. Lancastrians may well have suffered more than Londoners, or the people of, say, East Anglia, which saw little actual fighting. Some prisoners, such as Colonel Cuthbert Clifton – who was captured by parliament in 1644, and later died of 'hard usage' – undoubtedly suffered abuse. Many were neglected or failed to receive medical aid. Nevertheless this does not prove that by modern standards the war in Lancashire was unlimited, nor that war crimes, as defined by the standard of the time, were usual. Indeed, the deliberate killing of prisoners was exceptional. It was far more common for exchanges to take place, or for captives to be released on 'parole' not to fight again. Where identified prisoners were released upon their honour, and had given such undertakings, only to be seized again, the enemy had every legal right to put them to death. Yet such summary executions appear to have been rare. Indeed in the early days of the war in Lancashire some captured soldiers were simply disarmed, given a good talking-to, in an effort to make them see the error of their ways and the beneficence of their captors, before being sent off home. The discipline of one's own side was sometimes more to be feared than the enemy – and accounts of malefactors being hanged for desertion, mutiny, and other contraventions of the laws of war certainly occur.

The specific targeting of women and children in atrocities was almost unheard of. It is certain that many women and children died in the war, and that the ravages of disease, for example, cut a swathe through the youth of the county. Women were certainly killed in bombardments or fires on a regular basis. Nevertheless the moral codes of the time were strongly against the abuse of women. In a few instances the deliberate slaughtering of female civilians is mentioned, yet such cases are very few and far between. Moreover even in the extreme case of the Sack of Bolton in 1644, it is difficult to demonstrate the death of more than a very small number of individual women. Rape – referred to as 'violation' at the time – did occur, and is specifically mentioned during the Scottish invasion of 1648. How widespread a phenomenon this actually was during the wars as a whole is extremely difficult to determine, because the stigma of having been raped was significant, and many probably went unrecorded. On the other hand, a lurid story of 'violation' in the popular press made good propaganda, and some instances may have been reported more than once. Torture is mentioned in accounts, but extremely rarely, and on the face of it would appear to have been much less common than in recent conflicts.

The Commonwealth and Protectorate, 1651–1660

Under the Commonwealth and Protectorate much of Lancashire would remain a relatively impoverished area, and the burdens of poor relief would be shared well beyond the districts worst affected. This was partly due to continued unrest. For though peace returned to Lancashire after 1651, this was no general period of quiet. Considerable standing armies were maintained, and there was naval warfare against France in 1652; forces were deployed against the highland clans in 1653; war with Spain occurred a couple of years later; and intermittent brigandage and unrest in Ireland required virtually constant attention. As John Morrill has put it, there was 'no let up in the sense of military crisis'.

Booth's rebellion of 1659 was unsuccessful, but did involve the northern counties and Lancashire specifically. Sir George Booth drew his support from Cheshire, Lancashire and north Wales, and was inspired, at least in part, by disillusionment with disintegrating central authority after the death of Cromwell. Supported by Charles, eighth Earl of Derby, Colonel Egerton, and Thomas Myddleton, Booth managed to raise 4,000 men. A proclamation was issued that the aim of the rising was to defend the freedom of parliament, although there can be no doubt that the episode was actually royalist-inspired. Chester was seized, and the insurgents marched on York. On the way uncomfortable news was received that the rest of the country had not burst into revolt. The rebels turned back to Cheshire. Yet again the man of the hour was Major General Lambert. Marching from London at the head of 2,000 men, he succeeded in linking up with reinforcements from Ireland and Yorkshire which gave him a local superiority of numbers. At Winnington bridge in Cheshire he fell upon the opposition, whose resistance quickly crumbled. Booth escaped dressed as a woman, but was discovered, so it was said, in an inn at Newport Pagnell, where his bulk and importunate request for a razor had given rise to suspicion. Happily for Sir George he survived a brief imprisonment in the Tower, and would later receive both financial reward and the title Lord Delamere from Charles II. The young Lord Derby was attainted by parliament. Such had been John Lambert's energy and military performance during the 1640s and 1650s that one is left wondering to what extent Cromwell had depended on Lambert for his greatest military triumphs, and indeed whether Lambert deserves a far greater degree of the credit for these victories than he has customarily received.

The impact of these later events may have been less obvious than the three civil wars, but Lancastrians were still heavily involved, and still being killed. Lancashire's contribution to the wars of the Commonwealth and Protectorate was tangible, and again probably out of scale with its relatively small population. In what was a sideways tribute to local military prowess, Firth noted that Cromwell's own regiment of foot for Irish service was raised in the county. Certainly one or more regiments were found from Lancashire in this period. The *House of Commons Journal* of June 1650 recorded that it was intended 'That a regiment of foot be forthwith raised in Lancashire, for the Lord Lieutenant of Ireland, under such officers as he shall be pleased to appoint'. As always, the fact that the county was convenient for access to Ireland had a bearing, but parliament might have had other motives for their approval. These might have included, on the positive side, the finding of employment for the menfolk of a devastated county. On the negative it was certainly a handy way to ship out potential trouble-makers.[14]

Newspaper reports of the fighting in Scotland in 1650–51 likewise refer to troops raised in Lancashire. These included 'the Lancashire Regiment under Colonel Worsley', and 'another raised in those parts'. Though there may have been earlier instances of units raised in Lancashire to serve England's interests overseas, these mentions are probably the earliest of a specific 'Lancashire Regiment'. As such they mark the beginnings of the county as a major recruiting ground for Britain's armed forces, a role that has continued to the present day.[15]

Following Penruddock's uprising in the south-west of England in the spring of 1655 Cromwell had come to the conclusion that stiffer measures were required and that civilian politicians were not best suited to deal with the new situation of the country. A new system of administration was therefore devised in August and September, and major-generals – answerable only to Cromwell himself as Lord Protector – were formally commissioned with the security of the land in October. The main duty of these senior soldiers during the so-called 'rule of the major-generals' would be to maintain the peace by the suppression of unlawful assemblies, the disarming of royalist sympathisers and the apprehension of criminals. Mounted troops, comprising loyal volunteers, would enforce the rule of law funded by a new 'decimation' or 10 per cent tax levied on royalists. Regulations imposed on royalists included a need to apply for permission to leave their home areas, and there was a general abolition of various sports and pastimes.

England was divided into areas under major-generals or their deputies, and Lancashire was united with Cheshire and Staffordshire as the fiefdom of Major General Charles Worsley, one of the more puritan-minded of his peers. Worsley had been born in Manchester in 1622, the son of a wealthy merchant. He was a captain in parliament's army in 1644, rising to the rank of lieutenant colonel by 1650. Serving under Cromwell in his regiment of foot, he had been quartered at St James's in 1652 when he received the order to put an end to the sitting of the Rump of the Long Parliament. Acting in concert with Major General Harrison he entered the Commons 'with five or six files of musketeers, about 20 or 30, with theyr musquets'. Harrison persuaded the Speaker to leave, and Worsley and Harrison together ejected Algernon Sidney

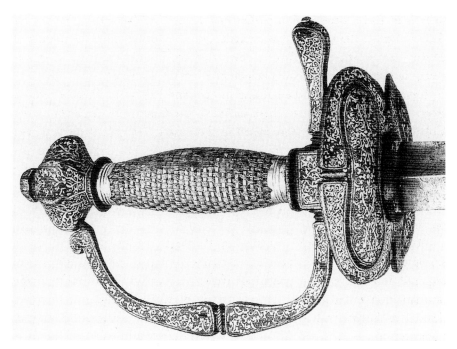

Detail of the small sword of Major General Charles Worsley, dated 1651. Charles Worsley (1622–56), Cromwellian major general. By the age of 22 Worsley was fighting as a captain on the side of parliament in Lancashire, and was still under 30 when he was colonel of the Lancashire regiment raised to serve under Cromwell in Scotland. From 1654 he was MP for Manchester and in 1655 was one of the major generals given local powers by the Protector. His fiefdom then extended over Lancashire, Cheshire and Staffordshire.

Major-General Charles Worsley was an important figure for a short time during the Protectorate. This drawing was made for the Chetham Society volume *The History of the Ancient Chapel of Birch* (1859).

who was refusing to move. Having locked the building, Worsley took away the key and the mace. It was perhaps paradoxical that the parliament which had encouraged Lancastrians to take up arms, was itself evicted by a Lancashire parliamentarian soldier. As a member of the political junta, Worsley was now himself faced with many of the problems hitherto confronted by parliament and committee. Tax-collecting was one of the most serious.

Just how little Lancashire had left to collect was made clear in a letter, written on Christmas Eve, 1655, from Worsley to the Lord Protector (interestingly, he began the letter, 'May it please your highnesse ...'). Many of those 'delinquents' whose property he had set on seizing were 'papist' and as such had already had most of their visible estates sold by the state in 1651–53. Worsley suggested lowering the bar so that delinquents with as little as £50 per annum from lands could have their property seized.

Ever the puritan, Charles Worsley boasted of ordering the closure of numerous alehouses, particularly those run by people who 'have been in armes against the parliament, and are looked upon to be enemies to the present government', as well as those 'of bad name and repute among their neighbours'.

I find it a difficult bussinese how to observe my instructions as to alehouses, and not weaken that revenew, though it's too visible that they are the very bane of the countrys ... we find that these alehouses are the very wombe, that brings forth all manner of wickedness; wee have ordered at least 200 alehouses to be thrown down in [Blackburn] hundred, and are catching up loose and vile persons.

Worsley also began a crackdown on vagrants or 'wandering idle persons' as well as the Quakers, who were seen as a 'great disturbance'. As he reported on 21 December 1655, 'We are much troubled with them, that are called quakers; they troble the markets, and get into private houses up and down in every towne, and drawe people after them. I have and shall take what course I can, but I could wish to have some further power or direction from you in that case.'

Another report, of 12 November 1655, written by Worsley to Secretary of State Thurloe in London is fairly typical of the enthusiastic major-general's work at this time:

... we have appointed a time to put in execution the ordinance for ejecting of scandelouse and insufficient ministers and scoolmasters. I have since bene in some corporations with the mayor and aldermen, and the best of the people, to stir up and quicken to be puttinge in effectual execution the laws against drunkennese, sweringe, profaininge the Lord's day, and other wickedness.

Wherever Worsley travelled he claimed to find a great deal of local support for the good work of puritan reformation. In March 1656, for example, he wrote:

> Wee are in a very good condition in this county. This worke stirs up the good people to informe us of the conversation of all men, their carridge and behaviour; soe that truly I thinke the good sober people never were in better hart then now, and soe much owned; nethere was more cordiall to present proceedings then att this time. I find noe man of what sperit soever, that apears in word or action against our present worke; some out of feare, and some by reason of the encouragement they receive, makes all quiet.

Whether the wider populace were quite as enthusiastic for the major-general's hounding of 'delinquents', replacing of 'scandalous schoolmasters', tax-collecting and the suppression of alehouses is unclear.

Worsley's puritanical campaign was actually part of a broader attempt during the 1650s to see God's work put into action. Of course, a handful of puritans in power for a short time at the county level could never really have hoped to effect a permanent 'reformation of manners' in Lancashire or elsewhere. For at the local level most communities probably escaped the attentions of the Interregnum reformers altogether, partly because Lancashire consisted of widely dispersed communities, most of which had no resident gentry, let alone JP or high constable. Thus, even if county officials or major-generals wanted to impose strict standards of social behaviour and morals on the population – and it seems certain that not all did seek to do such a thing – their efforts would be largely ineffectual or futile.

Indeed, it has been argued that in one important sense the townships of Lancashire were more or less self-regulating, if not self-governing, in the mid-seventeenth century. In the many small townships of the county most heads of household were themselves in positions of minor authority as petty constables, overseers of the poor or churchwardens. In many townships local custom was that minor local offices should pass around householders in turn, by 'hedge-row' or 'house-row'. Each resident would serve in rotation. The quarter sessions petitions for this period are full of complaints about the onerous nature of local office-holding. Some townships such as Ribbleton near Preston complained that they were obliged to find almost as many local officials each year to serve their communities as there were households in the township, with the result – they claimed – that almost everyone was obliged to be an office-holder every year.

In these circumstances, with at least the prominent householders serving office regularly, there was a strong incentive to resolve conflicts without recourse to the county authorities. Time and again local communities claimed at quarter sessions that no crime had taken place, and the suspicion has to be that most petty constables in particular would rather that minor transgressions be resolved close to home, without invoking the wrath or even exciting the attention of higher authorities. After all, if the neighbour you report at one session is appointed constable in his turn the following year it is not unlikely that you, too, will find yourself reported in your turn.

All of this did not necessarily amount to some form of incipient democracy at township level, but it certainly did mean that the 'concept of order' held by Worsley or the county JPs was rather different to the reality on the ground of keeping your head down, resolving disputes locally and taking care not

Soldiers turned iconoclasts on their way to York, pulling down 'Popish pictures', breaking altar rails and removing the altars from their places of veneration. From a contemporary print.

to antagonise neighbours who would be officeholders themselves in the near future. Worsley himself recognised the importance of appointing 'honest, faithfull, and judicious men' to the petty constableship, although he frequently despaired of being able to find enough such men. In one letter of 3 December 1655, indeed, he complained bitterly about the standard and conduct of many petty constables:

> the market day being either on the saturday or monday, ocations the Lords day to be much violated about constables, that are swerers, and drunken idle persons themselves, and of the meanest sort of men ... as also by a custom they have in this countye to goe by house-rows ...

Despite the difficulty of the task and the very limited real powers of enforcement at his command – no doubt suppressed alehouses in remote parts did not remain suppressed for very long – Charles Worsley undertook his duties at major-general with enormous vigour; the series of letters he wrote to the Secretary of State every few days from different parts of the three counties shows that he must have spent long hours in the saddle traversing the region under his authority. In each letter he listed with care all of the actions he had taken, recommending men for preferment, others for censure.

Some believed that Worsley worked himself into an early grave. Certainly, as perhaps the most committed of the Cromwellian major-generals, Worsley might well have had more impact on the history of the North West had he not died in his mid-thirties, in London, in 1656. On 17 June 1656 the major-general's Cheshire commissioners described Worsley's death as

> a loss we cannot but be deeply affected with, having had so large and manifest experience of his sincere, zealous, and upright endeavours, both to the discharge of his trust, and comfort and satisfaction of good mens spirits.

His value to the regime was recognised by his burial with full honours in Westminster Abbey. He was replaced, albeit briefly, by Tobias Bridge.[16]

Gloomy as the picture of death, destruction, financial ruin and imposed austerity undoubtedly was, it has to be said that rural society in Lancashire in the seventeenth century was more resilient and flexible than we might think. Compared to recent times the birth rate was high, and although infant mortality was also high, demographic recovery is likely to have occurred within a couple of generations, certainly by 1700. Both contemporary continental and more recent models suggest that while marriages might have been delayed by war, the churches were again busy when hostilities had ceased.

We also need to set Lancastrians' own apprehension of their misfortunes against a background of strong, and often very literal, religious belief. For the different shades of Protestant believers, suffering was commonly seen as a part of God's plan, or just punishment; for Catholics salvation and paradise were there for the asking. In either case 'corporal' things were just one part of a broader picture, and not the most important part at that. People who believed otherwise, including hedonists and atheists, certainly existed, but the overwhelming climate of opinion was against them. The former were generally regarded as unseemly if not sinful, the latter punishable or unspeakable. The bible was real and solid, largely unchallenged by other literature in the minds of the many. It was sworn on with the utmost solemnity, and to blaspheme was a crime; for the masses such transgressions were largely indistinguishable from crimes such as assault and theft. The ten Commandments were written on church walls, and roundly sermonised. Lancastrians were expected to know what they were. By comparison the law of the land was relatively obscure, the

George Monk, Duke of Albemarle (1608–70), from the frontispiece of Thomas Skinner's *Life of General Monk*. After fighting on the side of parliament, Monk was influential in the restoration of Charles II. Monk received the lordship of Clitheroe from the new king, and to this day the white lion's head of the Monk family is represented in the crest of the town.

preserve of officials with access to books, learning and money; and in any case many of the basic tenets of law were based on those of the Commandments. Catholics relied less on sermons and the written word, but this was balanced by pictures, images and ritual, in which the clothes and settings of the saints were often those of the world around them.

In the minds of Protestants 'the Word' was vivid, and for a majority the mental landscape was largely unclouded by concepts of history, archaeology, or notions or knowledge of other faiths. The presence or absence of church art and symbols was an issue provoking serious debate, and often iconoclasm. God was heard to speak directly, and sometimes the message was hard.

Alongside religion, there were other reasons why the depredations of the wars were perhaps more readily healed than we might think. Famine and plague were ever-present in society; the concept of public healthcare was unknown; sanitation was primitive if not non-existent. The rich might have been able to afford doctors, but then death was accepted as an ever-present companion, and the ministrations of the medical profession of uncertain efficacy. The idea of science was as yet hazy, being cautiously explored by philosophers far beyond the ken of most of rural Lancashire. The sea was an untamed beast, 'tempests' practically unexplained, except by reference to scripture or folklore. Life could certainly be 'nasty and brutish' for many – and arguably the civil wars merely made it potentially shorter. Some of the puritan-minded welcomed paradise with open arms; others did so with stoic resignation.

Surprisingly Lancashire's relatively backward nature, and its dependence on agriculture, may have helped to make for a swifter recovery. Crops had failed in certain years, and buildings had been burned or neglected, but replanting and the refurbishment of simple wooden buildings was more straightforward than rebuilding a great city or an urban landscape. With effort rough stone could be relaid. Horse power, human muscle power, and the healing of three or four decades were the primary requirements, while the capital investment needed was relatively modest. The material expectations of the poor had never been great, even in the good times. Much of the effort to put things right was sourced locally: help, support or resources from outside were at best few and sporadic. In 1663 Charles II's list of officers identified over 5,000 impecunious former royalist officers in England: of those in Lancashire 91 per cent received nothing from the new king. The charitable interpretation was that he had little to hand out.[17]

There was almost certainly a general population loss in Lancashire during the 1640s and 1650s. Detailed statistical work is available only for certain areas, but research does tend to confirm an excess of deaths over births in Amounderness, for example, from 1640 for some time onwards. A similar excess of deaths also occurred in south-west Lancashire from a point in the 1640s through to the 1680s. South-east Lancashire was also affected, but to a lesser extent, during three of the decades in the same period. Nevertheless this phenomenon has proved difficult to quantify with precision, or even to place chronologically with exactitude. Moreover population decrease was fairly short-lived, and appears less significant when viewed within a wider context. The general trend in Lancashire's population had been inexorably upwards; one calculation is that in the century from 1563 to 1664 the population rose from a little over 82,000 to about 142,000, an increase in excess of 70 per cent. Such, indeed, was the growth of the population that some commentators have referred to a 'population crisis', an uncontrolled increase leading to instability and greater incidence of poverty. Lancashire's woes of the period 1642 to 1651 are thereby put into perspective. There is also great doubt as to which disease-related deaths should be classified as side-effects of war and which would have occurred anyway, irrespective of conflict.

Lonsdale and Leyland showed the lowest percentage population increase during the century up to 1670, although still in double figures. Moreover it may be argued that Lonsdale's relatively poor showing was due to the prevalence of sheep, mountain and moor rather than the impact of war. Curiously, however, claims have also been made that Furness actually benefited from the civil wars, with progress and prosperity beginning after 1661, when the lordship passed from the crown to George Duke of Albemarle, the former General Monk. Amounderness and Salford hundreds showed the biggest population increases in the century to 1670, that of the former more than doubling. The growth of towns such as Manchester, Bolton and Preston, as well as the early stirrings of economic development (and even change towards early forms of industrial production), certainly contributed. In an age when statistics were collected erratically, and when only heads of households were enumerated, we search in vain for more exact measures. Against such a backdrop it is difficult to argue that the civil wars, miserable and bloody though undoubtedly were, were more than a relatively short hiccup or dislocation in Lancashire's economic and demographic journey through the early modern era. The population was probably the same size in 1664 as it had been in 1642.[18]

Though wartime hardships had been severe Manchester quickly recovered its former status and went on developing economically. At the end of the seventeenth century Celia Fiennes found Manchester a land of plenty, 'a thriving place'. Taking plans and contemporary statements into account it appears incontrovertible that the town grew physically somewhat between 1650 and 1672, with larger increases in area thereafter. Trade and cloth manufacture doubtless played their parts, but general migration to towns and enclosure cannot be ruled out as contributory factors. The hearth tax of 1666 found 1,368 dwellings with three or more hearths. In the same year over 700 Mancunians were wealthy enough to be caught in the tax net, at least an indirect indication of the revival of the town. The post of beadle now attracted a fixed salary of 2s. per week 'and no more', the incentive to beat as many vagrants as possible being thereby, and probably unintentionally, reduced.

In 1660 the Restoration was apparently greeted with joy in Manchester. Almost 600 townsmen signed an oath of allegiance to Charles II, and those who disagreed kept quiet. Warden Heyrick – the one-time puritan preacher – discovered, or remembered with the benefit of hindsight, that, in fact, he had always supported the monarchy and liturgical worship. On 23 April 1661 soldiers loyal to the crown and former royalist officers heard him preach at the collegiate church, and it is said that in addition to bonfires and fireworks the conduit ran with wine. The restored prayer book and ordination by bishops were made mandatory. In 1662, however, Heyrick refused to subscribe to the Act of Uniformity. This was obviously going further than Heyrick was prepared to countenance: yet despite refusing to sign, he kept his job. This was, perhaps, a sign that intolerance of Protestant nonconformity was beginning to decline. Just a decade later under the Declaration of Indulgence Henry Newcome received the first licence issued here to preach in his own house. He soon extended this privilege to his barn.

Very few people were better off after the wars than they had been before, but there were notable exceptions. Mancunian Humphrey Chetham died an undeniably wealthy man in 1653. Significant bequests from his estate included £7,000 to endow the Chetham hospital and school, and more than £1,000 for the eponymous library which still contains manuscripts dating back to before the wars.[19]

Bolton, one of the towns worst hit by war, also made what seems to have been a surprisingly rapid recovery. A new school, planned as early as 1641, was actually built in 1655. Though former royalist properties had been sequestered, and some of Lord Derby's holdings had been purchased by Major-General Worsley, much had to be returned after the Restoration. By 1671 Bolton could be described as 'a fair well built town, with broad streets', which had 'a market on Mondays, which is very good for clothing and provisions, and is a place of great trade for fustians'. Poverty had not been banished, but the late war did not seem to cast a long shadow over the town or its economy. By the mid-1650s poor relief was being provided locally, and marriages appear to have been on the increase by 1657. Coal mines had attracted the unemployed, or under-employed, and outlying hamlets were now growing, with the addition of new cottages. Thirty years on, the civil wars had likely become the tales of old men.[20]

Lancaster, another town particularly badly ravaged by war, also recovered in time, although circumstantial evidence suggests that the process was much slower here. Some of the destroyed structures appear to have been replaced in a temporary manner fairly quickly. A new town hall, a wooden edifice atop stone columns, appeared in 1668. Nevertheless a plan of 1684 shows that the street layout of Lancaster was little altered from 1610 – and that there were actually fewer buildings at the later date. In the 1690s Celia Fiennes described the town as 'old and much decay'd', but some thoroughfares were more prosperous than others, and certain businesses were doing well, some of them through the newly developing trade with the Americas. It has been suggested that, in contrast to the rebuilding of Wigan and Preston, Lancaster remained for decades 'in large part a temporary town built in haste to replace the devastation' which had taken place. Even so we have to be cautious about apportioning all of Lancaster's misfortunes to the civil wars. Long before 1642 the town's relative position in the county had been in decline. Nor were the wars Lancaster's only limiting factor, as a great fire in 1698 undid much of the good work that had been done in the time since the wars.[21]

If Lancashire remained a relatively poor county for many years it was by no means insignificant politically. As early as 1650 the number of Lancashire MPs was fixed at twelve – as many as London and Cheshire, with seven and five respectively, put together – in terms of populations an entirely disproportionate total. Despite the blood-curdling sermons and apocalyptic visions of the 1640s the post-war period in Lancashire was no bloodbath of retribution either. Even for Catholics, identified by the most vitriolic of their enemies as the very spawn of Satan, the future was not completely bleak. Further penal sanctions against Catholicism were introduced, and there was no denying that for many life would be tough. Whether it was any worse than what went before is questionable. Although there were a few who died for their beliefs, 'martyrdom' remained highly exceptional. There were however a relatively few high-profile executions. One such, at Lancaster in 1646, saw the execution and dismemberment of Edward Bamber, Thomas Whitaker and John Woodcock, their limbs and entrails being afterwards, 'exposed upon the towers of the Castle'. Even in violent times this would have had considerable impact; but it was the exception rather than the rule. Catholics who kept quiet – or could even bring themselves to attend established churches occasionally, were extremely unlikely to suffer such horrors.

In demographic terms it is unlikely that the civil war period had any very serious impact upon the old religion in Lancashire. Post-war lists of recusants still show hundreds of persons living openly as Catholics within the county, and there were probably even greater numbers who practised the faith in secret, or led double lives. Isaac Ambrose, appointed vicar of Garstang in 1654, was surprised to discover that though he was the official minister there were four or five Catholic priests that had 'their constant residence' within the parish. His conclusion was that there were still 'multitudes of papists'.[22]

Interestingly research in recent decades suggests that perhaps four in ten of the Catholic gentry of the county had regained their estates by 1665. Additionally some property that did not come back to the original owners was purchased by other Catholics. Agents or trustee bodies could also hide *de facto* Catholic ownership or control of specific lands. Perhaps surprisingly the Leveller John Wildman was later identified as 'a manager of papists' interests' in the north of England. Major-General Worsley seized upon this as corruption in 1655. In some instances the children of Catholics appear to have been able to retain a proportion of an estate if they allowed themselves to be 'educated in the Protestant religion', but whether they converted was very much another matter. An interesting case in point were the children of William Blundell of Crosby, who, under the terms dictated by the committee at Manchester in August 1646, were allowed to retain a tenth, with a further tenth for the use of their mother Ann. The family was thus reduced to poverty by 1649 – along with much of the population – and was still labouring under sequestration in the early 1650s. William served time in prison. Nevertheless he still managed to buy back his estate in 1653, and the children remained Catholics. For non-Catholic royalists the number regaining their lands was proportionately greater, with more than three-quarters back in their old estates soon after the Restoration.[23]

The wily Colonel Richard Shuttleworth had made his peace with the new regime by 1662. When he died at Gawthorpe, seven years later, he was 82 years of age, and had outlived most of his family. This was quite an achievement for a man who had once been so prominent an enemy of royalism. His estates were passed on to his grandson, Richard. The Shuttleworths again became stout pillars of their community. Unlike some of the religious and political radicals who had come to power and prominence in the 1650s, moderate presbyterians, particularly elderly ones, could appear quite harmless. The rehabilitation of many of them began early, even as soon as 1651, and was virtually complete after Charles II took up his throne.

Like some roundheads who later decided they had not been supporters of parliament at all, there were also Catholic royalists under the Commonwealth who were quick to try and demonstrate that they were unacquainted with 'delinquency' – or strangely pacifist warriors. Nicholas Anderton of Lostock is an interesting case in point. Accused as a former royalist in arms, he protested that he had not fought in the skirmish at Westhoughton at all, having been at home in Wigan at the time. Far from picking a quarrel with parliament, he had attempted to make his peace in 1643. Witnesses were produced to corroborate his story and to claim that he had never been seen with anything more warlike than his stick. These testimonies, from his daughter and his servant, might or might not have been credible; his own picture of himself as an unfortunate buffoon was, however, believed.[24] Interestingly Charles the

The Derby Chapel, also known as the 'Memorial' or 'Warriors Chapel', Ormskirk parish church. Endowed as a Chantry chapel about 1500 the Derby Chapel contains several effigies. The vault below contains the mortal remains of many of the earls, included those of James, the seventh earl, beheaded in 1651.

PHOTOGRAPH: AUTHOR

Detail of the 'Eagle and Child' crest of the Derby family on the font at Ormskirk parish church. The font was presented by Charlotte, Lady Derby, widow of the Seventh Earl in 1661 – it also bears the cipher of King Charles II.

PHOTOGRAPH: AUTHOR

eighth Earl of Derby was not left completely bereft by the situation after the execution of his father. Some of the Derby lands were sold by him, despite the technicality of a long-standing disinheritance, and the confiscation of so much by parliament.

Charlotte Countess of Derby, the defender of Lathom, was admitted to 'compound' for her estates in October 1653, although she had to pay a particularly large fine to the Liverpool mercer, Robert Massey, who had been held prisoner on the Isle of Man. She claimed to be destitute, but appears to have lived well enough, and her daughters all made politic matches with wealthy families. Catherine married the Earl of Dorchester, a wealthy if desperately unhappy match. Mary wed Viscount Wentworth, and Amelia the Earl of Atholl. However, Charlotte fell out with her son, a dispute at least partly tied up with the fate of the family lands. Though Lady Derby died in 1664, Lathom House was completely rebuilt in the early eighteenth century according to the latest fashions, following designs of the celebrated architect Giacomo Leoni (1686–1746). The new house was no medieval fortress, but a gentleman's country house, spacious and with large windows. The civil wars and the perceived shabby treatment of Derby and his immediate descendents were not forgotten. According to Guizot de Witt an inscription was placed over the door which read:

> This was erected by James, earl of Derby, Lord of Man and the Isles, grandson of James, Earl of Derby, by Charlotte, daughter of Claude, Duke of Tremoille, who was beheaded at Bolton, October 15th, 1651, for strenuously adhering to Charles II, who refused a Bill unanimously passed by both Houses of Parliament, for restoring to the family the estates which he had lost by his loyalty to him.

CHAPTER FOURTEEN

Conclusion:
the civil wars in perspective

L ANCASHIRE can claim to have had an important, even unique, role in
the civil wars. Two of the factors which led up to the war – religious
division, and the fear of Irish Catholic invasion – were at their strongest in
the county. These notions also weighed heavily on the minds of the men
in London who made many of the fateful decisions. As the first county to
receive the commission of array, and also to have suffered the first named
fatality, it might even be reasonably claimed that the English civil wars
started in Lancashire. However, as one contemporary put it, it was extremely
difficult to tell 'in what Shire this Egge was layed'. Certainly the final
impetus to arms came from the centre: the king personally directed Lord
Derby to raise troops, and it was parliament which had directed local men
to call out the militia.

Parliament had stated that its primary reason for taking up arms was
the maintenance of religion; and the case of Lancashire supports this claim.
Whether individuals really believed that religion was the reason they fought
is a different question entirely, and one that we will probably be unable to
answer definitively. Many were doubtless genuine in their stated beliefs and
reasons for going to war. That some were not – and cynical in their adoption
of a religious pose – is occasionally glimpsed in the satire and propaganda of
the period. As one ditty about the Scots put it in 1646,

> Religion is made a covering
> For every wicked and Rebelious thing,
> Errors are hid heer on the right and left
> Rebelion, Idolitry, and Theft
> Plunders, and Rapins, Whordoms, Fornications,

Disimulations, Flateries, and Invasions,
By Time this Cloake is torn from off their Back
So their's discovered many a Knavish Knack.

Sir James Turner summed it up: it was 'hipocrits' who made the church a symbol of war and 'bloody broyles'. Interestingly Lord Derby applied precisely the same argument to parliament. They not only mocked the king, but mocked God, by 'pretending to fight his quarrel'.[1]

Religious concerns were certainly in many men's minds when they marched to war, and perhaps even when they actually pulled the trigger. Ian Gentles has suggested that religious motivations to fight took a number of different forms. Fear was certainly one of them: fear of Catholic domination or rampage; fear of what the enemy might impose in terms of prayer books or liturgy; fear that one's church – indeed, salvation – might be taken away, subverted or banned. Striving to do God's work was another: good works for the Catholics, fulfilling God's designs or prophesies for others. Revenge was also sometimes a motive that could be religiously inspired. Belief in heaven was one of the few defences against musket balls, and one which was apparent in fighting men both before and after the civil wars. Generals, often parliamentarian ones, frequently put forward the view that they were God's instruments. The flags of the combatants, especially the 'guidons' and 'standards' of the dragoons and horse, were covered in religious iconography: promises to uphold religion and to do God's bidding.

Group loyalty has been identified as a motivating factor for troops in modern war, and similar thoughts and feelings might well have existed among the seventeenth-century soldiery, though often couched in religious terms - the 'union' of the troops being blessed by God, or described as a 'gathered church' in the face of an impious enemy. Sometimes, when really moved, men felt the actual 'presence of God' with them and their comrades upon the battlefield. The parliamentarian battle cry 'God with us' was certainly heard in Lancashire, and doubtless was comforting in time of adversity. Anthony Fletcher has suggested religion was the prime motivation for the major-generals. Certainly in the North West Charles Worsley was apt to describe himself as moved by 'the spirit' and directed by the 'finger of God'. On 3 November 1655, for instance, he wrote from Manchester:

The sense of the worke, any my unworthynes and insufficiencie as to the right management of it, is my only present discouragement. Yet however this is the ground of my hope and comforth, that the Lord is able to

Cartoon from *Truths Discovery of a Black cloud in the North; Shewing some Anti Parliamentary, Inhumane, Cruell and Base Proceedings of the Scotch Army Against the Well Affected in the North of England, 1646.* The critical point is that religion is depicted as the cloak for actions such as persecution, rape and cruelty.

supply my wants, and will appeare in weake instruments for his glory, to the perfectinge of his work.[2]

Interestingly the popular 'explanations' advanced for the civil wars have tended to mirror the preoccupations of times in which they were put forward. Thus, it might be argued, the concept of a 'puritan revolution' was first formulated in the nineteenth century when concerns about revolution and religion were to the fore; social and econometric theories that talked about 'rising' and 'declining' gentry and 'class' in the twentieth century were linked to the growing intellectual influence of Marxism; the idea of the wars as British, in which Ireland and Scotland were crucial, can be seen as a reflection of a continuing debate about devolution and the integrity of the United Kingdom. Yet our seventeenth-century ancestors did not think in such compartmentalised terms. For most people religion was not just part of life, but suffused the whole of life. It was a way of behaving, a way of expressing oneself, and a badge of allegiance. Where religious feeling was strong it is therefore likely that all feeling was strong. As Anthony Fletcher once observed, religion 'penetrated the interstices of family, community and national life. Thus it almost always has to be at the centre of the historical story.'[3]

Clarendon the royalist commentator certainly saw religion as a mainspring of parliament's fighting spirit in all counties,

> though it must be confessed, that the public safety and liberty wrought very much with most, especially with the nobility and gentry who adhered to Parliament; yet it was principally the difference about religious matters that filled up the Parliament's armies, and put the resolution and valour into their soldiers, which carried them on in another manner than mercenary soldiers are carried on. Not that the matter of Bishops was the main thing ... But the generality of the people through the land (I say not all or everyone) who were then called Puritans, Prescians, religious persons, that used to talk of God, and heaven, and scripture, and holiness, and to follow sermons, and read books of devotion, and pray in their families, and spend the Lord's day in religious exercises, and plead for mortification and serious devotion and strict obedience to God, and speak against swearing, cursing, drunkenness, prophaneness, etc. I say, the main body of this sort of men, both preachers and people, adhered to Parliament.

This does not mean however that religious differences made war inevitable. Lancashire did have a unique part in the commencement of hostilities, and was divided by religious concerns in a way unparalleled elsewhere, but it would be quite wrong to see Lancastrians as having been intent on conflict. From the county there certainly came petitions warning of the danger of 'papists' and the Irish; there was a tangible air of nervousness, in which several real or imagined plots were uncovered; but there were also petitions urging accommodation between king and parliament. Many leading parliamentarians within the county refused to take the fatal step of taking up arms until threatened by force. For a long time some parliamentarians would continue to hope that Lord Derby would see the sense of their position, and perhaps even lead a united, moderate, parliamentarian Lancashire. Even among Manchester parliamentarian sympathisers of a 'puritan' disposition there were many who were not particularly keen to go to war.

Nor did Lord Derby react with unbridled, militaristic enthusiasm to the king's call to arms. Though loyal to the king throughout, Derby had as his first objective the holding together of his estates and dynasty. To do this effectively meant adopting a middle way. Though Protestant himself, there is little or no evidence that he sought to root out Catholicism; to do so, indeed, would have led to greater instability in the county and a potential diminution of family interests. He also took the Irish problem just across the water seriously, seeing it, at least in 1641 and 1642, as a threat in very much the same vein as did those who would soon become his enemies.[4]

While few Lancastrians actually wanted to fight in the early summer of 1642, widespread 'neutralism' of the sort that has been identified at certain points in other places would be a deeply inadequate way to describe the county situation. Many, if not most, harboured a residual loyalty to the king and status quo. When asked the vital question of allegiance on the moor outside their town in July 1642, most Prestonians answered that they supported the king, and quite possibly were surprised and insulted to have been asked, feeling their loyalty was being impugned. Similarly, asking the same question of those who were now taking up arms for 'king and parliament' would very probably have elicited the same answer. The problem for both sides, and most particularly for the Lancashire royalists, was to convert nascent sympathy into practical support, keep military resources in the county – and keep them paid for.

The Catholics, a major pool of potential strength, were a problematic issue. At first the king banned them from taking up arms – later he allowed them to join his colours, which added troops but handed the enemy a propaganda coup. None of this was easy. Recruiting efforts began in an old-fashioned way, with the call-out of the militia and the securing of the munition stores in the hundreds which had been formally established about half a century earlier. With no standing army and no significant private force to hand it is difficult to see how it could have been otherwise. Within a few weeks or months other avenues began to open up, most obviously with royalist noblemen recruiting and supporting their own companies or regiments outside the existing lieutenancy system. Some parliamentarian leaders were both deputy lieutenants and committee men, and the one seems to have merged into the other fairly rapidly. Several were also MPs with good connections to London. In the Lancashire of late 1642 the fighting soldiers were either militia men fulfilling time-honoured obligations, or volunteers. Conscription was formally recognised in 1643.

'Club men' certainly existed in Lancashire, but never in the sense of being an independent or 'third force'. In the Lancashire arena they were, rather, the poorly armed local levies on either side, often conscripted at short notice, and with little prospect of being paid or enjoying any other form of army infrastructure. Club men could be very useful, providing overwhelming numbers at a specific point. On the other hand, they were not likely to be able to stay in the field for more than a few days; they were not usually well trained, if at all; and, as their name suggested, commonly lacked firearms. Capable of providing an impressive and often unexpected show of numbers, club men could just as easily melt away back into the general population at the first alarm or minor reverse. Interestingly it is the club men who provide the most obvious explanation for the wildly inflated numbers which one side or the other claimed were facing them in the field at various junctures. As conscripts, the same club men might well also appear on both sides at different points in the war.

Looking at the map of Lancashire in January 1643 would have given the impression of a large royalist county with a beleaguered minority of roundheads with their backs to Manchester. This was misleading, for geographical predominance was not commensurate with strength. Lord Derby had raised perhaps three or four thousand men by this time, but the majority had left Lancashire to fight for the king in the national struggle, and with the troops had also gone many of the muskets that would be sorely needed at home. The Mancunians, by contrast, were constrained within a narrow compass, and had started the war with relatively small numbers of troops, but their men and treasure were reserved for their own defence. Until April 1643 the struggle was thus far more equal than we might imagine, with both sides striving primarily to capture enemy towns and supplies. It was also the case that, until at least mid-1643 if not later, the influence of outside conditions and resources was negligible.

The horrors of war seventeenth-century style, from a contemporary woodcut. Although property destruction, requisition and looting were commonplace in Lancashire, the deliberate slaughter of non-combatants was in fact rare.

From the flashpoint at Manchester the war spread gradually north, south, and west until most of Lancashire had seen fighting. If some of the early engagements were almost comical, with poorly trained troops panicking, and magnanimous victors sometimes more than generous with the neighbours they had defeated or captured, war was still a very serious business. Looting and requisitioning were widespread, and marches long and gruelling. Slowly but inexorably the casualties and destruction mounted. For parliament everything appeared to come good on 20 April 1643 with the crucial defeat of Lord Derby at Read Bridge and the departure of a number of leading royalists and seasoned troops from the county. The parliamentarians now had almost a year in which to wear down, constrain and besiege their enemy into submission, and by the end of this period their job was all but complete, with Lathom House the only conspicuous stronghold still resisting.

Terrible as the war soon became, it was not unlimited, and most of the protagonists continued to recognise and honour existing 'laws of war'. There were some examples of massacre, and occasional killings of captives – Irish Catholics being perhaps most at risk due to long-standing fears stoked further by the bloody Irish rebellion of 1641. Yet, like torture and rape, these were exceptions to the general rule. Very few women or children were killed deliberately, although many died by the indirect consequences of war. Civil war differs, of course, from conflicts between nation states: protagonists on both sides come from the same place, the same society. Thus, the recognition of laws of war was supported by the feeling that both sides were fighting ultimately for the preservation of existing norms and orders, that acts contrary to these rules undermined authority and the ability to maintain discipline among one's own troops, and that, in the end, the wars would be over and fighting men would once again become neighbours, contacts, trading partners, even friends. Arguably there was one episode, in the summer of 1648, when the laws of war did break down. The Scots may have regarded Lancashire as part of a 'foreign' nation and therefore fair game: or it may simply have been that the supply train was so poor that the soldiery had no choice but to steal or starve. In either instance this military phenomena soon had the effect of uniting the New Model and many Lancastrians very efficiently. The course of war itself thus adjusted politics to circumstance as it unravelled.

Perhaps surprisingly plunder, requisitioning and repeated taxation turned out to be among the worst aspects of the war for most of the people of Lancashire in the long run. Once ready money, luxuries and 'spare' horses were gone it was fodder, crops and cattle that began to disappear. Once seed and breeding animals were denuded, and with many young men away under arms, the vicious cycle of hunger and disease was bound to begin. Though Lancashire's woes may never have been as deep as those experienced in parts of Thirty Years War Europe, there are obvious parallels in its burning towns and plagues. Arguably Lancashire suffered rather more than many parts of England. The similarity to Europe may extend further. In the case of Denmark, for example, it has been suggested that the Thirty Years War marked a point on the progression from a 'feudal' financial organisation to a tax-based state. There are at least echoes of this movement in Lancashire – with the rise of the excise and contributions to armies in other parts of the kingdom, and the decline in the influence of local nobles. The case of the Netherlands also has some parallels, in its religious and financial problems, and in its powerful provincialism. Nowhere did it prove possible to fund wars entirely out of current revenues. Borrowing against the future, by promises, loans from noblemen and merchants, underpayments, and outright theft, was common across Europe, and certainly extended to that European fringe that was Lancashire.

It is sometimes said that wars are won by the side that makes the fewest mistakes. This appears a truism in the case of Lancashire during the period

1642 to 1644. The royalists failed to reduce Manchester when it seemed open for the taking; failed to collaborate with their allies across the Pennines (as Peter Newman has long since determined); failed to establish trust between Derby and other royalist generals; failed to establish lasting and reliable supplies; failed to establish a strategy to access Catholic support effectively. The parliamentarians mobilised poorly, got little or nothing from their friends in London, failed to impress their worth upon Thomas Fairfax, never became effective players in the Northern Association, and at times moved with glacial slowness. Their worst failure was arguably in not adhering to a clear leadership; going from lack of clarity, to leaders – good and bad – foisted from outside, and then back to multiple leadership. In sum, however, the royalist mistakes were greater than those of the parliamentarians who now looked much the more likely to come out on top.[5]

From about mid-1643 the Lancashire committee did also benefit from help from the centre in a way that was not matched by the king assisting local royalists. This was not, however, simply a case of parliament being richer or better organised fiscally. There is scant evidence, for example, of any net inflow of funds from London to Manchester or Preston. Money coming out of London was channelled by inefficient routes, and its appearance relied on middlemen who expected to take a profit. It was sometimes almost as if the Members expected that the war could be supported by a private finance initiative. Conversely parliament gathered taxes in Lancashire, such as the excise, which were highly unpopular and expected to flow to the centre. Parliament also demanded contributions from Lancashire to support armies fighting elsewhere in Britain, and this tended to balance out any financial help which was received. Where Lancashire parliamentarians did reap real identifiable rewards was when the navy, gunpowder or other resources could be diverted to its direct assistance during campaigns. Supplies of powder were thus sent to Manchester, and the navy helped cut off Liverpool and made it difficult for the royalists to establish a steady and reliable conduit from Ireland and elsewhere. Lancashire and Cheshire parliamentarian forces were similarly able to help each other from time to time, although this did not always run smoothly, particularly when money was involved.

If there is some evidence for a case that the Lancashire parliamentary committee maintained a rough equilibrium between incoming assistance and outgoing efforts, the demands of the king's national war effort remained almost entirely one-sided. The notion, once formed, that the national always took precedence over the local proved impossible to break. In Ronald Hutton's memorable phrase, the king 'drained Lancashire rather than supplied it'. After

Read Bridge in 1643 more of Lancashire's key royalist commanders and troops rallied to the queen and left the county virtually bereft of men and resources – leaving only a few garrisons, notably Lathom, to carry on the fight. It may not be overstating the case to suggest that from a Lancashire perspective loyalty to the king's cause meant essentially loyalty to the king's person, and willingness to rally upon command to the king's field army. Lord Derby was also highly significant, but his place depended to an important extent upon his relationship with the monarch. Until at least 1646 loyalty to the cause of 'king and parliament' remained somewhat more abstract, and certainly not vested in any one person. Largely it was expressed through the local forces, doing the vital job of protecting the county, as they saw it, in the time-honoured way. To this extent at least there was an element of 'court' and 'country' animating what happened in Lancashire – though it is difficult to demonstrate that this was motivated in any conscious way.

That throughout the war Lancashire royalist assistance for the king's main field army was significant, and that most Lancashire parliamentarian effort was put into Lancashire, is obvious from the generalised facts long since known about regiments and campaigns. Recently, however, there have been attempts to quantify this phenomenon. Gratton, for example, has followed the movements of as many Lancashire officers as possible. The result, perhaps predictably, is the discovery that most royalist officers spent most of their time outside the county, while most parliamentarians were in, or close to, Lancashire. In many ways Prince Rupert's Lancashire campaign of May and June 1644 was an aberration. For not only were the tables abruptly turned on the Lancashire parliamentarian colonels, but for the first time the war in Lancashire and the civil war were essentially one and the same thing. The king's strategy to raise the siege of York and bring the north back under control was now central to his war effort. At first it looked as though this would work. Liverpool fell and the bloody storm of Bolton appeared to have put back the clock on the Lancashire parliamentarians by two years. Royalists who had virtually given up hope and secreted themselves away re-emerged to take part in what looked like a victory ride. Marston Moor brought this dashing and violent procession to an abrupt halt, and although it could be argued that Rupert still had adequate resources left to make a stand in Lancashire, he did not. His lieutenants did fight at Ormskirk in August 1644, but this 'battle' was at best half-hearted, with the eyes of the royalist commanders and the Northern Horse focused more upon living to fight another day than administering a bloody nose to the enemy. With Marston Moor and the royalist command abandoning Lancashire, late 1644 and early

1645 were essentially a re-run of late 1643 and early 1644. Royalist strongholds were knocked out one by one, and the hard core of opposition was pushed back inexorably on Lathom.

Parliamentarian victory in the North was crucial to the outcome of the war as a whole for several reasons. It allowed Scots' intervention to the South without significant prejudice to their supply lines; it removed a major enemy power base; and allowed the Lancashire and Cheshire parliamentarians relatively free rein, with a degree of active mutual cooperation that previously had been impossible. Perhaps even more significantly, as Stuart Reid has pointed out, it extinguished what was arguably the king's key recruiting ground. Approximate statistical comparisons certainly support this contention, suggesting that while about a fifth of the royalist armies came from the West Country, more than a third were raised in the North. Cutting off this supply of human resources was a body blow to the royalist cause. The only factors of doubt now standing in the path of obvious defeat were the king's 'new armies': bankruptcy; plague; starvation; war weariness and bloody-mindedness.

By late 1645 parliament's main enemy in Lancashire was no longer the royalists, but the war itself. There was no longer any glittering purse to claim, but the winner would be the fighter who succeeded in slugging, and in standing, the longest. Perhaps fortunately Lathom surrendered just before parliament's resources were totally extinguished – but the paralysing wrangle over the spoils of Lathom, which Cheshire men appeared to have pocketed at the eleventh hour, was a serious crisis.

The Lancashire committee was remodelled in August 1645, and the Lancashire parliamentarian forces remodelled with it. Against the national picture, and the attention since attracted by the national 'New Model Army', this mini-revolution went virtually unnoticed. Interestingly, though Lancashire's troops may have become more professional, and perhaps even more politically aware after 1645, they never became infected with the independent zeal that characterised Fairfax's army. Lancashire's militia remained staunchly presbyterian and essentially moderate in character. Two factors seem to have had particular influence upon this stance. The first was that though Lancashire MPs were no longer colonels in the field, strong family connections were maintained between local politicians and the fighting troops. The second was the 'local' character of the force – soldiers could return to their homes and families, and to their communities, which were also their paymasters. Unlike the New Model the Lancashire militia was never displaced and anonymous, and its men were never characterised as 'mercenaries' without a stake in the society from which they were drawn. Unpaid Lancashire troops might well have felt the same acute sense of unfairness, and taken action to back their claims, but this was never translated into anything akin to the revolutionary demands of the Levellers.

Parliament's victory of 1646 did not solve many of the issues that had been fought over during the preceding four years. Moreover, little political change was apparent in Lancashire at the end of the first civil war, since the parliamentarian committee had effectively been in power since late 1644. It may, however, be argued that this apparent stasis is illusory, since, in addition to the reform of the committee which had attempted to separate its civil and military functions, religious change was sweeping. The motivation behind this change was not a will to fragment, but an attempt to unify. The presbyterian 'province' of Lancashire, first convened at Preston in February 1647, not only formalised the removal of bishops, but effectively placed control of the Church in the hands of local elders and the committee, which, at least at first, dominated the synod. Lancashire's reform was all the more significant because it predated that carried out in London. Committee and synod started as close, or closer, than committee and militia.

Though the Lancashire parliamentarian group effectively suppressed both royalists and Catholics they saw themselves as no extremists; being a pragmatic centre between the old ways and the Independents and religious schismatics which were now emerging. They were presbyterians, and enduring supporters of the League and Covenant, but in their own portrayal also an expression of consensus and moderation. As in 1642 the ruling parties had no driving desire to go to war with anybody, but this pacific intent was rudely overtaken by national events. The Second Civil War of 1648 presented Lancashire a dreadful dilemma: side with the New Model Army with all its implications of religious chaos and political agitation, or be raped, possibly literally, by a rampaging Scottish army allied to their old enemy. Put like this the relatively disciplined New Modellers appeared thoroughly acceptable, if not actually desirable. The committee abruptly knuckled down and their Lancashire troops supported Cromwell and Lambert in a brilliant campaign which shattered the Scots and their allies at a single blow.

The role of the Lancashire militia in the campaign of 1648 was neither the most important nor the most conspicuous. Nonetheless, the decision of the local parliamentarian–presbyterian regime to fight alongside the New Model was vital. With Ashton's men at his side the numerical odds against Cromwell were roughly 2:1. If the Lancashire committee had hung back, the position would have been 3:1 against. Had the local leadership sided with the Scots – as most had done under the Solemn League and Covenant – the numbers would have been worse still, at 5:1 or more, and Lancashire would have been conceived of as an hostile environment. These odds might well have been too great, even for a commander of the stature of Oliver Cromwell. Then again perhaps the decision of the Lancashire committee had less to do with the nation, and more to do with the fate of the county.

The divergence between the wider conflict and the 'local' is natural enough, given the way that armies were raised, and the fact that the London parliament itself was a centralised body. It is therefore understandable that modern commentators may think of the fighting in Lancashire between 1642 and 1651 as not one war, in three episodes, but two entirely different conflicts, which periodically overlapped in the same territory. These two wars were the national: in which the king's major field forces battled with the associations and the New Model; and the local, in which Lancashire's own ancient forces fought it out for their own county, for their families, estates and religion. What is less well appreciated is that contemporaries occasionally thought in exactly these same terms. So it was that the author of the *Discourse*, reflecting upon the Preston campaign, drew a clear distinction between what pertained to the 'nation', and what to the county. Thus it was that the 'expedition of Duke Hamilton' against 'the Nation' was seen as contrary to the wishes of 'the shire' – but fortunately for local parliamentarians Cromwell left them in 'good posture' as a result of his campaign; and Lancashire, 'was freed of this much feared evill. Though this was not any of the Lancashire Warrs yet was it acted in this County and God's goodness therein is to be kept in remembrance.'[6]

As in mid-1644, the war in Lancashire in mid-1648 and the civil wars were briefly the same thing. Victory at Preston decided the Second Civil War and led finally to the death of the king and the birth of the republic. Less obviously Cromwell's role over this vital period elevated him from one of the most politically active senior officers of the New Model to the man of the hour. His performance in the campaign of 1648 was arguably the watershed which made him at least a potential national leader, and ultimately monarch material. Indeed, not only did Major-General Worsley refer to him as 'highnesse', but Cromwell was offered the crown by a desperate parliament in 1657.

Though Lancashire was much less intimately involved in the governmental experiments of 1648 to 1651 than London, the local scene was far from tranquil. New-fangled ideas spread out from the centre, and many of Lancashire's parliamentarian 'old guard' were replaced. A combination of famine, resistance to taxation, and an undercurrent of royalist sympathy led to disturbances in the central and southern parts of the county. In July 1649 there were even attempts to proclaim Charles II as king: that this could have happened in old royalist Wigan should have come as no great surprise – but the same trick was also tried in Manchester. This should have given a clear indication that Mancunian radicalism was not dead, and that dissatisfaction with the centre was running high. As had been the case throughout 'God's War', it was 'pulpit incendiaries' who were held to be the prime culprits in these new waves of unrest.

By 1651 the republicans had truly discovered that power brought with it unenviable responsibility. In what we might regard as a precursor of the Orwellian paradox in *Animal Farm*, the pigs had become the farmers; or, at the very least, the rebels had become the tax farmers. Some presbyterians now found that they had common cause with royalists: radical preachers, who had spoken against the Catholic and the king, now preached against the new authority, and sometimes even against too much freedom in religion. If there had been much stomach left for war among its potential enemies the Commonwealth experiment might have been ended with the Worcester campaign, and the local rule of the committee concluded with the triumphant return of the Earl of Derby to Lancashire. Worcester, like Preston, however was a punctuation mark of history which turned the tide again in favour of parliament – and perhaps even more importantly, was a 'crowning mercy' for Oliver Cromwell. The road was open to the rule of the major-generals and to the Protectorate. God had won his war.

If men should say they took up arms for anything but religion, they might be beaten out of it by reason; out of that they never can, for they will not believe you whatever you say. The very Arcanum of pretending religion in all wars is that something may be found out in which all men may have interest. In this the groom has as much interest as the lord. Were it for land, one has one thousand acres, and the other but one; he would not venture so far as he that has a thousand. But religion is equal to both.

John Selden 1584–1654

County forces abstracted from the Certificate of the Musters For the County of Lancaster in Annon Dom, 1639

Trained men

	Captain	Shot	Corsletts	Lances	Light horse
Derby hundred	Unspecified	70	30	7	24
Salford	Henry Byrom	70	30	6	14
Leyland	Robert Charnocke	70	30	3	12
Blackburn	Roger Nowell	70	30	4	11
Amounderness	William Farington	70	30	3	7
Lonsdale	George Dodding	70	30	2	9

Plus three 'Petronells' one each from Derby, Salford and Lonsdale Hundreds

Other officers: Captain of lances, Richard Shuttleworth; Captain of light horse, John Atherton; Provost marshal, Henry Dattine.

Untrained

		Muskets	Corsletts	Bills	Pioneers
Derby hundred	1,995	346	133	130	1,346
Salford	1,224	242	110	80	792
Leyland	669	104	46	30	489
Blackburn	1,214	129	73	62	950
Amounderness	1,186	165	63	60	898
Lonsdale	1,112	137	56	51	868

Mis-totalled in the original: actual totals 705 'trained', 7,400 'untrained'

8,105 'other ranks' plus officers.

(Gratton, citing LRO DDn 64, suggests that the Lancashire trained band strength in 1642 was 600 foot, 109 horse, and an 'untrained reserve' of 7,000, figures close to the above)

Information taken from MCA L1/40/2.

Membership of Lancashire commissions, committees and councils, 1642–1645

Lancashire royalist Commissioners of Array, June 1642

Name	Hundred of residence
James, Lord Strange	West Derby
Richard, Lord Molyneux	West Derby
Sir Gilbert Houghton	Leyland
Sir George Booth	(Cheshire)
Sir Edward Mosley	Salford
Sir Robert Bindloss	Lonsdale
Sir Alexander Radcliffe	Salford
Sir John Girlington	Lonsdale
Francis Leigh	(Cheshire)
Ralph Standish	West Derby
William Norris	West Derby
Richard Sherburn	Amounderness
Peter Bold	West Derby
Roger Kirkby	Lonsdale
Robert Holt	Salford
Gilbert Middleton	Lonsdale
Thomas Tyldesley	Amounderness
William Farington	Leyland
Thomas Preston	Lonsdale
John Atherton	West Derby
Edmund Assheton	Salford
John Fleetwood	Leyland
Thomas Prestwich	Salford
Alexander Rigby de Burgh	Amounderness
Roger Nowell	Blackburn

| John Greenhalgh | Salford |
| Edward Rawstorne | Salford |

Based on the table given in J.M. Gratton, *The Parliamentarian and Royalist War Effort in Lancashire*, unpublished Ph.D. thesis, Manchester, 1998, p.136.

It is notable that the vast majority of these gentlemen were normally resident south of the Ribble. While two appear to have lived normally in Cheshire, there are none from other adjoining counties. The Hundreds of West Derby and Salford are particularly prominent in the list, whilst Blackburn is remarkably under represented. The commissioners included obvious choices, such as Lords Strange (Derby) and Molyneux, Sir John Girlington and Gilbert Houghton. Also listed were at least one man with puritan sympathies, as well as Peter Bold, who was only 15. Two of the named commissioners for the king, Sir George Booth and Robert Bindloss, later sided with parliament. Booth thus has the unique distinction of appearing as both a commissioner for the king and a member of the parliamentarian committee.

The parliamentarian county committee meeting, 4 July 1642

Ralph Ashton (MP)

Alexander Rigby (MP)

Richard Shuttleworth (MP)

Sir George Booth

Sir Thomas Stanley

Thomas Holcroft (or Howcroft)

Richard Holland

Nicholas Starkie

As given in *A True and Perfect Diurnall of the Chiefe Passages in Lancashire from the 3 July to the 9. Sent to five Shopkeepers in London*, 9 July 1642.

It would seem that John Moore MP, named by parliament as an original member of the committee, was elsewhere at this time. Interestingly the *True and Perfect Diurnall* speaks of Ashton, Rigby, Shuttleworth, 'and the gentlemen that were with them' at this date. The clear suggestion is that initially at least the Lancashire MPs working on parliament's behalf were regarded a 'committee' of the London parliament whom others assisted. Later anywhere between 12 and 21 persons serving on the committee would be identified.

Royalist 'Council' at Preston and county finance collectors

As given in *Orders Concluded by the Lord Strange* 29 December 1642. *Orders Concluded* is a parliamentarian publication, but is probably reasonably accurate since it appears that Lord Derby's orders were made public with the intention of achieving wide compliance with the measures designed to support the royalist war effort. The royalist 'Council' at

Preston might have become more significant, were it not for the subsequent fall of the town which reduced the definition of 'permanent' to a few weeks. In mid-1644 royalist governance would be based on Liverpool – but again this would be but short-lived.

The permanent 'certaine Counsell' at Preston

Sir John Girlington

Adam Morte (mayor of Preston)

James Anderton

Roger Kirkby

The royalist 'Council' could be assisted by Sir Gilbert Hoghton; Thomas Clifton; William Farington; John Fleetwood or any of the Commissioners of Array as required. The idea of a sitting council in Preston was of course abruptly terminated by the fall of the town in early 1643.

Royalist 'Collectors' for the Lancashire hundreds

Lonsdale:	Sir John Girlington; Roger Kirkby
Amounderness:	Adam Morte; Alexander Rigby of Burgh
Leyland:	William Farington; John Fleetwood
West Derby:	Henry Ogle; John Bretherton; Robert Mercer
Salford:	Robert Holt; Francis Sherrington
Blackburn:	John Talbot; Radcliffe Ashton

The membership of the parliamentarian Lancashire committee following the reform of 1645

Sir Ralph Ashton

Sir Robert Binlosse

Richard Hoghton

Ralph Ashton

Richard Shuttleworth

John Moore

Alexander Rigby

William Ashurst

Gilbert Ireland

Peter Egerton

Chistopher Banister

John Bradshawe

George Dodding

John Starkie

Edward Butterworth

Thomas Fell

Rowland Hunt

Richard Howarth

James Ashton of Chaderton

Edward Rigby

Thomas Birch

Alexander Rigby the younger

Nicholas Rigby of Horrock

Richard Ashton

Nicholas Cunliff

Henry Fleetwood

Robert Cunliff

William Knipe

As given in the *House of Commons Journal*, 29 August 1645.

APPENDIX III

Extracts from Manchester's 'Resolution Against the Lord Strange', 12 July 1642

'Such are the severall distempers and distractions of this Kingdome, that former ages could hardly parallel the like. Every day produces heavy newes, and sad novelties of warres, and rumours of wars, proceeding from the Malignant Party of this Kingdome, such as are open and protest enemies to the peace of great Brittaine, and such (I am sure) as beare no good will to sion nor to the tranquility of Jerusalem. What hainous, and never the like heard of insolencies they have already acted ? what impudent affronts they have offered the kings Majestie, and his good government ? what horrid plots and hideous conspiracies they have contrived and attempted, both by Forraigne invasion and domestick insurrection, the history of these times doth sufficiently testifie ...

Upon the fourth day of this instant month of July there was a skirmish between the Lord Strange and the Inhabitants of Manchester in Lancashire; the occasion whereof was ... through Lord Strange's Resolution to take away their Magazine by force, having received for that purpose many forces from Yorke. Tis very strange, if this be true; I wish it may be false; if it be not, I am certaine it is an ill omento the peace of England, and doth prognosticate no good tidings to the City of London. If this be the beginning of Civill Warre, God knowes (and no mortall but he) when the ending will be: When that dreadfull time is once come (as God forbid it ever should) many a weake wife will bee husbandlesse, and many a poore childe fatherless: then will be mourning and lamentation in our Cities and Countries, many Rachels mourning for their children, because they are not: Many thousands will then lose their lives before this Kingdome be agine settled in peace.

A Civill Warre will teare in pieces our flourishing Kingdome, be a meanes for invasion of a forraigne foe, exposing us to the fury and derision of our enemies, to the pitty and deploration of our friends. *Bellum Dei flagellum*, warre is the scourge of God ...'

Printed in London, for A. Coe. From an original in the Harris Library, Preston.

Extracts from 'A True and Faithfull Relation of the Besieging of the Towne of Manchester in Lancashire, upon Saturday 24 of September. Together with the Manner of the Severall Skirmishes and Passages Betwixt the Earle of Derby the Besieger with his 4500 Men, and the Soldiers of the Town, being only 1000 or Thereabout' (1642)

'The Towne of Manchester having some malignants in it, and multitude of Papistes neere unto it, and being reputed a religious and rich towne, hath been much envied and often threatened by the Popish and Malignant partie, and therefore the Townes-men being incouraged first by some Justices of the Peace, afterwards by the Ordinance for the Militia, did in a peaceable manner exercise and traine up their youth in feates of armes, whereby sundry of them became skillfull musquetiers and active pikemen, and afterwards when the Lord Strange began to declare his opposition to the Lords and Commons in Parliament by raising of forces, and uttering divers menaces and threats against us and others that refuse to join with him, (which were farre the greater part of all Salford hundred) Mr Holland of Denton, Master Egerton of Shagh, Mr Eride of Denton, Deputie Lieutenants by the Ordinance of Parliament, did advise and consult with the Towne what was fittest to be done for the safetie of the Towne and Country adjacent, the result of which consultation was to provide for their own safety by securing the Towne, to encourage and assist them in which service, God by his providence had a quarter of a yeere before sent a German engineer amongst them, to whose skill, industry, faithfulnesse and valour, we owe (under God) much of our late preservation. He was often solicited by letters, messengers, and promises of great preferment and rewards, to serve the Lord Strange, but being unwilling to serve against the Parliament, he accepted of farre lesse encouragement from us, and he gave directions for the chaining up and fortifying the severall ends of the Towne, which was begun with diligence, but found opposition from divers of the malignant party, which threatened to hinder the setting downe of the stoopes. But God by his providence so disposed, that on 13 September, the Souldiers in Cheshire, under the Command of Sir Edward Fitton and Master leigh of Adlington, did plunder, pillage, and disarme his Majesties loyall, Protestant subjects, even of such armes as they had provided for the necessary defence of their own houses, which so awakened and affrighted the countrey, that many hundred men were suddenly up in armes in the Town of Manchester, which gave opportunity and facility for the setting downe of the stoopes, and the perfecting of the fortifications, which were not finish till about a day before his Lordship came against the Towne. Though we had no certain notice of the time of his coming, on Saturday night certain intelligence came to the Towne, that great forces were coming from Warrington against it, conducted by the Lord Strange, and (as we hear) by the Lord Molineux, Master Sheriffe, Sir Gilbert Haughton, Sir Alexander Radcliffe, Sir Gilbert Gerrard, Master Tildisley, Master Standish of Standish, Master Prestwich, Master Windebanke, Sergeant Major Danvars, Sergeant Major Sanders, Master Downes of Wardley, Master Townly of Townely, Master Ashton of Penkett, junior, Master Ogle, Master Byrom of Birom, Master Nowell of Read, Master Standish of Duxburie his eldest sonne, Master Chernock, Master Farington of Merthen, Master Holt of Ashurst, Master Rosterne of Newhall, junior, Mr Tarbuck of Tarbuck, Mr Montague with many others, which assisted with men and munition ...

... But his requests were not granted: his threats were not feared: about twelve of the clock he began to play with his cannon shot upon the Deans gate and Salford Bridge; the bullets that were found weighed between foure and six pounds weight. This afternoon the fight was hot on both sides, most of our men constantly charging and discharging, to the great admiration and terror of the enemies. The fight was first begun by Lord Strange his forces, which were in and about an house of Sir Edward Mosleys called the Lodge, where they planted some of their ordnance; and at the same time were seconded by an assault they made on Salford Bridge, they have possessed themselves of the towne of Salford, which adjoyneth to Manchester, save only the water betwixt, but did not joyne with them in a common defence. But God so ordered the matter, that the cannons plaid in vain, and therefore they assaid to enter the Towne, and to beat our men from their works, which being not able to doe, they sent some of their souldiers to fire two barnes and eight or ten dwelling houses about twelve roods from our Workes, which being effected, the enemies with a great shouting ("the towne is our owne, the towne is our owne") renued their assault, but by their valour and courage of Captain Bradshaw and his souldiers were beaten back, and many of them slaine. The wind at first blew the flame and smoke into the faces of our Souldiers, to their great annoyance and the endangering of the Towne. But God that rides on the wings of the wind did very seasonably turn the wind till the rage of the fire was abated. Those forces that were in Salford endeavoured the bridge, where they found so hot entertainement at the hands of Captain Rosworme, the German engineere before spoken of, and his Souldiers, that they were forced to retreat with the losse of some men; but having possessed themselves of an house at the foot of the Bridge, they continued shooting all night at our men. In this dayes fight, blessed be God, we lost not one man. On Tuesday morning a souldier was taken being mortally wounded, which confessed that he was one of the seven which set the barne on fire; he lived but a day after his apprehension. This day there was an assault made at the other ends of the towne, especially at the Market Street-lane end, but were valiantly resisted by Captain Radcliffe and his company. Our men likewise sallied out, took divers prisoners, slew and put to flight divers that were that were stragling in the fields. About five of the clock his Lordship sounded for a parley, and sent a message in writing, which was as followeth: "In obedience to his Majesties commands, I have drawne some forces hither, with no intention of prejudice to your Town or any person in it, to require your readie obedience to his Majestie in yielding yourselves dutifully and cheerfully into his protection; which I once more (so great is the value I sett upon the effusion of one drop of my countreys bloud) sommon you to, under this assurance that no mans person or goods shall be harmed, as you give up your armes to be disposed of by me, according to his Majesties commands.

But if you shall yet continue obstinate in your disobedience, and resolve to stand it out, I will in that way proceed with all honour, by offering you a safe convoy of your women and children out of the Towne, so as it be done immediately. – I Derby" The gentlemen desired ten of the clock next day to give their answer; he granted till seven. They promised mutually that all acts of hostility should cease during that time, which was carefully performed on our side, and by meanes of thereof our Souldiers being much wearied with watching three dayes and three nights before, got comfortable refreshing. But that very same night the Enemie was very busie plundering and pillaging many houses about the Towne, to their great prejudice, if not utter undoing, and slew two of our neighbours of Boulton, which were coming peaceably with about 150 more to assist the Towne, and planted two ordnances in Salford, from which they were beate the next day by musket shot from the church-yard ...

... Some few houres after., the Lord Strange sent Sir John Mounson to mediate, who said his Honour would be content with part of the armes; the Gentlemen referred it to the Souldiers, who all resolutely answered that they would not give him a yard of match, but would maintain their cause and armes to the last drop of bloud. After this message was returned, his Ordnance played upon the towne again, but did no harme, save onely that they killed one that stood gazing on the top of a stile. Thursday, Captaine Standish was slaine by a bullet in Salford, who (as we heare) was reproaching his Souldiers because they would not fall on. Vpon his death his Souldiers fled, and other Souldiers by scores, yea by hundreds, daily fled away from the Lord Strange. There were slaine of his side, as we heare, 100 or 200, and some commanders of note, three whereof were buried at Didsbury, upon Thursday. We lost but foure men, two by accident, two by the Enemie. Friday was little done, onely the Lord continued playing upon the Towne with the Ordnance and musket shot from Salford and the Lodge, and cast up a trench before the end of the Deanes gate, as if he intended a long siege. The Ordnance did make holes in divers houses and battered downe a piece of chimney, but did little harme. This night his cannons were removed ...'

Reprinted in *Ormerod Tracts Relating to Military Proceedings in Lancashire*, Chetham Society, Manchester, 1844.

APPENDIX V

The Battle at Whalley (Read Bridge), from 'A True Relation
of a Great and Wonderfull Victory Obtained by Captain
Ashton and the Parliaments forces Against the Earl of Derby
at Whalley in Lancashire', by 'EF', dated Padiham 24 April,
1643

'We marched with our horse towards Whalley, where we tooke a man and 2 geldings of Mr Lathams the great Papist, and retreated to Read bank, here we discovered above 150 horse to follow us, and when our foot was come thither to us, our horse retreated more, our foot advanced close under a wall, only myself stood and faced the enemy: I made as though I fled, they pursued me, when I knew they were in the command of our men, I advanced again and shot off my pistol (being the signe for our foot); whereupon our men discharged with a great showt; the enemies horse fled in great disorder, we wounded many, took forty prisoners, some horse and 60 musquets, our firemen pursued them to Whalley, where the earl of Derby and the rest were in the Abbey, much ado we had to keep our souldiers back, the enemy(who were ten for one of us) discharged his Cannon 5 times, but hurt not a man of us, (blessed be our good God) he drew into a body, we being out of order ran under hedges, played upon them with our muskets, and routed their foot, which fled over the water, their horse still facing us, our men pursued them to Langho Green, where Captain Ashton and myself with much ado caused our first men to stay until more came up and pursued them through Salisbury Park, and to Ribchester, and most of their great ones had some touch, or narrow escape as they themselves report. And having thus driven them out of the Hundred, we retreated to Padiham.'

Prince Rupert's march into Lancashire, May and June 1644

'After 10 daies march by reason of the roughness of the wayes, and weather wee came to Stopford [Stockport], a large village in the confines of Lancashire Mannour with the enemy without fortificacions, saveing a river with high bancks and a bridge devideing Cheshire from Lancashire, there the Prince intended to quarter that night, which after a little dispute from hedges and ditches, upon an universall assaulte was abandoned by the enemy, who fled towards Manchester some 6 myles distant, and by reason the sunn was downe, the night made way to theyr escape, though they were pursued a great way, and as was beleived noe man lost of eyther side; the goods of the towne was the souldiers rewarde. Upon the 28th of May the army marched towards Bolton, a large country towne in Lancashire, some 16 myles from Stopford [Stockport] as wee marched, mann'd likewise with 4,000 meen (as was informed) there the Prince intended to quarter that night, onely gates ang highways fortifyed lightly, the rayne was some immoderate that it cost an howre or two dispute, but being impetuously stormed it was taken with fall of 1,000 men of the enemy in the streetes and feilds, above 20 cullors, 600 prisoners, 50 officers, 20 barrells of powder, match and armes a great quantity; the towne [was the] souldiers rewarde.

As wee lay in the country about Bolton Generall Goreing came with his northerne army, partely from Marques of New Castle, partely from Newark, consistinge of 5,000 horss and 800 foote, not soe well appointed as was expected, with a great drove of cattle out of the enemyes quarters as they march. All this while great numbers of horss and foote resorted to the Prince, brought in by the Earle of Derby his meanes and Sir Thomas Tinsley, but unarmed most of them. Wigan a large town some 20 myles from Bolton received the Prince and his army with great tokens of joy, the streetes being strowed with rushes, flowers and boughs of trees.

Wee pitched before Liverpoole with our whole army, having beleaguered it with our horss the day before; it had mudd walls with barrs and gates, 14 peeces of ordnance, 1,000 souldiers (as was supposed); the matter disputed very hotly untill the tenth day of June with muskett and great shott without measure of the towne and from the shipps, upon which day our line approached within a coites cast of the gate where our great shott had almost filled the ditch with the ruines of the sod wall, and aboute noone a furious assaulte was made by our menn where a terrible fight was on both sides above the space of an houre uppon the workes, the enemy resolute, ours not seconded reatreated with some loss. The enemy whether dispayreing of releif, or of theyr owne strength against soe great power at Midnight they shipped themselves the chiefe of theyr menn and goods and left 12 collours on the workes, hoysted sayles, and road within halfe a league of the towne. Which Collonell Tillyer perceivinge haveinge the Guarde next the sea, supposeinge the enemy to bee gone, entred the towne with little or noe resistance, found about 400 of the meaner sorte of menn, wherof most were killed some had quarter ...'

Described in the Carte manuscript (x, 664), and reproduced in *Transactions of the Royal Historical Society*, London, 1898, pp. 69–71.

APPENDIX VII

Pay lists

Daily pay list published for Lord Derby's royalist forces raised in, and supported by, the county of Lancashire, 10 December 1642.

Infantry	
Captain of Foot	10s.
Lieutenant	4s.
Antient [Ensign]	3s.
Sergeant	28d.
Drummer	15d.
Corporal	12d.
Common Soldier	9d.
Cavalry	
Captain of Horse	15s.
Lieutenant	8s.
Cornet	6s.
Trumpeter	5s.
Corporal	4s.
Horseman	2s. 6d.
Dragoons	
Captain of Dragoons	12s.
Lieutenant	6s.
Cornet	4s.
Sergeant	3s.
Corporal	2s.
Dragoon	1s. 6d.
Supernumeraries	
Commissary	5s.
Kettle Drummer	2s.

Pay of royalist cavalry, as set by the 'Councell of warre at Oxford' 13 October 1643, presided over by the king, Prince Rupert, Lords Percy and Byron and others of the royalist command.

'It was then ordered that the Queen's Regiment of Horse, the Prince of Wales', Prince Rupert's, Prince Maurice's, the Lord Wilmott's, the Lord Percy's, and Sir Arthur Aston's regiment of Horse, Prince Rupert's Guard, the Horses allowed to all the Officers Generall of Horse and foote should be constantly payd out of the weekly loan contributed of £1,400 weekly of Oxfordshire and £1,000 out of Berkshire according to the pay hereafter exprest in which manner likewise all other Regiments of horse in other counties are to receive pay and noe more.

To every Colonel, Lieutenant Colonel, Sergeant Major and Captain of horse as captayne	xv *s.*
To every Lieutenant	xi *s.*
To every Cornett	vii *s.*
To every Quartermaster	v *s.*
To every Corporall	iii *s.*
To every Trumpet, Chyrurgeon and Smith each	ii *s.*
For every horse allowed to the officers Generall of horse and foote of the Army each per weeke	xii *s.*'

Extracted from *A Brief Collection of the Heads of Many Memorable Observations in the Practice of Military Discipline, 1643*, National Army Museum 7806–9.

This statement is relevant to Lancashire for a number of reasons. It directly includes not only many of Rupert's cavalry who fought in the county in 1644, but also contains the general direction that 'all Regiments of horse in other counties' are subject to these figures as a maximum. The impression is that the royalists in the main field army were paid somewhat less than their parliamentarian equivalents in the New Model, but as well as, or better than, many local forces.

Pay of parliamentarian troops in the New Model Army.

	Foot soldier	*Dragoon*	*Horse trooper*
1645	8*d.*	1*s.* 6*d.*	2*s.*
1649	9*d.*–10*d.*	1*s.* 9*d.*	2*s.* 3*d.*
1651	10*d.*	2*s.*	2*s.* 6*d.*
1655	8*d.*–9*d.*	1*s.* 8*d.*	2*s.* 3*d.*

Extracted from C.H. Firth, *Cromwell's Army* (1962 edn), pp. 182–207.

Firth explained these changes over time essentially in terms of reaction to the cost of living, as for example the price of wheat, which fluctuated up and down between 21*s.*

and 67s. a quarter over the period between 1645 and 1655. At some periods officers agreed to go on half pay, trusting that these arrears – as well as others accrued by all other ranks – would be paid later.

Daily pay of Parliament's Northern Association army

Foot	
Colonel	8s.
Lt Colonel	7s.
Major	6s. 6d.
Captain	5s.
Captain-Lieutenant	3s. 6d.
Lieutenant	3s.
Ensign	2s. 4d.
Quarter Master	3s. 6d.
Drum Major or Sergeant	9d.
Drummer, Corporal, or Gentleman at Arms	7d.
Soldier	6d.
Horse	
Colonel	9s.
Major	8s. 6d
Captain	8s.
Captain-Lieutenant	7s.
Lieutenant	6s.
Cornet	5s.
Quartermaster	4s.
Trumpeter, Corporal, Chyrurgeons mate	1s. 8d.
Trooper (mounted)	1s. 6d.
Trooper (unmounted)	9d.

Extracted from General Lambert's list, York Minster Library Mss BB 53.

Figures given assume that soldiers had to find their own quarters: reductions would apply where accommodation was supplied.

Pay of the infantry of the Lancashire militia in the service of parliament, August–September 1648.

Captain	7s. 6d.	per day
Lieutenant	4s.	per day
Ensigne	3s.	per day
Sergeant	1s. 6d.	per day
Drummer	1s.	per day
Corporal	1s.	per day
Private soldier	8d.	per day

According to Captain Samuel Birch, in HMC Fourteenth Report, Appendix, Part II, *The Manuscripts of the Duke of Portland*, Welbeck Abbey, Vol. III, p176.

Pay required for the expansion of the army of parliament by four regiments of foot, for three months, 1651

Army Estimate, &c.

Sir *Henry Vane* reports from the Council of State,

An Estimate of the Pay of Four thousand Men, with complete Officers, for three Months; *viz.*

	£.	s.	d.
The Pay of Four thousand private Soldiers of Foot for Twenty-eight Days, according to the present Establishment for Pay for the Field Forces, at 10 d. per diem	4,666	13	4
Which for Three Months, will be	14,000	—	—
The said Four thousand Men being made Four Regiments, with complete Officers, the Pay of the said Officers, for One Month, is	1,550	5	4
Which, for Three Months, will be	4,650	16	—
The Whole, both Officers, and Soldiers, for One Month, will be	6,216	18	8
Which, for Three Months, will be	18,650	16	—
Incident Charges of the said Forces, by Estimate	1,500	—	—
In all	20,150	16	—

From the *House of Commons Journal*, vol. 6, 5 August 1651 pp. 615–17.

'The Pay Allowed To the Parliaments Army'.

The pay of a regiment of foot

Colonel (as Colonel)	£1	10s.
Leiutenant Col. (as Leiut. Col.)		15s.
Sergeant Major, (as Major)		9s.
Quarter Master		5s.
Provost Marshal		5s.
Carriage Master		3s.
Preacher,		8s.
Chirurgion		4s.
2 Mates, each		2s. 6d.
Captain (since but 8s.)		15s.
Lieutenant		4s.
Ensign		3s.
Sergeants, each		1s. 6d., sometimes 1s. 8d.
Drum Major		1s. 6d.
Drum		1s.
Corporal		1s.
Souldiers		8d., since 10d. and now 9d., each

Dragoons paid as infantry except that 1s. is allowed per horse for officers and non commissioned officers and soldiers are paid 1s. 6d.

Extracts from William Barriffe, *Militarie Discipline: or The Young Artillery-Man*, 1661.

The depredations inflicted by the Scots on north Lancashire during the Second Civil War, 1648

'We spare to speak the worst of them, lest we should forfeit that credence which you have towards us, and not be believed, but assure yourselves; they by their daily incursions into our poor country, between this and their quarters, have left nothing in all the world that is portable.

In divers places some whole families have not left them wherewith to subsist a day, but are glad to come hither for meer subsistence. They have taken forth of divers families all, the very racken crocks and pot hooks; they have driven away all the beasts, sheep, and horses, in divers townships, all, without redemption, save some poor milch kine. They tell the people they must have their houses too, and we verily believe it must be so, because Duke Hamilton hath told them it should be so. Their usage of some women is extreamly abominable, and of the men very barbarous, wherein we apprehend nevertheless something of God's justice towards very many, who have abundantly desired and rejoiced at their advance hither: old extream cavaliers, whom they have most oppressed in their acts of violence and plunder, to our great admiration.

They raile without measure at our Ministers, and threaten the destruction of so many as they can get. Many Cavaliers have sent into Furness and Cartmel to Sir Thomas Tilsley for protections, but the Scots weigh not their protections a rush, and Tilsley himself tells the Cavaliers he can do them no good, but wishes them to use their best shifts in putting their goods out of the way. They say they'll not leave the country worth any thing; they take no account of Lambert, they say he is run away. They are yet in quarters at Burton, Kirby, Whittington &c and the English at Encross and Furness. They have driven away above 600 cattle and 1500 sheep. They have given such earnest of their conditions that the Country have wholly driven away their cattel of all sorts towards Yorkshire and the bottom of Lancashire; forty great droves at least are gone from us ...'

As described by Henry Porter and William West in a letter to the Lancashire committee at Manchester, 17 August 1648. A part of the tract *The Last Newes from the Prince of Wales*, reprinted in Ormerod, p.254.

Samples from the church 'inquisition' surveys of 1650

Turton, in the parish of Bolton, Salford Hundred

'Alsoe we present that there is within Turton ... two Chappells, one of them called Turton Chappell and the other called Walmesley Chappell, distant the one from the other two statute myles and a halfe, and distant from the Parish Church of Bolton five myles, and some part of Turton is distant from Boulton nyne myles or thereabouts, and that the said two Chappells are fit to bee made a parish, and to have theire boundaries and severall precincts allotted to them as formerly they have had, and maye be for the most conveniencies and benefits of the Inhabitants resorting to them; And that Mr James Livesay officiates at Turton, a painfull godly orthodox minister, And was elected by the unaminous consent of the congregation of Turton, and hath in parte of his sallery the intrest of twenty shillings, now in the hand of John Wood, and given towards mainteynce of a Minister at Turton by one Widowe Haighe, deceased, and that the residue of his wages and sallery are payed unto him by free gifte and contrbucion of the congregation; And that Mr Michaell Briscoe, a godly and painfull Minister did officiate at the said Chappell by order from the Comittie of plundered ministers, and was outed by some of the Cappelry that did not effect him, And hath forty pounds or thereabouts allowed him by the said Committee from Walmsley Chappell aforesaid. And that there is in stocke sixty pounds or thereabouts, to be disposed of towards mainteynce of a minister at Walmsley Chappell, in the hands of William Stones, of Sharples, John Welch, of Turton, James Sharrocke, of Turton, and others; and that the tyths within Turton and Longworth aforesaid are (as we conceive) worth forty pounds per annum, And are received by Mr Humffrey Cheetam and Mr Thomas Longworth, or their Assignes, and payes thirty five shillings by way of prescription.'

Winwick, in the parish of Winwick, West Derby Hundred

'Wee do present that within the Towneshipp of Winwicke there is a parish Churche called Winwicke Church, and that there is a parsonage house, and certaine howseinge thereunto belonginge, and alsoe glebe lands thereunto belonginge, of the yearely value of One Hundred Sixtie one pounds; And that there are Three Water Corne Milnes thereunto belonginge worth Thirty pounds per annum, And that the rentes off the Tennants thereunto belonging are of the yearly value of Twenty eight pounds; And wee present that the Tyth Corne within the said parish of Winwicke and the smale Tythes within Winwicke aforesaid are worth fower hundred Forty Fyve pounds and two shillinges per annum, All which proffittes aforesaid ... Mr Charles Herle, being the present Incumbent att Winwicke aforesaid, hath had received to his own use, And that he is an orthodox godly preaching Minister, But did not observe Thursday 13th of this instant June, beinge a daie of Humiliacion appoynted by Acte of Parliament, And was presented unto the said parsonage by the Earle of Derby, who clames to be patron of the said Church; And that the Tythes of the said Towne of Winwicke are worth Thirtie poundes and five shillinges per annum, which is part of the before mencioned sume of Fower hundred forty five poundes and 2s'.

Cockerham, in the parish of Lancaster, Lonsdale Hundred

'And the said Jurors doe further say upon their Oathes, That the Parish Church of Cockerham, within the said Hundred of Loinsdale and the County of Lancaster is a Vicaradge Presentative, John Calvert Esq. a Papist Delinquent, Patron; that the Tythes of Corne and graine within the whole parish are Impropriate to the said Mr Calvert and to Mr Bradshaw, another Delinquent papist, worth One Hundred and sixteene poundes per annum, viz Eighty pounds per annum in Ellell, sixteene pounds per annum on Cockerham, and Twenty pounds per annum in Forton; And that there is another Tyth of Corne in part of Thornham [Thurnam] within the said parish, impropriate to Mr Bradshaw, worth Ten pounds per annum; And the said parish of Cockerham doth containe within it the severall Townshipps, hamlets, or Villages of the severall distances from the said Parish Church heretofore following, viz Cockerham, where the Church is seated; Ellell, distant as aforesaid Three miles; Forton, one mile, part of Clevely Three myles; part of Thurnham Three myles; one howse in Lower Wyersdale, viz Robert Websters, of the Holmes; And that there is belonging to the said Church a Vicarage howse and Six acres & a halfe of Glebe land, and also Tyth of Salt & Wooll, lambe & pigg, Goose, hay, hempe, flax and smale Tythes, in most of the places within the said Vicaradge; That there is some Composicion Rent from Thurnham Hall, about Six shillings per annum; That the profits thereof were anciently reputed to be about Sixty pounds per annum, but by reason of the decay of Sheepe the said Vicaradge hath beene Farmed the last yeare for Thirty five pounds. And the said Jurors likewise say That the said Parish of Cockerham doth containe within it the severall Chappelles distant from their said parish Church as followeth, viz Ellell, Three myles, Shierside [Shire's Head Chapel] Three Miles; And that the Incumbent officiating att the said Parish Church for the Tyme being is one Mr Thomas Smith during the Sequestracion of Mr William Calvert, the Vicar, for delinquency. And the said Jurors further say That the said severall Chappells belonging to the said parish Church of Cockerham are provided for as followeth; viz, Fifty pounds per annum by order from the Committee of plundered Ministers to the said Chappell of Ellell; the Minister there Mr Peter Atkinson; And that the Chappell of Shierside hath no certaine maintenance to their knowledge, the Minister there for the Tyme being Mr John Fisher.'

These three surveys are just a sample of an extensive set of records covering 63 parish churches and 118 chapels in Lancashire. For some reason North Meols parish was omitted, bringing the total of parishes in the county to 64 at that time. On average Lancashire appears to have had an average of one recognised place of worship per 800–850 inhabitants, although the distributions of both people and churches varied considerably.

Reproduced from H.Fishwick (ed.), *Lancashire and Cheshire Church Surveys*, Record Society, vol. 1 (1879), pp. 32–3; 46–7; 128–9.

APPENDIX X

Lancashire civil war coin hoards

In the north and north midlands of England, coins are known to have been minted for the king at Shrewsbury, York and Chester. Siege pieces were also manufactured at Pontefract, Carlisle, Scarborough and Newark. Although Lancashire lacked its own mint, or 'siege' tokens during the period, a number of coins of the late Tudors and early Stuarts have been found in the county. At least eight Lancashire civil war hoards have been documented, the largest being a substantial assemblage of 383 coins. While this is significant, neighbouring Yorkshire holds the record in terms of sheer numbers, with a hoard of over 5,000 coins having been found at Middleham in 1993. The hiding of hoards in Lancashire during the war is explicitly mentioned in the *Discourse*, in the context of the Scottish invasion of 1648. It is likely, however, that caches were deposited in Lancashire at various times between 1642 and 1651 when the original owners of coins were threatened with violence or requisition, or had to flee at short notice. Some never returned to retrieve their money.

Up to the 1990s hoards could be declared 'treasure trove' by the coroner and acquired by museums. In 1996 a new Treasure Act was introduced, but again in cases where hoards are declared 'treasure' an opportunity is given for museums to buy them. In either instance finders were, and still are, paid for their good fortune or get to keep their find. In partnership with the British Museum based 'Portable Antiquities Scheme' Lancashire Museums in Preston is host to a 'Finds Liaison Officer' to whom treasure and other finds can be reported in the first instance.

The St Annes Hoard. Discovered in 1961 at Beauclerk Gardens, St Annes, by Mr D. Jeffrey, a council workman, this hoard was declared 'treasure trove' and later acquired by the Harris Museum, Preston. It consisted of 383 coins, of which 376 were silver and seven gold with a total face value of £19 5s. 2d. Three of the coins were Scottish and one Irish, and dated from the reign of Edward VI through to the reign of Charles I. Two of the Charles coins were so called 'false shillings' or copies. Many of the pieces were worn or clipped, suggesting that they had been in circulation for some time. The latest coins in the group dated from 1643 or 1644, indicating a likely time of deposit of 1644 or 1645. This would fit well with the campaigns in the area and the movements, for example, of the Northern Horse. The coins were contained in a small red-coloured chamber-pot with a brown internal glaze, which it has been suggested was intended for use by a child.

The Whittingham Hoard. This hoard, much of which survives in the Harris Museum Preston, was labelled as discovered 'in the thatch of a cottage at Whittingham, near Preston, in 1848'. However, an article in the *Preston Guardian* of January 1853 also refers to a hoard recently found in this village, so it likely that these are one and the same, and that the discovery was made certainly no earlier than 1848, and probably as late as the first two weeks of 1853. The museum documentation is likely to have been inexact because the Harris was established after the finding of the hoard, part of which had already been given to the Institution for the Diffusion of Knowledge. A total of 207 coins was finally deposited in the museum, of a total originally recorded as 301. The extant coins date from the reign of Elizabeth I, through to the middle 1640s. One coin was minted as late as sometime between 1646 and 1648, and it has reasonably been suggested that the whole were deposited 'about 1647'. The *Preston Guardian* opined that the hoard was hidden 'in the troublesome times of the Commonwealth'. However, since about a third of the coins are now missing, it is not possible to fix the date of deposition with any certainty. The remaining coins have a face value of £10 15*s*., so it may be that the total of the entire hoard was about £15.

The Formby Hoard.   Recorded as discovered in the thatch of a cottage in Formby in February 1870, and written up in the Transactions of the Historic Society of Lancashire and Cheshire, volume 22, this hoard is now lost. However, it was listed as comprising a collection of 19 coins contained in a pig's bladder. Strangely all the coins were noted as shillings dating to the reign of Charles I at the latest, except one piece which was noted as a Charles II crown of 1660. This leaves open several possibilities. The hoard may have been hidden about 1660; or alternatively the odd coin may have been mis-recorded or introduced to the bag at a later date. If the odd coin was not originally part of the group the hoard could well have been originally concealed about 1645 or 1646.

The Fulwood Hoard.   Recorded only in Whittle's History of Preston, this hoard was stated to have been found in April 1812. It was concealed 'a little below the surface' under the floor of a gentleman's house 'near Fulwood Moor', and comprised 'a quantity of silver coins, of various sizes'. They dated from the reign of Edward VI through to the reign of Charles I. The precise composition is not stated, but it would seem probable that the coins would have been hidden sometime during the period 1642 to 1648.

The Barton Hoard.   Found in 1967, a small hoard consisting of five silver coins, totalling 10*s*. 3*d*. in value. Only two of the coins were English, the other being a Spanish dollar and two Low Country 'quarter patagons'. The latest coins are dated to 1643–44.

The Salford Hoard.   A group of 31 silver coins found in 1928, total value £1 14*s*. Latest coins dated to 1645–47.

The Barton upon Irwell Hoard.   Discovered about 1880, this totalled 131 silver coins, value £7 13*s*. 11½*d*. The latest coins are dated to 1645–47.

The Hopwood, Middleton, Hoard.   Discovered in 1851, this hoard comprised 19 Charles I half-crowns, with a latest possible minting date of 1649. Total value £2 7*s*. 6*d*.

This information abstracted from R.F. Taylor 'The St Annes Hoard and other Civil War Coin Hoards in Lancashire', *Transactions of the Historic Society of Lancashire and Cheshire*, vol. cxviii (1967), pp. 39–50; E. Besly, *Coins and Medals of the English Civil War* (National Museum of Wales, 1990); J.J. North, *English Hammered Coinage*, vol. 2 (London, 1991), E. Besley, *English Civil War Coin Hoards* (British Museum 1987), and the data of the Portable Antiquities Scheme (NW, and Lancashire and Cumbria), British Museum, Liverpool and Preston 1997–2006 (www.finds.org.uk)

Cromwell in Lancashire

Oliver Cromwell has exercised the popular imagination more than any other character of mid-seventeenth-century England. He has also been adopted as a symbol – of democracy, bigotry, equality, religion, authoritarianism or freedom depending upon one's perspective. An internet search for 'Oliver Cromwell' produces over 2 million hits, and 12 million for the surname entered alone. Almost all civil war damage, and at least some that has nothing at all to do with the civil wars, is commonly ascribed directly to Cromwell. As John Aubrey observed, not long after the wars, Cromwell was sometimes thought of as 'England's Atilla'. He has also become, in many instances, a shorthand cipher for the wars in general. In the Lancashire case, though many parts of the county were indeed ravaged by the civil wars, very little of the destruction can actually be blamed specifically on Cromwell. Nevertheless, many places are associated with Cromwell, or bear his name. Virtually every town in the North West has a Cromwell Street, Cromwell Avenue or Cromwell House. The Greater Manchester area alone has 17 thoroughfares in which Cromwell forms part of the name. Only some have credible connections, and some are named after other historical figures. Salford, for example, has a Cromwell Road, with a Cromwell House, recently an optician's shop – though Oliver Cromwell never went to the town.

Where Cromwell slept has long been a bone of contention between a number of stately homes and tourist attractions. As far as can be determined, he came to Lancashire only once in person, remaining in the county just under two weeks from about 15 to 27 August 1648. His victory at Preston had considerable impact upon the history of England, but this was not matched by any prolonged presence in Lancashire then or at any other time. Even so many strong local traditions remain.

Contemporary documentary evidence gives us quite a good picture of his movements. Cromwell's letters record that he reached Gisburn (then in the West Riding of Yorkshire, now in Lancashire) on 15 August 1648. The commonly held belief is that he stayed with Sir John Ashton at Gisburn Park, then known as Lower Hall, and portraits of Cromwell and John Lambert are indeed recorded as being displayed in the Lodge. It has been stated that some of the parliamentarian cavalry were stabled in the church and that the stained glass was broken – though the evidence for this detail is unclear. Given that his previous day's ride had taken him from Skipton, a distance of perhaps ten or eleven miles, it is perfectly likely that Cromwell spent the entire night – and several waking hours – in and around Gisburn.

The following day, 16 August, Cromwell accompanied his army to the Hodder bridge. This still stands, at least in part, though it bestrides the Hodder, rather than the Ribble itself, as was reported by Cromwell. It is still referred to as 'Cromwell's bridge'. Following the council of war here the march was continued 'on the north side of Ribble' as far as 'Stonyhurst Hall, being Mr Sherburn's House'. Here Cromwell spent the night of the 16th, rising 'very early' the next morning. It is about a dozen miles from Gisburn to Stonyhurst, depending on the exact route taken. The council of war at the bridge, and the crossing, must have taken some time: but in August the days are long, and this still leaves Cromwell some time at Stonyhurst. One extraordinary legend surrounds an old table at Stonyhurst manor, which has now become Stonyhurst College. This suggests that Cromwell slept on the table, still wearing his clothes and armour. While there is no documentary evidence to support this it is likely that Cromwell and his men were already exhausted by the time they arrived at Stoneyhurst. Nodding off at the table in the midst of eating or conferring with his officers thus appears quite plausible, if unproven. A bed at Stonyhurst is also referred to as 'Cromwell's bed'.

The march of the New Model, Northern Association, and Lancashire forces from Stonyhurst to Preston resulting in the climactic battle of 17 August is well documented. Cromwell states that the distance between the two places is nine miles. Using modern statute miles the distance is more than ten as the crow flies, and rather more again by road. Both Longridge and Foulridge have in the past claimed Cromwell connections – though the stories that he named them on his march through the Lancashire mud are clearly apocryphal or wishful thinking. Cromwell Street, Foulridge, might, however, have some vague connection with the civil wars as it is claimed that the street is named after 'Cromwell's Croft' where parliamentarian troops were once billeted. Cromwell certainly passed through Longridge, but seems to have left little evidence of his passing.

There is impeccable documentary evidence for Cromwell's presence at Preston during the battle, with his letter of the evening of 17 August being headed with the name of the town. An enduring local tradition is that he stayed in a house south of the Ribble bridge, which has subsequently been used as a public house and restaurant – variously known as the Unicorn Inn, and Pinocchios. Although he might have stopped here briefly that Thursday evening in 1648, intelligence was received of the Scots' departure during the night, and Cromwell's army set off again as soon as it could be organised. Argument as to Cromwell's precise association with this location will doubtless continue; for though his letter is noted as written in Preston, and technically anything south of the Ribble is not Preston, spending time with his soldiery in the front line is very much what we might expect of Cromwell the general.

Another location in the area which claims Cromwell associations is 'Cromwell's Mound' in Fulwood, located in a field between the aptly named 'Oliver's Place', Eastway and D'Urton Lane. This tiny hillock, 37 metres long and 2 metres high, certainly predates the battle, and is man-made – piled up as part of the drainage scheme for Moss Leach Brook, which still runs around its side. The feature is now a scheduled ancient monument, and has been interpreted as a 'water control dam' or 'pond bay' for Broughton Tower moat. Although views from the mound are now obstructed by industrial units and housing, this would once have been a useful vantage point, especially for officers of the parliamentarian command who were attempting to determine the position and direction of march of the Scottish army moving to the west and south about mid-day. The mound is about two miles from the main axis of the march of the New Model Army on the Longridge Road, but would have been much closer to the right flank of the parliamentarian forces once they had deployed for battle. Cromwell's use of this observation point is therefore extremely likely, but remains unproven. Cromwell Road, also in Fulwood, is essentially nineteenth- and twentieth-century in date; nevertheless it runs obliquely across part of the battlefield just behind what was the royalist forward position, making it almost certain that Cromwell was indeed in this neighbourhood at some time in the early afternoon of 17 August 1648.

Between the early hours of 18 August and that evening Cromwell and the main body of his army covered upwards of 20 miles, from Preston to the outskirts of Wigan, part of the time fighting a running skirmish with the fleeing Scots. Again Cromwell used antiquated and very long miles as a measure of the distance, stating in his letters that the march was twelve miles, 'of such ground as I never rode in all my life the day being very wet'. We know that the main advance was down the Chorley road. Astley Hall, Chorley, retains very strong Cromwell connections with a bed in which he is believed to have slept, and a pair of boots, long known as 'Cromwell's boots', were also displayed here for many years. These boots were examined by Lancashire County Museum Service conservators in 1991, and photographs circulated to various footwear experts. The unanimous opinion was that the boots had nothing in common with any known mid-seventeenth-century design, and that they were made sometime during the eighteenth century. That Cromwell would have found time to go to bed in the midst of the pursuit of the enemy would appear unlikely. However, it has been pointed out that it is perfectly possible, that since Cromwell had very little sleep on the night of 17 August, followed by an exhausting ride, he might well have stopped at Astley for a brief rest or food. As we shall see, there was perhaps more chance that Cromwell spent time at Astley a few days later once the Scots were defeated, rather than during the pursuit. Commissary Farm, near Euxton, has also had claims for a Cromwell connection advanced in its favour, and while no documentary evidence has so far been presented, geography alone would suggest that one army, or both, could hardly fail to have been here.

The night of 18 August, by Cromwell's own account and confirmed by others, was spent 'in the field close by the enemy' near Wigan. A local tradition suggested that Cromwell had an association with the Rose Inn, Standishgate: but this has since been disputed on grounds of the date '1690' over the door. Passing through the town of Wigan much of 19 August was spent *en route* to Warrington, still pursuing the enemy. After ten or eleven miles the Scots stopped to dispute the way at Winwick, leading to a battle that Cromwell states took 'many hours' – though perhaps 'several' might be a more accurate. Later that day the surrender of Baillie's Scottish infantry was accepted at Warrington bridge.

Cromwell's sojourn in Warrington (then in Lancashire, now Cheshire) is well documented, his lengthy dispatch of 20 August 1648 to the Speaker of the Commons being headed with the name of the town. This missive runs to about 3,000 words, much longer than most known Cromwell letters, and is thoughtfully constructed, suggesting that he must have spent some time in its production. A second, much shorter letter of the same date was also written to the Committee at York. There is no good reason to doubt that 'Cromwell's Lodgings', Church Street, or at least very close to this spot, is where he stayed. A plaque on the surviving building in this street reads 'Oliver Cromwell lodged by this cottage on 20th August 1648 from where he sent his dispatches to Parliament to report his victories at Preston, Winwick and Warrington against King Charles Army'. Tradition states, credibly, that he actually slept in an inn nearby which was later known as 'The Spotted Leopard' or the 'General Wolfe'. Warrington retains numerous other connections with the Lord Protector, including a Cromwell Avenue and a 'Cromwell' junior football team. Scotland Road is said to have been so named because of the enemy prisoners who were marched along it.

Perhaps the town's most controversial piece of memorabilia is the larger-than-life Cromwell statue which stands in Bridgefoot, by the Old Academy. Fittingly enough this colossal Oliver couches a sword and bible in the crook of his left arm. The piece was sculpted by John Bell, and is mentioned in the International Exhibition catalogue of 1862, although it does not appear to have come to Warrington until over 30 years later. Local legend has it that Queen Victoria saw the statue and a set of gates intended for Sandringham together, and was so displeased by the figure of Cromwell that she rejected the gates. Both gates and statue were later donated to the town by Frederick Monks, and the bronzed cast-iron gates now adorn Warrington Town Hall.

The statue has been associated with Warrington since 1899 and the tri-centenary of the Lord Protector's birth. Monks, a convinced Cromwell supporter, suggested that it should be erected 'in front of the Town Hall or in the gardens behind'. Warringtonians did not all agree, and there was sharp and sometimes acrimonious debate about the merits of both Cromwell and the sculpture. Dr Cannell, one of Warrington's aldermen, characterised Cromwell as both murderer and 'diabolical scoundrel', and there was intimation that the town's Irish community was also much disquieted. In the event the pro-Cromwell lobby outvoted those seeking to reject the Monks gift, and Warrington accepted the statue. Even so the town's representatives chose a less obtrusive place for its display, and in so doing upset the Cromwell die-hards. The sculpture was listed in 1973, but renovated and moved a few yards in the early 1980s during road-widening operations.

Cromwell probably stayed in Warrington for three, or possibly four, nights from 19 to 22 August. His next extant correspondence is from Wigan on the 23rd, in which he explains to the York Committee that he is now 'marching northward with the greatest part of the army'. This he did quite smartly. Very probably he spent this night at Wigan, being a comfortable ride from Warrington, but exactly where is yet to be discovered. One source claims that he stayed 'near Ashton Cross'. We know that Cromwell had reached Skipton by the 27th, but this leaves at least a couple of 'missing nights' in his verified itinerary, when he can only have been somewhere in Lancashire, north of Wigan, or in Yorkshire. His most obvious route would appear to been back via Preston and the Ribble valley. Harry Wardale in his article *Cromwell in Lancashire* (1934) says that he did precisely this, spending a night at Astley Hall, another at Stonyhurst, and returning into Yorkshire via Gisburn. Nonetheless, Shadsworth Hall near Blackburn had a long tradition of a visit from Cromwell, to the extent that a later building nearby was named 'Cromwell Lodge'. Other places advancing claims for a stay, which are perhaps less likely, but still possible, include Heskin Hall near Eccleston, and Blakey Hall Farm near Colne. Similar claims made for Bradleigh Old Hall, five miles from Warrington, and for Prescot would appear less credible given the letter from Wigan, and the distance that Cromwell would have had to cover to get to Skipton within the established timeframe.

Oswaldtwistle in east Lancashire also maintains a somewhat tenuous Cromwell connection. Thomas Belasyse (or Bellasys), second Viscount Fauconberg, who married Mary (1637–1713), one of Oliver and Elizabeth Cromwell's nine children, at Hampton Court in 1657, also came into possession of the manor of Oswaldtwistle. Despite his relations Fauconberg flourished after the Restoration, and his 'spirited and strong willed' wife lived on into the reign of Queen Anne.

The idea of monumentalising Oliver Cromwell in Manchester was first suggested by a group of local Liberals in 1860. However, the death of Thomas Goadsby, one of the leading lights in this enterprise, delayed the production of a suitable statue. A model was finally produced by the sculptor Matthew Noble some years later, as was a bust which found its way into the town hall. The statue itself, probably based on the paintings by Samuel Cooper and Lely, was finally unveiled at the intersection of Cateaton Street and Deansgate on 1 December 1875. The site was said to have been chosen to allow the bronze figure, mounted on its granite pedestal, to look down Victoria Street towards the Royal Exchange, as well as marking the approximate spot where the first blood of the civil wars had been spilt. As in Warrington there were voices raised in opposition to the statue, Conservatives depicting its arrival as 'a preposterous whim', and an insult to the Irish and Scots. Traffic congestion finally achieved what political objection failed to do, and in 1967 it was decided to move the by-then listed statue. It now stands far less prominently in Wythenshawe Park, where it has been subjected to several episodes of vandalism.

'The White Church' at Clifton Drive, Ansdell, a seaside suburb of Lytham, boasts a stained-glass window of Cromwell by Abbot & Co. of Lancaster. This forms part of a group of lights celebrating the reformed and non-conformist traditions. Other persons depicted include Milton, Bunyan and Tyndale. The inscription with the Lord Protector, with no little understatement, identifies Cromwell as 'Saviour of his Country' and its civil and religious liberty. The church itself was opened in 1912. Interestingly, Ansdell itself was named after the Victorian painter Richard Ansdell (1815–85), who was famous for painting animals, but also an artist responsible for a number of canvases depicting scenes from the civil war.

A number of Lancashire 'Cromwell' objects have credible connection with the armies of Parliament, or other events of the period, even though they can never have been seen or touched by Cromwell himself. Among these we might include Cromwell's Door at Cartmel Priory, and Cromwell's Stone at Lathom. Cromwell is similarly supposed to have given a bell to Toxteth Chapel, but again there is no evidence that the Lord Protector ever actually visited the town of Liverpool.

One example of Cromwellian myth-creation comes from the publisher of this present work, who relates that during a talk he was giving to a local history class in Preston around 1982 he related a fanciful story he had heard from a tour guide in Chingle Hall some months earlier. The guide had claimed that before the battle of Preston Cromwell had climbed up inside the grand ingle-nook fireplace of Chingle Hall, emerging at the top to view the enemy's dispositions. After the lecture a shy young woman came forward and let it be known that her mother had been the tour guide in question. 'Mum was impressed by the size of the fireplace, but couldn't think of anything very interesting to say about, so she made up the story about Cromwell!'

For Cromwell's movements see P. Gaunt, *The Cromwellian Gazetteer* (Stroud, 2000); H. Wardale, 'Cromwell in Lancashire', *Transactions of the Lancashire and Cheshire Antiquarian Society*, vol. xlviii (1934), pp. 76–93; W. Harrison, 'Ancient Fords, Ferries and Bridges in Lancashire', *Transactions of the Lancashire and Cheshire Antiquarian Society*, vol. xii (1894), pp. 1–29; R.A. Irwin, 'Cromwell in Lancashire: The Campaign of

Preston, 1648', *Army Quarterly*, vol. xxvii (October 1933), pp. 72–87; T. Carlyle, *Oliver Cromwell's Letters and Speeches* (London, 1846–49); W.C. Abbott, *Bibliography of Oliver Cromwell*, Harvard 1929 (reprinted New York, 1969); www.stonyhurst.ac.uk

Notes and references

Chapter 1: *People, county, military: Lancashire in the seventeenth century*

1. In C.B. Phillips and J.H. Smith, *Lancashire and Cheshire from AD 1540* (Longman, 1994), a figure of about 142,000 is suggested, by means of multiplying the number of households by the likely number of persons in each household.

2. R.C. Shaw, *The Royal Forest of Lancashire* (Preston, 1956).

3. Transactions in *Manuscripts of Lord Kenyon*, HMC 14th Report, Part IV (1894), pp. 44–7; J. Richardson, *History and Antiquities of Furness*, vol. 2 (1880), p. 50.

4. *Manuscripts of Lord Kenyon*, HMC, 14th Report, Part IV (1894), p. 55; K. Thomas, *Religion and the Decline of Magic* (London, 1971), pp. 39, 83, 215, 261, 277, 537.

5. C. Webster, 'Richard Towneley (1629–1707), 'The Towneley Group and Seventeenth-Century Science', *Transactions of the Historic Society of Lancashire and Cheshire*, vol. cxviii (1967), pp. 51–76. Richard Towneley's library catalogue is preserved in the John Ryland's Library, R.72649.

6. LRO, QSB 1/269d/5,7; DDKe 5/123.

7. J.K. Walton, *Lancashire: A Social History* (Manchester, 1987), p. 40.

8. G. Chandler, *Liverpool Under Charles I* (Liverpool, 1965), *passim*. See also J. Hollinshead, *Liverpool in the Sixteenth Century: A Small Tudor Town* (Carnegie, 2007). The early economic history of Wigan has recently been explored by A.J.H. Latham, 'Wigan, 1540–1640: Pre-industrial growth and development in south Lancashire', in J.F. Wilson (ed.), *King Cotton: A tribute to Douglas A. Farnie* (Crucible Books, Lancaster, 2009), pp. 247–79.

9. A.P. Wadworth and J.L. Mann, *The Cotton Trade and Industrial Lancashire, 1600–1800* (Manchester UP, 1931), pp. 54–64.

10. J.P. Earwaker (ed.), *The Court Leet Records of the Manor of Manchester* (Manchester, 1887), vol. 3, p. 324; vol. 4, pp. 19–25. See also W.H. Thomson, *History of Manchester to 1852* (Altrincham, 1967), pp. 96–106.

11. See O. Ashmore, *Household Inventories of the Lancashire Gentry 1550–1700*, Transactions of the Historic Society of Lancashire and Cheshire, vol. 110 (1958–59), pp. 59–105.

12. H. Fishwick (ed.), *Lancashire and Cheshire Church Surveys, 1649–1655*, in Lancashire and Cheshire Record Society, vol. 1 (1878–79), pp. xvii–xxvi; R.C. Richardson, *Puritanism in North-West England* (Manchester, 1972), p. 3. Similar conclusions are reached by J.K. Walton in *Lancashire: A Social History* (Manchester, 1987), pp. 36–59.

13. Fishwick, *op. cit.*, p. 126; Richardson, *op. cit.*, p. 4.

14. Ibid., p. 5. See also K. J. Lindley, 'The Part Played by the Catholics in the Civil War in Lancashire and Monmouthshire', unpublished MA thesis, University of Manchester, 1965, pp. 5–6, 57–134.

15. P. Collinson, *English Puritanism*, Historical Association pamphlet, General Series, 106 (1983), pp. 25–39; P. Toon, 'Puritan Eschatology, 1600–1648', in *The Report of the 1968 Puritan and Reformed Studies Conference* (Cambridge, 1969), pp. 1–12. See also J. M. Gratton, 'The Parliamentarian and Royalist War Effort in Lancashire', unpublished Ph.D. thesis, University of Manchester, 1998, pp. 31–50.

16. See F. Tyrer, 'A Star Chamber Case: Ashton v. Blundell, 1624–31', *Transactions of the Historic Society of Lancashire and Cheshire*, vol. cxviii (1967), pp. 19–37.

17. LRO, QSB 1/271; Gratton, *op. cit.*, p. 188.

18. 'Liverpool Town Book', reprinted in Chandler, *op. cit.*, pp. 105–423.

19. See L. Boynton, *The Elizabethan Militia, 1558–1638* (Newton Abbot, 1967), *passim*.

20. LRO, DDX 1294/1; DDKe 6/7; Historical Manuscripts Commission, 14th Report, Appendix IV, *Manuscripts of Lord Kenyon* (1894), p. 594.

21. MCA, L1/40/1; British Library, Add. Ms 36924, ff. 24–5.

22. See C. L. Hamilton (ed.), *The Muster Master By Gervase Markham*, Camden Miscellany, vol. 26 (1975), pp. 54–76; Historical Manuscripts Commission, 14th Report, Appendix IV, *Manuscripts of Lord Kenyon* (1894), p. 35.

23. MCA, L1/40/1 and L1/40/2; see appendix I.

24. LRO, DDB 85/14 f. 12, 16; 85/19; 85/25.

25. J. Harland (ed.), *The Lancashire Lieutenancy*, Chetham Society (1859), pp. 316–17. Parts of Lancashire muster rolls for the period 1619–39, amounting to a few companies in total, survive in national collections: as for example PRO, SP 16/46 and SP 16/419; and, specifically for West Derby, British Library, Add Ms 36924, ff. 6–8, 10–12, 14–15, 18–20, 24–5.

26. Historical Manuscripts Commission, 14th Report, Appendix IV, *Manuscripts of Lord Kenyon* (1894), pp. 587–9. See also D. Blackmore, *Arms and Armour of the English Civil War* (London, 1990), *passim*; T. Richardson, *London Armourers of the Seventeenth Century* (Royal Armouries, 2004), *passim*; and J. Smith, *Men and Armour For Gloucestershire, 1608* (reprinted 1902, and Gloucester 1980).

27. From accounts reprinted in A. Fell, *A Furness Military Chronicle* (Ulverston, 1937), pp. 57–9.

28. See L. G. Schwoerer, 'The Fittest Subject for a King's Quarrel: an Essay on the Militia Controversy 1641–1642', *The Journal of British Studies*, vol, xi, number 1 (1971), pp. 45–76.

Chapter 2: *'The fittest subject for a King's quarrel': the causes of civil war*

1. The literature on the causes of the wars is varied and extensive. Key texts demonstrating the divergence of opinion include: C. Russell, *The Causes of the English Civil War* (Oxford, 1990); L. Stone, *The Causes of the English Revolution* (London, 1972); P. A. M. Taylor (ed.), *Problems in European Civilisation: The Origins of the English Civil War* (Boston, 1960); C. Hill, *The Century of Revolution*, 2nd edn (Wokingham, 1980); A. Hughes, *The Causes of the English Civil War* (Basingstoke, 1991); H. Tomlinson (ed.), *Before the English Civil War* (Basingstoke, 1983); J. Reeve, 'The Politics of War Finance in an Age of Confessional Strife: A Comparative Anglo-European View', in *Parergon*, 14.1 (1996), pp. 86–109. A number of other works relating to the origins of the wars are listed in the bibliography.

2. *The Times*, 15 October 2004, p. 35, obituary of Earl Russell; C. Russell, 'Why did People Choose Sides in the English Civil War?', *The Historian*, number 63 (Autumn, 1999), pp. 4–9. C. Russell, *op. cit.*, p. 14.

3. J. D. Maltby (ed.), *The Short Parliament Diary of Sir Thomas Aston*, Camden Fourth Series, Royal Historical Society, London (1988), p. 37.

4. G. H. Tupling, *The Causes of the Civil War in Lancashire*, Transactions of the Lancashire and Cheshire Antiquarian Society, vol. 65 (1955), *passim*. J. Morrill, *The Revolt of the Provinces* (London, 1976), p. 25.

5. LRO, QSB I/213/20; see also R. C. Shaw, *The Royal Forest of Lancaster* (Preston, 1956), pp. 445−58. *Humble Petition of Divers Recusants* (H) 49, also the king's reply, 27 September 1642, in Ormerod, *Tracts Relating to Military Proceedings in Lancashire* (1844), pp. 39−40.

6. *A True and Full Relation of the Troubles*, 1642, reprinted in Ormerod, *Tracts Relating to the Military Proceedings in Lancashire* (1844), p. 65.

7. C. O'Riordan, *Popular Exploitation of Enemy Estates in the English Revolution*, in *History*, vol. 78 (1993), pp. 184−200; Malbon in J. Hall (ed.), *Memorials of the Civil War in Cheshire and Adjacent Counties*, Lancashire and Cheshire Record Society, vol. xix (1889), p. 32.

8. R. Lockyer (ed.), *Clarendon's The History of the Great Rebellion* (Oxford, 1967), p. 43; C. Cross in G. E. Aylmer (ed.), *The Interregnum* (London, 1974), pp. 114−16.

9. B. G. Blackwood, *The Lancashire Gentry and the Great Rebellion*, pp. 37−71.

10. F. O. Blundell, *Old Catholic Lancashire, passim*; *Manuscripts of Lord Kenyon*, 14th Report, Part IV (1894), p. 59.

11. C. Hudson, 'The Triumph of God's Grace Over Sinne', in *Severall Sermons*, 1641, LRO, DP 353.

12. See B. W. Quintrell, 'The Practice and Problems of Recusant Disarming, 1585−1641', *Recusant History*, vol. xvii (1985), pp. 208−22.

13. R. C. Richardson, *Puritanism in North-West England* (Manchester, 1972), pp. 5−12; A. Fletcher *The Outbreak of the English Civil War* (London, 1981), p. 5; R. N. Dore, *The Civil Wars in Cheshire* (Chester, 1966), pp. 5−10; *Journal of the House of Lords*, vol. 4, pp. 369−370; see also J. K. Walton, *Lancashire: A Social History* (Manchester, 1987), pp. 36−59.

14. *House of Lords Journal*, vol. 4, 22 February 1642, pp. 602−7. BL Add MS 28000, cited in Fletcher, *op. cit.*, p. 410.

15. Richardson, *Lancashire Gentry, passim*.

16. Tupling, *op. cit.*; CSPD 26, 25 April 1636. A number of relevant artefacts and a portrait of father Arrowsmith are preserved at Stonyhurst College. Some of this material was exhibited at the Museum of Lancashire, Preston, in 2000 to 2002, as part of the AD 2000 Story of Christianity exhibition.

17. See P. Collinson, *English Puritanism*, Historical Association general series pamphlet 106 (1983), pp. 5−11, 25−39; C. Hill, *The Century of Revolution* (Wokingham, 1980), pp. 15−29, 103, 106; A. Woolrych, 'Puritanism, Politics and Society', in E. W. Ives (ed.), *The English Revolution 1600−1660* (London, 1975), pp. 87−100. On the Ashtons (Asshetons), see MCA, E7/27/2/10.

18. See R. C. Richardson, *Puritanism in North-West England* (Manchester, 1972), pp. 28−50, and J. K. Walton, *Lancashire: A Social History* (Manchester, 1987), pp. 48−55. LRO, DP353, *Severall Sermons Upon Divers Occasions*, by Christopher Hudson, 1641.

19. Walton, *op. cit.*, pp. 56−8; Hughes, *op. cit.*, pp. 9−61; D. Underdown, *Revel, Riot and Rebellion* (Oxford, 1985), p. 241; *House of Commons Journal*, vol. 1, 10 February 1626, pp. 817−18.

20. A. Fletcher in, J. Morrill (ed.), *Reactions to the English Civil War* (London, 1982), p. 35.

21. J. P. Earwaker (ed.), *The Constables Accounts of the Manor of Manchester*, 3 vols (Manchester, 1891−93), pp. 92−113.

22. See also J. Barratt, *Cavaliers* (Stroud, 2000), pp. 133−41; *House of Commons Journal*, vol. 2, 13 April 1642, pp. 524−6.

23. *House of Lords Journal*, vol. 4, 7 March 1642, pp. 629–34.

24. Ormerod, *Tracts Relating to Military Proceedings in Lancashire* (1844), pp. 2–12.

25. R. Ashton, *The English Civil War* (London, 1978,) pp. 247–67; C. Russell, *The Causes, op. cit.*, pp. 26–57.

26. L. G. Scwoerer, 'The Fittest Subject for a King's Quarrel: an Essay on the Militia Controversy, 1641–1642', *The Journal of British Studies*, vol. xi, number 1 (1971), pp. 45–76.

27. See B. G. Blackwood, 'Parties and Issues in the Civil War in Lancashire', in J. I. Kermode and C. B. Phillips (eds), *Seventeenth-Century Lancashire: Essays Presented to J. J. Bagley* (Liverpool, 1983), pp. 103–26; A. Fletcher, 'Factionalism in Town and Countryside: The Significance of Puritanism and Arminianism', in D. Baker (ed.), *The Church in Town and Countryside, Studies in Church History*, 16.

28. J. J. Bagley, *The Earls of Derby* (London, 1985), pp. 80–4.

29. *House of Lords Journal*, vol. 4, 16 November 1641, pp. 441–3.

30. B. Coward, *The Social and Political Position of the Earls of Derby in later Seventeenth-Century Lancashire*, in J. I. Kermode and L. B. Phillips (eds), *Seventeeth-Century Lancashire*, p. 128; P. Newman, *The Old Service* (Manchester, 1993), *passim*.

31. LRO, DDKe 1/20; 25; 26.

32. A. Hughes, *op. cit.*, p. 125.

33. J. Harland (ed.), *The Lancashire Lieutenancy*, Chetham Society (1859), pp. 283–4.

34. P. R. Newman, 'The Royalist Army in Northern England', unpublished D.Phil. thesis, York 1978, p. 31; R. Robinson (ed.), *The Life of Adam Martindale Written by Himself*, Chetham Society vol. iv (1845), pp. 31–2.

35. *House of Commons Journal*, vol. 2, 24 October and 22 November 1642.

36. Blackwood, *op. cit.*, pp. 58–66; Newman, 'Royalist Army', *passim*; I. Gentles, 'Why Men Fought in the British Civil Wars, 1639–1652', *The History Teacher*, vol. 26, number 4 (August 1993), pp. 407–18; J. M. Gratton, p. 385. J. Harland, *op. cit.*, p. 296.

37. See K. J. Lindley, 'The Part Played by the Catholics in the Civil War in Lancashire and Monmouthshire', unpublished MA thesis, Manchester University, 1965, pp. 57–78.

38. W. Bennett, *The History of Burnley* (Burnley, 1947), pp. 190–1; J. Harland (ed.), *The Lancashire Lieutenancy*, Chetham Soc. (1859), p. 287; *Discourse of the Warr in Lancashire*, p. 15.

Chapter 3: *'Up in arms': the siege of Manchester, 1642*

1. *House of Commons Journal*, vol. 2, 28 May 1642. See also C. V. Wedgwood, *The King's War* (London, 1958), pp. 59–101; Anthony Fletcher states that 'a select group of Lancashire gentry' were actually the 'first to receive the commission of Array' at the end of May; *The Outbreak of the English Civil War* (London, 1981), pp. 322–3.

2. *House of Lords Journal*, vol. 5, 9 June 1642, pp. 120–3; ibid., 13 June, pp. 127–30; see also R. Hutton, 'The Failure of the Lancashire Cavaliers' in *Transactions of the Historic Society of Lancashire and Cheshire*, vol. 129 (Liverpool, 1980), pp. 47–8.

3. As Alexander Rigby clearly refers to 'Preston Moor', it is fairly certain that the meeting happened in the area of what is now known as 'Moor Park' – not Fulwood Moor as is suggested in Broxap and elsewhere. See Ormerod, *Tracts Relating to Military Proceedings in Lancashire* (1844), p. 326.

4. *Lamentable and Sad Newes*, and Rigby's letter, reprinted in Ormerod, *Tracts Relating to Military Proceedings in Lancashire* (1844), pp. 13–15, 324–30; Brereton's letter to Hampden in *House of Lords Journal*, vol. 5, 1 July 1642; J. L. Malcolm, *A King in Search of Soldiers*, *Historical Journal* 21 (1978), *passim*.

5. Letter to the Speaker William Lenthall, reprinted in Ormerod, *Tracts Relating to Military Proceedings in Lancashire* (1844), pp. 15–18. Fletcher, *op. cit.*, p. 361.

6. *A True and Perfect Diurnall; The Beginning of the Civil Warres; News from Manchester; Lancashire's Valley of Achor* and *A Verie True and Credible Relation*, all reprinted in Ormerod, *Tracts Relating to Military Proceedings in Lancashire* (1844), pp. 20–35, 107–42. *Manchester's Resolution* (H)21. See also P. R. Newman, 'The Royalist Army in Northern England', unpublished D.Phil. thesis, York, 1978, pp. 65–82.

7. The claim regarding Parcival (or Percival) being the first fatality of the wars has been repeated many times over the years, and is widely regarded as fact. See J. Kenyon, *The Civil Wars of England* (London, 1988), p. 34.

8. *An Impeachment of High Treason*, in Ormerod, *Tracts Relating to Military Proceedings in Lancashire* (1844), pp. 35–7.

9. *J. Rosworme's Good Service Hitherto Ill Rewarded* (London, 1649), reprinted in Ormerod, *Tracts Relating to Military Proceedings in Lancashire* (1844), pp. 215–44.

10. *A True and Faithfull Relation of the Besieging of the Towne of Manchester*, and, *A True and Exact Relation*, in Ormerod, *Tracts Relating to Military Proceedings in Lancashire* (1844), pp. 49–56, 332–3. *A True and Full Relation of the Troubles* (H) 515; *Several Letters From Committees* (H) 23; *A True and Perfect Relation* E 121(13).

11. Shuttleworth correspondence in J. Harland (ed.), *The Lancashire Lieutenancy*, Chetham Soc. (1859), pp. 272–3, 275–7, 303.

12. Ormerod, *Tracts Relating to Military Proceedings in Lancashire* (1844), pp. 115, 333; see also *A Description of the Memorable Battles in the North of England that Happened During the Civil War* (Bolton, 1785), pp. 68–77.

13. Broxap, p. 54; Ormerod, *Tracts Relating to Military Proceedings in Lancashire* (1844), pp. 66, 70; Harland, *op. cit.*, p. 281.

14. *House of Commons Journal*, vol. 2, 22 November 1642.

15. Sutherland Manuscript, cited in Broxap, pp. 44–6. *True and Faithfull Relation of the Besieging*, *op. cit.*; *Perfect Diurnall*, in Ormerod, *Tracts Relating to Military Proceedings in Lancashire* (1844), pp. 56–7; R. N. Dore, *The Great Civil War in the Manchester Area* (Manchester, 1971), pp. 12–14; *House of Commons Journal*, vol. 2, 5 October, 17, 22 and 24 November 1642.

16. *Discourse of the Warr in Lancashire*, pp. 19–20; Broxap, pp. 55–7; Ormerod, *Tracts Relating to Military Proceedings in Lancashire* (1844), p. 61.

17. B. Holland, *The Lancashire Hollands* (London, 1917), pp. 275–6; J. J. Bagley, *The Earls of Derby 1485–1985*, pp. 83–5.

Chapter 4: *'All barbarous crueltie': the struggle for Lancashire, 1642–43*

1. Ormerod, *Tracts Relating to Military Proceedings in Lancashire* (1844), p. 70.

2. See Dean, *Gawthorpe Hall* (London, 2002), pp. 48–58; the Shuttleworth 'House and Farm' accounts for the period up to 1621 are reprinted in four parts in the Chetham Society volumes (1854, 1856, 1857 and 1858). By happy coincidence the present writer acted as Keeper of Gawthorpe Hall during the early part of 2005.

3. J. Harland (ed.), *Lancashire Lieutenancy*, Chetham Soc. (1859), pp. 290–5, 298, 303, 315–16. The actual, and very low, numbers of royalist troops in Lancashire in 1643 contrast sharply with some of the wild estimates made in the past, as for example the 60,000 'efficient men' mustered in Lancashire by Lord Derby cited in J. Croston, *County Families of Lancashire and Cheshire* (London, 1887), p. 81. These huge discrepancies would appear to be the result of counting the 'able men' of the whole county, rather than troops actually under arms for

one side at a specific time. It is possible that the entire male population of Lancashire, aged between 16 and 60, was about 60,000.

4. LRO, QDV/11. *Lists of Delinquents in Blackburn Hundred*.

5. T. Jesland, *A True and Full Relation of the Troubles in Lancashire* (London, 1642), (H) 515; JJ Bagley and A. S. Lewis, *Lancashire at War*, pp. 20–2.

6. See R. Hutton, *The Royalist War Effort* (Harlow, 1982), pp. 155–65; J. Morrill (ed.), *Reactions to the English Civil War* (London, 1982), p. 21.

7. Shuttleworth papers cited in G. C. Miller, *Hoghton Tower* (Preston, 1954), p. 54; J. Harland (ed.), *Lancashire Lieutenancy*, Chetham Soc. (1859), pp. 312–14.

8. *A True and Full Relation*, Ormerod, *Tracts Relating to Military Proceedings in Lancashire* (1844), pp. 63–6.

9. *Lancashire's Valley of Achor* in Ormerod, *Tracts Relating to Military Proceedings in Lancashire* (1844), pp. 124–5; *Discourse of the Warr in Lancashire*, p. 20; Broxap, pp. 60–1.

10. *Rosworme's Good Service* in Ormerod, *Tracts Relating to Military Proceedings in Lancashire* (1844), p. 224; *Discourse of the Warr in Lancashire*, pp. 20–1.

11. See W. A. Abram, *A History of Blackburn* (Blackburn, 1877), pp. 118–22, with particular thanks to Mr Max Simon of Carnforth for the reference.

12. *Orders Concluded by the Lord Strange and His Adherents at Preston*, (H) 28; *Discourse of the Warr in Lancashire*, p. 17 (The full pay list appears in the appendices of this volume.) *House of Lords Journal*, vol. 5, 26 January 1643, pp. 570–4. Gratton, *Parliamentarian and Royalist War Effort in Lancashire*, citing Anderton and Houghton Green Papers, pp. 145–64.

13. *Discourse of the Warr in Lancashire*, pp. 16–19.

14. Extract reprinted in G. C. Miller, *Hoghton Tower* (Preston, 1954), pp. 57–8; see also P. R. Newman, 'The Royalist Army in Northern England', unpublished D. Phil., York, 1978, pp. 24–31.

15. Ashmolean manuscript 830, f. 289, cited in Broxap, p. 57; *Lancashire's Valley of Achor* in Ormerod, *Tracts Relating to Military Proceedings in Lancashire* (1844), p. 127.

16. *Discourse of the Warr in Lancashire*, pp. 18–19.

17. Tilsley, *The True Relation* in Ormerod, *Tracts Relating to Military Proceedings in Lancashire* (1844), p. 73.

18. *Discourse of the Warr in Lancashire*, pp. 23–4: John Tilsley, 11 February 1643, *Perfect Relation*, 10 February 1643, and *Lancashire's Valley of Achor*, in Ormerod, *Tracts Relating to Military Proceedings in Lancashire* (1844), pp. 71–6, 126–7.

19. Ibid., pp. 80–1, 127–8: an original *Punctuall Relation* survives in the British Library, Thomason collection, E 91 (1).

20. Ormerod, *Tracts Relating to Military Proceedings in Lancashire* (1844), pp. 81–2; W. Eldred, *The Gunner's Glasse* (London, 1646), p. 141; D. Ufano, *Trato de Artilleria* (Brussels, 1613), *passim*.

21. G. Pendlebury, *Aspects of the English Civil War in Bolton and its Neighbourhood*, Manchester 1983, p. 8; Ormerod, *Tracts Relating to Military Proceedings in Lancashire* (1844), pp. 74–8, 82–4, 129.

22. Ormerod, *Tracts Relating to Military Proceedings in Lancashire* (1844), p. 84; *Discourse of the Warr in Lancashire*, p. 24.

23. Ibid., pp. 25–6; *God's Lift Up Hand For Lancashire*, in Ormerod, *Tracts Relating to Military Proceedings in Lancashire* (1844), pp. 88–90.

24. *Discourse of the Warr in Lancashire*, pp. 26–7; Broxap, pp. 71–4; *Lancashire's Valley of Achor*, in Ormerod, *Tracts Relating to Military Proceedings in Lancashire* (1844), p. 130; T. Heywood (ed.), *Letter From Sir John Seaton*, Chetham Soc. (1862), pp. 12–13.

25. H. Peters, 'Observations on Three Pieces of Iron Solid Round Shot Found in Fleetwood', unpublished manuscript, Lancashire County Museums, 1976, *passim*. The shot were weighed and measured by Ian Gibson, then Keeper of Technology. Peters also contains additional references to Porter's *History of the Fylde*, and other secondary material. Several other civil war cannon balls are preserved in local public collections, notably Warrington Museum and Art Gallery (accession numbers 21.03; 43.33; 682; 686; 689; 691).

26. *Discourse of the Warr in Lancashire*, pp. 28–9; *Mercurius Aulicus*, 26 March–2 April 1643; S. Reid, *The Finest Knight in England* (Aberdeen, 1979), *passim*.

27. *Mercurius Aulicus*, and *Lancaster's Massacre*, in Ormerod, *Tracts Relating to Military Proceedings in Lancashire* (1844), pp. 84–8; F. R. Raines (ed.), *The Papers of James Stanley*, Chetham Soc., vol. lxvi (1867), f. lxxiv, 22 March 1643. See also Sir William Dugdale (ed.), *History and Antiquities*, (introduction), and E. Warburton, *Memoirs of Prince Rupert and the Cavaliers* (London, 1849), p. 143.

28. Ibid.; T. Heywood (ed.), *Letter From Sir John Seton*, pp. 10–15.

29. *Discourse of the Warr in Lancashire*, pp. 28–30; Broxap, pp. 74–7.

30. Heywood, *op. cit.*, pp. 14–15.

31. J.C. Scholes and W. Pimblett, *History of Bolton* (Bolton, 1892), pp. 404–6; *Lancashire's Valley of Achor* in Ormerod, *Tracts Relating to Military Proceedings in Lancashire* (1844), pp. 133–4. Denbigh manuscript, cited in Broxap, p. 78.

32. A comparison with the activities of the New Model can be made against the lists and tables provided in J. Sprigge's *Anglia Rediviva* (London, 1647), pp. 332–5. See also I. Gentles, *The New Model Army* (Oxford, 1992), pp. 28–52, and R. Hutton, *The Royalist War Effort* (London, 1982), pp. 29, 41–2, 50, 61–2.

33. *Discourse of the Warr in Lancashire*, p. 31; *Rosworme's Good Service* in Ormerod, *Tracts Relating to Military Proceedings in Lancashire* (1844), pp. 225–8; *Lancashire's Valley of Achor* in Ormerod, *Tracts Relating to Military Proceedings in Lancashire* (1844), p. 134; *Manchester's Joy*, in Ormerod, *Tracts Relating to Military Proceedings in Lancashire* (1844), pp. 92–4.

34. *Discourse of the Warr in Lancashire*, p. 31; R. N. Dore (ed.), *The Letter Books of Sir William Brereton*, vol. 1 (1984), pp. 17–18, 528; R. N. Dore, *The Civil Wars in Cheshire* (Chester, 1966), pp. 11–39. See also S. Harrison *et al.*, *Loyal Chester* (Chester Record Office, 1984), *passim*.

35. Thomas Malbon's account in J. Hall (ed.), *Memorials of the Civil War in Cheshire and Adjacent Counties*, Lancashire and Cheshire Record Society, vol. xix (1889), pp. 25–32.

36. *Mercurius Aulicus* and *Providence Improved*, cited in Ormerod, *Tracts Relating to Military Proceedings in Lancashire* (1844), pp. 94–5.

37. Interestingly the word 'hubbub' – meaning 'confused din' – is thought to have been derived from Irish war cries. On the subject of uniforms and field signs see C. H. Firth, *Cromwell's Army*, 4th edn (London, 1962), pp. 230–50; see also P. J. Haythornthwaite, *The English Civil War* (Poole, 1983), pp. 24–55, 133–49; C. Carlton, *Going to the Wars* (London, 1992), pp. 96–7, 237–8; K. Roberts, *Soldiers of the Civil War (1): Infantry* (London, 1989), pp. 24–7.

Chapter 5: *'Brave and victorious': the war turns for parliament*

1. *A True Relation*, in Ormerod, *Tracts Relating to Military Proceedings in Lancashire* (1844), pp. 95–8; *Discourse of the Warr in Lancashire*, pp. 31–2; see also *A Description of the Memorable Sieges and Battles in the North of England that Happened During the Civil War* (Bolton, 1785), pp. 82–4.

2. Captain Ashton of Whalley was a kinsman of Colonel Ashton of Middleton; both fought for parliament.

3. *Discourse of the Warr in Lancashire*, pp. 32–4. I am particularly grateful to Mr Martyn Lucas of Clayton-le-Woods, and to Dot Bruns, Finds Liaison Officer Lancashire and Cumbria, for bringing the Read Bridge shot finds to attention.

4. Ormerod, *Tracts Relating to Military Proceedings in Lancashire* (1844), pp. 97–8; Broxap, pp. 81–5, and S. Reid, *The Finest Knight in England* (Aberdeen, 1979), *passim*.

5. *Discourse of the Warr in Lancashire*, p. 34; *Lancashire's Valley of Achor*, in Ormerod, *Tracts Relating to Military Proceedings in Lancashire* (1844), pp. 135–6.

6. *Speciall Passages*, in Ormerod, *Tracts Relating to Military Proceedings in Lancashire* (1844), pp. 98–9. A pair of Fleetwood family helmets is retained in the old church atop the hill at Penwortham. In 2000 these were displayed at the Museum of Lancashire.

7. *The Kingdom's Weekly Intelligencer*, in Ormerod, *Tracts Relating to Military Proceedings in Lancashire* (1844), pp. 101–2. J. Wilson, *Fairfax* (New York, 1985), pp. 28–32; J. J. Bagley, *The Earls of Derby* (London, 1985), pp. 86–8; *Discourse of the Warr in Lancashire*, pp. 36–40; Fairfax, *Short Memorials* in C. H. Firth (ed.), *Stuart Tracts* (New York, 1964), pp. 375–9; *A Miraculous Victory*, E 104 (13).

8. J. P. Earwaker, *Local Gleanings*, p. 259; Ormerod, *Tracts Relating to Military Proceedings in Lancashire* (1844), p. 101; Kendrick, *An Account of Warrington Siege AD 1643*, Historic Society of Lancashire and Cheshire (1852).

9. R. Lockyer (ed.), *Clarendon's History of the Great Rebellion*, p. 102; J. J. Bagley *The Earls of Derby* (London, 1985), p. 87; Guizot de Witt, *The Lady of Latham* (London, 1869), pp. 68–71: P. Draper, *A History of the House of Stanley* (Ormskirk, 1854). See also Derby Papers CO32, f. 88.

10. *Discourse of the Warr in Lancashire*, p. 38.

11. Fairfax, *Short Memorials*, reprinted in C. H. Firth, *Stuart Tracts* (New York, 1964), pp. 378–83; P. Gaunt, *The Cromwellian Gazetteer* (Stroud, 1987), pp. 167–8; D. Cooke, *The Civil War in Yorkshire* (Barnsley, 2004), pp. 61–78; J. Wilson, *Fairfax* (New York, 1985), pp. 31–4; *A Declaration and Summons*, in Ormerod, *Tracts Relating to Military Proceedings in Lancashire* (1844), pp. 143–6.

12. Ibid., p. 40; *House of Commons Journal*, 3 June, 1643.

13. *Lancashire's Valley of Achor*, in Ormerod, *Tracts Relating to Military Proceedings in Lancashire* (1844), pp. 139–40; *Certaine Informations* and Rigby's Letter in Ormerod, *Tracts Relating to Military Proceedings in Lancashire* (1844), pp. 106, 148–9; Broxap, p. 95.

14. Broxap has it, apparently on Ormerod's authority, that Thurland Castle was besieged twice: briefly and successfully in the early summer of 1643, and then again in August and September. From the sources this seems unlikely. It is certainly not mentioned in the *Discourse of the Warr in Lancashire*, where the author was present at 'the siege against Thurlum'. *Lancashire's Valley of Achor* does mention, confusingly, that the day after Ashton took Hornby 'Thursland Castle was delivered upon unkept conditions, which would be a wonder here and elsewhere, did we not know the principle, *"No faith is to be kept with Heretikes"*.' From this is seems probable that the rendering of Thurland was promised initially, and, the deal being reneged upon, the parliament troops proceeded to besiege it – just once. See Ormerod, *Tracts Relating to Military Proceedings in Lancashire* (1844), pp. 140, 151.

15. Rigby's letter of 17 October 1643, reprinted in Ormerod, *Tracts Relating to Military Proceedings in Lancashire* (1844), pp. 148–51; *Discourse of the Warr in Lancashire*, pp. 41–2. 'God with us' – 'Gott mit uns' – was later the motto of the German army in two world wars.

16. S. Taylor, *Cartmel People and Priory* (Kendal, 1955), *passim*. Peter Gaunt has attempted to track Oliver Cromwell's personal routes around the country during the civil wars, suggesting that he did not reach Lancashire at all until 1648, see P Gaunt, *The Cromwellian Gazetteer*

(Stroud, 2000), pp. 224–35. This point is explored more fully in Appendix XI.

17. *House of Commons Journal*, vol. 3, 18 November 1643. Park's account is reprinted in A. Fell, *A Furness Military Chronicle* (Ulverston, 1937), pp. 50–1.

18. *Discourse of the Warr in Lancashire*, pp. 42–5; Ormerod, *Tracts Relating to Military Proceedings in Lancashire* (1844), pp. 146–7; *House of Lords Journal*, vol. 6, 27 October 1643, pp. 274–82.

19. R. N. Dore and J. Lowe, 'The Battle of Nantwich, 25 January 1644', *Transactions of the Historic Society of Lancashire and Cheshire*, vol. 113 (1961), pp. 97–123.

20. R. N. Dore, *The Civil Wars in Cheshire* (Chester, 1966), pp. 30–9; Ormerod, *Tracts Relating to Military Proceedings in Lancashire* (1844), pp. 152–4; A. M. Robinson, *Cheshire in the Great Civil War* (1895), pp. 144–50.

21. See R. Hutton, 'The Failure of the Lancashire Cavaliers', *Transactions of the Historic Society of Lancashire and Cheshire*, vol. 129 (1980), p. 58.

Chapter 6: *'Stealing the earl's breeches: the first siege of Lathom House, 1644*

1. *A Briefe Journall of the Siege Against Lathom* was discovered bound up with British Museum, Harleian Manuscript 2074: another version is Wood Manuscript D.16 in the Ashmolean at Oxford. Reprints are found in Ormerod, *Tracts Relating to Military Proceedings in Lancashire* (1844), pp. 155–86, and as an appendix to Lucy Hutchinson's *Memoirs of the Life of Colonel Hutchinson*, Bohn edition (London, 1846), pp. 487–516. The *Briefe Journall* has been variously attributed to Edward Halsall, Colonel Chisnall, or Chaplain, later Bishop, Brideoake. The only surviving parliamentarian account of any substance is in the *Discourse of the Warr in Lancashire*.

2. Madame Guizot de Wit, *The Lady of Latham* (London, 1869), p. 15; C. Pilkington, *To Play the Man* (Preston, 1991), pp. 31–5. An extremely useful recent study is S. Kmec, 'Royalist Noblewomen and Family Fortunes During the Civil War', *Journal of the Oxford History Society* (Hilary term, 2004). See also P. R. Newman, 'The Royalist Army in Northern England', unpublished D.Phil. thesis, York, 1978, pp. 316–31; and C Petrie (ed.), *King Charles, Prince Rupert and the Civil War* (London, 1974), pp. 27–36.

3. J. Barratt, *Cavaliers* (Stroud, 2000), p. 180; J. Wilson, *Fairfax* (New York, 1985), pp. 43–7; Broxap, pp. 100–13. See also M. C. Rowsell, *The Life Story of Charlotte de la Tremoille* (London, 1905), pp. 32–9.

4. *Briefe Journall* in Ormerod, *Tracts Relating to Military Proceedings in Lancashire* (1844), pp. 159–66, 184–6; see also J.M. Lewis, 'Lathom House, Lathom, near Ormskirk', unpublished typescript, Lancashire County Council Environment Department files, 1990.

5. From Harleian Manuscript 293,367, cited in Hutchinson, *Memoirs*, p. 489.

6. Seacome, *House of Stanley*, p. 90; also reprinted in Hutchinson, *Memoirs*, pp. 489–90. See also P. Young and W. Emberton, *Sieges of the Great Civil War* (London, 1978), pp. 58–64, and their *Cavalier Army* (London, 1974), pp. 151–7.

7. T. Buxton, *The History, Traditions, and Antiquities of South West Lancashire … and the Siege of Lathom* (LRO, 1889); M. Fletcher *et al.*, *Lathom House, Ormskirk: Survey and Evaluation Report*, 1997–98/024/AUA7559, Lancaster University Archaeology Unit; N.J. Neil, *Lathom House: Documentary Research for Archaeological Evaluation*, Lancaster University Archaeology Unit, 1996; *Lathom Park Near Ormskirk: Desk Based Archaeological Assessment*, West Yorkshire Archaeology, report 802, May 2000; N. Nayling, *Tree-Ring Analysis of Timbers From Lathom House*, English Heritage Report 5/2000; *Land East of the West Wing, Lathom House Near Ormskirk*: Archaeological Evaluation, Matrix Archaeology Report 2002–12, Manchester 2002.

8. Repton's manuscript, *Red Book*, with its many illustrations and overlays of intended works on the grounds was purchased from America by Lancashire Record Office in 2004. It was later displayed in the Museum of Lancashire. See also C. Pilkington, *To Play the Man* (1991), pp. 19–30. The idea that Spa Roughs could have been the site of the house, proposed in the nineteenth century, hinted at by Broxap in 1910, and later supported by Mike Lawson, has hopefully now been laid to rest. See also P. Harrington, *Archaeology of the English Civil War* (Princes Risborough, 1992), *passim*, and G. Lea, *Handbook to Ormskirk* (Ormskirk, 1893), p. 79. Particularly useful comparisons for the Lathom works appear in *Newark on Trent: The Civil War Siegeworks* (RCHM, London, 1964), and M. Stoyle, *Exeter City Defences Project*, Exeter Archaeological Field Unit, reports 88.12 (1988) and 90.26 (1990).

9. The author is especially indebted to Peter Iles of Lancashire's Sites and Monument Record (SMR) in Lancashire County Council's Environment Department for access to the latest archaeological evidence, as also to Gill Chitty, former county archaeologist, for arranging an extremely useful symposium on the site. A useful reference for finds identification is P. Courtney, *Small Arms Accessories of the mid-Seventeenth Century*, Datasheet 11, 1988, reprinted in *Finds Research Group 700–1700*, consolidated data sheets, University of Oxford (1985–98).

10. *Briefe Journall* in Ormerod, *Tracts Relating to Military Proceedings in Lancashire* (1844), pp. 168–70; *Discourse of the Warr in Lancashire*, p. 46; *Cromwell's Trench, Spa Roughs, Lathom: A Report Upon the Archaeological Evidence and Possibilities for Future Survey* (Lathom and District Archaeological Society, 1997). See also Rowsell, *op. cit.*, pp. 120–48; G. Lea, *op. cit.*, p. 79.

11. T. Fairfax, *Short Memorials*, reprinted in C.H. Firth (ed.), *Stuart Tracts* (New York, 1964), pp. 351–98, particularly p. 392.

12. *House of Commons Journal*, 20 May 1644; S. J. Guscott, *Humphrey Chetham* (Manchester, 2003), pp. 224–7.

13. CSPD, vol. DI, 18 April 1644, p126. Another mention of the shortages at Lathom appears in vol. DII, 5 June 1644.

14. *Briefe Journall*, in Ormerod, *Tracts Relating to Military Proceedings in Lancashire* (1844), p. 173; Derby Papers CO32, ff.87–8.

15. Ibid., pp. 174–5; see also S. Bull, 'The Furie of the Ordnanc', unpublished Ph.D. thesis, University of Wales, Swansea, vol. II, pp. 339–95; *Mercurius Aulicus*, 18 May 1644, E 50 (6).

16. *Briefe Journall*, in Ormerod, *Tracts Relating to Military Proceedings in Lancashire* (1844), pp. 175–81.

17. Ibid., pp. 182–6; *Discourse of the Warr in Lancashire*, pp. 47–9; Guizot de Witt, *The Lady of Latham*, pp. 92–5; J. J. Bagley, *The Earls of Derby* (London, 1985), pp. 88–91; *Mercurius Aulicus*, 18 May 1644, E 50 (6), and E 49 May 1644 (3).

Chapter 7: *'Prince Robber' in Lancashire, 1644*

1. C. V. Wedgwood, *The King's War* (London, 1958), pp. 283–300; J. Barratt, *Cavaliers* (Stroud, 2000), pp. 84–8; C. Petrie (ed.), *King Charles, Prince Rupert and the Civil War* (London, 1974), pp. 112–15; Byron and Derby letters cited in Broxap, pp. 115–17; Lockyer (ed.), *Clarendon's History of the Great Rebellion*, p. 196.

2. P. Morrah, *Prince Rupert of the Rhine* (London, 1976), *passim*; Malcolm Rogers, *William Dobson* (National Portrait Gallery, 1984), pp. 58–61; R. N. Dore, *The Civil Wars in Cheshire* (Chester, 1966), pp. 40–2; J. E. Bailey, *The Life of a Lancashire Rector During the Civil War*

(Leigh, 1877), *passim*; F. R. Raines (ed.), *The Stanley Papers*, Chetham Soc, vol. lxvi (1867), f. xcix.

3. *House of Lords Journal*, vol. 6, 3 August 1644, pp. 651–7.

4. *Discourse of the Warr in Lancashire*, p. 51; S. Reid, *The Finest Knight in England*, *passim*; Seacome, *Memoirs*, reprinted on Ormerod, *Tracts Relating to Military Proceedings in Lancashire* (1844), pp. 196–8; also *Prince Rupert's Diary*, extract reprinted in P. Young, *Marston Moor*, pp. 212–14.

5. J. C. Scholes and W. Pimblett, *History of Bolton* (Bolton, 1892), pp. 400–17.

6. *An Exact Relation of the Bloody and Barbarous Massacre at Bolton*, in Ormerod, *Tracts Relating to Military Proceedings in Lancashire* (1844), p. 192.

7. G. Pendlebury, *Aspects of the English Civil War in Bolton and Its Neighbourhood, 1640–1660* (Manchester, 1983), pp. 12–13. Carte manuscript, cited in P. Young, *Marston Moor*, p. 211. On parish registers, death, and identification in war, see also M. P. Gutman, *War and Rural Life in the Early Modern Low Countries* (Princeton, 1980), pp. 151–73.

8. R. Heyrick, *Prince Roberts Bloudie Carriage at Bolton*, 7 June 1644, Bolton Reference Library, also Ormerod, *Tracts Relating to Military Proceedings in Lancashire* (1844), pp. 198–9.

9. Earls of Leven and Manchester and Lord Fairfax to the Committee of Both Kingdoms, 5 June 1644, CSPD, pp. 206–7.

10. Ibid., 1644, pp. 187, 192; Young, *Marston Moor*, p. 195: see also A. Woolrych, *Britain in Revolution* (Oxford, 2002), pp. 281–8.

11. 'An Account of the Siege and Taking of Liverpool' from Seacome's *Memoirs of the House of Derby*, reprinted in Ormerod, *Tracts Relating to Military Proceedings in Lancashire* (1844), pp. 199–201. *House of Commons Journal*, vol. 3, 15 December 1643; PRO, W0 47/1 ff. 44–5; see also J. Barratt, *Cannon on the Mersey* (Birkenhead, 1996), and *The Siege of Liverpool* (Bristol, 1993), *passim*.

12. E. M. Platt, 'Liverpool During the Civil War', in *Transactions of the Historic Society of Lancashire and Cheshire*, vol. lxi (1910), pp. 183–202. J. Barratt, *Cavaliers* (Stroud, 2000), p. 197. See also P. Harrington, *English Civil War Fortifications, 1642–51* (Oxford 2003), *passim*.

13. Carte cited in J. Barratt, *The Siege of Liverpool*, p. 13; T. Royle, *Civil War* (London, 2004), p. 289. On Rupert and Liverpool see also James Stonehouse, *The Streets of Liverpool* (Liverpool, 1869), pp. 36, 91, 208, 215–16.

14. *House of Commons Journal*, vol. 3, 13 June 1644.

15. J. Hall (ed.), *Memorials of the Civil War in Cheshire and Adjacent Counties*, Lancashire and Cheshire Record Society, vol. xix (1889), p. 132.

16. *Rosworme's Good Service*, reprinted in Ormerod, *Tracts Relating to Military Proceedings in Lancashire* (1844), pp. 229–231; CSPD, 1644, p. 205. Broxap, pp. 119–20, refers to the incident as 'Heywood's plot'.

17. Letter reprinted in C. Petrie (ed.), *King Charles, Prince Rupert, and the Civil War* (London, 1974), pp. 113–14. Broxap, pp. 127–30. See also R. Hutton, *The Royalist War Effort*, pp. 141–2.

18. R. T. Spence, *Skipton Castle in the Great Civil War* (Skipton, 1991), pp. 58–64.

19. Brigadier Peter Young was of the opinion that the following of Rupert's force were mainly raised in Lancashire: Molyneux's foot; Tyldesley's (horse and foot); Chisenall's foot. Additionally the Marquis of Newcastle's forces included the horse regiments of Bradshaw; Gerlington; Malham; Preston, and Tempest all of which were partly Lancashire. Newcastle's foot included Gerlington's and Towneley's which were wholly or mainly Lancashire troops. P. Young, *Marston Moor* (Kineton, 1970), pp. 53–60. J. M. Gratton makes a case for twelve royalist units with Lancashire troops in the ranks, as well as suggesting a stronger Lancashire

parliamentarian presence at the great battle: 'The Parliamentarian and Royalist War Effort in Lancashire', unpublished Ph.D. thesis, Manchester, p. 110. See also P. R. Newman, *Marston Moor* (Chichester, 1981), pp. 21–2.

Chapter 8: *'A fatal blow': the aftermath of Marston Moor*

1. A. D. H. Leadman, *Battles Fought in Yorkshire* (1891), p. 141; P. R. Newman and P. R. Roberts, *Marston Moor* (Kineton, 2003), pp. 123–7; P. Young *Marston Moor* (Kineton, 1970), pp. 143–7; T. C. Smith, *History of the Parish of Chipping* (Preston, 1894), pp. 241–2. J. M. Gratton, *The Royalist and Parliamentarian War Effort in Lancashire*, p. 107.

2. C. E. H. Healey (ed.), *Bellum Civile: Hopton's Narrative*, Somerset Record Society (1902), pp. 62–3; *House of Commons Journal*, 1 August 1644; R. N. Dore, *Letter Books of Sir William Brereton*, vol. 2, pp. 594–602.

3. P. Wenham, *The Great and Close Siege of York, 1644* (Kineton, 1970), pp. 85–107; D. Cooke, *The Civil War in Yorkshire* (Barnsley, 2004), pp. 121–59.

4. See A. Fell, *A Furness Military Chronicle* (Ulverston, 1937), pp. 46–8.

5. The general chronology of Rupert's retreat through Lancashire in mid-July 1644 is agreed, but the dates given of his visits to specific places differ by a day or two depending on the source. For slightly varying interpretations see J. Kenyon, *The Civil Wars of England* (London, 1988), pp. 109–11, and P. Newman, *Marston Moor* (Chichester, 1981), pp. 131–4, as well as Broxap, pp. 130–3. John Kenyon goes rather further regarding Rupert's lack of direction in late July 1644, saying that he 'wandered up and down Lancashire to no apparent purpose'. See also A. Fell, *Furness Military Chronicle* (Ulverston, 1937), pp. 45–8.

6. See F. H. Sunderland, *Marmaduke Lord Langdale* (London, 1926), pp. 23–43, 57–93; J. Barratt, *Cavaliers* (Stroud, 2000), pp. 152–4; D Lloyd, *Memoirs of the Lives, Actions etc.* (London, 1668), p. 550; P. R. Newman, *Royalist Officers* (New York, 1981), pp. 221–3.

7. R Lockyer (ed.), *Clarendon's History of the Great Rebellion* (1967), pp. 219–20.

8. S. Reid, *The Finest Knight in England* (Aberdeen, 1979), *passim*; P. Young, *Marston Moor* (Kineton, 1970), pp. 97–8; P. R. Newman and P. R. Roberts, *Marston Moor* (Pickering, 2003), pp. 59–61.

9. *London Post* and *Perfect Diurnall*, in Ormerod, *Tracts Relating to Military Proceedings in Lancashire* (1844), pp. 206–7; J. J. Bagley, *The Earls of Derby*, pp. 90–2; F. J. Leslie *James, Seventh Earl of Derby*, Transactions of the Historic Society of Lancashire and Cheshire, v (1889), *passim*.

10. *DNB*, 'Meldrum'; Royal Commission on Historical Monuments, *Newark on Trent: The Civil War Siege Works* (London, 1964), pp. 18–19, 61; L. Hutchinson, *Memoirs of the Life of Colonel Hutchinson* (reprinted London, 1846), pp. 218–20.

11. *Perfect Diurnall*, reprinted in Ormerod, *Tracts Relating to Military Proceedings in Lancashire* (1844), pp. 204–6; *Discourse of the Warr in Lancashire*, pp. 54–6.

12. Broxap, p. 132; *Discourse of the Warr in Lancashire*, p. 55; See also C. Pilkington, *To Play the Man* (Preston, 1991), pp. 111–12, and Ormerod, *Tracts Relating to Military Proceedings in Lancashire* (1844), p. 205. The spot where the 'portly' Cavalier died is occupied by, or immediately beside, the Bridge Inn.

13. *Discourse of the Warr in Lancashire*, pp. 55–6.

14. Ibid.

15. This account of Ormskirk follows essentially the lines first laid down by J. Barratt in his monograph, *The Siege of Liverpool and the Lancashire Campaign, 1644* (Bristol, 1993), pp. 14–21. For Byron's account see British Library, Additional Ms 18981.

16. *Perfect Occurrences*, reprinted in Ormerod, *Tracts Relating to Military Proceedings in Lancashire* (1844), p. 204.

17. *Discourse of the Warr in Lancashire*, p. 58; Ormerod, *Tracts Relating to Military Proceedings in Lancashire* (1844), p. 204; see also J. Barratt, *Cannon on the Mersey* (Birkenhead, 1996), pp. 37–40.

18. *Prince Rupert's Diary*, Carte Ms, x, 664, transcribed in P. Young, *Marston Moor* (Kineton, 1970), pp. 210–11.

19. The full list of officers taken in addition to the Colonels were listed as Captains, James Anderton; Ecclestone; Butler; Brooks; Lee and Atherton: Lieutenants, Sturbane; Thomas Massock; John de Hurst; John Mogrow; Walter Chamberlain and Nathaniel Jones: Cornets, Will Johnson; Edward Stanley; Richard Wright and Henry Gillibrand. See also S. Reid, *The Finest Knight in England* (Aberdeen, 1979), *passim*, and Gratton, *op. cit.*, p. 236.

20. *Discourse of the Warr in Lancashire*, pp. 58–9.

21. R. Lockyer (ed.), *Clarendon's History of the Rebellion* (Oxford, 1967), pp. 220–2; Firth Ms C7 f. 146, cited in Barratt, *Siege of Liverpool*, p. 21.

Chapter 9: *The end of the first civil war, 1645–46*

1. In Peter Newman's analysis lack of coordination across the Pennines is one of the defining features of the royalist war effort in the north: see his 'Royalist Armies in Northern England', unpublished D. Phil. thesis, University of York, 1978, *passim*. *Discourse of the Warr in Lancashire*, p. 59.

2. Reprinted in Ormerod, *Tracts Relating to Military Proceedings in Lancashire* (1844), pp. 206, 229. Rosworm's account is difficult to follow chronologically, but it appears that he received his orders to go to Liverpool on 16 August, probably arriving there after the battle of Ormskirk a few days later. Another account of the battle at Montgomery is given in P. Gaunt, *A Nation Under Siege: The Civil War in Wales* (London, 1991), pp. 46–51.

3. *House of Lords Journal*, vol. 6, 23 September 1644; see also R. N. Dore, *The Civil Wars in Cheshire* (Chester, 1966), pp. 42–3.

4. CSPD, DIII 2 October 1644, pp. 5–6; R. N. Dore (ed.), *Letter Books of Sir William Brereton*, vol. 2 (1990), p. 479.

5. Meldrum's summons to Liverpool, 30 September 1644, in J. Barratt, *Cannon on the Mersey* (Birkenhead, 1996), p. 42.

6. *Perfect Diurnall* in Ormerod, *Tracts Relating to Military Proceedings in Lancashire* (1844), pp. 207–8; CSPD, cited in Broxap, p. 136; Barratt, *op. cit.*, pp. 43–9.

7. R. N. Dore (ed.), *The Letter Books of Sir William Brereton*, vol. 1 (1984), p. 127; R. Lockyer (ed.), *Clarendon's History of the Great Rebellion* (London, 1967), pp. 253–4. S. Harrison, *Loyal Chester* (Chester City Record Office, 1984), pp. 22–4, 35–6. *House of Commons Journal*, vol. 3, 9 November 1644.

8. *Discourse of the Warr in Lancashire*, p. 60; *House of Commons Journal*, vol. 3, 4 November 1644; Broxap, pp. 136–7.

9. See C. V. Wedgwood, *The King's War* (London, 1958), pp. 385–7, 393–4; P. Gregg, *King Charles I* (London, 1981), p. 391, and C. Carlton, *Charles I* (London, 1984), pp. 278–85. Broxap, pp. 138–9. The Uxbridge propositions are replicated in Gardiner, and in brief in Anne Hughes (ed.), *Seventeenth-Century England, A Changing Culture* (London, 1980), vol. 1, pp. 101–4. See also R. Hutton, 'The Failure of the Lancashire Cavaliers', in *Transactions of the Historic Society of Lancashire and Cheshire*, vol. 129 (1980), pp. 58–62. Derby Papers CO31, f. 42.

10. *Discourse of the Warr in Lancashire*, p. 60; see also E. Collinson, *Greenhalgh Castle, Garstang and the Earls of Derby* (1993), *passim*.

11. *Discourse of the Warr in Lancashire*, p. 61.

12. Reprinted in Ormerod, *Tracts Relating to Military Proceedings in Lancashire* (1844), p. 209. See also C. Pilkington, *To Play the Man* (Preston, 1991), pp. 118–22, and H. Fishwick (ed.), *Lancashire and Cheshire Church Surveys*, Record Society (1879), pp. 38–9.

13. *House of Commons Journal*, vol. 4, 27 February 1645; P Young and W Emberton, *Sieges of the Great Civil War* (London, 1978), pp. 59–64.

14. *Brief Memorials of the Unfortunate Success of His Majesty's Army and Affairs in the Year 1645*, reprinted in P. Young, *Naseby* (London, 1985), pp. 312–20; J. Sprigge, *Anglia Rediviva* (London, 1646), pp. 26–46; R. N. Dore (ed.), *Letter Books of Sir William Brereton*, vol. 1 (1984), pp. 421, 482. See also M. Ashley, *Naseby* (Stroud, 1992), pp. 54–66. J. P. Earwaker (ed.), *The Constables Accounts of the Manor of Manchester* (Manchester 1891–93), pp. 120–30.

15. Ormerod, *Tracts Relating to Military Proceedings in Lancashire* (1844), pp. 209–10; *Discourse of the Warr in Lancashire*, p. 62.

16. G. de Witt, *The Lady of Latham* (London, 1869), pp. 110–11; E. Besly, *Coins and Medals of the English Civil War* (National Museum of Wales, 1990), p. 74.

17. Broxap, pp. 144–6; Ormerod, *Tracts Relating to Military Proceedings in Lancashire* (1844), pp. 211–12.

18. *Discourse of the Warr in Lancashire*, pp. 62–3.

19. Ormerod, *Tracts Relating to Military Proceedings in Lancashire* (1844), p. 211.

20. R. N. Dore (ed.), *Letter Books of Sir William Brereton*, vol. 2, items 1013, 1031, 1062, 1074–1075, 1117, 1141. Broxap, pp. 148–9, makes surprisingly little of the near collapse of the Lancashire parliamentarian war effort in December 1645.

21. For Lancashire there is a Deputy Lieutenancy Letter Book within Manchester Archives, L1/40/1, mainly covering Lonsdale and Amounderness, 1625–87, and fragmentary letters, as within Brereton's correspondence. There is nothing so far discovered that matches the scope of the Kent account books, or the minute books of Dorset and Staffordshire.

22. See S. Roberts, 'Local Government Reform in England and Wales During the Interregnum', in I. Roots (ed.), *Into Another Mould* (Exeter, 1983), pp. 24–41.

23. R. N. Dore, *The Civil Wars in Cheshire* (Chester, 1966), p. 28.

24. See J. M. Gratton, 'The Parliamentarian and Royalist War Effort in Lancashire', unpublished Ph.D. thesis, Manchester University, 1998, pp. 164–81.

25. C. B. Phillips, 'County Committees and Local Government in Cumberland and Westmorland' 1642–1660, in *Northern History*, vol. v (1970), pp. 34–66.

26. See R. N. Dore (ed.), *Letter Books of Sir William Brereton*, vol. 2, pp. 183, 194, 277, 402, 403, 561–4, and Ormerod, *Tracts Relating to Military Proceedings in Lancashire* (1844), pp. 210–11. See also Broxap, pp. 152–5.

27. *House of Lords Journal*, vol. 7, 29 August 1645. The full list of Lancashire committee members is given in Appendix II. See also B. G. Blackwood, *The Lancashire Gentry*, Chetham Soc., (1978), pp. 13, 73, 92.

Chapter 10: *War without conclusion and the 'Province' of Lancashire*

1. G. E. Aylmer (ed.), *The Interregnum: The Quest for Settlement 1646–1660* (London, 1974), is a particularly useful background synthesis.

2. Lancashire's relatively good situation appears to agree with the continental picture for 1646. At Maastricht rye prices were at their lowest for 25 years: throughout the Low Countries

grain prices were roughly half what they would be in 1648. In many other parts of England the harvest was poor. See J. Kenyon, *The Civil Wars of England* (London, 1988), p. 160; see also R. I. Rotberg and T. K. Rabb (eds), *Climate and History* (Princeton, 1981), pp. 32, 54, 63–83, 261.

3. *Discourse of the Warr in Lancashire*, pp. 63–4. We lack detailed evidence as to which Lancashire units were disembodied at what dates, but in other counties committee expenditure plunged in 1647 – in Kent, for example, to a tenth of its former level – suggesting that a majority of the local forces went home. *House of Commons Journal*, vol. 5, 25 March 1647, pp. 123–5.

4. Cited in J. Tonzeau, *The Rise and Progress of Liverpool* (Liverpool, 1910), pp. 203, 208, 228.

5. On the New Model see J. Sprigge, *Anglia Rediviva* (London, 1647), *passim*; I. Gentles, *The New Model Army* (Oxford, 1992), pp. 1–52; C. H. Firth, *Cromwell's Army* (London, 1962), pp. 34–67, and M. Kishlansky, *The Rise of the New Model Army* (New York, 1979), *passim*.

6. G. E. Aylmer (ed.), *The Interregnum*, pp. 2–3.

7. I. Gentles, 'The New Model Officer Corps in 1647: a Collective Portrait', in *Social History*, vol. 22, number 2 (May 1997), pp. 127–44; D. Massarella, 'The Politics of the Army and the Quest for Settlement', in *Into Another Mould*, Exeter Studies in History, number 3 (1981), pp. 42–69.

8. Broxap, pp. 154–7. I. Roots, *The Great Rebellion* (London, 1966), pp. 102–21; C. Cross, 'The Church in England, 1646–1660', in G. E. Aylmer (ed.), *The Interregnum*, pp. 99–120.

9. See also C Hill, *Puritanism and Revolution* (London, 1968), pp. 197–211, and J. Morrill (ed.), *The Impact of the English Civil War* (London, 1991), pp. 50–66.

10. The most convenient single source on the remarkable Lancashire Presbyterian 'Province' is W. A. Shaw, *Materials for an Account of the Provincial Synod of the County of Lancaster, 1646–1660* (Manchester, 1890).

11. BM, (E) 372 in Shaw, *op. cit.*, pp. 18–20; on London see C. Cross in G. E. Aylmer (ed.), pp. 108–9. Individual classes met earlier, but according to Cross the London synod itself did not meet until May 1647.

12. See G. Pendlebury, *Aspects of the English Civil War in Bolton* (Swinton, 1983), pp. 17–20.

13. Shaw, *op. cit.*, pp. 52–3. See also H. Fishwick (ed.), *Lancashire and Cheshire Church Surveys, 1649–1655*, Lancashire and Cheshire Record Society (1879), pp. xvii–xxviii.

14. C. Hill, *The World Turned Upside Down* (London, 1972), pp. 73–86, 184–258.

Chapter 11: *'Routed and defeated': the Second Civil War, 1648*

1. Fairfax, *Short Memorials*, Fairfax Ms. 36, British Library, also reprinted in C. H. Firth (ed.), *Stuart Tracts* (New York, 1964), pp. 352–64; J. Morrill, *Revolt of the Provinces* (London, 1976), pp. 204–8. This chapter is inspired by S. Bull and M. Seed, *Bloody Preston* (Lancaster, 1998); see also S. Bull, *The Battle that Led to the English Republic? Preston, 1648*, in Centre for North-West Regional Studies *Regional Bulletin*, Lancaster University, number 14 (Summer 2000). The opportunity has been taken here both to correct minor errors in earlier work, and to integrate the fruits of additional research.

2. A. Woolrych, *Britain in Revolution* (Oxford, 2002), pp. 403–4.

3. J. D. Jones, *The Royal Prisoner* (Carisbrooke, 1965), *passim*; F. Bamford (ed.), *A Royalist's Notebook: The Commonplace Book of Sir John Oglander* (London, 1936), pp. 111–29; I. Roots, *The Great Rebellion* (London, 1966), pp. 112–34; G. Burnet, *The Memoirs of the Lives and Actions of James and William, Dukes of Hamilton* (Oxford, 1852), *passim*.

4. Langdale's declaration is reprinted in F. H. Sunderland, *Marmaduke Lord Langdale* (London, 1926), pp. 111–14.

5. *Discourse of the Warr in Lancashire*, p. 64; S. Jefferson (ed.), *A Narrative of the Siege of Carlisle in 1644 and 1645 by Isaac Tullie ... to Which are Added A Preface; an Historical Account of Carlisle During the Civil War; and Biographical, Historical and Explanatory Notes* (Carlisle, 1840), pp. ix–xxiv; Lockyer (ed.), *Clarendon's History of the Great Rebellion*, pp. 389–401.

6. *Letters and Declaration*, reprinted in Ormerod, *Tracts Relating to Military Proceedings in Lancashire* (1844), pp. 248–52.

7. Ibid., pp. 250–2.

8. *Commons Journal*, vol. 5, 16 May 1648, pp. 559–62. For the embodiment and first moves of the Lancashire forces J. Rushworth, *Historical Collections of Private Passages of State* (London, 1659–1701), part iv, vol. ii, p. 123.

9. E. M. Furgol, *A Regimental History of the Covenanting Armies 1639–1651* (Edinburgh, 1990), pp. 1–15, 296–359. S. Bull and M. Seed, *Bloody Preston*, pp. 32–44, 104–9; S. Reid, *The Scots Armies of the Seventeenth Century*, 4 vols (1985–90), *passim*; D. Stevenson, *Scottish Covenanters and Irish Confederates* (Belfast, 1981), pp. 253–68; F. Maurice, *The Adventures of Edward Wogan* (London, 1945), pp. 83–106.

10. Cited in D. Scott, *The Barwis Affair: Political Allegiance and the Scots During the British Civil Wars*, undated pamphlet.

11. *House of Lords Journal*, vol. 10, 19 May 1648, pp. 264–72.

12. CSPD, 1648, vol. DXVI, pp. 136–7.

13. Carlyle (ed.), pp. 267–79; S. Bull and M. Seed, *Bloody Preston*, pp. 51–62; D. Farr, *John Lambert* (Woodbridge, 2003), pp. 31–76.

14. 'Diary of Samuel Birch' in Historical Manuscripts Commission, 14th Report, Appendix Part II, *Manuscripts of his Grace the Duke of Portland*, vol. 3 (London, 1894), p. 175; BL, E 454 (10); WH Dawson *Cromwell's Understudy*, London, 1938, pp. 68–78; CSPD, 1648, vol. DXVI, p. 203.

15. Turner *Memoirs*, vol. II, pp. 61–2.

16. NYCRO MIC 1320/1221, 1498

17. Reprinted in Ormerod, *Tracts Relating to Military Proceedings in Lancashire* (1844), pp. 252–4.

18. *An Impartiall Relation of the Late Fight at Preston, Being a Copy of a Letter ... by Sir Marmaduke Langdale* (1648).

19. Ibid. See also Ormerod, *Tracts Relating to Military Proceedings in Lancashire* (1844), pp. 256–73 and A. Woolrych, *Battles of the English Civil Wars* (new edn, London, 1991), pp. 153–84.

20. Turner, *Memoirs*, p. 63.

21. Thomas Sprigge, *Anglia Rediviva* (London, 1646), pp. 30–43; Hodgson, *Memoirs*, pp. 115–16; *Moderate Intelligencer*, 1648, British Library B 58/84 (72).

22. Cromwell's letter of 20 August 1648 in Carlyle, vol. 1, pp. 289–90; S. Bull and M. Seed, *Bloody Preston*, pp. 63–6, 82. Though much of the battlefield has been built up, parts of the royalist first defensive position along Eaves Brook can still be seen, notably in Brookfield Park.

23. J. P. Earwaker (ed.), *The Constables Accounts of the Manor of Manchester*, 3 vols (Manchester, 1891–93), p. 173.

24. Hodgson, *Memoirs*, pp. 115–16.

25. Ibid., pp. 116–18; S. Bull and M. Seed, *Bloody Preston*, pp. 63–8, 136.

26. G. Burnet, *The Memoirs of the Lives and Actions of James and William Dukes of Hamilton and Castle Herald* (Oxford, 1852), pp. 454–5; Turner, *Memoirs*, p. 63; *Discourse of the Warr in Lancashire*, p. 65; Lockyer (ed.), *Clarendon's History of the Great Rebellion*, p. 402.

27. Carlyle (ed.), p. 291; Hodgson, *Memoirs*, pp. 118–19; see also Farr, *op. cit.*, pp. 40–4.

28. HMC 14th Report, vol. 3, Appendix Part II, p. 175.

29. Turner, *Memoirs*, pp. 64–5; see also W. H. Dawson, *Cromwell's Understudy* (London, 1938), pp. 74–80.

30. *Discourse of the Warr in Lancashire*, p. 67.

31. Ibid.; Burnet, *op. cit.*, p. 457.

32. *Moderate Intelligencer*, British Library B 58/84 (72); Carlyle (ed.), pp. 282–3; S. Bull and M. Seed, *Bloody Preston*, pp. 39, 77–8. For many years Sir James Turner's statement that the Scots had no artillery at Preston was accepted at face value, despite the fact that this was contradicted by at least two other accounts. In recent years the presence of guns on the hills above Walton-le-Dale has also been supported by finds of shot in this general area. In 1999 an iron ball 47 mm in diameter found at Cinnamon Hill was reported to the Museum of Lancashire by Mr P. Childs of Clayton-le-Woods. In 2002 a second small cannon ball, similar in size, and some pistol and carbine shot, were discovered at different locations near Walton Summit, and near Walton church, and referred to the Portable Antiquities Scheme.

33. CSPD, 1648, vol. DXVI, p. 263.

34. L. Hutchinson, *Memoirs of the Life of Colonel Hutchinson* (reprinted London, 1846), pp. 320–1. It is thought that these memoirs were produced between 1664 and 1670.

35. Burnet, *op. cit.*, p. 457; Carlisle (ed.), p. 292; Turner, *Memoirs*, p. 65.

36. Carlyle (ed.), p. 293.

37. *Discourse of the Warr in Lancashire*, p. 66; G. Ashby, 'Terribly Obscure Battles of the Civil War: 10, Winwick Pass', in *Civil War Notes and Queries*, vol. 13 (1985), pp. 2–4; *Moderate Intelligencer*; see also R. Holmes *Preston, 1648* (Market Drayton, 1985), pp. 38–51 and W. H. Dawson, *Cromwell's Understudy* (London, 1938), pp. 78–80.

38. CSPD 1648, DXVI, p. 256.

39. J. D. Jones, *The Royal Prisoner* (Carisbrooke, 1964), *passim*; C. V. Wedgwood, *The Trial of Charles I* (London, 1964), pp. 62–165; A. Woolrych, *Battles of the English Civil War*, new edn (1991), pp. 153–84.

40. C. V. Wedgwood, *The Trial of Charles I* (London, 1964), pp. 146–93; R Lockyer (ed.), *Clarendon's History of the Great Rebellion* (London, 1967), pp. 456–8.

Chapter 12: *The search for peace and the Third Civil War, 1649–51*

1. *Discourse of the Warr in Lancashire*, p. 68; *House of Commons Journal*, vol. 6, 25 September 1648, pp. 30–3.

2. Ormerod, *Tracts Relating to Military Proceedings in Lancashire* (1844), p. 278.

3. *House of Commons Journal*, vol. 6, 8 November 1648, p. 71, and 16 December 1648, pp. 98–9.

4. *House of Lords Journal*, vol. 10, 20 December 1648, pp. 635–6.

5. Ibid., vol. 6, 10 February 1649, pp. 136–8. It is worth noting that Broxap, p. 174, confuses these events of early 1649 with those of 1650.

6. *House of Commons Journal*, vol. 6, 23 July 1650, pp. 444–5; J. J. Bagley, *The Earls of Derby* (London, 1985), pp. 94–5; F. H. Sunderland, *Marmaduke Lord Langdale* (London, 1927), pp. 155–6; *A Declaration of the Earl of Derby*, E.566 (5); T. Carlyle, *Oliver Cromwell's Letters and Speeches*, vol. 2 (London, 1869), pp. 31–96. See also S. Kmec, 'Royalist Noblewomen and Family Fortunes', in *Journal of the Oxford History Society* (2004), pp. 7–9. Derby Papers, CO34, f. 38.

7. A. Craven, *Coercion and Compromise: Lancashire Provincial Politics and the Creation of the English Republic, c. 1648–1653*, pp. 22–3; I. Gentle, *The New Model Army* (Oxford, 1992), pp. 15, 258, 320.

8. *House of Commons Journal*, vol. 6, 6 August 1649, p. 275; C. V. Wedgwood, *The Trial of Charles I* (London, 1964), pp. 40–4, 97–8, 176.

9. Gratton, *Parliamentarian and Royalist War Effort*, pp. 216–17; D. L. Smith in J. Morrill (ed.), *The Impact of the English Civil War* (London, 1991), pp. 39–41.

10. On this debate see Craven, *Coercion and Compromise*, pp. 105–8; Gratton, *Parliamentarian and Royalist War Effort*, p. 393.

11. H. Fishwick (ed.), *Lancashire and Cheshire Church Surveys*, Record Society for Lancashire and Cheshire, vol. 1 (1879), pp. 23–9, 47, 57, 61, 77–93, 150, 154, 186, 189.

12. R. Williams, *Montrose* (London, 1975), pp. 344–68; R. Hutton, *Charles II* (Oxford, 1989), pp. 49–70; J. Kenyon, *The Civil Wars of England* (London, 1988), pp. 208–11.

13. Sir James Turner, *Memoirs* (1670; reprinted 1829), p. 94; I. Gentle, *The New Model Army* (Oxford, 1992), pp. 402–11; W. S. Douglas, *Cromwell's Scotch Campaigns* (London, 1899), *passim*. G. Burnet, *Memoirs of the Lives and Actions of James and William Dukes of Hamilton* (Oxford, 1852), p. 541.

14. Carlyle (ed.), *Cromwell's Letters*, vol. 2, p. 286.

15. *Mercurius Politicus*, 21 August 1651, reprinted in Ormerod, *Tracts Relating to Military Proceedings in Lancashire* (1844), pp. 287–8; F. Maurice, *The Adventures of Edward Wogan* (London, 1945), *passim*; Broxap, pp. 182–4.

16. *Discourse of the Warr in Lancashire*, pp. 70–2.

17. *Mercurius Politicus*, 63, 21 August 1651, p. 1004, reprinted in Ormerod, *Tracts Relating to Military Proceedings in Lancashire* (1844), p. 286.

18. *Perfect Diurnal*, and other documents reprinted in Ormerod, *Tracts Relating to Military Proceedings in Lancashire* (1844), pp. 289–93; *House of Commons Journal*, vol. 7, 19 August 1651, pp. 2–3.

19. Sir James Turner, *Memoirs*, p. 95; W. H. Dawson, *Cromwell's Understudy* (London, 1938), pp. 136–8.

20. *House of Commons Journal*, vol. 6, 12 August 1651, pp. 619–21. On the career of Edward Massey see M. Atkin and W. Laughlin, *Gloucester and the Civil War* (Stroud, 1992), pp. 173–6.

21. Ormerod, *Tracts Relating to Military Proceedings in Lancashire* (1844), pp. 301–2.

22. *Discourse of the Warr in Lancashire*, pp. 72–7; Lilburne letters reprinted in Ormerod, *Tracts Relating to Military Proceedings in Lancashire* (1844), pp. 300–7.

23. Details of the Tyldesley memorial are given by the Public Monument and Sculpture Association on the internet at www.pmsa.cch.kcl.ac.uk; S. Reid, *The Finest Knight in England* (Aberdeen, 1979), *passim*.

24. J. J. Bagley, *The Earls of Derby* (London, 1985), pp. 96–7; *Discourse of the Warr in Lancashire*, p. 76; Lilburne letter in Ormerod, *Tracts Relating to Military Proceedings in Lancashire* (1844), p. 305.

25. C. V. Wedgwood, *Cromwell* (London, 1973), pp. 65–78; Carlyle (ed.), *Cromwell's Letters*, vol. 2, pp. 293–4; J. E. Bailey, *The Life of a Lancashire Rector During the Civil War* (Leigh, 1877), p. 13; *House of Commons Journal*, vol. 7, 5 September 1651, p. 12; F. Maurice, *The Adventures of Edward Wogan* (London, 1945), pp. 128–44. See also W. H. Dawson, *Cromwell's Understudy* (London, 1938), pp. 138–43.

26. Charles II, *Account*, reprinted in W. Matthews (ed.), *Charles II's Escape from Worcester* (London, 1967), pp. 38–80; D. Farr, *John Lambert* (Woodbridge, 2003), pp. 79–80; 90–1; I. Gentles, *op. cit.*, pp. 403–11; R. Hutton, *op. cit.*, pp. 62–70.

27. Hodgson, *Original Memoirs* (Edinburgh 1806), p. 154; J. J. Bagley, *op. cit.*, pp. 97–9; Ormerod, *Tracts Relating to Military Proceedings in Lancashire* (1844), p. 311.

28. Ibid., pp. 312–14; Bagley, *op. cit.*, p. 98; Whitelock, *Memorials*, p. 511.

29. Ormerod, *Tracts Relating to Military Proceedings in Lancashire* (1844), pp. 311–20.

30. *The Earle of Derby's Speech Upon the Scaffold* (London 1651), reprinted in Ormerod, *Tracts Relating to Military Proceedings in Lancashire* (1844), pp. 320–3.

31. Baggerly (sometimes rendered 'Bagguley') and other accounts appearing in *A Description of the Memorable Sieges and Battles in the North of England that Happened During the Civil War* (Bolton, 1785), pp. 191–204.

Chapter 13: *The aftermath of war*

1. *Discourse of the Warr in Lancashire*, pp. 77–8; Dugdale (ed.), *History and Antiquities*.

2. C. Carleton, *Going to the Wars* (London, 1992), pp. 201–29, and Carleton in J. Morrill (ed.), *The Impact of the English Civil War* (London, 1991), pp. 17–21, where he gives estimates of 84,738 killed in battle; 117,534 taken prisoner; 100,000 'indirect' deaths; and 300 killed 'by accident'. Carleton's figures may be faulted as impossibly precise, as he himself admits, and in certain instances might be exaggerated, but the point about general magnitude is a good one. His final computation is that between 3.6% and 3.7% of the population of England died in the civil wars. Interesting continental comparisons can be drawn with M. P. Gutman, *War and Rural Life in the Early Modern Low Countries* (Princeton, 1980), *passim*; M. S. Anderson, *War and Society in Europe of the Old Regime* (London, 1988), pp. 136–7, and G. Parker, *The Military Revolution* (Cambridge, 1988), pp. 52–60. See also J. P. Kenyon and J. Ohlmeyer, *The Civil Wars* (Oxford, 1998), pp. xix, 273–8. On demographic structures of the period see C. M. Cipolla (ed.), *Fontana Economic History of Europe: The Sixteenth and Seventeenth Centuries* (London, 1974). The comparative figure for Preston in World War I is drawn from *The Unveiling of the Preston War Memorial* (Preston, 1926), p. 3. See also A. Woolrych, *Britain in Revolution* (Oxford, 2002), pp. 335–41; Gratton, *Parliamentarian and Royalist War Effort in Lancashire*, p. 230.

3. Ormerod, *Tracts Relating to Military Proceedings in Lancashire* (1844), pp. 213, 232–3; J. P. Earwaker (ed.), *The Constables Accounts of the Manor of Manchester* (Manchester, 1891), p. 126; see also W. G. Howson, 'Plague, Poverty and Population in Parts of North-West England, 1580–1720', *Transactions of the Historic Society of Lancashire and Cheshire*, vol. 112 (1960–61), pp. 29–55. S. J. Guscott, *Humphrey Chetham* (Manchester, 2003), p. 227. G. Pendlebury, *Aspects of the English Civil War in Bolton and its Neighbourhood* (Manchester, 1983), pp. 13–17. Derby Papers, CO30, f.13.

4. *Discourse of the Warr in Lancashire*, pp. 28–9; S. Porter, *Property Destruction in the English Civil Wars* (Stroud, 1994), pp. 86, 126; Ormerod, *Tracts Relating to Military Proceedings in Lancashire* (1844), pp. 131–2; Broxap, p. 75.

5. M. Gray, *The History of Bury, 1660–1876* (Bury, 1970), pp. 5–18.

6. J. Touzeau, *The Rise and Progress of Liverpool* (Liverpool, 1910), pp. 223–4, 228.

7. H. Padfield. *The Story of Ormskirk* (Ormskirk, 1978), *passim*: many reprints, as well as original parish registers are available at LRO.

8. *House of Commons Journal*, vol. iv, 3 March 1647; J. Hall (ed.), *Memorials of the Civil War in Cheshire and the Adjacent Counties*, Lancashire and Cheshire Record Society, vol. xix (1889), p. 192; LRO, QSP 23/29; M. Fletcher (*et al.*), *Lathom House, Ormskirk: Survey and Evaluation Report*, 1997–98/024/AUA7559, Lancaster University Archaeology Unit, *passim*; A. Fell, *A Furness Military Chronicle*, p. 61.

9. SP, 23.180. 2223, f. 600.

10. J. E. Bailey, *The Life of a Lancashire Rector During the Civil War* (Leigh, 1877), *passim*;

M. Blundell, *Cavalier, Letters of William Blundell* (London, 1933), p. 13; R. C. Shaw, *Kirkham in Amounderness* (Preston, 1949), pp. 310, 473.

11. Accounts reprinted in A. Fell, *A Furness Military Chronicle* (Ulverston, 1937), p. 57; J. Barratt, *Cavaliers* (Stroud, 2000), p. 22.

12. S. Barber, 'The People of Northern England and Attitudes Towards the Scots, 1639–1651', *Northern History*, vol. xxxv (1999), p. 116.

13. R. Somerville, *History of the Duchy of Lancaster* (London, 1970), p. 241.

14. C. H. Firth, *Cromwell's Army* (London, 1962), pp. 38–9; *House of Commons Journal*, vol. vi, p. 428.

15. *The Modern Intelligencer* (E) 613, and *Mercurius Politicus*; see W. S. Douglas, *Cromwell's Scotch Campaigns* (London, 1899), p. 143.

16. Secretary of State Thurloe's correspondence from the 1650s was published as the *Thurloe State Papers* in seven volumes in 1742 under the editorship of Thomas Birch (copy in Lancaster University library); parts are also now available online at www.british-history.ac.uk. For Ribbleton, see LRO, QSP 62, fols 13–14 (Easter 1652). See also K. Wrightson, 'Two concepts of order: Justices, constables and jurymen in seventeenth-century England', in John Brewer and John Styles (eds), *An Ungovernable People: The English and their Law in the Seventeenth and Eighteenth Centuries* (London, 1980); much of Wrightson's early work, and his doctoral thesis on this topic, explored the 'reformation of manners' in Lancashire during the 1650s.

17. Carleton, *op. cit.*, pp. 339–41.

18. See C. B. Phillips and J. H. Smith, *Lancashire and Cheshire from AD 1540* (London, 1994), pp. 14–25; J. K. Walton, *Lancashire: A Social History* (Manchester, 1987), pp. 20–35. See also A. J. H. Latham, 'Wigan, 1540–1640: Pre-industrial growth and development in south Lancashire', in J. F. Wilson (ed.), *King Cotton: A tribute to Douglas A. Farnie* (Crucible Books, Lancaster, 2009), pp. 247–79.

19. See W. H. Thomson, *History of Manchester to 1852* (Altrincham, 1967), pp. 120–40.

20. Pendlebury, *op. cit.*, pp. 12–17.

21. See K. H. Docton, 'Lancaster 1684', *Transactions of the Historic Society of Lancashire and Cheshire*, vol. 109 (1957–58), pp. 125–42.

22. R. C. Richardson. *Puritanism in North-West England* (Manchester, 1972), pp. 154–66; N. Gardner (ed.), *Lancashire Quarter Sessions Records: Register of Recusants 1678*, North West Catholic History Society (1998); F. O. Blundell, *Old Catholic Lancashire*, 3 vols (London, 1925–38).

23. B. G. Blackwood, *The Lancashire Gentry* (Manchester, 1978), pp. 122–6.

24. At least in part such stories were financially inspired, since not being classified a former malignant would help to avoid fines or confiscations.

Chapter 14: *Conclusion: the civil wars in perspective*

1. From *Truths Discovery of a Black Cloud in the North* (London, 1646); Dugdale (ed.), *History and Antiquities*; Sir James Turner, *Memoirs of his Own Life and Times* (1670; reprinted 1829), p.55.

2. See I. Gentles, 'Why Men Fought in the British Civil Wars, 1639–1652', *The History Teacher*, vol. 26, number 4 (August 1993), pp. 407–18. Worsley's letters to London can be found in Thomas Birch (ed.), Thurloe State Papers (1742). This letter of 3 Nov. 1655 may be found in vol. 4, p. 149.

3. A. J. Fletcher, 'New Light on Religion and the English Civil War', *The Journal of Ecclesiastical History* (Cambridge, 1987), p. 106.

4. For a kinder interpretation regarding the Catholic position see K. J. Lindley, 'The Part Played by the Catholics in the Civil War in Lancashire and Monmouthshire', unpublished MA thesis, University of Manchester, 1965.

5. See P. R. Newman, 'The Royalist Army in Northern England', unpublished D.Phil. thesis, York, 1978, p. 12, and R. Hutton, 'The Failure of the Lancashire Cavaliers', in *Transactions of the Historic Society of Lancashire and Cheshire*, vol. 129 (1980), pp. 47–62.

6. *Discourse of the Warr in Lancashire*, pp. 68–9.

Bibliography

There are still significant gaps in our knowledge of the civil war period, but there is a surprising amount of written material extant. Among the primary sources are not only contemporary books and personal manuscripts, but the myriad pamphlets, broadsheets and journals that were published following the lifting of censorship under the Long Parliament. Many of the pamphlets filled the same sort of role as the modern newspaper, but in the absence of other media were arguably more important. Like modern newspapers they were not always accurate, and while some were remarkably well informed and up to date, sometimes with eyewitness accounts, others were sensationalist or ill informed. Some were unashamed propaganda organs for one party or another. This makes them one of the most colourful sources of information, but one which needs careful evaluation and corroboration. The largest collection of civil war pamphlets anywhere is the 'Thomason Tracts', 22,000 items originally collected by London bookseller George Thomason and now preserved in the British Library at St Pancras. This was comprehensively catalogued in 1908. References to this collection are denoted by the prefix 'E' in the following bibliography. Locally a much smaller collection, originally assembled by Dr Shepherd, is held in the Harris Library, Preston. Here references to this collection are prefixed 'H'. A vital third source of such material is George Ormerod's *Tracts Relating to Military Proceedings in Lancashire During the Great Civil War*, a collection printed in 1844 as part of the Chetham Society series.

There are also many civil war manuscripts. Some take the form of personal memoirs, letters, diaries and unpublished accounts; others are legal documents or financial papers. The manuscript sources are widely scattered, from the great national collections at one extreme, to very small private collections at the other. Some of the most significant have been published, notably in the publications of the Chetham Society, the Lancashire and Cheshire Record Society, and the Historic Society of Lancashire and Cheshire. Perhaps the greatest number of relevant items are held within the various county collections – those within the Lancashire Record Office being referred to here by the abbreviation 'LRO'. The National Archives (formerly known as the Public Records Office) also has useful items, material from this collection being indicated by the prefix 'PRO'. The state papers similarly have a bearing on our story. The abbreviation 'CSPD' in the text is a reference to the *Calendar of State Papers Domestic*, the printed volumes that give summaries of the actual documents. The Chetham Library in Manchester has some unique manuscripts of local significance, including Broxap's papers, ship money and other documents: these are listed hereunder prefixed with the letters 'CL'. Manchester

City Archives above the central library at St Peter's Square similarly contains a number of relevant items, here cited with the prefix MCA. The papers of the seventh Earl of Derby are located in the family archive at Knowsley. The internet has allowed certain manuscripts, including the important House of Commons and House of Lords *Journals*, to become available in electronic form.

Only one approximately contemporary written source attempted to tackle the war in the county as a whole. This is the famous *Discourse of the Warr in Lancashire*, penned by the hand of a parliament man, probably Captain Edward Robinson, who attempted, but usually failed, to be impartial. Dating from December 1655, it originally existed in manuscript form, but is now known primarily through its nineteenth-century reprint. Though an extremely important testament, the *Discourse* is very uneven in its coverage. More importantly we need to be aware that the events which the *Discourse* does cover are not presented in strict chronological order, and that some of the dates given are either obviously wrong, or at variance with those presented in other documents. As a vivid, and often first-hand, account the *Discourse* is remarkable and uniquely valuable: as a source for narrative reconstruction it has to be used with extreme care.

No bibliographical note would be complete without a brief mention of the major national histories. Though published later Clarendon's great *History of the Rebellion*, was actually begun during the war. Bulstrode Whitelock's *Memorials of the English Affairs* emerged in 1682. The major, and highly influential, Victorian history is S.R Gardiner's four-volume *History of the Great Civil War*, which was followed by a similar three-volume history of the *Commonwealth and Protectorate*. Since then it is arguable that only C.V. Wedgwood's *The King's Peace*, and *The King's War*, can claim similar scope – though these only carry the narrative as far as 1647. In the more strictly local context there has really only been one comprehensive history of note, Ernest Broxap's *The Great Civil War in Lancashire*, published in 1910. This was a remarkable breakthrough, succinct and intelligible, and one of the best of a number of such county histories produced at about the same time. Yet Broxap's brevity limited his coverage mainly to campaigns, and the book was not without minor flaws. A number of these were later addressed by R.N. Dore in a new edition of Broxap's work, published by Manchester University Press in 1973, and more in the recent Partizan Press edition. A few additional corrections are addressed in this volume as far as they are relevant to the narrative.

Derby Collection papers

CO30	*Commonplace Book*	
CO31	*Discourse Concerning the Government of the Isle of Man*	
CO32.1	*Book of Prayers* by James 7th Earl of Derby with and Almanac of Important Events, *c.*1647	
CO32.2	Contemporary copy of the *Book of Prayers*	
CO33	*Prayers and Meditations*	
CO34	*Private Devotions*	
CO35.1	*Private Devotions*	Copy W. Strange 1676
CO35.2	*Private Devotions*	Copy H. Charlotte Colchester
CO35.3	*Private Devotions*	Copy Mr Duloy
CO35.4	*Private Devotions*	Copy Charlotte Hornby

Other primary sources (original and reprinted)

Anderton Papers, *Inhabitants of Great Charnock that are Able Bodied*, and *Orders at Wigan*, January 1643, Wigan Archives Service, D/D An 16

Anon., *A Brief Account of the Several Plots, Conspiracies and Hellish Attempts of the Bloody Minded Papists … With a More Particular Account of Their Plots in Relation to the Late Civil War*, 1678. CL M.9.71

Anon., *A Continuation of Certaine Remarkable Passages*, London, October 1642. E 121(24)

Anon., *A Declaration and Summons Sent by the Earl of Newcastle to the Town of Manchester*, London, 1643. (H) 532

Anon., *A Great Victory at Appleby by Col-General Ashton*, 9 October 1648. E 468(7)

Anon., *A Message Sent From His Highnesse the Prince of Wales … Also Another Bloudy Fight Between the Scots and English*, London, 1648. E 454(21)

Anon., *A Perfect Relation of the Taking of the Town of Preston in Lancashire*, London, 1643. E 89(22)

Anon., *Petitions of the Gentlemen, Ministers and Inhabitants of Lancashire Against the Earl of Derby and Sir Thomas Tilsley*, 1648. MCA BR F942.062.P13

Anon., *A Punctuall Relation of the Passages in Lancashire*, London, 1643. E 91 (1)

Anon., *Severall Letters from the Committees in Severall Counties*, London, 1642

Anon., *A Sprituall Snapsacke For the Parliament Souldiers*, London, 1643. (H) unnumbered

Anon., *A True and Faithfull Relation of the Besieging of the Town of Manchester*, London, 1642

Anon., *A True and Full Relation of the Troubles in Lancashire Between Lord Strange, now Earle of Derby; and the Well Affected People of That County*, London, 1642. (H) 515

Anon., *A True and perfect Relation of the Proceedings at Manchester*, London, 1642. E 121(13)

Anon., *An Answer to Prince Ruperts Declaration*, 1643. (H) 18

Anon., *An Exact Relation of the Siege Before Yorke*, London, 12 June 1644. E 50(30)

Anon., *Another Great and Bloudy Fight in the North*, London, 1648. E 456(5)

Anon., *Colchester Surrendered to the Lord General … Also a List of the Names of the Lords, Collonels and Other Officers, Taken with the Duke of Hambleton at Utoxertor*, London, 1648. E 461(15)

Anon., *Eikon Basiliske, The Portraiture of His Sacred Majestie in His Solitude and Sufferings*, 1648

Anon., *Knowne Lawes. A Short Examination of the Counsells and Actions of Those That Have Withdrawne the king From the Government and Protection of His People*, London, 1643. (H) 9

Anon., *Manchester's Resolution Against Lord Strange*, London, 1642. (H) 21

Anon., *Mercurius Aulicus*, Oxford, May 1644. E 49(3)

Anon., *Mercurius Aulicus*, Oxford, 18 May 1644. E 50(6)

Anon., *Mercurius Aulicus*, Oxford, 15 June 1644. E 53(5)

Anon., *Orders Concluded by Lord Strange and His Adherents at Preston in the County of Lancaster, 1642.* (H) 28

Anon., *Packets of Letters from Scotland and the North Parts of England, to Members of the House of Commons*, 17 October 1648. E 468(7)

Anon., *Preston November 17 1646. The Deliberate Resolution of the Ministers of the Gospel Within the County Palatine of Lancaster*, London, 1647. (H)

Anon., *Strange Newes From Yorke, Hull, Beverly and Manchester*, London, July 1642

Anon., *The Cavaliers Catechisme*, London, 1643. (H) 11

Anon., *The Game at Chesse*, London, 1643. E88(2)

Anon., *The Kingdomes Weekly Intelligencer*, London 6–12 November, 1644. E 16(27)

Anon., *The Kingdomes Weekly Intelligencer*, London 2–9, July 1644. E 54(9)

Anon., *The Lord Strange His Demands*, London, October 1642. E 121(25)

Anon., *The Petition of Divers of his Majesties Faithfull Subjects, of the True Protestant Religion in the County of Lancaster: Presented to his Majestie at York*, London, 1642

Anon., *The True Informer*, 25 November – 1 December, 1643. E 77(22)

Anon., *A True and Perfect Book of All Rates and Exacions*, (Lancashire) 1649. CL A.6.15

Anon., *Severall Letters From the Committees … Wherein is Related How the Townesmen of Manchester Put Themselves into Arms*, London, 1642. (H) 23

Anon., *Three Letters Concerning the Surrender of Many Scottish Lords*, London, 1648

Anon., *To the King's Most Excellent Majesty the Humble Petition of Divers Recusants*, London, 1642. (H)

Assheton (Ashton), *Letter Books of the Ashton Family of Middleton and Whalley*, CL A.3.90–1

Assheton (Ashton), Assheton of Middleton Papers, MCA E7

Barriffe, W., *Militarie Discipline: or the Young Artillery-Man*, London, 1661

Beamont, W. (ed.), *Discourse of the Warre in Lancashire*, Chetham Society (vol. 62), Manchester, 1864

Beamont, W., *Beamont Collection*, Warrington Library, Museum and Archive Service, Cheshire County Council

Birch, S., *Diary of Samuel Birch*, Historical Manuscripts Commission, 14th Report, vol. 3, London, 1894

Blundell, M (ed.), *Cavalier: Letters of William Blundell To His Friends, 1620–1698*, London, 1933

Burghall, E., *Memorials of the Civil War in Cheshire and the Adjacent Counties*, Record Society of Lancashire and Cheshire, 1889

Burnet, G., *The Memoirs of the Lives and Actions of James and William Dukes of Hamilton*, 1673, reprinted Oxford, 1852

Carlyle, T. (ed.), *Oliver Cromwell's Letters and Speeches*, three vols, London, 1846–49

Chandler, G., *Liverpool Under Charles I* (containing a transcription of the 'Liverpool Town Book', 1625–1649), Liverpool, 1965

Chetham Papers, *Ship Money Collection*. (CL) A5

Collectors Accounts, *The County Commission to Examine Collectors Accounts of Funds Received During the Civil War: Addenda, Lancashire*. PRO E 178/7339

Committee of Both Kingdoms, *Letter from the Committee of Both Kingdoms to the Lancashire Committee*, 27 September 1645. CSPD vol. DX, pp. 165–6

Cromwell, O., *A Letter Written by Lieut. Gen Crumwell to the Honourable Committee of Manchester*, London, 21 August 1648. E 460(6)

Cromwell, O., *Lt. General Cromwel's Letter Concerning the Total Routing of the Scots Army*, 1648, LRO DP 223

Cromwell, O., *A Copy of Lieutenant General Crumwels Letter, Read in the House of Commons and Other Letters of a Great and Bloody Fight Neere Preston*, London, 1648. (H) 11497

Dore, R.N. (ed.), *The Letter Books of Sir William Brereton*, Record Society of Lancashire and Cheshire, vols cxxiii, cxxviii (1984 and 1990)

Draper, P., *A History of the House of Stanley*, Ormskirk, 1854

Dugdale, W. (ed.), *History and Antiquities of the Isle of Man, By James Stanley Earl of Derby; Earl of Derby and Lord of Man*. Reprinted in Manx Society, vol. 3 (and reproduced electronically at www.isle-of-man.com, 2001.)

Earwaker, J.P. (ed.), *The Constables Accounts of the manor of Manchester*, 3 vols, Manchester 1891–93

Earwaker, J.P. (ed.), *The Court Leet Records of the Manor of Manchester*, vols 3 and 4, 1618–62, Manchester, 1887

Farington, S.M., *The Farington Papers*, Chetham Soc. vol. 39, Manchester 1856. (LRO DDF 2387–2474)

Farrer, Dr (collector), *Deputy Lieutenancy Letter Book for Militia, Lonsdale and Amounderness*, 1625–87. MCA L1/40/1 (NRA 17338)

Farrer, Dr (collector), *The Certificate of the Musters For the County of Lancaster in Anno Dom 1639*, MCA L1/40/2

Firth, C. (ed.), *Narratives Illustrating the Duke of Hamilton's Expedition to England in 1648*, Miscellany of the Scottish History Society, vol. 2, Edinburgh, 1904

Firth, C. (ed.), *Stuart Tracts, 1603–1693*, New York, 1964

Fishwick, H., *Lancashire and Cheshire Church Surveys, 1649–1655*, Lancashire and Cheshire Record Society, vol. I, 1878–79

Gardiner, S.R., *The Hamilton Papers*, Camden Society, 1880

Gardner, N., *Lancashire Quarter Sessions Records: Register of Recusants 1678*, Catholic History Society, Wigan, 1998

Harland, J. (ed.), *The Lancashire Lieutenancy Under the Tudors and Stuarts*, Chetham Society vols xlix and l, Manchester 1859

Heywood, T. (ed.), *Letter from Sir John Seton*, Chetham Society, 1862

Hodgson, J., *Memoirs of Captain John Hodgson* (reprinted with the memoirs of Sir Henry Slingsby) Edinburgh, 1806

House of Commons, *House of Commons Journal* (available on line at www.british-history. ac.uk) University of London and Parliament History Trust, 2003

House of Lords, House of Lords Journal (available on line at www.british-history.ac.uk)

Hutchinson, L., *Memoirs of the Life of Colonel Hutchinson ... To Which is Now First Added, An Account of the Siege of Lathom House*, London, 1846

Hyde, E. (Earl of Clarendon), *History of the Rebellion*, Macray, W.D. (ed.), London 1888

Kuerden, R., *Kuerden's Map of Preston*, 1684, LRO, DDX 194/28

Kuerden, R., *History of the Dukedom or County Palatine of Lancashire*, unpublished manuscripts, CL A.7.8, and C.6.1.3

Laing, D. (ed.), *The Letters and Journals of Robert Baillie*, three vols, Edinburgh, 1841

Lancashire Record Office, *The Civil War in Lancashire*, including 21 reprinted documents, Preston 1969

Langdale, M., *An Impartiall Realation of the Late Fight at Preston*, 1648. (H) P942721

Maltby, J.D. (ed.), *The Short Parliament (1640) Diary of Sir Thomas Aston*, Royal Historical Society, London, 1988

Musgrave, P., Musgrave's account, in British Library, Clarendon Ms 2867, reprinted in *Miscellany of Scottish History*, vol. 2, Edinburgh, 1904

Northern Association Army, *Order Book of the Council of the Northern Parliamentary Army*, York Minster Library, BB53

Ordnance Office, *Journall Booke: Minutes of the Ordnance, Copies of Letters, 1644–1645*, PRO WO 47/1

Ormerod, G.W. (ed.), *Tracts Relating to Military Proceedings in Lancashire During the Great Civil War*, Chetham Society, old series, vol. II (1844)

Parker of Browsholme, *Papers Relating to the Bowland Militia*, 1642, LRO DDB 85/14 and DDB85/25

Raines, F.R. (ed.), *The Papers of James Stanley, 7th Earl of Derby*, Chetham Soc. three vols, 1865–67

Rigby, A., *Letter from Alexander Rigby to Sir William Brereton*, 18 April 1644. CSPD vol. DI, p. 126

Rosworme, *Rosworme's Fortifications on Blackstone Edge*, MCA Ms 942.72.S154, vol. 1, p. 60

Sanderson, J., Major 'Sanderson's Diary' in R. Blair (ed.), *Proceedings of the Society of Anitquaries*, third series, vol. IX, 1921, pp. 8–24

Shaw, G. (ed.), *An Assessment Levied in the Year 1641 Upon all Persons … in Oldham, Royton and Crompton*, Oldham, 1904

Shaw, W.A., *Materials for an Account of the Provincial Synod of the County of Lancaster, 1646–1660*, Manchester, 1890

Sprigge, J., *Anglia Rediviva; England's Recovery*, London, 1647

Stanning, J.H. (ed.), *The Royalist Composition Papers Being the Proceedings of the Committee for Compounding, AD 1643–1660 so Far as They Relate to the County of Lancaster*, in *Lancashire and Cheshire Record Society*, vol. 29, 1896

Taylor J. (ed.), *A Brief Description of the Borough and Town of Preston … Originally Composed Between the Years 1682 and 1686*, Preston, 1818

Thomson, T. (ed.), *Turner, Memoirs of his Own Life and Times*, Bannatyne Club, 1829 (reprinted Tonbridge, 1991)

Vicars, J., *Magnalia Dei Anglicana or Englands Parliamentary Chronicle*, London, 1646

Walton, J., *A Perfect Relation of A Great Victory in the North*, London, 1648

Walton J., *The Bloudy Battel at Preston in Lancashire*, London 1648. E 460(20)

Whitelocke, B., *Memorials of the English Affairs*, London, 1682

Wythenshawe, *Inventory of the Goods of Robert Tatton taken at Wythenshawe Hall*, seized 1643, MCA Misc 208

Secondary sources

Anon., *Historical Sketches of Ormskirk*, Ormskirk, 1881

Anon., *A Short History of Lathom*, St Helens (undated)

Anon., *A True Description of the Memorable Sieges and Battles in the North of England that Happened During the Civil War*, Bolton 1785, CL M.9. 71/7818

Anon., *An Historical and Descriptive Account of the Town of Lancaster; Collected from the Best Authorities*, Lancaster, 1811

Anon., *Cromwell's Trench Spa Roughs, Lathom; a Report Upon the Archaeological Evidence and Possibilities For Future Survey*, Lathom and District Archaeological Society, 1997

Abbott, W.C., *A Bibliography of Oliver Cromwell*, Harvard University, 1929

Abram, W.A., *A History of Blackburn*, Blackburn, 1877

Ackers, N., *The Civil War in the Leigh and Makerfield Area*, Leigh Local History Society, 1988

Adamson, J.S.A., 'The English Nobility and the Projected Settlement of 1647', *The Historical Journal*, vol. 30, number 3, 1987, pp. 567–602

Adamson, J., 'The Triumph of Oligarchy: the Management of War and the Committee of Both Kingdoms, 1644–1645', in C.R. Kyle and J. Peacey (eds), *Parliament at Work,*

Woodbridge, 2002, pp. 101–27

Ashby, G., 'Terribly Obscure Battles of the English Civil War: 10, Winwick Pass', *Civil War Notes and Queries*, issue 13, Leigh on Sea, 1985, pp. 2–4

Ashton, R., *The English Civil War*, London, 1978

Ashton, R., *Counter Revolution: The Second Civil War and its Origins*, Yale, 1994

Aylmer, G.E. (ed.), *The Intrregnum: The Quest For Settlement*, London, 1972

Aylmer, G.E. and Morrill, J.S., *The Civil War and Interregnum: Sources for Local Historians*, London, 1979

Aylmer, G.E., *Rebellion or Revolution*, Oxford, 1986

Bagley, J.J., *Roundheads and Cavaliers, a Paper Read to the Burnley Historical Society*, Burnley, 1963

Bagley, J.J., *The Earls of Derby, 1485–1985*, London, 1985

Bagley, J.J and Lewis A.S., *Lancashire at War: Cavaliers and Roundheads, 1642–1651*, Clapham, 1977

Bailey, J.E., *The Life of a Lancashire Rector During the Civil War*, Leigh 1877, CL 4c3–38

Barber, S., 'The People of Northern England and Attitudes Towards the Scots, 1639–1651', in *Northern History*, vol. xxxv (1999), pp. 93–118

Barratt, J., *The Siege of Manchester*, Bristol, 1993

Barratt, J., *The Siege of Liverpool and Prince Rupert's Campaign in Lancashire*, Bristol, 1994

Barratt, J., *Cavaliers: The Royalist Army at War 1642–1646*, Sutton, Stroud, 2000

Bennett, M., *The Civil War Experienced*, London, 2000

Billington, W.D., *Halliwell During the Civil War*, Bolton Education Department, 1976

Blackwood, B.G., 'The Lancashire Cavaliers and Their Tenants', in *Transactions of the Historical Society of Lancashire and Cheshire*, vol. 117, 1965

Blackwood, B.G., *The Lancashire Gentry and the Great Rebellion*, Chetham Society, vol. xxv (Manchester, 1978)

Blundell, F.O., *Old Catholic Lancashire*, 3 vols, London, 1925–38

Boynton, L., *The Elizabethan Militia, 1558–1638*, London, 1967

Broderick, K., *The Impact of the First Civil War on the Township of Rishton*, Manchester, undated

Broxap, E., *The Great Civil War in Lancashire*, Manchester, 1910 (new edn with introduction by R.N. Dore, Manchester 1973; new edn with introduction by S. Bull, Leigh-on-Sea, 2007)

Broxap, E., *Broxap Papers, Lectures and Correspondence Pertaining to 'The Great Civil War'*, 1910–1924. CL 7.54.39161

Bull, S., *The Civil War in Lancashire*, Preston, 1991

Bull, S., 'The Battle that Led to the English Republic … Preston 1648', in *Centre for North-West Regional Studies Regional Bulletin* (no. 14) Lancaster University, Summer 2000

Bull S. and Seed M., *Bloody Preston: The Battle of Preston, 1648*, Lancaster, 1998

Bullock, H.A., *History of the Isle of Man*, London, 1815

Buxton, T., *The History, Traditions and Antiquities of South West Lancashire … and the Siege of Lathom House* (LRO) 1889

Carlton, C., *Charles I the Personal Monarchy*, London, 1983

Carlton, C., *Going to the Wars: The Experience of the English Civil Wars*, London, 1992

Carter, C.F. (ed.), *Manchester and its Region*, Manchester University, 1962

Childs, J., *Warfare in the Seventeenth Century*, London, 2001

Collinson, P., *English Puritanism*, Historical Association pamphlet general series, 106, 1983

Cooke, D., *The Civil War in Yorkshire*, Barnsley, 2004

Craven, A.J., *Coercion and Compromise: Lancashire Provincial Politics and the Creation of the English Republic c1648–1653*, unpublished Manchester University Ph.D. thesis, 2004

Croston, J., *County Families of Lancashire and Cheshire*, Manchester, 1887

Cunliffe Shaw, R., *The Royal Forest of Lancashire*, Preston, 1956

Dawson, W.H., *Cromwell's Understudy: The Life and Times of General John Lambert*, London, 1938

De Witt, G., *The Lady of Latham, Being the Life and Original Letters of Charlotte de la Tremoille, Countess of Derby*, London, 1869

Dean, R., *Gawthorpe Hall*, National Trust, London, 2002

Dore, R.N. and Lowe, J., 'The Battle of Nantwich, 25 January 1644', *Transactions of the Historic Society of Lancashire and Cheshire*, vol. 113, 1961, pp. 97–123

Dore, R.N., *The Civil Wars in Cheshire*, Chester, 1966

Dore, R.N., *The Great Civil War in the Manchester Area*, Manchester, 1971

Douglas, W.S., *Cromwell's Scotch Campaigns*, London, 1899

Duffy, M., *The Military Revolution and the State 1500–1800*, Exeter University, 1980

Earwaker, J.P. (ed.), *Notes on the Life of Dr John Hewytt*, Manchester, 1877

Earwaker, J.P., *Local Gleanings*, Manchester, 1880

Everitt, A.M., *Change in the Provinces*, Leicester University, 1969

Everitt, A.M., *The Local Community and the Great Rebellion*, Historical Association pamphlet 70, London, 1969

Farr, D., *John Lambert*, Woodbridge 2003

Fassnidge, J., *English Civil War Documents*, 4 vols, London, 1984

Fell, A., *Furness Military Chronicle*, Ulverston, 1937

Firth, C.H., *The Regimental History of Cromwell's Army*, Oxford, 1940

Firth, C.H., *Cromwell's Army* (fourth edn) London, 1962

Fishwick, H. and Ditchfield, P.H., *Memorials of Old Lancashire*, two vols, London, 1909

Fletcher, A., *The Outbreak of the English Civil War*, London, 1981

Fletcher, A., 'Factionalism in Town and Countryside: the Significance of Puritanism and Arminianism' in D. Baker (ed.), *The Church in Town and Countryside*, Studies in Church History, 16, pp. 291–300, 1979

Fletcher, A., 'New Light on Religion and the English Civil War' in *The Journal of Ecclesiastical History*, Cambridge, vol. 38, number 1, January 1987, pp. 95–106

Fletcher, M. *et al.*, *Lathom House, Ormskirk: Survey and Evaluation Report*, 1997–98/024/ AUA7559, Lancaster University Archaeology Unit, 1998

Fletcher, M., *Land North of West Wing, Lathom House Near Ormskirk; Archaeological Watching Brief*, Report 2001–09, Matrix Archaeology, Manchester, 2001

Fletcher, M., *Land East of West Wing, Lathom House Near Ormskirk; Archaeological Evaluation*, Report 2002–12, Matrix Archaeology, Manchester, 2002

Fleury C., *Historic Notes on the Ancient Borough of Lancaster*, Lancaster, 1891

Forshaw, D.M., *An Economic and Social History of Liverpool*, unpublished dissertation, Nottingham University, 1953

Gardiner, S.R., *History of the Great Civil War*, four vols, London, 1891–93

Gaunt, P., *The Cromwellian Gazetteer*, Stroud, 1987

Gentles, I., 'The Struggle For London in the Second Civil War', in *The Historical Journal*, 26, number 2, 1983, pp. 277–305

Gentles, I., *The New Model Army*, Oxford, 1992

Gentles, I., 'Why Men Fought in the British Civil Wars, 1639–1652', *The History Teacher*, vol. 26, number 4, August 1993, pp. 407–18

Gentles, I., 'The New Model Officer Corps in 1647: a Collective Portrait', in *Social History*, vol. 22, number 2, May 1997, pp. 127–44

Gibson, J. and Dell, A., *Tudor and Stuart Muster Rolls*, Federation of Family History Societies, Birmingham, 1989

Gibson, J. and Dell, A., *The Protestation Returns, 1641–1642: and other Listings*, Federation of Family History Societies, Birmingham, 1995

Gratton, J.M., *The Earl of Derby's Catholic Army During the English Civil War*, Lancashire and Cheshire Historic Society, 1988

Gratton, J.M., *The Parliamentarian and Royalist War Effort in Lancashire*, unpublished Ph.D. thesis, Manchester University, 1998

Gregg, P., *King Charles I*, London, 1981

Guizot, F., *History of the English Revolution*, London, 1846

Guscott, S.J., *Humphrey Chetam*, Chetam Society Manchester, 2003

Haller, W., *Liberty and Reformation in the Puritan Revolution*, New York, 1955

Halley, R., *Lancashire: Its Puritanism and Nonconformity*, 2 vols, Manchester, 1869

Hampson, F.S., *Ye Olde Man and Scythe Inn: a Brief History of the House and Execution of James, Seventh Earl of Derby*, Bolton, 1914

Hardwick, C., *Antient Battles in Lancashire*, Manchester, 1882

Harrington, P., *Archaeology of the English Civil War*, Princes Risborough, 1992

Harrington, P., *English Civil War Fortifications*, Oxford, 2003

Harris, E., *The Participation of the Gentry of Central Lancashire in the Civil War*, Didsbury Training College, 1955

Hawkes, A.J., *Wigan's Part in the Civil War*, Manchester, 1932

Hewitson, W., *Captain Kay, Royalist: a Bury Hero at the Siege of Lathom*, in Bury and Rossendale Historical Review, 1909

Hill, C., *God's Englishman: Oliver Cromwell and the English Revolution*, London, 1970

Hill, C., *The Century of Revolution 1603–1714* (Second ed.) Wokingham, 1980

Holcroft, F., *The English Civil War Around Wigan and Leigh*, Wigan Heritage Service, 1993

Holland, B., *The Lancashire Hollands*, London, 1917

Holmes, R., *Preston 1648*, Market Drayton, 1985

Horrocks, S. (ed.), *Lancashire History*, vol. 8, Stuart period, Joint Committee on the Lancashire Bibliography, Manchester, 1976

Huehns, G. (ed.), *Clarendon: Selections From the History of the Rebellion and the Life By Himself*, Oxford, 1978

Hughes A., *The Causes of the English Civil War*, London, 1991

Hughes A. and Owens W.R. (eds), *Seventeenth-Century England; A Changing Culture*, 2 vols, London, 1980

Hume, D. *et al.*, *The History of England*, vol. VII, London, 1828

Hutton, R., 'The Failure of the Lancashire Cavaliers', in *Historic Society of Lancashire and Cheshire*, vol. 129, 1980

Hutton, R., *The Royalist War Effort*, London, 1982

Hutton, R., *Charles II*, Oxford, 1989

Irwin, R.A., 'Cromwell in Lancashire', *Army Quarterly*, vol. xxvii, no. 1, London, October 1933

Jones, J., *The Army of the North, 1642–1645*, unpublished Ph.D. thesis, York University, Toronto, 1991

Kmec, S., 'Royalist Noblewomen and Family Fortunes During the Civil War and Commonwealth: the Survival Strategies of the Countess of Derby', *Journal of the Oxford University History Society*, 2004

Kendrick, J., 'An Account of Warrington Siege A.D. 1643', in *Historic Society of Lancashire and Cheshire* vol. IV, 1852

Kenyon, J.P., *The Civil Wars of England*, London, 1988

Kenyon, J.P. and Ohlmeyer J., *The Civil Wars: A Military History of England Scotland and Ireland, 1638–1660*, Oxford, 1998

Kermode, J.I. and Phillips, C.B. (eds), *Seventeenth-Century Lancashire: Essays Presented to J.J. Bagley*, Historic Society of Lancashire and Cheshire, Liverpool, 1983

King, W.J., *Prosecution of Illegal Behaviour in Seventeenth Century England with Emphasis on Lancashire*, unpublished Ph.D. thesis, University of Michigan, 1977

Kishlansky M., *The Rise of the New Model Army*, New York, 1979

Latham A.J.H., 'Wigan, 1540–1640: Pre-industrial growth and development in south Lancashire', in J.F. Wilson (ed.), *King Cotton: A tribute to Douglas A. Farnie*, Lancaster, 2009), pp. 247–79.

Leslie, F.J., 'James, Seventh Earl of Derby', in *Transactions of the Historic Society of Lancashire and Cheshire*, vol. V, 1889

Lewis, J., *Lathom House, Lathom Near Ormskirk*, unpublished typescript, Lancashire County Council Environment Department, 1990

Lewis, J., *The Medieval Earthworks of the Hundred of West Derby*, unpublished Ph.D. thesis, Nottingham, 1991

Lindley, K.J., *The Part Played by the Catholics in the Civil War in Lancashire and Monmouthshire*, unpublished MA thesis, University of Manchester, 1965

Locke, J.W., *A Socio Economic History of 17th Century Poulton-le-Fylde*, Poulton, 1968

Lunn, J., *The Tyldesleys of Lancashire*, Altrincham, 1966

Maurice, F., *The Adventures of Edward Wogan*, London, 1945

McMullen, R and I., *Brindle in the Years of Civil War*, Preston, 1999

Miller, G.C., *Hoghton Tower*, Preston, 1948

Miller, G.C., *Hoghton Tower in History and Romance*, Preston, 1954

Morrah, P., *Prince Rupert of the Rhine*, London, 1976

Morrill, J., *The Revolt of the Provinces*, London, 1976

Morrill, J., 'The Northern Gentry and the Great Rebellion', in G. Forster (ed.), *Northern History*, vol. xv, University of Leeds, 1979

Morrill, J. (ed.), *Reactions to the English Civil War*, London, 1982

Morrill, J. (ed.), *The Impact of the English Civil War*, London, 1991

Morrill, J., 'The Causes of the British Civil Wars', *Journal of Ecclesiastical History*, vol. 43, number 4, October 1992, pp. 624–34

Nayling, N., *Tree Ring Analysis of Timbers From Lathom House*, Report 5/2000, English Heritage, 2000

Neil, NJ., *Lathom House; Documentary Research for Archaeological Evaluation*, Lancaster University Archaeological Unit, 1996

Nevell, M., *A History and Archaeology of Tameside*, Manchester, 1991

Newman, P.R., *Marston Moor, 2 July 1644: The Sources and the Site*, University of York,

Borthwick Papers, 35, 1978

Newman, P.R., *The Royalist Armies in Northern England 1642–1645*, unpublished D.Phil. thesis, University of York, 1978

Newman, P.R., *The Battle of Marston Moor*, Chichester 1981

Newman, P.R., *Royalist Officers in England and Wales*, New York, 1981

Newman, P.R., *Companion to the English Civil Wars*, New York, 1990

Newman, P.R., *The Old Service*, Manchester 1993

Newman, P.R. and Roberts, P.R., *Marston Moor 1644; The Battle of the Five Armies*, Pickering, 2003

O'Riordan, C., *Popular Exploitation of Enemy Estates in the English Revoultion*, in History, vol. 78, 1993

Ormerod, G.W., *First Blood is Drawn in the Civil War: Lord Strange and the Siege of Manchester*, Manchester, 1878

Page, W. (ed.), *The Victoria History of the Counties of England: A History of Lancashire*, eight vols, London, 1907–14

Palmer, J., *The History of the Siege of Manchester*, Manchester, 1822

Parker, G., *The Military Revolution*, Cambridge, 1988

Parry, R.H. (ed.), *The English Civil War and After 1642–1658*, London, 1970

Pendlebury, G., *Aspects of the English Civil War in Bolton and its Neighbourhood, 1640–1660*, Swinton, 1983

Petrie, C., *King Charles, Prince Rupert and the Civil War*, London, 1974

Phillips, C.B., 'The County Committees and Local Government in Cumberland and Westmorland, 1642–1660', *Northern History* vol. V (1970), pp. 34–66

Phillips C.B. and Smith J.H., *Lancashire and Cheshire from AD 1540*, London, 1994

Pilkington, C., *To Play the Man: The Story of Lady Derby and the Siege of Lathom House, 1643–1645*, Preston, 1991

Porter, S., *Destruction in the English Civil Wars*, Stroud, 1994

Postlethwaite, R., *Christopher Preston of Peacock Hall, Leyland and his Brother Richard Preston of the Folly, Settle, and their Relatives, Friends and Associates, who Fought for the king in the English Civil War*. Privately published, Haslingden, 2005

Quintrell, B.W., 'The Practice and Problems of Recusant Disarming, 1585–1641', *Recusant History*, vol. xvii, 1985

Reeve, J., 'The Politics of War Finance in an Age of Confessional Strife: A Comparative Anglo-European View', in *Parergon* number 14.1, July 1996, pp. 85–109

Reid, S., *The Finest Knight in England: Being a History of the Regiments of Horse, Foot and Dragoons of Sir Thomas Tyldesley*, Aberdeen, 1979

Richardson, R.C., *Puritanism in North West England*, Manchester, 1972

Robinson, A.M., *Cheshire in the Great Civil War*, 1895, reprinted Doncaster, 1990

Rogers, C.D., *Education in Lancashire and Cheshire, 1640–1660*, Historic Society of Lancashire and Cheshire, vol. 123, 1972

Roots, I., *The Great Rebellion*, London, 1966

Roots, I. (ed.), *Into Another Mould: Aspects of the Interregnum*, Exeter Studies in History, number 3, Exeter, 1981

Ross, W.G., 'Military Engineering During the Great Civil War 1642–9', *Professional Papers of the Corps of Royal Engineers*, vol. xiii, edited by F.J. Day, 1887–88

Rowsell, M.C., *The Life Story of Charlotte de la Tremoille Countess of Derby*, London, 1905

Royle, T., *Civil War*, London, 2004

Russell, C., *The Causes of the English Civil War*, Oxford, 1990

Russell, C., 'Why Did People Choose Sides in the English Civil War?' *The Historian*, number 63, Autumn 1999, pp. 4–9

Scally, J., *The Hamilton Papers as a Source for the History of the British Civil Wars*, Scottish Archives, Journal of the Scottish Records Association, vol. 4, 1998

Scholes J.C. and Pimblett, W., *History of Bolton*, Bolton, 1892

Schwoerer, L.G., 'The Fittest Subject for a King's Quarrel: an Essay on the Militia Controversy, 1641–1642', in *The Journal of British Studies*, vol. xi, number 1, 1971, pp. 45–76

Shaw R.C., *The Royal Forest of Lancashire*, Preston, 1956

Seacome, J., *Memoirs; Containing a Genealogical and Historical Account of Antient and Honourable House of Stanley*, Liverpool, 1741

Seacome, J., *The History of the House of Stanley*, Preston, 1793

Sinclair, D., *The History of Wigan*, two vols, Wigan, 1882

Sinclair, D., *The Battle of Wigan Lane*, Wigan (reprinted), 1987

Spence, R.T., *Skipton Castle in the Great Civil War*, Skipton, 1991

Stone, L. and Kearney, H., *Social Change and Revolution in England, 1540–1640*, London, 1965

Stone, L., *The Causes of the English Revolution, 1529–1642*, London, 1972

Stonehouse, J., *The Streets of Liverpool*, Liverpool, 1869 reprinted 2002

Sunderland, F.H., *Marmaduke Lord Langdale*, London, 1926

Tait, J., *Medieval Manchester and the Beginnings of Lancashire*, Manchester University, 1904

Taylor, P.A.M. (ed.), *Problems in European Civilization: The Origins of the English Civil War*, Boston (USA), 1960

Thomson, W.H., *History of Manchester to 1852*, Altrincham, 1967

Tomlinson, H., *Before the English Civil War*, Basingstoke, 1983

Toon, P., 'Puritan Eschatology: 1600–1648', in *The Report of the 1968 Puritan and Reformed Studies Conference*, Cambridge 1969,

Tupling, G.H., 'The Causes of the Civil War in Lancashire', in *Transactions of the Lancashire and Cheshire Antiquarian Society*, vol. 65, 1955

Tyrer, F., 'A Star Chamber Case: Ashton v. Blundell, 1624–31', *Transactions of the Historic Society of Lancashire and Cheshire*, vol. 118, Liverpool 1967, pp. 19–37

Walton, J.K., *Lancashire, a Social History*, Manchester University, 1987

Wanklyn, M. and Jones F., *A Military History of the English Civil War*, London, 2005

Wardale, H., 'Cromwell in Lancashire', in *Transactions of the Lancashire and Cheshire Antiquarian Society*, vol. xlviii, 1934

Wedgwood, C.V., *The King's Peace, 1637–1641*, London, 1955

Wedgwood, C.V., *The King's War, 1641–1647*, London, 1958

Wedgwood, C.V., *Thomas Wentworth, First Earl of Strafford*, London, 1961

Wedgwood, C.V., *The Trial of Charles I*, London, 1964

Wedgwood, C.V., *Oliver Cromwell* (revised edition) London, 1973

Wenham, P., *The Great and Close Siege of York*, Kineton, 1970

West Yorkshire Archaeology, *Lathom House Near Ormskirk; Post Fieldwork Assessment and Project Design* (compiled for the British Academy), West Yorkshire Archaeology, Report 613, 1998

West Yorkshire Archaeology, *Lathom Park Near Ormskirk: Desk Based Archaeological Assessment*, West Yorkshire Archaeology, Report 802, May 2000

White A. (ed.), *A History of Lancaster*, Keele University, 1993

Wilson, F., *The Effects of the Civil War on Burnley and Surrounding Districts*, Burnley, 1980

Woolrych, A., *Battles of the English Civil War*, London, 1961 (with new introduction, 1991)

Woolrych, A., 'Puritanism, Politics and Society', in E.W. Ives (ed.), *The English Revolution, 1600–1660*, London, 1975, pp. 87–100

Woolrych, A., *England Without a King*, London, 1983

Woolrych, A., *Britain in Revolution*, Oxford, 2002

Worden, B., 'Toleration and the Cromwellian Protectorate', in *Studies in Church History*, number 21, 1984, *Persecution and Toleration*, pp. 199–233

Wrighton, K.E., *The Puritan Reformation of Manners, with Special Reference to the Counties of Lancashire and Essex, 1640–1660*, unpublished Ph.D. thesis, University of Cambridge, 1974

Wythenshawe, *Notes on Wythenshawe Hall Siege*, MCA, Misc 227/2

Young, P., *Edgehill 1642*, Kineton, 1967

Young, P., *Marston Moor 1644: The Campaign and the Battle*, Kineton, 1970

Young, P. and Emberton, W., *Sieges of the Great Civil War*, London, 1978

Index